THE INSIDERS' GUIDE

TO

NORTH CAROLINA'S
TRIANGLE

Cary, Chapel Hill, Durham, Raleigh & Surrounding Towns

THE INSIDERS' GUIDE

TO

NORTH CAROLINA'S

TRIANGLE

Cary, Chapel Hill, Durham, Raleigh & Surrounding Towns

by

J. Barlow Herget

&

Rich Weidman

BCK Publishing Group

BCK

PUBLISHING GROUP

Published and distributed by:

BCK Publishing Group
P.O. Box 14154
Research Triangle Park, NC 27709
(919) 467-4035

•

TENTH EDITION
1st Printing, Fall 2000

•

Copyright © 2000
by BCK Publishing Group

•

This publication is available from BCK Publishing at special discounts for bulk purchases by human resource and relocation departments, Realtors®, schools, libraries and companies. Special editions, including personalized covers, can be created for large quantity orders. For more information contact BCK Publishing.

•

ISBN 0-9705760-0-5

BCK Publishing Group

President
Barbara King

Copy Editor
David McNally

Graphic Designers
Judy Huyser
Bob Koski
Evelyn Ward

Office Manager
Jim Harrop

Account Executives
Judith Carlton
Kerin Politis
Marianne Truitt

Administrative Assistants
Julie Pender
Gerry Pollard
Tiffany Reeves

Maps
Bob Koski
Shawn McClafferty
Evelyn Ward

Photographers
Tim Johnson
Rich Weidman

Cover Photos
Carolina Cobras
**N.C. Division of Tourism,
Film and Sports Development**
**Durham Convention and
Visitors Bureau**

•

Produced under license of
The Insiders' Guide®
An imprint of Falcon® Publishing, Inc.
A Landmark Communications company.
P.O. Box 1718
Helena, MT 59624
(800) 582-2665
www.insiders.com

Preface

Consider this book your own private tutor. It will tell you about the need-to-know things like schools, utility services and auto tags, but it also has exciting electives such as barbecue, basketball and beaches. It's a guide for newcomers as well as residents who have been watching too much TV and need to get out more.

You will enjoy the comprehensiveness that has always made this *the* guide to the Triangle. The guide has been painstakingly researched, completely revised in format and totally updated in content. However, things do change. By the time this edition is printed, some information will need updating. Your comments are always appreciated, so please drop us a note if you have any suggestions or find any factual discrepancies.

The Triangle is not a city nor a county nor any governmental jurisdiction. It's a place (and some will say, a state of mind) that takes its name from the private, non-profit Research Triangle Park that was established in the late 1950s by Governor Luther Hodges. The three counties that comprise the Triangle are Durham, Orange and Wake, and their respective cities are Durham, Chapel Hill and Raleigh.

These cities are also the homes to the area's three large research universities—Duke University in Durham, the University of North Carolina at Chapel Hill and North Carolina State University in Raleigh. In the middle of the Triangle sits the 7,000-acre Research Triangle Park or as we Insiders call it, RTP or simply, "The Park." Governor Hodges' dream was to build a place to attract research companies that would pay better wages than the state's traditional industries of textiles, apparel and furniture. And the dream has come true!

Today, RTP has its own zip code, 27709, and the three original cities, once separated by piney woods and meadows, are bumping up against each other. More than a million people call the Triangle home. Cary, once a small bedroom suburb of Raleigh, is larger than Chapel Hill and is likely to have 100,000 people by the year 2001. The three big research universities have entered the 21st century as among the best in the country, with rankings to prove it. UNC-Chapel Hill and NCSU in particular are two of the best bargains among major public universities with annual tuition under $3,000 for 2000-01.

Individually and together, the Triangle cities have won a string of awards and ratings. To brag about a few, this guide cites *Money* magazine's recent ranking of the Triangle as the second-best metropolitan area in the South; other accolades include its selection by *U.S. News & World Report* as one of the 50 Fabulous Places to Raise Your Family; *Money* and *PC World* magazines' titles as the No. 1 mid-size area in the country for people who work at home and telecommute; *Child* magazine's recognition of Raleigh as among the top five places to raise children in the U.S.; rankings as the No. 1 place in the country to live; the No. 1 place for business; a Top Hot Spot for starting a business; and as they say in *The King and I*, etceteras, etceteras, etceteras. Keep reading!

About the Authors

J. Barlow Herget

J. Barlow Herget is a writer who lives in Raleigh's Cameron Park neighborhood with his wife, Millie. They have two grown children. Barlow received his B.A. in English and history from the University of Arkansas and his M.A. in history from the University of Virginia. He was a Nieman Fellow ('70) at Harvard University. Barlow has worked for the *Daily Press* of Paragould, Arkansas, and Raleigh's *The News and Observer*. His articles have appeared in *The Atlantic, The New York Times* and numerous other publications. He was special assistant to the N.C. Secretary of Commerce, '77-'79, and worked for Data General Corporation. Barlow is a commentator on public radio in the Triangle. He has been a resident of the Triangle since 1973 and served on the Raleigh City Council for two terms. Barlow was one of the champions in the 1992 Rex Tennis Classic and can be found hobbling around the racquetball courts at the Hillsborough Street YMCA. He operates a writing and media consulting business in Raleigh.

Rich Weidman

Rich Weidman moved to the Triangle from Florida in 1994 and has served as the editor of several regional guidebooks, including *The Insiders' Guide to the Triangle, The Insiders' Guide to Charlotte, Daytrips and Weekend Vacations in North Carolina* and *Daytrips and Weekend Vacations in South Carolina*. He has also worked as an account executive for a Florida marketing company, a staff writer and sports editor at *The News of Orange County* in Hillsborough and a researcher and proofreader for a Raleigh advertising agency. Rich received his B.A. in English from Stetson University and his M.A. in English from the University of Florida. He lives in Cary's Brookgreen Forest neighborhood with his wife Nadine, daughter Hailey and cats Scamp and Kenya. Rich enjoys hiking in the Umstead and Eno River state parks, exploring the Blue Ridge Mountains, visiting North Carolina historic sites, vacationing in the Outer Banks (especially Ocracoke Island), eating Eastern-style barbecue and cheering the Duke Blue Devil basketball team to victory.

ACKNOWLEDGMENTS

This book includes information and insight from our authors and dozens of individuals who offered encouragement, as well as their thoughts and ideas about the Triangle. We especially want to thank all the Chambers of Commerce, Convention and Visitors Bureaus, Boards of Realtors and many other companies, organizations and individuals who helped us compile and update this 10th edition.

YOUR COMMENTS

Please take a few moments to share your comments and suggestions on our "More Information" reply card and we will be happy to forward your requests for information.

Table of Contents

Directory of Close-ups

Directory of Maps

STATE OF NORTH CAROLINA
OFFICE OF THE GOVERNOR
RALEIGH 27603-8001

JAMES B. HUNT JR.
GOVERNOR

Dear Friends:

As Governor of the State of North Carolina, it is indeed my pleasure to welcome you to the Triangle, that vast metropolitan area that connects Raleigh, Cary, Durham, Chapel Hill and Carrboro.

This area is home to more than 50 corporate, academic and governmental research facilities. What sets it apart from other great research centers, however, is the superior quality of life. Unlike most metro areas, the Triangle consists of medium-sized cities which offer all the amenities of big-city living without the high costs. One can easily go from urban to suburban to rural settings within the area, experiencing Southern Hospitality at its very best all along the way.

Having been named America's best city for business by *Fortune* magazine, Raleigh/Durham continues to live up to its industrious reputation. Contributing to the area's top ranking is the presence of three top universities—Duke, UNC and N.C. State—and the 7,000-acre Research Triangle Park. We are extremely proud of this recognition and feel that it is well deserved.

On behalf of all our citizens, I again welcome you and invite you to enjoy all that the Triangle has to offer.

My warmest personal regards,

Sincerely,

James B. Hunt Jr.

Welcome Home!
to the Triangle

Photo courtesy of the Carolina Hurricanes

We just keep getting better!

Check us out!

CitySearch
www.triangle.citysearch.com

The News & Observer Online
www.newsobserver.com
www.triangle.com

Cary Chamber of Commerce
www.carychamber.com

**Chapel Hill-Carrboro
Chamber of Commerce**
www.chapelhillcarrboro.org

Chapel Hill Visitors Bureau
www.chocvb.org

Durham Chamber of Commerce
www.durhamchamber.org

Durham Convention & Visitors Bureau
www.Durham-NC.com

Raleigh Chamber of Commerce
www.raleighchamber.org

Raleigh Convention & Visitors Bureau
www.raleighcvb.org

Triangle Cities

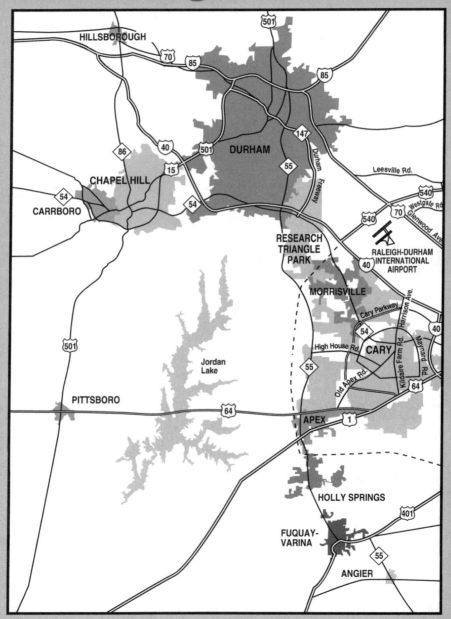

and Towns

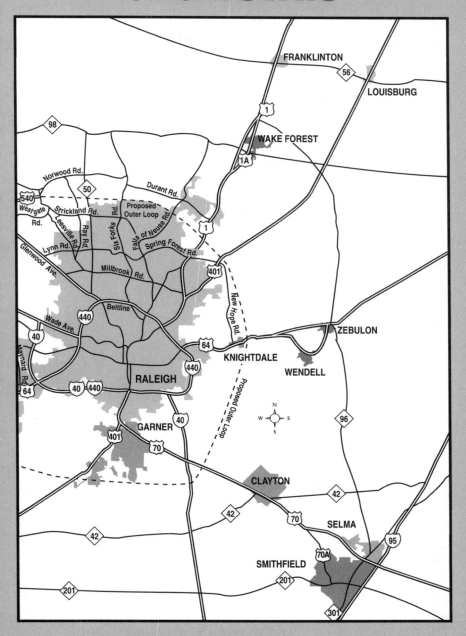

Cary

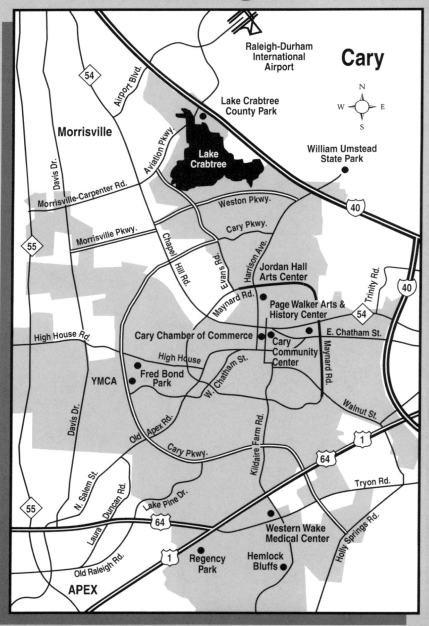

Chapel Hill

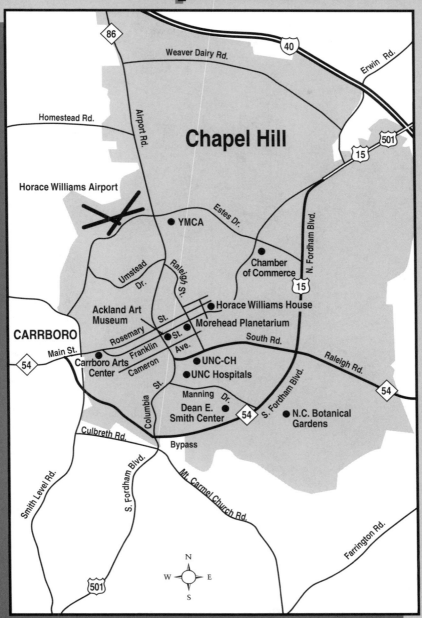

Durham

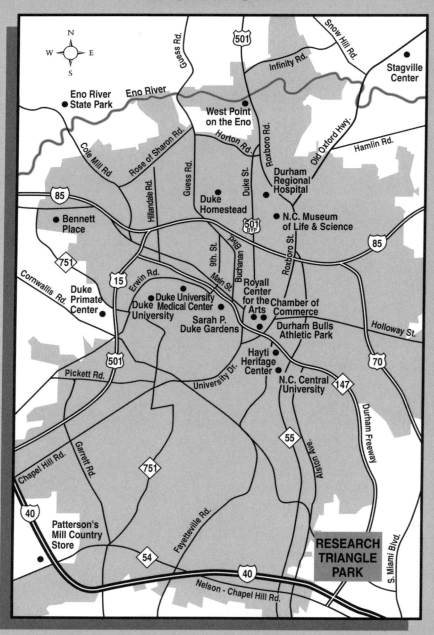

Raleigh

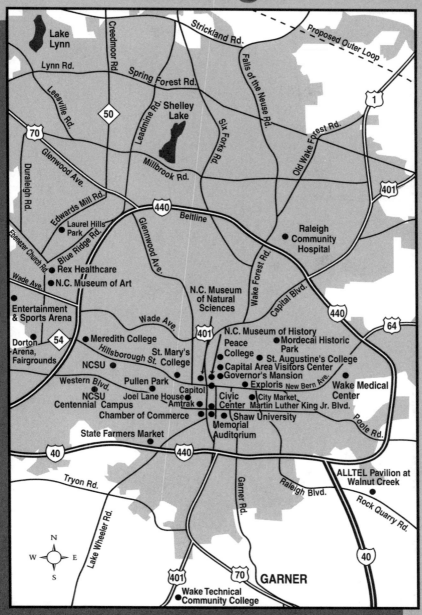

Research Triangle Park

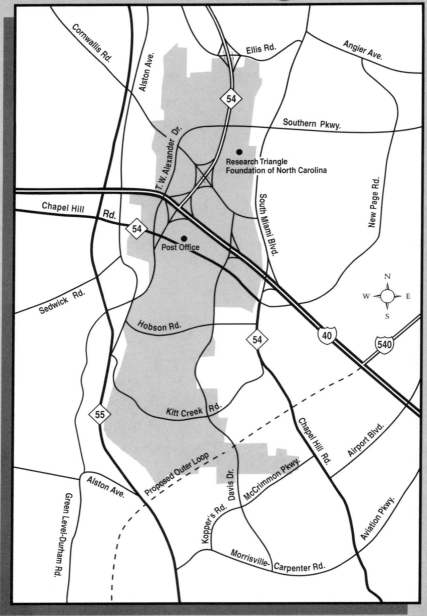

How to Use This Book

We're proud of the Triangle and our *Insiders' Guide* provides a one-stop source of information about this dynamic region. The guide has been designed for residents, newcomers, visitors and anyone else who wants a comprehensive overview of the Triangle. No matter where you travel throughout the area, take this guide along with you. Keep it in your glove compartment, briefcase or backpack.

Newcomers will certainly find the chapter on the *History of the Triangle* insightful. Our *Triangle Overview* chapter highlights Cary, Chapel Hill, Durham and Raleigh. The *Triangle Towns* section includes information on the smaller neighboring towns of Angier, Apex, Carrboro, Clayton, Franklinton, Fuquay-Varina, Garner, Hillsborough, Holly Springs, Knightdale, Louisburg, Morrisville, Pittsboro, Selma, Smithfield, Wake Forest, Wendell and Zebulon.

If you're just getting to the area and want to know how to navigate our highways and byways, our *Getting Around* chapter provides you with the information you'll need.

Visitors also will appreciate the chapters on *Accommodations and Temporary Housing, Annual Events, Arts and Culture, Attractions, Inns and B&Bs, Night Life, Restaurants* and *Triangle Shopping*. Our *Employment*

Opportunities chapter is for those individuals considering relocating to the Triangle. Newcomers will find the chapters on *Apartments, Real Estate and Neighborhoods* (with information on buying or building), *Colleges and Universities, Golf in the Carolinas, Health Care, Media, Retirement* and *Public Services and Utilities* especially helpful in making decisions associated with moving to a new area.

Our *Spectator Sports* chapter gives you an Insider's view of the Wolfpack, Blue Devils, Tar Heels, Bulls, Mudcats, Hurricanes, Cobras, Braves, Capital Express, Wings and local stock-car racing. We've even provided you with a variety of destinations in the mountains and along the coast in the *Daytrips and Weekend Vacations* chapter for those of you with a yearning to hit the road. Parents will appreciate the chapters on *Kidstuff and Camps, Parks and Recreation* and *Schools and Child Care*.

Each chapter has Insider's tips to provide you with some of the secrets we've gleaned as longtime residents of the Triangle. In-depth "Close-ups" on such regional topics as North Carolina barbecue and March Madness are also included throughout the guide.

Please note that the area code for all phone numbers listed in this guide in 919, unless otherwise noted.

History of North Carolina

(Excerpted from an article by Dr. Jerry C. Cashion, Research Branch, Division of Archives and History, North Carolina Department of Cultural Resources)

Before the arrival of European explorers, Native Americans inhabited the territory that is now North Carolina. Major tribes included the Tuscaroras, the Catawbas and the Cherokees. Beginning with Giovanni de Verrazzano in 1524, various French, Spanish and English explorers visited the area. In 1585 and 1587, English colonies were sponsored by Sir Walter Raleigh. These attempts at settlement failed. In 1629, Charles I of England declared all lands south of Virginia to be part of the British Empire. The first permanent settlement started in the 1660s when farmers settled around Albemarle Sound.

In 1677, economic and religious quarrels with the provisional governor in Virginia led to restrictions on shipping from North Carolina. These restrictions added to ill feelings in the state and hampered the growth of the state's significant tobacco crop. The settlers continued to resist the colonial rulings from England and Virginia and, in an attempt to restore order, the British formed the separate state of North Carolina in 1729 and sent a deputy governor to the area.

Meanwhile, the first town had been settled in 1700 and it was called Bath. After this, the population rose rapidly and settlements spread across the eastern and central (or Piedmont) part of the state.

Royal oppression mounted and American patriots talked, preached and fought for independence. Moores Creek, Halifax, Hillsborough and Fayetteville drew gatherings of North Carolinians who would be free to make their own laws and unite with the other American colonies to form the United States of America. With the famous Halifax Resolves, April 12, 1776, North Carolina became the first colony to instruct its delegates to the Continental Congress to vote for independence. General Cornwallis invaded the state in 1780 and his forces were substantially weakened at the Battle of Guilford Courthouse. The British army later surrendered in neighboring Virginia.

North Carolina representatives declined to ratify the new United States Constitution until assured that a Bill of Rights was to be added. In 1789, North Carolina became the 12th state of the United States of America.

Development in the state after the American Revolution was very slow. The state's economy was unable to grow due to poor transportation and communication systems. A reawakening occurred after 1835 when constitutional revisions gave more power to the western half of the state. Plank roads, canals and railroads helped solve the problem of transportation. Improved access to markets stimulated agricultural and industrial growth.

Education proved to be the major key to the development of the state. The University of North Carolina, which opened in 1795, became one of the leading institutions in the nation. The state was the first in the South to establish a tax-supported system of public schools.

When the Civil War started, North Carolina was somewhat reluctant to leave the Union, but the state fought on the side of the Confederacy. The state supplied more troops and suffered more losses than any other in the Confederacy. The state's ports drew much Union fire, but the Port of Wilmington remained open until the fall of Fort Fisher in January 1865. Confederate General Joseph E. Johnston surrendered to the Federal army under General William T. Sherman in April 1865 at the Bennett House, near the present city of Durham.

Reconstruction saw much internal upheaval. Partisan discord marked much of the remainder of the century. Industrial development outpaced a resurgence of agriculture at this time.

During the early 20th century, the foundation was laid for the state's rapid progress. Dedication to public education and highway construction became hallmarks of generations of legislators.

North Carolina devoted its human, industrial and agricultural resources to engage in two World Wars. Gearing up for wartime production, the state became more educated, urban and internationally connected. Developments in agriculture made it possible for highly efficient farms to produce an abundance of food and fiber that found its way to the national and global market.

The Research Triangle Park was established in 1958 to boost growth in research-related fields. Located in close proximity to the University of North Carolina at Chapel Hill, Duke University in Durham and North Carolina State University in Raleigh, the Triangle contains the South's greatest concentrations of scientists, research sources, laboratory facilities and cultural resources. Industrial growth has followed the growth in research.

North Carolina covers nearly 53,000 square miles and is divided into 100 counties. The state has three distinct regions:

Coastal, Piedmont and Mountains. The Coastal region comprises about 45 percent of the state's area. A long chain of islands called the Outer Banks is located on the northern coast. It includes the Cape Hatteras National Seashore, the longest strand of undeveloped beach in the country. The town of Manteo on Roanoke Island is home to The Lost Colony, America's oldest outdoor drama, which depicts the struggles of the first English settlers in the New World during the late 16th century. It takes place at the Waterside Theatre each summer. The nearby town of Kitty Hawk is where the Wright brothers, Orville and Wilbur, ushered in the age of flight in 1903. Other islands extend as far south as South Carolina.

The Piedmont, or central part of the state, is approximately 38 percent of the area of the state. It is the prime symbol of the "New South" in which modern industry and technology have replaced agriculture as the main source of income. Industry is prevalent in Raleigh, Chapel Hill, Durham, Greensboro and Charlotte (which is also the second-largest banking center in the country).

The Mountain region of North Carolina is bounded by two ranges of the southern Appalachians, The Blue Ridge Mountains and the Great Smoky Mountains. Established in 1934, the Great Smoky Mountains National Park is the most visited park in the United States. The nearby 56,000-acre Qualla Boundary Reservation is home to the Eastern Band of Cherokee Indians. The mountains are renowned for a variety of crafts including pottery, wood carving, basketry, needlework, handmade rugs and bedspreads. Today, the mountains have become a well-known year-round resort and Asheville is the center of activity.

The Democratic party dominated state government for the first half of the twentieth century, but in 1972 both a Republican senator and governor were elected. Democrat James B. Hunt served as Governor from 1977-1985. Republican James G. Martin then served two terms. In 1992, Governor Hunt was elected to serve a third term and in 1996 was reelected to a record fourth term.

The *Three Presidents* statue in front of the State Capitol honors three of North Carolina's most famous native sons: Andrew Jackson, James Polk and Andrew Johnson.

History of The Triangle

If you're going to be an Insider, here's the place to start. Past is prologue, remember. Our history lesson is short and designed to get you past that first social conversation with your neighbors, churchgoers or business contacts without embarrassment.

Many of North Carolina's history makers and historic places belong to the area we now call the Triangle. It includes, after all, the capital city Raleigh and the repository for North Carolina's story, the state Museum of History and Archives. We encourage you to visit both, the sooner the better, and for the truly dedicated, check out Lefler's and Newsome's *North Carolina, The History of a Southern State.*

Meanwhile, for the rest of us, the minimalist version that follows will suffice. It tells you the highlights and proper names of who got things started here and how we remember them. For example, we tell you how Cary got its name, when Chapel Hill and UNC-CH were born, why Duke University is not still called Trinity College, who lost the Lost Colony and how the idea for Research Triangle Park evolved. There's a brief history of the principal cities in alphabetical order: Cary, Chapel Hill (and Carrboro), Durham and Raleigh. The following Overview chapter includes the neighboring towns. Pay attention: There will be a pop quiz when you're finished reading.

Cary

Unlike some ersatz post-World War II suburbs, Cary has a past. It's been around for more than 125 years on the state's legislative books. Citizens are especially proud of Cary's record for establishing the first public school in the state, the original Cary Academy for which Academy Street is named.

Before Cary was a town, it was the busy home and gathering place for business friends and family of A. Francis (Frank) Page. He was the founder of the town and father to five sons, one of whom was to become one of the state's famous sons—writer and diplomat Walter Hines Page. Indeed, some citizens then and later believed Cary should have been named Page, after Frank. It was Page who, in the mid-1850s, set up a sawmill, store and inn along the main road between Raleigh and the University of North Carolina in Chapel Hill. He also ran the post office and began raising his family there. But it was the coming of the railroads in 1868 and the junction they formed at Page's place that literally put it on the map. That same year, he sold some of his lots: one 70-acre parcel went for $140 and a 10-acre piece sold for the grand sum of $50.

In 1871, the General Assembly incorporated the various enterprises and railroad crossing as the town of "Carey," a misspelling on the town clerk's part that was later corrected. The name was selected to honor one Samuel F. Cary, a famed Ohio temperance orator who reportedly stayed at Page's inn on one of his speaking tours in the South and greatly impressed his host. The selection must have been a brave choice for the times. Cary was not only a teetotaling Yankee outsider, he also had been a general in the Union Army, not a recommendation for honors in the South of 1871.

Photo by Rich Weidman

Built next to the railroad tracks by Frank Page around 1870, the Page-Walker Hotel in Cary was converted into the Page Walker Arts and History Center in 1991.

Cary began to make strides in the late 1800s and early 1900s. Cary High School (formerly known as Cary Academy) became the first state-assisted public high school in North Carolina in 1907. In 1909, the Bank of Cary was chartered. By 1917, the "Western Wake Highway" (now East Chatham and Hillsborough streets) was paved between Cary and Raleigh, and the town received power from Carolina Power and Light Company the following year.

Cary's population grew by more than 60 percent in the 1920s, but the Great Depression put an end to all of the prosperity. The Bank of Cary closed its doors in 1931 and the town defaulted on its bonds and declared bankruptcy the following year. Cary managed to bounce back after World War II, firmly establishing itself as a Raleigh bedroom community. However, few jobs were available, with the notable exception of the Taylor Biscuit Company (now known as Austin Quality Foods), which opened in 1947. The development of Research Triangle Park in the late '50s changed everything, generating new industries and housing for Cary.

In 1960, Cary developed a comprehensive growth plan that is updated annually. The first issue of *The Cary News* rolled off the presses in 1963. The town's first major housing development, MacGregor Downs, was incorporated in 1966. By the time Cary celebrated its Centennial in 1971, the town's population had reached 7,640 and it had begun to step outside of Raleigh's shadow and establish its own identity.

The success of MacGregor Downs led to the construction of other developments along Kildaire Farm Road, including Kildaire Farms (Cary's first planned unit development), Wimbledon and Lochmere. The arrival of industrial and business parks such as MacGregor Park, Regency Park and Weston brought in thousands of additional jobs. SAS Institute, which started in 1976 with less than a dozen employees, took off in the 1980s and currently employs approximately 3,500 people. Formerly known as Cary Village Mall, Cary Towne Center opened in 1979 and by 1991 had tripled in size, the same year that Cary's first regional shopping center, Crossroads Plaza, opened for business.

Today, Cary has become a favorite among many new Triangle residents who have moved here from the North, as evidenced by the population growth over the past 10 years from 43,858 to nearly 100,000.

Chapel Hill and Carrboro

It's not clear just when UNC-CH and Chapel Hill picked up their reputations for being scandalously tolerant. Some would say it goes back to that fateful day in April 1865 when General Atkins of the Union forces then occupying Chapel Hill paid a visit to the home of University President Swain. It was there that the Yankee General met Swain's young daughter, Eleanor, and fell instantly in love. The two were married in August while students hung the General and the President in effigy. Later, someone recalling the disgrace scribbled on a classroom blackboard, "This old University ... has busted and gone to hell."

If Chapel Hill's identity is inescapably intertwined with UNC-CH's, it is because, like twins, their births occurred simultaneously. Legend has it that the location of both UNC-CH and Chapel Hill was sealed one warm summer day in 1792 when a committee entrusted with selecting a site for the first state university embarked on its search mission. They stopped to rest in the shade of a great tulip poplar, not far from the New Hope Chapel. Refreshed by a picnic lunch and a few rounds of "exhilarating" spirits, the group agreed this was the perfect spot for their university. It was beautiful, served by pure water from a nearby spring and, most importantly, "inaccessible to vice" (or so they thought). More likely than not, the site was really chosen because the property had been donated to the cause by some wealthy benefactors. At any rate, on October 12, 1793, a formal ceremony was held for laying the cornerstone of Old East, the university's first

building. That same day, taking advantage of the crowd that had assembled, an auctioneer offered 22 large lots for sale in what would soon become the surrounding town.

Prior to the opening of the university, Chapel Hill was nothing more than a muddy crossroads in the wilderness, a hamlet of Scottish and English families who had arrived in the mid-1700s. The community took its name from the New Hope Chapel located on a hill overlooking a valley to the east. The hamlet contained perhaps a half-dozen houses, a blacksmith shop and an inn. The town of less than 1,000 inhabitants was incorporated in 1851 and elected its first mayor in 1879. The Bank of Chapel Hill opened its doors in 1896.

Meanwhile, west of Chapel Hill, another community had sprung up around the only railroad station that served the university. One student, on a train he thought was destined for the UNC-CH campus, wrote of finding that he had been dropped off "in the middle of nowhere."

Eventually a settlement grew up around the railroad depot, consisting of a flour mill, a blacksmith shop and a cotton mill built in 1898 by Chapel Hillian Tom Lloyd. The community was known as West End, then West Chapel Hill and later Venable, for former UNC-CH President Francis P. Venable. Finally, after Lloyd's mill was purchased by the Julian Carr family of Durham, the town took the name of Carrboro, as it is still known today.

Although they grew up side by side, Chapel Hill and Carrboro were distinct communities for years. Chapel Hill evolved as a university village and a haven for liberal intellectuals, while Carrboro's population was made up of blue-collar workers employed to service the university and the cotton mill. When Carr Mill shut down after the Great Depression, the town became more of a small bedroom community for people who worked at the university or its hospital. Right up through the 1970s, Chapel

Hill and Carrboro maintained their distinct identities, one as the university village, the other as a small historic town. With the continuing surge of growth in the county, the two towns have grown together; however, merger of the two municipalities is not on the current agenda.

Today, the "Southern Part of Heaven," as Chapel Hill is affectionately known, boasts a bustling downtown centered around Franklin Street, a wealth of cultural attractions, eclectic restaurants and a vibrant music scene. The population stands at 45,000 with an additional 24,600 college students during the school year. Chapel Hill is a diverse mix of professionals, students, professors, musicians, artists and retirees. With a population of more than 15,500, Carrboro has become quite an artists' community in its own right. A variety of specialty shops and restaurants are sprouting all over downtown near Carr Mill Mall, Julian Carr's old cotton mill.

Durham

Back in the middle of the 19th century, Durham was not much more than a whistle-stop on North Carolina's east-west railroad line. Today the "City of Medicine" has become world renowned for its health-care facilities, cutting-edge research and development companies and educational institutions.

The forces that built this town—tobacco, textiles, medicine and education—also shaped its uniquely diverse character. Once heavily populated by blue-collar tobacco and textile workers, it is as much a home today for doctors and dancers, high-tech execs and entrepreneurs.

It all started at the corner of Peabody and Corcoran streets where Bartlett Snipes Durham, a local physician, built his country estate and called it, some would say prophetically, "Pandora's Box." In 1852, Dr. Durham offered four acres of his homesite to the North Carolina Railroad Company for a depot along its Goldsboro-to-Charlotte line. Thus was born the hamlet known as Durham's Station, Durham Depot, Durhamville and finally, just plain Durham. Durham's official birth date is April 26, 1853, when its first post office opened. By 1860, three stores, two saloons and a carpentry shop had sprung up on what was still an agricultural landscape inhabited by fewer than 100 persons. Dr.

Photo courtesy of the N.C. Division of Archives & History

The nation's oldest state university, UNC-Chapel Hill, opened its doors in 1795. The above photo shows UNC's Gerrard Hall, ca. 1881.

Durham's homesite was purchased by R. F. Morris, whose small tobacco factory nearby would add another significant chapter to the community's development.

Durham played a relatively minor role in the Civil War until the very end, when Confederate General Joseph Johnston surrendered to Union General William Sherman in 1865 at a nearby farm owned by James Bennett. The event marked the end of the Civil War in the Carolinas, Georgia and Florida. Ironically, it also launched the beginning of Durham's prosperity.

While Sherman and Johnston were taking care of business out on the Bennett farm, the boys in blue and gray were swapping war stories and smoking the peace pipe down at the Durham depot. Seems that soldiers from both sides had gotten a bit restless, broken into the nearby tobacco factory, then owned by John R. Green, and made off with what turned out to be the finest Bright Leaf weed any of them had ever smoked. When the honorable terms of surrender were finally consummated, the troops took their tobacco and went home.

It wasn't long before orders for Green's tobacco began pouring into the Durham post office from as far away as Maine and Texas. To meet the sudden demand, Green cranked up production on a brand of tobacco he named "Bull Durham" after the picture of a bull on the jar of Coleman's Mustard manufactured in Durham, England. Pretty soon the image of that bull was appearing in advertisements on walls and rooftops around the world, even on one of the Great Pyramids of Egypt. An ad painted behind the New York Yankees' dugout inspired a new baseball term—"bullpen." Durham was on the map and the "Bull City" shifted into high gear.

The demand for Durham tobacco prompted other entrepreneurs to get into the business, including Washington Duke and his sons Brodie, Ben and James. With the introduction of the cigarette rolling machine, the Dukes became the leading cigarette makers in the nation. Their powerful American Tobacco Company, founded in 1890, was later broken up by antitrust legislation into Liggett & Myers, P. Lorillard and R.J. Reynolds.

Photo by Rich Weidman

The Horton Grove Slave Quarters can be toured at Historic Stagville, once one of the South's largest working plantations.

Durham's population grew to more than 2,000 by the mid-1870s. Tobacco profits provided the capital for other ventures, including cotton and flour mills, banks, trucking firms and more railroads. Notable enterprises included Erwin Mills, the first mill in the South and one of the nation's largest manufacturers of denim, and Durham Hosiery, the world's largest maker of stockings.

The tobacco that built the city also had a hand in shaping what would be Durham's next major industries: education and medicine. Tobacco magnate James Buchanan Duke thought it would be a good idea to endow Trinity College. With the aid of an $85,000 gift from James' father and land donated from tobacco-textile executive Julian Shakespeare Carr, Trinity College moved to Durham from Randolph County in 1892. In 1924, James B. Duke gave the college $40 million. As you might expect, it was warmly received; the college was promptly renamed Duke University. The Duke University Medical School opened in 1930.

Durham is full of many other success stories. While the Dukes were striking it rich in tobacco, Durham's African-American leaders were also thriving. Beginning around 1905, West Parrish Street turned from an industrial to a commercial district when the black-owned-and-operated North Carolina Mutual

Completed in 1840, the North Carolina State Capitol is considered one of the best-preserved examples of Greek Revival architecture in the United States.

and Provident Association purchased several lots there. After the insurance company prospered and attracted other businesses, the block became known as the "Black Wall Street." The company, now known as North Carolina Mutual Life, remains the largest African-American managed financial institution in the world.

Meanwhile, North Carolina Central University (NCCU), founded in 1910 as a religious training school, went on to become the first state-funded liberal arts college for African-Americans and is now part of the University of North Carolina system.

In 1977, Durham became the first North Carolina city to have its downtown district placed on the National Register of Historic Places. Today, Durham's population is rapidly approaching 200,000 people and Durham County is home to 75 percent of Research Triangle Park. The last tobacco company, Liggett & Myers, closed shop here in the summer of 2000. However, the future looks bright for the downtown area, where old tobacco warehouses are being converted into apartments, offices, specialty shops and restaurants. Downtown Durham is also home to the Durham Bulls Athletic Park. Little did

Dr. Bartlett Durham realize when he opened "Pandora's Box" to the railroads and tobacco merchants, that a muddy, country whistle-stop would evolve into the eclectic "New South" city that it is today.

Raleigh

The city takes its name from the 16th-century English gentleman and explorer, Sir Walter Raleigh. It was Sir Walter, according to romantic lore, who spread his cloak before Queen Elizabeth to spare her feet from stepping in a mud puddle. Unfortunately for Sir Walter, Elizabeth was not around in 1618 to spare his head when James I asked for it. It was also Sir Walter who lost a colony on North Carolina's coast in 1587 and, despite three years at Oxford, had trouble spelling his name, using Rawleyghe in his youth, then Ralegh and sometimes Raleigh. Such a checkered reputation, however, did not deter admiring North Carolinians in 1792 from naming their new capital after him.

The selection of the new capital city's site in Wake County was a political decision. Members of the state's General Assembly were tired of meeting in various cities and were anxious for an "unalterable seat of government." They purchased 1,000 acres of "woodland and old field" from Revolutionary War veteran and state Senator Joel Lane for 1,378 pounds (under $3,000). A planned city was mapped and lots were auctioned to raise money for the new Capitol building. The parcels sold for $60 to $263.

The city in its early years was dependent on the legislature for many of its public works and conduct. The city's commissioners, for instance, were instructed in 1801 to fine merchants who did business on the Sabbath; in 1803, city fathers were empowered to keep hogs from running at large; in 1820, they were given authority to establish a fire department; and in 1825, they were urged to keep infectious diseases from spreading. Members of today's General Assembly continue the tradition of giving advice to Raleigh and its residents. In turn, Raleigh residents are fond of the saying, "The legislature is in session; let us pray."

The city grew and shrank in spurts during the years before the Civil War. The first railroad puffed into town in 1840—the same year that the State Capitol was completed—and the city's population doubled during the decade, totaling 4,518 by 1850. Not surprisingly, its commerce centered around state government and one of its largest private businesses was based on the state's printing contract and book binding. The best beds in town for travelers were at the Yarborough House, sometimes called the legislature's "third house" because of the off-hours business conducted there. The city had adopted the slogan "City of Oaks" and it was under such a tree on North Street that Whig presidential candidate Henry Clay wrote the "Raleigh letter" opposing the annexation of Texas. The North Carolina State Fair opened in October 1853 to capacity crowds, a tradition that hasn't diminished since.

The Civil War left its mark on Raleigh as it did other Southern capitals. It was in Raleigh that "the scourge of the South," General William Tecumseh Sherman, was quartered with 60,000 restless Union troops when news of President Lincoln's assassination arrived. Luckily, the city escaped any vengeful wrath, thanks to Sherman's rein on his soldiers, but his good deed failed to improve his reputation among Raleigh residents. Indeed, the story persists to this day that Sherman's brief occupation of the governor's mansion so tainted the place that no respectable North Carolina governor would set foot in it. The empty house finally burned and in its place today stands the city's graceful Memorial Auditorium, home of the North Carolina Symphony.

By 1910, Raleigh's population was 19,218 and it had become a flourishing academic center as well as the seat of government. St. Mary's School for Girls, begun in 1842, had been joined by two of the nation's first colleges for blacks, St. Augustine's Normal School and Collegiate Institute (1867) and Shaw University (1875), as well as by Peace College for women (1872). The Baptist Female Seminary, which is today's Meredith College, was founded in 1889, the same year as the North Carolina College of Agriculture and Mechanical Arts, now the renowned North Carolina State University (whose current enrollment is approximately 28,000).

The city turned on electric street lights in 1885 and at least 1,900 people were gossiping over the telephone by 1910. A count of manufacturers the same year produced a list of six cotton mills and 33 other manufacturing operations.

Suburbia came early to Raleigh with the pre-World War I subdividing of the Boylan Plantation into Boylan Heights and the promotion of Cameron Park as a place to enjoy quiet country pleasures in the shadow of city lights. Both are considered downtown neighborhoods today.

In 1925, the state decided to sell its Raleigh fairgrounds and asked the newly formed Raleigh Board of Realtors to auction the property. The fairgrounds growth required a move farther west of the city. The state,

INSIDERS' TIP

The location of the state's capital was finally decided at Isaac Hunter's Tavern after a full evening of drinking by the committee of legislators assigned the task. Some things never change.

however, restricted the sales. For example, if you bought a lot on Hillsborough Street, you agreed to build a suitably grand home on the property—one that cost at least $7,500! The farther away from Hillsborough Street, the less demanding the restrictions. On Brooks Avenue, you could get by with a $5,000 home and east of Chamberlain Street, $2,500. The area is today called Fairmont after the fairgrounds. In its center is the Raleigh Little Theater and park grounds, which include the city's Rose Garden and amphitheater. If you look hard enough, you will see that they sit in what used to be the old fairgrounds racetrack.

By 1930, Raleigh's population reached 37,379, a 10-year increase of more than 50 percent. However, the city's prosperity came to an abrupt halt with the arrival of the Great Depression. Housing starts dwindled and no major commercial building was erected until 1942. Even fancy, new neighborhoods such as Hayes-Barton, named after Sir Walter's English home, did not escape foreclosures. A young real estate agent of the times recalled being offered by a banker friend the chance to live in one of Hayes-Barton's largest, newest homes rent free. He would have to pay only the utilities. The bank had foreclosed on the home, then had second thoughts when the vacant house began to deteriorate. The young real estate agent was sorely tempted until he discovered that the house's heating bill alone was more than his annual salary.

The New Deal brought public housing to town along with public works, among them Halifax Court, Chavis Heights and the Raleigh Little Theater. World War II brought the city a full employment economy and the city has grown ever since. FHA and VA loans financed whole neighborhoods following the war as Raleigh builders such as E.N. Richards and J.W. "Willie" York put up small, but affordable $6,000 homes with four percent mortgage rates. In 1949, York built the region's first shopping center, Cameron Village, about a mile from the downtown business district, which was thought of as a "crazy, wild" venture at the time.

In the 1960s, city government moved to meet new challenges, including the explosive issue of civil rights. Mayor W.G. Enloe used his office in 1963 to encourage better community relations and the shedding of institutional segregation. Amazingly, within a year of Enloe's initiative, most of Jim Crow's noxious feathers had been plucked and the era of separate black and white restaurants, hotels, parks, etc., faded. The city also moved to a city manager form of government as its population grew from 93,931 in 1960 to 122,830 in 1970. A highway Beltline across its northern half gave Raleigh a new profile on road maps and accelerated growth in North Raleigh.

Today, Raleigh's tremendous growth continues in all directions as the population nears 300,000. The city's first major league franchise, the NHL Carolina Hurricanes, calls the new Entertainment and Sports Arena its home, as do the NCSU men's basketball team and the Carolina Cobras arena football squad. The downtown area has also experienced quite a revival lately with attractions such as City Market, Exploris children's museum, the new Museum of Natural Sciences and Museum of History, as well as new restaurants and nightclubs opening up on a regular basis. The downtown Memorial Auditorium is being transformed into the state-of-the-art BTI Center for Performing Arts, scheduled to open in early 2001.

Research Triangle Park

Insiders generally agree that the establishment of a vast research complex midway between the University of North Carolina at Chapel Hill, N.C. State University and Duke University was a good idea. But getting a consensus on just whose idea it was is another matter.

Our research leads us to conclude that the development of the now world-famous Research Triangle Park grew from the dreams of more than one creative individual. There was the late Dr. Howard W. Odom, founder in 1924 of UNC's Institute for Research in Social Science; he envisioned an academic

Photo by Rich Weidman

Burroughs Wellcome (now known as Glaxo SmithKline) opened its unique honeycomb-shaped facility at Research Triangle Park in 1970.

center for research in the social sciences and human relations. Beginning in 1952, Odom wrote a series of proposals for the establishment of research institutes that would involve programs affiliated with the consolidated University of North Carolina.

About the same time that Odom was envisioning an academic center, Greensboro builder Romeo H. Guest was dreaming of ways to attract research and industrial development to the area. It was Guest who in 1953 coined the name "Research Triangle" to describe the triangular-shaped area lying among the state's three major research universities.

Guest was concerned that the influx of northern industries was slowing down. As a graduate of MIT in Cambridge, Massachusetts, he was familiar with the now famous research and industrial complex growing up along Boston's Route 128. Guest believed that the development of similar research facilities here would eventually spawn new industrial growth.

In 1955, Guest talked with Governor Luther H. Hodges about the idea. The Governor went for it and the rest is history. By the spring of that year, Hodges appointed a committee composed of prominent bankers, business executives, industrialists and university heavyweights. The committee eventually established a nonprofit organization known

today as the Research Triangle Foundation. The Foundation was entrusted with the task of acquiring land and finding appropriate tenants for the park. Its first executive director was Dr. George L. Simpson, a UNC sociology professor and former colleague of Dr. Odom. Plans were soon made that forged the dreams of both Odom and Guest: there would be a vast research-industrial complex, including a separate Research Triangle Institute to be owned by the three universities.

By 1958, the Research Triangle Foundation had raised enough money to begin purchasing and developing the land that would soon be known as Research Triangle Park. The following year, the Chemstrand Corporation purchased a 100-acre site to build the Park's first research campus.

Things moved along slowly but steadily after that, with about one or two new tenants added each year until 1965 when both the National Institute of Environmental Health Sciences and IBM Corporation announced plans to construct major facilities here.

IBM put Research Triangle Park on the map. The number of organizations located here has grown from 10 in 1965 to 137. The number of RTP employees has grown dramatically as well, from 8,000 employees in 1970 to 17,500 in 1980 to 32,500 in 1990 to more than 43,000 today.

Getting Around

As the Triangle continues to grow to accommodate thousands of new residents each year, getting around has become more and more of a challenge. Fortunately, getting to and from the Triangle has never been easier. By plane, the Raleigh-Durham International Airport (known as RDU), one of the nation's fastest-growing airports, offers approximately 600 daily arrivals and departures. By train, Amtrak provides service from Cary, Durham and Raleigh. By automobile, the Triangle is conveniently located near I-40, I-85 and I-95. In addition, rental cars are readily available at the airport and you can also take advantage of the Triangle's growing regional and municipal bus service.

Gone are the days when traffic jams were limited to the State Fair in October. Weekday traffic in the heart of the Triangle can sometimes be a true nightmare. However, relief is on the way. Although the $1.2-billion, six-lane Outer Loop expressway is scheduled for completion around 2025, a section has already opened from I-40 to Leesville Road in North Raleigh. In addition, plans are in the works for a $350 million commuter rail system between Raleigh and Durham to begin service around 2005.

The following chapter provides you with in-depth information on the RDU airport, rental car agencies, private air charters, ground transportation and rail service. For additional information and a free state map, contact the North Carolina Department of Transportation, 733-2520, P.O. Box 25201, Raleigh, NC 27611.

As you take to the highway, bring along a good road map and don't hesitate to stop and ask for directions. Before no time, you'll be buzzing around like a native (or sitting in a traffic jam if you're caught near Research Triangle Park during rush hour).

Air Transportation

Raleigh-Durham International Airport

Located off Interstate 40 (Exit 284-B or Exit 285) between Raleigh and Durham and accessible from I-540 and U.S. 70, the Raleigh-Durham International Airport (RDU) is only a 20- to 30-minute drive from most points in the Triangle. We'd offer a word of caution, though. It helps to allow extra time, since traffic delays on I-40 can sometimes lengthen your trip en route to RDU, especially during morning and afternoon rush hour. You also need to plan on a few extra minutes to park and ride to your terminal when you are leaving your vehicle for an extended trip.

When the airport opened in what was an old Army barracks in 1943, its location was considered in the middle of nowhere. It remained out in the boondocks for the next couple of decades. But those days are now a distant memory. RDU has grown dramatically from its beginnings, with much of the growth coming in the last 20 years. In 1982, the airport added the $9.6 million Terminal A. In 1986, another $2.5 million was spent expanding the terminal's passenger waiting areas, gate space and aircraft parking, as well as building a new 10,000-foot runway. The $60 million Terminal C opened in 1987, after American Airlines made RDU one of its major north-south connecting hubs (American closed its hub operations in 1995). An $18 million expansion of Terminal A has been completed that contains new aircraft gates for Continental and AirTran. Across the street from Terminal

A, construction was completed on a $40 million, 2,700-space parking garage in the spring of 2000. In addition, construction began on a $75 million, 6,150-space parking garage between Terminal A and C in early 2000. The number of parking spaces available at RDU will ultimately reach 16,000. The airport has nearly completed Phase I of a $10 million, five-year program to overhaul its general aviation facilities. In early 2000, RDU embarked on a $500 million expansion to Terminal A, doubling the number of boarding gates over the next seven to 10 years.

Some benefits for air travelers have emerged from the changes. The average price of a ticket has declined, due to more competition among the airlines for RDU's business. Passenger traffic continues to increase and that growth is expected to continue. Today, RDU International is served by more airlines than at any time in its history, offering service to both domestic and international destinations. In fact, approximately 8.9 million passengers passed through the airport's gates to their business and pleasure destinations in 1999, up nearly 24 percent from 1998. According to *Airlines International* magazine, RDU is the fifth fastest growing airport in North America.

Thanks to this continuing growth and expansion of the airport, you can take your pick of a variety of flights—many nonstops to most major U.S. metropolitan areas, including Atlanta, Baltimore, Boston, Chicago, Cincinnati, Dallas-Ft. Worth, Kansas City, Miami, Minneapolis/St. Paul, New Orleans, Newark, New York City, Orlando, Philadelphia, San Jose, St. Louis and Washington D.C. Direct flights are also available to some international destinations, including the Bahamas, London, Ottawa and Toronto.

RDU's leading carrier, Midway, moved its headquarters from the Chicago area to Raleigh-Durham in 1995. Midway Airlines is Raleigh-Durham's hometown airline and now serves more than 20 major cities along the East Coast. Low-fare carrier Southwest, the country's fourth-largest airline, began flights out of RDU in 1999. United and USAirways have announced merger plans, which should take effect in early 2001.

Overlooking RDU's 10,000-foot runway, Observation Park offers a free picnic and play area. Visitors to the park can also hear direct communication from the control tower to pilots. It's a perfect spot to take the kids on a Sunday afternoon. The park is open daily from 7 AM to dusk.

Photo courtesy of Raleigh-Durham International Airport

Raleigh-Durham International Airport, which provides approximately 600 flights daily, is the fifth fastest growing airport in North America.

LOCAL WISDOM

Baseball–**The Durham Bulls**

Pizza–**Lilly's**

Airline–**Midway**

...t traveling ought to be...
Take the Train!

*T*reat yourself to a trip worth remembering. Climb aboard, sit back and relax. Whether enjoying a weekend away or visiting friends or family, the train is the way to go.

The Piedmont and Carolinian provide convenient daily service to twelve North Carolina cities with easy connections to Florida and the Northeast.

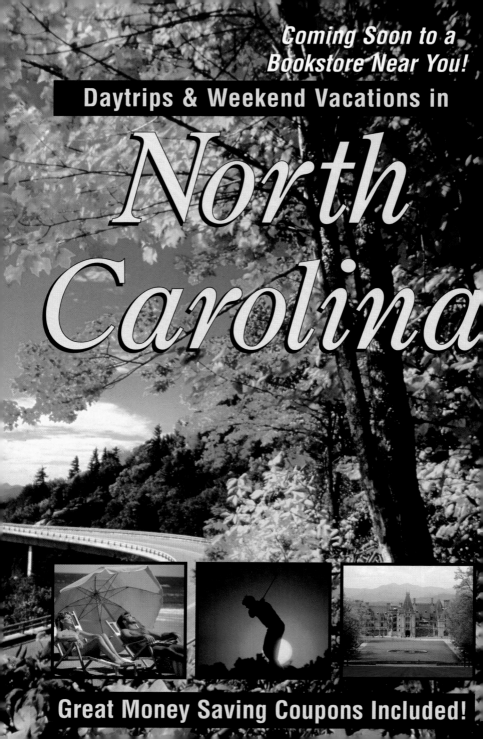

Coming Soon to a
Bookstore Near You!

Daytrips & Weekend Vacations in

North
Carolina

Great Money Saving Coupons Included!

Airport Parking

All lots charge $1 per hour with varying daily maximums, including $18 for hourly lots and $6 for daily lots. Park and Ride lots 1 and 2, which are located closer to the terminals, cost $4 per day. The overflow and Park and Ride 3 and 4 lots are $3 a day. Payment by cash, credit card or traveler's check is accepted. Allow at least an hour to park before your flight.

Airport Transportation

Bus service from the airport to major cities of the Triangle is available from Triangle Transit Authority (TTA) Monday through Friday. In addition, there are rental cars, taxis and limousine services. The airport limousine services (usually a van) will charge about $22.50 per person to get you to downtown Raleigh, Chapel Hill or Carrboro. That's cheaper than local taxis that will charge $25 to $30 for the same trip. But if you are sharing a ride to one location with one or more riders, you'll probably do better in a cab, since cabs charge by the trip and add only moderate surcharges for additional passengers. RDU is served by a number of cab companies and shuttle services to the cities of the Triangle. The major rental car companies also offer pick-up at the airport. Check with the airport information desk or in the Yellow Pages for cab companies offering service to and from RDU and for rental car information. Many hotels and motels offer free shuttle service to and from the airport, so check with them when you make your reservations.

General Aviation Services

North State Air Service, Inc.
• **(800) 831-8208**

North State provides air charter, air courier, aerial photography and scheduled weekend services to the Outer Banks.

AIRPORT INFORMATION

RDU Airport Information (www.rdu.com)	840-2123
Airport Parking Information	840-2110
Airlines	
Air Canada (www.aircanada.ca)	(888) 247-2262
AirTran (www.airtran.com)	(800) 247-8726
American Airlines (www.aa.com)	(800) 433-7300
Canadian Regional (www.cdnair.ca)	(800) 426-7000
Continental Airlines (www.continental.com)	(800) 525-0280
Delta Air Lines (www.delta.com)	(800) 221-1212
Delta Express (www.delta.com)	(800) 325-5205
Midway Airlines (www.midwayair.com)	(800) 446-4392
Midwest Express (www.midwestexpress.com)	(800) 452-2022
Northwest Airlines (www.nwa.com)	(800) 225-2525
Southwest Airlines (www.southwest.com)	(800) 435-9792
TWA (www.twa.com)	(800) 221-2000
United Airlines (www.ual.com)	(800) 241-6522
USAirways (www.usairways.com)	(800) 428-4322
Airlines (Commuter)	
American Eagle (www.aa.com)	(800) 433-7300
Continental Express (www.continental.com)	(800) 525-0280
Corporate Airlines (www.midwayair.com)	(800) 555-6565
Delta Connection (www.delta.com)	(800) 221-1212
United Express (www.ual.com)	(800) 241-6522
USAirways Express (www.usairways.com)	(800) 428-4322

Piedmont Charters
• 840-2700, (800) 807-4616

Piedmont offers air charter services from Raleigh-Durham International Airport using a variety of aircraft, from piston twins to intercontinental jets. Services are available 24 hours a day.

Southern Jet
• 840-4400

Southern Jet offers air charters, aerial photography, sight-seeing flights, aircraft service and flight training.

Horace Williams Airport

The Horace Williams Airport, just north of downtown Chapel Hill, started out as a grass landing strip in the 1920s. The airport was constructed by the Navy just before World War II. Owned by the University of North Carolina, it has a 4,000-foot paved and lighted runway. Pilots can give five signals on the 123.0 radio frequency to raise the intensity of the lights for landing. 100 octane, low-lead fuel and jet fuel are available. Hours of operation are 8 AM to 9 PM Monday through Friday and 9 AM to 9 PM Saturday and Sunday. For more information on the airport, call 962-1337.

Ground Transportation

Bus Service

Greyhound Bus Lines
Durham • 687-4800
Raleigh • 834-8275

Triangle Transit Authority
• 549-9999 • www.ridetta.org

Regional Service

Triangle Transit Authority is a growing transportation catalyst that expedites service among and within the area's municipal bus systems. Approximately 2,370 passengers a day take advantage of TTA's regional bus service, which offers a comfortable commute

at a reasonable rate. Bus fares run $1 to $2. Monthly passes are available, as well as special rates for seniors and the handicapped. TTA also offers evening and Saturday service via its hub in Research Triangle Park (near the intersection of Davis Drive and N.C. 54) to Chapel Hill, Durham and Raleigh. During the evenings, hourly service runs until 11:45 PM and on Saturdays buses run between 6:45 AM and 6:45 PM. TTA also provides fixed shuttle service between Raleigh-Durham International Airport and the RTP hub every half hour during peak times and every hour during other times.

Plans are in the works for TTA to expand service to RTP from South Cary, Apex and North Raleigh along Interstate 540, as well as routes from Raleigh to Garner and Durham to Hillsborough. TTA is also planning to start a $350 million, 16-stop commuter rail system between Raleigh and Durham to begin service around the year 2005. For TTA information, call 549-9999.

Chapel Hill

Chapel Hill Transit provides bus and shared-ride service throughout Chapel Hill. Buses run regularly from as early as 6:30 AM to as late as 11 PM on busy weekday routes, with less frequent service on weekends. Buses also run less often when the university is not in session. The fare is 75 cents. Annual and semiannual passes are available. Call 968-2769 for route and schedule information. The Triangle Transit Authority runs weekdays year round from 6 AM to 7 PM between UNC and Chapel Hill to Durham and Duke University. The fare is $1. The Chapel Hill Trolley does not run on a regular basis but may be rented out for weddings and other events.

TRIANGLE RENTAL CAR AGENCIES

Alamo Rent A Car (www.alamo.com)	800-327-9633
Raleigh-Durham International Airport	840-0132
Avis Rent A Car (www.avis.com)	800-331-1212
Raleigh-Durham International Airport	840-4750
Budget Car and Truck Rental (www.drivebudget.com)	800-527-0700
Raleigh-Durham International Airport	840-4775
Dollar Rent A Car (www.dollar.com)	800-800-4000
Raleigh-Durham International Airport	840-4850
Enterprise Rent-A-Car (www.enterprise.com)	800-325-8007
1859 N. Harrison Ave., Cary	677-1266
100 Ephesus Church Rd., Chapel Hill	967-5128
2603 Chapel Hill Blvd., Durham	493-2683
5105 Capital Blvd., Raleigh	790-1900
Hertz (www.hertz.com)	800-654-3131
Raleigh-Durham International Airport	840-4875
National Car Rental (www.nationalcar.com)	800-227-7368
Raleigh-Durham International Airport	840-4350
Thrifty Car Rental (www.thrifty.com)	800-367-2277
Raleigh-Durham International Airport	840-0583
2804 Durham Chapel Hill Blvd., Durham	688-1147
103 Lee Ct., Clayton	359-1716
Triangle Rent-A-Car (www.trianglerentacar.com)	800-643-7368
Raleigh-Durham International Airport	832-9381

Photo by Tim Johnson

Amtrak's Piedmont and Carolinian trains make daily stops at the Cary Depot.

In some areas where buses do not run, residents can call Chapel Hill Transit at 968-2772 and request a ride to the nearest bus stop for the price of the regular bus fare. This service, called "shared-ride feeder service," is available in a number of areas in town. A special "E-Z Rider" service is provided for people who are unable to use regular bus service because of handicaps.

Chapel Hill Transit offers a bus service called the "Tar Heel Express" during every UNC home basketball and football game, as well as most concerts at the Dean Smith Center. Call 968-2769 for more information.

Durham

Durham is served by DATA (Durham Area Transit Authority), an intracity bus system that transports approximately 3 million passengers annually. The fare is 75 cents. Schedules are available at many locations, including municipal offices and public libraries. Call 683-DATA (3282) for route, rate and schedule information.

A special bus service, Duke University Transit, is operated Monday through Friday between Duke's East, Central and West campuses. Call 684-2218.

Raleigh

Raleigh's municipal bus system serves the city and some outlying areas such as Cary and Garner in peak hours and goes by the acronym of CAT (Capital Area Transit). The system doesn't make change, so have the exact fare of 75 cents. The buses are safe, clean and rarely crowded. There can be a long wait between rides and the routes are limited. Once a year, the system is jammed during State Fair week when every vehicle that rolls is used to ferry people to and from the Fairgrounds. CAT travel is a bargain and you escape the traffic jams. For CAT information, call 828-SCAT (7228).

Narrated trolley tours of downtown Raleigh are available every Saturday (except in January and February) from noon to 3:45 PM (the last trolley departs at 3 PM). Call 834-4844 for more information. The trolley also operates a downtown route on weekend evenings.

Trains

Amtrak
320 W. Cabarrus St., Raleigh
• 833-7594
211 N. Academy St., Cary (not staffed)
400 W. Chapel Hill St., Durham
• 956-7932
Information • (800) 872-7245
• www.amtrak.com

Amtrak offers a full schedule from its depot in Raleigh. Of special interest to many Triangle business people is the Carolinian—a daily train that runs between Charlotte and Raleigh. It then travels on to New York with stops in Virginia, Washington, D.C., and Philadelphia. The Piedmont departs daily from Raleigh, Cary and Durham to Greensboro, Charlotte and some cities in between.

Navigating Your Way Through the Triangle

Inside the Beltline, the Inner Beltline, the Outer Beltline, the Outer Loop, I-40, I-440, I-540. What does it all mean? Newcomers to the Triangle may be confused by the terms used to describe the roads they are traveling in the area. Let's start with Inside the Beltline. The Beltline, also known as I-440, encompasses downtown Raleigh and the surrounding vicinity within 1 mile of the State Capitol to the south and 3 miles to the north. This geographic area encircled by The Beltline (I-440) is known as "Inside the Beltline."

This area is rich in history, containing the aforementioned State Capitol (circa 1840), the beautiful Governor's Mansion (built between 1883 and 1891), Historic Oakwood (established in the mid to late 19th century), the State Legislative Building, City Market (1914), the State Farmers Market, several colleges, and many other renovated buildings and homes. Many native Raleighites also live Inside the Beltline, as have generations of their families. Occasionally, you may hear a native refer to Inside the Beltline as "Old Raleigh." To the north, however, and still "inside the beltline" are many new subdivisions and shopping plazas. This is sometimes referred to as "New Raleigh."

The Beltline (I-440 that encircles downtown Raleigh and its environs) is divided into the Inner Beltline and the Outer Beltline. This can be confusing, especially when trying to figure out which way to go when you want to get on the Beltline as you're traveling 60 miles an hour with traffic surrounding you. Just keep in mind—on the Inner Beltline, cars travel in a clockwise motion; on the Outer Beltline, cars travel in a counterclockwise motion.

The Outer Loop (also known as I-540) is relatively new and only partially completed. When it is finished, sometime around 2025, it will encompass almost all of the Wake County towns of Raleigh, Cary, Morrisville, Apex and Garner. The completed portion currently extends from I-40, by RDU International Airport, northeast to Leesville Road in North Raleigh. I-40 extends from Wilmington at the coast and blends with I-440 south-

Photo courtesy of N.C. Dept. of Transportation

I-40 and the Durham Freeway

east of downtown Raleigh. It winds west through Cary, becoming I-40 once again when it passes over U.S. 1 (also known as U.S. 64). I-40 then continues west to the North Carolina-Tennessee border.

So, now you should be able to navigate some of the highways and byways of the Triangle; but just to be on the safe side, it might be a good idea to keep a map handy.

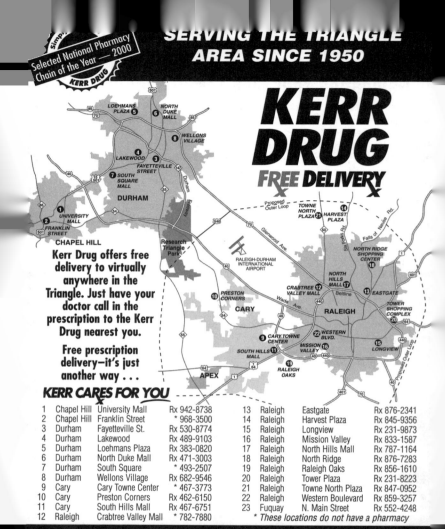

Triangle Overview

When you fly into Raleigh-Durham International Airport (RDU to frequent flyers), you see a seamless, green, rolling landscape. But when you land, you'll find some very distinct cities and places. You're in an area soaked in politics; then again, you're in one of the country's top medical research centers; and you're also in the shady calm of the oldest public university in the country. They, and much more, are here, a mixed, myriad menu of people, places and pastimes. Why has the Triangle grown so popular for relocating families? First of all, people are drawn here by the low unemployment rate and the proximity to Research Triangle Park, Centennial Campus and three major universities: University of North Carolina at Chapel Hill, Duke University in Durham and North Carolina State University in Raleigh. Other drawing cards include world-class healthcare facilities and top-notch school systems.

In addition, the Triangle has become known for its burgeoning arts community—from Broadway shows to regional theater to nationally renowned art museums to local art galleries. Each city holds at least one major arts festival annually: Lazy Daze in Cary, Apple Chill in Chapel Hill, Centerfest in Durham and Artsplosure in Raleigh. Other exciting events include the 10-day North Carolina State Fair, American Dance Festival, North Carolina International Jazz Festival, Summerfest at Regency Park, July 4th Festival for the Eno and Labor Day Weekend Pops in the Park.

Recreational opportunities also abound in the region. Popular parks and recreation areas include Eno River State Park in Durham, Falls Lake north of Raleigh, Jordan Lake in Chatham County, Lake Crabtree in Morrisville and Lake Wheeler in Raleigh. In addition, all of the major cities have their own parks and recreation departments, providing acres of park land and a wide variety of activities for all ages. Golfers will also find a variety of semiprivate and public courses here.

College basketball, minor league baseball and stock car racing have always been popular diversions in the Triangle. However, new spectator sports here include the Carolina Cobras of the Arena Football League and the Carolina Hurricanes of the National Hockey League.

Another benefit is the Triangle's convenient location about halfway between the mountains and the coast, offering numerous opportunities for weekend getaways. See the "Daytrips and Weekend Vacations" chapter for suggestions.

Speaking of regional benefits, let's not forget Eastern-style barbecue, the ACC Tournament, the Durham Bulls and the Carolina Mudcats, City Market, N.C. Museum of Art, Duke Chapel, Raleigh's downtown museums, Entertainment and Sports Arena, Morehead Planetarium, Duke Homestead, Walnut Creek, Memorial Auditorium, Hemlock Bluffs, N.C. State Capitol, Brightleaf Square, Pullen Park, Cameron Village, Carolina Theatre, Franklin Street and Duke Forest.

This chapter provides an overview of the four major cities in the Triangle: Cary, Chapel Hill, Durham and Raleigh, as well as Research Triangle Park, followed by profiles of 18 surrounding towns.

Cary

Cary is one of the nation's fastest growing cities. Its population rose from 1,500 in 1950 to 7,640 in 1970 to 43,858 in 1990. Today, the population is nearly 100,000. And through the use of Planned Unit Developments (PUDs), the city has become a model for good living that keeps people coming despite the current political mood to slow down the pace. With an abundance of educational and recreational opportunities, as well as the lowest crime rate of the state's 10 largest cities, Cary has solidified its reputation as a great place to raise a family.

Today, Cary shows off one planned community after another, many of them with their own golf courses, swimming pools, tennis courts and greenways. MacGregor Downs subdivision led the way in the 1960s, followed by such planned unit developments as Kildaire Farms, Lochmere and Preston, the Triangle's largest golf course community with more than 20 neighborhoods.

The Town Council in the 1970s deliberately sought to increase its nonresidential tax base with businesses and industry. The policy has been stunningly successful. With beautiful research and business parks such as Weston, Regency Park and SAS Institute's serene, rolling campus, the city's job base makes the home-to-work drive a short commute for many Cary residents. Major Cary employers include SAS, one of the country's premier software developers, MCI WorldCom, American Airlines' Reservation Center and Austin Quality Foods. Many of the nation's big-name employers also have offices here: IBM, Union Carbide and Lucent Technologies, to name a few. Cotton Incorporated recently moved its world headquarters to Weston Park.

The town of Cary is governed by the Cary Town Council. Although the town is currently in a slow-growth phase, there's still plenty of action in Cary. A variety of new businesses and restaurants continue to open and prosper.

New public school construction is on the top of Cary's agenda. Green Hope High School opened in 1999, followed by Green Hope, Salem and Yates Mill elementary schools in 2000. Plans for additional schools are in the works, including Middle Creek High School, which is scheduled to open in the fall of 2001 at the intersection of Optimist Farm and West Lake roads. Cary Academy, a private school founded by the leaders of SAS, opened in 1997, and St. Michael the Archangel Catholic School made its debut on Tryon Road in the summer of 2000. Wake Tech Community College recently opened a Business and Industry Center in a new business park on Tryon Road.

Healthcare options in Cary also have increased to meet the growing demand. Western Wake Medical Center, an 80-bed community hospital located off Kildaire Farm Road, is the site of the Women's Pavilion and Birthplace, Cary's only obstetrical center, and the state-of-the-art Wake Radiology Center. Rex Healthcare's 62,000-square-foot health and wellness center is located off Cary Parkway.

Cary's downtown includes a main street drugstore, a railroad station, specialty shops, historic buildings and churches, a post office, a public library, one of the oldest elementary schools in the state and a modern Town Hall complex. Amtrak's Piedmont and Carolinian trains both make daily stops at the Cary Depot, which doubles as a driver's license bureau. Ashworth Village Center, located on the corner of Chatham and Academy streets, contains a variety of unique shops and two popular restaurants: Serendipity Gourmet-Deli and Vespa Italian restaurant. West on Chatham Street lie two small shopping complexes: Olde Cary Commons, home to Assaggio Italian restaurant, and the new Chocolate Smiles Village. Cary Parkway shows off some of the city's prime residential real estate and its shopping centers, such as Cary Towne Center and Crossroads Plaza, rival Raleigh's malls and discount power centers in retail revenue. The new Centrum Shopping Center recently opened across from Crossroads with a discount grocery store warehouse, specialty stores and chain restaurants.

Photo by Rich Weidman

Downtown Cary offers an old-fashioned drugstore, specialty shops, restaurants, a post office, a public library and a train depot.

Currently, Cary has more than a dozen city parks, including the 310-acre Fred G. Bond Metro Park, which is the largest municipal park in Wake County, and the 150-acre Hemlock Bluffs Nature Preserve, which features a grove of Canadian hemlocks. Cary's expanding network of greenway trails now extends more than 12 miles. The Cary YMCA, located off Cary Parkway, has proven extremely popular with the fitness crowd. The Cary Community Center on North Academy Street offers classes and special events for all ages. A Kids Together Playground is located at Wellington Park, near the corner of Tryon Road and Cary Parkway.

For the artistically inclined, Jordan Hall Arts Center offers visual and performing arts classes. The Page-Walker Arts and History Center, built in 1868 as a hotel to serve train passengers, contains a fine arts gallery that displays the works of local and regional artists, and sponsors a Starlight Concert series each summer. It also houses the Cary Heritage Museum, which displays a variety of interesting exhibits that trace the town's history.

Downtown Cary is the site of the annual Lazy Daze Arts and Crafts Festival that takes place on the last Saturday in August, featuring approximately 400 craftspeople and artisans from all over the region. Other popular events include the Cary Road Race and Spring Daze Arts and Crafts Festival in April, Summerfest at Regency Park in June and July, the Jimmy V Celebrity Golf Classic at Prestonwood Country Club in August and Cary Band Day in November. The Cary Downtown Farmers Market takes place on Tuesday afternoons and Saturday mornings from April through November.

There's also plenty of activity with Cary's award-winning high school band, high school sports teams (it's a wrestling powerhouse with 10 state championships) and some of the finest golf courses in the Triangle.

It's not brag but fact when Cary leaders declare: Cary, it's a great place to live.

For More Information

Cary Chamber of Commerce
307 N. Academy St., Cary, NC 27519
800-919-CARY or 467-1016
www.carychamber.com

Chapel Hill

With a diverse population of students, professors, business people and retirees, Chapel Hill is not your ordinary small Southern town. First of all, there is nothing ordinary about the people who live here: there are more Ph.D.'s per capita living in Chapel Hill than just about any other place on the planet.

Secondly, it's not all that Southern. Believe it or not, a higher percentage of the population here reads *The New Yorker* magazine than in the Big Apple. That's not to say that everyone who lives here comes from New York; they come from everywhere, many of them to study or teach at the University of North Carolina, to work in the Research Triangle Park or to retire in the hospitable climate.

Come to think of it, Chapel Hill is not really very small as North Carolina towns go. While the vibrant downtown still feels like a village, the town's population and borders have expanded considerably. Today, there are about 45,000 residents, with another 24,600 or so students when the university is in session.

Finally, although Chapel Hill is geographically situated in the conservative Bible Belt, it has long been considered an oasis for liberals and one of the most tolerant communities in the state. Perhaps that's why our notoriously conservative U.S. Senator Jesse Helms is said to have once suggested that instead of wasting tax dollars on a state zoo, we simply build a fence around Chapel Hill.

So it is that the "Southern part of heaven" has grown into a most unusual and appealing community. Chapel Hill is the home of UNC-CH—the oldest state university in the nation, which first opened its doors in 1795. In fact, in most parts of North Carolina, the words Chapel Hill and UNC-CH are synonymous and, therefore, used interchangeably. For instance, if you sit at a lunch counter in any small town around the state and loudly express your fondness for the politics of Ralph Nader, someone will undoubtedly raise an eyebrow and observe that you "must have

University of North Carolina at Chapel Hill's most famous landmark, the Old Well, once provided the only source of water for students.

gone to Chapel Hill." That doesn't mean they think you went shopping here; it means they are assuming you must have picked up your liberal views while attending the University of North Carolina in Chapel Hill. State and county elections are held every even year, with city and school board elections every odd year. Primaries are held in May. The mayors of Chapel Hill and Carrboro are elected for two-year terms; the council members of each town, members of the Chapel Hill-Carrboro school board and County Commissioners hold four-year overlapping terms. Members of the Orange County school board in Hillsborough are elected to six-year overlapping terms. Chapel Hill is governed by the Chapel Hill Town Council.

Bustling, downtown Chapel Hill still has a "village" feel even though a boom in residential construction over the last two decades has brought many new citizens to the community. Development has recently begun on the massive 435-acre Meadowmont community, which is located off N.C. 54 in eastern Chapel Hill. The interest in Chapel Hill can be linked to several factors. First, it offers the charm of small-town life with the sophistication of a university community tied to a booming metropolis. Second, it is accessible to a number of desirable jobs nearby in Research Triangle Park. Finally, Interstate 40 puts Chapel Hill within convenient commuting distances to Raleigh.

Residents of Chapel Hill, like their counterparts in the other cities of the Triangle, worry that runaway development will destroy what is unique about their community. These folks may have a reputation for tolerance, but one thing they will not accept is unsightly development, hence some rather restrictive zoning laws. Today, citizens and elected officials are continuing to work together to ensure the preservation of those qualities that make their towns such attractive places to live and work.

Chapel Hill offers a wide variety of attractions, most centered around UNC-CH, such as Ackland Art Museum, Coker Arboretum, Morehead Planetarium and North Carolina Botanical Garden. All visitors and new residents should take UNC-CH's half-hour "Walkman" tour of the historic campus to view the Old Well, Old East (UNC-CH's first building, constructed in 1793), the Forest Theatre and the 172-foot-tall Morehead-Patterson Bell Tower, among other sights. Of course, die-hard sports fans will want to take a peek at Kenan Football Stadium and the Dean E. Smith Center—known throughout the Triangle as "The Dean Dome"—which the Tar Heel men's basketball team calls home. (As the new Chapel Hill motto states, "You'll Be A Fan for Life.")

Chapel Hill also boasts a thriving night life scene along Franklin Street, mostly directed at the college crowd. Legendary establishments include Bub O'Malley's, The Cave, He's Not Here, Linda's, Local 506, North Carolina Original Sports Bar and Zog's. Popular Chapel Hill festivals are the Apple Chill and Arts Downtown in April, the Family Fourth of July Festival at UNC-CH's Kenan Stadium, La Fiesta del Pueblo in September and Festifall in October.

For More Information

**Chapel Hill-Carrboro
Chamber of Commerce**
104 S. Estes Dr.
Chapel Hill, NC 27514 • 967-7075
www.chapelhillcarrboro.org

**Chapel Hill-Orange County
Visitors Bureau**
501 W. Franklin St., Ste. 104
Chapel Hill, NC 27516 • 968-2060
www.chocvb.org

INSIDERS' TIP

Normally (not during rush hours), it takes about 10 minutes to drive from Chapel Hill to Durham, 35 minutes from Chapel Hill to Raleigh and 25 minutes from Durham to Raleigh.

Durham

Durham offers something for everyone: excellent cultural and recreational opportunities, world-renowned healthcare facilities, superb educational institutions, award-winning restaurants, a Triple-A baseball team and a prime location near Research Triangle Park.

With the influx of new businesses and industries have come changes in the nature of Durham's work force. Tobacco and textiles were once the leading industries. Not so today, as the top employers include Duke University and its Medical Center, as well as some of the large research facilities in and around Research Triangle Park. Liggett Group, the last remaining manufacturer of cigarettes in Durham, moved its operations to the nearby town of Mebane in 2000.

So it is that tobacco warehouses and cotton mills downtown have been converted into chic shops, restaurants, condominiums and office spaces. Downtown attractions—such as Brightleaf Square, a cluster of former tobacco warehouses that has been converted into trendy shops, galleries and restaurants; the Royall Center for the Arts; the 10,000-seat, state-of-the-art Durham Bulls Athletic Park (DBAP); and the $9 million, 46,000-square-foot YMCA—are steadily helping to bring businesses back downtown. Concerts, plays and movies can all be viewed at the restored 1926 Carolina Theatre.

New downtown developments have already been constructed or are in the planning stages. The $9.6 million Diamond View office building lies adjacent to DBAP. West Village, a $36-million complex of offices, apartments, specialty shops and restaurants, is being constructed within walking distance of Brightleaf Square. The immense American Tobacco Complex across the street from DBAP also has been the focus of revitalization efforts. A $200 million plan is in the works to transform the vacant buildings into offices, shops, restaurants and a hotel. Built in 1937, the old downtown Durham Armory may be converted into a dinner theater.

Another major project underway in southern Durham is The Streets at Southpoint, a huge regional mall that will encompass 1.3-million square feet at the intersection of Fayetteville Road and I-40. The mall will contain five anchor department stores, about 120 specialty shops, five restaurants and an 18-screen movie theater when it opens its doors in spring 2002.

Durham residents are never lacking for something fun to do, especially with the Durham Bulls Athletic Park and Duke University at their doorstep. Duke boasts the Neo-Gothic towers of the Duke Chapel; the beautiful Sarah P. Duke Gardens with its dazzling displays of flowers and shrubs; Duke Primate Center, home to more than 250 endangered species of primates; and, of course, Cameron Indoor Stadium where the famous Blue Devil basketball team plays its home games. Other popular Durham attractions include the Museum of Life and Science with its Magic Wings Butterfly House; Bennett Place, site of the largest troop surrender of the Civil War; Duke Homestead, the restored home of tobacco magnate Washington Duke; and Historic Stagville, a cluster of several 18th- and 19th-century plantation buildings

Photo by David Haring, courtesy of Durham Convention & Visitors Bureau

The Duke Primate Center is home to more than 250 endangered primates.

Photo courtesy of N.C. Division of Tourism

The Gothic towers of Duke Chapel rise majestically over West Campus.

that once made up one of the South's largest working plantations.

Durham is also home to a diverse and thriving arts community. The Royall Center for the Arts contains the Durham Arts Council Building, which is home to the Durham Art Guild, one of only five continuously operating guilds in the United States. The Duke University Museum of Art has a unique collection that includes African, Pre-Columbian, Classical, Medieval and Renaissance, Old Masters, Russian, contemporary, American and European painting, sculpture and decorative arts. The Hayti Heritage Center on Old Fayetteville Street displays African-American works and artifacts.

Eclectic annual events abound in the Bull City. Durham is the site of the world-renowned American Dance Festival and the Centerfest celebration, an immensely popular two-day street festival in September. Other popular events include North Carolina Jazz Festival, DoubleTake Documentary Film Festival, Greater Durham International Festival, Bimbe Cultural Arts Festival, Edible Arts Festival, American Dance Festival, July 4th Festival for the Eno and Bull Durham Blues Festival, among others.

Outdoor enthusiasts will find a variety of recreational activities to keep them busy.

Three of Durham's most popular parks are Eno River State Park, West Point on the Eno and Lake Michie Recreational Area. The Durham Trails and Greenways Commission has established miles of hiking, jogging and biking trails that snake throughout the county. Public and semiprivate golf courses in Durham County include The Crossings at Grove Park, Duke University Golf Course, Falls Village, Hillandale, Lakeshore, Lake Winds and Willowhaven.

The city of Durham, with a population of about 178,000, is the only municipality in the county (which numbers about 218,000). The city operates on a council-manager form of government with an elected mayor and 12 council members. The county is governed by a five-member board of commissioners and administered by a county manager. A possible consolidation of the city and county governments is currently under review.

State and county elections are held every even year. City elections are held every odd year. Primaries are held in May. The Mayor is elected to a two-year term; city council members to four-year staggered terms. County commissioners hold office for two years at a time. State senators and representatives serve two-year terms. Duke University is Durham's largest private employer and one of the top private colleges and medical research facilities in the nation. Duke's reputation, as well as its proximity to three other universities and Research Triangle Park, helped to eventually establish Durham as an ideal location for high-tech research companies.

For More Information

Greater Durham
Chamber of Commerce
300 W. Morgan St.
Durham, NC 27701 • 682-2133
www.durhamchamber.org

Durham Convention
& Visitors Bureau
101 E. Morgan St.
Durham, NC 27701 • 687-0288
www.Durham-NC.com

Raleigh

Raleigh makes a perfect capital city. It's in the middle of the state. It's connected to a major east-west Interstate freeway, I-40, and it's less than an hour from the East Coast's major north-south roadway, I-95. It's served by an international airport, Raleigh-Durham International. Amtrak stops here. Eastern North Carolina shops here. The North Carolina Symphony and the North Carolina Art Museum play and show here. While North Carolina history wasn't started here, this is where we keep it—in the state's Archives and History Museum. And where we make a lot of it, thanks to the Governor, the General Assembly, Council of State members and the Supreme Court. It's home to more than 283,600 people.

There are some names and phrases that you need to know in your education as an Insider. For example, Beltline is a proper noun here. It is the circumferential highway that splits Raleigh into two real estate markets—Inside the Beltline and the rest of Raleigh. It has other official highway names such as I-440, but most directions you will hear for getting around town will include the word, "Beltline." The new road around North

Raleigh that is under construction is called the Northern Wake Expressway or "Outer Loop." The $1.2-billion, six-lane Expressway is scheduled for completion in 2025 but a portion of the road is already open. When people say they're going to Crabtree, that's not a suburb. It's Raleigh's largest and second-oldest mall. You may also hear the term "old Raleigh," which has to do more with genealogy than geography as in "his family is 'old Raleigh'." The designation North Raleigh (that part of the city north of the Beltline) covers a range of things such as neighborhoods and shopping centers, as well as a state of mind and the intimation that you may have ties north of the Mason Dixon Line. The *N&O* refers to the city's venerable newspaper, *The News and Observer,* just as RDU is the airport and ACC is the Atlantic Coast Conference, whose college sports provide approximately half of all Raleigh conversation topics. The Creek is the popular outdoor amphitheater at Walnut Creek where you can see the Back Street Boys or Jimmy Buffett. When friends offer you barbecue, they mean pork, soaked in distinctive eastern North Carolina vinegar-based sauce, and if you're invited to a 'pig pickin,' go. If you're going to Jones

Raleigh has staked its claim as the political *and* cultural capital of North Carolina.

Photo courtesy of N.C. Division of Tourism

Street, it's a polite way of saying you're going to seek the company of ... legislators at the General Assembly on Jones Street.

For those who are shopping for homes, which were selling in Raleigh and Wake County for an average of $182,380 at the start of 2000, it will be comforting to know that their purchase is likely to appreciate. Consider that the first lots in town sold for $60 to $263; inside the Beltline lots can sell today for more than $150,000. Raleigh's established neighborhoods reflect the city's history as a place of moderate and broad affluence. Real estate, indeed, was one of the strongest segments of the Raleigh economy during the '90s. It is a city of neighborhoods, most of them stuffed with comfortable homes of traditional design. From the air, it looks like a park with a city in it. These verdant neighborhoods reflect the city's history as a place of moderate and broad affluence. Indeed, visitors and newcomers are struck by how one lovely neighborhood simply leads to another.

The demand for houses and nonresidential projects, however, means builders struggle to find skilled craftsmen in all construction sectors. Unemployment in the Triangle repeatedly falls under 2 percent and many shops and restaurants display faded "Help Wanted" signs. It is not uncommon to find people who, having heard about the comfortable living and strong economy, move here without first finding a job. The 1,000-acre Centennial Campus adjacent to North Carolina State University's main campus has lured top-name companies and generated thousands of jobs in the area. A unique technological community that blends public academic and private sector research, Centennial Campus is slated for development over the next 15 years. It will eventually employ more than 25,000 people.

Speaking of NCSU, it's one of the state's and nation's premier research institutions. Founded in 1887 as a land-grant school for agriculture and the mechanical arts, it has evolved into North Carolina's largest school with approximately 28,000 students. NCSU is among the nation's leaders in engineering, textiles, forestry, architecture, wood and paper science, biotechnology and veterinary

medicine. Raleigh is also home to Peace College (founded in 1857), Shaw University (1865), St. Augustine's College (1867) and Meredith College (1891). Wake Tech, the second-largest community college in the state, allows area residents to upgrade skills in fields such as computer programming and nursing. The Wake County Public School System, which serves more than 97,500 students, is the second-largest system in the state and the 27th largest in the nation. The system includes more than 40 magnet schools that draw students from all over the county.

Activities abound throughout Raleigh as the other chapters of this book spell out. Raleigh is a lively city that legitimately claims itself the cultural as well as the political capital of the state. Sparked by a youthful population that includes students from six colleges and universities, Raleigh bubbles with art shows and shops, music and museums, flea markets and the Farmers Market, tournaments and concerts. There is enough music that the city sings all year. There are classical and pops performances at the Symphony and free rock and jazz music downtown in the summer. The North Carolina Theatre is the state's largest musical production company and the City of Raleigh's Best of Broadway Series offers national tours of current hits such as *Les Miserables* and *The Phantom of the Opera*. The North Carolina Museum of Art hosts major exhibitions such as "Monet to Moore," "Festival Rodin" and the upcoming "In Praise of Nature: Ansel Adams and Photographers of the American West." Popular annual festivals include the Artsplosure Spring Jazz and Art Festival in May, the Sunday in the Park concert series from June through September, the July 4th Celebration at the State Fairgrounds, Labor Day Weekend Pops in the Park with the North Carolina Symphony, the 10-day North Carolina State Fair in October and First Night Raleigh on New Year's Eve. The city has earned a reputation as a popular waystation for bands and performers working toward the Big Time. For instance, the Connells and Corrosion of Conformity both have roots in a single Raleigh neighborhood, and country western stars and bluegrass bands enjoy strong followings in Raleigh.

Just over a decade ago, downtown Raleigh's night life was practically nonexistent. However, the restored 1914 City Market in the Moore Square Arts District started a mini-renaissance with the opening of the city's first brewpub, Greenshields, as well as a comedy club, ComedySportz. Popular night clubs—such as Jillian's Billiards Cafe, The Warehouse and Humble Pie—soon started sprouting up in the nearby area of renovated warehouses known as The West End. Today, the hottest new downtown area is "Glenwood South," which offers such lively night spots as RiRa Irish Pub, Southend Brewery and 42nd Street Oyster Bar.

Like big cities that rally around professional teams and players, Raleigh loves its college and amateur sports. Ah, to be in Raleigh when the North Carolina State Wolfpack wins a national basketball championship (twice since 1974) is to rise toward Rapture! In 1987, Raleigh was the center for the Summer Olympic Festival, and in 1999, it hosted the International Special Olympics. The city has opened the new Entertainment and Sports Arena that is home to NCSU's men's basketball team, the National Hockey League Carolina Hurricanes (Raleigh's first major league franchise) and the Arena Football League Carolina Cobras. Other popular spectator sports include the Raleigh Wings professional women's soccer team (which has captured two out of three league championships), the Raleigh Capital Express professional men's soccer team and stock car racing at Wake County Speedway.

Recreational opportunities also abound in the "City of Oaks." For boating, water skiing, windsurfing and fishing, residents flock to Falls Lake to the north or Lake Wheeler to the south. Lake Johnson in southwest Raleigh offers boat rentals and a hiking trail that circles the lake. Umstead Park has nature trails, fishing, rental rowboats and canoes, 19 miles of horseback riding and bicycling trails, campsites and a visitors center. Pullen Park near NCSU is a favorite with kids for its miniature passenger train and celebrated Dentzel Carousel. A 612-acre educational park is being developed around historic Yates Mill, Wake County's only remaining grist mill.

Shoppers will have a field day in Raleigh. For years, the city has served as a regional shopping area for eastern North Carolina. Cameron Village started it all back in 1949 when it opened as the Southeast's first outdoor shopping center. Crabtree Valley Mall, which opened on Glenwood Avenue in 1972, has more than 240 stores, restaurants and services. Triangle Towne Center is a new, 1.2-million-square-foot regional mall being developed at the intersection of Capital Boulevard and Old Wake Forest Road. It is scheduled to open in early 2002.

For political junkies, Raleigh is their fix. It's a rite of spring to watch school children from all over the state parade between the Capitol and the Legislature, observing their elected representatives at work. Tour the 1840 Capitol, which is considered one of the best-preserved examples of Greek Revival architecture in the country. (If you are really tall, you can peek in the windows on the southwest corner of the Capitol and see the Governor at work.) The State Legislative Building was designed in the early 1960s by Edward Durrell Stone, the renowned architect who also planned the John F. Kennedy Center for the Performing Arts in Washington, D.C. Raleigh's government complex also includes its most popular museums, namely the new, 200,000-square-foot Museum of Natural Sciences, the History Museum and the state Archives and Library. The nearby Executive Mansion, completed in 1891, is a prime example of Queen Anne Cottage-style Victorian architecture, also known as gingerbread style. President Franklin D. Roosevelt

INSIDERS' TIP

Visit the North Carolina Division of Tourism, Film and Sports Development at 301 North Wilmington Street, 733-4171, in downtown Raleigh for an official *North Carolina Travel Guide*, area maps and brochures.

Photo courtesy of N.C. Division of Tourism

The 1891 Executive Mansion in downtown Raleigh is considered one of the United States' outstanding examples of Queen Anne Cottage-style architecture.

once referred to it as "the most beautiful governor's residence in America."

Nearby attractions include Raleigh's Exploris, a children's museum of the world that opened in Moore Square in 1999, featuring hands-on exhibits, daily performances and programs for all ages. The Joel Lane House at Hargett and St. Mary's streets was once part of a 1,000-acre plantation known as Wakefield. The house was built by the Revolutionary War veteran and state senator who sold 1,000 acres of "woodland and old field" to the General Assembly, which selected it as the site of the new capital city. Mordecai Historic Park contains a variety of historic structures, including the 1785 Mordecai House, an 1847 plantation chapel and the humble cabin where Andrew Johnson, 17th president of the United States, was born in 1808. Other popular area attractions include the African American Cultural Complex; Historic Oakwood, a 20-block Victorian neighborhood with more than 400 restored homes; the Raleigh City Museum, housed in the 1874 Briggs Building on Fayetteville Street Mall; Raleigh Rose Garden, which boasts

1,200 roses of 60 different varieties; and the Haywood Hall House, a Federal-style dwelling built in 1799 and considered to be the oldest house within Raleigh's original limits. For more information about Raleigh attractions, stop by the Capital Area Visitor Center at 301 North Blount Street.

We could go on ... and on some more, but you get the picture. Raleigh is a city that's not too provincial. Not too sophisticated. Not too busy. Not too slow. Not too hot. Not too cold. Not too big. Not too small. For many, it's just right.

For More Information

Raleigh Chamber of Commerce
800 S. Salisbury St.
Raleigh, NC 27601 • 664-7000
www.raleighchamber.org

Raleigh Convention & Visitors Bureau
421 Fayetteville St. Mall, Ste. 1505
Raleigh, NC 27601 • 834-5900
www.raleighcvb.org

Research Triangle Park

The Research Triangle Park or RTP or simply, The Park, is the engine that drives the Triangle's economy. The Park's founding is one of those select examples of public-private partnership at its best. RTP was established in the 1950s, the result of visionaries and practical politicians. Credit is due a number of people: Dr. Howard Odom, founder of UNC's Institute for Research in Social Science; Romeo H. Guest, a Greensboro builder and developer; and Governor Luther Hodges, the man who made it happen. They all wanted to develop an industrial or business park that would attract good paying research jobs and provide employment for the state's best and brightest students who were leaving home to go elsewhere. RTP, contrary to some notions, is not a government project; it is a private, nonprofit research park—that has good government connections. By 1958, the Research Triangle Foundation was in business buying land. The Research Triangle Institute became The Park's first tenant in 1959.

Today, RTP occupies about 7,000 acres and is the site for some 137 organizations that employ more than 43,000 people. It is estimated that more than 50,000 people will be employed in RTP by the year 2010. The average salary of an RTP employee is more than $55,000. Three fourths of The Park is located in Durham County and one fourth is in Wake County. About 1,300 acres of Park land remains to be developed. Foundation directors no longer have to take their show on the road to trade shows and industry fairs. Companies come to RTP looking for land where they can build research and science-oriented manufacturing facilities. States and countries send delegations to learn how RTP works. The late Executive Director Ned Huffman, for instance, told of one week's worth of visitors that included representatives from Kansas, Texas, Indiana, Germany, Netherlands, Japan and Singapore. If you want to build your facility here, you'll need to stop by the Foundation office at 2 Hanes Drive. You can get more information there—including history brochures and maps.

RTP is located almost in the middle of the triangle formed by Chapel Hill, Durham and Raleigh. Most of the land is in Durham County and it is only five miles from Raleigh-Durham International Airport. Interstate 40 bisects the Park and is the principal commute artery. A drive through the park reveals jogging paths, landscaped sites and glimpses of facilities among the pine trees. There are some architectural standouts, the most famous of which is the Glaxo SmithKline building, which was a film location for the movie, *Brainstorm*. Other show stoppers include the National Humanities Center, the National Institute of Environmental Health Sciences and the fortress-like U.S. Environmental Protection Agency's research center (a new EPA facility is being constructed here at a cost of $272 million).

Until recently, there were few restaurants or gas stations close by so you had to go off campus to fill up. Restaurants, gas stations and shops are prohibited in RTP except in the 100-acre Triangle Service Center, which includes commercial operations such as Radisson Governors Inn, Bank of America, Centura Bank, Wachovia Bank, Triangle Transit Authority and Arty P's Cafe. There are, however, many businesses and shopping centers on the Park's edges and many companies operate their own cafeterias.

But you don't go to the Park for fine dining or Broadway shows. The jobs and the work are the featured attractions here. It was at the former Burroughs Wellcome laboratories in the Park, for instance, that scientists won Nobel Prizes in chemistry. The virtual reality, computer-created, special effects in today's Hollywood movies were spawned here and at UNC-CH. Nortel Networks, the Canadian telecommunication powerhouse, and Sweden's mobile telephone giant,

INSIDERS' TIP

RTP has established a special group, Smart Commute@RTP, to reduce single-passenger auto commuting traffic. To get information or to participate, visit www.rtp.org.

Photo courtesy of Picturesque Photography and Durham Convention & Visitors Bureau

Founded in 1958, Research Triangle Park is home to 137 organizations that employ more than 43,000 people.

Ericsson, work here and in offices close by. The biggest presence is IBM's site where 14,000 full-time employees work in one million square feet of building space. One of the nation's 24 supercomputers lives here at MCNC, and the Supercomputing Center and Foreign Trade Zone No. 93 are also here. Other tenants include such familiar names as BASF (agricultural products), Biogen (biotechnology), Cisco Systems (enterprise networking equipment and software), DuPont Technologies (electronics), EMC Corporation (software), Eisai Inc. (pharmaceuticals), Glaxo SmithKline (pharmaceuticals), National Institute of Environmental Health Sciences (biomedical research), Sphinx (pharmaceuticals), Sumitomo (fiber optic cable) and Verizon (telecommunications products). In addition, the University of North Carolina Center for Public Television, North Carolina's only statewide broadcasting system, maintains its headquarters here. One of the newest tenants is German drugmaker Schwarz Pharma

AG, which recently opened a research and development office here called Schwarz Biosciences. The RTP office will run trials on drugs for Parkinson's disease and epilepsy.

If you're going to live in the Triangle but not work at the Park, take a Sunday drive to inspect the region's namesake. Do not, we repeat, do not go during the morning or evening rush hours on weekdays. It's about 20 minutes from Raleigh, 10 minutes from Durham and 15 minutes from Chapel Hill. Since RTP's payrolls put more than $2.7 billion dollars into the Triangle economy, most residents endure the traffic jams.

For More Information

Research Triangle Foundation
2 Hanes Dr., P.O. Box 12255
RTP, NC 27709 • 549-8181
www.rtp.org

Triangle Towns

When you move to a new neighborhood, you like to know that you have nice neighbors. Well, the Triangle is filled with good neighbors in the smaller towns that make up Orange, Durham and Wake counties as well as those in adjacent counties. These places enjoy a growing popularity among newcomers and with those who like a small-town pace of life—and lower real estate prices!

Companies are locating their facilities there and you might be closer to work living in Wake Forest or Hillsborough than Raleigh or Durham. Some, like Garner, border on Raleigh's southern city limits, while others, such as Smithfield, are farther out. New housing developments and strip shopping centers keep sprouting up along the N.C. 55 corridor, which runs south of Cary to such bustling towns as Apex, Holly Springs, Fuquay-Varina and Angier. East of Raleigh toward I-95 lie Clayton, Smithfield and Selma. Another cluster of developing towns, Knightdale, Wendell and Zebulon, lies off U.S. 64 East. Southern charm can be found in Pittsboro, south of Chapel Hill, and north of Raleigh in such small towns as Franklinton and Louisburg. None of these towns are more than 30 to 45 minutes away from Research Triangle Park. Each has its own identity:

• *Angier* is a bustling little town on the Wake-Harnett County border, known for its beautiful crape myrtles.

• *Apex* grew up around the railroad tracks and its recent growth is a result of its proximity to Cary.

• *Carrboro*, once a mill town and then a bedroom community of Chapel Hill, has quietly transformed into a community of artists and craftspeople.

• *Clayton* is known for its small-town atmosphere and affordable housing.

• *Franklinton* has become popular with Raleigh commuters as a tight-knit community with rural ambience.

• *Fuquay-Varina*, located in southern Wake County, offers a recently renovated downtown historic shopping district on Broad Street and a new park around its famous springs.

• *Garner*, located south of Raleigh and known as the "Most Promising Corner in the Triangle," blends new economic development with a strong sense of history.

• *Hillsborough* offers a colonial past with more than 100 buildings dating from the 1700s, 1800s and early 1900s.

• *Holly Springs* is one of the fastest-growing towns in North Carolina and home to the popular Sunset Ridge golf course development.

• *Knightdale*, a former country crossroads, has grown into a thriving residential community of 5,000 people.

• *Louisburg*, the seat of Franklin County, is home to Louisburg College, the nation's oldest two-year college.

• *Morrisville*, nestled between Research Triangle Park and Cary, continues to develop at a rapid pace.

• *Pittsboro* is known for its restored 1881 county courthouse and its downtown antique shops.

• *Selma*, located in Johnston County, is also known for its antique shops and charming downtown district, as well as the American Music Jubilee variety show at Rudy Theater.

• *Smithfield*, the seat of Johnston County, is one of the 10 oldest towns in the state and home to a number of popular shopping outlet centers.

• *Wake Forest* (one-time home of Wake Forest University) is a college town, home to Southeastern Baptist Theological Seminary.

• *Wendell* grew up with railroads and tobacco, and its downtown is listed in the National Register of Historic Places.

• *Zebulon* is known for Five County Stadium, home to the Carolina Mudcats minor league baseball team.

All of these towns are great places to visit on a weekend drive. Many have quaint downtowns full of antiques, specialty shops and cafes. They offer the pleasant rhythm of small-town living and easy access to the cultural offerings of the larger Triangle cities. The towns are listed alphabetically.

Angier

Population: 3,000
Commute to Raleigh: 20 mi.
Commute to RTP: 18 mi.
Chamber of Commerce: 639-2500
www.angierchamber.org

For years, Angier was a quiet crossroads town; however, over the past decade, new subdivisions and strip shopping centers have sprouted in former tobacco fields. The town's population has risen from 2,235 in 1990 to more than 3,000 today, with another 11,000 people living in the surrounding area. The little farming community has quickly transformed itself into a bedroom community for Raleigh and the Research Triangle Park.

Named for one of its founders, Col. John C. Angier, the town is located off N.C. 55 in Harnett County about 2 miles south of the Wake County line. Town leaders are currently working toward turning the downtown area along Broad Street into a trendy commercial district with restaurants and specialty shops.

The old town depot, built around 1900, has been renovated and is the site of festivals, parties and other town get-togethers. Angier's friendly small-town charm is

Photo by Rich Weidman

Angier's Broad Street has been transformed into a charming commercial district.

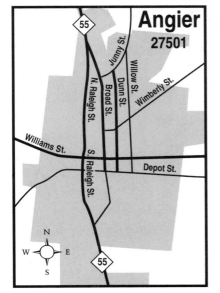

demonstrated at the annual Crape Myrtle Festival in September, featuring arts and crafts, food and live entertainment. Started in 1974, the festival has grown in attendance from 1,500 in the early years to more than 15,000 today. The festival is named for the abundance of beautiful crape myrtles that were planted in the 1930s by the Angier Women's Club. In fact, Angier's slogan is "The Town of Crape Myrtles."

Angier is governed by a Town Council that meets the first Tuesday of every month. Angier students are served by the 24-school Harnett County Public School System. Area schools include Angier Elementary, which serves about 265 students in grades 1 to 5, Harnett Central Middle and Harnett Central High.

The Barnes Paddock Equestrian Center, which lies between Angier and Coats, offers riding lessons for all ages and skill levels, as well as equestrian events throughout the year. It is located on Carson Gregory Road, just south of Angier.

Apex

Population: 21,700
Commute to Raleigh: 12 mi.
Commute to RTP: 10 mi.
Chamber of Commerce: 362-6456
www.apexchamber.com

If recent years are indicators, Apex is definitely poised for continued strong growth. Today, the population stands at approximately 21,700, compared to 4,789 in the 1990 census, and is expected to reach 32,000 by 2004. In fact, over the past decade, Apex has vaulted past Carrboro, Garner, Smithfield and Wake Forest and is currently the Triangle's fifth-largest municipality. The town is growing by approximately 12 new residents a day.

Apex is adjacent to Cary and particularly close to Regency and MacGregor office parks, only minutes from the Raleigh Beltline and a 15-minute commute to RTP. In addition to the "small-town" feel, what has caught the eye of many new homebuyers is Apex's proximity to Jordan Lake on U.S. 64. To find Apex, go south on U.S. 1 or take Old Apex Road (which turns into North Salem Street) coming out of Cary. Located at the crossroads of N.C.

55, U.S. 1 and U.S. 64 and near Interstate 40, Apex offers residents easy access to Cary, Raleigh, Chapel Hill, Durham and Research Triangle Park.

Apex's history is tied to the growth of the railroads, in this case, the Chatham Railroad Company. The rail tracks still run through the city, but they're now the CSX line. The land on which the tracks ran was one of the highest points along the line at 504 feet above sea level, hence the town's name, Apex, and its motto, "The Peak of Good Living." The community was incorporated in 1873.

Locals believe Apex was the obvious choice of *Business North Carolina* when the magazine named it "The Best Small Town in North Carolina" in 1994. Townspeople and those nearby have taken to the ambience evident in Apex's historic downtown. The Town Depot, the downtown centerpiece, has been renovated to reflect its 1914 origins. Now on the National Register of Historic Places, it houses the Apex Chamber of Commerce. During the spring, summer and fall, the Depot is the site of concerts sponsored by the Apex Chamber and Apex Department of Parks, Recreation and Cultural Resources.

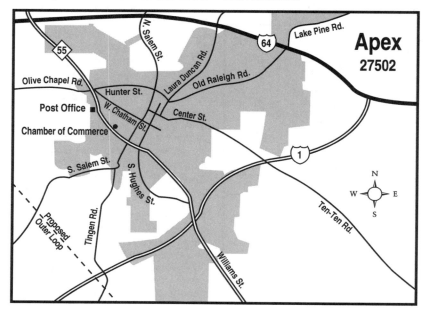

Photo by Rich Weidman

Listed on the National Register of Historic Places, the 1914 Town Depot now houses the Apex Chamber of Commerce.

Neighborhoods have quickly sprouted in Apex over the past few years. Popular developments include Abbington, Walden Woods, Amherst, Holly Glen, Haddon Hall, Greenbrier and Scott's Mill. Apex is also home to the only Mormon Temple in the state. The intersection of U.S. 64 and N.C. 55 north of downtown is turning into a true retail corridor with the introduction of a Home Depot, Lowes Foods and Apex/Cary Auto Mall, and more businesses to follow.

The town's spectacular growth has also increased the demand for public school space. Apex High School is currently one of the largest high schools in the state. A new public high school, Green Hope, opened in fall 1999, followed by Green Hope Elementary in 2000.

Leisure activities are important to Apex residents. Residents approved a $6 million bond referendum to renovate existing parks and build new ones. Located at 23-acre Apex Kelly Road Town Park, KidsTowne is one of the Triangle's newest and largest playgrounds. A new community center is also being developed. The 160-acre Apex Community Park off Laura Duncan Road offers a playground, ballfields, picnic shelters, tennis and basketball courts and a paved walking path around a serene lake. The new 56,000-square-foot Dream Sports Center provides indoor soccer and roller hockey facilities. The Eva Perry Regional Library, which opened in 1996 to serve southwest Wake County, leads the state in circulation with more than 1 million books checked out annually.

Some popular Apex restaurants include House of China and Daniel's on N.C. 55 North. Salem Street is still the center of town with its small retail shops, antique stores, offices and popular eateries such as La Rancherita. The town celebrates an annual downtown festival during the first week of May called "Peak Week." It offers arts and crafts, musical entertainment, food concessions, children's activities, road races, historic home tours and other events. Apex's "Today and Yesteryear Festival," which commemorates the town's history, takes place each September. Other popular town events include the Olde-Fashioned Fourth of July celebration, the Christmas Parade and the Historic Homes Tour in December.

Carrboro

Population: 15,500
Commute to Raleigh: 25 mi.
Commute to RTP: 20 mi.
Chamber of Commerce: 967-7075
www.chapelhillcarrboro.org

Nicknamed the "Paris of the Piedmont," Carrboro has become one of the fastest-growing municipalities in the Triangle and one of the most densely developed communities in the state. One of the reasons for Carrboro's popularity is its convenient proximity to Chapel Hill and the University of North Carolina. Retirees have also discovered the area; in fact, Carrboro was named one of the top five retirement "hotspots" in the nation in a recent *U.S. News & World Report* survey.

The history of Carrboro can be traced to 1882 when a portion of the Durham-Greensboro Southern Railroad was extended here. Incorporated in 1911 as Venable, after UNC President Francis P. Venable, the town was soon renamed after Julian S. Carr (1845-1924), owner of Durham Hosiery Mills. Today, vacant farmland and mill houses are rapidly being replaced by apartments and condominiums. Listed in the National Register of Historic Places, the old cotton mill has been converted into Carr Mill Mall, a quaint shopping mall housing specialty shops and trendy restaurants.

Carrboro has become known throughout the Triangle as a community of artists and craftspeople. The back-to-back galleries, North Carolina Crafts Gallery and North Carolina Arts Gallery, feature a diverse selection of art from craftspeople around the state. Begun as a loft designed for painting classes in 1975, The ArtsCenter on East Main Street has rotating art exhibits and offers classes in the visual, literary and performing arts. In addition, concerts, theater, children's programs and summer day camps take place here. Carr Mill Mall contains a number of art galleries, including the eclectic Animation and Fine Art Galleries. The Carrboro Town Hall also has a gallery that displays the works of local artists. It is open Monday through Friday from 8:30 AM to 5 PM. The popular band, Squirrel Nut Zippers, got its start in Carrboro. The town is also home to the North Carolina Writers' Network, a statewide organization that supports fiction and nonfiction writers and poets.

Photo by Rich Weidman

Once a cluster of textile mills, downtown Carrboro has evolved into a unique artistic community with shops, galleries and eclectic restaurants.

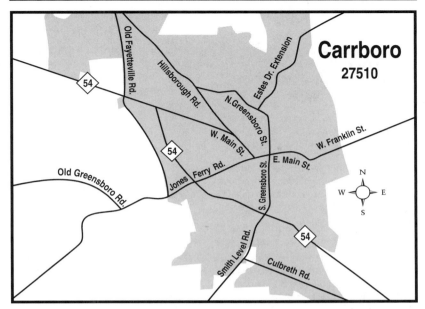

Carrboro has its own Parks and Recreation Department that provides a variety of recreational facilities and activities for all ages. Residents have two nearby choices for fishing and boating: University Lake on South Old Fayetteville Road and Cane Creek Reservoir on Stanford Road. Carrboro also boasts one of the most extensive bikeway systems in the entire state. Stop by the Carrboro Parks and Recreation Department at 301 West Main Street to pick up a copy of *Carrboro Bikeways Map: A Guide for Commuting and Recreational Cyclists.*

One aspect visitors to Carrboro always note about the town is the strong sense of community that still prevails here even with rapid growth in the area. A number of lively festivals take place throughout the year to bring residents together. Carnaval Brasileiro is a Brazilian version of Mardi Gras held in The ArtsCenter each February. Carrboro Day takes place in May, celebrating the town's rich history with arts and crafts, historical exhibits, live music and children's activities. Fete de la Musique is an international celebration of the summer solstice held each June with free musical performances. Practically the whole town turns out for the old-fashioned Fourth of July Celebration. From April through December, Carrboro holds an Arts, Crafts, Antiques and Flea Market at the Town Commons every other week from 1 to 5 PM. The Carrboro Farmer's Market runs from March through December.

A number of popular restaurants have opened up in downtown Carrboro, including ACME Food and Beverage Company, Armadillo Grill, El Chilango, The Spotted Dog Restaurant and Bar, The Trains Cafe and Tyler's Restaurant and Tap Room, among others. In addition, Carr Mill Mall is home to Elmo's Diner, Weaver Street Market Cafe and the new Panzanella Restaurant and Bakery. The Sunday brunch at Weaver Street Market—complete with live jazz—has turned into a community event. Bon's Bar-B-Q in the Carrboro Plaza offers traditional Southern recipes. For night life, the Cat's Cradle on East Main Street features the best of new and local touring bands.

Carrboro students are served by the 14-school Chapel Hill-Carrboro School System, one of the best public school systems in the state and nation. Although Chapel Hill and Carrboro share the same school system, they are separate towns run by two different mayors and town councils.

Clayton

Population: 16,000
Commute to Raleigh: 15 mi.
Commute to RTP: 35 mi.
Chamber of Commerce: 553-6352
www.claytononline.com/ccc

Just a few miles beyond Garner lies Clayton, which was incorporated in 1869. Originally known as Stallings Station, the town changed its name to Clayton after the Civil War in honor of John M. Clayton, a senator from Delaware. To reach Clayton, travel east on U.S. Highway 70. It's convenient to N.C. Highway 42, U.S. 70 and I-40 on the western edge of Johnston County.

A small but growing town with friendly people and affordable housing, Clayton has begun to feel the Triangle's boom in population and economic growth. For Clayton, the growth spurt has taken place over the past five years or so when the town experienced a 50 percent increase in population. In 1996, it was named to *Money* magazine's list of top 50 suburban growth towns. Today, Clayton is one of the fastest growing towns in the county with a population of about 16,000.

Clayton has a quality school system, excellent roads, a low crime rate and a good mix of newcomers and residents whose families have lived in the area for generations. New home communities abound with reasonable prices. The average new home price is $145,150 and home prices list anywhere from the low $90,000s to more than $500,000. No longer is Clayton simply "that little town on the way to the beach." Officials have good reason to use the slogan, "Clayton—the Complete Community."

Commercial and retail growth is on the rise. Winn-Dixie has built a distribution center that contains more than 1 million square feet. Other large employers include Bayer Labs and Caterpillar. The Rockin' Comet Diner on U.S. 70 has become a favorite among locals.

Clayton also boasts a vital downtown where older business buildings are getting a face-lift for use as retail space and offices. The Chamber of Commerce renovated its headquarters in the First Citizens Bank building, which is on the National Register of Historic Places. The vibrant downtown area features antique shops, specialty boutiques, jewelry stores, a coffee shop, restaurants (including the ever-popular Jones Cafe, which

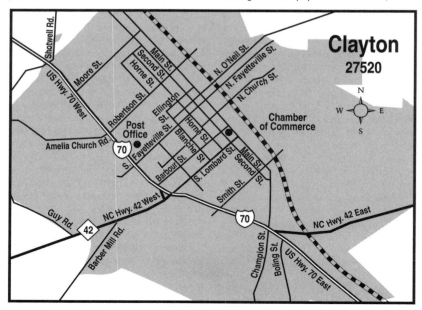

The Clayton News-Star

P. O. Box 157 • Clayton, NC 27520 • 553-7234 • Fax 553-5858

The only newspaper in the world dedicated solely to the Clayton community. Get involved in your community and stay informed. Read the Clayton News-Star.

opened its doors in 1958) and more. Downtown is abuzz with activity. In the long term, many envision old-fashioned street lamps, buried power lines and park benches here.

Clayton has a council-manager form of government that consists of a mayor and five council members. The Clayton Town Council meets at Town Hall on the first and third Monday of the month at 7:30 PM. All meetings are open to the public. Clayton has already outgrown its Town Hall and a new one is in the process of being built. The weekly *Clayton News-Star*, published every Tuesday, keeps locals apprised of developments in this burgeoning town.

Area public schools, which are operated by the Johnston County School System, include West Clayton Elementary, East Clayton Elementary, Cooper Elementary, Clayton Middle and Clayton High. The town's Hocutt-Ellington Memorial Library is located at 100 South Church Street.

Clayton is home to three semiprivate golf courses: The Neuse Golf Course, which is part of the upscale Glen Laurel subdivision; and Pine Hollow Golf Club and Riverwood Golf Club,

both championship courses with Bermuda fairways and bent grass greens.

The annual Steeplechase at Brookhill Farm and Clemmons Educational State Forest are major draws from across the region and the state. The Steeplechase runs each May and offers a purse of $60,000, with proceeds benefitting the Raleigh Jaycees. The race draws approximately 20,000 spectators. The Clemmons Forest on Old U.S. 70 West functions as a living environmental education center with nature and hiking trails (including a "Talking Tree" trail), campsites and picnic facilities. Explore the trails, picnic on the grounds, visit the exhibit center or join an environmental education class. The Clayton Municipal Park on Stallings Street contains a ballfield, basketball court, tennis court, volleyball court, playground and horseshoe pits. Both Front Street Park and Legend Field have basketball courts and playgrounds. Clayton hosts the popular Harvest Festival in September with crafts, live music, an antique car show, carnival rides, a barbecue cookoff, golf tournament, auction, food and rides. A town Christmas Parade takes place during the second Saturday of December.

Franklinton

Population: 4,200
Commute to Raleigh: 25 mi.
Commute to RTP: 35 mi.
Chamber of Commerce: 496-3056
www.franklinconcchamber.com

Located about 25 miles northeast of Raleigh off U.S. 1 in the western part of Franklin County, Franklinton (named for Benjamin Franklin) was built around a cotton mill and rail line during the early 1800s. It was originally known as Franklin Depot. Incorporated in 1842, Franklinton is currently the second-largest town in Franklin County. Growth is definitely making its way to Franklinton. The town is becoming popular with commuters who want to enjoy a small-town ambience. The population has risen from 1,615 in 1990 to 2,126 in 1996 to approximately 4,200 today. Franklin County has a growing mix of housing options, including subdivisions, farm houses, lakefront lots and golf course communities. The average price of a new home is $109,000.

Franklinton has always been known as a tight-knit community. Local residents flock to

Photo by Rich Weidman

Originally known as Franklin Depot, Franklinton grew around a rail line in the 1800s.

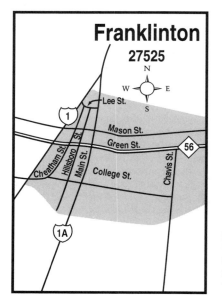

Franklinton
27525

the antique auction downtown Tuesday and Thursday nights. The town's popular Fun in the Sun Festival, which is held each May, draws people from all over the Triangle. Franklinton also hosts an annual Christmas Parade in December.

The town is run by a mayor-council form of government that includes a five-member Board of Commissioners, a mayor and a town administrator. The Town Council meets on the third Thursday of each month at 7 PM. Meetings are open to the public. Over the past few years, Franklinton has completed $1.8 million in water and sewer improvements, constructed a new water plant and added a new shopping center along U.S. 1 with a Food Lion and specialty stores.

Franklinton students are served by the Franklin County Public School System. Two public schools are located in town: Franklinton Elementary and Franklinton High. The town lies just west of Louisburg, home to Louisburg College and the Franklin County campus of Vance-Granville Community College.

A Primer of Triangle Movers and Shakers

Frank Porter Graham. Charles Brantley Aycock. Asa Spaulding. Terry Sanford. Bill Friday. Frank Jr. and Frank III. Mary Duke Biddle Seamans. If you're a long-time Triangle resident and haven't been living in a refrigerator, you will recognize these names. They are names that Triangle citizens know or will need to know at some point in their stay. These names belong to people in all walks of life, some living, some not. Their names, however, live on, and they are important entries in the Triangle's vocabulary. This is not a Who's Who list, but rather a useful primer for newcomers. If you're already an Insider, you, no doubt, may add to the names below, but no subtractions are allowed!

Frank Porter Graham, for example, is deceased but his name is invoked at almost every University of North Carolina function and often appears in any noteworthy political commentary. He was the happy president of UNC in the years before and after WWII, and his race for the U.S. Senate was one of the great watersheds in North Carolina politics. (That race also launched the political career of Jesse Helms, who opposed Graham, and Terry Sanford, who supported him.)

Aycock was elected governor in 1900 and is remembered annually by state Democrats at the Vance-Aycock gathering as the state's father of public education. Asa Spaulding founded one of America's most successful black-owned businesses during the early part of the 20th century, and his name lives on in several of Durham's current leaders. Sanford was a war hero paratrooper, governor, Duke University president, U.S. Senator and a good guy. Bill Friday is not a detective; he is the respected and wise builder of today's unified University of North Carolina System. And Frank Jr. is Frank Daniels Jr., former publisher of The News & Observer and grandson of Josephus, who founded the paper. Which should explain Frank III. Okay, you got a clue on Mary Duke Biddle Seamans. She is a Triangle philanthropist, former Durham City Councillor and the only Duke living in town.

Photo by Tinka Deal, courtesy of UNC-TV

William Friday

Here are some other need-to-know names: J.W. and Smedes York are father and son who have long records in Raleigh business and politics. J.W. shaped Raleigh's future after WWII, and Smedes, a former mayor, airport authority chairman, chamber chairman, etc., continues J.W.'s tradition. The Kenans, as in Kenan Transport, are known for UNC's Kenan Institute and the many endowed Kenan Chairs across the country. The late Frank Kenan of Durham was one of the state's most generous benefactors. John Motley Morehead was the famed chemist whose largess lingers in the coveted Morehead Scholarships and UNC's Morehead Planetarium. Similarly, NCSU alums like to remember the late John Caldwell, the Yazoo, Mississippi, transplant who transformed the university into a premier research university and for whom the Caldwell Scholarships are named.

Jim Goodnight is founder of Cary's SAS Institute and Cary Academy and, by the way, the richest man in the state ($8 billion). Don't confuse him with Jim Goodmon, head of Capital Broadcasting (WRAL-TV and radio) among other businesses, and one of the Triangle's Fletcher family who run the Fletcher Foundation. Dan Blue, who was the first African-American House Speaker, practices law and politics in Raleigh. Jeannette Hyde, that's Ambassador Hyde to you, is the "fundraising fairy godmother" to Democratic politicians. Clarence Lightner, Raleigh's first African-American mayor, is a name to note as is attorney Mickey Michaux in Durham, a veteran House member.

At some point, you will be asked, "Did you see Powell this morning?" That's Dwane Powell, the N&O's wickedly accurate cartoonist. Similarly, you will be asked if you've read Crowther, as in Hal Crowther, the unarmed but dangerous commentator for the weekly Independent.

There are some names that even people outside the Triangle recognize, so we don't include them. You know—Jim Hunt, Jesse Helms, Dean Smith, Billy Graham and Michael (that's Jordan, of course).

Fuquay-Varina

Population: 8,150
Commute to Raleigh: 17 mi.
Commute to RTP: 20 mi.
Chamber of Commerce: 552-4947
www.fuquay-varina.com

Fuquay-Varina is a southern Wake County town of 8,150, located on U.S. 401 about 17 miles from Raleigh's Beltline. It not only has a double name, but two main streets since the town grew up as two communities— Fuquay Springs and Varina, after the pen name of the postmaster's wife.

The area was long famous for its mineral springs, discovered in 1858, and developed in the earlier part of the 20th century as a tourist destination and health spa. The town was first incorporated in 1909 as Fuquay Springs. The two communities joined names in 1963.

City leaders believe that Fuquay-Varina's future is linked to the growth of Research Triangle Park and the town boasts of its proximity to Raleigh and Research Triangle Park. The town's hospitality impressed the likes of such large employers as Guilford Fibers. Other businesses that have found homes here

are Berk-Tek, a maker of fiber optics; Bob Barker Company, which specializes in institutional supplies; John Deere, a producer of commercial equipment for residential and golf course use; Johnson Concrete; Raychem, a manufacturer of telecommunications cable accessories; Betts Tackle, distributor of fishing lures; In-Serv, industrial contractors; and Tomsed Corporation, a manufacturer of turnstiles. The town has a 50-50 split between residential and commercial/industrial growth.

There is a comfortable feel about Fuquay-Varina. Local folks gather along South Main Street, which has several restaurants, a busy drug store, a hardware store and the historic Ben-Wiley Hotel, which is under renovation to celebrate Fuquay-Varina's past. Restaurants, boutiques, specialty shops and offices are rapidly opening their doors in the newly renovated Broad Street historic shopping district. Other new projects under development include the 275,000-square-foot Main Street Market, which will include the town's first Wal-Mart, and Club 1, Wake County's largest private recreation and sports facility.

Subdivisions such as Crofts at Brackenridge, Crooked Creek Country Club, Marcom Place, Northwyck, Sandy Springs and the Village of Sippihaw lure homeowners from all over, from the chill of northern latitudes and from the bustle of Raleigh. Residential properties range from starter homes at $90,000 to a golf community house at $600,000. Occasionally, homes are available in the Jones-Johnson-Ballentine Historic District.

People find a relaxed pace in places like Nil's Bakery Cafe, Hyphen Coffeehouse and The Gold Leaf Tea Room, a popular lunch spot located on Main Street. The local newspaper, *The Fuquay-Varina Independent,* keeps track of town events such as the Tournament of Bands and the Heritage Festival in October, the Annual Draw Down for Autos in the spring, the Celebration of the Outdoors in May and the annual Christmas Parade and Christmas Tree Lighting. Fuquay-Varina is also home to the last working tobacco warehouse in the area and the region's largest Latino flea market.

For the outdoor enthusiast, 20-acre Carroll Howard Johnson Environmental Education Park offers a variety of nature programs. Fuquay Springs Park opened in the spring of 2000 around the fabled springs. Golfers have a choice of four local courses: Crooked Creek County Club, Devil's Ridge Country Club, Bentwinds Country Club and Hidden Valley Country Club.

Photo by Rich Weidman

A variety of businesses is sprouting up in Fuquay-Varina's newly renovated Broad Street historic shopping district.

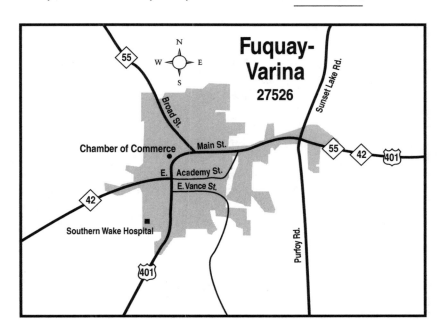

Garner

Population: 20,000
Commute to Raleigh: Adjacent
Commute to RTP: 12 mi
Town of Garner: 772-4688
Chamber of Commerce: 772-6440
www.garnerchamber.com

The town billed as the "Most Promising Corner In The Triangle," was founded in 1883 as "Garner's Station" and rechartered in 1905 as Garner (named for town's founder H.C. Garner).

Garner is located immediately south of Raleigh and shares some of its southern city limits with Raleigh at the fork of U.S. 401 South and U.S. 70. Garner currently has a population of more than 20,000. For years it was a stopping point for eastern North Carolinians who were drawn to jobs in Raleigh, but wanted to live in a smaller town. Today, Garner is home to many families from other states.

Perhaps because of its proximity to Raleigh, Garner has diversified as shopping, entertainment and employment opportunities grow at a rapid pace. The town's largest shopping center, the 475,000-square-foot Garner Towne Square, is anchored by a Kroger grocery store and also includes a 10-screen United Artists Theater.

The completion of the southern link of the Raleigh Beltline and the extension of Interstate 40 helped spur Garner's growth. The I-40/U.S. 70 Interchange has become a prime industrial location, known as Greenfield Industrial Park, which is an 850-acre business and office park. Perstorp Flooring Inc.'s $20 million North American Headquarters and Manufacturing Plant is located here. Just north along I-40 is the $28 million plant of Goodmark Foods, maker of Slim Jims.

Garner business and town officials have forged a favorable business climate, underscored by their lapel buttons saying "Garner is a Great Place to do Business." Officials have identified a goal of a 60 percent residential to 40 percent nonresidential tax base, which is being realized due largely to the boom in commercial development of manufacturing and distribution firms in the industrial corridor.

Through a unique public-private partnership, Olde School Commons, formerly Garner Elementary School, has become a 45-unit residential apartment building for senior

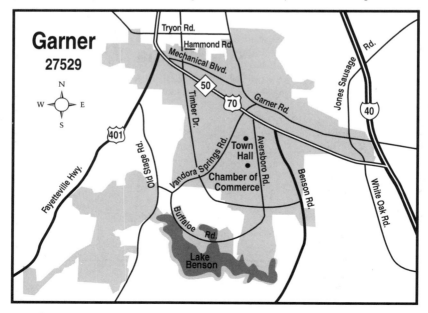

SELMA, NORTH CAROLINA

AMERICAN MUSIC JUBILEE

"An Evening of Southern Hospitality, Great American Music & Side-Splitting Comedy."

Musical Variety Shows January thru November
Southern Christmas Show Thanksgiving thru Christmas

The American Music Jubilee, Rudy Theatre, Selma, NC
From Raleigh take I-40 East to 70 East-Exit 306 through Clayton to
Exit 334-Benson/Wilson to Selma-Hwy 301 North. Turn left on 301 North,
turn right on Oak Street, go to the corner of Oak and Raiford Streets.

Shows weekly—for Show Schedule, Ticket Information or Reservations
call Toll Free 877-843-7839 or 919-202-9927
www.amjubilee.com

Garner Is A Great Place To Do Business

GARNER ★

Discover The Most Promising Corner In The Triangle.

Mary Lou Rand
Town Manager
Town of Garner
P.O. Box 446 • Garner, NC 27529
(919) 772-4688 • Fax (919) 662-8874
email: mlrand@ci.garner.nc.us

Dale M. Bouldin
President
Garner Chamber of Commerce
401 Circle Drive, Garner, NC 27529
(919) 772-6440 • Fax (919) 772-6443
www.garnerchamber.com

Garner ranks second in Wake County and fifteenth statewide on work force, business climate, infrastructure and quality of life, according to Business North Carolina magazine's rating of the state's 50 largest cities in its "Best Cities for Business" issue, 2/98.

citizens in the heart of town. The old auditorium is maintained by the town and used for community events organized by the Garner Arts Association. Olde School Commons, the 19th-century Banks House and the restored Garner Depot constitute portions of the Garner Historic District, which is listed on the National Register of Historic Places.

Part of the Wake County School System, Garner is a "Community Involved In Its Schools." Community leadership through the Garner Educational Foundation has resulted in one of the strongest high school science programs in North Carolina. Timber Drive is a new year-round elementary school. The town proudly rallies around its high school academics as well as its sports programs. Friday night football is a town ritual.

As commercial development spreads south along U.S. 401 and U.S. 70, residential growth is increasing in prestigious areas, such as Arbor Greene, Avery Park, Heather Springs, Heather Woods, Lee's Plantation, Landings at Lakemoor, Kenwood Meadows, Kenland Trails, Turner Farms, South Meadow, Hampton Ridge, Highland Ridge and Holland Farms. The 18-hole River Ridge Golf Community lies along Auburn-Knightdale Road. Eagle Ridge is the largest residential development in Garner. Timber Drive, Garner's garden parkway, also provides greater accessibility to the town's growing neighborhoods.

Popular area restaurants include Stephenson's Barbecue, Gypsy's Shiny Diner and Toot-n-Tell, a country-cooking eatery that has been packing customers in since 1946. The North Carolina Symphony holds an annual Fourth of July concert at Lake Benson Park, Garner's largest park, complete with an impressive fireworks display. The Historic Garner Festival celebrates the town's heritage with arts and crafts, food and live music.

Townspeople say their family-oriented tradition has met and mingled with new ideas and technology. That harmony and diversity has drawn thousands to Garner.

Hillsborough

Population: 5,200
Commute to Chapel Hill: 12 mi.
Commute to Durham: 15 mi.
Commute to RTP: 22 mi.
Chamber of Commerce: 732-8156
www.hillsboroughchamber.com

Founded in 1754, Hillsborough was the site of both the Regulator tax revolt and the most successful Tory raid on Colonial forces during the Revolutionary War. The town functioned as the Colonial Capital of North Carolina and then as the Capital during the Revolutionary Period. Several royal governors and elected governors lived here as did William Hooper, a signer of the Declaration of Independence. The War of the Regulation ended here in 1771. Hillsborough hosted the Third Provincial Congress in 1775 and the state's Constitutional Convention of 1778, which demanded the inclusion of a Bill of Rights in the U.S. Constitution. It is also said to have been the starting point of Daniel Boone's journey west to Kentucky. The town was laid out by the Earl of Granville, William Churton, near a village once inhabited by the Occaneechi Indians.

Today, residents find a pleasing mixture of modern conveniences and rural ambience. Despite the phenomenal growth taking place all around it, this bustling county seat has retained much of its historic charm. In fact, *Outside* magazine recently named Hillsborough as one of the top three places in North America to raise a family. Buildings of Colonial, Antebellum, Victorian and other architectural styles dot the landscape with gardens that enhance the town's visual history. Wood-frame homes dating back hundreds of years line the town's narrow streets. More than 100 buildings date to the 1700s, 1800s or early 1900s. More than a dozen are found in the National Register of Historic Places and one, the Nash-Hooper House, is a National Historic Landmark. The downtown area has been designated a National Historic District.

Antique stores, small shops and a 19th-century courthouse frame the central business district, with nearby bed and breakfast inns such as the 1759 Colonial Inn, Hillsborough House Inn and The Inn at Teardrop. Hillsborough is the self-proclaimed "Antique Capital of North Carolina." Dozens of antique shops are found in town—both downtown and in the Daniel Boone Village antique mall, a few blocks south. LU-E-G's Sandwich Shop is a

Photo by Rich Weidman

Built in 1821, Hillsborough's historic Burwell School served as the site of the Rev. and Mrs. Burwell's School for Young Ladies from 1837 to 1857.

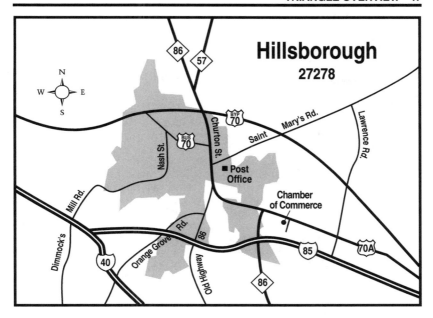

casual downtown gathering place with delicious sandwiches and baked goods. The Triangle SportsPlex on U.S. 70-A East in the Meadowlands business park offers a fitness center, ice skating and indoor swimming pools. The annual Hog Day festival in June draws folks from all over to eat barbecue, listen to music and buy local crafts. Other popular events include the annual Christmas Candlelight Tour of the historic district and the Spring Cultural Festival and Pow Wow. Art galleries reflect a burgeoning artist community. Novelists Lee Smith and Allan Gurganus make Hillsborough their home.

In addition to antique shopping and strolling through the historic district, Hillsborough has a number of attractions to make for an enjoyable daytrip. Visit the reconstructed 17th-century Occaneechi Indian Village that lies downtown on the banks of the Eno River. Take a hike to the top of the 860-foot summit of Occoneechee Mountain, now a State Natural Area, which provides a spectacular view of Hillsborough and the surrounding countryside. Tour the Orange County Historical Museum, housed in the Confederate Memorial Building, which contains a variety of unique exhibits, including Occaneechi Indian

artifacts and Civil War items such as the battle flag of the Orange Guard. Don't miss the late-18th-century Alexander Dickson House, which served as the headquarters for Confederate generals Joseph E. Johnston and Wade Hampton in April 1865 and is now home to the Orange County Visitors Center; the 1815 Ayr Mount plantation house; the circa 1821 Burwell School; the 1845 Old Orange County Courthouse; and Montrose Gardens.

Students in Hillsborough and surrounding northern Orange County are served by the Orange County Public School System, which contains seven elementary schools, two middle schools and Orange High School, home of the Panthers.

Hillsborough is about a 15-minute drive north of Chapel Hill, along N.C. 86, and 20 minutes from Durham via I-40 or I-85. While Hillsborough has managed to preserve its small-town character, it is perhaps more receptive to growth today than ever before. This former rural outpost is only about a 20-minute commute to the heart of the Triangle via I-40. A new water reservoir is in the planning stages. Many developers are already busy transforming Hillsborough into the next suburban frontier.

Holly Springs

Population: 9,000
Commute to Raleigh: 13 mi.
Commute to RTP: 15 mi.
Chamber of Commerce: 567-1796
www.hollyspringschamber.org

Before the Civil War, Holly Springs was a promising little town on one of the main roads to Raleigh. The Chatham Railroad changed that when the tracks were laid north of Holly Springs through Apex and Cary and the town was incorporated in 1876. The town was named for the abundance of holly trees growing near a spring in the area. Holly Springs, which encompasses a little more than six square miles in size, is now one of the hottest residential communities in Wake County as its population continues to skyrocket—from 900 in 1992 to 3,000 in 1996 to more than 9,000 today. The population is expected to reach 20,450 by the year 2010.

The formula is simple: small-town atmosphere, better utility and road systems, and reasonably priced homes, all within driving distance of RTP and Raleigh. Holly Springs is part of the corridor of growth extending along N.C. 55 from Cary down to Angier in Harnett County. The challenge for town leaders is to find a way to encourage growth while preserving the town's rural charm.

The Holly Springs Methodist Church and the First Baptist Church (founded by freed slaves) are two of the oldest churches in town. The town had a general store, a liquor store, two turpentine distilleries and four flour and grist mills during its early years. In keeping with the need to retain the "small-town" feel, plans are in the works to turn a 38-room mansion that was built in the 1840s into a museum.

Today, the town has its own Chamber of Commerce, a weekly newspaper, *The Holly Springs Sun,* and one of the most popular golf course communities in Wake County, Sunset Ridge, home to Devils Ridge Golf Club, one of the best semiprivate courses in the area. The largest employer in town is yarn manufacturer Warp Technologies with 150 workers. Much of Holly Springs' work force is found in service-oriented businesses. Other major employers in the Holly Springs area include Holly Springs Elementary School, the Town of Holly Springs, Food Lion and Holland Grill Company.

Town leaders are striving to maintain the town's traditional Southern image by developing building

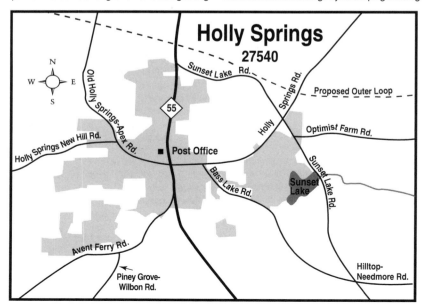

Photo by Rich Weidman

Holly Springs is home to the massive Sunset Ridge residential development, which contains the 18-hole Devils Ridge Golf Club.

and landscaping guidelines. The town's new slogan is "Where Tradition and Vision Meet," replacing the old slogan, "Unity for Growth." Revitalization of the downtown area, including plans for shops, offices, an amphitheatre, bicycle paths and walkways is a part of the town's plan for growth. Holly Springs' newest park will incorporate the freshwater springs that gave the community its name.

Holly Springs is located southwest of Raleigh on N.C. 55 between U.S. Highways 1, 64 and 401. Harris Lake County Park and Jordan Lake, located nearby, provide water activities, including boating, fishing and swimming, and the town's parks have baseball fields, basketball courts and tennis courts. A new 46-acre recreational park is being built with ballfields, tennis courts, playgrounds and hiking trails.

Holly Springs offers a wide range of housing options, from as low as $90,000 to as high as $750,000. The average home sales price is about $167,000. The single-family neighborhood of Somerset Farms offers homes from $130,000 to more than $170,000, and custom homes in Arbor Creek start at $120,000. Homes at Braxton Village are priced from $110,000 to the $160,000s, at Holly Glen from $150,000 to the mid $200,000s, and at Sunset Ridge from $160,000 to more than $700,000.

The town uses a council-manager form of government with a mayor and five commissioners. The board meets on the first and third Thursdays of each month at 7 PM at Town Hall, which is located on Main Street. Holly Springs' students attend schools in the Wake County Public School System, the second-largest system in the state with 120 schools and more than 97,500 students. The town is home to one public school: Holly Springs Elementary at 401 Holly Springs Road. Middle and high school students attend Apex schools. A new middle school is in the planning stages and a charter high school is also coming to town.

Annual events include the Holly Days Parade and the Labor Day Festival. The Holly Days Parade is held on the second Saturday in December. Live entertainment and the traditional lighting of the Town Christmas Tree follow the parade. The Labor Day Festival offers beach music, carnival rides, food and a fireworks display. In May, the Chamber hosts a Superball Golf Tournament at Devils Ridge Golf Club.

Knightdale

Population: 5,000
Commute to Raleigh: 6 mi.
Commute to RTP: 20 mi.
Chamber of Commerce: 266-4603
www.knightdalechamber.com

The history of the community dates back to 1701 when the Tuscarora Indians inhabited the Knightdale-Marks Creek area. The development of the downtown area began in 1907 when Henry Haywood Knight donated land for a depot for the newly completed Norfolk and Southern Railroad, and in 1927 the town of Knightdale was incorporated. In 1989, the town moved a caboose to the downtown area and constructed a park to commemorate the town's heritage.

Since then, Knightdale has experienced a great deal of growth, from one bank and little else to a thriving community, complete with three elementary schools, a public library, national retail stores and eateries. The 22,000-square-foot Wake County East Regional Library opened here recently, and Wake Tech Community College is planning to locate a campus nearby.

Photo by Rich Weidman

A restored caboose in downtown Knightdale serves as a constant reminder of the town's railroad heritage.

About 6 miles east of Raleigh on U.S. Highway 64, the town of Knightdale is evolving from a rural farming community into one of the fastest growing communities in the Triangle. In fact, its population more than tripled between 1983 and 1994. Today, Knightdale is the seventh-fastest growing town in North Carolina. The town is close to Raleigh and RTP, has one of the lowest tax rates in the Triangle, boasts a low crime rate and offers quality housing at reasonable prices. The town has also developed a comprehensive program to improve its park and recreational programs. Residents enjoy the Eugene F. Harper Memorial Park, which contains a playground and basketball and tennis courts.

The average price of a new house in Knightdale is $125,000. Construction continues apace on hundreds of single-family and multifamily homes. Major developments include Mingo Creek, Ashley Hills, Planters Walk, Parkside, Emerald Pointe and Carrington Woods.

Residents flock to Knightdale Seafood and Barbecue restaurant, a converted gas station that offers traditional chopped barbecue and fried catfish, as well as such exotic cuisine as bear, alligator and rattlesnake on Tuesday "Sportsman's Night."

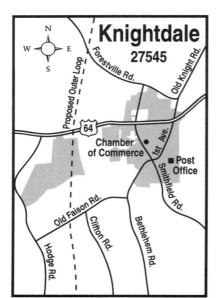

Louisburg

Population: 4,500
Commute to Raleigh: 45 mi.
Commute to RTP: 55 mi.
Chamber of Commerce: 496-3056
www.franklinconcchamber.com

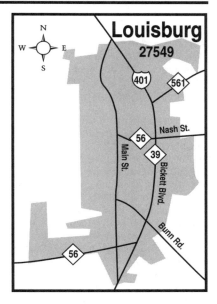

Founded as the Franklin County seat in 1779, Louisburg was named for France's King Louis XVI. The town, which is located along the Tar River, contains a number of quaint Greek revival and Victorian houses along its shady avenues as well as Louisburg College, the nation's oldest two-year college, which was chartered in 1789. Louisburg College offers an annual concert series and presents plays using local talent. The Franklin County campus of the Vance-Granville Community College is also located here. In addition, Louisburg is home to the 85-bed Franklin Regional Medical Center, an acute care medical surgical hospital.

The town hosts two popular annual events: the Tar River Festival at River Bend Park and the International Whistler's Convention, held on the campus of Louisburg College. The popular Murphy House restaurant, which opened in 1951, is famous for its authentic North Carolina pork barbecue.

Located in the geographical center of the county, Louisburg is governed by a mayor and six-member Town Council with a Town Administrator that oversees general government operations. The average price of a new home is $109,000. Students are served by the Franklin County Public School System. Local schools include Laurel Mill Elementary, Louisburg Elementary, Terrell Lane Middle and Louisburg High.

Named for France's King Louis XVI, Louisburg serves as the seat of Franklin County.

Morrisville

Population: 3,644
Commute to Raleigh: 8 mi.
Commute to RTP: Adjacent borders
Chamber of Commerce: 380-9026
www.morrisvillenc.com

History records show that Governor Tryon's army camped "at Jones on Crabtree Creek" on May 7, 1771, on the way to fight the Regulators in Hillsborough. Nathanial and Tingnall Jones were landowners and plantation operators where the town of Morrisville is now situated. In 1852, Jeremiah Morris, then a landowner, gave the railroad a right-of-way and three acres of land for a "water station, woodshed and other buildings and a yard." For his generosity, the railroad named the town Morrisville.

Morrisville, another "railroad" town that began as a depot on what is now the Norfolk Southern Railroad, lies between Cary and Research Triangle Park, about 8 miles from Raleigh. Its population has grown from 251 in 1980 to 3,644 today and is expected to reach 14,500 by 2009. While people have

relocated from all parts of the country to live or work in Morrisville, the town has pride in its roots: the Shiloh community was founded by freed men and women after the abolition of slavery. The community began in 1867 when Reverend Ed Cole organized the congregation of Shiloh. In 1925, Reverend James Dunston divided 2,000 acres into farms for the 12 original major church members, the descendants of whom developed the community. More than 150 descendants still live in the community.

In comparison to its neighbors, Morrisville's growth has been nonresidential and has resulted in a healthy tax base. However, new apartment complexes and single-family housing developments have recently begun to sprout up everywhere. The town has changed from a sleepy country village straddling N.C. 54 to a community with industrial parks, planned neighborhoods and even a lovely community center and park. While other communities, especially Cary, attracted residential newcomers, this little town near RDU busied itself attracting businesses such as EDS, Kaiser Permanente, AT&T, Radian and MCI. Along the roads linking

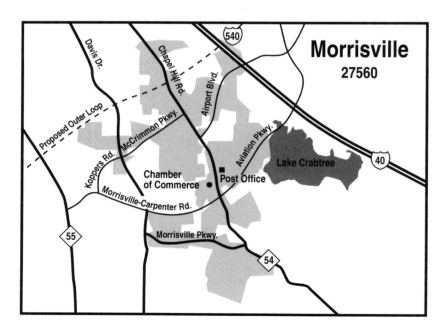

Photo by Rich Weidman

The Town of Morrisville hosts an annual Day at the Park Festival in June.

downtown to Interstate 40, one finds office parks with innumerable tenants. Morrisville has also added Midway Airlines and the Carolina Hurricanes to its stable of businesses headquartered in town.

Morrisville's commercial growth includes Prime Outlets-Morrisville, a mall of more than 40 manufacturer-owned outlet stores located just off I-40. The Northern Wake Expressway, a new highway that will pass through the northern portion of the town and move traffic from the Airport around the capital faster, will create two exits within the town limits and add further polish to Morrisville's image as a hub for business.

Morrisville is governed by a council-manager form of government that consists of a mayor and five town commissioners. The town's tax base has grown from $85 million in 1987 to more than $580 million today. Its land use plan, revised in 1990, envisions an ultimate tax base that has roughly a mix of 30 percent residential and 70 percent commercial/industrial growth. Its residential population, although small, continues to grow due to its central location between Durham and Raleigh, and its proximity to Research Triangle Park and RDU International Airport. About 70 percent of the land within the town limits remains undeveloped.

Development of Huntington, a 680-acre planned community, doubled the town's population and companies such as Bristol-Myers Squibb, which has a plant near Huntington's industrial park, have added to the town's job market.

With the airport a nearby neighbor, Morrisville occupies about 13.2 square miles; it has five parks on 51 acres, allowing townspeople the opportunity to enjoy outdoor activities. A greenhouse in the downtown area boasts poinsettias that bloom year round, and the recently renovated Town Hall houses Civil War artifacts.

The town even purchased a health club and converted it into a community center complete with municipal pool, tennis courts and exercise facility. Morrisville also has the distinct honor of having one of the largest year-round elementary schools in the country located within its boundaries.

With the opening of the 16-screen Park Place Cinema on Chapel Hill Road, the small town nestled near the airport has become a small pocket of night life, attracting people from across the Triangle, especially on weekends. The adjacent Park Place Shopping Center includes a Golden Corral, Food Lion, Bear Rock Cafe and a handful of specialty shops. The Morrisville Square Shopping Center has been constructed near Town Hall on Morrisville-Carpenter Road. Morrisville is also home to the Hindu Society of North Carolina, the largest Hindu temple in the Triangle.

Pittsboro

Population: 2,100
Commute to Chapel Hill: 18 mi.
Commute to RTP: 30 mi.
Chamber of Commerce: 742-3333
www.co.chatham.nc.us

When you arrive in Pittsboro, located along U.S. 15-501, the first thing you'll notice is the restored 1881 courthouse situated squarely in the middle of a traffic circle. Nearby, you'll find the Pittsboro General Store and Cafe, a local institution.

Incorporated in 1787, Pittsboro was named for William Pitt, Earl of Chatham (1708-78). This Chatham County seat, 18 miles south of Chapel Hill, still feels like a small Southern town. Historic homes line its streets. Town inhabitants include a blend of longtime natives and newcomers drawn to the area because of its charm, proximity to UNC-CH and Research Triangle Park, and, of course, lower land prices and property taxes. Pittsboro, like the other small towns on the edges of the Triangle, faces the challenge of balancing growth pressures against the desire to preserve the qualities that make this such a pleasant place to live.

Pittsboro has become a mecca for antique and crafts hunters, as well as a home for many artists and craftspeople. If you're driving from Chapel Hill, you'll pass the Fearrington Market, a good place to stop for a casual lunch. Also located at Fearrington Village is Pringle's, a shop featuring hand-thrown stoneware,

Photo by Rich Weidman

Built in 1881, the Chatham County Courthouse is listed on the National Register of Historic Places.

jewelry and fine crafts. As you cross the Haw River at Bynum, you'll see Stone Crow Pottery, located in a rebuilt log cabin and Cooper-Mays Pottery just across the road. Bynum is home to the famed Clyde Jones, who fashions rustic wood art.

Outdoor recreational activities abound within a short driving distance of Pittsboro. Nearby is Jordan Lake, a state recreational area with 150 miles of shoreline. Take a boat out on the lake, fish, water-ski, camp out or just enjoy the scenery. The nearby Haw River offers canoeing and kayaking opportunities. Rock Rest Adventures is a popular local outfitter for such excursions.

The Pittsboro Fall Festival celebrates the area's strong agricultural roots. The Pittsboro Farmers Market takes place on Thursday afternoons from April through October at the Chatham County Fairgrounds. Premiere Motorsports has a facility here that contains the Pitt Stop Cafe and Race Shop. The Carnivore Preservation Trust was founded in Pittsboro in 1981 to preserve endangered species. Located on 55 acres, it is home to more than 240 animals from 14 species of threatened carnivores such as tigers, jaguars, leopards, ocelots and cougars. Although the Preservation Trust is not a zoo, it does provide community outreach programs.

Pittsboro
27312

Selma

Population: 5,500
Commute to Raleigh: 30 mi.
Commute to RTP: 45 mi.
Chamber of Commerce: 934-9166
www.smithfieldselma.com

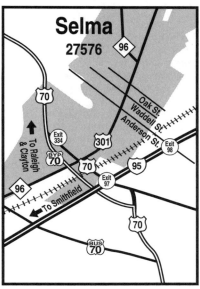

Established in 1867 as a rail center and originally called Michener's Station, Selma was named after Selma, Alabama, another well-known rail center at the time. The town is conveniently located just north of Smithfield and near U.S. 70 and interstates 40 and 95.

Today, Selma bills itself as "The South's Antique Mecca." The town is known for its "uptown" antique stores with names like Alice's Wonderland Antiques and Collectibles, Reid's Country Sampler, Collected Treasures, Granny's Attic and Simpler Times. Here you can find heirloom quilts, old books, glassware, antique toys, furniture and estate jewelry. Selma also contains a working blacksmith's shop, Hickory Forge, which sells a variety of specialty items.

Every Friday and Saturday night, Selma's American Music Jubilee provides quality entertainment in the form of a rousing musical extravaganza of singing, dancing and comedy at the 576-seat Rudy Theatre, similar to the kinds of high-energy shows that can be found in Myrtle Beach, South Carolina, and

Selma is home to the American Music Jubilee at the 576-seat Rudy Theatre.

Branson, Missouri. Locals flock to the Rocket Room Deli and Coffeehouse, which is open for lunch Tuesday through Saturday. Creech Drug Store has been serving up hand-dipped ice cream since 1939. Located at the Town Depot, the Selma Railroad Museum showcases the town's railroad history. Tours are available of the nearby Atkinson Mill (built in 1757), the only water-powered grist mill still operating in the region.

The town's most popular festival is Selma Railroad Days Festival, held on the first Saturday in October. A celebration of Selma's railroad heritage, the festival includes railroad displays, arts and crafts, live music, a parade, road races and beauty pageants.

Selma operates under a council-manager form of government with a mayor and four council members, all elected at-large. Students from Selma attend schools in the Johnston County Public School System, which serves more than 21,300 students. The main campus of Johnston Community College is located in neighboring Smithfield.

A nearby attraction worth a visit is the Tobacco Farm Life Museum in Kenly, a restored farmstead that celebrates the area's farming heritage with exhibits, outbuildings, farming equipment and a gift shop.

Smithfield

Population: 11,476
Commute to Raleigh: 30 mi.
Commute to RTP: 45 mi.
Chamber of Commerce: 934-9166
www.smithfieldselma.com

Founded in 1777 as the seat of Johnston County and originally known as Smith's Ferry and then Johnston Court House, Smithfield is one of the 10 oldest towns in North Carolina. It was named after John Smith Jr., the son of one of the area's earliest settlers, who operated a ferry at the Neuse River. Smithfield was actually considered as a site for the State Capital but lost out to Raleigh. The 1921 Johnston County Courthouse is listed on the National Register of Historic Places.

Smithfield is conveniently located near interstates 40 and 95. Downtown Smithfield includes a variety of specialty shops and restaurants such as The Willow Oak Tea Room, housed in the restored 1910 Dupree House; and Cafe Monet, which serves delicious cuisine in a relaxing atmosphere. The walls of the Cafe are covered with the work of local artists. Another popular local restaurant is

Becky's Log Cabin for seafood and steaks. Smithfield's famous Ham Shop and Jones Brothers Furniture—the largest furniture showroom in eastern North Carolina—draw customers from all over the region.

Shoppers from all over the state travel to Smithfield's Carolina Outlet Center, which is home to more than 85 stores, including Ralph Lauren, Polo, Gap, Nike, Liz Claiborne and Tommy Hilfiger. Other nearby outlets include J.R.'s Tobacco & Fragrance Outlet and a Fieldcrest-Cannon Store. The downtown Johnston County Heritage Center contains historic artifacts and a genealogical research center full of family histories, old newspapers and photographs and court records. Film star Ava Gardner, who appeared in such memorable movies as *Showboat* and *The Sun Also Rises*, was born and raised near Smithfield. The Ava Gardner Museum at 325 East Market Street holds a collection of more than 100,000 items, including costumes, original scripts, photos and Gardner's personal belongings. Gardner is buried in Smithfield's Sunset Memorial Park.

Smithfield's most popular annual event is the Ham and Yam Festival in April with an open cooking contest, arts and crafts, live music, carnival rides, children's activities and agricultural

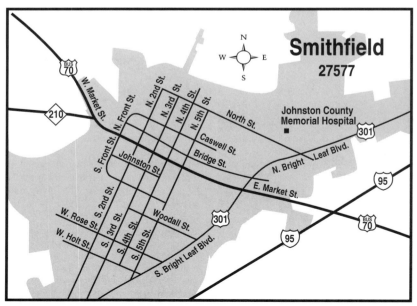

Photo courtesy of Johnston County Visitors Bureau

The 1880 Yelvington-Lee House is home to the Smithfield-Selma Chamber of Commerce and the Johnston County Visitors Bureau.

exhibits. A local theater group, Neuse Little Theater, performs four annual productions, including musicals, comedies and dramas. The town has nine parks, including the 50-acre Town Commons, which lies along the banks of the Neuse River. It is the site of the historic Hastings House, which now serves as the administrative center for the Parks and Recreation Department. A municipal swimming pool is located adjacent to Smith-Collins Park. The popular Bob Wallace Jaycee Kiddie Park off South Second Street has been completely renovated. InterSKATE is an area roller hockey arena located at 350 Components Drive that provides skating sessions and league play. It is a popular spot for birthday parties. Race fans can enjoy KART racing at the Johnston County Speedway or NASCAR racing at the Southern National Speedway in nearby Kenly.

Johnston County has traditionally served as an agricultural center and today contains more than 1,700 farms. The county leads the country in sweet potato production and is ranked second in North Carolina in harvested tobacco. The Smithfield Tobacco Market has operated for more than 100 years. However, the area has also diversified its industry base and now includes a number of major corporations among its largest employers such as Channel Master, Bayer Laboratories, Caterpillar, Eaton Corporation and Burlington Industries.

Smithfield operates under a council-manager form of government with a mayor and seven council members—four elected in districts and three elected at-large. The Town Council meets on the first Tuesday of each month at 7:30 PM at Town Hall on East Market Street. The Johnston County Board of Commissioners consists of seven members, each elected from a district. The Board meets on the first Monday of each month at 10 AM at the Courthouse Annex, 307 East Johnston Street. The Smithfield-Selma Chamber of Commerce is located in the renovated 1880 Yelvington-Lee House. Established in 1951, the Johnston Memorial Hospital is a 180-bed, nonprofit facility with more than 40 physicians on staff.

Students from Smithfield attend schools in the Johnston County Public School System, which serves approximately 21,300 students. The main campus of Johnston Community College is located in Smithfield. Thecampus includes the $4-million Paul Johnston Auditorium, which contains more than 1,000 seats and hosts an annual concert series.

Civil War buffs will want to visit the nearby Bentonville Battleground in Four Oaks, site of the largest and bloodiest Civil War battle fought in North Carolina. It was here that Confederate General Joseph E. Johnston's 4,500 troops tried to slow down Union General William T. Sherman's massive army of 60,000 as it made its way toward Virginia. The site contains the restored Harper House (which served as a Union field hospital), reconstructed and original trenches, hiking trails and a picnic area.

Wake Forest

Population: 15,287
Commute to Raleigh: 12 mi.
Commute to RTP: 30 mi.
Chamber of Commerce: 556-1519
www.wakeforestnc.com/chamber

A lovely old college town established in 1838, Wake Forest sits about 12 miles northeast of Raleigh's outskirts off U.S. 1. Its small-town charm and proximity to the Triangle have been enhanced by the development of Falls Lake a few miles to the west. The challenge to city leaders is to keep Wake Forest's small-town pace and grace while accommodating growth.

The town's history is intertwined with education, beginning with three private academies that operated nearby in the early 1800s and the founding of Wake Forest College in 1834 by the state's Baptist Convention. Dr. Calvin Jones, founder of the Wake Academy, described the town's early inhabitants as "sober, moral, thriving in their circumstances, educated and intelligent."

When the college moved to Winston-Salem in 1956, its buildings were occupied by

Photo by Rich Weidman

Southeastern Baptist Theological Seminary is located on the former campus of Wake Forest College.

an older crowd of Southeastern Baptist Theological Seminary students. Wake Forest, in the words of one town historian, became "a

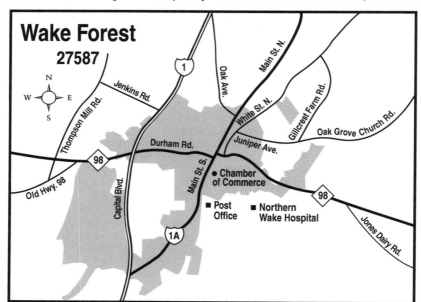

Wake Forest
27587

much quieter and more sedate place." It also became an attractive residential town.

The average sales price of a new home is about $159,000. Starter homes at The Village of the Olde Mill Stream start in the low $100,000s; Tarlton Park lists homes from $200,000 to $300,000; and The Oaks at Waterfall Plantation, from $280,000 to more than $600,000. Nearby Wakefield Plantation is a 2,260-acre housing and commercial development on Falls of Neuse Road. The largest residential development in Wake County, it features the Tournament Players Club, an 18-hole golf course designed by Hale Irwin, as well as a plantation-style clubhouse, an equestrian facility, 85-acre town park, tennis courts and an outdoor pool. Prices for this new home community range from $130,000 to more than $2 million. Adjacent to Wakefield lies Crenshaw Hall Plantation, with homes from $170,000 to $250,000. Construction began recently at the southern end of town on a 944-acre development called Heritage, which will eventually contain 2,200 homes.

Older homes in the Wake Forest Historic District offer a variety of architectural styles, including Greek Revival, Queen Anne and bungalow. A two-story Victorian home in the historic district might sell for considerably less than homes in a nearby, newer neighborhood. The Wake Forest College Birthplace Museum is housed in a circa-1820 structure located within the Historic District.

Wake Forest's revitalized downtown area contains specialty shops, bookstores (including the immensely popular Not Just for Kids) and restaurants. The 60,000-square-foot Ligon Mill Business Center, an office and retail center, is located just a mile outside the downtown area. The town has six parks, including a baseball park and two swimming pools. The Historic Dubois School is in the process of being transformed into a community center. The beautiful Wake Forest Country Club offers graceful amenities to its members. Kids will love ZooFauna, a nature park with more than 200 animals from around the world. Wake Forest is also just 5 miles from Falls Lake, which offers opportunities for boating, swimming, fishing, hiking and picnicking. The

Border restaurant is a popular gathering place for breakfast and lunch. Other popular eateries include Shorty's, located downtown, and The Fork Lunchroom, a country cooking hotspot located near Wakefield Plantation.

Wake Forest offers a variety of community activities, the largest of which is the Fourth of July celebration at the Wake Forest-Rolesville High School stadium. Meet in the Street is a popular street fair held in May with arts and crafts, food, entertainment and exhibits. Other annual events include a Spring Concert Series in April and May, Autumn in Wake Forest festival, Historic Homes Tour and a Christmas Parade. The Wake Forest Chamber of Commerce sponsors a Superball Golf Tournament at the Wake Forest Country Club each September.

Wake Forest's population has skyrocketed from 6,839 in 1993 to more than 15,200 today. With the completion of I-540 (the Northern Wake Expressway or Outer Loop) over the next couple of years and Wakefield Plantation, Wake Forest will undergo significant growth, providing a host of new opportunities and challenges for town planners.

Photo by Rich Weidman

Wake Forest's bustling downtown area has undergone extensive renovations.

Wendell

Population: 4,000
Commute to Raleigh: 13 mi.
Commute to RTP: 25 mi.
Chamber of Commerce: 365-6318
www.wendellchamber.com

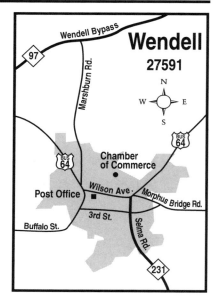

First settled during the early 1800s, Wendell was named after poet Oliver Wendell Holmes. However, residents pronounce the name Win-DELL, since that's the way the train conductor called out the stop during the town's early years.

Incorporated in 1903, Wendell's economy was tied to tobacco. Warehouses were built in 1907 for the first tobacco market in Wake County. Today, Wendell has prospered from the Triangle's explosive growth and the town has refurbished its downtown with a small, municipal park that includes a gazebo at J. Ashley Wall Town Square. The downtown area is listed in the National Register of Historic Places. Some of the stores here have been in business for many decades such as Kannon's Clothing, Inc., which opened its doors in 1916. Perry's Hardware, a local

Wendell's charming downtown contains a number of stores that have been in business for decades.

institution, has been transformed into a gun and sporting good shop.

Wendell's last tobacco market, Liberty Warehouse, closed in early 2000. However, several manufacturing operations, such as Siemans Energy & Automation, have located close by, bringing jobs and demands for housing. There is a solid core of professional services whose practitioners have deep roots in the community. Wendell's motto is "Home of Progress and Opportunity."

Eastern Wake Senior Center, a joint public and private venture, provides a unique social and cultural facility for older adults in the community. The new Wendell Community Center has been constructed on the edge of town. It is the only community center in eastern Wake County. Wendell also boasts the first indoor soccer facility in eastern Wake County. A favorite attraction in Wendell is St. Eugene's Catholic Church, one of the few in mostly protestant eastern Wake County. The annual Bright Leaf Folk Festival, held the first weekend in October, celebrates Wendell's rich heritage surrounding the flue-cured tobacco leaf. Musicians from all over the state flock to Zepp's Country Music Store for Thursday-night bluegrass jam sessions.

Zebulon

Population: 5,000
Commute to Raleigh: 17 mi.
Commute to RTP: 42 mi.
Chamber of Commerce: 269-6320
www.zebulonchamber.com

The Carolina Mudcats compete
at Zebulon's recently renovated
Five County Stadium.

A short distance from Wendell, Zebulon serves as a hub for those commuting to Johnston, Wilson, Nash and Franklin counties. Its central location near Raleigh and Rocky Mount, its affordable housing and its industrial growth mark the town as an outstanding relocation choice for professionals and families moving to the Triangle area from both in-state and out-of-state.

In 1907, the town was chartered and laid out into "lots, blocks, streets, alleys, avenues and parks" by the Zebulon Company, which took its name from North Carolina Governor Zebulon Baird Vance (1830-94). According to the *Historic Architecture of Wake County*, Zebulon's core business district is one of the "largest intact historic commercial districts among Wake County's 11 small towns."

The town has embarked on a downtown revitalization project at a cost of more than

$1 million, complete with banners proclaiming "Discover Downtown Zebulon." Town officials hope the revitalization efforts will draw more specialty shops and restaurants to the business district.

Zebulon enjoys a solid economic base. Glaxo SmithKline (formerly Glaxo Wellcome), the pharmaceutical giant; Nomaco, a foam manufacturing company; PYA/Monarch, one of the Southeast's largest food distributors; and Blount Industries have operations in Zebulon, spurring more growth and drawing interest by other companies.

Zebulon's older residential homes sit among tree-lined streets and display Victorian, Craftsman and Colonial Revival styles. Many of them are still occupied by longtime Zebulon families. In 1998, the town annexed the 260-acre community of Wakefield, adding about 400 residents to its population.

Zebulon's recently renovated Five County Stadium is home to the Carolina Mudcats baseball team, a minor league AA affiliate of the Colorado Rockies. The town's other big draw for Triangle homeowners is Whitley's Furniture Gallery near downtown.

In the early 20th century, there was a large pine forest, a one-room school and three houses where Zebulon stands today. Today, it's a thriving community. The town motto— "The town of friendly people"—says it all.

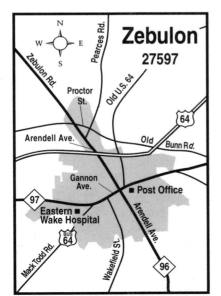

Photo by Rich Weidman

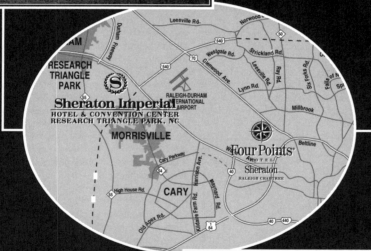

Accommodations & Temporary Housing

From budget motels to luxury hotels, the Triangle offers leisure and business travelers numerous lodging choices. New accommodations seem to be sprouting up everywhere, reflecting the area's dynamic population growth.

In this chapter, we've listed a cross-section of accommodations, from family-owned motels to economy chains to mid-priced hotels aimed at the business traveler to convention-sized name brand hotels such as Holiday Inn, Marriott, Embassy Suites and Hilton. Most of the full-service hotels can be found in clusters near Research Triangle Park and on Glenwood Avenue in North Raleigh. A variety of budget motels can be found just off of I-40, I-85 and U.S. 70. We've also included a few hotels that reflect a more Southern flavor such as the Carolina Inn in Chapel Hill, the Washington Duke Inn in Durham and the Plantation Inn in Raleigh.

Since bed and breakfast inns have become so popular, they have been given their own chapter. If you are intending to stay more than a week, you may want to consider residing at an extended-stay facility (see our "Temporary Housing" section at the end of this chapter). Check out our "Restaurants" chapter for hotels that have become just as well known for their dining rooms such as the award-winning Il Palio in the Siena Hotel.

North Carolina law prohibits pets in hotels and motels, although some lodgings make provisions for them. Call ahead to make arrangements. Also keep in mind that during special events, especially college graduation in May and big football weekends in the fall, the availability of rooms in certain areas may be limited or in some cases nonexistent.

Price Code

We have categorized accommodations with one to four dollar signs ($), based on the typical daily rates charged for a standard room with two double beds:

$	Under $50
$$	$51-$75
$$$	$76-$100
$$$$	$101-up

Keep in mind that this is a guide and rates may change. What doesn't change is the Southern hospitality for y'all.

Cary

Best Western Cary Inn & Suites
$$-$$$ • 1722 Walnut St.
• 481-1200, (800) CARY INN
• www.bestwestern.com

Like all units in the Best Western chain, this one is independently owned and the chain gives it a top rating. It is located at one of Cary's busiest exits off I-440 and if you're coming from RDU airport, you will exit I-40 at Exit 293. Many of Cary's motels are clustered at this exit. The Best Western has suites, mini-suites and standard rooms. It has two conference rooms, a satellite dish receiver, an outdoor pool, indoor whirlpool and fitness center. A free continental breakfast buffet is served daily and complimentary transportation for business guests is provided to and from the airport and to some local business parks. Other amenities include a manager's reception and complimentary weekday newspaper.

Staff Photo

Designed for the business traveler, Holiday Inn and Suites in Cary
is conveniently located in Crossroads Corporate Park.

Courtyard by Marriott
$$$ • 102 Edinburgh Dr. • 481-9666
• www.courtyard.com

One of Cary's upscale accommodations, the Courtyard offers 149 rooms and suites. Like other Courtyards, it's designed for business travelers and is conveniently located in southwest Cary, where U.S. 1 intersects U.S. 64 at MacGregor Village Shopping Center. It offers an outdoor pool, laundry, exercise room, whirlpool and restaurant open for breakfast.

Embassy Suites Hotel And Convention Center
$$$$ • 201 Harrison Oaks Blvd.
• 677-1840 • www.embassy-suites.com

Located off Harrison Avenue (I-40, Exit 287), this hotel offers 280 two-room suites that include kitchen appliances. Meeting space totals 21,000 square feet in gracious, flexible ballrooms and break-out areas. The Bistro in the Park restaurant, a gift shop, indoor pool, sauna, Jacuzzi, fitness room and access to a business center with audiovisual equipment are among the hotel's amenities. It also offers guests a complimentary full breakfast and airport shuttle service.

Fairfield Inn by Marriott
$$ • 1716 Walnut St. • 481-4011
• www.fairfieldinn.com

A member of the Marriott chain, the 125-room Fairfield Inn features cable TV, a complimentary continental breakfast, exercise facilities, an outdoor pool and sun deck.

Other Fairfield Inn locations in the Triangle include Crabtree Valley at 2201 Summit Park Lane, Raleigh, 881-9800; Durham/RTP at 4507 N.C. 55, Durham, 361-2656; 3710 Hillsborough Road, Durham, 382-3388; and Raleigh Northeast, 2641 Appliance Court, Raleigh, 856-9800.

Hampton Inn
$$ • 201 Ashville Ave. • 859-5559
• www.hampton-inn.com

An affiliate of the popular chain, the Hampton Inn caters to the mid-range customer. Like most of the town's other accommodations, the Hampton is located in southwest Cary, near the Western Wake Medical Center and has 131 rooms. It offers a free continental breakfast, weekday newspaper, nonsmoking rooms, swimming pools and exercise room. Children stay free.

Holiday Inn Hotel & Suites
$$$-$$$$ • 5630 Dillard Dr. • 851-1220
• www.holiday-inn.com

The Holiday Inn, which is located in Crossroads Corporate Park, offers 120 deluxe guest rooms especially suited for the business traveler. Amenities include a heated indoor pool and whirlpool, fitness room, conference and banquet facilities, on-site guest laundry and same-day valet service. The Cafe Sage serves breakfast and dinner. The Holiday Inn is conveniently located off I-40, Exit 293A.

Homewood Suites
$$$-$$$$ • 100 MacAlyson Ct. • 467-4444
• www.homewood-suites.com

Homewood Suites is an "all suites hotel" located near MacGregor Village off U.S. 1. It opened in 1994 and offers 120 suites in three sizes. The typical tenant stays a week and all suites include bedrooms and living rooms with daily maid service and a complimentary breakfast buffet. Guests are invited to a reception in the late afternoon every Monday through Thursday. Amenities include an outdoor pool and fitness center.

Chapel Hill

Best Western University Inn
$$$ • N.C. 54 E. • 932-3000
• www.bestwestern.com

The University Inn has been a Chapel Hill landmark since 1952. Located minutes from downtown, the UNC campus, UNC Hospitals, the Friday Center and Finley Golf Course, it is an excellent choice for those who are traveling for business or for pleasure. The 84-room Inn offers a pool, complimentary continental breakfast and cable television with HBO. The well-known Aurora Restaurant, specializing in fine northern Italian cuisine, is adjacent to the Inn and open daily for lunch and dinner.

The Carolina Inn
$$$$ • 211 Pittsboro St.
• 933-2001, (800) 962-8519
• www.carolinainn.com

A lot of history lives in this building, which underwent a $16.5 million renovation and addition in 1995. The old New Hope Chapel, from which Chapel Hill derives its name, once stood about where the Inn's parking lot is

Photo by Rich Weidman

Built in 1924, The Carolina Inn is listed on the
National Register of Historic Places.

today. The original Inn was built in 1924 by John Sprunt Hill, an industrialist, financier and graduate of the UNC class of 1889. His family deeded it to the university in 1935. It has been enlarged twice prior to the recently completed project. The Inn is listed on the National Register of Historic Places.

The Inn, which contains 184 rooms, is located on the UNC-CH campus and is one block from the town center. Many upgrades in services and facilities have been added to the natural charm and tradition of the Inn. Rooms have two telephone jacks, allowing use of modems. There is a gift shop and exercise room. Meals are a delightful experience. Enjoy innovative Southern-style cuisine with an Italian influence at Carolina Crossroads restaurant.

Hampton Inn
$$$ • 1740 U.S. 15-501 Bypass
• 968-3000, 800-HAMPTON
• www.hampton-inn.com

A two-story, 122-room hotel, this Hampton Inn is part of a national chain offering comfortable accommodations at lower-than-average prices. The Inn eliminates a few "frills" such as restaurants, lounges and meeting spaces—a minor concession to economy given its location near the many eateries and shops at Eastgate and along

U.S. 15-501. You still get an outdoor pool, television, movie channels, free local calls and a complimentary continental breakfast and newspaper. Eighty percent of the rooms are nonsmoking.

Holiday Inn of Chapel Hill
$$-$$$$ • 1301 N. Fordham Blvd.
(U.S. 15-501 Bypass) • 929-2171
• www.holiday-inn.com

Convenient to downtown Chapel Hill, the UNC-CH campus and close to the Interstate 40 interchange, the Holiday Inn has 135 comfortable rooms with color cable TV and an outdoor pool. Teddy's Grill and Pub is open for breakfast and dinner.

Sheraton Chapel Hill Hotel
$$$$ • 1 Europa Dr. (U.S. 15-501 Bypass)
• 968-4900, (800) 325-3535
• www.sheraton.com

The 168-room Sheraton Chapel Hill Hotel sits on six rolling acres with lighted tennis courts, an outdoor pool, fitness center and more than 16,000 square feet of meeting and banquet space. As soon as you walk in the door you'll see the highlight of the well-appointed lobby, a wall-sized bas-relief sculpture called "The Dream," commissioned for this location.

Photo courtesy of The Siena Hotel

Designed to resemble a Tuscan villa, Chapel Hill's luxurious Siena Hotel is furnished throughout with fine European antiques and rich fabrics.

Enjoy an elegant dinner in Ruben's Restaurant or more casual fare in the Lobby Lounge. Take the glass elevator to the King's Club lounge on the top floor for late-night entertainment.

The Siena Hotel
$$$$ • 1505 E. Franklin St. • 929-4000
• www.sienahotel.com

Named for a small Italian city, this luxurious addition to Chapel Hill was designed to recall the intimate hotels of Europe. The Siena's 80 spacious guest rooms are individually appointed with hand-selected fine antiques and French doors opening onto European balconies.

Il Palio, the Siena's restaurant, features Northern Italian and Mediterranean cuisine. Internationally acclaimed Executive Chef Gennaro Villella offers an exceptional menu in a refined atmosphere. A complimentary full buffet breakfast, daily newspaper delivery and nightly turndown service round out the hotel's special amenities.

Durham

Brookwood Inn at Duke
$$-$$$ • 2306 Elba St.
• 286-3111, (800) 716-6401

An eight-story high rise near Duke University and area hospitals, Brookwood Inn at Duke has 150 spacious rooms with double or king-size beds and color satellite TV. The Brookwood Inn Grille restaurant serves breakfast, lunch and dinner. Kids stay free.

Brownestone Inn
$$-$$$ • 2424 Erwin Rd. • 286-7761,
(800) 367-0293

The Brownestone is conveniently located next to the Duke Medical Center and Duke University. Complimentary shuttle service to and from the Medical Center is available. The Inn has 138 rooms with double or king-size beds and color cable TV with HBO. Upscale amenities are available on the Executive level, a floor with its own limited-access elevator and special services such as a complimentary morning newspaper and a deluxe continental breakfast.

Other services and facilities include a heated indoor pool, Jacuzzi and sauna, handicap-access rooms, nonsmoking rooms, self-service laundry and same-day dry cleaning and complimentary afternoon tea in the Williamsburg-style lobby. A full-service restaurant and a pub feature daily lunch, dinner and drink specials.

Carolina Duke Motor Inn
$ • 2517 Guess Rd. (off I-85)
• 286-0771, (800) 438-1158
• www.citysearch.com/rdu/carolinaduke

The Inn provides a free shuttle to Duke University Hospital and the Veterans Affairs Medical Center. It offers 180 rooms, each with a color TV and HBO, and your choice of queen- or king-size beds. Other amenities include an outdoor pool, free continental breakfast and two conference rooms for meetings that accommodate up to 30 persons.

Comfort Inn University
$$-$$$ • 3508 Mt. Moriah Rd. I-40 at
U.S. 15-501 • 490-4949, (800) 221-2222
• www.comfortinn.com

Conveniently located near Duke University and UNC-Chapel Hill, Comfort Inn has 138 rooms (including 18 suites with whirlpools, wet bars and VCRs) that are carefully planned for business and leisure travelers. Facilities include an outdoor pool, an exercise room, a guest laundry and valet services, handicap-access and nonsmoking rooms. A complimentary deluxe continental breakfast is served. Meeting space is available to accommodate up to 160.

Days Inn-Durham
$-$$$ • 3460 Hillsborough Rd.
• 383-1551, (800) 238-8000
• www.daysinn.com

Located just off I-85 at the U.S. 15-501 Bypass, the 100-room Days Inn (formerly known as the Forest Inn) is convenient to the Durham Freeway. It has a restaurant, lounge and meeting rooms that accommodate up to 250 people. Other amenities include a complimentary continental breakfast, an outdoor pool, weekday newspaper and a rose garden courtyard.

Washington Duke Inn is home to Duke University Golf Club, an 18-hole, Robert Trent Jones-designed golf course.

Durham Marriott at the Civic Center
$$$$ • 201 Foster St. • 768-6000
• www.marriott.com

Located downtown, the hotel complex includes the Durham Civic and Convention Center, which contains more than 40,000 square feet of meeting space. It offers 187 beautifully refurbished rooms and three suites. A restaurant, lounge and exercise room are on the premises. In addition, the Downtown YMCA is just a block away. It is a great place to stay when you have business downtown or at Duke University.

Hampton Inn & Suites
$$-$$$$ • 6137 Farrington Rd. • 403-8700
• www.hampton-inn.com

Located off U.S. 15-501 between Durham and Chapel Hill, the Hampton Inn boasts 92 rooms and suites, a pool, exercise room, business center and free continental breakfast. Kids stay free. Meeting and business facilities are available for up to 100 people.

Hilton Durham
$$$-$$$$ • 3800 Hillsborough Rd.
(off I-85) • 383-8033, (800) 445-8667
• www.hilton.com

A six-story facility with 194 rooms and suites, the Hilton Durham also offers an outdoor pool and complete healthclub facilities, including a sauna, a Jacuzzi, a VCR for Jazzercise tapes and lots of exercise equipment. Tipton's Restaurant, which features fine dining and a piano bar, can accommodate private parties and banquets. The Hilton offers more than 5,000 square feet of meeting and banquet space.

La Quinta Inn & Suites Durham-Chapel Hill
$$$-$$$$ • 4414 Chapel Hill Blvd. • 401-9660
• www.laquinta.com

La Quinta Inn and Suites boasts 130 two-room suites and king rooms with microwaves and refrigerators. Amenities include an indoor heated pool, spa, fitness center and complimentary continental breakfast.

Regal University Hotel
$$$$ • 2800 Campus Walk Ave.
• 383-8575, (800) 222-8888
• www.regal-hotels.com

Only one mile from Duke University, this hotel offers 318 spacious rooms and suites. Guests on the VIP floor receive complimentary hors d'oeuvres, a continental breakfast and a morning newspaper. Discount rates are available on holidays, during summer months and for extended stays. Special rate plans are offered for hospital patients and their families.

The Bel Gusto restaurant has an all-you-can-eat breakfast and lunch buffet seven days a week, plus a la carte dining. The Executive Club offers the traveling business person a place to work (personal computers, printers and desks are provided), network or just unwind and relax. The Varsity Lounge in the lobby is a handy place for a drink or a bite to eat. The hotel also contains a spa and fitness center.

Washington Duke Inn and Golf Club
$$$$ • 3001 Cameron Blvd.
• 490-0999, (800) 443-3853
• www.washingtondukeinn.com
Located on the edge of Duke University's West Campus, this award-winning hotel has 171 rooms and suites. It faces a Robert Trent Jones-designed 18-hole championship golf course, which was redesigned by the architect's son, Rees Jones, in 1994. The course has been selected to host the 2001 NCAA Men's Golf Championship.

The Washington Duke Inn has many amenities that include an outdoor pool and jogging trails. For fine dining, guests enjoy the Fairview Restaurant. Terrace-on-the-Green features more casual alfresco dining and the Bull Durham Bar serves cocktails. Meeting facilities include the Duke University Room for small conferences and the Ambassador Ballroom for groups up to 600.

Raleigh

Brownstone Hotel
$$$ • 1707 Hillsborough St.
• 828-0811, (800) 331-7919
• www.brownstonehotel.com
The Brownstone is located downtown, about one mile from the State Capitol, and is popular with politicians, legislators and lobbyists when the General Assembly is in session. It is also next to the NCSU campus and contains banquet facilities for moderate-sized conventions and meetings. It has a restaurant, Chambers, a lounge and pool. A color TV with HBO is in each of its 192 spacious rooms. Guests enjoy a complimentary

breakfast buffet. The Hillsborough Street YMCA is conveniently located next door.

Country Inn & Suites by Carlson
$$ • 2715 Capital Blvd.
(U.S. 1 N. & I-440 Beltline)
• 872-5000, (800) 456-4000
• www.countryinns.com
Popular with traveling business people because of its reasonable rates, Country Inn is close to a number of restaurants as well as the Highwoods business park. It has 156 standard rooms, suites and two-room suites. Amenities include an outdoor pool, complimentary continental breakfast, meeting space and an open bar Monday through Thursday evenings. It sits across the highway from the Parker Lincoln office building.

Courtyard by Marriott
$$-$$$ • 1041 Wake Towne Dr.
(Wake Forest Rd. and the I-440 Beltline)
• 821-3400 • www.courtyard.com
Located near Raleigh Community Hospital, this is one of the Marriott chain's six Courtyards in the Triangle and if you've seen one Courtyard, you know to expect a high level of service. It has 153 rooms and is very popular with business travelers who want more than a light left on for them. Amenities include an outdoor pool, exercise room and complimentary breakfast buffet.

Crabtree Summit Hotel
$$-$$$ • 3908 Arrow Dr. • 782-6868
• www.crabtreesummithotel.com
The Crabtree Summit offers 85 rooms and suites, all with coffee makers and other amenities to make your stay a comfortable one. Some suites are equipped with refrigerators and whirlpool baths. A weekday stay in any room gets you a full breakfast buffet and free van service to and from the airport. Every Monday through Thursday from 5 to 7 PM, this establishment offers The Manager's Reception with complimentary drinks and hors d'oeuvres to all guests and their guests. An outdoor pool and fitness center provide a means for exercise and relaxation while away from home. The Crabtree's restaurant and lounge are open nightly.

Embassy Suites Raleigh/Crabtree Valley
$$$$ • 4700 Creedmoor Rd. • 881-0000
• www.embassy-suites.com

Embassy Suites Raleigh, which was named the best Embassy Suites in the world in 1995, offers 225 spacious, two-room suites; a complimentary breakfast and manager's reception; and a garden atrium. It also has an indoor pool, outdoor sundeck, fitness facility and sauna. Guests can also enjoy authentic Italian cuisine at the hotel's restaurant, Nicola's. The Embassy Suites is located across the street from Crabtree Valley Mall.

Four Points Hotel Raleigh Crabtree
$$$$ • 4501 Creedmoor Rd. • 787-7111
• www.fourpointsraleigh.com

The 10-story Four Points provides several amenities, including an indoor pool, fitness room, an upscale restaurant called Seby's and a lobby bar. With 318 rooms, this is one of the largest hotels in the city, located adjacent to Crabtree Valley Mall. It caters to business clients with convention-size facilities in the form of 10 spacious meeting rooms for up to 300 people.

Hampton Inn & Suites Raleigh/Cary
$$-$$$ • I-40, Exit 290 • 233-1798
• www.hampton-inn.com

Conveniently located between Raleigh and Cary, the all-suite Hampton Inn features 124 suites with fully equipped kitchens and luxurious whirlpool suites. Amenities include an outdoor pool, fitness room, garden courtyard, library and complimentary breakfast buffet.

Hilton North Raleigh
$$$$ • 3415 Wake Forest Rd. • 872-2323
• www.hilton.com

One of Raleigh's most popular spots for hosting meetings and conferences, the Hilton is located right off the I-440 Beltline and across the road from Raleigh Community Hospital. It contains an indoor pool with sun deck, restaurant and an upscale night spot, Bowties. The large convention and meeting facilities

The Holiday Inn State Capital is within walking distance of downtown attractions.

accommodate up to 1,500 people—one of the largest such centers on the East Coast—and its 338 rooms lodge plenty of guests.

Holiday Inn Crabtree
$$$ • 4100 Glenwood Ave. • 782-8600
• www.holiday-inn.com

The 12-story Holiday Inn Crabtree features an outdoor pool, separate men's and women's saunas, a fitness center, Carolina Jacks Restaurant, C.J.'s Lounge and 4,500 square feet of state-of-the-art meeting and banquet facilities. It is conveniently located across from the Crabtree Valley Mall off the I-440 beltline (Exit 7).

Holiday Inn State Capital
$$$ • 320 Hillsborough St. • 832-0501
• www.holiday-inn.com

Within a short stroll of many downtown attractions, the recently renovated Holiday Inn is known for its distinctive cylindrical shape. From the Top of the Tower restaurant, you have a panoramic view of the city. It has 202 rooms and two suites. Here you'll find the amenities one expects at a Holiday

Inn, including an outdoor heated pool on the second floor and a fitness center. Banquet and meeting facilities are available for up to 350 people.

Homewood Suites
$$$$ • 5400 Homewood Banks Dr.
• 785-1131 • www.homewood-suites.com

Located in Crabtree Valley within walking distance from the mall, Homewood Suites features 136 two-bedroom suites with spacious bedrooms, living rooms and kitchens. Guests can enjoy a pool, fitness center, weekday newspaper, complimentary breakfast buffet and evening manager's reception.

Marriott Crabtree Valley
$$$$ • 4500 Marriott Dr. • 781-7000
• www.marriott.com

One of Raleigh's national chain hotels, this 375-room Marriott sits off Glenwood Avenue, across from Crabtree Valley Mall and is the largest hotel in the city. The hotel's central location to northwest Raleigh has made it a popular business meeting place. It's also only 18 minutes from RTP and RDU. Amenities include an indoor-outdoor pool, tennis courts, a fitness room and a restaurant, the Crabtree Grill. Also check out the Marriott's less expensive Courtyard, at the intersection of the I-440 Beltline and Wake Forest Road. The Fairfield Inn, Marriott's least expensive chain, is located at the I-440 Beltline and U.S. 1 North.

Plantation Inn Resort
$$-$$$ • 6401 Capital Blvd.
• 876-1411, (800) 521-1932
• www.plantationinnraleigh.com

Built in the early 1950s, this is one of the city's grand old motels and the place to stay when it offered travelers the luxuries of a large outdoor pool, playground, putting green and even a fishing pond! The Inn has seen Raleigh grow well past its doorstep, yet it retains its green landscape and serene, Southern plantation motif. The buffet at

Jacqueline's restaurant has been popular for years. Enjoy lakeside dining each evening at the Carriage Club. The Inn has 90 rooms and offers bargain rates for travelers as well as meetings and/or private dining.

Quality Suites
$$$-$$$$ • 4400 Capital Blvd. • 876-2211
• www.qualityinn.com

Located in North Raleigh, Quality Suites offers 114 two-room suites, complete with refrigerator, microwave oven, coffee maker, cable TV and VCR. Other amenities include a pool, fitness room, complimentary breakfast, newspaper and evening cocktail reception Sunday through Thursday.

Ramada Inn, Crabtree
$$-$$$ • 3920 Arrow Dr. • 782-7525
• www.ramada.com

This locally owned Ramada Inn is one of the best and has the awards to prove it. The Colonnade Restaurant has a great reputation and serves many homemade specialties. Stay alert when nearing this inn, since the entrance is somewhat obscured by the traffic jamming the I-440 Beltline and Glenwood Avenue interchange. (The entrance is off the eastbound lane of Glenwood Avenue, immediately before the I-440 Beltline interchange.) It has 174 rooms, an outdoor pool, fitness center and spa. Another Ramada Inn is located on Blue Ridge Road, 832-4100.

Residence Inn
$$$-$$$$ • 1000 Navaho Dr. • 878-6100
• www.residenceinn.com

Another establishment in the Marriott Hotel group, this one is aimed at the person who is planning to stay longer than a single night. The rates vary according to stay and it's popular with corporate visitors. There are 144 units, including suites with fireplaces, free continental breakfasts, heated pool, whirlpool and sports courts. Another Residence Inn is located at 2200 Summit Park Lane, 279-3000.

INSIDERS' TIP
The championship golf course at the Washington Duke Inn has been selected to host the 2001 NCAA Men's Golf Championship.

TRIANGLE ACCOMMODATIONS

Hotel/Motel	Address	$-$$$$	Airport Shuttle	Phone
CARY				
Best Western	1722 Walnut St.	$$-$$$$	Y	481-1200
Comfort Suites	350 Ashville Ave.	$$-$$$$	N	852-4318
Courtyard by Marriott	102 Edinburgh Dr.	$$$	N	481-9666
Embassy Suites	201 Harrison Oaks Blvd.	$$$$	Y	677-1840
Fairfield Inn by Marriott	1716 Walnut St.	$$	N	481-4011
Hampton Inn-Cary	201 Ashville Ave.	$$	N	859-5559
Holiday Inn Hotel & Suites	5630 Dillard Dr.	$$$-$$$$	N	851-1220
Homewood Suites	100 MacAlyson Ct.	$$$-$$$$	N	467-4444
La Quinta Inn & Suites	191 Crescent Commons	$$$-$$$$	N	851-2850
Ramada Inn	U.S. 1 & N.C. 55, Apex	$-$$	N	362-8621
Red Roof Inn	1800 Walnut St.	$$	N	469-3400
Residence Inn	2900 Regency Pkwy.	$$$-$$$$	N	467-4080
CHAPEL HILL				
Best Western University Inn	N.C. 54 E.	$$$	N	932-3000
The Carolina Inn	211 Pittsboro St.	$$$$	N	933-2001
Days Inn	1312 N. Fordham Blvd.	$$$	N	929-3090
Hampton Inn	1740 U.S. 15-501	$$$	N	968-3000
Holiday Inn of Chapel Hill	1301 N. Fordham Blvd.	$$-$$$$	N	929-2171
Sheraton Chapel Hill	1 Europa Dr.	$$$$	N	968-4900
The Siena Hotel	1505 E. Franklin St.	$$$$	Y	929-4000
DURHAM				
Best Western Skyland Inn	5400 U.S. 70 W.	$-$$	N	383-2508
Brookwood Inn at Duke	2306 Elba St.	$$-$$$	N	286-3111
Brownestone Inn	2424 Erwin Rd.	$$-$$$$	N	286-7761
Carolina Duke Motor Inn	2517 Guess Rd. at I-85	$-$$	N	286-0771
Comfort Inn University	3508 Mt. Moriah Rd.	$$-$$$$	N	490-4949
Courtyard by Marriott	1815 Front St.	$$$-$$$$	N	309-1500
Days Inn	3460 Hillsborough Rd.	$-$$	N	383-1551
Days Inn of Durham	5139 Redwood Rd.	$-$$$	N	688-4338
Durham Marriott	201 Foster St.	$$$-$$$$	N	768-6000
Fairfield Inn	3710 Hillsborough Rd.	$$	N	382-3388
Hampton Inn & Suites	6137 Farrington Rd.	$$-$$$$	N	403-8700
Hampton Inn & Suites	1816 Hillandale Rd.	$$-$$$	N	471-6100
Hilton Durham	3800 Hillsborough Rd.	$$$-$$$$	Y	383-8033
Holiday Inn Express	2516 Guess Rd.	$$-$$$	N	313-3244
Homewood Suites	3600 Mt. Moriah Rd.	$$$-$$$$	N	401-0610
Howard Johnson Inn	1800 Hillandale Rd.	$-$$$	N	477-7381
Innkeeper South	4433 N.C. 55	$-$$	N	544-4579
La Quinta Inn & Suites	4414 Chapel Hill Blvd.	$$-$$$$	N	401-9660
The Luxury Inn	600 Willard St.	$$-$$$	N	956-9444
Red Roof Inn	1915 North Pointe Dr.	$$	N	471-9882
Red Roof Inn	4405 N.C. 55 E.	$-$$	N	361-1950
Regal University Hotel	2800 Campus Walk Ave.	$$$$	Y	383-8575
University Inn	502 Elf St.	$$	N	286-4421
Washington Duke Inn	3001 Cameron Blvd.	$$$$	Y	490-0999

TRIANGLE ACCOMMODATIONS

Hotel/Motel	Address	$-$$$$	Airport Shuttle	Phone
RALEIGH				
AmeriSuites	1105 Navaho Dr.	$$-$$$	N	877-9997
Best Western Crabtree	6619 Glenwood Ave.	$$-$$$	N	782-8650
Best Western Hospitality Inn	2800 Brentwood Rd.	$$	N	872-8600
Brownstone Hotel	1707 Hillsborough St.	$$$	Y	828-0811
Claremont Inn	2639 S. Saunders St.	$$	N	828-5151
Comfort Inn North Raleigh	2910 Capital Blvd.	$-$$	N	878-9550
Comfort Inn Six Forks	4220 Six Forks Rd.	$$	N	787-2300
Country Inn & Suites by Carlson	2715 Capital Blvd.	$$	N	872-5000
Courtyard by Marriott	1041 Wake Towne Dr.	$$-$$$	N	821-3400
Crabtree Summit Hotel	3908 Arrow Dr.	$$-$$$	Y	782-6868
Days Inn-Crabtree	6329 Glenwood Ave.	$$	N	781-7904
Days Inn-North	2805 Highwoods Blvd.	$$	N	872-3500
Days Inn-South	3901 S. Wilmington St.	$$-$$$	N	772-8900
Embassy Suites, Crabtree	4700 Creedmoor Rd.	$$$$	Y	881-0000
Fairfield Inn Crabtree	2201 Summit Park Ln.	$$	N	881-9800
Fairfield Inn N. Raleigh	2641 Appliance Ct.	$$	N	856-9800
Four Points Hotel by Sheraton	4501 Creedmoor Rd.	$$$$	Y	787-7111
Hampton Inn Capital Blvd. N.	3621 Spring Forest Rd.	$$-$$$	N	872-7111
Hampton Inn Crabtree	6209 Glenwood Ave.	$$-$$$	Y	782-1112
Hampton Inn N. Raleigh	1001 Wake Towne Dr.	$$-$$$	N	828-1813
Hampton Inn Raleigh/Cary	111 Hampton Woods Ln.	$$-$$$	Y	233-1798
Hilton North Raleigh	3415 Wake Forest Rd.	$$$$	Y	872-2323
Holiday Inn Crabtree	4100 Glenwood Ave.	$$$	Y	782-8600
Holiday Inn Express	4716 New Bern Ave.	$$$	N	231-2727
Holiday Inn State Capital	320 Hillsborough St.	$$$	N	832-0501
Homewood Suites	5400 Edwards Mill Rd.	$$$-$$$$	Y	785-1131
Howard Johnson Lodge	3120 New Bern Ave.	$	N	231-3000
La Quinta Crabtree	2211 Summit Park Ln.	$$$	N	785-0071
Marriott Crabtree Valley	4500 Marriott Dr.	$$$$	Y	781-7000
Microtel Inn & Suites	1209 Plainview Rd.	$	N	231-0002
Milner Inn	1817 Capital Blvd.	$-$$	N	834-0717
Motel 6-Crabtree	3921 Arrow Dr.	$	N	782-7071
Motel 6-Raleigh/Cary	1401 Buck Jones Rd.	$	N	467-6171
Plantation Inn Resort	6401 Capital Blvd.	$$-$$$	Y	876-1411
Quality Suites	4400 Capital Blvd.	$$$$	N	876-2211
Ramada Inn Blue Ridge	1520 Blue Ridge Rd.	$$$	Y	832-4100
Ramada Inn Crabtree	3920 Arrow Dr.	$$-$$$	Y	782-7525
Red Roof Inn	3201 Old Wake Forest Rd.	$-$$	N	878-9310
Residence Inn	1000 Navaho Dr.	$$$-$$$$	N	878-6100
Residence Inn	2200 Summit Park Ln.	$$$-$$$$	N	279-3000
Sheraton Capital Center	421 S. Salisbury St.	$$$$	Y	834-9900
Sleep Inn	2617 Appliance Ct.	$	N	755-6005
Sundown Inn	3801 Capital Blvd.	$-$$	N	790-8480
Super 8 Motel	3804 New Bern Ave.	$$	N	231-8818
Velvet Cloak Inn	1505 Hillsborough St.	$$-$$$	Y	828-0333
Wingate Inn	2610 Westinghouse Blvd.	$$-$$$	N	821-0888

TRIANGLE ACCOMMODATIONS

Hotel/Motel	Address	$-$$$$	Airport Shuttle	Phone
RESEARCH TRIANGLE PARK				
Baymont Inn & Suites	1001 Aerial Center Pkwy.	$$-$$$	Y	481-3600
Comfort Suites	5219 Page Rd.	$$$-$$$$	Y	314-1200
Courtyard by Marriott	2001 Hospitality Ct.	$$$-$$$$	Y	467-9444
Courtyard by Marriott	301 Residence Inn Blvd.	$$$-$$$$	Y	484-2900
Days Inn Airport	1000 Airport Blvd.	$$$	Y	469-8688
Doubletree Guest Suites Hotel	2515 Meridian Pkwy.	$$$-$$$$	Y	361-4660
Fairfield Inn	4507 N.C. 55	$$	N	361-2656
Fairfield Inn RDU Airport	2750 Slater Rd.	$$-$$$	Y	468-2660
Hampton Inn	1010 Airport Blvd.	$$$	Y	462-1620
Hawthorn Suites	300 Meredith Dr.	$$$$	Y	361-1234
Hilton Garden Inn	1500 RDU Center Dr.	$$-$$$$	Y	840-8088
Holiday Inn	4810 Page Rd.	$$$$	Y	941-6000
Holiday Inn Express-RDU	1014 Airport Blvd.	$$$	Y	653-2260
Homewood Suites	I-40 at Miami Blvd.	$$$-$$$$	Y	474-9900
La Quinta Inn & Suites	1001 Hospitality Ct.	$$$-$$$$	Y	461-1771
La Quinta Inn & Suites-RTP	1910 West Park Dr.	$$$-$$$$	Y	484-1422
Marriott at RTP	4700 Guardian Dr.	$$-$$$$	Y	941-6200
Microtel Inn	104 Factory Shops Rd.	$$	N	462-0061
Radisson Governors Inn	I-40 at Davis Dr.	$$$-$$$$	Y	549-8631
Residence Inn	1919 N.C. 54 E.	$$$-$$$$	Y	361-1266
Residence Inn	2020 Hospitality Ct.	$$$-$$$$	Y	467-8689
Sheraton Imperial	I-40 & Page Rd.	$$$-$$$$	Y	941-5050
Wellesley Inn & Suites	4919 S. Miami Blvd.	$$-$$$	Y	998-0400
Wingate Inn	5223 Page Rd.	$$$-$$$$	Y	941-2854
Wyndham Garden Hotel	I-40 & Miami Blvd.	$$-$$$$	Y	941-6066

Sheraton Capital Center Hotel
$$$ • 421 S. Salisbury St.
• 834-9900 • www.sheraton.com

Formerly known as the Raleigh Plaza Hotel, the 359-room Sheraton Capital Center underwent $7 million in renovations in 1998, including the addition of a restaurant, The Grove Cafe. The 17-story downtown hotel is located next to and is connected through the underground parking lot with the city's Civic Center and the BB&T York-Hannover skyscraper and is a block from Memorial Auditorium (soon to be BTI Center for the Performing Arts) and the City Market. The Sheraton Capital Center offers business meeting facilities for groups ranging from 12 to 600 and its indoor pool features a whirlpool. Other amenities include an exercise facility and complimentary daily newspaper.

Velvet Cloak Inn
$$-$$$ • 1505 Hillsborough St.
• 828-0333 • www.velvetcloakinn.com

Built during the 1960s, the Velvet Cloak has been a fixture in the city's hotel life ever since. The Velvet Cloak and its restaurants set the standard for many years. The 172-room inn has an indoor pool and atrium and is next to the YMCA where visiting members can play racquetball and work out. Enjoy fine dining in The Charter Room, which features a seasonal menu with nightly specials. The Velvet Cloak's location near NCSU and downtown makes it popular both with academic and government leaders. By the way, the Inn is named after Sir Walter Raleigh's gallant gesture of placing his velvet cloak over a mud puddle so Queen Elizabeth wouldn't dim the shine of her shoes.

Research Triangle Park/Airport

Doubletree Guest Suites
$$$-$$$$ • 2515 Meridian Pkwy.
• 361-4660, (800) 222-8733
• www.doubletree.com
Well situated in the Research Triangle Park, the 203-suite Doubletree Guest Suites offers travelers spacious accommodations in a conveniently located, first-class hotel. The hotel offers three flexible meeting and banquet rooms, a health club, an indoor/outdoor pool, a tennis court and jogging trails. The guest library is available for small meetings or for relaxing with a good book or magazine. The Piney Point Grill & Seafood Bar is a comfortable place to enjoy good food.

Hawthorn Suites
$$$$ • 300 Meredith Dr. off N.C. 55
• 361-1234, (800) 527-1133
• www.hawthorn.com
These luxury accommodations include 100 fully furnished and equipped suites geared to business travelers, visitors planning an extended stay or people relocating to the area. Each suite contains a kitchenette, living room and one or two bedrooms. Hawthorn Suites has an outdoor lap pool, fitness center, meeting and conference rooms and audio/visual equipment. A complimentary breakfast buffet is served, and catered lunches, dinners and bar services are available. Guests enjoy a weekday evening manager's reception.

Hilton Garden Inn-RDU
1500 RDU Center Dr. • 840-8088,
(800) HILTONS • www.hilton.com
A refrigerator, microwave and coffee maker are available in each of the Hilton Garden's spacious rooms. Other amenities include a restaurant, a heated indoor pool, 24-hour business center, complimentary airport transportation and meeting facilities.

Holiday Inn/RDU Airport
$$$$ • 4810 Page Rd. at I-40 (Exit 282)
• 941-6000 • www.holiday-inn.com
The Holiday Inn in the Research Triangle Park has 249 rooms and suites, all with TVs and VCRs. The hotel has a fine restaurant, Remington's, as well as the more casual Cafe, a lobby bar and a popular area night spot, Horsefeathers. Other amenities include a pool, sauna and exercise room. Meeting facilities are available for up to 300 people.

La Quinta Inn & Suites
$$$ • 1001 Hospitality Ct. • 461-1771,
(800) 531-5900 • www.laquinta.com
Opened in the fall of 1996, La Quinta has 135 rooms, an exercise room and a pool. Continental breakfast, free local calls, laundry service and a shuttle service are offered to guests. The hotel is near the airport and is just across the street from Prime Outlets mall.

Marriott Research Triangle Park
$$-$$$$ • 4700 Guardian Dr.
(South Miami Blvd. at I-40) • 941-6200,
(800) 228-9290 • www.marriott.com
This six-story Marriott is just off I-40, a few miles from the airport. Features include 224 rooms, spacious meeting and banquet facilities and a conference center. The hotel also offers two executive boardrooms, the Parkside restaurant and lounge, a lobby bar, gift shop, indoor pool, health club and sauna.

Radisson Governors Inn
$$$-$$$$ • I-40 at Davis Dr. (Exit 280)
• 549-8631, (800) 333-3333
• www.radisson.com
Adjacent to Research Triangle Park and convenient to RDU International Airport, the

INSIDERS' TIP
Some hotels are worth a trip just to experience their popular dining rooms such as Carolina Crossroads in the Carolina Inn, Il Palio Ristorante in the Siena Hotel, the Fairview Restaurant at the Washington Duke Inn, The Charter Room at the Velvet Cloak Inn and, of course, the buffet at Jacqueline's in the Plantation Inn Resort.

Radisson Governors Inn is one of the nicer accommodations in the Triangle and the only hotel in RTP catering to the business traveler. It offers 193 recently renovated spacious rooms with queen-size beds. Dining is elegant in the remodeled Galeria or grab a quick bite to eat in the Quorum Lounge. It also features meeting space and banquet facilities. A swimming pool, tennis and basketball courts, exercise room and workout stations are some of the leisure activities available.

Sheraton Imperial Hotel
$$$-$$$$ • 4700 Emperor Blvd.
(I-40 at Page Rd., Exit 282)
• 941-5050, (800) 222-6503
• www.sheratonrtp.com
This 10-story, 331-room hotel offers luxurious accommodations for tourists and traveling business executives. The 19-acre hotel and convention center complex includes two restaurants and a nightclub/lounge. Tennis courts, a jogging trail, indoor and outdoor pools and a Jacuzzi round out the amenities. It also offers plenty of space for meetings, conferences and private parties. The Imperial Athletic Club is on the premises.

Wingate Inn
$$$-$$$$ • 5223 Page Rd.
• 941-2854, (800) 228-1000
• www.wingateinns.com
The Wingate Inn boasts spacious rooms designed for the business traveler with mini refrigerators, microwave ovens and coffee makers. Guests can also enjoy a deluxe continental breakfast buffet, 24-hour business center with complimentary faxing and copying, outdoor pool, fitness center and whirlpool.

Wyndham Garden Hotel
$$-$$$$ • 4620 S. Miami Blvd.
• 941-6066, (800) 972-0264
• www.wyndham.com
The Wyndham features 172 rooms and many unique amenities and features. The Wyndham has a 50-foot lap pool, a cardiovascular room, sauna and whirlpool. Enjoy the Garden Cafe and Patio Lounge. The hotel can provide catering and imaginative themed events for up to 120 people.

Corporate Temporary Housing

Bridgestreet Accommodations
• 481-3663, (800) B-STREET
• www.bridgestreet.com
Bridgestreet provides fully furnished apartments throughout the Triangle. Most apartments contain washers and dryers, Jacuzzis, outdoor pools, exercise rooms and clubhouses.

Campus Arms Motel Apartments
2222 Elba St., Durham • 286-9133
• www.campusarms.citysearch.com
Weekly/Monthly
The Campus Arms is frequented by people using or visiting nearby Duke University, or the VA or Durham Regional hospitals and traveling business executives who need to stay in town for more than a week. Each of the 29 furnished apartments contains a living room, kitchen, bedroom and bathroom. Four are efficiencies equipped for the handicapped. Apartments can be rented by the week or month and include a telephone, cable TV and weekly maid service.

Candlewood Suites
1818 E. N.C. 54, Durham • 484-9922
1020 Buck Jones Rd., Raleigh
• 468-4222, (888) 226-3539
• www.candlewoodsuites.com
Candlewood is an extended-stay hotel chain with spacious rooms that contain a variety of amenities such as a fully equipped kitchen, microwave, range, dishwasher, coffee maker, television with VCR and compact disc player. Business guests can take advantage of personalized voice mail, a speaker phone, computer data port and conference calling capabilities. Candlewood also offers a fitness center and free laundry facilities.

Chapel Hill Inntown
609 Hillsborough St., Chapel Hill
• 967-3743, (800) 996-7575
• Weekly Rates
Tucked into a cul-de-sac within walking distance of town are 11 extended-stay apartments reserved for out-of-town guests needing a place to stay for at least a week. It's

As the Triangle's only full service rental relocation company we are able to accommodate all temporary housing budgets!

A Rental Solution

Serving All Your Temporary Housing Needs

Looking For An Apartment?

Call today and request a FREE copy of
Apartment Finder or pick one up at area
**Kerr Drugs, Wachovia Banks, Phar-Mor,
Winn Dixie** or **Pantry Stores.** And remember...
we're the book with the RED cover!

Color Photos
Prices
Maps & Directions
Over 200 Pages

**Call today for
your FREE copy!**

(919) 782-7819

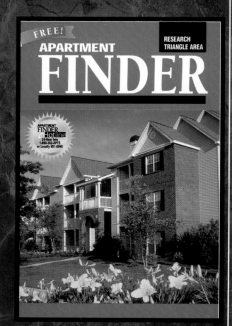

perfect for traveling business executives or families visiting for a short time. You can choose between spacious one-bedroom and two-bedroom units, each fully furnished and equipped with washer and dryer, cable color television, central air conditioning, linens, towels, all cooking utensils and appliances. Theme suites now include Indonesian, Mexican and Arabian Nights condos. Pets are allowed (for a small fee).

Corporate Apartments By CORT
1820 New Hope Church Rd., Raleigh
• **876-7550**
Chapel Hill • 929-5075
Durham • 493-2563 • www.cort1.com
CORT offers furnished apartments for long- and short-term rentals. CORT can also provide design assistance as well as housewares and electronics.

Crossland Economy Studios
5008 N.C. 55, Durham • 484-1878
• **www.crosslandstudios.com**
Crossland is designed specifically for extended-stay travelers. Each of the 132 studios offers a kitchen, cable TV, free local calls, voice mail, computer data port, coffee maker and weekly housekeeping. A 24-hour coin laundry is on the premises.

Duke Tower Residential Suites
807 West Trinity Ave., Durham
• **687-4444 • www.duketower.com**
A furnished all-suite hotel for extended stays, Duke Tower Residential Suites is located near Duke University Medical Center and Northgate Mall and 15 minutes from RDU Airport. It offers 111 spacious suites. Exercise facilities, an outdoor pool, laundry room, fully equipped kitchen and office services are available. Pets are permitted for an additional charge.

Execustay, Inc.
308D W. Millbrook Rd., Raleigh
• **518-1707, (800) 959-7829**
• **www.execustay.com**
Execustay is a quality service that requires a 30-day minimum stay. It offers fully furnished one-, two- and three-bedroom apartments, townhouses and private homes.

Extended StayAmerica
1500 Regency Pkwy., Cary • 468-5828
3105 Tower Blvd., Durham • 489-8444
2700 Slater Rd., Morrisville • 380-1499
911 Wake Towne Dr., Raleigh • 829-7271
• **www.extstay.com**
Extended StayAmerica efficiency suites offer queen-size beds; fully equipped

Photo by Rich Weidman

Extended Stay America offers efficiency suites
in four locations throughout the Triangle.

kitchens with refrigerators and microwaves; free local calls, voice mail and data port; and laundry service. A weekly housekeeping service is also available.

Globe Corporate Stay International
- **851-1511, (888) 900-1992**
- **www.globecsi.com**

Thirty locations serve Cary, Chapel Hill, Durham, Raleigh and RTP. No minimum stay is required. Apartments are furnished and have a kitchen with cookware, microwave and a washer/dryer. Most Globe Corporate Stay International complexes have pools, fitness centers and tennis courts.

Home Suite Home
5840 McHines Pl., Raleigh
- **954-0349, (888) 824-0349**

Locally owned and professionally managed, this firm advertises that one phone call does it all. Home Suite Home offers one-, two- and three-bedroom suites throughout the Triangle.

Homestead Village
4515 N.C. 55, Durham • 544-9991
1920 Ivy Creek Blvd., Durham • 402-1700
4810 Bluestone Dr., Raleigh • 510-8551
3531 Wake Forest Rd., Raleigh • 981-7353
- **www.stayhsd.com**

Homestead Village offers extended-stay lodging at an affordable weekly rate. Amenities include a fully equipped kitchen, well-lighted work area, coffee maker, iron and ironing board, personalized voice mail, telephone with data port, twice weekly housekeeping and free local phone calls.

Homewood Suites
100 MacAlyson Ct., Cary • 467-4444
4603 Central Park Dr., Durham • 474-9900
3600 Mt. Moriah Rd., Durham • 401-0610
5400 Homewood Banks, Raleigh • 785-1131
- **www.homewood.suites.com**

Homewood contains spacious suites with separate sleeping and living areas, as well as fully equipped kitchens. Most suites also include microwaves, refrigerators, dishwashers and coffee makers. Guests can enjoy an outdoor pool and fitness center. Meeting facilities are also available.

MainStay Suites
2601 Appliance Ct., Raleigh • 807-9970

MainStay offers single-, double- and queen-size bedroom suites with fully equipped kitchens. Amenities include an indoor pool, fitness center, complimentary continental breakfast, courtyard grill and social hours on Monday, Tuesday and Wednesday evenings.

Marriott Residence Inn
2900 Regency Pkwy., Cary • 467-4080
201 Residence Inn Blvd., Durham
- **361-1266, (800) 331-3131**
2020 Hospitality Ct., Morrisville • 467-8689
1000 Navaho Dr., Raleigh • 878-6100
2200 Summit Park Ln., Raleigh
- **279-3000**
- **www.marriott.com**

Residence Inn offers one- and two-bedroom studios with comfortable living room areas and fully equipped kitchens. Other amenities include laundry facilities, pool and whirlpool. Daily maid service is also available.

Meredith Corporate Housing
2603 Village Ct., Raleigh
- **781-5088, (800) 237-9363**

If you need more amenities than a hotel room, you may want to consider a guest house. The Meredith Guest House offers 30 suites that are nothing less than small, well-furnished apartments. It has one-, two- and three-bedroom units and is conveniently located off the I-440 Beltline at the Lake Boone Trail exit on Wycliff Road. Included is a 24-hour message center and maid service. The units rent by the day or month and many Triangle companies lodge employees on temporary assignments in this facility. Relocating families with children find the guest houses less cramped than motel rooms. Pool and fitness center privileges are available.

Oakwood Corporate Housing
- **460-4550, (800) 888-0808**
- **www.oakwood.com**

Oakwood is a temporary housing service that has locations in Raleigh, Durham, Chapel Hill and Cary. An economical alternative to

Photo by Rich Weidman

Extended-stay hotels such as Residence Inn offer
a variety of amenities for the business traveler.

hotels, it is ideal for business travelers, transferees and relocating individuals and families. Housing is provided for extended stays of 30 days or more and all accommodations are fully furnished. Oakwood has 1,000 locations across the nation.

Rental Resources
4205 Wake Forest Rd., Ste. 202, Raleigh
• 863-5200, (800) 319-0089

Rental Resources specializes in single family and townhomes, filling a niche left void by apartment communities. Its Executive Service includes picking up the prospective client, showing currently available accommodations that meet specific needs, assisting with the leasing process, facilitating school registration for children and more.

A Rental Solution
8541-A Glenwood Ave., Raleigh
• 781-9925, (888) 869-RELO
• www.arentalsolution.com

A Rental Solution offers temporary housing locations throughout the Triangle area. All apartments include furnishings, utilities, housewares, appliances and amenities such as a pool, tennis and exercise facilities. Offering both economy and luxury options, A Rental Solution can accommodate most budgets.

StudioPlus Corporate Suites
3100 Regency Pkwy., Cary • 460-4800
600 Weston Pkwy., Cary • 677-9910
2504 N.C. 54, Durham • 361-1853
4610 S. Miami Blvd, Durham • 941-2878
921 Wake Towne Dr., Raleigh • 546-0879
• www.studioplus.com

Conveniently located throughout the Triangle, StudioPlus features such amenities as a fully equipped kitchen, cable TV, voice mail/data port, weekly housekeeping, on-site laundry facility, fitness center and outdoor pool.

Walden Executive Suites
103 Melville Loop, Chapel Hill
• 929-8634

Walden Executive Suites is located 3 miles from UNC Hospitals and 6 miles from Duke University Medical Center. Walden's fully furnished suites offer a full kitchen, washer and dryer and free local calls. An outdoor pool is on the premises. Maid service is available. A seven-day minimum stay is required. Pets are allowed for a small fee.

Wynne Residential Suites
Raleigh • 781-6922, (800) 477-6922

This service offers convenient locations throughout the Triangle and can provide everything from furniture, washer and dryer and kitchen necessities to optional maid service.

Apartments

The Triangle area has thousands of apartments for rent at nearly every price level—along with a variety of amenities to fit just about anyone's needs. Thanks to an ongoing construction boom, vacancy rates are at their highest level in nearly a decade. More than 4,000 apartment units were built in 1999 alone.

Some apartments boast furnishings, balconies, fireplaces, vaulted ceilings, walk-in closets and ceiling fans. Some complexes offer pools, clubhouses, fitness centers, tennis courts and playgrounds. Of course, the more amenities you seek, the higher the rent!

In addition to amenities, factors to consider when embarking on your apartment search include location, price, space, furnishability and security. Location should be one of your first priorities since you'll want a reasonable commute time (somewhere in the range of 15 to 20 minutes). Note: If you decide to live near one of the universities, beware of late-hour revelry that may lead to sleepless nights. Lease agreements are usually for 12 months, although six-month and shorter-term leases are available. Security deposits also vary but are usually half of the monthly rent. Many places allow pets, but some complexes have size limits and most require a deposit or a fee.

For a temporary residence, furnished corporate apartments provide all the comforts of home. Most offer fully furnished rooms and include services for business travelers and families relocating to the area. A minimum one-week stay is usually required (see our chapter on "Accommodations and Temporary Housing"). In this chapter, we highlight free apartment publications and apartment locator services that will assist you in your search.

Apartment Publications

The Apartment Book
516 Brickhaven Dr., Raleigh
- **834-2665, (800) 849-APTS (2787)**
- **www.aptbook.com**

This book and apartment locator service can be found at locations throughout the Triangle, usually at big grocery stores next to newsstands. It's free, as is the locator service. An online edition of *The Apartment Book* is also available.

Apartment Finder
2626 Glenwood Ave., Ste. 120, Raleigh
- **782-7819, (888) 360-2787**
- **www.apartmentguide.com**

A free, quarterly, color, digest-sized publication from HPC Publications, the *Apartment Finder,* is available at most large retail centers, banks, hotels and other visitor centers. It's a comprehensive guide serving the Triangle. The magazine has locator maps and gives a detailed description of the larger apartment communities.

Triangle Area Apartment Guide
4000 Westchase Blvd., Ste. 140, Raleigh
- **743-0805 • www.aptguides.com**

Another informative publication for the apartment hunter, this easy-to-use guide provides locations, prices, features and maps. It can be found at your local grocery store. An online edition is available.

Newspapers, Real Estate Ads

The local newspapers are always a good source for current rental properties. Also, check the Triangle's weekly publications

INSIDERS' TIP
The high level of apartment vacancy rates has forced many landlords to freeze rates and to offer rent concessions such as reduced security deposits. Shop around for special offers.

Staff Photo

Triangle apartments offer a wide variety of amenities and price levels.

(see "Media" chapter). If you're looking for a room, house or an apartment in a private home a block from campus and you have the time, you'll find the dailies and weeklies are a good bet. *The Herald-Sun* and *The News and Observer* both offer apartment listing information on their web sites.

The Cary News
212 E. Chatham St., Cary • 460-2600

The Chapel Hill Herald
106 Mallette St., Chapel Hill
• 967-6581 • www.herald-sun.com

The Chapel Hill News
505 W. Franklin St., Chapel Hill
• 932-2000
• www.chapelhillnews.com

The Herald-Sun
2828 Pickett Rd., Durham
• 419-6500 • www.herald-sun.com

The News & Observer
215 S. McDowell St., Raleigh
• 829-4500 • www.newsobserver.com
• www.triangle.com

Locator Services

Apartment Book Locator Service
516 Brickhaven Dr., Raleigh
• 755-6030, (800) 365-5755
• www.caraptloc.com
Lone Wolf Publishing offers this free apartment locator service in conjunction with its *Apartment Book*. The service utilizes a Triangle-wide database of furnished and unfurnished apartments to find the appropriate location, features, amenities and price to meet your needs. Relocation packages are also available with floorplans, maps and directions, rental rates and current specials. The relocation center is located off the I-440 beltline near Hillsborough Street.

Drucker & Falk Welcome Center
7200 Stonehenge Dr., Ste. 105, Raleigh
• 870-0777, (800) 849-FIND
• v;ww.druckerandfalk.com
With more than 7,000 units, Drucker & Falk is the largest single owner of apartments in The Triangle. The group is well organized and knows the area and needs of relocating clients. Its locator services are free and can help you find an apartment in Apex, Cary, Chapel Hill, Clayton, Durham, Garner, Holly Springs, Knightdale, Morrisville, Raleigh or Wake Forest. The Drucker & Falk Welcome Center is located off of Creedmoor Road in North Raleigh.

A Rental Solution
8541-A Glenwood Ave., Raleigh
• 781-9925, (888) 869-RELO
• www.arentalsolution.com
A Rental Solution is the Triangle's only full-service rental relocation company specializing in apartment locating, temporary/ corporate housing and rental touring. The firm's relocation counselors provide floorplans, images, prices and availability for hundreds of Triangle area apartments. A Rental Solution also offers a fee-based roommate referral service.

With more than 200 artists and craftspeople, along with dozens of musicians, Artsplosure offers a spectacular celebration of the arts.

Annual Events

Triangle residents will find almost any excuse to throw a party. On most weekends throughout the year, but especially in the spring and summer, you'll discover lively festivals and special events going on somewhere in the area.

Events in the Triangle run the gamut from the internationally acclaimed American Dance Festival to the historic North Carolina Renaissance Faire to the bizarre Hillsborough Hog Day with its best-dressed pot-belly pig contest. Art lovers will enjoy Apple Chill in Chapel Hill, Artsplosure in Raleigh, Lazy Daze in Cary and Centerfest in Durham. Celebrities like Michael Jordan can be seen teeing off at such charity events as the Duke Children's Classic at Croasdaile Country Club in March and the Jimmy V Celebrity Golf Classic at Prestonwood Country Club in August. Festivals with an ethnic flavor have also become popular over the past few years, reflecting the Triangle's ever-changing population. Carnaval Brasileiro in Carrboro, Festival de la Americas in Raleigh, Cinco de Mayo throughout the Triangle, Fete de la Musique in Carrboro, La Fiesta del Pueblo in Chapel Hill and International Festival in Raleigh are just a few such examples. Of course the grandaddy of all Triangle festivals is the 10-day North Carolina State Fair, held annually since the mid-19th century. The action continues right up through the end of December with First Night Raleigh when the famous copper acorn drops to bring in the New Year, signaling the onset of a whole new round of festivities.

Good sources for information on upcoming festivals include the Friday entertainment sections of both the *News & Observer* and the *Herald-Sun*, the weekly arts and entertainment publications *Independent* and *Spectator*, and the monthly *Triangle Pointer* magazine.

January

KwanzaaFest
Durham Marriott Convention Center
• **560-2729**
Presented by Chuck Davis and the African American Dance Ensemble, KwanzaaFest consists of a Kwanzaa ceremony, dance, music, poetry, children's activities and vendors.

N.C. International Jazz Festival
Baldwin Auditorium, Duke University
• **684-4444**
North Carolina International Jazz Festival, which started in 1983, features musicians from such countries as Italy, Monaco, Portugal and The Netherlands. The festival runs from late January through April at Duke University's Baldwin Auditorium. Single tickets for the festival are general admission, $15; students, $12. Series tickets run $60; students, $50.

Raleigh Antiques Extravaganza
Raleigh Convention & Conference Center, Fayetteville Street Mall
• **(336) 924-8337**
More than 175 exhibitors from all over the East Coast display their wares at this three-day event that offers the finest in country and Americana, Victorian, wicker, dolls, toys, clothing and much more. Admission fee is $4.50 for one day, and weekend passes are available for $5.50. The Raleigh Antiques Extravaganza is also held in July.

February

Carnaval Brasileiro
The ArtsCenter, Carrboro • 929-ARTS
A Brazilian version of Mardi Gras, this event features traditional and new Carnaval and Samba sounds. Costumed and masked

participants contribute to the festivities. Tickets are $10 and include a complimentary sampling of Brazilian food.

Home, Garden & Flower Show
Raleigh Convention & Conference Center, Fayetteville Street Mall
• **831-6011**

Each year, local and regional garden centers, garden clubs, landscapers, contractors and remodelers turn the Raleigh Convention and Conference Center into an indoor wonderland of gardens, featuring water gardens and thousands of plants and flowers. Decks, spas and many other related garden and home products are also on display.

Native American Pow Wow
N.C. School of Science & Mathematics, Durham
• **286-3366**

Traditional Native American dancing, singing, storytelling, crafts and food highlight this popular pow wow sponsored by the Native American Club at the N.C. School of Science and Math. About 25 tribes are invited from North Carolina, South Carolina and Virginia. Admission is $3 (free for ages 5 and under).

Ringling Brother's Circus
Entertainment & Sports Arena, Raleigh
Ticketmaster: 834-4000

Mark your calendar for the annual return of the "Greatest Show on Earth" to Raleigh. Once held at the State Fairground's Dorton Arena, the Circus has a new home at the state-of-the-art Entertainment and Sports Arena on Edwards Mill Road.

March

ACC Tournament

Okay, we're cheating. This event does not take place in Chapel Hill, Durham or Raleigh. But it is still very much a Triangle attraction because when tournament time arrives in March, the Atlantic Coast Conference basketball tournament is THE event. As Tournament week begins, the local media will run stories and features; there will be private parties to watch the games; bars and clubs will host special ACC TV nights; and it becomes difficult to get your business phone calls returned during game times. In fact, practically the whole Triangle closes down as everyone scrambles to the nearest TV to root for their favorite team.

Photo by Jeff Camarati, courtesy of Duke University

The Duke Blue Devils captured back-to-back ACC Basketball Tournament championships in 1999 and 2000.

ANNUAL EVENTS • 85

The Tournament was once held at NCSU's Reynolds Coliseum but these days, the playing sites—supposedly neutral arenas—have been in larger coliseums such as the Greensboro Coliseum, Atlanta's Omni and the Charlotte Coliseum. Atlanta will host in 2001, Charlotte in 2002 and Greensboro in 2003 and 2004. The format has been changed for the 2001 season to bring back the dreaded "play-in" game that pairs the two teams with the worst season records in the opening round on Thursday night. Tickets are sometimes available and the trip is worth their cost.

N.C. Antiquarian Book Fair
Kerr Scott Building, State Fairgrounds
• 933-9585

Bibliophiles will not want to miss this popular book fair that boasts antiquarian book dealers from across the country. Subjects include Americana, art, Civil War, history, travel, regional, gardening, religion and much more.

N.C. Renaissance Faire
State Fairgrounds • 755-8004

Step back in time to the Medieval/Renaissance era where lords and ladies, knights in armor, a royal court and much more congregate in a magical village during this entertaining two-day festival. Activities include jousting competitions, children's activities, arts and crafts, live entertainment, fencing and "live steel" sword demonstrations, "unicorn" pony rides, a petting zoo, medieval games and food. Admission is charged.

Southeastern Microbrewers Invitational
Durham Marriott at the Civic Center
• 484-1128

The Microbrewers' Invitational has grown substantially since its humble beginnings in 1994. It now boasts about 150 beers from 30 of the country's best microbreweries. The festival includes food, live music and information booths. Admission is charged.

St. Patrick's Day Parade
Downtown Raleigh • 571-7869

Activities for all ages can be found at this Irish-style celebration, which takes place in the Moore Square Arts District in downtown Raleigh. Enjoy traditional Irish music, Irish step dancing and Scottish Highlands dancing. After the festivities, be sure to head over to Tir na nOg for a green beer.

April

Apple Chill
Franklin St., Chapel Hill
• 968-2784

Up to 28,000 people from all over the Triangle converge on Chapel Hill for this famous street fair, which offers a variety of arts and crafts, live music, clogging, magicians, puppet shows, jugglers, potters, incredible edibles and more. Shuttle service is available from the University Mall on U.S. 15-501.

Art Springs to Life Arts Festival
Chapel Hill • 929-9700

Art Springs to Life debuted in the spring of 2000, offering a series of free events throughout the month, including music recitals, art symposiums and exhibits, a garden tour, dancing and live music. The festivities culminate with the extremely popular Arts Downtown and Apple Chill festivals at the end of the month.

Arts Downtown
Chapel Hill • 929-9700

Arts Downtown is a children's celebration of the arts that features performances by area schools—choral, band music, drama and art, as well as food and children's activities. It takes place on the Rosemary Street parking deck in downtown Chapel Hill.

Cary Road Race
Cary High School, Cary • 469-4061

Sponsored by the *Cary News* and Cary Parks, Recreation and Cultural Resources Department, the Cary Road Race attracts approximately 1,120 runners each year. The event features a 5K (3.1 miles) race, a 10K (6.2 miles) run and a one-mile fun run. All of the courses wind through Cary. Proceeds from the Cary Road Race benefit the preservation and expansion of greenways in the Cary area.

The immensely popular Artsplosure Spring Jazz and Art Festival takes place in downtown Raleigh.

Chapel Hill Spring Garden Tour
Chapel Hill • 962-0522

Celebrate the arrival of spring by taking a walking tour of 10 private gardens in Chapel Hill's historic Gimghoul neighborhood. Organized by the Chapel Hill Garden Club, the tour benefits the North Carolina Botanical Garden.

DoubleTake Documentary Film Festival
Carolina Theatre, Durham • 660-3699
www.doubletakemagazine.org/filmfestival

DoubleTake, the largest event of its kind in the United States, celebrates the power and artistry of documentary cinema with four days of film screenings. The festival also features seminars led by acclaimed documentary directors such as D.A. Pennebaker, Ken Burns, Albert Maysles, Michael Apted and Ross McElwee. Call ahead for ticket prices.

Greater Durham International Festival
Durham Civic Center Plaza • 560-4107

The International Festival is held in conjunction with the Festival Viviendo en America at the Durham Athletic Park. Highlights include a multicultural parade, live entertainment on four stages, children's activities, arts and crafts and culinary creations from around the world.

Piedmont Farm Tour
Orange, Chatham & Alamance Counties • 542-2402

Take a self-guided tour of about 25 small family farms in this unique two-day event cosponsored by Weaver Street Market, *Independent Weekly* and the Carolina Farm Stewardship Association. Participating farms include an organic food processor, a working dairy farm, cut-flower and herb growers, an all-natural chicken ranch, an apple orchard, organic vegetable farms, a goat farm and an oriental vegetable farm. Weaver Street Market kicks off the event with a night of live music, food and beverages on its front lawn.

Southern Ideal Home and Garden Show
State Fairgrounds, Raleigh • 851-2911

If you want to remodel your home or just get some ideas for a future project, this is the place to visit. You'll find many of the area's home improvement specialists, home decorators and specialty vendors at the show, which is sponsored by the Home Builder's Association. The Home Show is also held the last week in September.

Southern Women's Show
Raleigh Convention & Conference Center, Fayetteville Street Mall • (800) 849-0248

The Southern Women's Show is a very popular event that has become a traditional outing for many women in the area. Exhibits include jewelry, clothing, fashion accessories, healthcare, fitness, cosmetics, books, food and decorative items.

Spring Daze
Town Hall Campus, Cary • 469-4061

Handmade crafts from dolls' clothes to stained glass are sold at this outdoor event, which features more than 150 local artists and craftspeople. Free shuttle buses run from the Cary Towne Center to the festival.

May

Artsplosure Spring Jazz & Art Festival
Downtown Raleigh • 832-8699 • www.artsplosure.org

More than 200 artists and craftspeople combine with dozens of musicians to mix art, international jazz and regional blues into a spectacular celebration of the arts. Artsplosure also features 150 juried art exhibits and children's exhibits. The event draws approximately 75,000 people.

Bimbe Cultural Arts Festival
Durham Athletic Park, Durham • 560-4355

Started in 1969, the two-day Bimbe Cultural Arts Festival celebrates the traditional West African end of harvest and the spirit of hope with music, dance, storytelling, crafts, art displays, food, rides, children's events and much more. It takes place downtown in the old Durham Athletic Park.

Brookhill Steeplechase
Brookhill Farm, Clayton • 510-7915

We're so uptown in the Triangle that we started a nationally sanctioned steeplechase in 1992. Sponsored by the Raleigh Jaycees, Brookhill is held the first Saturday in May on Brookhill Farm outside of the Johnston County town of Clayton, east of Raleigh. Brookhill is offered as the Triangle's answer to the older, more famous Stonybrook race near Southern Pines. This race draws approximately 20,000 spectators. Tailgating and picnicking are welcome.

Carrboro Day
Carrboro Town Hall Grounds • 968-7703

Celebrate Carrboro's rich heritage with historical exhibits, arts and crafts, live music, storytelling, poetry readings, children's activities, a potluck dinner and street dance.

Celebration of the Outdoors
Falcon Park, Fuquay-Varina • 552-1430

Fuquay-Varina's four-acre Falcon Park comes alive for this celebration, which includes crafts, food, music, carnival rides and a petting zoo.

Duke Children's Classic
Croasdaile Country Club • 667-2560

The Duke Children's Classic has evolved into one of the Triangle's biggest spectator attractions since its humble beginnings in 1974. Recently, the event has been selected as a stop for the Celebrity Players Tour. The event raises money for the Duke Children's Hospital and Health Center. More than $10 million has been raised for the hospital over the years.

In addition to golf, the Classic also includes tennis, entertainment, a celebrity autograph tent and a sumptuous banquet. It is held in late May and tickets for participants usually are sold out before Christmas. Celebrities at past events have included the late Frank Sinatra, former President Gerald Ford, Michael Jordan, Bill Murray, Dan Marino,

Steve Spurrier, Jim McMahon, Terry Bradshaw, Arnold Palmer and, of course, Perry Como, the founding chairman. Comedian Jeff Foxworthy is the current tournament chairman.

Eno River Old Time & Bluegrass Music Festival
West Point on the Eno • 990-1900

This entertaining bluegrass music festival and competition draws talented musicians from all over the state. It takes place at the West Point on the Eno Amphitheater.

Festival de la Americas
Kiwanis Park, Raleigh • 831-6854

A Latin American festival and soccer tournament, Festival de la Americas made its debut in 1999. The festival includes food, crafts and a carnival.

Great Raleigh Road Race
Downtown Raleigh • 831-6011

The Great Raleigh Road Race is the City of Oaks' largest single participant sporting event with as many as 2,000 runners and joggers lining up for the starting gun on Wilmington Street next to Memorial Auditorium. A 5K race (about 3.1 miles) is just one of the highlights of a whole weekend of activities, including the city's Artsplosure. The course winds its way through downtown and then up Hillsborough Street—and that's UP, too, folks—past NCSU and then back downtown, finishing at the Civic Center. Although it is a sanctioned event, the participants are those same men, women, boys and girls you see plugging along the Triangle's byways and sidewalks year round. The registration fee runs about $12 or

$17 if you would like to receive a commemorative T-shirt.

Landmark Tours
Downtown Raleigh • 833-6404

Spend the day exploring some of the most interesting historic homes and buildings in Raleigh on this self-guided tour. From Mordecai Historic Park (1785) to Montfort Hall (1858) to Nordon Grocery Store (1917), you'll find a variety of architectural styles that are sure to educate and enlighten you. Individual tickets are $20 and family tickets are $40. Ticket price includes a one year introductory membership in Capital Area Preservation, Inc.

Meet in the Street
Downtown Wake Forest • 556-1519

Hosted by the Wake Forest Chamber of Commerce, this street fair offers arts and crafts, food, entertainment and exhibits.

Old Durham Home Tour
Durham • 682-3036

The Historic Preservation Society of Durham Houses in downtown Durham sponsors a self-guided tour of historic houses in the Forest Hills and Fayetteville Street areas. Tickets cost $12 in advance; $15 the day of the tour.

Peak Week Festival
Downtown Apex • 387-3065

Sponsored by the Apex Chamber of Commerce, this entertaining, day-long festival celebrates the arrival of spring with arts and crafts, food concessions, children's activities, information booths, musical groups and much more.

INSIDERS' TIP

North Carolina festivals worth a daytrip or weekend getaway include the North Carolina Azalea Festival in Wilmington (April), Merlefest in Wilkesboro (April), Cameron Antique Fair (May and October), Eastern Music Festival in Greensboro (June-August), Grandfather Mountain Highland Games (July), Folkmoot in Waynesville (July), Summer Festival of Music in Brevard (July), Mountain Dance and Folk Festival in Asheville (August), Woolly Worm Festival in Banner Elk (October) and Carolina Renaissance Festival in Charlotte (October-November).

Photo by Rich Weidman

The streets of Apex come alive for Peak Week,
the town's celebration of the arrival of spring.

June

American Dance Festival
Page Auditorium, Duke University
• 684-6402
• www.americandancefestival.org
(See "Dance" section in our "Arts" chapter.)

Carolina Classic
Raleigh • 380-0011

The Carolina Classic, which started in 1994, boasts some of the PGA Tour's up-and-coming pros as well as some older players who are trying to get back on the tour. Previously known as the NIKE Tour, the event has a new sponsor, BUY.COM. The Classic has been played at Raleigh Country Club but will reside at the Wakefield Planta-tion Tournament Players Club course start-ing in 2001. The Classic, one of 30 events on the BUY.COM Tour, features a $400,000 purse. Tournament tickets cost $15 in ad-vance. All net proceeds are donated to the Boys and Girls Clubs of Wake County.

Day At The Park Festival
Morrisville Community Park, Morrisville
• 469-9760

Live music, arts and crafts, food, clowns, pony rides, a children's stage and much more make up this entertaining festival. You'll even find a dunk tank, with local officials volun-teering to get wet. Free admission, free carnival rides and fireworks make this a very popular event.

Edible Arts Festival
Durham Arts Council, Durham
• 560-2787

Edible Arts is a festival of food and art that features a wide assortment of delectable food from the Triangle's restaurants and cafes. Past festivals have included Magnolia Grill, Pop's Trattoria, Fowler's, Carolina Brewery and Sitar India Palace. A silent auc-tion includes travel and dining packages, artwork, wine and gifts. All proceeds benefit the Durham Arts Council's Arts Education Program. Tickets are $35 in advance; $40 at the door.

Fete de la Musique
Downtown Carrboro • 990-1225

Enjoy a diverse range of musical talent at this lively outdoor festival that celebrates the summer solstice. Dozens of live music and performance acts take the stage with styles that include Latino folk, country, rock, reggae, ska, jazz and more.

Hillsborough Hog Day
Downtown Hillsborough • 732-8156

One of the Triangle's most unusual events, Hog Day takes place every June in downtown Hillsborough, 15 minutes north of Chapel Hill and Carrboro. If you like to eat eastern North Carolina pork, you'll feel at home here. It features a highly competitive barbecue cook-off, with the results to be enjoyed by those attending this event. In addition to Carolina barbecue, other foods are there for you to enjoy. A best-dressed pot-belly pig contest, arts and crafts, music and dance, an antique car show, games and activities for kids round out the offerings of the festival.

Spring Cultural Festival & Pow Wow
Hillsborough • 304-3723
• www.occaneechi-saponi.org

The Occaneechi-Saponi Tribe share their culture with all on the banks of the Eno River in downtown Hillsborough. The festival features traditional dancing, music, samples of native foods, primitive weapon demonstrations and arts and crafts from tribes such as Abanaki, Cherokee, Coharie, Haliwa and Lumbee. A reconstructed 17th-century Occaneechi village opened recently, enabling visitors to learn more about the lifestyle of this Piedmont tribe.

Summerfest at Regency Park
Regency Park, Cary • 733-2750, ext. 260

The North Carolina Symphony's Summerfest at Regency Park in Cary has become the informal, fun, family event all the Triangle looks forward to every Saturday night in June (7:30 PM), two June Thursday nights (6:30 PM) and the Fourth of July (8 PM). You can picnic on the lawn with food you've

Photo by Rich Weidman

The Fourth of July Capitol Celebration in downtown Raleigh features costumed demonstrators, military encampments, crafts and live music.

brought or purchased. If you're not a grass and blanket fan, some seats are available under a tent where you can sit at a table with friends and enjoy the concert in comfort. The venue will boast a new $12-million amphitheater for the year 2001. Recent highlights have included Dixieland jazz from the New Reformation Band, R&B singer Ben E. King, Red Clay Ramblers, jazz vocalist Carol Sloane and folk singers Arlo Guthrie and Tom Chapin. Adult tickets are $12 when purchased in advance and $15 at the gate (the Fourth of July concert is free). Children 12 and under are admitted free of charge. Single tickets are available at the gate or call 831-6060 or (800) 292-7469.

Sunday in the Park
Fletcher Park, Raleigh • 831-6854

Sunday in the Park is a popular, laid-back and free concert series held every Sunday at 6 PM from early June until mid-September. It showcases such area talent as the Steel Creek Bluegrass Band, the Raleigh Concert Band, Triangle Wind Ensemble and the Blues in the Night Jazz Orchestra. It's the perfect chance to picnic with the whole family.

Tar Heel Regatta
Lake Wheeler Park, Raleigh • 662-5704

The Tar Heel Regatta offers national competition boat races at Lake Wheeler, the largest of Raleigh's city parks. Tickets for the Regatta run about $5 per person; $20 per carload.

July

Carrboro Community Fourth of July Celebration
Carrboro • 968-7703

This old-fashioned July 4th celebration is presented each year by the Carrboro Recreation and Parks Department. It features a kid's parade, food, games, face painting and many more activities.

Durham Fireworks Celebration
Wallace Wade Stadium • 560-4355

Held at the football stadium on Duke's West Campus, this popular free event features a classical pops concert followed by fireworks at 9 PM.

Family Fourth at Kenan Stadium
Kenan Stadium, UNC-CH
• 968-2784

If you like fireworks, live music and big crowds, this is where you ought to celebrate Independence Day in Chapel Hill. It is jointly sponsored by the towns of Chapel Hill and Carrboro and Orange County.

Garner Independence Day Festival
Lake Benson Park, Garner
• 772-4688

Get a jump on the Fourth of July crowd by attending this fun-filled extravaganza, which consists of a lively pops concert starring the North Carolina Symphony and an impressive fireworks display. It takes place on the third of July.

July 4th Celebration
State Fairgrounds, Raleigh • 831-6640

Raleigh celebrates the Fourth in a big way, starting about 3 PM at the State Fairgrounds at the intersection of Hillsborough Street and Blue Ridge Road. Admission is free. It's a relaxed day in which you can toss horseshoes, test your basketball free throws or football passes in contests sponsored by the city's Parks and Recreation Department, WRAL 101.5 FM radio and the North Carolina State Fairgrounds. Enjoy live music from popular local bands. Games and rides are spread out throughout the grounds. Concession stands sell Fourth of July specials such as hot dogs and soft drinks. Cold watermelon is usually free.

The big show—and the one that draws more than 40,000 people to the Fairgrounds and another 100,000 spectators parked all along Interstate 40, Meredith College and any street, road or highway within sight of the Fairgrounds—is the fireworks display around 9:15 PM. The city spends thousands of dollars to light up the sky with the rockets' red glare. It's a show that would make Francis Scott Key proud and brings thrills to contemporary patriots.

Staff Photo

Triangle residents come out in droves for the Lazy Daze
Arts and Crafts Festival in downtown Cary.

July 4th Celebration
with N.C. Symphony
Regency Park, Cary • 733-2750

Everything about the free Fourth of July concert and fireworks extravaganza is Americana at its best—American pops favorites, flags waving, families and friends together and a sky exploding with spectacular sights and sounds. The Symphony performs at a new $12 million amphitheater overlooking Symphony Lake.

July 4th Festival for the Eno
West Point on the Eno • 477-4549
• www.enoriver.org

Every year since 1979 the Eno River Association has sponsored a Fourth of July extravaganza at West Point on the Eno city park. It's three days jam-packed with crafts, exhibits, food, fun and most of all, music. Styles include big-name gospel, folk and bluegrass. There's an admission charge ($8 in advance, $10 at the gate and children 12 and under free) and proceeds go to preservation of the park and the Eno River. A free shuttle bus service runs from Durham County Memorial Stadium. A detailed schedule of events is published in the local newspapers in advance of the event.

N.C. State Capitol Celebration
Capitol Square, Downtown Raleigh
• 733-4994

Costumed demonstrators, military encampments, live music, cloggers and concessions round out the festivities at this patriotic and educational Fourth of July celebration.

Raleigh Antiques Extravaganza
Raleigh Convention & Conference Center, Fayetteville Street Mall
• (336) 924-8337
(See write-up in January section.)

Tobacco Harvest Festival
Duke Homestead • 477-5498

Tobacco was what first put Durham on the map back in the mid-18th century. The Tobacco Harvest Festival highlights the tradition of tobacco harvesting and curing and other related activities.

Triangle Triathlon
Lake Crabtree County Park, Morrisville
• (800) 4JIMMYV

Nearly 800 athletes test their endurance skills in this multifaceted event that includes swimming, cycling and running. In 2000, the triathlon drew 2,000 spectators and raised $20,000 for cancer research.

August

Italian Festival: "A Taste of Italy"
Siena Hotel, Chapel Hill • 929-4000

Inspiration for the Siena Hotel's Italian Festival, begun in 1994, came from the pageantry of the medieval horse race held twice each summer in Siena, Italy. The festival features a culinary journey through Italy, including a Murder Mystery Dinner, Lessons in Italian Class, Tuscan Table dinner, Italian Wine Tasting Class, Cooking Demonstration, Kid's Day and more.

Jimmy "V" Celebrity Golf Classic
Prestonwood Country Club, Cary
• 319-0441 • www.golfclassic.org

The Classic honors legendary North Carolina State basketball coach Jim Valvano, who died of cancer. His family started the Classic in 1994 to raise money for the "V" Foundation, which sponsors cancer research. The tournament generates more than $1 million for cancer research annually. It attracts big name sports and entertainment celebrities such as Michael Jordan, Mia Hamm, Charles Barkley, Meatloaf, Mike Krzyzewski, Ric Flair, Dean Smith and Kevin Costner to the Triangle for two days of parties and golf. Expect 30,000 fans to attend. Spectators park at Carter-Finley Stadium and receive shuttle service to Prestonwood. Pay $6 in advance or $10 on tournament day to stroll the links with the celebrities. Tickets can be ordered through Ticketmaster at 834-4000.

Lazy Daze Arts & Crafts Festival
Downtown Cary • 469-4061

Lazy Daze, which has become a real Triangle attraction, is held the last Saturday in August in downtown Cary. Started in 1976, the festival draws approximately 500 craftspeople and artisans from all over the region. They show their wares and paintings from booths set up along Academy and Chatham streets. It's a great place to look for handmade items, some of them at very good

prices. Live entertainment from mountain cloggers to bluegrass music is featured on a bandstand set up near the intersection. Catch a free shuttle bus from Cary Towne Center to the festival.

September

Bull Durham Blues Festival
Durham Athletic Park, Durham
• 683-1709 • www.hayti.org

Some of the country's best-known blues artists descend on historic Durham Athletic Park for two days of blues standards and new blues variations. The festival's "Marketplace" includes eclectic regional and international foods, arts and crafts by North Carolina artists and unique specialty items. Such legendary bluesmen as Wilson Pickett, Buddy Guy, Lightnin' Wells and Clarence Carter have taken the stage at the Blues Festival in recent years.

Centerfest
Downtown Durham • 560-2787
• www.centerfest.org

The Durham Arts Council and the City Parks and Recreation Department co-sponsors this two-day street festival. It draws more than 80,000 people downtown for high-quality, beautiful arts-and-crafts exhibits, kids' activities, theatre, dancing, music, all kinds of food and more. It's fun for all ages.

Well-known celebrities like Gary Busey turn out for the Jimmy V Celebrity Golf Classic at Prestonwood in Cary.

La Fiesta del Pueblo
Chapel Hill High School, Chapel Hill
• 835-1525 • www.elpueblo.org

Started in 1994, this two-day festival celebrating Latino culture continues to grow in popularity. Traditional dancing, music, food and crafts are enjoyed annually by close to 20,000. A soccer tournament, which features teams from the state's Latino leagues, adds to the excitement and festivities.

Gourd Festival
State Fairgrounds, Raleigh • 362-4357

This two-day event, co-sponsored by the Cary Gourd Village Garden Club and Cary's Parks, Recreation and Cultural Resources Department, was first held in 1941. The festival showcases dried gourds made into a variety of one-of-a-kind jewelry and decorative accessories, including bowls, birdhouses, pitchers, lamps, clocks, masks and three-dimensional puzzles.

Grecian Festival
State Fairgrounds, Raleigh • 781-4548

Greek dancing and entertainment, food, pastries and coffee, cooking demos and a gift shop are all part of the fun at this 3-day event sponsored by the Holy Trinity Greek Orthodox Church. A portion of the net proceeds are donated to Habitat for Humanity.

Labor Day Weekend Pops In The Park
Meredith College • 733-2750

"Pops in the Park" is the Labor Day Weekend Concert with the North Carolina Symphony that's the Triangle's unofficial salute to the end of summer. Thanks to the graciousness of Meredith College in Raleigh, the concert is held on the college's beautiful front campus and is televised by WRAL-TV.

Families and friends start gathering about 4 PM Sunday to spread their blankets, set up tables and partake of the biggest community picnic (25,000 picnickers) of the summer. It's a great time for people who have been away on vacations or off to summer camp to get back together and swap news or gossip and listen to beautiful music. Meanwhile, you can watch the orchestra set up, tune its instruments and then hear light classical and show tunes with a rousing finale of Tchaikovsky's "1812 Overture," punctuated with booming fireworks. What follows is Raleigh's most mellow traffic jam of the year as thousands

Photo courtesy of N.C. Division of Tourism

Discover North Carolina's true flavor at the State Fair,
which takes place over 10 days in mid-October.

patiently load up their cars and station wagons and slip into the night and into the start of another autumn.

Oktoberfest
North Hills Mall, Raleigh • 828-0890

Despite its name, Oktoberfest is held in late September. German beer, food and entertainment become part of North Hills Mall for four days to raise funds for Hospice of Wake County.

Today & Yesteryear Festival
Downtown Apex • 387-3065

Historic downtown Apex comes alive for two days of good old-fashioned fun at the Today & Yesteryear Festival, which features arts and crafts, live entertainment, food, a Civil War reenactment, children's activities and more. Sponsored by the Apex Downtown Merchants Association, the festival draws more than 10,000 people each year.

October

Bright Leaf Folk Festival
Downtown Wendell • 365-6318

Held the first weekend in October, this festival features family-centered activities and entertainment, including arts and crafts, children's games, a parade, food and face painting.

Festifall
Franklin St., Chapel Hill • 968-2784

Join the crowds in downtown Chapel Hill for this popular street fair that celebrates fall with arts and crafts, music, dancing, magicians, puppet shows, jugglers, potters, food and more.

International Festival
Raleigh Convention & Conference Center, Fayettevillle Street Mall
• 832-4331 • www.internationalfestival.org

The International Festival is a celebration of all the different nationalities that now call the Triangle home. The food is the tastiest part of the festival—sample everything from Armenian Meesahatz to Vietnamese Spring Rolls—but dancing, singing and native crafts are also on display. A $6 admission fee is charged ($5 in advance); $3 for children 3-12.

N.C. State Fair
Hillsborough St. & Blue Ridge Rd.
• 733-2145 • www.ncstatefair.org

For newcomers, the State Fair is a great place to taste, touch, see and smell all those things that reveal the richness of North Carolina's people and culture. It's all here for you and your family to enjoy year after year—agriculture, technology, traditional arts and crafts, horse shows, livestock exhibits, great food, carnival rides, tractor pulls and even a demolition derby or two.

Founded in 1853 by the State Agricultural Society, the fair lasts 10 days in mid-October; in 2000 it ran from October 13 to October 22. Check at fair time for admission prices, which are under $10 for adults, less for children 6 to 12 and free for children under 6 and adults over 65. Each ticket is good for the entire day, including the Dorton Arena's evening performances of popular stars such as The Oak Ridge Boys, Merle Haggard, Little Richard, Tanya Tucker and The Charlie Daniels Band.

It's the kind of fair where judges still hand out blue ribbons for the best cakes, pies, preserves, pigs and cows. If you're looking for really good down-home food at the fair, try the restaurants across from the Dorton Arena staffed by volunteers from local organizations. The big attractions are the rides and tents on the midway that arrive by rail. A fireworks display brings every fair night to an end—with a BANG.

Gates open at 9 AM. Expect a crowd, even if it rains. Avoid the traffic jam if you can by taking a CAT bus from several outlying locations. Buses run regularly down Hillsborough Street every 15 minutes.

A Shopping Spree
Raleigh Convention and Conference Center, Fayetteville Street Mall
• 787-7480

Organized by the Junior League of Raleigh, this four-day event offers the perfect opportunity to start your holiday shopping.

Photo by Rich Weidman

The International Festival includes dancing, singing, crafts and food from different cultures around the world.

Food and entertainment are also provided. Admission is $5 in advance; $7 at the door.

November

Carolina Christmas Show
Raleigh Convention and Conference Center, Fayetteville Street Mall
• (800) 232-4936

A wonderful shopping experience, the Christmas Show features many of the state's craftspeople and their wares.

Carolina Designer Craftsmen Fine Crafts Show
State Fairgrounds • 460-1551

Started in 1969, this acclaimed craft show provides a showcase for more than 100 talented regional craftspeople displaying jewelry, sculpture, wood furniture, photography, print making, fiber arts, blown glass and more. Admission is $4 per person.

Cary Band Day
Downtown Cary • 460-3572

The largest high school band competition in the South, Cary Band Day starts with a parade of high school bands through downtown Cary and winds up at the Cary High School for competition among participating bands. Since 1958, Cary Band Day has drawn high school bands from throughout the United States.

Durham Art Guild Juried Art Show
Durham Arts Council Building
• 560-2713

Started in 1953, this prestigious show boasts more than 100 talented local and regional craftspeople who compete and display in a variety of media.

Raleigh Christmas Parade
Downtown Raleigh • 420-0120

Sponsored by the Greater Raleigh Merchants Association, this is the city's biggest parade of the year. Starting at the intersection of Hillsborough and St. Mary's streets, 40 floats, 20 bands and a cast of thousands march down Hillsborough Street toward the Capitol. If you're used to attending Thanksgiving parades in New York City or Detroit, you're in for a Sunbelt treat—no mittens, woolen underwear, thermal socks or pocket handwarmers are needed down here. Just find a good place along the street before the 10 AM starting time.

Several traditions keep the crowds—estimated at 150,000—coming back. One of them is the competition between children marchers in costume. Another competition is held for children with costumed pets. Reflecting the city's more cosmopolitan makeup, the parade also has floats from different nationalities, including Scandinavian, Indian and Latin American. You'll see some of the country's best baton twirlers and in the last float, guess who? Santa Claus himself, who always gets the biggest cheer of the day.

December

Executive Mansion Holiday Open House
200 N. Blount St., Raleigh • 733-3456

In early December, the governor and his family invite Triangle residents over for a tour of the 1891 Queen Anne Cottage-style Victorian house.

First Night Raleigh
Downtown Raleigh • 832-8699
• www.raleigh-nc.org

Held in downtown Raleigh, First Night is an artistic and alcohol-free community celebration of New Year's Eve that keeps getting bigger each year. First Night's full schedule of activities include live music and drama, original works of art, a parade and children's events. Recent highlights have included performances by Chuck Davis and the African-American Dance Ensemble, the Red Clay Ramblers, Shady Grove Band and The Connells, as well as the Burning Coal Theatre Company's rendition of Samuel Beckett's *Krapp's Last Tape*. You will especially want to be part of the crowd of thousands in front of the Civic Center when the famous copper Raleigh Acorn drops to bring in the New Year.

Historic Oakwood Candlelight Tour
Historic Oakwood Association
• 821-7276 • www.historicoakwood.org

A walking tour of Oakwood, the Victorian neighborhood near the Governor's Mansion, organized in 1972, has turned into an annual public event. The two-day Historic Oakwood Christmas Tour, one of the capital city's showplaces, usually begins on the first or second weekend of December, starting at 1 PM and ending at 7 PM each day. Advance tour tickets cost $10 for adults; $15 on the day of the tour. It's free for children 12 and under. Group discounts are available.

The Christmas Tour lets you inside the wonderful old homes, many of them decorated in period greenery. There are from six to 11 homes on the tour (it changes each year) and the homeowners will usually greet you and give you the history of the house. Refreshments, tea and homemade cookies may be offered. The hosts and hostesses need rest and refreshment too, since 2,000 to 3,000

people usually make the tour. This is great entertainment for your visiting grandmother or mother-in-law or the cousin who is renovating an older home. A walking garden tour of the neighborhood is offered in September.

Holly Days Parade & Festival
Holly Springs • 557-3900

Held on the second Saturday of December, the event begins with a community parade, followed by live entertainment ranging from beach music to rock 'n' roll, food and the traditional lighting of the Town Christmas Tree.

Light-Up Durham & Holiday Parade
Durham Bulls Athletic Park
• 687-6561 • www.lightupdurham.org

Light-Up Durham is a festive downtown celebration that includes seasonal music, performers, a tree lighting, parade food and much more. It's fun for all ages. Light-Up Durham is sponsored by the Durham Parks and Recreation Department.

New Year's Eve Concert
Raleigh Marriott Crabtree Valley
• 733-2750, Ext. 260

The North Carolina Symphony's New Year's Eve concert is one of the Triangle's most pleasant ways to ring in the new year. The concert is billed as a "Viennese evening" of light music and waltzes. Those who want the full treatment can begin the evening with a pre-concert sip of champagne at a local hotel and end it with a post-concert dinner and dancing. The concert begins about 8 PM and lasts for about two hours. After the concert, the crowd is bused to the hotel and guests dine sumptuously while a dance band picks up the beat and continues the mood with waltzes and other rhythms. Check with the Symphony's box office for ticket prices. Make reservations through the hotel.

INSIDERS' TIP

Get your Christmas shopping done early at the annual Seagrove Pottery Festival, which is held the Sunday before Thanksgiving. Call (336) 873-7887 for more information.

"Where Art Works"

Artspace is a non-profit center for visual and performing arts, recognized for offering high quality programming for children and adults, award winning exhibitions and critically acclaimed artists.

- *40 Artists Working in Open Studios*
- *Exhibition & Sales Galleries*
- *First Friday Gallery Walks*
- *Summer Art Classes for Children & Adults*
- *Award Winning Art Education Programs*

artspace

201 E. Davie Street
919-821-2787
Tuesday-Saturday
10am-6pm
First Friday of each
month until 10pm

www.artspace.citysearch.com

Arts and Culture

The Triangle has become quite a treasure trove of the arts over the past 20 years. From youth orchestras to the North Carolina Symphony, from regional theater to big-budget Broadway shows, from local art galleries to the North Carolina Museum of Art, from downtown gallery walks to citywide art festivals and from folk dance to the American Dance Festival, the Triangle offers cultural opportunities for all ages and tastes.

View popular theater productions such as *The Sound of Music* and *South Pacific* through the City of Raleigh's Best of Broadway Series and the North Carolina Theatre at Memorial Auditorium. Longstanding regional theater groups like Raleigh Little Theatre and Theatre in the Park continue to play to packed houses. Cutting-edge independent theater groups include WideAwake in Chapel Hill, Manbites Dog in Durham and Burning Coal in Raleigh. In addition, all of the colleges and universities have their own theatrical offerings.

If it's music you want, nationally known performers take the stage at the ALLTEL Pavilion at Walnut Creek and the Raleigh Entertainment and Sports Arena. However, if you're looking for music that has a little more depth than Britney Spears or the Backstreet Boys, you can find it throughout the Triangle. The North Carolina Symphony calls Raleigh home even though it performs throughout the state. Orchestras, symphonies and choruses abound here as well. The Triangle also has a growing list of opera companies that includes the National Opera Company (founded in 1948!) in Raleigh, Triangle Opera in Durham, Opera Company of North Carolina in Raleigh and the new Long Leaf Opera Company in Durham.

In the area of visual arts, galleries and museums can be found everywhere. The North Carolina Museum of Art recently hosted two major exhibitions that drew record crowds: "Monet and Moore" and "Festival Rodin." College and university galleries include UNC's Ackland Art Museum, Duke University Museum of Art and NCSU's Gallery of Art and Design.

The list of offerings continues to grow. The critically acclaimed Carolina Ballet, a dynamic professional company, made its debut in 1999. The BTI Center for the Performing Arts is set to become the Triangle's premier arts facility when it opens in early 2001 as the new home of the North Carolina Symphony.

Theater

Chapel Hill and Carrboro

ArtsCenter
300-G E. Main St., Carrboro
• 929-ARTS

The ArtsCenter started in 1974 as a modest community venture located in a one-room loft in Carrboro. Its current home on East Main Street in Carrboro contains two theaters, including an intimate 335-seat theater, six classrooms, a gallery with skylights, offices and studios for ceramics, dance, television and recording.

Among the many activities that take place at the ArtsCenter are theatrical events geared to participants of all ages, interests and levels

Photo by Rich Weidman

UNC-Chapel Hill's Forest Theatre is the site of the innovative
Forest Theatre Festival each summer.

of experience. A recent highlight was a production of Shakespeare's *All's Well That Ends Well* with actors from the London stage and a musical version of *Peter Pan*. In addition to offering performances and events, the ArtsCenter occasionally sponsors theater classes for students of all levels and ages. Adults can learn about scenes, play writing and improvisational techniques. There are classes for children from ages 6 to 17 in creative drama, improvisation and fantasy. Two drama groups housed at the ArtsCenter are the Transactors and New Plays Rising.

Classes and performances are offered to the public at very reasonable prices, with discounts available to Friends of the ArtsCenter.

University of North Carolina
www.unc.edu/depts/union

Whether it's a production by the PlayMakers Repertory Company or an experimental piece by the Drama Department, UNC-CH provides Triangle audiences with an array of theatrical possibilities and facilities.

Formed in 1919, the PlayMakers Repertory Company, 962-7529, is the state's only year-round professional resident theater. Famous Playmakers have included Thomas Wolfe, Paul Green, Andy Griffith and Louise Fletcher. Since joining the national League of Resident Theatres in 1976, PlayMakers has been committed to preserving the classics,

as well as performing more modern works. Recent productions include Tennessee Williams' *The Glass Menagerie*, Margaret Edson's *Wit*, Noel Coward's *Hay Fever*, Tazewell Thompson's *Constant Star* and Edward Albee's *The Zoo Story*. The company also presents a special holiday show each year: *An O. Henry Christmas* was the 2000 production. All shows are produced in the modern Paul Green Theater, named in honor of the late Pulitzer Prize-winning playwright and UNC alumnus. The theatre seats 500 people on three sides of its thrust stage. The Playmakers make their home at the $10-million Center for the Dramatic Arts, which opened in 1998.

In addition to working with the PlayMakers company, UNC's drama department also stages plays six times a semester in its Laboratory Theatre, 962-1132. "The Lab's" productions range from classic modern drama (Tennessee Williams, Neil Simon) to original works written and directed by the undergraduate drama students themselves.

WideAwake Theatre Company
P.O. Box 1674, Carrboro, 25710
• www.ibiblio.org/wideawake

Wide Awake is a relatively new alternative theater company in Orange County that hosts the Forest Theatre Festival each summer at the University of North Carolina at

Chapel Hill's Forest Theatre. The festival consists of eight shows performed by five area theater companies.

Durham

Duke University
Page Box Office • 684-4444
• www.duke.edu/web/drama

Of course we don't always get the big plays before they hit Broadway, but we can always catch them when they come this way on tour—and for usually about half the price—thanks to the Theater Preview series. One of the nicest places to enjoy that level of theater, as well as music and dance, is at Duke's $16 million Bryan Center on West Campus. Performances take place in the 600-seat Reynolds Theater or the 150-seat Sheafer Laboratory Theater. Recent productions have included *A Midsummer Night's Dream* and *Birdy*.

Duke Drama, 660-3343, is a group of drama students at Duke who produce theater for the university, the community and the state. It stages close to a dozen plays a year in the Bryan Center theaters. The Duke Institute of the Arts, 660-3356, is breaking the boundaries of convention with its new directions in performance art. Hoof 'N' Horn, 684-2072, is a Duke student organization that produces one to three musicals a year. Duke also offers dramatic productions and dance, music and film during its annual Summer Festival of Arts.

Durham Arts Council
120 Morris St. • 560-ARTS
www.durhamarts.org

Founded in 1954, the Durham Arts Council makes grants to and houses a number of outstanding local arts organizations, including community theater groups such as the Durham Savoyards, the Little Big Theatre Company and the Young People's Performing Company. It also helps with art programs in the Durham Public Schools, produces the annual CenterFest and Edible Arts Festival and provides more than 350 classes in the arts for the community. Call the council for more information or a schedule of upcoming events.

Durham Savoyards
120 Morris St. • 688-4168

If you enjoy the operas of Gilbert and Sullivan, you'll love the Durham Savoyards. This community theater group has devoted itself to presenting at least one major G&S production a year since the 1960s. Recently, the Savoyards produced *The Grand Duke*, Gilbert and Sullivans' last collaboration. Call for more information.

Manbites Dog Theater
P.O. Box 402, Durham, NC 27702
• 682-3343

As the name suggests, the establishment of this innovative local group in 1988 was exciting news for downtown arts patrons seeking something different. Manbites Dog's theater is located at 703 Foster Street in downtown Durham. This offbeat laboratory focuses on timely and controversial subjects that otherwise might not be dramatically addressed in our neck of the woods. Manbites Dog produces four to five shows a season. Recent productions have included Mike Wiley's *One Noble Journey* and Michael A. Smith's *A Mouthfulla Sacco and Vanzetti*. Call or write for performance information.

North Carolina Central University
Fayetteville St. • 560-6242
• www.nccu.edu/campus/theatre/index.html

North Carolina Central University's Department of Dramatic Art sponsors the Ivan-Dixon Players, a student group that puts on at least four major productions a year. NCCU also has featured appearances by guest artists such as James Earl Jones. The Triangle Performance Ensemble focuses on works by African-American playwrights. Performances are at the University Theatre in the Farrison-Newton Building at North Carolina Central University.

Royall Center for the Arts
120 Morris St. • 560-ARTS

Royall Center for the Arts, named for State Senator Kenneth Royall, is actually a plot of land in downtown Durham, bounded by

Morris, Chapel Hill, Foster and Morgan streets, on which stand the Durham Arts Council Building, the Carolina Theatre and the Civic Center Plaza. Thanks to the fund-raising efforts of the Council itself, the persistence of several leaders in the local arts community and the passage of a bond referendum in the 1980s, the theater and adjoining building were renovated into a vast multipurpose complex.

The Durham Arts Council Building opened in September 1988. And in 1994, the restored Carolina Theatre reopened after five-plus years of design and construction work. The Carolina Theatre, built in 1926, holds a 1,016-seat main hall for films and live performances and a 3,700 title video rental shop. The Carolina Theatre screens films and hosts concerts, opera, dramatic productions and other special events. The box office number is 560-3030.

Young People's Performing Company
120 Morris St. • 560-2745

As the name suggests, this community theater group offers classes and performance opportunities for young people from in grades K to 12. Financial aid for tuition is available. The Company calls the Durham Arts Council Building its home.

Raleigh and Cary

The Raleigh-Cary area is a stage full of theater. If the stage is your world, you will find parts aplenty. If you like the critic's seat, we have a variety of venues. You want to start, however, with the basic arts organizations. They are the Raleigh Arts Commission, 857-4372, the Raleigh Fine Arts Society (which is more social), the Cary Parks,

Photo by Rich Weidman

The downtown Durham Royall Center for the Arts encompasses the Durham Arts Council Building, the Carolina Theatre and the Civic Center Plaza.

Recreation & Cultural Resources, 469-4061, Visual Art Exchange, 828-7834, and the United Arts Council, 839-1498, a private, non-profit agency founded in the 1980s to provide financial support to the arts much the way the United Way supports human services agencies. The United Arts Council publishes a quarterly calendar and the news weeklies, *The Spectator* and *The Independent,* publish weekly calendars; these publications and *The News and Observer* are the best sources for information on Raleigh and Cary cultural activities. The Wake County Public Library also maintains a list of clubs, many of which are involved in the arts. The associations and organizations listed here are major and minor groups, but ones that Insiders will know.

Best of Broadway Series
Memorial Auditorium, 1 E. South St.
• 831-6060
Ticketmaster: 834-4000
• www.bestofbroadway.net
Through the Best of Broadway Series at Memorial Auditorium, the City of Raleigh offers national tours of current hits such as *Les Miserables, Cats* and *The Phantom of the Opera.* 2000 productions in the Best of Broadway Series include *Jekyll & Hyde, Beauty & the Beast, The Buddy Holly Story, The Sound of Music, Cabaret* and *Peter Pan.*

The Memorial Auditorium complex is currently undergoing a $38 million expansion that will include a 1,700-seat symphony hall for the North Carolina Symphony and a 600-seat multipurpose theater. The new complex, which will be called the BTI Center for the Performing Arts, is set to open in early 2001.

Burning Coal Theatre Company
P.O. Box 90904, Raleigh, NC 27656
• 388-0066 • www.burningcoal.org
Since debuting in 1997 with the intense and disturbing drama, *Rat in the Skull*, the Burning Coal Theatre Company has taken the independent theater scene by storm with its innovative productions. Formed by the husband and wife team of Jerome Davis and Simmie Kastner, Burning Coal was voted "Best New Ensemble in Raleigh" by *The News and Observer.* Recent productions have included *Saint Nicholas, Romeo and Juliet* and Tom Stoppard's *Night and Day,* the Company's 1999-2000 season finale.

North Carolina Theatre
Memorial Auditorium, 1 E. South St.
• 831-6950 • www.nctheatre.com
The North Carolina Theatre, the state's largest musical production company, is located in the beautiful 2,300-seat Memorial Auditorium. It is sponsored in part by the City of Raleigh and produces professional theater for the capital city. Auditions are held for each production in New York and Raleigh. The group traces its roots back to 1972 and Chapel Hill; but in 1983 with partial funding offered by the City of Raleigh, it made its home in Memorial Auditorium downtown. Since then, it has produced well-known musicals such as *Grease, South Pacific, La Cage Aux Folles* and *The Music Man.* 2000 productions include *Oklahoma!, The Best Little Whorehouse in Texas, Steel Pier* (the first of the Theatre's shows to go on tour) and *Cinderella.* Season tickets are available. The 2001 season will feature *The Wizard of Oz, Oliver!, Guys and Dolls* and *Evita.*

Raleigh Ensemble Players
Artspace, 201 E. Davie St.
• 832-9607
• www.realtheatre.org
The Ensemble Players began in 1983 and is a community theater group that specializes in contemporary plays and musicals in a second-floor gallery at Artspace in downtown Raleigh. Four to five "Mainstage" productions are performed each season. Recent productions have included *The Clearing, Unidentified Human Remains* and the *True Nature of Love* and *As Bees in Honey Drown.*

INSIDERS' TIP
The Joseph J. Bryan Jr. Theater, an outdoor amphitheater at the North Carolina Museum of Art, plays host to concerts, drama, dance and films. Call 715-5923 for a schedule of events.

The group sponsors acting classes through-out the year. REP holds open auditions for all productions. For a schedule, tickets or infor-mation, give the Ensemble Players a call.

Raleigh Little Theatre
301 Pogue St. • 821-3111
www.mindspring.com/~rallittletheatre

Raleigh Little Theatre is one of the country's oldest community theaters, born in the Great Depression, and the building is vin-tage WPA architecture. The theater, known to Insiders as RLT, is comprised of volunteer performers, with a paid artistic director, man-aging director and technical staff. RLT's productions range from comedies to musi-cals to dramas. Each season, the Main Stage Series includes five well-known Broadway shows, the City Stage Series presents four contemporary works and the Family Series includes four shows for family audiences. Recent productions have included *The Old Settler, Oklahoma, Man of La Mancha, The Lion in Winter, Antony and Cleopatra* and *The Taming of the Shrew*. For individual ticket prices at the door, call the box office.

Theatre in the Park
107 Pullen Rd. • 831-6058
• www.theatreinthepark.com

Theatre In The Park has earned a repu-tation as one of the state's most exciting and innovative community theater centers since its start in the early '70s. TIP annually presents a wide range of productions in its intimate and totally flexible performance space. The best in comedy, musicals, Shakespeare, contemporary drama and children's theater are offered as mainstage productions. Recent productions have in-cluded *Look Homeward, Angel, Moon Over Buffalo, The Merry Wives of Windsor, Enrico IV, Visiting Mr. Green, Anastasia* and *Good Ol' Girls*. TIP also offers theater classes and workshops for all ages.

A Christmas Carol, starring Ira David Wood III as the miserly Ebenezer Scrooge, has been a traditional sellout at Raleigh's Memorial Audi-torium since making its debut in 1975. Sign up or become a season member of TIP if you want to be guaranteed a seat!

University Theatre
NCSU • 515-2405
• www.fis.ncsu.edu/arts

North Carolina State University's Theatre consists of the student-run University Play-ers and the Center Stage professional series. Performances are held at the 200-seat Thompson Theatre and the 816-seat Stewart Theatre.

University Players productions are student-oriented, with an emphasis on ex-perimentation. Each production is open to all NCSU students, whether experienced or not, as actors, technicians, crew members and directors. Student Studio Series productions are completely student run, and African-American and children's theater are also available for all students. The tickets are among the best value in the Triangle: $10 for adults and $9 for senior citizens. Recent pro-ductions have included Stephen Schwartz's *Pippin*, William Smith's *The Drunkard* and *Ten Little Indians*, based on the Agatha Christie novel. NCSU's annual Theatrefest, a sum-mer season that features local professional and student artists, takes place in June.

The Center Stage series offers over 30 professional events each year. Every sea-son includes music, modern dance, comedy, mime, children's theater, jazz, international events, drama and more. Recent performers have included The Reduced Shakespeare Company, The Billy Taylor Trio, Shenandoah Shakespeare Express, Native American flut-ist R. Carlos Nakai and Canadian entertainer Tomas Kubinek, billed as "Certified Lunatic and Master of the Impossible." Ticket prices range from $5 to $22. Call 515-1100 for tickets.

Music

Whether you like the jazz sounds of the Gregg Gelb Swing Band, the rousing folk bal-lads of troubadour Mike Cross, the sassy lyrics of The Red Clay Ramblers, the croons of Nnenna Freelon or the harmonic strains of the North Carolina Symphony, you can hear them and other musical notes regularly in Triangle clubs and music halls. For more information on the night life scene, see our "Night Life" chap-ter. Here's a look at other kinds of live musical presentations available in Chapel Hill and Carrboro, Durham, and Raleigh and Cary.

Chapel Hill and Carrboro

If you've read the "Chapel Hill" section of "Night Life," you know that you can find great music at lots of clubs and restaurants in this town. But those aren't the only places you should look. A variety of musical performances are regularly scheduled on the UNC-CH campus and at the ArtsCenter in Carrboro. And there are several community groups you may want to join yourself. Here's a guide to what you can expect.

ArtsCenter
300-G E. Main St., Carrboro • 929-ARTS

Most weekends, the ArtsCenter sponsors one or more musical concerts at reasonable admission prices. A diverse selection is offered, from jazz to folk, Cajun to country, rock to reggae and everything else in between. Recent performers to take the stage here have included Shady Grove Band, Red Clay Ramblers, Stacey Earle, David Wilcox, Robin and Linda Williams, John Gorka and Terence Blanchard, as well as the reunion of Arrogance, the preeminent North Carolina-based rock band of the 1970s. What's more, the ArtsCenter has an ongoing Sunday jazz series, featuring popular local artists and groups like Tony Galiani and the ArtsCenter Rhythm Section. In addition, a Swing Big Band Jazz Concert takes place on the third Thursday of the month. Ticket prices are in the $3 to $15 range for local performers, more for national performers on tour. Friends of the ArtsCenter receive a discount on ticket prices.

Chapel Hill-Carrboro Community Chorus
• 490-1626

This group is made up of individuals at all levels of musical achievement who share a common interest in choral music. The Chorus practices at 7:30 PM on Tuesdays at Binkley Baptist Church off U.S. 15-501. The group usually performs public concerts twice a year.

Piedmont Youth Orchestra
229 S. Elliott Rd. • 968-8099

The Piedmont Youth Orchestra offers experience in playing standard orchestral pieces for students from elementary through high school grades. The orchestra rehearses weekly.

University of North Carolina
www.unc.edu/depts/union

UNC-CH's Student Union sponsors a slew of music acts each year. All concerts are open to the public. Major concerts are held at the Dean Smith Center or Memorial Hall for faculty and student concerts are held at Hill Hall. Recent performers have included Bobby McFerrin, David Dorfman Dance and Dance Theatre of Harlem. Occasionally, there are concerts outdoors on campus, like the annual North Carolina Symphony Pops performance in June. For information, call the Carolina Union at 962-1449.

During the school year, the Department of Music presents dozens of free concerts by students, faculty and occasional guest artists, including the William S. Newman Artists Music Series. The annual UNC Jazz Festival takes place in February. Student music groups sponsored by the department include the following: Carolina Choir, Jazz Lab, Wind Ensembles, Men's and Women's Glee Clubs, Mixed Chorus, Chamber Singers, Symphony and Chamber Orchestra, and others. For more information, contact the Department of Music, University of North Carolina, Chapel Hill, NC 27514.

In addition, the Black Student Movement sponsors a Gospel Choir that performs on campus. For more information, contact the

---

INSIDERS' TIP

Don't miss the monthly First Friday Gallery Walk, held in and around the Moore Square Arts District in downtown Raleigh from 6 to 9 PM. Participating art galleries include Artspace, Raleigh Contemporary Gallery, Sally Huss Gallery and Sweet Tea & Grits, among others.

Black Student Movement, UNC, Chapel Hill, NC 27514.

Village Symphony Orchestra
• 929-5487, 489-1587

The Village Symphony Orchestra is a private, nonprofit group for adults who get together to play and further the tradition of community music. The orchestra rehearses Thursdays at 7:30 PM at Hill Hall (the music building) on the UNC-CH campus.

Durham

In addition to clubs and restaurants (see "Durham" section of "Night Life"), you can regularly find live music at a number of other locations in Durham, including Duke University, North Carolina Central University and the Carolina Theatre. In the summer, there's Jazz in the Parks, a series of concerts in community parks sponsored by the Durham Recreation Department, 560-4355. There's always live music at the July 4th Festival for the Eno, the Bull Durham Blues Festival and CenterFest, the downtown street festival. The Durham Alive Concert Series takes place at the Durham Civic Center Plaza during the summer. And throughout the year, you can attend concerts at St. Joseph's Performing Arts Center, a concert auditorium located at 804 Old Fayetteville Street.

Here's a guide to the musical groups and events you are likely to find in Durham.

Carolina Theatre
309 W. Morgan St.
Box Office: 560-3030
• www.carolinatheatre.org

In addition to screening foreign and independent films, the restored 1926 theater in downtown Durham hosts live performances in its historic Fletcher Hall, which seats more than 1,000 people. Performers who have graced the stage here include Mike Cross, Doc Watson, Steve Earle and Guy Clark. In addition, The Long Leaf Opera and Chamber Orchestra of the Triangle both stage productions here. Carolina Theatre hosts the North Carolina Shakespeare Festival in October and is the site of the DoubleTake Documentary Film Festival in April.

Chamber Orchestra of the Triangle
309 W. Morgan St. • 560-3040

Founded in 1982, this professional, nonprofit group is conducted by Lorenzo Muti. Chamber Orchestra concerts take place at the Carolina Theatre.

Choral Society of Durham
120 Morris St. • 560-2733

Formerly known as the Durham Civic Choral Society, which was founded in 1949, the Choral Society of Durham gives local residents an opportunity to perform large and small works accompanied by an orchestra. The Society usually presents at least two concerts a year, including the annual Christmas concert in Duke Chapel. A recent highlight was the Choral Society's collaboration with the Duke Chorale on *Carmina Burana*. Auditions for new members are held each fall. Rodney Wynkoop has served as conductor and artistic director since 1986.

Duke University
www.duke.edu/music

The quantity, quality and diversity of musical offerings on the Duke University campus is enough to keep anyone busy. Here's a quick look at some of what is available. Except where noted, additional information on any of the following may be obtained by writing the Duke University Music Department, P.O. Box 90665, Durham, NC 27708-0665, or by calling 660-3300.

Since it beginnings in 1931, the Duke University Artists' Series has brought to campus a string of nationally and internationally renowned musical artists and performances, including Itzhak Perlman, Yo-Yo Ma, Martha Graham, Vladimir Horowitz and Sergei Rachmaninoff. Recent performers include pianist Alicia de Larrocha and violinist Midori.

FYI

Unless otherwise noted, the area code for all phone numbers listed in this guide is 919.

Constructed in 1926, the restored Carolina Theatre hosts
live performances in its historic Fletcher Hall.

Since 1965, the Ciompi Quartet, a resident chamber music quartet, has provided classes and concerts at Duke as well as worldwide. It emphasizes variety, offering pieces from Mozart to Ward to Brahms to Copeland, in four formal concerts a year.

The Chamber Arts Music Society brings to the Duke campus internationally acclaimed artists, such as the St. Petersburg String Quartet, the Onion String Quartet and the Tokyo String Quartet.

The 65-piece Duke Symphony Orchestra is composed of Duke students, faculty and local residents. Led by conductor Lorenzo Muti, it performs about four concerts during the academic year. Individual members often perform with Duke choral groups such as the Duke Chorale, which performs several concerts each year.

Lovers of vocal and instrumental music from the Medieval, Renaissance and Baroque periods will enjoy performances by the Duke University Collegium Musicum, a select group of Duke students, faculty and local residents. It gives at least one concert each semester.

The 20-member Duke Jazz Ensemble is composed of students and performs several times during the academic year with a repertoire that includes big band, jazz-rock and swing.

And if that's not enough, each year the Duke University Wind Symphony selects a group of about 60 musicians who perform two formal concerts and several informal concerts held outdoors in the Sarah P. Duke Gardens.

Durham Symphony
120 Morris St. • 560-2736
• www.durhamsymphony.org

The Durham Symphony is a 65-member, community orchestra that annually presents a Classical Concert Series, a Holiday Pops Concert and an Outdoor Family Pops Concert. The Symphony also sponsors a Young Artists' Competition and a concert featuring the winners. It celebrated its 25th anniversary during the 2000-01 season and frequently collaborates with groups such as the Durham Public Schools' Durham Youth Orchestra, Orange County Charter School Symphony, the Duke Strings School and the Durham School of the Arts Chorale at different sites throughout the Triangle. The Symphony is conducted by Alan Neilson, who also leads the Raleigh Symphony Orchestra.

Durham Youth Orchestra
• 544-2364

This group provides quality orchestral training for aspiring musicians throughout Durham County. It contains approximately 70 members who rehearse once a week during the school year. The Orchestra hosts a

Christmas holiday concert, spring concert and community outreach performances at locales throughout the Triangle.

Long Leaf Opera Company
Carolina Theatre • 968-9595
• www.longleafopera.org

Long Leaf is a new opera company that reflects North Carolina and the American experience in opera. In its inaugural season in 1999, the Company produced Kurt Weill's *Down in the Valley* and Carlisle Floyd's *Susannah*. It has also produced William Grant Still's African-American drama *Highway 1, USA* in conjunction with the North Carolina Central University Department of Theatre.

Mallarme Chamber Players
120 Morris St. • 560-2788
• www.pair.com/mallarme

The Mallarme Chamber Players performs its Music Series of five Sunday afternoon concerts at the Peoples Security Insurance Theatre in the Durham Arts Council Building on Morris Street. The group, which was founded in 1984 and named for the French Symbolist poet Stephane Marllarme, draws mostly from early 20th-century, classical and Romantic pieces not typically performed by other groups in this area. The Mallarme Players also presents two Family Concerts during the fall and spring.

North Carolina Boys Choir
Contact: Bill Graham • 489-0291
• www.ncboyschoir.org

Founded in 1972 as the Durham Boys Choir, this choir of more than 40 musically talented boys between the ages of 9 and 14 performs about 50 concerts a year, including major Christmas and spring concerts in Duke Chapel, television appearances and programs for local nursing homes, hospitals, schools, churches and other groups. The choir takes an annual two-week tour of the United States and Canada. It also offers workshops, scholarships and summer camps. The choir features a training choir for beginning singers and a choir of high-school-aged tenors and basses.

North Carolina Central University
560-5252 • www.nccu.edu

NCCU's Department of Music sponsors several groups and concerts each year. They include the NCCU Jazz Ensemble and the NCCU Choir. The annual Grady Tate/NCCU Jazz Festival is held here in April. For additional information, contact the Department of Music, North Carolina Central University, Durham, NC 27707.

Triangle Opera
3333 Chapel Hill Blvd.,
Durham, NC 27707
• 493-7880 • www.triangleopera.org

The Triangle Opera has usually hosted two performances a season since 1985. Recent productions include *Luyala*, a collaboration with the African American Dance Ensemble, and Beethoven's only opera, *Fidelio*. The company works in conjunction with the Durham Arts Council to provide a wide variety of educational programs to both students and adults in the Triangle.

Raleigh and Cary

Wake County is home to a number of cultural treasures, most notably the North Carolina Symphony, which calls Raleigh's Memorial Auditorium its home base. If you're searching for a more contemporary sound, check out name acts at the ALLTEL Pavilion at Walnut Creek and the Raleigh Entertainment and Sports Arena (see "Attractions" chapter for details).

Cary School of Music
127 W. Chatham St. • 460-0052

Instructor Pam Mole saw her lifetime dream come true when the doors of the Cary School of Music opened in May of 1993. The school offers private lessons for strings, guitar, piano, orchestra and flute choirs, brass and woodwinds, voice and percussion. The school draws its 35 instructors from such organizations as the North Carolina Symphony, the North Carolina School of the Arts and others. Student ensembles perform every other Friday night at the Glenaire retirement complex. The school

The North Carolina Theatre's

PRODUCING BROADWAY MUSICALS AT MEMORIAL AUDITORIUM SINCE 1984

2001 Season
OF BROADWAY MUSICALS
The Shows You've Always Wanted to See!

February 9 - 18, 2001

July 13 - 22, 2001

September, 14 - 23, 2001

November 9 - 18, 2001

ON SALE NOW
Season Ticket Prices From $54 - $204

Going To The Prom 48"x72"

JANE FILER
ACRYLIC PAINTINGS ❧ VISIONARY EXPRESSIONIST

Band Wagon 43"x43"

Visit the Studio
919•942•5372

website: www.janefiler.com
email: janefiler@earthlink.net

Painting Instruction Available
Through the ArtsCenter
929•ARTS

Represented
At Tyndall Galleries
Brightleaf Square
683•8489

Also At Museums &
Galleries Nationwide

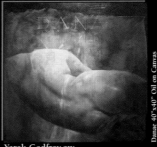

The North Carolina Symphony performs during an annual Fourth of July extravaganza at Regency Park in Cary.

performs with the Raleigh Symphony and holds a series of music camps.

Concert Singers of Cary
P.O. Box 1921, Cary, NC 27512
• 481-3745
• www.concertsingers.org

Formed in 1991, this Cary group of singers now has more than 175 singers and performs three or four concerts each year. The chorus is directed by Lawrence Speakman and meets at the Cary Community Center at 404 N. Academy Street, behind the Town Hall Annex on Monday nights from 7:30 until 9:30 PM. Concerts are exciting events. An ensemble is available for performances at civic and corporate functions. Projects include additional community outreach and development of a children's chorus. The group has recorded an album of classical and popular music. Auditions are held in August and January.

Little German Band
Contact: Connie Varner • 363-8664
• www.prosit.org

Raleigh residents knew the city had attained a cosmopolitan status when the Little German Band began to play in 1971. Many of its members were raised around such ethnic music and the band members even put on lederhosen and feathered hats when they perform. The Little German Band has become a featured attraction at local Oktoberfest celebrations.

National Opera Company
P.O. Box 12800, Raleigh, NC 27605
• 890-6083

Started in 1948, the National Opera Company has survived and prospered. The company's mission is threefold: to introduce opera to public school students; to give experience to young singers; and to perform opera in a language the audience understands, namely English. The company has proven to be a good training ground and its alumni include such stars as Samuel Ramey, Jeanette Scovotti and Arlene Saunders. Recent productions include Mozart's *Cosi fan tutte* and the world premiere of J. Mark Scearce's *Kitty Hawk*, an opera about the Wright Brothers.

The National Opera Company has made tentative plans to reorganize and relocate to the North Carolina School of Arts in Winston-Salem in time for the 2001-02 season. The company will continue to put on two full productions in Raleigh at the new A.J. Fletcher Opera Theater in the BTI Center for Performing Arts in downtown Raleigh and make 20 to 25 appearances in Wake County schools annually.

North Carolina Symphony
Memorial Auditorium, 1 E. South St.
• Tickets & Information: 733-2750
• www.ncsymphony.org

The North Carolina Symphony is one of the state's treasures, dating from 1932. It was the first continuously state-supported symphony in the country and it lives up to that acclaim by performing nearly 200 concerts a year, including 65 in admission-free school performances. It truly is a "people's orchestra" and a special bonus for Triangle residents because many performances are in this area. It employs about 65 full-time musicians and is conducted by Gerhardt Zimmermann, who celebrated his 18th season as Music Director of the Symphony in 2000. William Henry Curry serves as Associate Conductor.

Most Raleigh performances are in Memorial Auditorium which, with its crystal chandeliers and improved acoustics, rivals any facility in the Southeast. The Memorial Auditorium complex is currently undergoing renovations that will add a new 1,700-seat concert hall, which will be completed in early 2001. The Symphony, which also offers series in Chapel Hill and Durham, has performed at Carnegie Hall, the Kennedy Center and Chicago's Orchestra Hall.

The Symphony offers several series, including classical concerts; a pops series; a children's series for young and old alike; and an outdoor "Summerfest" concert series at Cary's Regency Park. There is also an "Open Rehearsal" series for those who want a peek at stars and players before the curtain goes up. Three of the concerts in the Durham Series take place in the Carolina Theatre at 309 West Morgan Street. The fourth is in the majestic Duke Chapel. The Chapel Hill Classical Series of five concerts takes place in Memorial Hall on the UNC Campus. Guest performers have included Andre Watts, Henry Mancini, Nadja Salerno-Sonnenberg, Susan Starr, Horacio Gutierrez, Doc Severinsen, Burt Bacharach and Neil Sedaka.

You can sign up for season tickets or buy single tickets; call the box office for price ranges for the different series.

Opera Company of North Carolina
3600 Glenwood Ave., Ste. 101
• 783-0098
Since its debut in 1996, this Company has entertained audiences with a host of diverse performances such as the Southern premiere of singer Carly Simon's *Romulus Hunt* in 1999, Leonard Bernstein's *Trouble in Tahiti*, Mozart's *The Magic Flute* and Puccini's *Madama Butterfly*. The Opera Company of North Carolina boasts local as well as world-class talent and is known for its informative educational outreach programs.

Pinecone
P.O. Box 28534, Raleigh, NC 27611
Contact: Susan Newberry • 990-1900
• www.pinecone.org
The Piedmont Council of Traditional Music has brought a heaping helping of traditional North Carolina grassroots music, dance and singing to Raleigh and Cary residents. In conjunction with the city's Parks and Recreation Department, this nonprofit organization produces monthly concerts and sessions of traditional music and song. It also sponsors a monthly contra dance.

PineCone started the Fiddlers' Convention in 1990, which is now called the Eno River Old Time Fiddler and Bluegrass Convention, and it performs at Durham's West Point on the Eno Amphitheater. Admission is charged for some events; others, especially the outdoor shows, are free.

Raleigh Boychoir
1329 Ridge Rd. • 881-9259
• www.ipass.net/~rbc/
Since its beginning in 1968, Thomas E. Sibley has developed one of the finest boys' choirs in the region. More than 90 boys ages 8 to 15 raise their voices weekly in one of the three performing choirs and the training choirs. Their repertoire includes music from classics, musical theater, patriotic and folk. The 2000 concert series features a Celebration of American Music, Spring Concert, Music from Great Cathedrals, Fall Concert and the Carols of Christmas Concert.

The choir regularly performs with the North Carolina Symphony, the Raleigh Oratorio Society and the Durham Choral Society. Nationally and internationally recognized, the choir has performed at the White House, Carnegie Hall and the World's Fair, as well as in England, Austria, Germany, Belgium, France, the Netherlands, Switzerland and

OTHER TRIANGLE ARTS ORGANIZATIONS

THEATER

Actors Comedy Lab	873-1333
Applause! Cary Youth Theater	469-4069
Flying Machine Theater Company	954-8847
Kazoom Children's Theatre	829-0822
Meredith College Theater	760-2840
Open Door Theater Company	933-4650
Peace College Theater	508-2229
Rags to Riches Theater for Young Audiences	956-9891
Raleigh's Village Idiots (Improv)	546-0822
The Shaw University Players & Company	546-8420
St. Augustine's College Community Theatre	516-4000

MUSIC

Capital Area Chorale	779-2852
Cardinal Singers	781-5210
Carolina Harmony Chorus	467-1193
The Cary Town Band	467-7336
Chapel Hill Chamber Orchestra	408-0193
Durham Community Choir	806-8283
The Encore Singers	859-6954
Heart of Carolina Jazz Orchestra	933-3261
Hillyer Community Chorus	787-9458
Jim Marshall Chorale	876-0987
Leonard D. Wilson Community Chorus	828-1842
Martin Luther King Jr. Children's Chorus	833-1003
Raleigh Area Flute Association	781-3225
Raleigh Area Flute Choir	787-4142
Raleigh Music Club	829-8536
Triangle Blues Society	834-8667
Triangle Brass Band	870-9089
Triangle Folk Music Society	968-9600
Triangle Wind Ensemble	274-3921
Village Band	966-9919

DANCE

Capital Square Dancers Club	846-8240
Carolina Heartland Cloggers	254-4424
Dixie Twirlers Square Dance Club	772-4828
English Country Dancing Society	878-0114
EXPRESSIONS! Dance Troupe	471-2003
Millbrook Cloggers	872-4156
N.C. Square Dance Association	556-2685
Rainbow Dance Society	833-5218
Rainbow Square Dancers	876-1826
Raleigh International Folk Dancers	834-4172
Scandanavian Folk Dancers	787-2505
TNT Square Dance Club	362-6315
Triangle Latin Dance	929-7769

Italy, which included an audience with Pope John Paul II. Three auditions a year for new boys and a monthly membership charge help to support this nonprofit choir.

Raleigh Chamber Music Guild
Ravenscroft School • 821-2030

The Raleigh Chamber Music Guild started in 1941, and it brings to the Triangle a season of chamber groups. Guest artists have included the Juilliard String Quartet, New Zealand String Quartet and Leipzig String Quartet. Adult season tickets cost about $60 ($20 for students); call for the location of upcoming performances. Another chamber series of note is the Smedes Parlor performances at St. Mary's School. These concerts attract the devoted chamber music fan and are held Monday evenings, once a month. Call St. Mary's at 839-4045 for more information.

Raleigh Civic Symphony
Price Music Center, NCSU • 515-8279

For those who are not content to sit in their seats and listen, there is the Civic Symphony that is less a city group than an outgrowth of the NCSU Music Department. The orchestra is a combination of "town and gown" performers and meets weekly at NCSU's Price Music Center. It is a full symphony with 75 members and it performs two or three times each semester. The orchestra is the parent group for several other orchestras; for more information about where you and your flute might fit in, contact Professor Randolph Foy.

Raleigh Concert Band
Contact: Carl Van Cott • 872-2743
• www.RTPnet.org/~rcband

The Concert Band is another nonprofit, all-volunteer group. It is often asked to play at major civic functions where a little horn blowing and a few drum rolls are in order. Many of the 60 members are former high school and college band players who can't

put their instruments away. The band performs regularly throughout the Raleigh area.

Raleigh Conservatory of Music
3636 Capital Blvd. • 790-1533

The Raleigh Conservatory of Music was established in 1986 as a nonprofit organization dedicated to enriching the lives of individuals through music. Programs include "Kindermusik," the exposure of infants and preschool children to musical experiences; childhood through adult music instruction; special programs for the handicapped on an individual basis; community performances and accompanying; and outreach programs to expose all segments of the community to the joys of music.

Raleigh Oratorio Society
Contact: Michelle Hile • 856-9700
• www.raleigh-oratorio.org

The Society, which is under the direction of Dr. Alfred E. Sturgis, consists of a volunteer symphonic choir and a professional chamber choir. These are serious singers and they can hold a note with the best, including annual performances with the North Carolina Symphony and Carolina Ballet. Founded in 1941, the Society is considered to be perhaps the best of the Triangle's choral groups. It has performed at Memorial Auditorium and in some of the city's larger churches, and a sample of its work includes performances of Mendelssohn's *Elijah*, Beethoven's *Symphony No. 9*, Mozart's *Mass in C Minor* and Bach's *St. Matthew Passion*.

Raleigh Ringers
Contact: David M. Harris
• 847-RLRG (7574) • www.rr.org

Founded in 1990, Raleigh Ringers is an internationally recognized community handbell choir that consists of talented area musicians. The choir promotes the art of handbell ringing through sponsoring and participating in festivals, workshops, tours and other educational and performing opportunities. Rehearsals are held at the Abbotswood Retirement Community.

Raleigh Symphony Orchestra
336 Fayetteville Street Mall
• 832-5120

Created in 1979, the Raleigh Symphony Orchestra is not to be confused—although many do—with the Civic Symphony even though some of its members began there and left to form their own orchestra. More than half of the orchestra is comprised of volunteer musicians with a portion of paid players. It is a full, 65-member orchestra that performs 12 to 15 concerts annually, including one of its annual favorites, *The Messiah*. The Raleigh Symphony Orchestra is not afraid to tackle Beethoven, Brahms, Mozart, Tchaikovsky or Mussorgsky. It is led by Alan Neilson, who also conducts the Durham Symphony Orchestra.

Sunday in the Park
Fletcher Park, 820 Clay St. • 831-6854

Sponsored by the City of Raleigh Parks and Recreation Department, this laid-back concert series is held every Sunday at 6 PM

UNC-CH's Ackland Art Museum contains works ranging from ancient times to the 20th century.

Photo courtesy of Ackland Art Museum

from early June to mid-September. It features such bands as Raleigh Concert Band, Steel Creek Bluegrass Band and the Blues in the Night Jazz Orchestra.

Youth Orchestras
N.C. Symphony • 733-9536
Raleigh Children's Orchestra
• 781-3812
Wake County Schools • 850-1700

Raleigh and Cary children can play in several orchestras, and to find which one best suits their talents, they should contact the North Carolina Symphony, the Raleigh Children's Orchestra or the Wake County Public School system. All the orchestras give concerts and provide young musicians the experience of ensemble playing. The Symphony sponsors the Triangle Youth Philharmonic, 469-5287, which draws from the Triangle area. The group performs five concerts annually and young musicians receive coaching and advice from musicians in the North Carolina Symphony. The public schools sponsor the Raleigh Preparatory String Orchestra (K through 6th grade), the Capital Area Youth Orchestra (middle school grades) and the Raleigh Youth Symphony Orchestra (high school students). The Raleigh Children's Orchestra, for grades 1 through 7, is managed by the Pullen Arts Center.

Visual Arts

There must be more than 100 galleries and museums in the Triangle displaying the works of locally and nationally known painters, sculptors, photographers and craftspeople. But you definitely need a guide to help you find them all. Unlike some major urban centers, the cities of the Triangle don't have well-defined art districts. Instead you'll find worthwhile exhibits all over the place: from the North Carolina Museum of Art in Raleigh and college campuses in Durham and Chapel Hill, to displays at banks, restaurants and, of course, private galleries tucked into business districts and shopping centers throughout the area. Following is a brief synopsis of some of the best visual arts venues in the Triangle, plus some class listings.

Chapel Hill and Carrboro

Orange County has a thriving arts community with more than 1,200 artists calling the area home. Like other parts of the Triangle, the art exhibits in Chapel Hill and Carrboro are scattered about. But since Chapel Hill and Carrboro are relatively small towns, it's easy to find the museums and galleries. Both towns' public libraries, as well as the Orange County Public Library in Hillsborough, have public art galleries that feature the works of local artists. The Chapel Hill and Carrboro town halls also contain galleries. The annual Orange County Open Studio Tour takes place in November. For more information about arts in Orange County, contact the Orange County Arts Commission at 245-2325.

Ackland Art Museum
UNC, Columbia St. • 966-5736
• www.ackland.org

UNC's Ackland Art Museum's permanent collection includes the art of Asia, Africa, Europe and America, with works ranging from ancient times to the 20th century. Special exhibits change periodically. Hours are Wednesday through Saturday 10 AM to 5 PM and Sunday 1 PM to 5 PM.

ArtsCenter Galleries
300-G E. Main St., Carrboro • 929-ARTS

The ArtsCenter Galleries features exhibits by local and regional artists. It's open from 10 AM to 10 PM Monday through Thursday, 10 AM to 6 PM Friday and 10 AM to 4 PM Saturday. In addition to providing exhibit space for emerging artists, the ArtsCenter offers a variety of classes in the visual arts for all ages and all levels of experience. A recent schedule included classes in watercolor, drawing, printmaking, Chinese and Japanese painting, mixed media, sculpture and photography. The ArtsCenter also sponsors summer art classes for kids ages 6 and older. Call for a current class schedule.

Cameron's
University Mall • 942-5554

If you're looking for pottery and other functional craft items, you'll want to check out Cameron's 5,000-square-foot gallery and shop in University Mall. Danny Cameron chooses works from North Carolina and across the United States, focusing often on the whimsical or eccentric. Cameron's is open from 10 AM to 9 PM Monday through Saturday and 1 to 6 PM on Sunday.

Carolina Union Galleries
UNC, Carolina Union • Info: 962-2285
• www.unc.edu/depts/union

The galleries are located in the Student Union building on campus, where you'll find exhibits of student artists. The galleries are open from 8 AM to 11 PM when school is in session.

Green Tara Gallery
241 S. Elliott Rd., Village Plaza
• 932-6400 • www.greentaragallery.com

Green Tara Gallery offers one-of-a-kind handmade art. Its casually elegant environment is host to frequent art exhibits and poetry readings, as well as an extensive clay art collection and the only collection of Hispanic and Latino contemporary art in the state. It is open Monday through Saturday from 10 AM to 6 PM, Sunday from 12 to 4 PM and by appointment.

Hanes Art Center
UNC Art Classroom Studio Bldg. (next to the Ackland Art Museum)
• 962-2015 • www.unc.edu/depts/art

The Hanes Art Center features exhibits by students and emerging local artists. Admission is free. The gallery is open Monday through Friday from 8 AM to 5 PM.

Horace Williams House
610 E. Rosemary St. • 942-7818

One of Chapel Hill's oldest homes, the Horace Williams House is the headquarters of the Chapel Hill Preservation Society. It is also a cultural arts center and a place for wedding receptions, private parties, concerts and monthly art exhibits. Here you'll find paintings, sculptures and crafts by local and regional artists. Other special events include Historic Trolley Tours every Wednesday at 2 PM April through November, a Chamber

Photo by Rich Weidman

The historic Horace Williams House offers changing art exhibits
and hosts chamber music concerts regularly.

Concert series and an annual 4th of July band concert. The house is open from 10 AM to 4 PM Monday through Saturday and 1 to 4 PM on Sunday.

North Carolina Crafts Gallery
North Carolina Arts Gallery
212 W. Main St., Carrboro • 942-4048

These two back-to-back galleries were originally opened by Sherri Ontjes as a means to encourage and support North Carolina craftspeople; her mission has expanded to include painting and other fine arts. Both galleries sell quilts, pottery, jewelry, stained glass, blown glass, baskets, toys, knitting and weavings, and handmade wooden objects and paintings, drawings and other artwork. They are open Monday through Saturday from 10 AM to 6 PM and Sunday from 1 to 4 PM.

Somerhill Gallery
Eastgate Shopping Center • 968-8868

Since 1973, Joe Rowand has been bringing together emerging regional artists and enthusiastic collectors in his gallery. Here you'll find the paintings, sculptures and tapestries. Hours are Monday through Saturday from 10 AM to 5:30 PM.

Toktumee Art Gallery
200 W. Franklin St., Ste. 280
• 960-4004 • www.toktumee.com

The Triangle's own showcase for exciting original American and international, Toktumee,

opened its doors in downtown Chapel Hill in the fall of 1999. Located in the Pavilion II Building, the innovative, 1,500-square-foot gallery is the creation of Evanne and Jean-Claude Solvinto, two Parisian art lovers and collectors who have made their home in the Triangle for the past several years. The gallery displays the works of such talented artists as Yarek Godfrey.ow, Sibylle de Monneron, Christine Vidil, Francoise Denis and Barbara Goraczko. Hours are 11 AM to 7 PM Monday through Friday and 12 to 5 PM Saturday.

Womancraft
Eastgate Shopping Center • 929-8362
• www.womancraft.com

Womancraft offers all kinds of functional items by more than 60 area craftswomen, including splendid pottery, paintings, handmade jewelry, woven clothing and quilts. It is a co-op of artists and periodically juries new pieces for membership. Hours are Monday through Friday from 10 AM to 8 PM, Saturday from 10 AM to 6 PM and Sunday from 1 to 6 PM.

Durham

Thanks to the Durham Arts Council and Art Guild, Duke and North Carolina Central universities and several impressive private galleries, there are plenty of places to explore the visual arts, if you just know where to look. In addition, you'll discover original works by local artists regularly on display at many Durham restaurants. Don't miss the annual Durham Art Walk in May and December where more than 25 galleries and art studios downtown open their doors for tours, sales and demonstrations.

Cedar Creek Pottery & Gallery
I-85 at Creedmoor Exit • 528-1041
• www.cedarcreekgallery.com

If you like pottery and crafts, you'll enjoy the short trek out to Cedar Creek, which opened in 1968. Five resident potters and one glass blower work at Cedar Creek. In addition, artwork by more than 200 of the most accomplished craftspeople in the United States is on display here.

To reach Cedar Creek, drive 9 miles north of Durham on I-85 to Exit 186-A (Creedmoor Road and N.C. 50) and turn right at the top of the ramp. Go 1/2 mile and turn right onto Will Suitt Road. Take the first left onto Fleming Road, go 300 yards and turn in at the Cedar Creek sign. The gallery is open daily from 10 AM to 6 PM.

Duke Campus Galleries
East and West campuses • 684-2911
• www.duke.edu

In addition to the Duke Museum of Art, there are two galleries on the East Campus and two more on the West (main) Campus, featuring rotating exhibits of paintings and photography. They are open to the public free of charge. The Hanks Gallery and the Brown Gallery are located in the Bryan Center on the West Campus. They are open daily from 8 AM to 5 PM when school is in session.

The Duke University Institute of the Arts Gallery on the East Campus is open from 8 AM to 5 PM Monday through Friday. Exhibits by area artists change monthly. The East Campus Gallery is located in the East Campus Library and is open daily from 8 AM to 6 PM. It features exhibits of artworks by Duke faculty, staff and employees.

Duke University Museum of Art
East Campus, Main Street Entrance
• 684-5135 • www.duke.edu/duma

DUMA boasts a diverse collection that includes African, Pre-Columbian, Classical, Medieval and Renaissance, Old Masters, Russian, contemporary, American and European painting, sculpture and decorative arts. In addition, the museum has a long-term loan exhibition through June 2002 entitled "Southern Gate: African American Paintings from the National Museum of American Art, Smithsonian Institution." DUMA also has many exciting temporary exhibitions throughout the year, including the popular annual "Student Curated" exhibition featuring contemporary art selected and curated by Duke undergraduates. DUMA's active weekly schedule includes Wednesday night

Photo courtesy of Durham Convention & Visitors Bureau

The NCCU Museum of Art displays the works of students and local and regional African-American artists.

student-focused programs, Thursday evening "After Hours" programs and weekend family programs.

Construction on the new $15-million, 50,000-square-foot Nasher Museum of Art at Duke University is set to begin in 2001. The museum, which is scheduled to open in the fall of 2003, will be designed by internationally renowned architect Rafael Vinoly.

Admission to DUMA is free. Hours are 10 AM to 5 PM Tuesday through Friday (Wednesdays until 9 PM during the school year), 11 AM to 2 PM Saturday and 2 PM to 5 PM Sunday.

Durham Arts Council
120 Morris St. • 560-ARTS
• www.durhamarts.org

The Arts Council sponsors classes in painting, graphic design, fiber art, photography and video for students of all ages and experience levels, at various locations in the city. Recent classes include basic drawing and portraiture, graphic design and composition, drama, dance, performing arts, writing, sculpture, photography, quilting, weaving and spinning. Call for a current schedule. It sponsors the annual CenterFest in September.

Durham Art Guild
120 Morris St. • 560-2173
• www.durhamartguild.org

Headquartered in the Durham Arts Council Building, the Durham Art Guild is one of only five continuously operating guilds in the United States. Established in 1948, it exhibits the works of local and regional artists. The Guild also hosts an Annual Juried Art Show from late November through early January. Hours are Monday through Saturday from 9 AM to 9 PM and Sunday from 1 to 6 PM.

Hayti Heritage Center
804 Old Fayetteville St. • 683-1709
• www.hayti.org

The Hayti Heritage Center, which is located in Durham's historic Hayti community, displays a diverse selection of African-American art. The Center is operated by the St. Joseph's Historic Foundation. The Lyda Merrick Gallery showcases the Center's permanent collection, as well as major national touring exhibits and the work of local artists. The adjacent St. Joseph's AME Church is currently being converted into a 350-seat performance hall set to open in the fall of 2000. The Center's Artsquest Summer Camp focuses on creative expression through the arts for ages 6 to 15. The Center also sponsors the annual Bull Durham Blues Festival in September.

Horizon Gallery
Brightleaf Square • 688-0313
• www.horizongallery.citysearch.com

Horizon offers functional and wearable art: ceramic pieces, pottery by North Carolinian as well as national craftsmen, jewelry, blown glass, wooden bowls and cutting boards, mirrors and woven items. Hours are 11 AM to 7 PM Monday through Friday, 10 AM to 8 PM Saturday and 1 PM to 6 PM on Sunday.

James Kennedy Antiques, Ltd.
Brightleaf Square • 682-1040
• www.antiqnet.com/kennedy

James and Norvell Kennedy have had one of the most interesting antique shops in the Triangle for the past 25 years or so, showing a vast array of African and Oriental objects of art within their diversified inventory of antiques. In one of the few shops of its kind in the country, you can enjoy the sculptural beauty of a wide selection of 18th- and 19th-century scientific and nautical instruments usually seen only in museums. Located in Brightleaf Square, it is open Monday through Saturday from 10 AM to 6 PM.

North Carolina Central University Museum of Art
1801 Fayetteville St. • 560-6211
• www.nccu.edu

Located on the campus of North Carolina Central University, this museum features exhibits of the works of students and local and regional African-American artists. During the school year, it's open to the public free of charge from 9 AM to 5 PM Tuesday through Friday and 2 to 5 PM Sunday. In the summer, it's open from 9 AM to 5 PM Monday through Friday.

Semans Gallery
120 Morris St. • 560-ARTS
• www.durhamarts.org

The gallery offers a series of exhibits throughout the year that are open to the public free of charge. Exhibitions usually change monthly. The gallery is in the Royall Center for the Arts in the Durham Arts Council Building. Hours are Monday through Saturday 9 AM to 9 PM and Sunday 1 PM to 6 PM.

Thomas Kinkade Signature Gallery
Northgate Mall • 416-0996 • www.tknc.com

The new Signature Gallery at Northgate Mall is devoted exclusively to the art of Thomas Kinkade, America's most collected living artist. Known as the "Painter of Light," his paintings are characterized by a rich glow. Another Thomas Kinkade Gallery is located in Raleigh's Crabtree Valley Mall, 781-2727.

Tyndall Galleries
Brightleaf Square • 683-8489
• www.tyndall.citysearch.com

Jane Tyndall's gallery showcases painting, sculpture, prints and wearable art, primarily by local and regional artists. It also offers framing and art consultation services for corporate and individual clients and is open from 11 AM to 6 PM Monday through Saturday and 1 to 4 PM on Sunday.

Raleigh and Cary

Raleigh is home to the venerable North Carolina Museum of Art and many art galleries are scattered throughout Wake County. Don't miss the monthly First Friday Gallery Walk, held in and around the Moore Square Arts District from 6 to 9 PM. For information on the arts in Cary, contact the Cary Cultural Arts Association at 851-1809.

Altamira Galleries
409 W. Martin St. • 835-0992

When this innovative gallery opened in early 2000, its first major exhibit was an ambitious survey of surrealist art in the United States. Altamira also has a large collection of African arts and crafts. Hours are Tuesday through Thursday 10 AM to 5 PM, Friday

Photo courtesy of N.C. Division of Tourism

Located at City Market, Artspace contains 25 artist studios and three exhibition galleries.

10 AM to 9 PM, Saturday 12 to 7 PM and Sunday 12 to 6 PM.

Ant Farm
303 Kinsey St. • 828-2514

The Ant Farm is a true Insiders' place, located in a fading, downtown neighborhood, Boylan Heights, off Dupont Circle in a renovated 1925 warehouse. It is a private 2,200-square-foot studio for young artists and artisans who display their works from time to time in public showings. The works vary from sculpture to jewelry to painting to furniture to ceramics. If you are an art collector looking for new talent, take in the Ant Farm, but call first. It's by appointment only.

Arts Together
114 St. Mary's St. • 828-1713
• www.artstogether.org

Arts Together is a nonprofit community arts school and performance center that has developed a devoted following over the years, especially among young dancers. It has classes in visual arts, too.

Artspace
201 E. Davie St. • 821-ARTS
• www.artspace.citysearch.com

Artspace is a very special part of Raleigh's downtown renovation. It was conceived to be a community of artists with studios and performance areas housed under one roof. Today, it has become the heart of the city's

Art District, located in the old Sanders Ford building in the City Market block across from Moore Square. Artspace has three exhibition galleries, 25 artist studios and a small auditorium upstairs used for lectures, receptions and even political forums! You can stroll through the building and see the artists at work on jewelry, paintings or other artwork and they will sell you their art on the spot. Artspace also offers a variety of summer arts programs for youths and adults.

Artspace is unique in North Carolina and draws residents as well as visitors who find a lively hub of art and entertainment, including a comedy club, antiques and the city's first brewery at Greenshield's. Take a Gallery Walk the first Friday of each month when seven galleries, all near Artspace and Moore Square, put on a show.

Contemporary Art Museum
409 W. Martin St. • 836-0088
• www.camnc.org

The Contemporary Art Museum will contain a variety of galleries, a museum, a small theater, a sculpture garden, a museum shop and a bookstore. It is scheduled to open in a warehouse in downtown Raleigh in late 2000. It will be the only Triangle museum devoted to contemporary art and design.

Gallery A
1637 Glenwood Ave. • 546-9011

Gallery A, which is part of Dr. Steven Andreaus' dental office, offers mostly contemporary painting, pottery, sculpture and photography. A different artist is featured every six to eight weeks.

Gallery C
Ridgewood Shopping Center • 828-3165
• www.galleryc.net

Owner Charlene Newsom opened Gallery C in the 1980s. The emphasis is on contemporary art, mostly from Southeastern artists, along with a selection of vintage animation art. Don't miss the annual Holiday Crafts Exhibition. Hours are Monday through Friday from 10 AM to 6 PM, Wednesday from 10 AM to 8 PM and Saturday from 10 AM to 5 PM.

Gallery of Art & Design
NCSU Student Center • 515-3503
• www.fis.ncsu.edu/arts

Exhibitions of contemporary art and design that are related to the University's various curricula are featured in the Cannon and Foundations galleries. View collections of ceramics, textiles, photography, furniture, paintings and pottery. The Gallery is located on the second floor of the NCSU Student Center. The gallery hours are from noon to 8 PM Wednesday through Friday and 2 PM to 8 PM Saturday and Sunday.

Jordan Hall Arts Center
908 North Harrison Ave. • 469-4069

Jordan Hall hosts exhibits and offers visual and performing arts classes. The Cary Cultural Arts Association meets here at 7:45 PM on the fourth Thursday of the month.

Lee Hansley Gallery
225 Glenwood Ave. • 828-7557

Opened in 1993, the Gallery hosts 10 solo and group exhibitions a year featuring works from Southeastern and national artists in the areas of painting, sculpture, ceramics, drawings, photography and fine art prints. One of the Gallery's recent shows was "North Carolina's 20th Century Masters: A Retrospective of North Carolina Art in the 1900s."

Little Art Gallery
North Hills Mall • 787-6317

Little Art Gallery, which is co-owned by Ruth Green and Rosanne Minick, has been a fixture on the Raleigh art scene for years. It features original artwork and contemporary crafts, as well as custom framing. The owners are usually there, and like many of those from whom they buy, they have definite opinions about art. Don't be afraid to get their advice.

Lump Gallery
505 S. Blount St. • 821-9999
• www.lumpgallery.com

Owners Bill Thelan and Med Byrd opened Lump in 1996 as a showcase for emerging local artists creating cutting-edge art. Half of the gallery consists of three studios and the other half is reserved for a variety of shows from one-person exhibits to group displays to complex installations. Gallery hours are 1 to 5 PM Saturday and Sunday and by appointment.

NCSU Crafts Center
Lower level, Thompson Theater, NCSU
• 515-2457 • www.ncsu.edu/crafts

NCSU Crafts Center provides opportunities for hands-on experience in beginning through advanced crafts courses such as woodworking, pottery, jewelry-making and photography. Special interest classes range from flower arranging to telescope making—more than 150 multi-session courses in 30 disciplines each year. The Center's Gallery features local and national exhibitions and is open to the public afternoons and evenings.

North Carolina Museum of Art
2110 Blue Ridge Rd. • 839-6262
• www.ncartmuseum.org

The Museum of Art is the premier art museum in the state and has become one of North Carolina's treasure houses for the visual arts. Much of the state's fine art activities are centered here. Like the North Carolina Symphony, this is a tax-supported museum, and it reaches out to its people with a wide variety of free or inexpensive programs.

In 1983, the museum opened at its current address on Blue Ridge Road. It has more than 181,000 square feet, displaying its permanent collections in American, ancient and European art to maximum advantage. The European paintings are considered the museum's finest, particularly in Italian and Dutch and Flemish artists. Its American collection has a number of lush landscapes from the Hudson River School. The museum recently expanded its African, Ancient American and Oceanic collections.

Between eight and 10 special exhibitions are organized at the museum annually, some from other museums. Three spaces are set aside for these shows and student artwork from across the state is displayed in the lobby of the museum's education wing. Two recent major exhibitions, "Monet to Moore: The Millennium Gift of Sara Lee Corporation" and "Festival Rodin"—displaying more than 120

works by French sculptor Auguste Rodin (including "The Thinker," of course)—brought the museum record-breaking attendance. "In Praise of Nature: Ansel Adams and Photographers of the American West" will run until January 7, 2001.

The museum offers lectures, adult classes, children's workshops and film festivals. It also features an outdoor amphitheater for films and live entertainment.

The museum also operates a gift shop, a new restaurant called Blue Ridge and a new coffee shop, L'Express. Admission to the museum is free; hours are 9 AM to 5 PM Tuesday through Saturday (Friday, it's 9 to 9) and 11 AM to 6 PM Sunday.

Page Walker Arts & History Center
119 Ambassador Loop, Cary • 460-4963

The former Page Walker Hotel, built in 1868, fell into disrepair during the early 1980s, but was restored as the Page Walker Arts and History Center in 1991. Its fine arts gallery features the works of local and regional artists. Art classes are also available. It also

Photo by Rich Weidman

The N.C. Museum of Art's popular exhibit, "Festival Rodin," displayed more than 120 works by the famous French sculptor.

sponsors a summer Starlight Concert Series. The Cary Heritage Museum is located on the third floor of the Center. Hours are Monday through Wednesday from 10 AM to 9:30 PM, Thursday from 10 AM to 5 PM and Friday from 10 AM to 1 PM.

Pullen Park Arts Center
Hillsborough St. & Pullen Rd. • 831-6126

Pullen Park Arts Center offers a variety of art exhibits and classes for adults and children. It is open Monday through Thursday 9 AM to 10 PM, Friday 9 AM to 1 PM and Saturday 10 AM to 3 PM.

Raleigh Contemporary Gallery
323 Blake St. • 828-6500

Opened in 1985, this eye-catching gallery shows original paintings, sculpture, fiber art and limited edition graphics by local and national artists. It also features custom conservation frames and provides consulting services for individuals as well as for corporate clients.

Sertoma Arts Center
1400 W. Millbrook Rd. • 420-2329

The Sertoma Arts Center is part of Raleigh's Shelley Park and has become the center for most city-sponsored art activities, including a multitude of children's programs. It is listed under the visual arts because it's probably best known for art classes, programs and shows, but the Sertoma Center is equally a hub of interest for dance, music, drama, pottery, quilt making, photography and literature.

If you want to learn about the art scene in Raleigh and Cary at the grassroots level, this is a good place to start. Hours are Monday through Thursday, 9 AM to 10 PM; Friday 9 AM to 3 PM; and Saturday 10 AM to 3 PM (during the school year). The Center is also available Sundays for nonalcoholic private receptions for weddings, anniversaries and other events.

Sweet Tea & Grits
City Market • 834-7752
• www.sweetteaandgrits.com

Sweet Tea & Grits is a small studio in City Market that offers Southern pottery at its best.

The gallery also displays other handcrafted items, as well as picture frames, candles, T-shirts and much more. The coffee bar offers custom-blend gourmet coffees, sandwiches, baked goods, ice cream and smoothies. Sweet Tea & Grits is open Monday through Thursday 8:30 AM to 6 PM, Friday 8:30 AM to 10 PM, Saturday 9:30 AM to 10 PM and Sunday 1 to 5 PM.

Trillium
Olde Raleigh Village, Edwards Mill Rd. • 783-0030

Trillium, which contains a gallery and gift store, attracts a strong market among the upscale buyer and big city newcomers. It started as an art gallery and gift shop but added a clothing boutique in 1994. For the young working woman, it is one of the Triangle's special places for dressy or career fashions. The gifts include jewelry and ceramic pieces and it maintains a bridal registry when you want to give the bride a piece of her "best china."

Visual Art Exchange
City Market • 828-7834
• www.vae.citysearch.com

Founded in 1980, Visual Art Exchange supports local artists of all levels and gives them opportunities to exhibit and sell their work. The gallery hosts 10 to 12 exhibits annually and is a major venue for local artists. Visual Art Exchange also offers traveling exhibits throughout the area. The gallery is open Tuesday through Saturday from 11 AM to 4 PM.

West Side Furnishings
200 S. West St. • 829-0770
• www.westsidefurnishings.com

West Side offers artistically designed furniture, accessories, antiques, oriental rugs and brocades. The designs are classic, yet modern, and the shop features local artists in a variety of mediums. West Side is the spot to find some unique pieces for your home and a great place if you just want to browse. It is open Monday through Friday 10:30 AM to 5 PM, Saturday 10 AM to 6 PM, Sunday 1 to 5 PM and by appointment.

Dance

If you think you can only really find dance in the Big Apple, think again. Believe it or not, little ole' Durham is where you'll find the acclaimed American Dance Festival.

But the ADF is only part of the Triangle dance scene. If you really want to get a taste of Southern culture, you'll want to see the Apple Chill Cloggers and the Cane Creek Cloggers, both based in Chapel Hill. Aspiring dancers can hone their skills through various studios and organizations in the Triangle.

Chapel Hill and Carrboro

Chapel Hill has become a local mecca for American folk dance. Clogging and international folk dancing seem to be the favorite forms of dance activities taking place.

The Apple Chill Cloggers
P.O. Box 119, Carrboro, NC 27510

The Apple Chill Cloggers is a nonprofit group dedicated to preserving and promoting the art of clogging. This group performs and holds workshops all over the South and, occasionally, abroad. For a schedule of dances and appearances, write the Cloggers at the above address.

The ArtsCenter for Visual, Performing and Literary Arts
300-G E. Main St., Carrboro • 929-ARTS

The ArtsCenter periodically offers classes in both the appreciation and performance of a variety of dance styles.

The Ballet School of Chapel Hill
1603 E. Franklin St. • 942-1339

The Ballet School provides year-round classes in ballet, modern, tap and fencing for children and adults.

Bounds Dance Studio
157 Rams Plaza • 942-1088

The highly trained staff at Bounds has been teaching dance in the Triangle since 1952. Ballet, tap, jazz and modern instruction is available for ages 3 to adult. The Studio is home to the Triangle Youth Ballet.

Photo by Lois Greenfield, courtesy of ADF

The internationally acclaimed American Dance Festival features such notable companies as Paul Taylor.

The Cane Creek Cloggers
• 933-2440

Like The Apple Chill Cloggers, this troupe specializes in preserving and performing traditional Appalachian folk dance. The Cane Creek Cloggers appear regularly at square dances throughout the Triangle.

Carolina Song & Dance Association
• 967-9948

The Carolina Song & Dance Association sponsors dances and instruction in contra dance regularly at various local elementary schools. These popular dances are usually held once a month on Friday night. The association features instruction for beginners at 7:30 PM and dancing (with live music) at 8 PM.

The Chapel Hill Ballet Company
P.O. Box 3233, Chapel Hill, NC 27514
• 942-1339

The Chapel Hill Ballet Company is committed to developing the potential of area dance students through classes, while bringing an appreciation of ballet to the community through dance concerts and demonstrations. The Company sponsors two performances a year that are open to the public.

North Carolina Youth Tap Ensemble
The Ballet School, Chapel Hill
• 967-9624

Founded in 1983, the N.C. Youth Tap Ensemble, formerly the Children's Tap Company, was created to offer young dancers an opportunity to perform and refine their skills, and to offer audiences a chance to enjoy tap dancing entertainment. The company includes about 45 dancers ages 7 to 23, who perform approximately 35 times a year.

Durham

African-American Dance Ensemble
• 550-2729 • users.vnet.net/aade

Choreographer Chuck Davis started this innovative ensemble in 1980 to share the finest traditions of African and African-American dance and music. The professional touring company of dancers and musicians has performed throughout the country. It offers classes for all ages in ballet, jazz dance and African dance in conjunction with the Durham Arts Council.

American Dance Festival
Duke University • 684-6402
• www.americandancefestival.org

You could spend six weeks in New York City and still not catch as many internationally renowned modern dance performances as you can get right here in Durham every June and July as part of the six-week American Dance Festival.

Established in 1932 in Bennington, Vermont, the ADF chose Durham as its home in 1978, and has been thrilling local audiences ever since with the best modern dancers from the world over. Over the years, the ADF has featured such dance greats as Merce Cunningham and Martha Graham, and notable dance companies including those of Paul Taylor, Pilobolus Dance Theatre, Cleo Parker Robinson, Chuck Davis, Parsons Dance Company, Twyla Tharp Dance, David Dorfman and The Next Ice Age.

For six weeks, the ADF offers classes, workshops and nightly performances, many to sellout audiences. The schedule offers a blend of classics, old favorites, brand-new works and experimental variations. Local newspapers provide good previews of upcoming performances, which take place in Page Auditorium and Reynolds Theatre on Duke University's West Campus. Single tickets range from $17 to $34, with a few less expensive seats for special performances. Season tickets covering more than a dozen events range from about $60 to over $100. For tickets, call 684-4444.

Ninth Street Dance
1920 1/2 Perry St. • 286-6011

Located near Duke University's East Campus, Ninth Street Dance provides skilled instruction for dancers and non-dancers of all ages. Classes are available in ballet, modern dance, jazz, shag, hip-hop, Flamenco, salsa and ballroom, among others.

Triangle Swing Dance Society
220 Foster St. • 286-6624

Approximately 250 to 400 dancers of all skill levels from all over the Triangle and beyond descend upon the downtown Durham Armory twice a month on Saturday nights for a swing dance extravaganza.

Raleigh and Cary

Raleigh is home to the critically acclaimed Carolina Ballet, which has been immensely popular since its debut in 1999. A number of dance schools are available throughout the city. There is even a Triangle Youth Ballet, 932-2678. Meredith College sponsors the North Carolina Dance Festival each winter. Call 760-8388 for more information.

Arts Together
114 St. Mary's St. • 828-1713

While Durham is the recognized dance mecca in the Triangle, a number of teaching and community dance organizations serve Raleigh and Cary. Arts Together is one, and it is home to one of the city's better known groups, The Rainbow Dance Company. Arts Together offers instruction in modern dance, tap and jazz for children and adults. Call the above number for more information.

Carolina Ballet
3101 Glenwood Ave., Ste. 265
• 303-6303 • www.carolinaballet.com

The critically acclaimed Carolina Ballet made its debut in 1999 under the direction of Robert Weiss. This dynamic professional company presents the full range of ballet from the finest classics to fresh, contemporary new works. Recent productions have included *Romeo and Juliet*, Handel's *Messiah* and Bizet's *Carmen*, a collaboration with Duke University's Ciompi Quartet. The 2000-01 season includes productions of *Coppelia*, *Messiah* and *Carmina Burana*.

Cary Ballet Conservatory
3791 N.W. Cary Pkwy., Cary • 481-6509

The conservatory provides instruction in classical ballet for ages 3 1/2 years to adult and hosts many local benefits. It is also home to the semiprofessional Cary Ballet Company, which presents local and regional performances. The 18-member professional faculty also offers instruction in jazz, modern dance and tap dancing.

The Dancers Studio
6124 St. Giles St. • 782-0622

Started in 1974 by director Karen Edwards, this 20-member ballet includes apprentice, senior and concert dancers. It is the home of the Concert Dancers of Raleigh. It occasionally performs ballets in Triangle schools; the studio has classes in ballet tap and jazz as well.

The Raleigh School of Ballet
West Raleigh Studio: 3921 Beryl Rd.
• 834-9261
North Raleigh Studio: 3290 Gresham Lake Rd. • 873-1090
• www.raleighballet.citysearch.com

Founded in 1984, The Raleigh School of Ballet provides professional training in classical ballet. Raleigh Dance Theatre is the affiliate performing company of the School. Summer programs are available for ages 4 and older.

Raleigh School of Dance Arts
608 North Market Drive • 850-9030

The Raleigh School of Dance Arts offers lessons in ballet, jazz and tap dancing for ages 3 to adult. The School is also home to the Raleigh Civic Ballet, which holds performances, from classical ballet to modern dance, at such locales as the Raleigh Little Theatre. The School of Dance Arts also hosts free performances for schools and other local organizations.

Photo courtesy of Carolina Ballet

Founded in 1999, the dynamic Carolina Ballet presents the full range of ballet, from classics to more contemporary works.

Triangle Academy of Dance
2918 Kildaire Farm Rd., Cary
• 387-1298

Cary's classical ballet academy offers some of the finest instruction, facilities and programs in the Triangle. The professional staff includes guest teachers from the neighboring Carolina Ballet. Specialized programs are available for the very young such as tap, jazz and tumbling. The Academy also schedules master classes, summer workshops and multiple opportunities for students to perform.

Writing

The Triangle is home to a number of excellent writers, among the best in the land. An Insider knows that you can meet Doris Betts, the author of *Souls Raised from the Dead*, *The Sharp Teeth of Love* and other stories, at the University of North Carolina at Chapel Hill where she teaches in the English Department. Lee Smith, named as one of the South's best writers and author of *Saving Grace*, once taught writing at NCSU; her husband Hal Crowther writes a syndicated column in *The Independent*. Kaye Gibbons, whose books *Ellen Foster*, *A Virtuous Woman*, *On the Occasion of My Last Afternoon* and others have all gotten rave reviews, lives in Raleigh, and novelist Tim McLaurin, author of *Keeper of the Moon*, lives outside of Chapel Hill. Clyde Edgerton, the floatplane pilot and author of *Raney*, *Killer Diller* and *Where Trouble Sleeps* and others, lives in Orange County with his writer/editor spouse, Susan Ketchin.

Creedmoor is home to Charles Frazier, the author of *Cold Mountain*, which won the National Book Award and spent over a year on the bestseller list. And author Dan Gearino has a day job as a columnist for the *N&O*.

The dean of Triangle fiction writers, Reynolds Price, teaches at Duke University and seems to have produced almost a book a year lately. Durham is also home to poets Michael McFee and Jaki Shelton Green.

The North Carolina Writers Workshop is a literary showcase that features guest author readings, discussions, classes and receptions spread over four days during the summer at NCSU's Thompson Theatre. Recent participants have included such regionally acclaimed writers as Lee Smith, Tim McLaurin, Betty Adcock and Robert Bateman. Call 515-4118 for more information.

Outside of the college campuses and places such as the local arts centers, you can pursue the art of writing through the North Carolina Writer's Network. Contact information for the Network is listed below, along with some Triangle publishers.

Algonquin Books of Chapel Hill
P.O. Box 2225, Chapel Hill, NC 27515
• 967-0108 • www.algonquin.com

Algonquin Books, founded by UNC professor Louis Rubin and current editorial director Shannon Ravenel, is affiliated with New York's Workman Publishers. This house has published notable books, such as novels by acclaimed contemporary writers Clyde Edgerton, Jill McCorkle, Larry Brown, Lewis Nordan and Julia Alvarez. The publishing house received national attention recently after Robert Morgan's *Gap Creek* was selected for Oprah Winfrey's book club.

Carolina Wren Press
120 Morris St., Durham
• 560-2738

Supported by the Durham Arts Council, Carolina Wren Press publishes fiction, poetry and drama of writers, says the brochure, "who are working at the cultural edge." The press is nonprofit and dedicated to the cause of "meaningful contemporary literature."

N.C. Writers' Network
P.O. Box 954, Carrboro, NC 27510
• 967-9540 • www.ncwriters.org

The N.C. Writers' Network is a statewide organization that publishes a bimonthly newsletter, sponsors an annual conference and offers a wide variety of information and support for fiction and nonfiction writers and poets.

The 1,800-seat, Gothic Revival Duke University Chapel was built to fulfill James B. Duke's dream of "a great towering church which will dominate all the surrounding buildings."

Attractions

When we first wrote this book, we found there was a big attraction every month. Now, there's something all the time, whether it's high art like the Rodin exhibit at the North Carolina Museum of Art or low camp like a Cher concert at the new Entertainment and Sports Arena (ESA). This chapter is a starting point, with addresses and phone numbers. Some of the entries such as the General Assembly are command performances—if you're going to be an Insider, you must attend. (Often, once is enough. The debate to decide the "State Rock" is a case in point.)

We were very busy at the end of the 20th century and we have several new attractions such as Raleigh's ESA, the Museum of Natural Sciences and Exploris, and improved places like Durham's Museum of Life and Science's new Magic Wings Butterfly House.

Here's where you can find gardens, monkeys and yes, even the moon and the stars! All right here in Triangle attractions!

Chapel Hill

Ackland Art Museum
Columbia St. at Franklin St. • 966-5736
• www.ackland.org
(See our "Arts" chapter.)

Chapel Hill Museum
523 E. Franklin St. • 967-1400
• www.chmuseum.citysearch.com

The Chapel Hill Museum offers exhibits, demonstrations and programs on North Carolina history with a special emphasis on Chapel Hill and Orange County. The museum is open Wednesday through Saturday from 10 AM to 4 PM and Sunday from 1 to 5 PM. Admission is free.

Morehead Planetarium and Sundial Gardens
UNC Campus, 250 E. Franklin St.
• 962-1236, 549-6863 (Information Line)
• www.morehead.unc.edu

From watching the universe spin above your head to strolling through the elegant Rotunda Art Gallery to enjoying the beautifully cultivated sundial rose gardens, the Morehead Planetarium offers a day full of activities for the whole family. This Triangle treasure boasts both traveling and original shows about moon landings, space voyages and more. The staff also present special children's shows. Friday evenings, catch *Sky Rambles,* a live narrated show.

The Planetarium opened four new exhibits in 1999: "The History of Astronomy at UNC-CH," "How Big are the Planets?," "What Causes Daytime and Nighttime?" and "Why Does the Moon Change Shape?" Public Star Theater shows are offered Wednesday through Sunday. The Rotunda Art Gallery features portraits from the Morehead family's collection and a statue of President James Polk, a UNC alumnus.

The Planetarium is open every day of the year except December 24 and 25. Call for more information about show times, prices, group rates and special events.

North Carolina Botanical Garden
U.S. 15-501 • 962-0522
• www.unc.edu/depts/ncbg

Located on 600 acres, this is the largest natural botanical garden in the Southeast. As part of UNC's Totten Center, the Garden is set up for research and conservation of plants native to the

The largest troop surrender of the Civil War took place
at Bennett Place, west of downtown Durham.

Southeastern United States. The main visitor area features displays of native plants arranged by habitats and more than two miles of trails through the woods. Throughout the year, special programs and workshops are offered in the Totten Center. It is open from 8 AM to 5 PM daily except on winter weekends. The nature trail is open dawn to dusk year round.

UNC Walking Tour
Visitors Center • 962-1630
• www.unc.edu/depts/visitor

You can take a half-hour "Walkman" tour of the historic University of North Carolina, the nation's first state university. You'll see and hear about the Old Well (the symbol of UNC), the Davie Poplar (the spot where the site for the University was selected in 1792, according to legend), Old East (built in 1793, UNC's first building), the 1851 Old Playmakers Theatre and the five-acre Coker Arboretum, among other sights. The tours begin at the Rotunda of the Morehead Building Monday through Friday from 10 AM to 5 PM. A driver's license or credit card is needed as a deposit to ensure return of the equipment used on the free tour. The Rotunda is well supplied with informative brochures and

pamphlets and is staffed at most times by volunteers. Call the Visitors Center to arrange special tours.

While you're strolling the campus, stop by the second floor of the Wilson Library, which contains the North Carolina Collection Gallery, full of historical exhibits on the state and university. Sports fans won't want to miss the Memorabilia Room at the Dean E. Smith Center or the Kenan Football Center Hall of Honor. Other sites of interest include the 172-foot-tall Morehead-Patterson Bell Tower, built in 1931, and the Old Chapel Hill Cemetery with gravestones dating from 1798.

Durham

Bennett Place
4409 Bennett Memorial Rd. • 383-4345
• www.ah.dcr.state.nc.us/sections/hs/
bennett/bennett.htm

You don't have to be a Civil War buff to appreciate the significance of what occurred on the farm of James and Nancy Bennett in April 1865. It was in the Bennett's home that two battle-fatigued adversaries—Generals Joseph E. Johnston and William T. Sherman—met to work out a peaceful settlement. Their original agreement was nullified in the wake of hostilities surrounding Abraham Lincoln's assassination, but their talks continued and eventually resulted in Johnston's surrender. It was the largest troop surrender of the Civil War, ending the fighting in the Carolinas, Georgia and Florida.

The Bennett grandchildren lived on the farm until 1890. A fire destroyed the farmhouse and kitchen in 1921. The present buildings were reconstructed in the 1960s from Civil War sketches and early photos. A reenactment of the surrender is held each April. To get to Bennett Place, take the Hillsborough Road exit off U.S. 15-501 Bypass or Interstate 85 and follow the signs. It's open from 10 AM to 4 PM Tuesday through Saturday and from 1 AM to 4 PM Sunday. Call about extended summer hours. Admission is free and you can picnic on the grounds.

Downtown Historic District

In 1977, thanks to the Historic Preservation Society of Durham, downtown Durham became the first solely commercial district to be placed on the prestigious National Register of Historic Places. Take a walk in and around the downtown loop and just look up; you'll be amazed at the exquisite facades and cornices of buildings dating back to the late 19th century. Begin your tour at the Bank of America building at the intersection of Main and Corcoran streets. The 1914 building sits on the property once owned by the city's founder, Dr. Bartlett Snipes Durham. Proceeding up Main Street you'll take in the Kress Building, a 1932 art deco jewel featuring a facade of polychromed terra-cotta ornaments. Further up the street, you'll see the lovely arched pedimented doorway of a white marble, Beaux Arts-era building. The district also includes the beautifully restored Carolina Theatre (formerly the Durham Auditorium). A detailed brochure and map of the district is available from the Greater Durham Chamber of Commerce by calling 682-2133; it is also available at the Visitors Center.

Duke Homestead & Tobacco Museum
2828 Duke Homestead Rd.
• 477-5498 • www.ah.dcr.state.nc.us/ sections/hs/duke/duke.htm

You can't fully appreciate Durham until you understand how tobacco figured into the city's growth and development. The Duke Homestead and Tobacco Museum is where you go for a quick course in how the local industry began. Every year on the last weekend in July, you can attend the Tobacco Harvest Festival and see how tobacco was tied on sticks and cured over wood fires. The Duke Homestead also hosts a Christmas by Candlelight Tour each December. The museum is open free of charge April through October from 9 AM to 5 PM Tuesday through Saturday and 1 to 5 PM Sunday, and November through March from 10 AM to 4 PM Tuesday through Saturday and 1 to 4 PM Sunday.

Duke Primate Center
3705 Erwin Rd. • 489-3364
• www.duke.edu/web/primate

The world-renowned Duke Primate Center was established to promote the preservation of some endangered species of primates, including lemurs and bush babies. The Center is open for tours, which must be scheduled by appointment. It's a fascinating place full of more than 250 primates—a bit of the wild right in the heart of the Triangle. Admission is charged. Call for more information or to schedule a tour.

Duke University Chapel
Chapel Dr., West Campus • 684-2572
• www.chapel.duke.edu

Modeled after England's Canterbury Cathedral, the Gothic architecture of this breathtaking chapel is exquisite inside and out. The soft glow of light from 77 stained glass windows illuminates the interior and a organ with 5,200 pipes. The 210-foot bell

INSIDERS' TIP
If you've never been on a movie location, go visit the old Durham Athletic Park, the vintage baseball stadium where the movie *Bull Durham* was filmed and the old Class-A Durham Bulls played.

tower, which was completed in 1932, is no longer open to the public.

Historic Stagville
5825 Old Oxford Hwy. • 620-0120
• www.ah.dcr.state.nc.us/sections/do/ stagvill/default.htm

Several historic 18th- and 19th-century plantation buildings set on 71 acres make up Historic Stagville, once one of the South's largest working plantations. View the 1787 Bennehan House, the Horton Grove Slave Quarters and the 1860 Great Barn. This is the nation's first state-owned research center for the study of historic and archaeological preservation. Workshops and demonstrations are scheduled throughout the year. Don't miss the Christmas Open House in December. The Center is located 7 miles northeast of Durham on the Old Oxford Highway (S.R. 1004). It's open from 9 AM to 4 PM Monday through Friday. Admission is free.

Museum of Life and Science
433 Murray Ave. • 220-5429
• www.ncmls.org

The Museum of Life and Science, a 70-acre regional science-technology center, features two floors of hands-on exhibits and an outdoor Nature Park. Kids and adults alike will be fascinated with exotic butterflies in the Magic Wings Butterfly House, the 15-foot tornado in the ABC News Channel 11 Weather exhibit, the models of pumping hearts and demonstrations in BodyTech and the native animals in Carolina Wildlife. Explore the Science Arcade, the Tree House discovery room, the outdoor Loblolly Park complete with wind chimes and water play or lose yourself in the MegaMaze. The Ellerbee Creek Railway winds through Nature Park with views of black bears, red wolves and hawks. Other exhibits include Aerospace, Small Science (for the little ones), Geology, Data Earth and Discovery Rooms. Nationally touring exhibits, such as the popular "MarsQuest," stop here. The Museum also has developed exhibits that have gone on tour. The Magic Wings Butterfly House, one of only 10 permanent butterfly houses in the United States, opened in spring 1999, featuring about 1,000 exotic butterflies. A state-of-the-art insectarium opened in early 2000. Seasonal annual events include a moonlight train ride to the North Pole. School programs, community classes, summer camps and teacher workshops are also offered at the Museum. Annual memberships may be purchased that provide admission to

Photo courtesy of Museum of Life & Science

The Magic Wings Butterfly House at the Museum of Life and Science in Durham serves as the habitat for about 1,000 exotic butterflies.

the museum and discounts on classes. Group rates are available with reservations. Hours are 10 AM to 5 PM Monday through Saturday and noon to 5 PM on Sunday (open until 6 PM Memorial Day through Labor Day). The museum is wheelchair-accessible.

Patterson's Mill Country Store
5109 Farrington Rd. • 493-8149

In a rural setting, tucked on a wedge of land between highways and housing developments, lies a tribute to a simpler time. Patterson's Mill is a replica of a mom-and-pop country store, drugstore, doctor's office and tobacco shop all rolled into one. While antiques and North Carolina crafts can be bought from the store, 90 percent of what you'll see there is not for sale at any price. Considered one of the best collections of mercantile Americana in the United States, the Patterson's Mill Country Store is open from 10 AM to 5:30 PM Tuesday through Saturday and from 2 to 5:30 PM Sunday. It's located on Farrington Road, about 2 miles north of N.C. 54 between Durham and Chapel Hill.

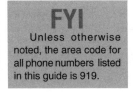

FYI

Unless otherwise noted, the area code for all phone numbers listed in this guide is 919.

Sarah P. Duke Gardens
Duke University West Campus
• 684-3698 • www.duke.edu

More than 300,000 visitors from all over the world annually flock to this spectacular spot on the edge of Duke's West Campus to catch dazzling displays of flowers and shrubs in season. Known as the "Crown Jewel of Duke University," the gardens were named for Sarah P. Duke (1856-1936), wife of Benjamin N. Duke, one of the University's founders. It is recognized as one of the premiere public gardens in the United States. Fifty-five acres of landscaped gardens and pine forest are open daily to the public. The Duke Gardens consists of three major sections: the original Terraces and their immediate surroundings, the Blomquist Garden of Native Plants and the Culberson Asiatic Arboretum. Seasonal blooms include pansies, tulips, daffodils, azaleas, wisteria, roses, daylilies and chrysanthemums as well

as flowering dogwood, magnolia, redbud, crab apple and cherry trees. The premises also include an azalea court, rock garden, rose garden, fish pond and Terrace Gift Shop. Sunday afternoon concerts and programs are held in the late spring and summer. It is a great place to picnic and spend a peaceful afternoon. Free public tours are available March 15 through May. The Doris Duke Visitors Center is set to open here in the spring of 2001. A children's amphitheater is also in the planning stages. The gardens are open daily from 8 AM to dusk.

Raleigh and Cary

African American Cultural Complex
119 Sunnybrook Rd. • 212-3598
• www.aaccmuseum.org

At this unique Raleigh museum, collections of artifacts, documents and photographs highlight the contributions of African Americans to the culture of North Carolina and the United States. The Complex also contains a replica of the infamous slave ship *Amistad* and a nature trail. A 90-minute outdoor drama, *The Amistad Saga: Reflections*, takes place here during the summer. The Complex also hosts a summer children's theater workshop. It is open for tours by appointment only. Admission is free but donations are accepted.

ALLTEL Pavilion at Walnut Creek
Sunnybrook and Rock Quarry Rds.
Concert Line: 831-6666
Ticketmaster: 834-4000
• www.alltelpavilion.com

Built in 1991, the $13.5 million amphitheater holds about 20,000 people, 7,000 under the roof. Other patrons are seated on a great, green sloping hill from which they can view and hear the stage via giant video screens and a state-of-the-art digital sound system.

The amphitheater is part of the city's 240-acre Walnut Creek Park that also features the city's largest softball complex. Walnut Creek is one of the top spots for national tours. Recent acts include Santana, Britney Spears, Shania Twain, Bob Dylan, Jimmy Buffett, Dixie Chicks, KISS, Red Hot Chili Peppers, Trisha Yearwood, Widespread Panic and OzzFest.

You can't bring lawn chairs, food or drink, so bring money for food and refreshments when you go. Parking is extra. Be sure to take a moment and stand on the top of the hill and soak up the glittering scene below you—it's where the stars come to shine!

Capital Area Visitor Center
301 N. Blount St. • 733-3456

You may want to start your downtown tour here because you'll sample our warm Southern hospitality along with generous helpings of information about the Capital City from the award-winning staff. The Center, which is located in the 1918 Andrews-London House, welcomes more than 100,000 walk-in visitors annually and provides maps, brochures, a 15-minute orientation film about Raleigh and true Insider tips on gifts, artwork, restaurants, accommodations and history.

Cary Heritage Museum
119 Ambassador Loop • 460-4963

Located on the third floor of the Page-Walker Arts and History Center, the Cary Heritage Museum contains a variety of interesting exhibits that trace the town's history. Highlights include a town timeline, biographies of famous local citizens, Civil War shells and a World War I uniform.

City Market
Management Office • 303 Blake St.
• 828-4555
• www.citymarket.citysearch.com

The 1914 City Market, located on the south side of Moore Square in downtown, began an exciting rebirth in 1988. Today, the cobblestone streets are home to a tantalizing array of restaurants, shops and art galleries. Try the homemade brew at Greenshields, visit galleries displaying crafts by local and regional artisans, shop for fresh produce, take in a comedy show at ComedySportz or eat a power breakfast at Big Ed's with local and state politicians and big-time lobbyists.

Mounted police and old-fashioned trolley cars, complete with bells and finished with brass and mahogany, recall the elegance and pace of days gone by.

College Attractions

All of the colleges and universities draw big-name entertainment and speakers to the Triangle. NCSU's Reynold's Coliseum, the Raleigh Entertainment and Sports Arena and UNC's Dean E. Smith Center ("The Dean Dome") are where the biggest entertainers show up during the winter months.

Exploris
201 E. Hargett St. • 834-4040
• www.exploris.org

The world's first global experience center opened its doors downtown in October 1999, featuring hands-on exhibits, daily performances and programs for all ages. Exploris' attractions are brought to life by an expert program staff, a host of interactive computer activities, video and videoconferencing, the Internet, and art, sculpture and artifacts from around the globe. Highlights include a four-ton section of the Berlin Wall, "Words on Water Sculpture," Marbles Wall and the Look-In-Look-Out Window. One of Exploris' newest exhibits is called "One Voice: From the Pen of Anne Frank." Plans for the center include an IMAX Theater. It is open Tuesday through Saturday from 9 AM to 5 PM and Sunday from 12 to 5 PM. Call for summer hours.

The General Assembly
16 W. Jones St., Downtown • 733-4111
• www.ncga.state.nc.us

Some consider this the best attraction in town. The General Assembly used to officially meet on a biannual basis; however, the legislators come to town every year now, for what's called a Short or Long Session. Sessions of the House and Senate begin at 1:30 PM with the ringing of bells to alert stray legislators.

Sitting in the comfortable, red plush seats in the galleries, you can watch legislation being made. There is drama; there is comedy; there is tragedy; there is intrigue; and there is oratory, vintage Southern style. You can hear

Photo courtesy of Exploris

Exploris, the world's first global experience center, provides interactive activities for all ages.

the Elizabethan accents of the state's Outer Banks, the rounded drawls of the coastal plains and the distinct twang of mountain vernacular. In one seat may sit the state's next governor and in another may sit the next subject of an FBI investigation. Where else in the state can you see a show that costs millions and spends billions and charges no admission? The General Assembly, up close and personal in Raleigh.

Historic Oakwood
Person, Franklin & Edenton Sts.
• www.historicoakwood.org

Stroll through this 20-block Victorian neighborhood that boasts more than 400 restored homes. It is listed on the National Register of Historic Places. Residents show off their homes and workmanship during the annual Historic Oakwood Christmas Tour in December. The Oakwood Garden Tour takes place each April. The Oakwood Cemetery contains the graves of more than 2,800 Confederate soldiers, as well as seven governors and a number of United States senators. Self-guided walking tour brochures of Historic Oakwood can be picked up at the Capital Area Visitor Center at 301 North Blount Street.

Historic Trolley Tours
Downtown • 834-4844

Narrated trolley tours begin at Mordecai Historic Park and wind through the heart of the Capital City, with stops at historical sites, art galleries, museums and City Market. The trolley runs every Saturday from noon to 3:45 PM (the last trolley departs at 3 PM) during the summer and the first and third Saturday of the month from September through December. The admission is $5 for adults, $2 for ages 7 to 17 and free for children 6 and under.

Historic Walking Tours of Raleigh
301 N. Blount St. • 829-4988

Take an entertaining and educational one-hour walking tour of downtown on Sundays at 2 PM from March through November (or by appointment). Tours originate at the Capital Area Visitor Center. Call ahead for reservations.

N.C. Museum of Art
2110 Blue Ridge Rd. • 839-6262
• www.ncartmuseum.org

(See the "Visual Arts" section of our "Arts" chapter.)

N.C. Solar Center
Western Blvd. & Gorman St.
• 515-3799

At the Solar Center on the campus of North Carolina State University, you can take a free tour of a fully furnished solar-operated house. The facility also contains a reference and video library. Hours are Monday through Friday 9 AM to 5 PM and Sunday 1 to 5 PM.

N.C. State Fairgrounds
Hillsborough St. & Blue Ridge Rd.
• 733-2145

Events occur throughout the year at the North Carolina State Fairgrounds. The most popular attraction of the year is the N.C. State Fair. The fair starts on the third Friday in October and runs for 10 days. Other popular attractions at the fairgrounds include the North Carolina Renaissance Faire, July Fourth Celebration, the Southern Ideal Home Show and numerous animal shows and civic events throughout the year. A lively Flea Market is held every weekend.

Raleigh City Museum
Briggs Building, Fayetteville St. Mall
• 832-3775
• www.raleighcitymuseum.org

The 10,000-square-foot museum features fascinating exhibits, which change regularly, relating to the history of the Capital City. It is housed in the 1874 Briggs Buildings, a former hardware store. The museum's first permanent exhibit documents Raleigh's role in the Civil Rights movement. It is open 10 AM to 4 PM Tuesday through Friday and 1 to 4 PM Saturday and Sunday. The museum's gift store contains a variety of unique items. Admission is free and group tours are available.

Raleigh Convention & Conference Center
500 Fayetteville Street Mall • 831-6011
• www.raleighconvention.com

The $18-million Civic Center, which offers 100,000 square feet of interior space and can seat up to 4,000 concertgoers, is home to a number of special shows each year,

Photo by Rich Weidman

The Raleigh Rose Garden, which boasts 60 varieties of roses, lies adjacent to the Raleigh Little Theater.

including the Raleigh Antiques Extravaganza, the Southern Women's Show and the Home, Garden and Flower Show.

Raleigh Entertainment & Sports Arena
1400 Edwards Mill Rd. • 861-2300
Ticketmaster: 834-4000
• www.raleigharena.com

Completed in the fall of 1999, this $158 million, 20,500-seat multipurpose arena serves as the home of the National Hockey League Carolina Hurricanes, the North Carolina State University Wolfpack men's basketball team and the new Carolina Cobras of the Arena Football League. The arena also functions as a regional entertainment showcase, hosting such diverse acts as The Judds, Harlem Globetrotters, WWF Wrestling, Stars on Ice and Bruce Springsteen and the E Street Band.

ZooFauna
U.S. 1 A, Wake Forest • 562-8899
• www.zoofauna.com

A 30-acre privately owned nature park opened by an exotic animal breeder, ZooFauna boasts about 225 animals, including camels, zebras, ostriches, bears, lemurs, emus and miniature donkeys. A petting area, snack bar and gift shop are on the premises. ZooFauna is located in Franklin County, just north of Wake Forest.

Gardens

Beautiful gardens abound in and around Raleigh, and some consider Fayetteville Street Mall and the adjoining Government Mall two of the best landscapes in the state. Four area gardens are of special interest: the Raleigh Rose Garden, WRAL-TV's gardens, Martin Luther King Jr. Memorial Gardens and NCSU's J.C. Raulston Arboretum located on Beryl Road, near the Fairgrounds. The Raleigh Rose and WRAL gardens are very popular for spring and

summer weddings. Another quiet and beautiful nursery and garden is the Niche Gardens at 1111 Dawson Road in Chapel Hill.

J.C. Raulston Arboretum
4301 Beryl Rd. • 515-3132
• arb.ncsu.edu

Founded in 1976, the arboretum is part of North Carolina State University's Horticulture Sciences Department. It is on Beryl Road, which runs parallel to Hillsborough Street just past Meredith College, toward the State Fairgrounds. The Arboretum is a wonderful collection of gardens and plants. It boasts a fabulous Perennial Border, a Japanese Garden and excellent plant diversity. The arboretum is open from 8 AM to 8 PM all year round.

Martin Luther King Jr. Memorial Gardens
Rock Quarry Rd. & Martin Luther King Jr. Blvd. • 834-6264

More than 5,000 colorful trees, shrubs and flowering plants surround a life-size bronze statue of the famous Civil Rights leader at this beautiful garden. A 12-ton water monument honors other pioneers of the Civil Rights movement.

Raleigh Rose Garden
301 Pogue St. • 821-4579

The Raleigh Rose Garden is on Pogue Street, two blocks off Hillsborough Street where it runs in front of the NCSU campus. It boasts 1,200 roses of 60 different varieties. The garden is maintained by some of the city's garden clubs and includes an outdoor amphitheater.

WRAL Gardens
2619 Western Blvd. • 821-8555
• www.wral-gardens.com

On the other side of the NCSU campus are the five-acre WRAL gardens, highlighted by more than 2,000 azaleas. A favorite location

INSIDERS' TIP
The Executive Mansion was constructed with many native materials and bricks made with local clay by prison laborers. Look for the names of prisoners in the bricks on the sidewalk surrounding the mansion.

for intimate weddings, the gardens are currently undergoing renovations until spring 2001.

Historic Homes

Five historic Raleigh homes are on any Insiders' list: The Governor's Mansion, Haywood Hall, the Joel Lane House (he's the fellow who sold the land that became Raleigh), the Mordecai House at Mordecai Park and Oak View.

Executive Mansion
200 N. Blount St. • 733-3456

Home to the Governor and his family, the Executive Mansion is a classic example of Queen Anne Cottage-Style Victorian architecture, known as gingerbread style. The building was started in 1883 and completed in 1891 at a cost of $58,843.01, using mostly native North Carolina materials. The 34,806-square-foot house is filled with antiques and crystal chandeliers, many manufactured in North Carolina. President Franklin Delano Roosevelt once referred to the mansion as "the most beautiful governor's residence in America." It is a "working" mansion in that the governor's family not only lives there but he also conducts much of the state's business and entertaining in the mansion and on the grounds.

Call the number above for planning your tour, not for chatting with the Governor. The ground floors are open to the public. Tours take about 30 minutes and are open to the public in the fall and spring. One of the most popular times for tours is during the December holiday season.

Haywood Hall House & Garden
211 New Bern Pl. • 832-8357

Built in 1799 by North Carolina State Treasurer John Haywood, this Federal-style dwelling is considered to be the oldest house within Raleigh's original limits. Haywood's descendents occupied the house until 1977. It is open Thursdays from 10:30 AM to 1:30 PM. An Annual Open House takes place during the second weekend of December.

Historic Oak View County Park
The Beltline & Poole Rd. • 250-1013

Take a step back in time and experience 19th-century North Carolina farm life at Historic Oak View. Some of the buildings date back to before the Civil War and the complex contains the 1855 farmhouse, plank kitchen, carriage house, cotton gin museum, gazebo, livestock barn, family cemetery and a still-productive pecan grove. It's open from 8:30 AM until one hour before sunset Monday through Saturday. Tours are available daily. Visitors can also enjoy fishing in the farm pond and picnicking. Oak View can be rented for special events.

Joel Lane House & Gardens
Hargett and St. Mary's Sts. • 833-3431

Built in the 1760s, this renovated home and grounds was once part of a 1,000-acre plantation (known as "Wakefield") and considered the finest house within a 100-mile radius in the late 18th century. Joel Lane was a Revolutionary War veteran who later sold the state the property on which the capital city grew. The house is now maintained by volunteers. Much of the interior woodwork and flooring is original. It is open to the public Tuesday through Friday from 10 AM until 2 PM and from 1 PM to 4 PM on Saturday. The house is also available for receptions and meetings.

Mordecai Historic Park
1 Mimosa St. • 834-4844

Part of the city's parks system, the Mordecai House and grounds are a quiet spot downtown. Built in 1785, the house remained in the same family until the 1960s. Its furnishings span two centuries of styles. When the

Photo by Rich Weidman

Built in the 1760s, the Joel Lane House in downtown Raleigh was once part of a 1,000-acre plantation called Wakefield.

city acquired the home, officials were amazed at the treasure trove of antiques found in the dilapidated barn out back. The country's Bicentennial Celebration spurred interest and contributions and with the city's acquisition, the home has been preserved.

The grounds also contain the humble cabin in which Andrew Johnson, 17th president of the United States, was born in 1808. There is a charming 1847 plantation chapel that can be reserved for small weddings. Colorful flower and herb gardens are scattered throughout the grounds. Hours are 10 AM to 4 PM Monday through Saturday and Sunday from 1 to 4 PM (the last tour each day starts at 3 PM). The Mordecai House is closed Tuesdays. Tours begin on the hour and last one hour.

Government Buildings

As the capital city, Raleigh's most enduring attractions, perhaps, are its capital buildings near the Government Mall. Several can be seen in a day's walking tour and all are deserving of closer inspection. They are not only attractions; they're the state's heritage. The state Museum of History and Museum of Natural Sciences are also within walking distance of the Capitol.

N.C. Museum of History
5 E. Edenton St. • 715-0200
• nchistory.dcr.state.nc.us

Completed in 1994, the museum's 170,000-square-foot facility houses both short- and long-term exhibits that describe how North Carolinians have lived from the state's beginnings to the present day. The collection includes artifacts, photographs and videos. Long-term exhibits focus on the state's chronological history, folklife, healing systems, struggles during the Civil War and the North Carolina Sports Hall of Fame. Special programs include dramatic presentations, demonstrations and family nights. Guided tours are available. The museum's gift shop is filled with items from North Carolina such as crafts, pottery, quilts, toys and regional fiction and history books. Hours are Tuesday through Saturday 9 AM to 5 PM and Sunday noon to 5 PM. The gift shop is open Monday through Saturday 9 AM to 5 PM and Sunday noon to 5 PM. Admission is free.

N.C. Museum of Natural Sciences
Bicentennial Plaza • 733-7450
• www.naturalsciences.org

Probably the most popular place in the capital among North Carolina's children, the

Museum of Natural Sciences was founded in 1879 as North Carolina's first public museum. The new $70.5-million, 200,000-square-foot facility opened its doors in April 2000 as the Southeast's largest natural history museum. The seven-story structure includes a variety of fascinating exhibit areas that showcase the state's natural diversity and global connections, including "Coastal Carolina," "Mountains to the Sea," "North Carolina's Natural Treasures," "Windows on the World," "Tropical Connections," "Prehistoric North Carolina" and "Underground North Carolina." Experience a prehistoric fight scene in the "Terror of the South" exhibit, the only place in the world to see a 110-million-year-old Acrocanthosaurus dinosaur skeleton. In addition, nearly 3,500 animals, representing approximately 270 species and subspecies, call the museum home.

The museum also houses an auditorium, classrooms, a fossil lab, an animal conservatory, a special exhibits gallery, a hands-on science experiment center, the Acro Cafe and an expanded museum store. Admission is free. The Museum is open Monday through Saturday 9 AM to 5 PM and Sunday 12 PM to 5 PM.

N.C. State Archives & Library
109 E. Jones St. • 733-3952
• statelibrary.dcr.state.nc.us

This shining white building serves several purposes: it holds the offices of the Secretary of Cultural Resources, the state's archives and the state library. The building also displays the original Carolina Charter of 1663. You will also find many people here researching their family trees. The Federation of North Carolina Historical Societies has its office here and there is a special section in the Library for genealogical research.

N.C. State Capitol
Capitol Square, Downtown • 733-4994

The recently renovated State Capitol building is the center of downtown, a landmark from the day it was completed in 1840. The current structure is considered one of the best-preserved examples of Greek Revival architecture in the country with its columns, moldings and the honeysuckle crown atop the dome carefully patterned after certain Greek temples. A replica of Antonio Canova's marble statue of George Washington stands in the center of the four-story rotunda (the original was destroyed during

Photo courtesy of N.C. Museum of Natural Sciences

The "Terror of the South" exhibit at the new Museum of Natural Sciences features a 110-million-year-old Acrocanthosaurus dinosaur skeleton.

Photo courtesy of N.C. Division of Tourism

According to legend, an escape tunnel was built beneath the North Carolina State Capitol for the governor's use during the Civil War.

a fire that burned the State House in 1831). The Capitol cost $532,682 to build which, at the time, was three times the state's annual income.

Looking around the Government Mall today, it's hard to believe that until the 1880s, the Capitol housed all of state government! The Capitol, which attracts more than 250,000 visitors a year, is still in use. The Governor and his press office work here as does the Lieutenant Governor. Several legends surround the building, including one involving an escape tunnel, an open bar on the second floor and secret rooms. A number of interesting statues and monuments surround the Capitol, including *Three Presidents* (honoring native sons Andrew Jackson, James Polk and Andrew Johnson), *After the Firefight* (a Vietnam veteran's memorial) and a 75-foot Confederate monument.

You can walk through the Capitol between 8 AM and 5 PM during weekdays, 10 AM to 4 PM on Saturday and 1 PM to 4 PM on Sunday. Guided tours may be scheduled through the Capital Area Visitor Center, 733-3456.

N.C. State Legislative Building
Corner of Jones and Halifax Sts.
• 733-7928

When the General Assembly outgrew the Capitol, the state employed famed Arkansas architect Edward Durrell Stone to design a new home for the legislators. Stone also designed the John F. Kennedy Center for the Performing Arts in Washington, D.C. The 206,000-square-foot building that resulted is every bit as classic as the Capitol. It has Stone's trademark colonnade of columns outside and soothing garden fountains inside. The building's native granite and its marble facing give it a sense of public majesty. Note the pyramid-shaped roofs and the mosiac of the Great Seal of North Carolina lies at the entrance. Inside, the House and Senate chambers are within view of public galleries overhead. Weekdays, the building is open to the public. Call ahead for hours. Unlike legislators, children must be accompanied by an adult.

N.C. State Supreme Court
Justice Building • Corner of Morgan and Fayetteville Sts.

The N.C. State Supreme Court is not one of your tourist hot spots, but as the third branch of state government standing quietly across Morgan Street from the Capitol, it's worth notice. Ask the security guard at the entrance for instructions and go take a look at the court chambers where even the most aggressive lawyers mind their manners when arguing before the seven-member court.

Colleges and Universities

The rich history of the Triangle has always been intertwined with the strength of its institutions of higher learning. Five universities and five colleges have made countless contributions to the area's vibrancy, culture, lifestyle and employment base.

Educational opportunities abound throughout the region for students of all ages. For instance, you can send your children to top-ranked public universities at bargain tuition rates. And you can choose from three MBA programs, three law schools and two medical schools. In addition, a half-dozen graduate schools offer courses in a variety of subjects. You can also take an array of credit and non-credit continuing education classes at area universities on just about every subject imaginable.

Whether or not you are enrolled at one of these schools, you can take advantage of their cultural and athletic facilities and programs. All of the colleges and universities draw big-name entertainment and speakers to the Triangle. Enjoy award-winning theatre and music events, libraries, art museums, botanical gardens, a planetarium, a primate center and, of course, sports arenas and stadiums. Nothing beats rooting your favorite football team to victory on a crisp fall afternoon. Don't forget the ACC basketball tournament in March when practically the whole area shuts down for a couple of days to participate in the madness. (For more information, see our chapters on "Arts and Culture," "Attractions" and "Spectator Sports.")

The following chapter briefly describes the colleges, universities and technical schools in Chapel Hill, Durham and Raleigh. For more information, write or call each school for catalogs and brochures.

Chapel Hill

University of North Carolina At Chapel Hill
Morehead Planetarium Bldg.
Franklin St., Chapel Hill, NC 27514
Visitors Center • 962-1630
• www.unc.edu

For more than 200 years, UNC-CH has been nationally acclaimed for its teaching, research and public service programs. New chancellor James Moeser, formerly of the University of Nebraska-Lincoln, said his goal is to make UNC-CH the nation's top public institution by the end of the decade.

The nation's oldest state university has been a leader in higher education since it opened its doors in 1795. The first student to register, Hinton James, was the University's only student for several weeks.

UNC-CH is consistently ranked as one of the top state universities in the country. In a recent survey, *U.S. News & World Report* ranked it third in the nation among public universities (with high marks for its Medical, Business, Law and Nursing schools). The tuition for state residents is about $2,711 per academic year; for nonresidents, it's about $11,877.

What started in one building with only a handful of students and two professors has mushroomed into a major research university with nearly 200 buildings, about 24,600 students and more than 2,400 faculty members, approximately 94 percent of whom have a doctorate or their field's terminal degree.

UNC offers students a wide choice of curriculums leading to nearly 400 different undergraduate, graduate or professional degrees. You can study in one of eight colleges in the Division of Academic Affairs (General, Arts and Sciences, Business Administration, Education, Journalism and Mass Communication, Law, Information and Library Science and Social Work), or one of five schools in the Division of Health Affairs (Dentistry, Medicine, Nursing, Pharmacy and Public Health). More than 1,500 courses are offered through special institutes, seminars and workshops.

In 1997, the Kenan-Flagler Business School moved into the $43 million, state-of-the-art McColl Building, which is named for Kenan Flagler alumnus Hugh McColl, chairman and CEO of Bank of America.

Even for nonstudents, UNC-CH is a fantastic resource to have in the neighborhood. With more than four million volumes, its libraries (www.ibiblio.org) are among the best in the Southeast. You'll enjoy the Rare Book Collection, the North Carolina Collection and the Southern Historical Collection housed in the Wilson Library, as well as the resources in the Davis graduate library. North Carolina residents can apply for library cards, which cost $10. For information, call 962-1053.

UNC-CH is also the site of the UNC Hospitals complex, the state's principal referral, diagnostic and treatment center (see our chapter on "Health Care"). UNC and the medical center are the largest employers in Chapel Hill.

What's more, UNC-CH's 729-acre main campus, known as "The Noble Grove," is rich in history, as well as just a nice place to stroll. Among the major attractions offered by UNC-CH are the Old Well, Davie Poplar, Old East Dormitory, Coker Arboretum, McCorkle Place,

FYI

Unless otherwise noted, the area code for all phone numbers listed in this guide is 919.

Morehead-Patterson Bell Tower, Forest Theatre, Polk Place, Morehead Planetarium, Ackland Art Museum, Louis Round Wilson Library, N.C. Botanical Garden, PlayMakers Repertory Company, Dean E. Smith Center (the "Dean Dome"), Memorial Hall and, of course, Atlantic Coast Conference Basketball (the Tar Heel men were the national champs in 1993 and made Final Four appearances in 1997, 1998 and 2000, and the Lady Tar Heels won the NCAA title in 1994), football and soccer. For more information on these attractions, see our chapters on "Arts," "Attractions" and "Sports."

Famous Tar Heel alumni include President James K. Polk, Watergate Hearings chairman Sam Ervin Jr., North Carolina Governor and Senator Terry Sanford, television journalists Charles Kuralt and Roger Mudd, writer Thomas Wolfe, North Carolina Central University Chancellor Julius Chambers, Oscar-winning actors Louise Fletcher and Jack Palance, actor Andy Griffith, soccer star Mia Hamm, golfer Davis Love and, of course, basketball star Michael Jordan.

Durham

Duke University
Box 90586, Duke University
Durham, NC 27708
Undergraduate Admissions
• 684-3214 • www.duke.edu

Duke has long been considered one of the finest private colleges in the nation. In a recent nationwide survey by *U.S. News & World Report*, Duke was ranked the eighth-best national university (public or private) in the country.

It all began in 1892 when Trinity College, a Methodist school located in rural Randolph County, was moved to Durham with the help of tobacco magnate Washington Duke. In

INSIDERS' TIP

Visitors to UNC-CH can take a "walkman" tour of the campus. Tours begin at the rotunda of the Morehead Planetarium building Monday through Friday from 10 AM to 5 PM.

Photo by Rich Weidman

A statue of Duke University benefactor and tobacco magnate Washington Duke stands guard at the entrance to East Campus.

1924, James Buchanan Duke endowed the institution and it was renamed in the family's honor.

Today, Duke encompasses 575 tree-shaded acres in Durham, including the Georgian architecture of the East campus off Broad Street and the Gothic towers of the Duke Chapel on the West campus 1.5 miles away. Here you'll find more than 11,000 students working toward a variety of graduate and undergraduate degrees. Nan Keohane, former president of Wellesley College, has been president of Duke since 1993.

Duke's admissions criteria are tough—only about 25 percent of the 14,000 students who apply eventually enroll and tuition is steep, more than $33,000 a year. Students who make the grade leave with prestigious credentials from one of Duke's highly acclaimed schools: Trinity College of Arts and Sciences, School of Engineering, Graduate School, School of Law, School of Medicine, School of Nursing, Divinity School, Nicholas School of the Environment and Fuqua School of Business (recently ranked fifth in the nation by *Business Week*).

Many students choose interdisciplinary programs such as Women's Studies, the Institute of the Arts or Technology and Liberal Arts. The Terry Sanford Institute of Public Policy offers graduates and undergraduates a chance to prepare for their chosen careers by studying under federal government officials and nationally respected journalists. Other special centers of learning and programs of study include the Mary Lou Williams Center for African-American Culture, the Center for Documentary Studies, the Center for Teaching and Learning, the Levine Science Research Center, the Center for Jewish Life and the Center for International Studies, among others.

Duke is known for its specialized research in science and medicine. Duke University Medical Center is engaged in highly sophisticated cancer research, among other things, drawing its patients from all over the world (see our "Health Care" chapter). The Center for the Study of Aging and Human Development is the first such facility in the country to study what happens biologically, psychologically and socially as people grow older. Duke's Primate Center is an active teaching facility devoted to the preservation and study of humanity's primate relatives.

Duke's 12,500-square-foot Botany Greenhouse holds the most diverse collection of plants under glass in the Southeast, including more than 2,500 different species. Visitors may tour the facilities from 10 AM to 4:30 PM every day except Friday.

Finally, there is the F.G. Hall Laboratory for Environmental Research, containing special high-pressure chambers for simulating deep-sea diving experiments. A research dive to 2,250 feet set a new world's record.

You don't have to be a research scientist or student to enjoy having Duke University in the neighborhood. Anyone can take advantage of the resources available at the Perkins Library, considered to be among the top 10 university libraries in the nation, with more than 4.5 million books and 33,000 periodicals.

You also can enroll in one of dozens of stimulating courses offered through Duke's Continuing Education program. A recent schedule included classes in foreign language studies, technical writing, cooking, line dancing, screenwriting, business skills and career counseling. For a schedule, call 684-6259. If you are age 50 or older, you might sign up for Duke's Institute for Learning in Retirement, a program of classes taught by peers and professionals, including history, language, literature, religion, science, current affairs, business and fitness. Call 684-2703 for more information.

Even if you don't want to study anything at all, Duke has something for you. You can hike, jog or picnic in Duke Forest, the 8,300-acre preserve that serves as a laboratory for Duke's Nicholas School of The Environment.

Other attractions open to the public include the Bryan University Center and Page Auditorium, where more than 500 events are presented each year, including the world-renowned American Dance Festival; the Art Museum and galleries on both the East and West campuses; and the 55-acre Duke Gardens. Of course, there's always Atlantic Coast Conference basketball, football, soccer and baseball brought to you by the Duke Blue Devils. To learn about the rich history of Duke sports, visit the new Duke Sports Hall of Fame, located along the northwest side of Cameron Indoor Stadium. For more information on these attractions, see our chapters on "Arts," "Attractions" and "Sports."

Famous Duke graduates include political figures Elizabeth Dole, Kenneth Starr and Richard Nixon (law school); authors Reynolds Price, Anne Tyler and William Styron; and basketball superstar Grant Hill.

N.C. Central University
1801 Fayetteville St., Durham, NC 27707
• 560-6100 • www.nccu.edu

Founded in 1910 by educator Dr. James E. Shepard, North Carolina Central University (NCCU) later became the first state-supported liberal arts college for African-Americans in the United States. Today, NCCU is part of the 16-campus University of North Carolina system and continues to provide educational opportunities to students of all races.

The campus is set on 103 acres southeast of downtown Durham. About 5,200 students work toward bachelor's and master's degrees in more than 55 fields. Students enroll in one of five schools: the Undergraduate and Graduate Schools of the Arts and Sciences, the School of Education, the School of Business, School of Law and School of Library and Information Sciences. Graduate programs also have been established for careers in criminal justice and public administration. The school recently added a Hospitality and Tourism program.

NCCU's law school is the only one in the state that offers working adults an opportunity to earn their degree through an evening program. NCCU also provides an extensive continuing education program, including courses of study available to many workers at their place of employment. NCCU's Academic Community Service Learning Program is only one of 10 university programs in the United States that requires a set number of volunteer community service hours as a requirement for graduation.

NCCU is also known for its radio station, WNCU (90.7 FM), which specializes in jazz; its literary magazine, *Ex Umbra*; and its internationally acclaimed jazz ensemble, as well as its award-winning theatre department and dynamic "SoundMachine" marching band. The NCCU Eagles compete in eight men's and women's sports at the Divsion II level.

Popular spectator sports include men's and women's basketball at McLendon-McDougald Gymnasium and football at O'Kelly-Riddick Stadium.

The tuition for in-state residents is about $1,907 per academic year; for nonresidents, it's about $9,157.

NCCU opened the $12 million Julius L. Chambers Biomedical Biotechnology Research Institute in 1998. It is named after the popular chancellor who led the school from 1993 to 2000. A new state-of-the-art School of Education building recently opened on the NCCU campus.

Durham Technical Community College
P.O. Drawer 11307, Durham, NC 27703
• 686-3333 • www.dtcc.cc.nc.us

As a charter member of the North Carolina Community College System, Durham Tech is a two-year institution that offers vocational and technical training to residents of Durham and Orange counties, as well as

fully transferable credit to four-year colleges and universities. More than 20,000 students attend Durham Tech annually. The school features more than 55 programs of study, 20 of them leading to an associate's degree. Courses of study include accounting, architectural technology, automotive systems technology, business administration, computer programming, criminal justice, dental laboratory technology, early childhood development, electronics, general education, occupational therapy assistant, office systems technology, opticianry, paralegal technology, pharmacy technology, practical nursing, real estate, respiratory care and more.

Day, evening and weekend classes are available. Durham Tech also offers short courses, workshops and seminars for continuing career development. It also customizes training programs for businesses and industries in the area. In addition, Durham Tech provides programs in adult basic education, high school completion and English as a Second Language. Tuition for residents is $26.75 per credit hour; out-of-state residents, $169.75 per credit hour.

Raleigh

North Carolina State University
Admissions: 112 Peele Hall, Box 7103
Raleigh, NC 27695 • 515-2011
• www.ncsu.edu

One of the three corners of the Research Triangle, NCSU is one of the state's and nation's premier research institutions, confirmed in 1995 by Phi Beta Kappa, which conferred chapter status to the University. The campus is on Hillsborough Street about 1.5 miles from the Capitol. With a 1,563-acre campus and nearby research stations and recreational facilities covering another 2,700 acres, NCSU comprises a big chunk of Raleigh's real estate and much of the area's economic, social and artistic life. There are other schools in the city, but "State," as it's often called, commands the most attention.

Founded in 1887 as a land-grant school for agriculture and the mechanical arts, it was long derided as a "cow college" by fans of arch-rival UNC-Chapel Hill. But NCSU is now

Photo by Rich Weidman

With approximately 28,000 students, NCSU is the state's largest school.

known as far more than an "ag and tech school." It is among the nation's leaders in engineering, textiles, forestry, architecture, wood and paper science, biotechnology and veterinary medicine. NCSU is now the largest school in North Carolina, with approximately 28,000 students who average 1090 on their SAT scores and earn about a 3.5 GPA in high school.

The tuition for an in-state student at NCSU costs about $2,692 a year; out-of state, $11,880. Considering the school's reputation, that's a bargain. The school maintains housing for about 7,000 students and tries to place all freshmen who are not commuting in campus housing. The school has about 19,000 undergraduates; it receives more than 12,000 applications a year, from which it accepts 3,500 freshmen. Average class size is 35. About 85 percent of the students come from North Carolina. The student body is composed of about 40 percent women and 60 percent men.

Dr. Marye Anne Fox became NCSU's chancellor in 1998. Fox, the first woman to hold the post in the school's history, is a nationally renowned scientist and former vice president for research at the University of Texas.

The university is divided into colleges; the largest is Engineering with about 5,100 undergraduates and 1,400 graduate students. The others are Agriculture and Life Sciences, Design, Education and Psychology, Natural Resources (formerly Forestry Resources), Humanities and Social Sciences, Textiles, Physical and Mathematical Sciences, Veterinary Medicine (ranked fourth in the country in a recent *U.S. News and World Report* survey) and Management. There is also a School of Design and a Graduate School. In the fall of 1999, NCSU added a master's of science degree program in computer networking.

NCSU offers more than 230 undergraduate, master's and doctoral degree programs. Former chancellor, Larry K. Montieth, put new emphasis on undergraduate programs, proposing a unique Freshman College for NCSU. The result is that undergrads at NCSU have access to world-class research facilities. In the field of engineering, the school maintains a close relationship with a number of Research Triangle Park companies—more than 150 Park employees hold adjunct professorships at NCSU. Its work in signal processing, communication and microchip technology is at the forefront in national research. One of the nation's premier software companies, SAS in Cary, was started by an NCSU professor in the statistics department of mathematical sciences.

NCSU's Centennial Campus, located on 1,000 acres adjacent to the main campus, is a research and advanced technology community where university, corporate and government partners interact in programs directed toward technological solutions to problems and the creation of new products. Slated for development over the next 15 years or so, this "technopolis" will ultimately consist of a dozen or more research clusters made up of university, corporate and government laboratories, an alumni center, a magnet middle school, a hotel conference center with an 18-hole golf course, retail stores and housing situated around a central lake. The first cluster, on the north side of Lake Raleigh, has more than 25 major buildings completed or in the planning/construction stage. A new $3-million Genome Research Lab recently opened here. A monorail will eventually link Centennial Campus to the main university campus. About 3,200 people currently work at Centennial Campus, which will eventually employ more than 25,000. Lucent Technologies has located a 120,000-square-foot research lab on the campus that employs about 500 employees.

Among public universities, NCSU has been ranked in the top 25 nationally in terms of industry-sponsored research and in terms of research expenditures. Its School of Textiles is not only the largest in the country, but is considered the best by many in the industry. Departments at NCSU that regularly rank among the top 10 of their kind in the nation include: plant pathology; entomology; horticulture; wood and paper science; natural resources; parks, recreation and tourism management; statistics; architecture; mathematics and science education; community college and adult education; food science and nuclear engineering. What's surprising is NCSU's record in the non-science areas. Its design school is also ranked among the top 10 in the country.

The main library, D.H. Hill, is especially strong in biological and physical science, engineering, agriculture and forestry.

Outreach and continuing education play a major role at NCSU, too. The Jane S. McKimmon Center is one of the largest continuing education centers in the nation, serving more than 110,000 people in about 1,600 different programs annually. The Japan Center, one of NCSU's institutes, conducts Japanese language programs for business people, as well as courses about Japanese customs for companies interested in doing business in Asia.

Life at NCSU is not all books. There are more than 25 social fraternities and sororities and an active intramural athletic program. In addition, there are hundreds of student organizations, including a radio station (WKNC 88.1 FM), a newspaper (*Technician*) and the University Theatre. Being in the center of Raleigh gives the school access to the capital city's cultural life, too. The campus becomes one big party when the Wolfpack teams are winning—like in '74 and '83 when the basketball teams captured the national championship. Victory celebrations center around the Brickyard, the historic gathering place for students in the heart of the campus.

Famous NCSU alumni include Governor Jim Hunt, Agriculture Commissioner Jim Graham, basketball great David Thompson and General Hugh Shelton, chairman of the Joint Chiefs of Staff.

There's an unpretentiousness about State students that's quite refreshing. Some are the first in their families to go to college and they tend to be diligent and hard working. NCSU is big, it's a bargain and it's among the best research universities in the nation.

Meredith College
3800 Hillsborough St.
Raleigh, NC 27607 • 829-8600
• www.meredith.edu

Meredith, founded in 1891, is a private, comprehensive college for women and one of the Triangle's best values for a good education at a good price. With an enrollment of more than 2,600 students in both undergraduate and graduate programs, Meredith is the largest private four-year women's college in

Photo by Rich Weidman

The 1,000-acre Centennial Campus at NCSU consists of research clusters made up of university, corporate and government laboratories.

Located in downtown Raleigh, Peace College was founded in 1857 and has a current enrollment of nearly 600 students.

the Southeast. In a recent survey of "America's Best Colleges," *U.S. News & World Report* ranked Meredith 17th among Southern colleges.

The school's 225-acre campus in west Raleigh is near the I-440 Beltline and I-40. Meredith provides the city with one of its loveliest architectural settings, complete with a tree-lined drive, columned brick buildings and flowering trees and shrubs and a master plan for future growth. Meredith's beautiful campus is the site of many community events, such as the Labor Day concert by the North Carolina Symphony, weddings, and civic and educational meetings.

Tuition, room and board cost about $14,100 per year. Tuition only for nonresident students is $9,840. The faculty-student ratio is 1 to 17. In the past two decades, the college has strengthened its reputation as a resource center for many nontraditional students (over age 23). The Continuing Education Community Programs offer short courses on a variety of topics such as computers, creative writing and financial planning. The college also offers a post-baccalaureate certification program for legal assistants.

With more than 36 majors, Meredith offers bachelor of arts, music and science degrees. Admissions officials consider both

SAT and high school records when admitting students. More than 65 percent of incoming freshmen rank in at least the top 25 percent of their class and the median SAT score for freshmen is between 810 to 1,000. The John E. Weems Graduate School (named after former Meredith President Weems) offers master's degrees in business administration, education, music and health administration. More than 200 women are currently enrolled in graduate programs. In addition, the growing graduate school has recently started accepting men in the program. The MBA program features evening classes year round and is tailored for the demanding schedules of professionals.

Meredith also offers students opportunities to participate in International Programs and in cooperative education and internships in and around Research Triangle Park.

Students have the opportunity to compete in five intercollegiate sports at the NCAA Division III level: soccer, tennis, volleyball, basketball and softball.

Longtime Meredith President John E. Weems retired in 1999 and was succeeded by Maureen Hartford, a former University of Michigan administrator who is the first woman to lead the women's college. Future plans for Meredith College include the construction of a new science building and a new graduate school building.

Peace College
15 E. Peace St., Raleigh, NC 27604
• 508-2000 • www.peace.edu

Peace is another of Raleigh's scenic college campuses, located on 15 acres in the downtown area close to the state government complex. It is the second oldest of the city's colleges, founded in 1857 and named for William Peace, who gave the land and $10,000 to help build Main Hall. Until 1995, it was a two-year, liberal arts college for women. While still a women's college, it currently offers 11 baccalaureate degrees in biology, business administration, communication, English, human resources, leadership studies, liberal studies, music performance, psychology, Spanish and Visual Communication. It continues its two-year Associate Degree's programs in music, the arts and science.

Peace College is affiliated with the Presbyterian Church (USA) and enjoys a strong relationship with the First Presbyterian Church of Raleigh. However, women of all denominations attend the school.

With an enrollment of nearly 600 students, Peace offers a faculty-student ratio of 1 to 14. The college's size allows young women to become involved in campus and community activities. The students often assume leadership positions not generally available to them at larger schools.

The cost of attending Peace is lower than at many comparable colleges. Tuition, room and board for the academic year is about $14,927; for day students, tuition is $8,040. If you reside in North Carolina, you can subtract from that the $1,300 tuition grant from the state. Peace students receive assistance through scholarships and need-based financial aid, totalling 2.5 million dollars annually. The fiscal strength of the college is based on a $33 million endowment, with no indebtedness.

The college considers both high school rank and SAT scores when admitting students. According to the admissions brochure, an applicant should rank in the top half of her graduating class and SAT scores should be average or above average when compared to the scores of all college-bound students. The college does not release SAT scores. Peace also offers early admission to exceptional students. In addition to its regular programs, Peace is a member of Cooperating Raleigh Colleges, a consortium that allows students from member colleges to take classes at other member colleges. Peace students thereby have the opportunity to take classes at a larger university such as NCSU while still enrolled at Peace. Students are also offered a summer international-study program in England and Mexico each year.

The president of Peace College, Laura Carpenter Bingham, is the first alumna and the second woman to hold the post in the college's history.

In the fall of 2000, Peace will open a new $4.5-million academic building featuring state-of-the-art classrooms and laboratories. In addition, a Spanish major and a Leadership Studies double major have been added to the degree programs for the fall 2000 semester.

Peace is known for the tradition of graduating its Associate Degree students in long, white dresses, carrying red roses. Four-year graduates created a new tradition by wearing green caps and gowns and bachelor's hoods. Graduates will agree the oldest tradition at Peace is the lasting friendships that develop among the students.

St. Augustine's College
1315 Oakwood Ave., Raleigh, NC 27610
• 516-4000 • www.st-aug.edu

St. Augustine's was founded two years after the Civil War by the Protestant Episcopal Church to educate freed slaves. In 1867, it opened its doors to its first four

---

INSIDERS' TIP

The Raleigh Entertainment and Sports Arena will host the CIAA Basketball Tournament in 2001 and 2002. The Tournament includes teams from NCCU, St. Augustine's and Shaw.

students. Today, St. Augustine's continues its affiliation with the Episcopal Church and its commitment to educate its predominately black student body. In 1995, it installed Dr. Bernard W. Franklin as college president to succeed Dr. Prezell Robinson, who led the school for 27 years. Franklin resigned in 1999 to lead Virginia Union University and was replaced by Dianne Boardley Suber, the college's first female president. During Franklin's short tenure, he attempted to raise academic standards for incoming freshmen and also increased computer access on campus.

The school's green, wooded campus is located in east Raleigh, near the Governor's Mansion. St. Aug's, as it is called, adds grace and energy to its 125 acres of the capital city.

Tuition, room and board cost about $12,859 a year. There are about 1,550 male and female students—with more men than women—enrolled, drawn from every state in the Union, the District of Columbia, three territories and 28 foreign countries. Many students board in one of the seven dormitories or 24 duplex apartments.

The college is one of two historically black colleges and universities to own and operate both commercial radio and television

stations, WAUG 750 AM and WAUG-TV 68, respectively. St. Aug's is the only historically black college to house a privately held, full-powered commercial television station (WRMY-TV 47) on its campus.

St. Aug's offers 35 baccalaureate degrees. The structure of its academic program consists of the following divisions: Business; Education; Liberal and Interdisciplinary Studies; Natural Sciences, Mathematics and Allied Health; Urban, Social and International Studies; and Military Science. Each division has its own faculty and offers a choice of majors leading to either a Bachelor of Arts or a Bachelor of Science degree. There are six Centers of Excellence designed to produce graduates that will be globally sophisticated, analytically adept and personally challenged. The centers focus on urban research and enterprise; mathematics and science; teaching; management science; visual and performing arts; and technological research. The division of visual and performing arts recently added a bachelor of arts degree in film production.

St. Augustine's is considered to be among the top 5 percent of black institutions in the country. Through the Cooperating Raleigh Colleges program, it maintains cooperative

Photo by Rich Weidman

Shaw University's landmark building, Estey Hall (1873), is listed on the National Register of Historic Places.

programs with other Raleigh colleges, including NCSU, where students interested in technical degrees can take engineering courses. It also offers an Army ROTC program and a co-op program that permits students to work in their field while attending college during alternating semesters. The school considers its small size an advantage. Students enjoy an active social life in clubs, fraternities, sororities and intramurals. Its lecture program has brought numerous national and international speakers to the school, including the Reverend Jesse Jackson, former Virginia Governor Douglas Wilder and the late Arthur Ashe. Famous St. Aug graduates include the Delany sisters, Bessie and Sadie, authors of the best-selling book, *Having Our Say*.

The school has an envious athletic record and boasts hundreds of world-class athletes among its alumni. It has won several national Central Intercollegiate Athletic Association (CIAA) championships in cross country, track, tennis and volleyball. The men's basketball team was the 1996 CIAA champion and the baseball team captured the 1999 CIAA Championship. St. Aug's student, Jerome Young, and his coach, Antonio Pettigrew, were on the 1,600-meter relay team that set a world record of 2:54.20 at the 1998 Goodwill Games. St. Aug's hosted the 2000 Division II Track and Field Championship during which the school's women's team captured the national title.

Shaw University
118 E. South St., Raleigh, NC 27601
• 546-8200 • www.shawuniversity.edu

Shaw is one of the country's oldest black four-year colleges. Shaw traces its beginnings to 1865 when a former Union Army chaplain began teaching theology to young blacks with the financial backing of Massachusetts industrialist Elijah Shaw. Its enrollment is about 2,670 men and women with a faculty to student ratio of 1 to 15. Black Baptist churches helped the University overcome financial difficulties in the 1980s. Under the leadership of President Talbert Shaw and alumni such as Willie Gary of Florida, who made a $10 million gift to Shaw, the school has survived

and progressed. Shaw has added many new programs, including the Institute for the Study of Ethics and Values and its $11 million northeast campus that has new residential halls. Dr. Shaw has encouraged more scientific courses, and degrees are offered in engineering and computer studies, radiotelevision (WSHA-FM 88.9 plays jazz), audiology and adaptive physical education. Boxing promoter Don King sits on Shaw University's board of trustees and has also made contributions to the school.

The campus is located downtown, just east of Memorial Auditorium. Shaw's landmark building, beautiful Estey Hall, was constructed in 1873 and named after Vermont philanthropist Jacob Estey. Listed in the National Register of Historic Places, it is believed to be the first building in the United States built to house women on a coed campus. It has been restored as a community building and was reopened in 1993. The school became a source of civil rights activity during the 1960s when Dr. Martin Luther King Jr. visited the campus.

The school offers 22 majors leading to a bachelor of arts or bachelor of science degree, three degree programs leading to an associate of arts degree and one program leading to a master's degree in divinity. Tuition, room and board is about $11,196 a year. Financial aid is available to most students.

Wake Technical Community College
9101 Fayetteville Rd., Raleigh, NC 27603
• 662-3500 • www.wake.tec.nc.us

Wake Tech, the second-largest community college in North Carolina, is part of the state's heralded technical and community college system established in 1958. Its main campus is located south of Raleigh, beyond Garner, on the highway to Fayetteville (U.S. 401). The school offers a wide variety of vocational, technical and continuing education courses. The college transfer program allows students to complete their first two years at Wake Tech and then transfer to a four-year school.

The Wake Tech campus has grown steadily over the years, with many area residents seeking to upgrade skills in fields such as computer programming and nursing. Indeed, the college is challenged to accommodate all comers. Enrollment at Wake Tech, including part-time students, is approximately 45,000!

Associate degrees are offered in a number of programs and graduates in such fields as electronic and computer technology and pharmaceutical technology have been vigorously recruited by Research Triangle Park companies. It also offers more traditional vocational programs such as auto mechanics and heating and air conditioning. The business administration curriculum is popular with clerical employees anxious to improve their job skills and prepare for supervisory roles. Other courses include office automation and computer graphics technology.

Its offerings are lifesavers to some and lifechangers to many, with courses such as the GED test (high school equivalency) and, for international students, "English as a Second Language" provided. Along with Durham Tech, it's also the best educational bargain in the Triangle. Courses for residents are $26.75 per credit hour; for nonresidents it's $169.75 per credit hour, with an additional fee of $18 if the course is taught off campus at one of the participating Wake County public schools.

Plans are in the works to build a $30-million Wake Tech north campus near Rolesville in northern Wake County by the year 2003.

Satellite Campuses

Campbell University
Raleigh Center
2050 National Guard Dr.
Morrisville, NC 27560
• 840-0062 • www.campbell.edu

Campbell is a private university affiliated with the Baptist State Convention of North Carolina. Both in and out of the classroom, the University endeavors to present Christian principles to students and to foster their application to daily life. The main University occupies a spacious 850-acre campus in the village of Buies Creek, located in Harnett County about 30 minutes south of Raleigh. In addition to four remote campus locations

Staff Photo

At its satellite campus in Research Triangle Park, Mount Olive College offers degree programs in Management and Criminal Justice.

in North Carolina, the University is involved in several off-campus and special programs, as well as foreign colleges and universities. Founded in 1887 by James Archibald Campbell, Campbell was originally known as Buies Creek Academy. The school began with 21 students and grew slowly over the years to its present standing among the state's largest church-related senior universities. Over the years, Campbell has added the following schools within the university: the Lundy-Fetterman School of Business, the Norman Wiggins School of Law, the School of Pharmacy and the Divinity School. Campbell students hail from all 100 North Carolina counties, all 50 states and more than 35 countries. Open to all qualified students, Campbell includes students from more than 40 denominations and faiths. Dr. Norman Wiggins is Campbell's president.

In 1975, Campbell University initiated a dramatic departure—extending University programs and classes into various communities within the state—an idea that has developed and flourished since. The University is a charter member of the Servicemembers Opportunity College (SOC), a coalition of more than 1,300 institutions of higher education dedicated to helping servicemembers and veterans determine and achieve their education goals. Campbell began its educational military affiliation with the U.S. Army at Fort Bragg and subsequently with the Marines and Sailors at Camp LeJeune, the Army National Guard in Raleigh and the U.S. Air Force at Pope Air Force Base.

At Campbell's Raleigh Center, students may earn a four-year degree in Business or Accounting in an accelerated evening program that is conducive to both work schedules and one's personal life. Most students qualify for federal and/or state assistance. Many Triangle companies participate in Campbell's tuition reimbursement program.

Mount Olive College at the Triangle
Central Park West, 5001 S. Miami Blvd.
Durham, NC 27703
- **941-2970, (888) 258-5188**
- **www.mountolive.edu**

Chartered in 1951 as a junior college, Mount Olive has been sponsored by the Convention of Original Free Will Baptists from its beginning. In 1986, Mount Olive became a four-year institution, awarding associate and baccalaureate degrees. Its main campus occupies 138 acres in the town of Mount Olive, which is located south of Goldsboro in eastern North Carolina. The College has also initiated degree programs in Goldsboro at Seymour Johnson Air Force Base (1975), New Bern (1993), Wilmington (1995) and the Triangle (1997).

At its satellite campus in Research Triangle Park, Mount Olive offers two degree programs: Management and Organizational Development and Criminal Justice for Professionals. Both programs span 57 academic weeks, consisting of one four-hour class meeting one night a week from 6 to 10 PM.

TO A CHILD USED TO SEEING THINGS ON A 19" TV SCREEN, IT CAN BE QUITE AN EXPERIENCE.

POLAR BEARS
AT THE NORTH CAROLINA ZOO, ASHEBORO
800.488.0444

Daytrips and Weekend Vacations

The Triangle lies about halfway between the mountains and the coast, making it the perfect point of departure for daytrip excursions and weekend getaways throughout the state. Just hop in your car and within a few hours you can be hiking the Appalachian Trail, whitewater rafting on the Nolichucky River, hang gliding at Jockey's Ridge State Park, scuba diving in the "Graveyard of the Atlantic" or sunbathing at the Cape Hatteras National Seashore.

Head east to discover bustling beach communities, animated boardwalks, historic lighthouses, pristine national seashores, maritime museums and aquariums, Civil War-era forts, a World War II battleship, legendary seafood restaurants and the nation's oldest outdoor drama.

Toward the west, you'll find a natural habitat zoo, pottery studios, Revolutionary War battlegrounds, an 18th-century Moravian village, lively theme parks, scenic parkways, state parks and national forests, picturesque waterfalls, busy ski resorts, the largest private residence in the United States, a 24-hour casino and 6,684-foot Mount Mitchell, the highest peak in the eastern United States.

For more information about North Carolina attractions, contact the N.C. Division of Tourism, Film and Sports Development, 301 North Wilmington Street, Raleigh, NC 27699-4324, 733-8372 or (800) VISITNC (www.visitnc.com). For information on historic sites, contact the N.C. Division of Archives & History, 532 North Wilmington Street, Raleigh, NC 27604, 733-7862.

Another quality travel resource is *Daytrips and Weekend Vacations in North Carolina*, a comprehensive guidebook that includes $1,000 in valuable coupons. The book may be purchased from your local bookstore or by calling (800) 777-4843.

Beaches and Ports

North Carolina offers some of the finest beaches on the East Coast. When people in the Triangle talk about the beach, they are usually talking about the area known as the Crystal Coast, the Cape Fear Coast or Wrightsville Beach at Wilmington. The Outer Banks are beautiful and definitely worth a visit, but will take more than one weekend to fully explore. The port cities of Wilmington, Morehead City, Beaufort and New Bern offer a blend of history and modern-day commerce.

The Northern Coast

Outer Banks

Nothing beats a summer excursion to North Carolina's Outer Banks. These barrier islands are marked with the names of American history—Kitty Hawk (where the Wright brothers took to the skies), Nags Head (the coast's first beach resort) and Roanoke Island (site of the first English settlement in the New World)—and they include Cape Hatteras National Seashore, the longest stretch of undeveloped beach in the country. Hang glide off Jockey's Ridge, the largest sand dune on the East Coast, or experience a blue fish blitz; these are just some of the luring pastimes of these beaches.

The Outer Banks are, at minimum, a 4-hour drive from Raleigh—longer to Cape

Photo courtesy of N.C. Division of Tourism

During the summer, hang gliders flock to Jockey's Ridge,
the largest natural sand dune on the East Coast.

Hatteras and its fabled lighthouse. Enjoy the drama of *The Lost Colony*, (252) 473-2127, at the Waterside Theatre near Fort Raleigh on Roanoke Island. The nearby Roanoke Island Festival Park, (252) 475-1500, is home to the state-of-the-art Outer Banks History Center and the *Elizabeth II* State Historic Site. Kids will love a trip to the recently renovated North Carolina Aquarium on Roanoke Island, (252) 473-3493, which boasts a 285,000-gallon tank.

Travel north along N.C. 12 to visit the Wright Brothers National Memorial, (252) 441-7430, which honors the achievement of Orville and Wilbur Wright, who made the first successful powered flight on the dunes of Kitty Hawk on December 17, 1903. Travel south along N.C. 12 to view the 1872 Bodie Island Lighthouse and the 1870 Cape Hatteras Lighthouse, which was moved 1,600 feet from the encroaching surf in 1999 through the use of advanced hydraulic technologies.

To get to the isolated, quaint village of Ocracoke where Blackbeard was caught and hanged in 1718, you take a free, state-operated ferry. Ocracoke is about as laid back as you can get—full of pristine beaches, sandy lanes, wild ponies, live oaks, pirate tales and old graveyards. To learn more about North

Carolina's Outer Banks, pick up a copy of *The Insiders' Guide To The Outer Banks*.

The Crystal Coast

The name "Crystal Coast" describes the area around Beaufort, Morehead City and the beaches of Bogue Banks, as well as the inland historic town of New Bern. Visitors can choose between the historic preservation area of Beaufort, Morehead City's famous seafood boardwalk, golf courses and shopping or any of the public beaches. A commercial ferry from Harkers Island leads to the 28,500-acre Cape Lookout National Seashore and its 1859 Cape Lookout Lighthouse. From the Triangle, the Crystal Coast is an easy 3 1/2-hour drive down U.S. 70. To learn more about this area, pick up a copy of *The Insiders' Guide to NC's Central Coast & New Bern*.

Beaufort

Incorporated in 1722, Beaufort is North Carolina's third-oldest town. This quaint seaport has a wide boardwalk along the waterfront and narrow streets lined with white frame houses. It has become a favorite dockage for seagoing yachts. Many of the town's beautiful historic homes have been restored and are nestled among grocery stores, gift shops, a wide variety of restaurants and several of North Carolina's most popular bed and breakfast inns. The Beaufort Historic Site, (252) 728-5225, encompasses the 1767 Joseph Bell House, the Mattie King Davis Art Gallery, the 1732 Rustell House, the 1829 county jail and the 1859 apothecary shop. Stroll through The Old Burying Ground, one of the few graveyards to be listed on the National Register of Historic Places. The North Carolina Maritime Museum, (252) 728-7317, exhibits the maritime history and coastal natural history of North Carolina with full-sized watercraft and models, decoys, tools, fossils, shells, aquariums and an impressive research library.

Bogue Banks
(Atlantic Beach, Pine Knoll Shores, Indian Beach, Salter Path, Emerald Isle)

Bogue Banks is one of 23 barrier islands off the North Carolina coast. Unlike most of the "outer banks," the 27-mile-long Bogue Banks runs from east to west. The Atlantic Ocean drums its southern shore while Bogue Sound laps its beaches to the north. This unusual orientation leads to one of the island's unique features: the sun both rises and sets over the ocean.

Atlantic Beach is the most highly developed of the Bogue Banks beaches. Its surf is mild, the beach is very wide and the sun-warmed shallow water is the most enjoyable of the state's beaches. This beach is traditionally THE BEACH for Triangle teenagers.

The North Carolina Aquarium at Pine Knoll Shores, (252) 247-4003, is one of the three nationally accredited state aquariums on the North Carolina coast. It is open daily from 9 AM until 5 PM. The Theodore Roosevelt State Natural Area lies adjacent to the aquarium.

Salter Path is a residential community making the transition to a tourist community with new restaurants, motels and campgrounds. West of Salter Path is Emerald Isle, which was incorporated as a resort town in the mid-50s and has been attracting North Carolina's sunlovers ever since. Emerald Isle features houses for rent—beachfront, soundside, modern, rustic, casual, elegant and in every price range.

Nearby is the Crystal Coast Amphitheatre where *Worthy is the Lamb,* an outdoor drama based on the Passion of Christ, is performed during the summer months. Call (252) 393-8373 for more information.

Fort Macon State Park

More people visit Fort Macon, (252) 726-3775, than any other state park. Fort Macon is a brick, pentagon-shaped garrison that was built between 1826 and 1834, then restored in 1936. Lieutenant Robert E. Lee designed the fort's stone jetties in the early 1840s. Fort Macon stood guard over Beaufort inlet during the Civil War and World War II. You can fish from the rock jetties, swim at the public beach or enjoy your lunch at the picnic areas.

Morehead City

Morehead City ("Morehead" to everyone at the coast) is an easy town to like. Fill the town with blocks and blocks of seafood restaurants, internationally renowned sport fishing fleets and scuba diving charters that explore the "Graveyard of the Atlantic" and you only have half the story.

The Morehead Waterfront is devoted to commercial fishing, sport fishing, preparing fish and eating fish. Enjoy fresh seafood at such legendary seafood restaurants as Sanitary Fish Market and Captain Bill's. Unlike most coastal waterfronts, the Morehead

---

FYI

Unless otherwise noted, the area code for all phone numbers listed in this guide is 919.

INSIDERS' TIP

The free, state-operated ferries that run along the North Carolina coast comprise the most extensive ferry system in the United States. Call 800-BYFERRY (293-3779) for more information.

Wharf is not devoted entirely to tourism. Shipping and fishing-related commercial activities keep the area bustling.

In addition, the waterfront offers scuba diving charters (Olympus Dive Center, (252) 726-9432, is world famous), sport fishing charters, boat rentals, sailboat excursions, party boat tours, daytrips to Cape Lookout and seafood sold fresh off the boats.

New Bern

Only about a two hour's drive from the Triangle sits this historic little town of lacy crape myrtle trees. Founded in 1710 and named for Baron Christopher de Graffenried's home of Bern, Switzerland, New Bern is located at the confluence of the Neuse and Trent rivers. Union Point Park is where most of the waterfront activity buzzes. It was New Bern's linkage to Pamlico Sound and the Atlantic that made this an ideal port. It became the first colonial capital of North Carolina.

When Royal Governor William Tryon began building his combined residence and government capitol offices, they took on the appearance of a palace more than a modest government home with offices. The original palace burned in 1798, but has been completely rebuilt and refurbished to its former splendor. The restoration includes the 19-room Tryon Palace, the 1780 John Wright Stanly House, the 1805 Dixon-Stevenson House that was occupied by Union troops during the Civil War and the Academy Museum.

A daytrip to Tryon Palace is a must-do on any Insiders' list. In the spring, the Latham Gardens are abloom with tulips. Costumed interpreters and craftspeople bring history alive about the everyday happenings in the 1700s and 1800s. After Thanksgiving, the Palace and historic homes are decorated to reflect two centuries of holiday traditions—a must-see holiday event. Call (252) 514-4900 for more information about Tryon Palace and the admission fees.

The Southern Coast

Some of the more popular Southern beaches of North Carolina include Topsail, Wrightsville, Carolina, Kure, Holden, Ocean Isle and Sunset. Though intimidating to early European explorers who named the area Cape Fear, today's traveler will enjoy the rugged beauty of the coast and the gracious hospitality of its people. From the Triangle, Wilmington is an easy 2-hour drive down I-40. To learn more about this area, pick up a copy of *The Insiders' Guide to Wilmington.*

Photo courtesy of N.C. Division of Tourism

Wilmington is the permanent home of the Battleship North Carolina, which covered over 300,000 miles during her World War II Pacific tour.

Wilmington

Wilmington, the state's largest port city, sits on the Cape Fear River and is really worth more than a daytrip. Founded in 1732, this historical city is well known for its growing film industry. In fact, Wilmington's nicknames include "Hollywood East" and "Wilmywood."

Wilmington is the permanent home of the Battleship North Carolina, (910) 350-1817, a 35,000-ton battleship memorial to the men and women who served in World War II. In town, Wilmington has a historic homes tour and Chandler's Wharf, which shows the city as it was in the 1800s. The restored Cotton Exchange building is home to a variety of unique shops and restaurants near the Wilmington Hilton. Other notable attractions include the 1861 Bellamy Mansion, the 1770 Burgwin-Wright House and Gardens, the Cape Fear Museum, St. John's Museum of Art, Wilmington Railroad Museum and the 1852 Zebulon Latimer House.

Timed to correspond with the blooming azaleas and dogwoods of spring, the city's annual Azalea Festival features a street fair, garden tours, workshops, a parade, horse show and beauty pageants. Started in 1947, Wilmington's biggest extravaganza takes place in early April.

Fort Fisher is located at Kure Beach, site of one of the country's largest land-sea battles in 1865 and a museum of items from Confederate blockade runners. The North Carolina Aquarium at Fort Fisher, (910) 458-8257, is less than 2 miles away. Note: The Aquarium is closed for extensive renovations until the spring of 2002.

Kids will enjoy the amusement park atmosphere of Carolina Beach, a short drive down U.S. 421 south. The Carolina Beach State Park, (910) 458-7770, offers five miles of hiking trails, campsites, fishing, a full-service marina and picnic areas.

Orton Plantation near Wilmington, (910) 371-6851, is one of North Carolina's best-known Southern plantations and rivals those of Virginia. It was an 18th-century rice plantation and the gardens are now open to the public. The best time to visit is in the spring when the plantation's dazzling azaleas are in full bloom.

Known as "North Carolina's Best Kept Secret," the nearby town of Southport is characterized by towering live oak trees, commercial fishing and shrimping, historic sites, eclectic restaurants, parks, art galleries and antique shops. The North Carolina Maritime Museum at Southport, (910) 457-0003, showcases the rich maritime history of Southport and the Lower Cape Fear area.

Catch a ferry from Southport for a 3.5-mile ride to 12,000-acre Bald Head Island, which offers vacationers 14 miles of sandy beaches, championship golf, tennis, fishing, watersports and thousands of acres of protected salt marsh, tidal creeks and maritime forest. A visit to Bald Head Island is not complete without a stop at "Old Baldy," the state's oldest standing lighthouse, built in 1817. For a free *Bald Head Island Vacation Guide,* call 1-800-432-RENT.

Wrightsville Beach

Wrightsville Beach, just over the bridge from Wilmington, is on the barrier islands, which protect the state's Atlantic coast. It is an upscale community with miles of beautiful sandy beaches perfect for long walks, swimming, surf fishing or most any water sport you may enjoy. Accommodations include quality hotels and motels, apartments and cottages, and there are many restaurants featuring, naturally, seafood. Popular lodging options include the Blockade Runner Beach Resort, (800) 541-1161, and the Holiday Inn Sunspree Resort, (877) 330-5050.

Piedmont

The region located between the coastal areas and the mountains is known as the Piedmont. Business and industry thrive here within North Carolina's richest agricultural region. Food, fiber, manufacturing, education, research and commerce enjoy the resources of the land and its people. The history and culture of the Piedmont is rich and diverse.

Bentonville Battleground
5466 Harper House Rd., Four Oaks
• (910) 594-0789

Civil War buffs must visit this state historic site, which is less than an hour's drive from the Triangle. The Battle of Bentonville was the last, full-scale action in the Civil

Civil War reenactments are occasionally held at Bentonville Battleground, the site of the largest and bloodiest battle fought in North Carolina.

War, fought over three days, March 19 through 21, 1865. There were over 4,000 casualties in the armies fighting under Union Gen. William T. Sherman and Confederate Gen. Joseph E. Johnston, who surrendered on April 26 at Bennett Place near Durham. The battleground today maintains a picnic area and visitors center. The Harper House, where a field hospital was established, still stands and is outfitted as it might have appeared during those bloody three days. Maps inside the center and a film presentation tell the history of the battle, the largest ever fought in North Carolina. On occasion, the battle's anniversary is observed by reenactments that give visitors a more realistic idea of conditions of the times. Visiting hours are 9 AM to 5 PM Tuesday through Saturday and 12 PM to 5 PM on Sunday.

Fayetteville

Fayetteville, home of Fort Bragg and Pope Air Force Base, also boasts a variety of other attractions, such as wonderful architecture, several colorful festivals and outstanding regional theater. For those who are interested in learning more about Fayetteville's place in military history, Fort Bragg is open for individual and group tours. Call (910) 396-5401 for information. The 82nd Airborne Division War Memorial Museum (at Ardennes and Gela streets at Fort Bragg), (910) 432-5307, is a great place for a military history buff. It houses more than 3,000 artifacts from World War I to Operation Desert Storm. Admission is free to the museum, which is open Tuesday through Saturday 10 AM to 4:30 PM and Sunday 11:30 AM to 4 PM. Also check out the John F. Kennedy Special Warfare Museum, (910) 432-4272, and the new Airborne and Special Operations Museum, (910) 483-3003.

Not to be missed is the Cape Fear Regional Theatre. Located on the corner of Hay Street and Highland Avenue, CFRT is housed in a beautifully renovated old movie house. CFRT consistently receives rave reviews from theatre critics across the state for its innovative productions. Call (910) 323-4233 for a schedule and ticket information.

Other notable Fayetteville attractions include the Cape Fear Botanical Garden, the Fayetteville Museum of Art and the Museum of the Cape Fear Historical Complex.

Those interested in historic architecture will want to view Fayetteville's Market House in the center of the downtown area. When Union General William T. Sherman and his men passed through Fayetteville in 1865, they destroyed the Confederate Arsenal and many other buildings but left the Market House intact, it is said, because of its beauty.

There are many other beautiful old buildings in Fayetteville and you can see some of the oldest homes, churches and other historic places during the Olde Fayetteville by Candlelight Tour held each December. The Dogwood Festival is Fayetteville's welcome to spring. Held over 10 days starting the first weekend in April, this event allows Fayetteville to show off its dogwood trees (more than 100,000) and thousands of blooming flowers. The many activities include parades, tours and street dancing. The International Folk Festival is held on the last Sunday in September. The festival centers around the Market House downtown and features a big parade, international foods and musical entertainment.

For information on Fayetteville, contact the Fayetteville Area Convention and Visitors Bureau, 245 Person Street, Fayetteville, NC 28301, or call (910) 483-5311 or (800) 255-8217.

Kerr Lake, Lake Gaston

These two man-made lakes provide excellent fishing, boating, picnicking and camping. Both are about an hour's drive north of the Triangle near the Virginia state line. Kerr Lake has a shoreline of 800 miles, more than 1,000 family campsites and three commercial marinas. For information, call Kerr Reservoir at (252) 438-7791.

Lake Gaston offers at least three access areas: Summit, Henrico and Stonehouse Creek. For more information on Lake Gaston, call the North Carolina Wildlife Resources Commission at 733-3633.

Morrow Mountain State Park
Off N.C. 740, Albemarle • (704) 982-4402

Just across Badin Lake from the Uwharrie National Forest is this scenic, 4,693-acre state park in Stanly County. It offers swimming, fishing, camping, boating and hiking.

N.C. Zoological Park
4401 Zoo Pkwy., Asheboro
• (336) 879-7000, (800) 488-0444
• www.nczoo.org

Like the famous San Diego Zoo in California, North Carolina's zoological park gives visitors the chance to observe animals while they roam in areas similar to their native habitats. This is a perfect outing for the whole family. Here you can observe more than 1,000 wild animals and birds amid 60,000 exotic plants. This ever-expanding facility is the largest walk-through natural habitat zoo in the nation.

You won't want to miss the R.J. Reynolds Forest Aviary, the only one of its kind anywhere. A 55-foot-high glass dome houses exotic plants and birds from all over the world. Walking through the aviary is like exploring a rain forest, complete with all the sights and sounds. The newest sections in the zoo are the Sonora Desert Habitat and the North American Region, which has everything from polar bears to alligators.

The zoo is located off of N.C. 220, south of Asheboro, and is open from 9 AM to 5 PM April through October and 9 AM to 4 PM November through March. The zoo is not open on Christmas Day. Admission is $5 for

Photo courtesy of N.C. Zoo

N.C. Zoological Park is the largest walk-through natural habitat zoo in the United States.

senior citizens and children ages 2 to 12 and $8 for adults. Traditionally, the zoo does not charge admission the second Monday of June, July and August and only charges half-price admission every day from December through February.

Pottery Country

One of our favorite daytrips is a trek through pottery country in Randolph and Moore counties. Here, just about 2 hours from the Triangle, you'll find pottery being made from native clays, just as it was in the 1700s. In fact, some of the local potters belong to the same families that were shaping this native clay two centuries ago. The town of Seagrove contains the largest community of working potters in the United States (more than 90 studios at last count).

Stop first at the North Carolina Pottery Center, (336) 873-8430, in Seagrove off of N.C. 220, south of Asheboro and the North Carolina Zoo. Here you'll see samples of the area's world-famous pottery from its earliest days to the present. At the museum, which is open Tuesday through Saturday, 10 AM to 4 PM, you can also pick up a map to the shops of some 95 local potters. Our personal favorites are Phil Morgan's Pottery, Jugtown, Turn and Burn, Ben Owens Pottery and Westmoore Pottery. The annual Seagrove Pottery Festival is held on the Sunday before Thanksgiving.

Raven Rock State Park
Off U.S. 421, Northwest of Lillington
• **(910) 893-4888**
• **ils.unc.edu/parkproject/raro.html**

Raven Rock is a 3,000-acre state park that makes a pleasant picnic outing for the family. It's about a 1 1/2-hour drive from the Triangle and boasts 11 miles of hiking trails. The 2.1-mile Raven Rock Loop Trail leads to a massive 152-foot outcropping that overlooks the Cape Fear River. A good time to go to Raven Rock is spring or fall when the climate is temperate. Take along water or something to drink because there are no fountains or facilities once you get down to the river.

Snow Camp
N.C. 1005 • (336) 376-6948

You'll want to visit this historic Quaker landmark in southwest Alamance County during the summer months when there are plenty of activities. Named by Cornwallis' soldiers following the snowy Battle of Guilford Courthouse, Snow Camp is known today as the site of *The Sword of Peace,* one of the state's most popular outdoor dramas. From late June through early August, *The Sword of Peace* portrays the conflict experienced by peace-loving Quakers confronted by events of the American Revolution. On alternate days, *Pathway to Freedom*, a drama that premiered in 1994, gives the African-American perspective of the "Underground Railroad" prior to the Civil War. A children's show, which changes each season, also runs from mid-June through July. Other summer activities at Snow Camp include a traditional Fourth of July celebration complete with a parade and crafts fair and a mid-August molasses festival that has demonstrations of pioneer cooking and crafts. Snow Camp is about a 30-minute drive from Chapel Hill.

Uwharrie National Forest
N.C. 1107, Troy • (910) 576-6391
• **www.cs.unca.edu/nfsnc**

Established as a national forest in 1961, Uwharrie National Forest is proof that you don't have to drive 4 hours to reach the mountains. Located on Badin Lake in Montgomery County, this wilderness includes 46,000 acres of piney forests, hiking and biking trails, campsites, watersports and more.

INSIDERS' TIP
The North Carolina Department of Transportation publishes a free *North Carolina Scenic Byways* **booklet that provides detailed descriptions of all 44 designated scenic byways. Write NCDOT, P.O. Box 25201, Raleigh, NC 27611 for your copy.**

Uwharrie National Forest encompasses the 8,000-acre Badin Lake recreation area.

The Triad

Little more than an hour west of the Triangle lies the Piedmont Triad, which includes Greensboro, the site of a famous Revolutionary War battle; High Point, known as the "Furniture Capital of the World;" and Winston-Salem, home to Old Salem, a restored living history town dating to the 1760s.

Guilford Courthouse National Military Park
**2332 New Garden Rd.,
Greensboro • (336) 288-1776
• www.nps.gov/guco**

Guilford Courthouse is the site of the March 1781 Revolutionary War battle that pitted General Nathanael Greene against British General Lord Charles Cornwallis. According to Greene, the battle was "long, obstinate and bloody." The park includes a visitors center, monuments and hiking trails. In mid-March each year, a mock battle is staged in adjacent Tannenbaum City Park by Redcoats and soldiers of the Revolution in uniform. It is open daily from 8:30 AM to 5 PM and admission is free.

Hanging Rock State Park
**N.C. 89, Danbury • (336) 593-8480
• ils.unc.edu/parkproject/haro.html**

A 6,457-acre state park in Stokes County, Hanging Rock is a great getaway for camping, hiking, rock climbing, swimming, fishing and picnicking. Hike past cascading waterfalls to the top of sheer cliffs for breathtaking views of the surrounding countryside. Popular hiking trails include the 1.2-mile Hanging Rock Trail and the 3.7-mile Indian Creek Trail. The park contains a visitors center and interpretive markers.

Museum of Early Southern Decorative Arts (MESDA)
**Old Salem, Winston-Salem
• (336) 779-6140 • www.mesda.org**

MESDA is adjacent to Old Salem and features 24 furnished rooms and six galleries, demonstrating the varied styles and periods of Southern furnishings. It's an antique lover's dream! Admission is charged.

Natural Science Center
**4301 Lawndale Dr., Greensboro
• (336) 288-3769
• www.greensboro.com/sciencecenter**

Adjacent to the Guilford Battleground, this fine museum for children has reproductions of dinosaur skeletons, rock and mineral exhibits, fish and reptiles, a small petting zoo and a planetarium show. The Center is open Monday through Saturday from 9 AM to 5 PM and Sunday 12:30 PM to 5 PM. There is an admission fee for the museum and the planetarium show.

Old Salem
Old Salem Rd., Winston-Salem
(336) 721-7300, (888) 653-7253
• www.oldsalem.org

About 1 1/2 hours west of the Triangle via I-40 is Winston-Salem's restored 18th-century Moravian village. There are almost 100 restored buildings here. Twelve are open to the public, including Winkler Bakery (where you can buy delicious Moravian sugar cake), the Salem Tavern, the Single Brothers' House and many other shops and restored homes. Other attractions include the Museum of Early Southern Decorative Arts, The Gallery at Old Salem and The Children's Museum. Don't miss the 1771 Moravian Cemetery, known as "God's Acre," and the World's Largest Coffee Pot (1858). A bed and breakfast, the Augustus T. Zevely Inn, and an authentic tavern restaurant, Old Salem Tavern, are available in the historic district. Special events are held at Christmas, Easter and July 4th. Old Salem is open Monday through Saturday 9 AM to 5 PM and on Sunday from 12:30 to 5 PM. Admission is charged.

Wood-burning ovens still churn out Moravian baked goods daily at Old Salem.

Reynolda House
Museum of American Art
2250 Reynolda Rd., Winston-Salem
• (336) 725-5325 • www.reynoldahouse.org

Reynolda House, the former home of R.J. Reynolds of tobacco fame, is now a museum of American art. The collection features paintings by diverse artists ranging from 19th-century landscape painter Frederic E. Church to Thomas Eakins and Mary Cassatt. The house contains many of its original furnishings and is fascinating in its own right. Admission is charged. It is open Tuesday through Saturday from 9:30 AM to 4:30 PM and from 1:30 to 4:30 PM on Sunday.

Southeastern Center for
Contemporary Art (SECCA)
750 Marguerite Dr., Winston-Salem
• (336) 725-1904 • www.secca.org

Housed in the 1929 English-style manor of the late industrialist James G. Hanes, SECCA is just down the road from Reynolda House and well worth a visit. It is a complex of galleries with rotating exhibits by contemporary Southern artists. It is open Tuesday through Saturday 10 AM to 5 PM and Sunday 2 PM to 5 PM.

Charlotte

The nation's second-largest banking center, Charlotte is a city of commerce and culture. Visitors come to the "Queen City" for education, entertainment and cultural events. To learn more about the Charlotte Metro area, pick up a copy of *The Insiders' Guide To Charlotte*. Once you arrive in Charlotte, stop by INFO! Charlotte at 330 South Tryon Street for free brochures on attractions, events, restaurants and accommodations.

Amtrak's Piedmont train is a fun and relaxing way to travel to Charlotte for a daytrip. The round-trip cost from the Triangle is only about $38. Call (800) 872-7245 for details.

Carolina Renaissance Festival
Hwy. 73, North of Charlotte
• (704) 896-5555

Each year, for seven weekends in a row from October to November, 10 acres of beautiful woods and meadows are transformed into a 16th-century European village. Hundreds of elaborately costumed performers, exhibits of period handiwork and renaissance food create the atmosphere of a European Market Faire.

Discovery Place
301 N. Tryon St. • (704) 372-6261
• www.discoveryplace.org

Discovery Place is one of the top science museums in the United States. This hands-on science and technology museum in downtown Charlotte welcomes more than 500,000 visitors annually and is open every day of the year except Thanksgiving and Christmas. Discovery Place offers an OMNIMAX theatre and planetarium combination that is unique to the United States. With a 79-foot dome, the Planetarium is the largest in the nation.

Among the permanent exhibits at Discovery Place are the Collections Gallery, the Aquarium and the Knight Rain Forest. "Hands-on" exhibits are also featured with a collection of experiments designed to teach basic principles of science through color, motion and perception.

The Challenger Learning Center simulates a rendezvous with Halley's Comet in the year 2061. Kid's Place, an early childhood learning area, features the Puppet Place stage with shows that delight visitors of all ages. The museum has hosted outstanding traveling exhibits such as Hunter's of the Sky and The International Space Station.

Open seven days a week, the Exhibit Hall hours are 9 AM until 6 PM Monday through Saturday and 1 to 6 PM on Sunday. Reservations for regularly scheduled OMNIMAX and Planetarium shows can be made by calling (704) 372-6261 or (800) 935-0553. Call for current rates and discounts.

Lowe's Motor Speedway
5555 U.S. 29 N., Concord
• (704) 455-3200
• www.lowesmotorspeedway.com

Twelve miles north of Charlotte is one of the nation's hottest stock car racing facilities. The lighted NASCAR track is home to many annual events, including the Coca-Cola 600, which is the longest Winston Cup race on the NASCAR circuit. The 2,010-acre, 1.5-mile speedway offers guided tours and a ride around the track (except during race weeks), a movie on the speedway's rich history, special exhibits and a huge gift shop. Twice a year, in April and September, the AutoFair, one of the nation's largest antique car shows, is hosted on the grounds. Tickets for races can be hard to come by, so make plans early.

Mint Museum of Art
2730 Randolph Rd. • (704) 337-2000
• www.mintmuseum.org

Originally this branch of the United States Mint served from 1836 until it closed at the outbreak of the Civil War. In 1936, the Mint reopened as North Carolina's first art museum. The 81,000-square-foot facility is one of the Southeast's finest museums with extensive collections of American and European paintings, furniture and decorative arts. In addition to its own shows, it also mounts larger, nationally prominent exhibits such as "Unseen Treasures: Imperial Russia and the New World." A small admission is charged. Call for hours and further information.

Mint Museum of Craft & Design
220 N. Tryon St. • (704) 337-2000
• www.mintmuseum.org

The sister facility of the Mint Museum of Art opened in 1999 at the former Montaldo's building on North Tryon Street, adjacent to Discovery Place. It features a permanent collection of international studio craft in ceramics, glass, fibers, metal and wood. The Museum originates and hosts major touring exhibitions, including "Turning Wood into Art: Masterworks from the Jane and Arthur Mason Collection" and "Out of the Ordinary: The Allan Chasanoff Ceramic Collection."

Paramount's Carowinds
Exit 90 off I-77 S.
• (704) 588-2600, (800) 888-4FUN (4386)
• www.carowinds.com

Paramount's Carowinds, which opened in 1973, is a 100-acre water and theme park along the North Carolina-South Carolina border that features 100 state-of-the-art rides, shows, movie-themed experiences, shops and restaurants. Nearly 2 million people visit the park annually. Although the park is generally open daily during the summer and on weekends in the spring and fall, hours and operating dates vary, so call ahead.

The Paladium Amphitheatre hosts big-name concerts and special events each season. Attractions range from a variety of thrill rides, like Drop Zone, to more easygoing attractions such as Animation Station, a cartoon fantasy land for young children. Each year, attractions are added or enhanced. The new attraction for 2000 was the Nickelodeon Flying Super Saturator, the ultimate water play adventure. Once on the ride, you'll glide along a unique suspended coaster track—dodging a gauntlet of gushing geysers, racing through a narrow net of nozzles and speeding past a series of rain curtains. Don't miss the heart-pounding roller coasters like the Top Gun: The Jet Coaster (the park's tallest and fastest coaster), Hurler or Thunder Road, Frenzoid and VORTEX, then cool off with Rip Roarin' Rapids and White Water Falls or the wave pool and you're off to a thrilling start. The DROP ZONE Stunt Tower offers a thrilling 56 m.p.h., 100-foot free fall. Other attractions include the Water Works entertainment complex and Zoom Zone children's area.

Carowinds' popular one-price ticket covers all rides and park shows. Palladium concerts, featuring big-name entertainers, are extra. Admission to Paramount's Carowinds for ages 7 to 54 runs about $34.99 and $22.99 for children ages 3 to 6 and senior citizens 55 and older. Children 2 and younger are admitted free. Groups, family and individual season passes are available.

Professional Sports

Charlotte is North Carolina's mecca for professional sports. It is home to the Lowe's Motor Speedway, the Charlotte Hornets, the Charlotte Sting, the Carolina Panthers and the Charlotte Knights. Watch for offers of special travel and ticket arrangements that deliver you directly to the game sites from the Triangle.

Reed Gold Mine
N.C. 24/27 to Reed Mine Rd., Stanfield
• (704) 721-4653

Long before the California Gold Rush, Reed Gold Mine became the site of the first authenticated gold find in the United States. It was here in 1799 that Conrad Reed discovered a 17-pound nugget. His father used the rock as a doorstop before selling it for $3.50, unaware of its true value. The site includes a visitors center, mining trails, a mill used to crush ore and a restored section of the underground mine shaft.

Young prospectors patiently sift through rocks and sand with dreams of finding a gold nugget at Reed Gold Mine.

Photo courtesy of N.C. Division of Tourism

From April through October, for a small fee, you can try panning for gold.

Mountains

Just three hours west of the Triangle you begin an ascent into the third distinct region of North Carolina. The mountains are divided into three regions: Northern Mountains, Central Mountains and Southern Mountains. Each area demands at least a long weekend to explore. For further reading on this area, order a copy of *The Insiders' Guide To The Mountains.*

The Northern Mountains

Blowing Rock

A lot of towns are dressed up to look quaint these days. Blowing Rock is the real deal. In summer, the main street is lined with pyramid-shaped planters spilling over with pink and white begonias. Since the days the rambling 1882 Green Park Inn was built over the center of the Continental Divide, the town has taken on an aristocratic appeal.

Window shopping on Main Street is a favorite pursuit with lots of antiques and Oriental rug houses. Evenings find folks at the auction house, which is a show in itself. The park on Main Street is a gathering place for tennis, people-watching and craft shows.

Enjoy horseback riding along the trails of Moses Cone Estate on the Blue Ridge Parkway. Make reservations with Blowing Rock Stables, (828) 295-7847. The adventurous will enjoy canoeing and whitewater rafting through Class 3 (fairly mild) to Class 5 (pretty wild) rapids down the Nolichucky.

Children in North Carolina grow up on trips to Tweetsie Railroad, (828) 264-9061, on U.S. 321/221 between Blowing Rock and Boone. The drawing card is a three-mile action-filled train ride on an original mountain train, complete with Indian attacks and settler rescues. The attraction has amusement rides, live entertainment, crafts, shops and picnic tables. It's open daily from May through Labor Day and on weekends in September and October.

Boone

In the heart of Boone lies the beautiful campus of Appalachian State University. Boone is also home to the Appalachian Cultural Museum, (828) 262-3117, where the evolving lifestyle of mountain people is displayed with artifacts and information on the abundant variety of rare and unusual herbs and plants. Unique artifacts include an authentic whiskey still, NASCAR great Junior Johnson's race car and memorabilia from Land of Oz, a defunct Beech Mountain theme park that operated from 1970 to 1980.

During the summer (June 16 until August 12), make reservations for the outdoor drama *Horn In The West,* which has run every summer since 1952. The musical drama revolves around life in Appalachia during the days of Daniel Boone. For reservations, call (828) 264-2120. Adjacent to *Horn In The West,* you'll find Hickory Ridge Homestead, which is an interesting tour of five representative homesites of the 1800s.

The 1883 Mast General Store, a tourist attraction in its own right, is located in the nearby town of Valle Crucis. Listed on the National Historic Register, the store retains a rustic decor, full of advertising posters and a pot-bellied stove. It contains a post office, clothing, footwear, camping gear, hardware, candy, toys and much more. Enjoy delicious Southern cuisine at the nearby Mast Farm Inn, an 1885 farmhouse listed on the National Historic Register.

About 30 miles east of Boone lies Wilkesboro, home to the annual MerleFest in late April. This four-day internationally acclaimed celebration of music honors the late Merle Watson, son of festival host Arthel "Doc" Watson. The festival, which started in 1988 with two stages and 6,000 spectators, has grown to include 13 stages, more than 100 performers and 65,000 spectators. Call (800) 343-7857 for more information.

Glendale Springs

It's a toss-up to know whether people go to the quaint community of Glendale Springs for the wonderful gourmet food at the Glendale Springs Inn or to see the frescoes. Ben

Long's world-famous frescoes at Episcopal Holy Trinity Chapel are among the most highly visited in the state. A number of craft shops have sprung up in town, which changes the area's once "hidden away" flavor but does not diminish its overall appeal.

Grandfather Mountain
www.grandfather.com

The privately owned Grandfather Mountain, which has been designated an International Biosphere Reserve by the United Nations, features natural habitats, an interpretive nature museum, 12 miles of hiking trails, scenic picnic sites and the famous Mile High Swinging Bridge, the highest swinging footbridge in the United States. The 5,964-foot mountain can be seen for miles around and looks like a giant sleeping grandfather. It is considered North Carolina's top scenic attraction. You'll want to visit the natural habitats for native black bear, white-tailed deer, cougars and bald and golden eagles. Stop in at the nature museum that offers state-of-the-art displays along with entertaining movies on native wildlife (especially the film on the red-tailed hawk). For those brave enough to cross it, the swinging bridge, which connects Linville's Peak with the visitors center, rewards you with a spectacular view.

The museum's restaurant is a great place for lunch. You can also picnic on the mountain. Grandfather Mountain is open daily from 8 AM to 7 PM. Call (828) 733-2013 for more information.

An exciting Grandfather Mountain experience is the annual Highland Games, the second weekend in July. You don't have to be a Scot to enjoy the bagpipes, dancing, saber-toss and watch Border Collies return lost sheep to the flock, as well as other games of skill. Another popular yearly event that comes the fourth Sunday in June is Singing on the Mountain, a day-long gathering of gospel music and preaching that began in 1924.

Linville Falls, Linville Caverns, Old Hampton Store

At Linville Falls and Gorge, there are three hiking trail options, from easy to rugged, depending on your energy and time. The gorge is the deepest slash in the earth's crust east of the Grand Canyon. The river tumbles into the gorge from its head to form a 90-foot fall of water. To reach the falls, you'll walk through a 1/2 mile tunnel of towering trees so dense that spatters of sunlight are rare. Waterfalls, some dramatic, others serene, draw visitors to watch their grand displays.

There are probably undiscovered caves all through the mountains. Linville Caverns, like others, was discovered by accident in 1822 when curious fishermen followed trout disappearing into the side of a mountain. Trout in this 20-million-year-old limestone cave have become blind due to the lack of a light source. During the Civil War, the Caverns served as a refuge for deserters from both sides of the conflict. Don't expect the splendors of Carlsbad or Luray, but the cavern, on three levels, is an interesting and enjoyable half-hour experience. It's open year round, but check times, (828) 756-4171.

The Old Hampton Store, (828) 733-5213, sits just outside the town of Linville. Constructed in 1921, this general store offers a wide assortment of notions that you need and some that you probably don't—such as horse hoof medication. Churns and washtubs hang from the ceiling and the back screened door is perpetually in motion. Out back, the stone gristmill grinds cornmeal and grits nearly every afternoon. These products are sold with apple butter, local jams and old fashioned tin cookware. Kids can buy marbles by the pound and sturdy clothes are available upstairs.

Best of all is lunch. The store serves the leanest and most delicious barbecue around and its root beer is excellent. Top this off with a slice of terrific carrot cake or your choice from assorted cheesecakes.

Ski Country

Each year thousands of Triangle skiers listen to weather reports, watch the sky, send up snow prayers and wax skis in hope of bringing on the first winter's snow. That's when you'll see packed cars bearing ski racks headed for one of the many North Carolina downhill ski resorts.

Appalachian Ski Mountain, (800) 322-2373, home of the French-Swiss Ski College outside Boone, has one of the best teaching schools for beginners. It has nine slopes and trails with a peak elevation of 4,000 feet. Ski Beech, (800) 438-2093, north of Banner Elk has 14 slopes and trails and a peak elevation of 5,505 feet, making it the highest in the East with a vertical drop of 830 feet. The resort also has a charming Swiss Village-type appearance with an outdoor ice skating rink encircled with shops and restaurants. Sugar Mountain Ski Resort, (800) 784-2768, just to the south of Banner Elk on N.C. 184, boasts 21 slopes and trails, peak elevation of 5,300 feet with a vertical drop of 1,200 feet, and needless to say, fairyland views. Ski Hawksnest, (888) 429-5763, is sometimes less crowded and has 12 slopes and trails, a peak of 4,819 feet and a vertical drop of 669 feet, plus night skiing.

All of these resorts have chair lifts, rope tows, lockers and restaurants. Beech and Sugar even have nurseries. High Country Host at (800) 438-7500 is a good source of mountain area information.

You can ski cross-country at Moses Cone Park on the parkway just outside Blowing Rock and at other gated-off areas by calling the Ranger's office at (828) 295-7591.

The Central Mountains

Asheville

Called the "Land of the Sky," this mountain city where wealthy vacationers once came for relief from the summer heat is still drawing visitors. The Downtown Asheville Historic District contains a superb collection of early 20th-century architecture, boasting more art deco-style buildings than any other Southeastern city except Miami Beach.

The centerpiece of the downtown historic district is Pack Place Education, Arts and Science Center. This bustling complex contains four museums, a performing arts theatre, courtyards, permanent exhibitions, a gift shop, restaurant and lobby galleries. Tickets are required for admission to theater events and to each of the four museums: the Asheville Art Museum, The Colburn Gem and Mineral Museum, The Health Adventure and the YMI Cultural Center. You may buy a one-day pass that is good for all four or you can buy single tickets. No admission charge is required for visitors to enter Pack Place and view the historic exhibit "Here is the Square," visit the Craft Gallery that spotlights regional crafts or shop in the Museum Gift Store. Call (828) 257-4500 for ticket information and hours.

Another must-see attraction in downtown Asheville is the Thomas Wolfe Memorial State Historic Site, which honors the acclaimed author of *Look Homeward, Angel*. Although the "Old Kentucky Home" boarding house that served as Wolfe's boyhood home is currently closed for restoration, a visitors center at the site remains open. Call (828) 253-8304 for further details. By the way, Wolfe's gravesite can be found at the Riverside Cemetery near the final resting place of another famous author, William Sydney Porter, better known as O. Henry.

Other notable Asheville attractions include the N.C. Arboretum, the 1840 Smith-McDowell House and the W.N.C. Nature Center. For more information, call the Asheville Area Convention and Visitors Bureau at (800) 257-1300.

Biltmore Estate and Winery
• www.biltmore.com

One of the best daytrip excursions is to the Biltmore Estate, Gardens and Winery, which remains the largest private residence in the United States. Between 1888 and 1890, George Washington Vanderbilt, grandson of the railroad promoter Cornelius Vanderbilt, purchased a total of 125,000 acres of land for the estate he planned to build. The architectural style was designed by Richard

Morris Hunt to resemble a chateau in France's Loire Valley and it rivals the grandest palace abroad. The castle-like house contains 255 rooms, which took 1,000 artisans five years to build for the six residents and their guests (not including the 100 servants). You can tour the main house with its beautiful antique furnishings, priceless paintings and ceiling frescoes that are kept in excellent repair. The servant's quarters, where even the butler had his own servant, are also interesting.

A favorite time is the Christmas season when the house is resplendent with thousands of poinsettias and Christmas trees trimmed with many original ornaments. Concerts fill the magnificent halls. The estate is open from 8:30 AM to 5 PM year round except Thanksgiving, Christmas Day and New Year's. Call (828) 255-1700 or (800) 624-1575.

Another enjoyable—as well as tasty—tour is that of the estate's winery. The old dairy barn has been renovated into a lovely open air restaurant, Deerpark, where you may see herds of deer roaming the land. Afterward, stop in Biltmore Village where the houses of the original construction workers have been converted into shops and restaurants.

Blue Ridge Parkway and Mount Mitchell
• **www.blueridgeparkway.org**

The scenic Blue Ridge Parkway meanders uninterrupted for 469 miles, connecting Virginia's Shenandoah National Park with Great Smoky Mountains National Park. Construction on the Parkway was begun in 1935 as a public works project during the Depression. It is considered to be one of America's most scenic parkways. The frequent overlooks afford breathtaking panoramas of high peaks, waterfalls and lakes tucked into lush valleys.

Spring is alive with color with mountain laurel and red rhododendron in awesome abundance. Fall plays the same game with "leaf-lookers" drinking in every ounce of autumnal beauty. An excellent daytrip is to Mount Mitchell State Park at Milepost 355. At 6,684 feet above sea level, Mount Mitchell is the highest peak east of the Mississippi River and you can hike through the park's many nature trails. To camp here, call

(828) 675-4611 to reserve one of the nine campsites. Other sites of interest on the Parkway include Brinegar Cabin (MP 238.5), E.B. Jeffress Park (MP 272), Parkway Craft Center (MP 294), Julian Price Memorial Park (MP 295), Linville Falls (316.4), Linn Cove Viaduct (MP 304), Museum of N.C. Minerals (MP 331), Crabtree Meadows Recreation Area (MP 339.5), Craggy Gardens (MP 363-369) and the Folk Art Center (MP 382).

Brevard

Surrounded by the Pisgah National Forest, Brevard offers a variety of activities from rugged outdoor adventures to communing quietly with nature or delving into the magical mountain lore through music, drama or local crafts.

You can spend the day locating a few of the 250 waterfalls in Transylvania County and Brevard. The best way to see them is to take the scenic 79-mile drive (U.S. 276) that loops through the Pisgah National Forest. Don't miss Looking Glass Falls, Sliding Rock and the Cradle of Forestry. You may also hike along the designated trails or explore the Pisgah Forest on horseback.

When you're ready to return to civilization, check out the annual summer Brevard Music Festival at the Brevard Music Center. Call (888) 384-8682 for dates. Drive back down U.S. 64 to Flat Rock and take in a play at the Flat Rock Playhouse, (828) 693-0731, the state theater of North Carolina. Flat Rock is also the site of Connemara, (828) 693-4178, the former home of famous poet Carl Sandburg.

Chimney Rock, Lake Lure
www.chimneyrockpark.com

The town of Chimney Rock, with a river running beside it, is a favorite of tourists. You can enjoy a climb up to the spectacular Chimney Rock Park, (800) 277-9611, or ride up in a 26-story elevator inside the mountain. You'll be at the top of the chimney-shaped rock with a panoramic view that is worth the trip all by itself. Below is Hickory Nut Gorge, which includes the French Broad River and Lake Lure. Pack a picnic lunch to enjoy at one of the park's many picnic areas. Lake Lure is a 1,500-acre man-made lake with 27 miles of shoreline and a variety of recreational opportunities and accommodation choices.

The Southern Mountains

Cashiers

Beautiful Cashiers (pronounced "Cashers"), high in the Blue Ridge Mountains, is a resort town, famous for its waterfalls, including Toxaway Falls (123 feet), High Falls (135 feet) and the beautiful Rainbow Falls, which plunges some 200 feet. Nearby Whitewater Falls drops 411 feet along the North Carolina-South Carolina border, making it the highest waterfall in the Eastern United States.

Cherokee

The 56,000-acre Qualla Boundary Reservation is home to the Eastern Band of Cherokee Indians. The rich history of the Cherokee Indians can be explored at the Museum of the Cherokee Indian, (828) 497-3481. The museum received $3.5 million in renovations a couple of years ago with new interactive exhibits documenting the history of the Cherokee people.

The not-to-be-missed Oconaluftee Indian Village, (828) 497-2111, is a reproduction of how the Eastern Band of the Cherokees lived 200 years ago. And the Qualla Arts and Crafts Mutual, (828) 497-3103, in the village is a shop that looks more like a museum. This shop of artisans' works is responsible for keeping alive the authentic arts and crafts of the Cherokee. It is also the only place that you'll find these distinct crafts.

Cherokee is also home to Harrah's Cherokee Casino, (800) HARRAHS, which offers 24-hour casino action in a facility the size of three football fields. About 2,400 video gaming machines can be found here, as well as three restaurants, a childcare center and a 1,500-seat theater.

Of course, no trip to Cherokee would be complete without attending *Unto These Hills*, (828) 497-2111, at the recently renovated Mountainside Theatre. The outdoor drama unfolds the tragic story of how the proud Cherokees were driven west on the "Trail of Tears" from their Smoky Mountain homeland.

Traditional crafts are demonstrated at Oconaluftee Indian Village in Cherokee.

Cherokee serves as the gateway to Great Smoky Mountains National Park, (423) 436-1200, the largest national park east of the Rocky Mountains. It is the most visited national park in the United States, drawing an estimated nine million visitors annually. Established in 1934, the park contains 140 native species of trees, 900 miles of trails and more than 700 miles of rivers and streams. An estimated 400 to 600 black bears live within the park's boundaries. Campsites, hiking trails, waterfalls, fishing spots and historic sites are located throughout the park.

Maggie Valley

A bustling tourist town, Maggie Valley is located off the Blue Ridge Parkway near the entrance to Great Smoky Mountains National Park. If you like gunfights in a mile-high Ghost Town in the Sky theme park and warm mountain hospitality, go to Maggie Valley. There's also a first-rate zoo in town called Soco Gardens Zoo. Maggie Valley is also home to the Cataloochee Ski Area, (800) 768-0285, North Carolina's first ski area.

TRIANGLE FINANCIAL INSTITUTIONS

Bank of America www.bankofamerica.com	829-6500
Branch Banking & Trust Company (BB&T) www.bbandt.com	716-9000
Capital Bank www.capitalbank-nc.com	878-3100
Central Carolina Bank (CCB) www.ccbonline.com	683-7777
Centura Bank www.centura.com	571-2400
Fidelity Bank www.fidelitybank.com	552-2242
First Citizens Bank www.firstcitizens.com	716-7000
First Union National Bank www.firstunion.com	881-6161
Hillsborough Savings Bank www.hsbebank.com	732-2143
Mechanics & Farmers Bank www.mfbonline.com	683-1521
Mutual Community Savings Bank SSB	688-1308
NBC Bank FBS www.nbcbank.com	954-0040
SOUTHBank	682-5531
SouthTrust Bank N.A. www.southtrust.com	872-4260
Wachovia Bank N.A. www.wachovia.com	755-2461
Wake Forest Federal Savings & Loan Association	556-5146

Bank of America

Pictured, Left to Right: Rob Hounshell, Frank Hooper, Brenda Seligmann, Gwen Baker, Dottie Brooks, Bill Smith, Mary Knight, Carolyn Hicks

Private Banking & Investment Management

One Hanover Square
Raleigh, NC
(919) 829-6751

Headquarters:
Bank of America
Corporate Center
100 North Tryon Street
18th Fl.
Charlotte, NC 28255
(704) 386-8486

www.bankofamerica.com

Building strong relationships with clients has been a hallmark of Bank of America through its evolution over the years, from its early days as North Carolina National Bank, to NCNB and then NationsBank. The merger between NationsBank Corporation and BankAmerica Corporation formed Bank of America, the largest bank in the United States. Today, the merger translates into a wealth of benefits for Bank of America customers. Everyone remembers the days when a customer traveling out of state was forced to stop by his or her local branch to load up on traveler's checks. However, interstate banking moved from concept to reality after NCNB bought a Florida savings and loan. Today, Bank of America customers can conduct their banking at 1,800 full-service branches throughout the United States and in certain international markets.

Bank of America's Raleigh Private Bank office provides comprehensive banking services for clients with a million dollar net worth. Even though the Raleigh Private Bank office primarily handles clients in the Triangle and Eastern North Carolina, they also assist clients all over the United States. Prior to the historic NationsBank and BankAmerica merger, Nationsbank managed $70 billion in assets for their clients, making it the largest manager of personal assets in the country. Once NationsBank became Bank of America, the figure skyrocketed to $120 billion. That's an impressive achievement, especially when you consider the reputation for banks being conservative investors. Although the portfolio managers at Bank of America Private Bank are very careful with their client's investments, they can also be as aggressive or as conservative as their clients want them to be.

Referrals from satisfied customers are a primary source of new clients for Bank of America. Portfolio performance and client focus are the primary reasons for this success. For instance, when a client contacts their personal "relationship manager," that manager will determine which member of the Bank of America Private Bank team is the most knowledgeable about the client's individual investments. The manager then seeks the advice of those experts for their client's benefit. If the client is heavily invested into oil and natural gas companies, the manager might bring in the bank's oil and gas expert from Texas. If the client is invested exclusively in just one stock, the manager might offer the advice of the bank's expert in alternative investment strategies to help the client create a more balanced portfolio.

Bank of America Private Bank has come a long way. The future looks even brighter. For more information about how Bank of America can help you formulate your investment strategies, call Brenda Seligmann at **919-829-6751.**

Some meetings are educational.

This one can get a kid into college.

Lots of events in life are learning experiences. But they don't supply what it takes to get into college. Meeting with one of our agents, however, can help you provide for your child's higher education—no matter what happens to you. Northwestern Mutual has always received the highest ratings for financial strength and security from Standard & Poor's, Moody's, A.M. Best, and Duff & Phelps. It could be the smartest move you ever make in looking after your child's future.

R. Michael Condrey, CLU, General Agent
The Carolina Condrey Agency
4020 WestChase Boulevard, Suite 275
Raleigh, NC 27607
919/834-7772

Northwestern Mutual™

GTE Wireless
s now **Verizon Wireless.**

Simple. Affordable. National.

Join in.

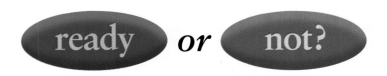

Employment Opportunities

Yes, we have jobs, jobs, jobs. At the beginning of 2000, unemployment was below 2 percent. Any lower and we'll be sacking groceries ourselves at the checkout lines.

For two decades, the Triangle has posted some of the best employment figures in the nation. The Research Triangle Park started the good times back in the '60s, and even in national recessions, the Triangle economy has grown. The most attention goes to the booming high-tech sector where software programmers and computer engineers are in short supply. But the skilled trade jobs of carpenters, plumbers, auto mechanics, electricians and bricklayers also go begging month after month. One of the hottest categories of late has been office administrators.

The Triangle also has become the entrepreneurial capital of North Carolina, a fact reflected by the presence of the Council for Entrepreneurial Development, the Kenan Institute for the Study of Private Enterprise at the UNC-CH and Duke University's Fuqua School of Business' annual Venture Fair that tries to match new businesses with venture capitalists. IPO is in the headlines as often as Dow Jones and venture capital funds are a growth industry here.

Still, if you or your trailing spouse is looking for your dream job, be prepared to wait a couple of months. A good way to start in the job market is to sign up as a temp and get a foot in the door. And in this market, a temp job can be anything from managing a computer manufacturing operation to conducting clinical research for a pharmaceutical giant. For the record, the largest employer in the Triangle is state government and the largest private employer is Duke University.

Employment Resources

Useful resources and publications you should explore when seeking employment in the Triangle are listed below. A number of these publications describe the major employers in the area. Contact your local Chamber of Commerce for more information on these and other publications that will assist you in your job search.

Major Employers in Orange Cty.
Chapel Hill-Carrboro
Chamber of Commerce
P.O. Box 2897, Chapel Hill, NC 27514
• **967-7075** • **Order by mail or phone.**
$10 (Visa/MC accepted)

Major Employers in Wake County
Greater Raleigh Chamber of Commerce
P.O. Box 2978, Raleigh, NC 27602-2978
• **(919) 664-7004** • **Order by mail or phone.**
$20 (Visa/MC accepted)

Organizations Employing Over 100
Greater Durham Chamber of Commerce
P.O. Box 3829, Durham, NC 27702
• **(919) 682-2133**
Order by mail or phone.
$10 (Visa/MC accepted)

MAJOR TRIANGLE EMPLOYERS

Name	Type of Business	# of Employees
CARY		
SAS Institute, Inc.	Computer Software	3,500
MCI WorldCom	Telecommunications	2,200
American Airlines	Reservation Center	1,600
Cary Towne Center	Shopping Mall	1,500
Midway Airlines	Reservation Center	1,500
Austin Quality Foods	Snack Foods	1,200
CDI Corporation	Computers	750
IBM Corporation	Computers and Software	750
Western Wake Medical Center	Health Care	700
Gregory Poole Equipment	Heavy Equipment	653
CHAPEL HILL		
UNC-Chapel Hill	Education	9,700
UNC Hospitals	Health Care	4,425
Blue Cross/Blue Shield	Insurance	2,260
Chapel Hill/Carrboro Schools	Public Education	1,500
General Electric Co., Inc.	Electrical Components	1,100
Orange Cnty. Bd. of Education	Public Education	900
Orange County Government	Government	620
Town of Chapel Hill	Town Government	575
Harris Teeter	Groceries	540
Food Lion	Groceries	400
DURHAM & RTP		
Duke University	Education, Medical Center	21,300
IBM Corporation	Computers and Software	14,000
Nortel Networks	Digital Switching Equipment	8,500
Glaxo SmithKline	Pharmaceuticals	5,300
Durham Public Schools	Public Education	4,000
Blue Cross & Blue Shield/NC	Health Insurance	2,600
Cisco Systems	Network Equipment and Software	2,500
Durham City Government	City Government	2,050
Durham Hospital Corporation	Health Care	2,000
Ericsson, Inc.	Digital Cellular Telecommunications	1,700
RALEIGH		
State of North Carolina	State Government	23,230
N.C. State University	Education	10,400
Wake County Schools	Public Education	9,200
City of Raleigh	City Government	5,500
WakeMed	Health Care	4,950
Rex Healthcare	Health Care	3,530
Carolina Power & Light	Utilities	3,125
Wake County Government	County Government	2,620
Winn-Dixie Stores	Groceries	1,950
United Parcel Service	Package Delivery	1,500

RTP Owners and Tenants
Research Triangle Foundation
• (919) 549-8181
Order by phone—no charge.

The classified section of a local newspaper is a cheap and easy source of many job listings and is an excellent place to begin your job hunt. The Sunday edition of the major local newspapers will provide the largest selection of opportunities and can also help you identify personnel agencies that may specialize in your field or give you access to small companies that don't use agencies. If you live in a large city, there may be a retailer near you that sells newspapers from across the country. Otherwise, a subscription to one of the area's largest papers might be a good investment.

The Cary News
212 E. Chatham St., Cary
• 460-2600

The Chapel Hill Herald
106 Mallette St., Chapel Hill
• 967-6581
• www.herald-sun.com

The Chapel Hill News
505 W. Franklin St., Chapel Hill
• 932-2000
• www.chapelhillnews.com

The Herald-Sun
2828 Pickett Rd., Durham
• 419-6500 • www.herald-sun.com

The News & Observer
215 S. McDowell St., Raleigh
• 829-4500
• www.newsobserver.com
• www.triangle.com

The N&O also offers *Employment Weekly* (available by special subscription and also distributed in the Wednesday edition of *The Chapel Hill News*). Two employment newspapers are available free at locations throughout the Triangle or by subscription: the biweekly *Carolina Job Finder,* 319-6816, and the weekly *Employment Guide,* 463-9144 (www.careerweb.com).

Temporary Placement

One of the best ways to explore career options is with the help of temporary or permanent staffing agencies. For the newcomer, a temporary position has the advantage of providing an opportunity to become more familiar with the area and with employment options before settling on a permanent position. In addition to placement, many agencies offer training and some even offer skill and personality testing to determine the best working situation for each individual.

TRIANGLE EMPLOYMENT AGENCIES

Company	Type	Phone
Ablest Staffing Services	Clerical, Light Industrial	388-0633
Accountants On Call	Financial Services	403-3330
Accountemps, Robert Half, Intl.	Financial Services	787-8226
Accounting Solutions	Financial Services	828-3940
Action Staffmasters	Manufacturing, Clerical, Technical	873-0567
Adecco	Clerical, Light Industrial	572-2662
Atlantic Staffing	Administrative, Clerical, Light Industrial	833-0407
Bullington Associates	Medical, Industrial	781-1350
Capital Temporaries, Inc.	Administrative, Clerical, Light Industrial	833-8367
Duke Temporary Service	Clerical, Technical, Service	681-3132
Executive Staffing Group	Administrative, Technical	481-0093
Express Personnel Services	Administrative, Clerical, Light Industrial	875-1268
Five Star Staffing	Administrative, Accounting	854-4488
Fortune Personnel Consultants	Executive, Manufacturing	848-9929
Global Software	Data Processing	872-7800
Greer Personnel Consultants	Administrative	571-0051
Griffin Staffing Services	Clerical, Technical	554-3811
Headway Corporate Staffing	Office, Technical	544-2600
Healthcare Recruiters	Medical Sales, Administration	319-6306
Information Systems Professionals	Computer Systems	954-9100
Interim Personnel	Technical, Medical	420-0026
Kelly Temporary Services	Technical, Light Industrial	781-8667
Labor Ready	General	831-1018
Legal Personnel Services	Legal Secretaries, Paralegals	787-0049
Longistics	Administrative, Industrial	872-2167
Manpower	General	755-5800
Monarch Services	Professionals, Health Care	490-0000
Norrell Services	Administrative, Clerical	850-0046
Pat Licata Associates	Medical, Pharmaceutical	859-0511
Personal Communications	Secretarial, Light Industrial	544-4575
Quality Staffing Specialists	Medical, Accounting, Clerical	481-4114
Radeco Technical Services	Technical	851-7630
Randstad	Clerical, Office Support	676-0068
Remedy Intelligent Staffing	Administrative, Accounting	783-6300
Renaissance Worldwide	Technical, Systems	678-1001
Sales Consultants	Sales, Sales Management	460-9595
Smither and Associates	Administrative, Office Support	493-5444
Snelling Personnel Services	Engineering, Medical Sales	876-0660
Staffmark	Clerical, Light Industrial	493-8367
Tandem	Industrial	828-4110
TRC Staffing Services	Administrative, Technical	481-2525
Triangle Temporaries	Administrative, Technical	876-0009
Unicorn Staffing	Administrative	844-1960
USA Staffing	Clerical, Light Industrial	806-8292
Westaff Services	Office, Industrial, Technical	781-7998
Volt Services Group	Technical, Administrative	829-1660

Located on 1,000 acres adjacent to NCSU, Centennial Campus blends public academic and private sector research.

NCSU's Centennial Campus

Although Research Triangle Park gets all the attention, Centennial Campus also has lured top-name companies and generated thousands of jobs in the Triangle. Located on 1,000 acres adjacent to North Carolina State University's main campus, Centennial Campus is a unique technology community that blends public academic and private sector research. Slated for development over the next 15 years, Centennial Campus will ultimately consist of a dozen or more research clusters made up of university, corporate and government laboratories, a hotel conference center, retail stores and housing situated around a central lake.

About 3,200 people currently work at Centennial Campus, which will eventually employ more than 25,000. Lucent Technologies has already located a 120,000-acre research lab on the campus that employs about 500 workers.

Research Triangle Park Companies

Research Triangle Park (RTP), the area's high-tech centerpiece, is home to 137 private, governmental and nonprofit companies, employing approximately 43,000 people—making it the largest research park in the United States. It is estimated that by the year 2010, more than 50,000 people will be employed in the Park. For more information about RTP, contact: Research Triangle Foundation, 2 Hanes Drive, RTP, NC 27709, 549-8181 (www.rtp.org). Here's a list and brief description of some of RTP's major employers.

Aventis CropScience
560 Employees
2 T.W. Alexander Dr.
• **549-2000**
• **www.aventis.com**
Formerly known as Rhone-Poulenc, this company conducts research and development, engineering and marketing of agricultural products.

BASF Corporation
Agricultural Products
254 Employees
26 Davis Dr. • 547-2000 • www.basf.com
RTP is the Agricultural Products Divisional Headquarters and Research Center for BASF. The company focuses its efforts on agricultural research and development and plant biotechnology.

BD Technologies (Becton Dickinson)
139 Employees
21 Davis Dr. • 549-8641
• www.bd.com
B-D conducts research related to medical devices and health-care products.

Biogen, Inc.
125 Employees
5000 Davis Dr. • 941-1111
• www.biogen.com
Biogen is a biotechnology company that manufactures AVOMEX, a treatment for multiple sclerosis. Biogen entered Research Triangle Park in 1995.

CheckFree Investment Services
65 Employees
68 T.W. Alexander Dr. • 549-0444
• www.secapl.com
Formerly known as Mobius, CheckFree is a leading developer and provider of information and software in the investment management, consulting and financial planning industry.

CIIT (Chemical Industry Institute of Toxicology)
144 Employees
6 Davis Dr. • 558-1200
• www.ciit.org
CIIT is an independent, not-for-profit research laboratory dedicated to developing an improved scientific basis for understanding and assessing potential adverse effects of chemicals, pharmaceuticals and consumer products on human health. CIIT has been located in Research Triangle Park since 1979.

Cisco Systems, Inc.
2,500 Employees
7025 Kit Creek Rd. • 392-2000
• www.cisco.com
RTP is the East Coast headquarters for Cisco, the leading global supplier of enterprise networking equipment and software. Cisco products comprise more than 80 percent of the backbone routers that currently make up the Internet. It's estimated that Cisco's RTP division will have 10,000 employees by 2004.

Photo by Rich Weidman

Cisco System's Technology and Mobile Wireless Business Unit is headquartered in Research Triangle Park.

Covance Biotechnology Services, Inc.
450 Employees
6051 George Watts Hill Dr.
• 468-9400
• www.covance.com

Covance Biotechnology provides process development, clinical and commercial manufacturing services for recombinant biotechnology products.

Delta Products Corporation
65 Employees
5101 Davis Dr. • 767-3800
• www.deltaca.com

Delta Products designs and develops data communication products and switching power supplies.

DuPont Technologies
270 Employees
14 T. W. Alexander Dr.
• 248-5000
• www.dupont.com

Research, development, applications engineering and sales support associated with materials and systems for the electronics industry are the focus here.

Eisai, Inc.
107 Employees
900 Davis Dr. • 941-6920
• www.eisai.com

Eisai, Inc. performs pharmaceutical formulation research and development, and manufacturing at its Research Triangle Park facility.

EMC Corporation
230 Employees
62 T.W. Alexander Dr. • 549-8421
• www.emc.com

Formerly Data General Corporation, EMC houses its Systems Software Development, the Software Qualifications and Support and the Customer Documentation divisions at RTP. EMC designs advanced systems, builds software alliances and provides integration solutions to design, implement and support total computing solutions.

Ericsson, Inc.
1,700 Employees
7000 Development Dr. • 472-7000
• www.ericsson.com

Digital cellular telecommunications, microcell base station research and

Ericsson, a world leader in telecommunications, has its headquarters for cellular and wireless products at Research Triangle Park.

Photo by Rich Weidman

Brainstorm, Natalie Wood's last movie, was filmed at Glaxo's RTP facility.

development are conducted here. RTP is its world headquarters for cellular and wireless products.

General Dynamics-Communication Systems
150 Employees
400 Park Plaza • 549-1111
• www.generaldynamics.com
General Dynamics maintains an engineering organization at Research Triangle Park responsible for software development and systems integration.

Glaxo SmithKline
5,300 Employees
5 Moore Dr. • 483-2100
• Job Line: 483-2565
• www.glaxowellcome.com
Glaxo SmithKline is a research-based pharmaceutical company that was formed in 2000 from the merger of Glaxo Wellcome and SmithKline Beecham, creating the world's largest drug company. A manufacturing plant is located in nearby Zebulon. Basic research is in cancer, as well as viral and metabolic disorders.

IBM
(International Business Machines Corp.)
14,000 Employees
3039 Cornwallis Rd. • 543-5221
• Job Line: (800) 964-4473
• www.ibm.com
The largest employer in RTP, IBM undertakes development, assembly and programming for its networking business products division here. The facility is also the headquarters for its personal computers division. IBM put RTP on the map when it arrived in the Triangle in 1965.

ISA
(International Society for Measurement and Control)
120 Employees
67 T.W. Alexander Dr. • 549-8411
• www.isa.org
RTP is the headquarters of an international society of engineers, scientists, technicians, managers and educators. The Society develops publications, standards and educational programs in instrumentation, control and automation.

Larscom, Incorporated
50 Employees
7030 Kit Creek Rd. • 991-9000
• www.larscom.com
Larscom manufactures telecommunications equipment, particularly equipment that provides access to wide area networks.

Lineberry Research Associates
68 Employees
79 T.W. Alexander Dr.
• 547-0970
• www.lineberryresearch.com
Lineberry is a contract research organization that provides high-level scientific and regulatory consulting services for pharmaceutical, biotechnology and other clients. It

With approximately 8,500 employees, Nortel Networks is the second-largest employer in Research Triangle Park.

Photo by Rich Weidman

also specializes in scientific writing and marketing communications.

Litespec, Inc.
N/A Employees
76 T.W. Alexander Dr.
• **541-8411** • **www.litespec.com**
Litespec develops and manufactures optical fiber. Located in RTP since 1989, it is a subsidiary of Lucent Technologies and Sumitomo Electric Industries.

Lockheed Martin Services
365 Employees
79 T.W. Alexander Dr. • **541-3351**
• **www.lmco.com**
Lockheed Martin's office provides support for the U.S. Environmental Protection Agency's National Data Processing Division.

MCNC
143 Employees
3021 Cornwallis Rd. • **248-1800**
• **www.mcnc.org**
MCNC is a private, nonprofit corporation that supports advanced education, research and technology programs in partnership with the state's universities, research institutes and industry. The N.C. Supercomputing Center and the N.C. Research and Education Network are based here.

Motor and Equipment Manufacturers Association
67 Employees
10 Laboratory Dr. • **549-4800**
• **www.mema.org**
Founded in 1904, MEMA represents and serves U.S. manufacturers of original equipment, replacement parts, services tools and chemicals for cars and trucks. It provides its members with market research, industry information, financial services, government representation and electronic data services.

National Humanities Center
25 Employees
7 T.W. Alexander Dr. • **549-0661**
• **www.nhc.rtp.nc.us:8080**
Founded in 1978, the National Humanities Center is a nonprofit institute that seeks to promote excellence in scholarship, to

strengthen teaching and to broaden public understanding of the humanities and their role in contemporary culture. Leading scholars from around the world come to the Center annually for individual research and seminars. The Center, which is associated with the American Academy of Arts and Sciences, also hosts seminars for students and teachers, and sponsors exhibitions, lectures and concerts for the general public.

National Institute of Environmental Health Sciences
1,000 Employees
Headquarters • 541-1919
South Campus: 111 T. W. Alexander Dr.
East Campus: 79 T. W. Alexander Dr.
North Campus: 104 T. W. Alexander Dr.
• www.niehs.nih.gov
NIEHS conducts biomedical research on the effects of chemical, physical and biological environmental agents on human health and well being. It is also the headquarters for the National Toxicology Program.

Nortel Networks
8,500 Employees
4008 E. Chapel Hill/Nelson Hwy.
• 992-5000 • www.nortelnetworks.com
RTP is the world headquarters for Public Carrier Networks. The company designs, develops, manufactures and supplies one of the industry's most complete lines of fully digital switching and transmission systems for the public telephone network. Nortel, which came to the Triangle in 1980, is the second-largest employer in RTP.

N.C. Biotechnology Center
45 Employees
15 T.W. Alexander Dr.
• 541-9366
• www.ncbiotech.org
The N.C. Biotechnology Center is a nonprofit corporation dedicated toward strengthening the state's leadership in biotechnology development.

North Carolina State Education Assistance Authority
10 T.W. Alexander Dr.
• 549-8614
www.ncseaa.edu
The State Education Assistance Authority plans, finances and administers statewide and inter-institutional student financial assistance programs. The NCSEAA opened it doors in RTP in 1979.

Novartis Biotechnology
260 Employees
3054 Cornwallis Rd.
• 541-8500
• www.novartis.com
Novartis Agribusiness Biotechnology Research, Inc. conducts research using biotechnology for more efficient crop production. Novartis' world headquarters is located in Basel, Switzerland.

Paradigm Genetics
111 Employees
104 T.W. Alexander Dr.
• 544-5578
• www.paradigmgenetics.com
Paradigm is industrializing the process of gene function determination in four major market areas: crop production, nutrition, human health and industrial products.

Reichhold, Inc.
550 Employees
2400 Ellis Rd. • 990-7500
• Job Line: 990-7805
• www.reichhold.com
RTP is the global headquarters and home for the research and development laboratories for Reichhold, a leading manufacturer of coating resins, emulsion polymers, polyesters and adhesives.

INSIDERS' TIP

One of the fastest growing cohorts of students in the Triangle's community colleges is that of four-year college graduates who turn to the schools for technical training, especially in computers.

At its Research Triangle Park facility, Novartis uses biotechnology to enhance crop production and create a more effective means of crop protection.

Research Triangle Institute
1,750 Employees
3040 Cornwallis Rd.
• **541-6000** • **www.rti.org**

Research Triangle Park's first tenant, the Institute is an independent, applied research institute serving government and industry in the U.S. and abroad. Disciplines at RTI include applied statistics, social engineering, chemistry and life sciences.

Resource Solutions, Inc.
27 Employees
3200 Chapel Hill Hwy., Ste. 100
• **558-8650** • **www.rsi-nc.com**

A contract research organization, Resource Solutions focuses on clinical trials management, project monitoring teams, client controlled monitoring services, medical monitoring and comprehensive audits.

Sigma Xi, The Scientific Research Society
40 Employees
99 T.W. Alexander Dr.
• **549-4691**
• **www.sigmaxi.org**

Sigma Xi, The Scientific Research Society engages in program activities to encourage scientific research, public understanding of science and technology, and science education through chapters at colleges and universities, government laboratories and industrial research centers.

Sigma Xi also sponsors international forums, awards grants and publishes *American Scientist* magazine.

Sphinx Pharmaceuticals
N/A Employees
20 T.W. Alexander Dr.
• **489-0909** • **www.elililly.com**

A division of Eli Lilly and Company, Sphinx Pharmaceuticals conducts research to identify new drug leads for a variety of disease areas.

Sumitomo Electric Lightwave Corporation
620 Employees
78 T.W. Alexander Dr.
• **541-8100** • **www.sumitomoelectric.com**

Sumitomo Electric Lightwave Corporation develops and manufactures fiber optic cable and sells fiber optics apparatus and video products to other manufacturers. Headquartered in Japan, Sumitomo opened its facility at Research Triangle Park in 1983.

Troxler Electronic Labs, Inc.
125 Employees
3008 Cornwallis Rd. • **549-8661**
• **www.troxlerlabs.com**

Troxler Electronic Labs develops, manufactures and distributes instruments and systems for measuring physical properties and characteristics of engineering materials through the use of radioactive isotopes.

UAI Technology, Inc.
35 Employees
68 T.W. Alexander Dr. • 541-9339
www.phoenixhecht.com

UAI Technology produces databases and software, provides consulting in the corporate cash management field, and performs market research.

Underwriters Laboratories, Inc.
558 Employees
12 Laboratory Dr.
• 549-1400 • Job Line: 549-5227
• www.ul.com

Underwriters Laboratories' Research Triangle Park facility conducts product testing for public safety.

U.S. Department of Agriculture, Forest Service
42 Employees
3041 Cornwallis Rd. • 549-4000
• www.rtp.srs.fs.fed.us

Part of the Forest Service's Southern Research Station, which is headquartered in Asheville, this facility provides forest research in the areas of economics, soils, global climate change, forest health and forest productivitiy and sustainability.

U.S. Environmental Protection Agency
1,734 Employees
86 T.W. Alexander Dr.
• Human Resources: 541-2201
• Job Line: 541-3014
• www.epa.gov

The U.S. Environmental Protection Agency conducts research on the health effects of exposure to air pollutants, pesticides and toxic substances and develops and evaluates techniques for monitoring and controlling air pollutants. The Research Triangle Park division will move to a new $272-million facility in the spring of 2001.

United Therapeutics Corporation
15 Employees
68 T.W. Alexander Dr. • 485-8350
• www.unither.com

Research Triangle Park is home to United Therapeutic's Clinical Development Center. The facility is involved in pharmaceutical research and development, as well as the licensing of technologies for life-threatening chronic diseases, including pulmonary hypertension and peripheral vascular disease.

University of North Carolina Center for Public Television
200 Employees
10 T.W. Alexander Dr.
• 549-7000
• www.unctv.org

Founded in 1955, North Carolina's 11-station statewide public television network has maintained its headquarters at Research Triangle Park since 1989. The facility is committed to producing and broadcasting programs for and about the state such as *North Carolina Now*, *North Carolina People* and *The Woodwright's Shop*.

Verizon Enterprise Solutions
275 Employees
50 Park Dr. • 549-0138
• www.verizon.com

Verizon, formerly known as GTE, is a full-service provider of telecommunications products and services solutions.

Xanthon, Inc.
30 Employees
104 T.W. Alexander Dr., Ste. 21
• 572-0707
• www.xanthoninc.com

Xanthon is a genomics company that utilizes patented molecular diagnostic technology for the direct analysis of DNA and RNA. It opened its doors in Research Triangle Park in 1996.

An excellent game
is just a matter of

COURSE

Play your best on the Triangle's
only fully-lit, 27-hole, par-3 course

Open 8 am - midnight • State-of-the-art lighted driving range • 27 well-sculpted holes • PGA teaching professionals on staff • Multiple tees for all levels of play • Junior and Senior discounts • Pro Shop • Sandwich Grill • Full-service Clubhouse

Knight's Play Golf Center

919-303-4653 • Open 8-am-midnight every day
Ten Ten Rd., Apex (between Kildaire Farm Rd. and U.S. I S.)
www.knightsplay.com

Golf In The Carolinas

North Carolina and golf go together like sand and trap. One of the nation's premier courses and site for the dramatic 1999 U.S. Open Championship, Pinehurst No. 2, lies in the state's rolling sandhills. And remember that fellow Arnold Palmer? He got his education and college golf lessons at Wake Forest University. So, yes, we have golf, and this chapter lists the public and private courses not only in the Triangle but elsewhere in the state (there are nearly 600!).

Pinehurst No. 2, for example, is about a 45-minute drive south and it is just one of a bag full of fabled fairways such as Pinehurst No. 7 and Mid Pines in and around the Village of Pinehurst and its neighbor, Southern Pines. We have golf in the mountains and all along the coast. The Greater Greensboro Open (which now has some sponsor's name in front of it) is 90 minutes away and an easy ticket. Duke University Golf Club will host the 2001 NCAA Men's Golf Championship. The U.S. Open Championship, by the way, will return to Pinehurst in 2005.

This chapter, however, is for the person who wants an Insider's head start on playing 18 holes on the weekend or during the week. And given our weather, you can usually play year round. Green fees, vary, but if you're a bargain hunter, you should be able to find some courses where green fees are only $12 during the week. On weekends, they cost between $18 and $25. We've also listed the private club courses such as Prestonwood in Cary and the Washington Duke Inn in Durham, two of the best in the Triangle.

The North Carolina Division of Tourism, Film and Sports Development publishes an annual *Official Golf Guide*. Call (800) VISIT NC to order your free copy. Every March, *North Carolina* magazine ranks the state's top 100 courses. There are the usual suspects but because of the recent boom in golf course building, the list changes. And now, it's time to say, FORE!

Triangle Courses

Cheviot Hills Golf Course
7301 Capital Blvd., Raleigh • 876-9920

Cheviot Hills is a veteran course that used to be on the outskirts of North Raleigh but has the city at its clubhouse door today. Noted for its scenic rolling hills, the semiprivate course opened in 1967 and was designed by acclaimed architect Gene Hamm. Rated near the middle for area courses, it's one of the better bargains and won't embarrass a beginner. Total yardage: 6475.

Crooked Creek Golf Course
4621 Shady Greens Dr., Fuquay-Varina • 557-7529 • www.crookedcreek.com

Chuck Smith designed Crooked Creek, an 18-hole, par-71 course that opened in 1994. It features complete practice facilities, a grill, pro shop and full-service conference center. Hole No. 12 is waiting for you. Total yardage: 6271.

The Crossings at Grove Park
4023 Old Wake Forest Hwy., Durham • 598-8686 • www.thecrossings.citysearch.com

With four sets of tees from 5000 to more than 6700 yards, this 18-hole, par-72

Popular Durham golf courses include Treyburn, which is part of a residential development, and Duke University Golf Club at the Washington Duke Inn.

championship course provides challenges for golfers of all skill levels. It was designed by Ron Garl. A full-service dining area is on the premises. Total yardage: 6700.

Devil's Ridge Golf Club
5107 Linksland Dr., Holly Springs
• 557-6100 • www.sunset-ridge.com

Built in 1991, this semiprivate course is rated among the best. Designed by John LaFoy, it is part of a residential real estate development located south of Cary in Holly Springs. Hole No. 17, a 388-yard par 4, is the signature hole. Total yardage: 7002.

Duke University Golf Club
N.C. 751 at Science Dr., Durham
• 681-2288
• www.washingtondukeinn.com

Located at the Washington Duke Inn, this classic championship course was designed by Robert Trent Jones in 1957 and redesigned by his son Rees Jones in 1994. In the recent *North Carolina* magazine survey, it ranked 20th among the state's best courses. The course has been awarded the 2001 NCAA Men's Golf Championship. It boasts a pro shop, hotel, driving range and 19th-hole restaurant. If you're coming to visit Duke University, stay here and work in a round. Hole No. 12 is considered one of the most beautiful in the area. Total yardage: 7054.

Eagle Crest Golf Course
4400 Auburn Church Rd., Garner
• 772-6104

John Baucom designed this course amid wooded, rolling hills. The 18-hole, par-71 course has been serving Triangle golfers since 1968. It includes a driving range/practice facility, clubhouse, pro shop and snack bar. Total yardage: 6514.

Finley Golf Course
Finley Golf Course Rd., Chapel Hill
• 962-2349

Finley, which is the University of North Carolina's backyard course, has been extensively renovated at a cost of approximately $8.5 million. It reopened in November 1999. Internationally renowned golf architect Tom Fazio redesigned the 18-hole, par-72 course. Finley has already been acclaimed as one of the top college facilities in the United States. It provides plenty of challenges for all skill levels. Total yardage: 7187.

Hedingham Golf Club
4801 Harbour Towne Dr., Raleigh
• 250-3030

Part of an attractive planned community in east Raleigh, north of U.S. 64, Hedingham was completed in 1993. It has a 18-hole, par-72 course, a well-equipped pro shop and a driving range. Hedingham is rated above average among the public courses and is a good place to find other newcomers. Total yardage: 6675.

Hillandale Golf Course
1600 Hillandale Rd., Durham
• 286-4211 • www.hillandale.com

Opened in 1913, Hillandale is the grandaddy of the public courses in the Triangle. George Cobb is responsible for the current design. The crowd that hangs out here doesn't put on any social airs. There's no charge for the philosophy or golf tales. You might even find a few golfers who will put a friendly wager on a friendly match. The course is kept in excellent condition and has some challenging holes. According to some, the pro shop is the best in the Triangle. Total yardage: 6339.

Knight's Play Golf Center
2512 Ten Ten Rd., Apex
• 303-4653
• www.knightsplay.com

Knight's Play opened in 1998 and features a state-of-the-art, fully lit 27-hole course and driving range open from 8 AM until midnight every day. David Postlethwait designed the course, which provides a variety of challenges for all skill levels. Knight's Play offers a driving range, a fully stocked pro shop and sandwich grill. Total yardage: 3810.

Lochmere Golf Club
2511 Kildaire Farm Rd., Cary • 851-0611

Lochmere is a favorite in Cary and was a hit when it opened in 1985. It is part of a very popular residential community and offers a beautiful, scenic landscape that includes two lakes. The challenging 18-hole, par-71 course, which was designed by Gene Hamm, has more that 40 bunkers and 10 water holes. It was the first home for the One Club World

Championships. The clubhouse includes a pro shop and a bar and grill. It has a driving range and it ranks above average in play. Total yardage: 6627.

Mill Creek Golf Club
1700 St. Andrews Dr., Mebane • 563-4653

A popular 18-hole, par-72 course located northwest of Chapel Hill, Mill Creek was named the best new course in the state by one survey when it opened in 1995. It hosted the prestigious Tar Heel Skins Challenge in 1999. Amenities include a clubhouse, driving range, putting green and pro shop. Total yardage: 7004.

The Neuse Golf Club
918 Birkdale Dr., Clayton • 550-0550
• www.glen-laurel.com/golf.html

Running parallel to the Neuse River, this scenic golf course designed by John LaFoy opened in 1993 in the Clayton development of Glen Laurel. Located about 15 to 20 minutes from the east side of Raleigh, it's ranked among the top 100 courses in the state. The course's signature hole is No. 14, with rocks on the left and water on the right. A well placed tee shot is critical on this 176-yard, par-3 hole. Total yardage: 7010.

Occoneechee Golf Club
1500 Lawrence Rd., Hillsborough
• 732-3435

Marvin Ray designed this semiprivate course, which opened in 1963. Although you can walk this course anytime, carts are very affordable. A clubhouse, pro shop, driving range and golf lessons are available. Total yardage: 6062.

Pine Hollow Golf Club
3300 E. Garner Rd., Clayton • 553-4554
• www.pine-hollow-golf.com

Pine Hollow has been around for a long time, and is located east of Raleigh amid rolling fields and tall pines. The semiprivate course has an informal, relaxed air and you can find industrial league players here during the week. It's also a great escape from household or weekend chores. The latter is reflected by very reasonable green fees on the weekend. The 18-hole, par-71 course is kept in good shape and offers a putting green, driving range, pro shop and snack bar. Total yardage: 6385.

Raleigh Golf Association
1527 Tryon Rd., Raleigh
• 772-9987

Raleigh Golf Association is another veteran course, perhaps one of the oldest in the Triangle. It was built in the country, south of Raleigh off Tryon Road, but is now within the city limits. Described by one player as a "nice member's course," it is unpretentious and plays fast. The fairways and greens are well-tended, especially Hole No. 13, which is a challenging 434-yard par 4. Amenities include putting and chipping greens, a pro shop and snack bar. Total yardage: 6276.

River Ridge Golf Club
3224 Auburn-Knightsdale Rd., Raleigh
• 661-8374

When River Ridge opened in 1997, it was named the best new public golf course in North Carolina by *Golf* magazine. Located in southern Wake County, the picturesque 18-hole, par-72 course was designed by Chuck Smith. It features putting and chipping greens, a driving range, cafe and pro shop. Total yardage: 6740.

Wake Forest Golf Club
13239 Capital Blvd., Wake Forest
• 556-3416

Gene Hamm designed this 18-hole, par-72 course, which opened in 1968. This very challenging course starts with an incredible 711-yard par 5—the longest in the world. It has a clubhouse, restaurant and lounge, driving range, putting green and pro shop. Total yardage: 6956.

Wildwood Green Golf Club
3000 Ballybunion Way, Raleigh
• 846-8376

Wildwood Green was one of the city's older public courses that underwent major renovations from architect John LaFoy in 1986 and emerged as part of a golf course community. It offers a number of membership options, including weekday plans for older golfers and junior cards for those under age 21. Hole No. 2, a 377-yard par 4, is a special challenge—short and scenic. Wildwood Green is rated among the average courses in play and is one of the shorter courses. Total yardage: 6502.

OTHER AREA COURSES

Bentwinds Golf Club	6536 Dornoch Pl., Fuquay-Varina	552-5656
Brevofield Golf Links	Camp Kanata Rd., Wake Forest	562-1900
Cedar Grove Golf Course	McDade Store Rd., Cedar Grove	732-8397
Eagle Ridge Golf Club	575 Competition Rd., Garner	661-6300
Falls Village Golf Course	115 Falls Village Ln., Durham	596-4653
Hidden Valley Golf Course	7900 N.C. 55, Willow Springs	639-4071
Lake Winds Golf Course	U.S. 501 N., Durham	471-4653
Lakeshore Golf Course	4621 Lumley Rd., Durham	596-2401
Par Golf	5715 Fayetteville Rd., Raleigh	772-5261
Riverwood Golf Club	400 Riverwood Dr., Clayton	550-1919
Twin Lakes Golf Course	648 Willow Way, Chapel Hill	933-1024
Wendell Country Club	180 Jake May Dr., Wendell	365-7337
Wil-Mar Golf Club	2300 Old Milburnie Rd., Raleigh	266-1800
Willowhaven Country Club	253 Country Club Dr., Durham	383-1022
Zebulon Country Club	2424 Pearces Rd., Zebulon	269-8311

Private Club Courses

The Triangle also has some of the best private country club courses in the state. While these courses are not open to the public, they should be part of every golfer's education about Triangle golf.

There are eight courses that rise to the top: Treyburn in Durham; Governors Club in Chapel Hill; Raleigh, North Ridge, Carolina and the new Tournament Players Club at Wakefield Plantation in Raleigh; and MacGregor Downs and Prestonwood in Cary.

Treyburn, a vast real estate community north of Durham's downtown, is a spectacular course that was designed by Tom Fazio and opened in 1988 to rave reviews by the golf press. It is one of the top-rated courses in the Triangle and across the state. The clubhouse is warm, beautiful and ranked by *Southern Links* as among the region's top five. It also has one of the finest croquet greens around. A number of Duke's and UNC's famous athletes are club members, including Michael Jordan. It features a super finishing hole, No. 18, a par 4.

Governors Club is a Jack Nicklaus design that opened in 1990 as part of a 1,600-acre planned community. The 27-hole course is ranked very high among the state's best courses. The setting is against Edwards Mountain and from the ninth tee, you get a spectacular view of the neighborhood. There are five sets of tees, so the course ranges from over 7085 yards to just under 6000 yards.

Among the private clubs in Raleigh, North Ridge usually gets top honors, although the venerable Raleigh Country Club over by Wake Medical Center gets good reviews and is notable as one of the last courses designed by golfing legend Donald J. Ross. Built in 1948, it features a 6700-yard, par-70 course. Raleigh Country Club hosted the annual Carolina Classic in 2000.

Today, North Ridge, which opened in 1970, has 36 holes—the original 18 holes were designed by George Cobb, who left his mark on courses at Linville Ridge and Bald Head Island, other courses in North Carolina. Its members are often connected to the Triangle's corporate establishment.

Surrounded by the Country Club Hills neighborhood on Glenwood Avenue, which was developed mostly in the 1950s, Carolina Country Club is the hub of the Old Raleigh Establishment. It features a 5502-yard, par-71 course.

Cary's MacGregor Downs dates back to 1968. It is considered a great "member's course" and was designed by Willard Byrd.

Prestonwood opened in the mid-'80s as part of Preston, one of Cary's trademark planned unit developments and the Triangle's largest golf course community. The clubhouse is elegant and the course is surrounded by some of the most attractive real estate in the county. The Nike Tour made its Triangle debut here in June '94 and the club pro is former PGA great Vance Heafner. Prestonwood is also home to the annual Jimmy V Celebrity Golf Classic in August. The course has 54 holes.

Other notable private country club courses in the Triangle include Chapel Hill, Hope Valley, Croasdaile and Tournament Players Club at Wakefield Plantation. Chapel Hill Country Club, located northeast of downtown, features a recently renovated 6752-yard, par-72 course. Hope Valley's 6148-yard, par-70 course is surrounded by some of the most colossal older homes in Durham. Built in 1966, Croasdaile's 6797-yard, par-72 course is located about 5 minutes from Duke University. Tournament Players Club opened in 2000 as part of a massive development just north of Raleigh called Wakefield Plantation. It will become the permanent home of the Carolina Classic starting in 2001.

Courses Elsewhere

Triangle residents may prefer to travel a relatively short distance to tee-up on some of the state's other great fairways. This is like jumping from Cloud Nine to Golfer's Heaven.

For instance, it's only an hour's drive to the village of Pinehurst, home of Pinehurst Resort and Country Club, (800) ITS GOLF (487-4653). The town dates back to 1895 when James W. Tufts bought 5,000 acres of North Carolina piney woods and hired Frederick Olmsted, the designer of New York's Central Park, to plan a private village. Tufts then hired Scotsman Donald Ross to build a course in 1899. Olmsted's concentric city plan continues today as the core of a town that Ross developed into the state's acknowledged golf capital and the first home of the PGA's World Golf Hall of Fame, which has since moved to Central Florida.

Queen of the eight courses (a 9th and 10th are in the planning stages) at the resort is Pinehurst No. 2, the masterpiece of legendary architect Donald Ross, which hosted the 1999 U.S. Open Tournament and has been awarded the 2005 tournament. Built in 1901, it easily captured the title as No. 1 course in the state in the recent *North Carolina* magazine survey. Guests at the resort can play here and entire articles have been written just about this one course. If you make the trip, just remember that as you line up your first shot you're playing the same course where Ben Hogan won his first pro tournament in 1940, and where golf legends Sam Snead, Byron Nelson and Jack Nicklaus played and won. Makes you want to go right for the flag, doesn't it?

Pinehurst No. 7 is also among the top-rated courses, listed at No. 22 out of the Top 100 courses in the state. Tom Fazio designed Pinehurst No. 8, which placed 8th overall in the *North Carolina* survey. Fazio also recently redesigned No. 4, another original Donald Ross layout.

The eight courses at the resort are just the beginning of the feast. There are many more courses in and around the towns of Pinehurst and Southern Pines. Most of them wear designer labels with names like Jack Nicklaus, Arnold Palmer, Tom and George Fazio, Dan Maples and Rees Jones.

An Insider's favorite is Mid Pines Resort, (800) 323-2114, in Southern Pines. This resort has a Donald Ross course that opened in 1921 and was ranked 14th in the *North Carolina* poll. The greens are small and the fairways are narrow.

Pine Needles Resort, (800) 747-7272, in Southern Pines is a 1927 Ross course. It is a challenging par 71 that hosted the 1996 Women's U.S. Open Championship and was awarded the tournament again in 2001. It's among the state's top courses and is operated by three generations of the same family.

Country Club of North Carolina, (910) 692-6565, has two private courses, but guests at Pinehurst Resort may play here. Insiders claim it is among the best in the state—with a notable membership. The recently renovated course is kept in immaculate condition, which helps explain why it's so highly rated.

Rees Jones designed the championship course Talamore, (910) 692-5884, which was nominated for best new public course in the nation in its debut in 1991. It offers a truly unique feature—llama caddies.

Carolina Trace Country Club, (919) 499-5611, which is in a private retirement community in nearby Sanford, features two 18-hole courses designed by Robert Trent Jones. Tournament group play is welcome.

The widely acclaimed Tobacco Road Golf Club, (877) 284-3762, also in Sanford, boasts a beautiful and challenging par-71, 18-hole layout. It was voted the Best New Course for 1999 in the *North Carolina* magazine survey. The unique Mike Strantz-designed course, which was carved out from an old sand pit, promises a rewarding and unforgettable golf outing.

When you travel to the coast, you will find more slices (pardon) of golf paradise. At Calabash, there is Pearl Golf Links, (910) 579-8132, designed by Dan Maples. It offers 72 holes of golf and a grand and informal clubhouse. Pearl Golf Links also has one of the best driving ranges in the state. Close by is Marsh Harbour Golf Course, (803) 249-3449. You can enjoy Calabash-style seafood and then work it off on these courses.

Brandywine Bay Golf and Country Club, (252) 247-2541, west of Morehead City, is set in dense woods and laced with streams and ponds. Originally designed by Bruce Devlin and redesigned by Ellis and Dan Maples, this coastal course plays 6609 yards from the championship tees, 6138 yards from the regular men's tees and 5196 yards from the women's tees. The 10th hole is a challenging 555-yard par 5. Golfers will find a pro shop, snack bar and putting greens.

Up north, on the Outer Banks, you can get a feel of Scottish moors and winds at The Village of Nags Head course, (252) 441-8073. You're surrounded by history and hang gliders, and, according to *Golf Digest*, perhaps the "longest, strongest and most irritating 6,100 yards you've ever encountered."

Traveling west, there is Tanglewood, (336) 778-6320, in Clemmons, outside Winston-Salem. Tanglewood rivals some of the state's finest courses for championship play and it is among Robert Trent Jones' best known courses. Lee Trevino won the 1974 PGA here and the 1986 Public Links Championship. Tanglewood currently hosts the PGA Senior Tour's annual Vantage Championship. It's a public course and considered by Insiders to be among the best 25 public courses in the country. The par 5, Hole No. 5, says *Golf* magazine, is one of the "most challenging" in the United States.

Golfers find summertime happiness in the mountains. Grandfather Golf and Country Club, (828) 898-4388, is at the center of the courses around Blowing Rock and Linville, North Carolina, in the northwest mountains. It is a private course designed by Ellis Maples. The championship course at Grandfather is always highly rated in the statewide survey and among the most challenging mountain courses in the country.

Guests at the Eseeola Lodge in Linville can enjoy the Linville Golf Club, (828) 733-4363, a classic Donald Ross design that ranks sixth in the state, according to the *North Carolina* magazine survey. Built in 1975, Burnsville's Mount Mitchell Golf Club, (828) 675-5454, also ranks highly.

Despite its name, Olde Beau, (800) 752-1634, opened in 1991 as part of a residential

Photo courtesy of N.C. Division of Tourism

Pinehurst Resort and Country Club is scheduled to host the 2005 U.S. Open Tournament.

mountain community about 20 minutes north of Elkin in the northwest mountains. The course is long, 6799 yards, and the signature hole is No. 15, a par 4 that overlooks the scenic Mitchell River Gorge. Play involves mastering the vertical, especially on the back nine, but golfers like its character.

The second hub of mountain golf is in the Highlands area south of Asheville. You will find a number of private clubs here such as The Cullasaja Club, (828) 526-3531, with a course designed by Arnold Palmer and down the road at Cashiers, there's the Wade Hampton Club, (828) 743-5950, by Tom Fazio, rated No. 12 among the Top 100 in the state in a recent survey.

Located in Cashiers, the High Hampton Inn & Country Club, (800) 334-2551, offers some of the most dramatic scenery of any of the mountain courses. It is an 18-hole, par 71 course designed by George W. Cobb. It features bent grass greens, a practice range with a covered hitting area, two putting greens and, during the season, it offers a series of golf schools. The Inn itself, once the home of Confederate General and Governor Wade Hampton, is in the National Register of Historic Places and the resort offers a variety of activities in addition to golf.

Golf is a natural in North Carolina. See you at the tee!

CARY PRIORITY CARE

URGENT CARE PROVIDED BY
Board-Certified
Emergency Physicians

Leslie McKinney, M.D., FACEP

Jennifer Swanson, M.D., FACEP

We specialize in providing urgent care to people of all age groups. Our main goal is to provide a convenient source of high-level medical expertise "for life's little emergencies."

- Injuries and Medical Illness
- Sports, Camp, DOT, Teacher Physicals
- Workers' Compensation
- Drug Screening • Flu Shots
- On-Site X-Ray and Lab

- Most Major Insurance Accepted, including: BC/BS, Cigna/Healthsource, Mamsi, MedCost & Partners, MediCare, UnitedHealthcare

8 AM - 8 PM
(Special Hours • Some Holidays!)
7 Days A Week
No Appointments Necessary

859-1136
212 Ashville Avenue, Suite 30
Cary, North Carolina 27511

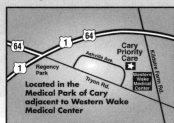

Located in the Medical Park of Cary adjacent to Western Wake Medical Center

www.caryprioritycare.citysearch.com

Health Care

You don't have to be an Insider to know that Triangle residents have access to some of the best medical care in the world. That's right, the world. There are two major medical centers here, one in Durham at Duke Medical Center and the other in Chapel Hill at the University of North Carolina Medical School and Memorial Hospital. Durham has three other general and specialty hospitals and Raleigh has three more general hospitals and two specialty hospitals. This lineup has been a big reason for the Triangle's high ratings in various magazines' quality of life surveys.

In this chapter, we provide you with an Insider's view of these health care resources and we also help you find a place to start when you select your own family physicians and specialists. As noted elsewhere in this book, because of the two large research hospitals here and the presence of major pharmaceutical companies, there are frequent calls for volunteers to participate in trials for new medicines and treatments. Normally, volunteers are paid for their services.

Finally, good health care is more than great ERs and operating rooms. It includes healthy diet, exercise and living so that you stay out of the operating rooms. This "wellness" trend has taken firm root in the Triangle. Joe and Terry Graedon, the people in The People's Pharmacy, broadcast from WUNC-FM, and medical centers such as Rex Healthcare in Raleigh offer "Wellness Centers" as part of their total health care mission. Also, Durham is know worldwide for its weight loss clinics, including the famous Rice Diet Clinic and the Duke University Diet and Fitness Center. Now, breathe deeply and start exercising your fingers by turning these pages!

FYI

Unless otherwise noted, the area code for all phone numbers listed in this guide is 919.

Hospitals
Cary

Western Wake Medical Center
1900 Kildaire Farm Rd., Cary
• **233-2300** • **www.wakemed.org**
In 1991, Wake Medical Center expanded into western Wake County with the opening of Western Wake Medical Center. This 80-bed community hospital offers a 24-hour emergency department, an intensive care unit, general medical/surgical and telemetry beds and outpatient diagnostic services. Western Wake is also the site of the Women's Pavilion and Birthplace, Cary's only obstetrical center, where about 1,300 babies are delivered annually. Wake Radiology Oncology Services, a state-of-the art, 65,000-square-foot cancer radiology center, opened at Western Wake in 1998. A $22-million expansion of Western Wake is scheduled for completion in early 2002. Among the additions will be the installation of a cardiac catheterization lab and an expansion of the Women's Pavilion.

Chapel Hill

UNC Healthcare System
101 Manning Dr. • 966-4131
• **www.unchealthcare.org**
Built in 1952 as a teaching hospital for the UNC School of Medicine, the UNC Healthcare complex has become one of the state's largest medical referral centers, drawing patients each year from throughout the Southeast for specialized diagnostic and treatment services. UNC Healthcare System

Duke University Health System provides a helicopter service for the quick transport of critically ill or injured patients.

contains 684 beds and serves as the community hospital for residents of Orange and adjacent counties. UNC Healthcare System also recently purchased Rex Healthcare in Raleigh.

The Healthcare System's staff is composed of faculty from the UNC Schools of Medicine and Dentistry. Many are recognized nationally and globally as experts in their fields. There are more than 900 attending physicians and about 560 interns and residents on the medical staff. Approximately 600,000 patients are treated here annually.

UNC Healthcare System was the first hospital in the nation to have an intensive care unit, and the present Adult and Pediatric Critical Care Center's services are among the most advanced facilities available. Accident and disaster victims from all over North Carolina use the services provided by the N.C. Jaycee Burn Center, the Trauma Center (designated as a Level 1 Center by the American College of Surgeons) and Carolina AirCare, the helicopter and ground patient transport service. UNC Healthcare System also has the UNC Lineburger Comprehensive Cancer Center, a nationally recognized Comprehensive Hemophilia Diagnosis and Treatment Center and an organ-transplant program.

UNC Healthcare System (which includes the main facility, the N.C. Women's Hospital, the N.C. Children's Hospital and the N.C. Neurosciences Hospital) and its medical staff

are recognized as leaders in the care of patients with diseases such as arthritis, cancer, digestive diseases, cystic fibrosis, growth disorders, neurological disorders, hemophilia and infertility. UNC Healthcare System is a major referral center for the care of premature infants and women with high-risk pregnancies. The new $140-million, state-of-the-art N.C. Children's Hospital and N.C. Women's Hospital are scheduled to open at UNC in December of 2000.

In a recent survey, U.S. News & World Report ranked UNC Healthcare System as one of "America's Best Hospitals" in the following categories: gastroenterology, geriatrics, gynecology, kidney disease, neurology, pulmonary care and urology.

UNC Healthcare System offers highly specialized care for patients with complex medical problems, as well as a complete range of high-quality, routine services for families. Expectant parents appreciate the family-centered maternal and infant care, including private delivery rooms with comfortable home-style furnishings and a visitation policy that allows siblings to visit as soon as the baby is born. More than 2,500 babies are delivered here annually.

UNC Healthcare System also offered one of the first outpatient surgery programs in the country, making it possible for more patients to avoid the necessity of a costly hospital stay for many types of surgery. The

Ambulatory Care Center offers an expanded outpatient surgery service, as well as more convenient and accessible acute and preventive medical care for children and adults. Elderly and home-bound patients can participate in the hospital's Lifeline program, which provides them with an electronic device so they can signal the hospital when they need emergency medical assistance.

UNC Healthcare Systems' staff physicians, who specialize in internal medicine, pediatrics, obstetrics and gynecology and family medicine, also provide day-to-day medical care. Call UNC HealthLink (966-7890) for information.

Durham

Durham is the City of Medicine. The medical industry is the town's top employer, utilizing almost a fourth of the city's work force. Here there are five major hospitals and a cadre of specialized diagnostic and treatment clinics. There are also a number of well-known weight-loss and fitness programs, most notably the world-famous Rice Diet Clinic.

Duke University Health System
Erwin Rd. • 684-8111
• www.mc.duke.edu
It all began in 1925 when tobacco magnate James Buchanan Duke bequeathed $4 million to the university named for his father for the purpose of constructing a medical school and hospital. Today, Duke University Medical Center is rated one of the best private tertiary-care facilities in the world. *U.S. News and World Report* recently ranked this teaching hospital sixth in the nation on an honor roll of top hospitals. Duke received top marks in the areas of digestive disorders, geriatrics, orthopedics, kidney disease and cancer treatment.

With more than 3 million square feet of space, Duke University Health System offers patient care, physician training and specialized research into the causes and treatment of disease. To give just one example, Duke is a major research and treatment center for pediatric and adult AIDS patients, one of a few sites in the nation (along with neighboring UNC Healthcare System) conducting clinical trials on new drugs used in the treatment of AIDS. Duke has also expanded its scope throughout the Triangle with recent acquisitions of Durham Regional Hospital and Raleigh Community Hospital.

Doctors and other hospitals refer patients from around the world to Duke University Health System. At the same time, it is a primary-care hospital for residents of the Durham area. Duke handles about 61,000 emergency department visits annually.

The original 400-bed facility opened in 1930 and today is licensed for 1,124 beds. The 870-plus bed North Division includes a 39-room operating suite, a burn-and-trauma unit and a helicopter service for the quick transport of critically ill or injured patients. In the Duke Children's Hospital, more than 132 beds are dedicated to children's services, making it one of the largest children's hospitals in the Southeast. Duke recently added a $34-million, Children's Health Center—a 65,000-square-foot outpatient facility.

Connected to the North Division is The Duke Eye Center, the only one of its scope between Baltimore and Miami, providing both patient care and research into the causes of eye disease.

The hospital's South Division includes nine buildings housing inpatients in psychiatry, medicine, surgery and obstetrics/gynecology, as well as outpatient clinics, an ambulatory surgery program, a rehabilitation unit and the Comprehensive Cancer Center, one of the only federally supported facilities of its magnitude between Washington, D.C., and Birmingham, Alabama. Other specialty facilities include the Heart Center, the Liver Center, the Alzheimer's Disease Research

Center, the Advanced Study of Epilepsy Center and the Sports Medicine Program.

Most doctors on the staff at Duke are also teachers in the School of Medicine here. The faculty of more than 2,000 clinical and research physicians includes many physicians who are world renowned in their fields. Duke University Health System's programs in surgery, cardiac care, obstetrics and gynecology, cancer treatment and AIDS research and treatment are among the many medical center services that are well known nationally and beyond.

Call 416-3853 to reach the Duke Consultation and Referral Center.

Durham Regional Hospital
3643 N. Roxboro Rd., North of I-85
• **470-4000**
• **www.drh.duhs.duke.edu**

Since opening its doors in 1976, this 447-bed facility has enjoyed a reputation as a fine community hospital. Duke University Health System took control of Durham Regional in 1998—negotiating a 20-year lease of the facility with Durham County.

Over the years, renovations at Durham Regional have improved access for outpatients and enhanced emergency room services and surgical capacity. A freestanding surgical facility called the Ambulatory Surgery Center lies across the street from Durham Regional and offers outpatient surgical services.

With about 450 medical staff members representing virtually all specialties of medicine (and about 700 nurses), Durham Regional Hospital offers personalized, quality health care services. Just ask a new mother. Durham Regional delivers more than 2,000 babies each year. Expectant parents are offered an orientation tour of the obstetrics facilities before the birth takes place. Many mothers are able to leave the hospital with their newborns within 24 hours of delivery.

Durham Regional Hospital's outpatient services are equally popular. For example, its day surgery program features a growing list of procedures that do not require an overnight hospital stay. The hospital offers special programs to help patients cope with a variety of problems, from asthma to backaches. There are even wellness classes to help you control your weight and to reduce stress through biofeedback.

Durham Regional Hospital, through its HomeCare health services, provides at-home nursing services for patients of all ages. The hospital also provides the Lifeline program that allows elderly, frail and handicapped patients to signal the hospital through an electronic device when they need emergency medical service.

Some of the other services affiliated with Durham Regional Hospital include: Lincoln Community Health Center, which offers a wide variety of outpatient medical services on a sliding fee scale; Oakleigh (309 Crutchfield Street, 470-6600), which provides treatment for adults and families suffering from alcoholism and drug dependency; Davis Center ambulatory surgery facility; Wellness Institute fitness facility; and Emergency Medical Services, which responds to medical emergencies with Advanced Life Support ambulances and can also provide non-emergency, Basic Life Support transportation. Its Wheelchair Van Service is for people confined to wheelchairs, or who do not have their own transportation. Durham Regional also operates the Watts School of Nursing, the oldest nursing program in North Carolina.

The Durham Regional Hospital Referral Service can be reached at 403-4374.

Lenox Baker Children's Hospital
3000 Erwin Rd. • 684-6669

An integral part of Duke University Health System, Lenox Baker provides pediatric rehabilitation services to patients from newborn through 18 years of age. Patients treated here have some type of physical, cognitive or medical disability that impairs their level of function. Services are provided by a multidisciplinary team to coordinate individual medical, surgical, therapeutic and/or psychosocial care. The hospital offers both inpatient and outpatient treatment through its clinics, inpatient units and the physical, occupational and speech therapy departments.

Specialized programs for children with brain injuries and physical disabilities are provided.

North Carolina Eye and Ear Hospital
1110 W. Main St. • 682-9341
911-A Ridge Rd., Roxboro • 597-2826

North Carolina Eye and Ear Hospital (formerly McPherson Hospital, founded in 1926) is a leading private hospital for treating the eye, ear, nose and throat. Today, it serves more than 70,000 patients a year from across the Southeast. A full-service eye clinic and ear, nose and throat clinic provide services ranging from routine eye and ear exams to more advanced treatments. The hospital provides overnight accommodations for patients requiring inpatient care.

Other services include allergy testing and treatment, pediatric eye and ear care, facial reconstructive and cosmetic surgery procedures, speech and hearing services and conveniently located optical centers at both its Durham and Roxboro locations.

Veterans Affairs Medical Center
508 Fulton St. • 286-0411 • www.va.gov

Established in 1953, this 502-bed general medical and surgical hospital shares many services and physicians with nearby Duke University Medical Center. It also operates a 120-bed nursing home unit. Through its affiliation with Duke, the VA Hospital participates in accredited residency training programs in psychiatry, internal medicine, general and thoracic surgery, anesthesiology, neurology, neurosurgery and ophthalmology, among other areas.

Specialized treatment for veterans is available in such areas as neurosurgery, plastic surgery, open-heart surgery, home dialysis and nuclear medicine. A 650,000-square-foot, $80-million expansion has been planned for the facility.

Raleigh

As throughout the nation, health care in Raleigh and Cary is changing. Physicians are consolidating practices and health care alliances are forming to offer families and patients lower medical costs. However, citizens' access to high quality medical care remains constant. Even when excluding UNC Healthcare System and Duke University Health System, Raleigh and Cary residents are served by three general hospitals and three specialty hospitals.

Dorothea Dix Hospital
820 S. Boylan Ave. • 733-5540

Dorothea Dix was a crusading Yankee who came South in 1848 and helped start the state's first programs for the mentally ill. In 1856, the state opened its first hospital for the mentally ill and it was appropriately named after the persistent Dorothea Dix. Today, the hospital occupies several hundred acres of rolling historic countryside southwest of downtown Raleigh, surrounded by highways and the Beltline, the Farmers Market and neighborhoods.

Dix Hospital has seen its resident patient load diminish as treatment of the mentally ill has de-emphasized institutionalization. With 442 beds, the hospital remains one of the state's

Photo by Rich Weidman

Duke University Health System recently negotiated a 20-year lease of Durham Regional Hospital with Durham County.

largest psychiatric hospitals for adults and adolescents, and it is accredited by the Joint Commission on Accredited Hospitals (JCAHO). It contains a full hospital staff with surgical and radiology units, a special children's psychiatric outpatient clinic and a new substance abuse treatment and rehabilitation center, as well as an adolescent education program and adolescent inpatient services.

The hospital often is the subject of news reports because it also provides forensic services and receives patients who are referred by the courts for one reason or another. As a state hospital, it accepts indigent patients and has a policy of billing patients according to their ability to pay.

Holly Hill/Charter Behavioral Health System
3019 Falstaff Rd. • 250-7000
Outpatient: 250-7206
Mental Health Options: (800) 242-7837

Founded in 1978, this system is a joint venture of Columbia Healthcare Corporation and Magellan Health Services. The combined facility offers a full continuum of mental health and chemical dependency services for adolescents, adults and older adults. The hospital has 108 beds and there are more than 50 psychiatrists who are active staff members.

Outpatient services include individual and group therapy, family therapy, day treatment programs and a chemical dependency intensive outpatient program. Inpatient services are provided for individuals with acute psychiatric or substance abuse problems. There is also a residential treatment center for adolescents, located at the North Raleigh site.

Holly Hill/Charter offers a 24-hour crisis intervention, assessment, information and referral service, free of charge to any individual seeking help for an emotional or chemical dependency problem.

Raleigh Community Hospital
3400 Wake Forest Rd. • 954-3000
• www.rch-hospital.org

Raleigh Community Hospital (RCH) opened its doors in 1978. It is conveniently located a block north of the I-440 Beltline exit onto Wake Forest Road. Formerly an affiliate of Columbia/HCA Healthcare Corporation, RCH was purchased by Duke University Health System in 1998.

Raleigh Community Hospital has 218 private and semiprivate beds, 15 of which are dedicated to intensive care. The hospital offers general medical and surgical services, and maintains an emergency room 24 hours a day with full-time emergency medicine physicians. An expansion of the Emergency Department is set for completion in the fall of 2001. The staff includes nearly 500 physicians, many of whom have offices located nearby.

Other services include The Childbirth Center, Level III Neonatal Intensive Care Nursery, Same-Day Surgery Center, Diabetes Treatment Center, Senior Health Center, Rehabilitation Services and Health Plus Wellness and Cardiac Rehab Center. RCH also offers Raleigh's only Psychiatric Unit within a full-service hospital. In addition, the hospital provides radiology, pathology, CT and MRI scanners, respiratory therapy and a sleep-study center. A full-service pharmacy, The Plaza Pharmacist, is located on the RCH campus, as well as Raleigh Sports Medicine and Physical Therapy.

A member of the American Hospital Association, Raleigh Community Hospital earned the distinction of being the only hospital in the Triangle to receive Accreditation with Commendation by the Joint Commission on Accreditation of Healthcare Organizations in 1995. Less than 5 percent of all hospitals in the nation receive this distinction.

INSIDERS' TIP

The health care community is very dynamic in the Triangle. Duke University Health System is now operating Durham's largest public hospital, Durham Regional, and has purchased the for-profit Raleigh Community Hospital. Meanwhile, the UNC Healthcare System in Chapel Hill recently purchased the private, nonprofit Rex Healthcare in Raleigh, the city's oldest (1894) and second largest hospital.

Photo by Rich Weidman

Rex Healthcare became part of UNC Health Care System in the spring of 2000.

RCH's Physician Referral Service can be reached at (800) 382-4095.

Rex Healthcare
4420 Lake Boone Tr. • 784-3100
• www.rexhealth.com

Rex is the city's oldest hospital and its board of directors has always included the names of Raleigh's power elite. It's more than a city hospital; it is Raleigh history as well, tracing its roots to John Rex, a merchant and property owner who left money and land in 1839 to establish a hospital for the capital city. It took city leaders until 1894, however, before they erected a hospital bearing the Rex name on South Street. Since then, Rex has migrated about town and, in 1980, moved to its current facilities on a 62-acre site at the intersection of Blue Ridge Road and Lake Boone Trail. It is both the city's oldest and newest hospital and takes pride in its history as a not-for-profit institution.

In April 2000, Rex became part of UNC Health Care System. The partnership strengthens Rex's ability to offer high-quality, cost-effective healthcare to the community. Rex also benefits from UNC's ability to introduce new treatment capabilities and advances in care.

Rex has 394 beds, all of them in private rooms, and includes a family birthing center with 40 rooms. More importantly, over 3,500 employees at Rex include some of the best physicians in the Triangle and its Cancer Center is as good as you will find, which is reflected in the 40,000 cancer treatments it performs annually. The Family Birth Center delivers nearly 5,000 babies annually, which is more than any other Triangle hospital. Rex's Wellness Centers, including the $8.5 million, 62,000-square-foot health and wellness center on Cary Parkway, have become popular with the fitness crowd.

As a full-service integrated health care organization, Rex provides care in obstetrics, pediatrics, surgery and the latest in 24-hour emergency-room care. It also has a same-day surgery unit. Rex's specialized departments include clinical laboratories, intensive care, cardiac care and rehabilitation, nursery, physical therapy, radiation and radiology, respiratory therapy and a telemetry unit. Rex's Heart Center offers cardiac catheterization, angioplasty, atheretomy and open heart surgery. It also has a 140-bed convalescent-care center. Rex's home care division, Rex Home Services, makes thousands of home visits to patients every year. Rex is fully accredited with the JCAHO and maintains the Rex Blood Plan, a not-for-profit community blood bank.

Rex recently completed construction of a new Emergency Department and also opened an adult day care and diabetes education center. A 107-bed convalescent care center, Rex Nursing Care Center of Apex, recently opened. Call 363-6011 for more information.

WakeMed
3000 New Bern Ave. • 250-8000
• **www.wakemed.org**

WakeMed is Wake County's largest general hospital, and as a public hospital, it maintains a high standard of care and serves all citizens regardless of their ability to pay. Today, it offers the most advanced technology available through its 746-bed, five-hospital system, 68-bed Rehabilitation Institute and the Medical Education Institute.

The state-of-the-art WakeMed Heart Center contains all of the latest technology and an experienced staff of cardiologists, cardiovascular surgeons and critical care nurses who perform the most advanced cardiology procedures. The Heart Center also provides a mobile cardiac care fleet, cardiac rehabilitation and an educational resource center. More than 1,000 open heart surgeries are performed annually at the Heart Center, one of the top three centers for the treatment of heart disease in the state.

Changing and growing according to community needs, Wake Medical offers vital services, including the only trauma center in the county, a Maternity Center where more than 3,600 babies are born every year, and a growing pediatric department that includes a children's emergency transport service, all on the central campus on New Bern Avenue just off I-440. A special $2 million Children's Emergency Department, one of only two in the state, opened in 1997. WakeMed recently proposed a $4.3 million expansion of its intensive-care nursery to address the growing numbers of premature and at-risk babies.

WakeMed opened Western Wake Medical Center in Cary in 1991. Southern Wake in Fuquay-Varina and Eastern Wake in Zebulon are short-term skilled nursing facilities. WakeMed also plans to build a $26-million medical complex in North Raleigh near Wakefield.

At WakeMed's Medical Education Institute are 45 outpatient clinics, the Area Health Education Center (AHEC) for continuing education programs and a full-service Medical Library. The Center features Healthworks, a cardiac rehabilitation center, and two mobile cardiac care units for specialized ground transportation of patients from eastern North Carolina. The 56-bed Wake Rehabilitation Hospital is the county's only inpatient rehab hospital serving patients recuperating from stroke, traumatic brain injury, multiple trauma, arthritis, neurological disorders and orthopedic conditions. After discharge, many patients continue treatment through the Rehabilitation Institute on Wake Forest Road.

The most advanced neonatal intensive care nursery in Wake County is at WakeMed, and a 38-bed maternity center offers family-centered, single-room care for women who want to labor, deliver and complete their hospital stay in the same room. In the Neuro-Intensive Care Unit, patients with back and neck problems have access to the area's only endovascular specialist, neuropathologist and neuroradiologist.

WakeMed's team includes more than 4,000 nurses, technologists and support staff, and an affiliated physician staff of over 700. The hospital is proud of its history of delivering quality care and was the first hospital in Wake County to have CAT scan and MRI services. A teaching hospital, WakeMed is affiliated with the University of North Carolina at Chapel Hill School of Medicine.

The WakeMed Physican Referral Service can be reached at 350-8900.

Medical Care

Triangle residents have access to a wide range of primary and specialty care. The medical delivery system here has been changing rapidly during the past decade. In some ways, there is more competition among doctors and dentists than ever before as urgent care centers and Health Maintenance Organizations (HMOs) have proliferated in our area. However, the growth of HMOs has resulted in some consolidation of medical services as practices have merged or been bought by local hospitals or HMOs. There are a large number of doctors, dentists and health care specialists, many of whom trained in the Triangle's nationally recognized teaching hospitals. Among the area hospitals, HMOs and private practitioners, you will easily find quality medical care.

For your family or "primary-care" physician, however, you want to find a family practitioner or an internist for the adults in your family and a pediatrician or family practitioner for the children.

How do you find such a physician? Many people ask a trusted friend or neighbor to recommend a doctor. If you know a staff member at a local hospital, he or she can often be a good, unofficial source. If you call a physician who is not taking new patients, ask his or her office staff to recommend someone else.

Some people may prefer a group practice that includes not only internists or primary care physicians but also specialists in other areas such as heart, lung, digestive and infectious diseases. A group practice can be a good choice for a family who knows it will need such specialty care because of existing medical conditions. If you're middle-aged or younger and healthy, an internist, family practitioner and (if you have kids) a pediatrician should be able to provide any needed care. The local telephone book's Yellow Pages, county medical societies and community hospitals all can provide some information about physicians in your town.

Chapel Hill

Chapel Hill medical care is impressive in both its quality and diversity.

UNC Healthcare Services
Manning Drive • 966-4131

Many Chapel Hill area residents go to the staff and clinics at UNC Hospitals and the UNC School of Medicine for their day-to-day medical care. Just call for an appointment. There are also walk-in clinics for people who do not have a regular doctor and need to see someone right away. If you need more information prior to making an appointment, call UNC HealthLink, 966-7890. HealthLink is staffed by registered nurses who provide health information and easy access to

medical services at UNC Hospitals. Here are brief descriptions of some of the services available:

The Ambulatory Care Center is on the corner of Mason Farm Road and South Columbia Street. The ACC features modern treatment and exam rooms and spacious waiting areas with playrooms for children. There is ample on-site parking. Other outpatient services available at UNC Hospitals include Internal Medicine Clinic, Surgery Clinics, Pediatrics, Outpatient Surgical Services and Pediatric Acute Care Service.

The Family Practice Center, 966-0211, on Manning Drive near U.S. 15-501 Bypass, houses family physicians who can provide general medical care for every member of the family, including obstetrics, pediatrics and minor surgery.

Chatham Crossing Medical Center (formerly Fearrington Medical Center), 960-6094, is a UNC Healthcare System outpatient center offering internal medicine and physical therapy at Chatham Crossing Shopping Center.

Durham

More than 1,500 licensed doctors make Durham's physician-to-patient ratio better than five times the national average.

UNC Healthcare System has grown into one of the state's largest medical referral centers.

How does a newcomer know where to turn for medical care? Probably the best way is to ask your friends or coworkers for recommendations. Or try one of the sources listed below.

Durham-Orange County Medical Society
• 383-2602

Durham Regional Hospital Referral Service
• 403-4DRH (4374)

Duke Family Medicine Center
2100 Erwin Rd. (Pickens Bldg.) • 684-6721

Sponsored by Duke University, this facility offers health care for the entire family, including OB/GYN, family counseling and substance abuse evaluation.

Lincoln Community Health Center
1301 Fayetteville St. • 956-4000

Lincoln Community Health Center offers an extensive range of medical services to patients on a sliding-fee basis. Services offered under the sponsorship of Durham Regional Hospital (see "Hospitals" section of this chapter) include medical care for the whole family, mental health counseling, dental care and health education.

Diet and Fitness Centers

Durham has a number of well-known weight-loss and fitness programs, earning Durham an international reputation as the Diet Capital of the World. Here are brief descriptions of three of the best known.

Duke University Diet and Fitness Center
804 W. Trinity Ave. • 684-6331
• www.dukecenter.org

Part of Duke's Health System's Center for Living, this program offers a comprehensive treatment and education plan for individuals with weight management problems. Long-term lifestyle changes are the goal here, and the center emphasizes nutrition, behavior and fitness. Psychologists and their staff of physicians work with patients to achieve and maintain weight-loss.

Rice Diet Clinic
4020 N. Roxboro St. • 286-2243
• www.ricediet.com

The Rice Diet is the reason that Durham has become a mecca for dieters and a spawning ground for dozens of innovative weight-reduction centers. At the Rice Diet Clinic, patients are put on a strict, six-phase eating plan calling for initial emphasis on rice and fruit, eventually followed by steamed vegetables, chicken, fish, eggs and an average weight loss of 15 to 25 pounds in 2 weeks.

Structure House
3017 Pickett Rd. • 493-4205
• www.structurehouse.com

Structure House claims to be the first intensive residential weight-control program in the nation to successfully combine psychology and lifestyle counseling with medicine, nutrition and exercise. Started in 1977, Structure House is the brainchild of Dr. Gerard Musante, the first psychologist in the United States to treat obesity as a psychological, rather than a physical problem.

Raleigh and Cary

We have combined Raleigh and Cary medical information since the subject spills over city lines; Cary residents, for example, may use Raleigh-based physicians and vice versa.

The free Physician Referral line is open from 10 AM until 5 PM Monday through Friday to provide names and phone numbers of local physicians who have indicated they are taking new patients. Information about a physician's medical education is available only if the physician is a member of the Wake County Medical Society.

The Wake Dental Society has a similar referral system and you can get that information by calling the state society's office and asking for the number of the current Wake County chapter president.

The Triangle United Way provides First Call, a free information and referral service, at 460-1811 (Wake County) or 688-2316 (Durham County). The Cary Chamber of Commerce also publishes a list of local physicians and dentists.

Meanwhile, if you sprain your ankle moving in or your child runs a fever before you've found a family physician, you may want to try one of the area's urgent care centers. For major emergencies you must go to the Emergency Room at one of Raleigh's three major hospitals.

Below are contact numbers for healthcare sources.

Wake County Medical Society
222 N. Person St., Raleigh • 821-2227

N.C. Dental Society
P.O. Box 4099, Cary, 27519 • 677-1396
• www.ncdental.org

N.C. Chiropractic Association
333 Fayetteville Street Mall, Raleigh
• 832-0611
• www.chirolink.com/ncca

The Alcoholism Treatment Center
3000 Falstaff Rd. • 250-1500

A Wake County Human Services agency, the center provides outpatient services and has 34 beds for inpatient services. If you're a member of AA and want to find a local chapter, the center can help you. It is a licensed psychiatric hospital with a full nursing staff and certified alcoholism counselors, and there is a substance abuse day-treatment program. Services also include family counseling for those who live with alcoholics and substance abusers.

Planned Parenthood
100 South Boylan Ave. • 833-7526

Located at the corner of West Morgan Street and South Boylan Avenue near downtown, the local chapter provides family planning programs for individuals as well as organizations such as church youth groups. It also conducts pregnancy tests and gynecological exams, but performs no abortions. It does make referrals.

Carolina Breast Cancer Detection Centers
300 Ashville Ave., Ste. 100, Cary • 233-5338
110 S. Estes Dr., Chapel Hill • 942-3196
3821 Merton Dr., Raleigh • 787-7411
4301 Lake Boone Tr., Raleigh • 781-6707

These local, state-of-the-art centers specialize in the detection of breast cancer. Physicians serving the branches are on staff at WakeMed.

Wake County Mental Health, Developmental Disabilities and Substance Abuse Services
3010 Falstaff Rd. • 250-3100
401 E. Whitaker Mill Rd. • 856-6400
Evaluation & Emergency Services: 250-3133
• web.co.wake.nc.us/humnserv

Services of this public service agency are delivered in many locations throughout Wake County by agency staff or through contract affiliates. Assistance is offered for children, adults and families affected by mental illness, developmental disabilities and/or substance abuse. Services include assessment and treatment, emergency care, case management, brief individual/family therapy, community support services, mobile crisis intervention, services for persons who are deaf or hearing impaired, vocational services, psychiatric services and medication monitoring. Court-ordered evaluation and treatment are offered here as well as an in-home assistance program, intervention services, housing assistance and services for the homeless. Regular hours for outpatient services are Monday through Friday, 8:30 AM until 5:15 PM. Evaluation and emergency services are available 24 hours a day, seven days a week. Fees vary according to the type of service provided.

INSIDERS' TIP

The Healing Place will open in 2001 on the campus of Dorothea Dix Hospital in Raleigh as a new, nonprofit treatment and rehabilitation center for poor people suffering from substance abuse.

Photo by Rich Weidman

Set amid the rolling countryside of Chatham County, Fearrington House provides luxurious quarters in the tradition of the 18th-century country retreat.

Inns and B&Bs

To experience true Southern hospitality, nothing beats a weekend stay at a bed and breakfast inn. Although the Triangle will never rival Charleston or New England for its bed and breakfast offerings, the area does boast more than a dozen delightful such places to stay. Most inns here occupy meticulously restored historic homes; a few are even listed on the National Register of Historic Places. One inn occupies the site of a 19th-century preparatory school and another once served as the home of noted playwright Paul Green (*The Lost Colony*). The Triangle's oldest inn, the 1759 Colonial Inn, once hosted the likes of Aaron Burr, Dolley Madison and Lord Cornwallis. The most recent entry to the list, the Cameron Park Inn, is located in a newly renovated 1916 house near downtown Raleigh.

Always call ahead for specific questions you may have about children, pets, smoking and methods of payment. Also ask what constitutes breakfast and clear any special dietary needs. Innkeepers are also typically knowledgeable about the area and will usually assist you with directions and useful tips on restaurants, shopping and attractions.

Each bed and breakfast inn listed below promises a unique experience; each is a destination in itself. For more information on bed and breakfasts throughout the state, contact the North Carolina Bed and Breakfast Association, (800) 849-5392, P.O. Box 1077, Asheville, NC 28802 (www.ncbbi.org) and request a copy of the annual *Guide to North Carolina Bed & Breakfasts and Inns*.

Price Code

We have categorized bed and breakfasts with one to four dollar signs ($), based on the typical daily rates charged for a standard room with two double beds:

$	Under $50
$$	$51-$75
$$$	$76-$100
$$$$	$101-up

Keep in mind that this is a guide and rates may change.

Apex

B&B's Country Garden Inn
$$$-$$$$ • 1041 Kelly Rd. • 303-8003
www.b-and-b-country-inn.com

Located in a secluded country setting, this very modern, three-room Inn is surrounded by beautiful ponds and gardens. Innkeepers Bud and Beth McKinney opened B&B's Country Inn in 1997. Guests can enjoy the cozy family room, complete with TV and games. Other amenities include a home-cooked breakfast, large sun deck with grill and picnic table and a hot tub. The Inn is also available for small weddings, bridal showers, church groups and meetings.

Pearson Place Bed & Breakfast
$$-$$$ • 1009 North Salem St. • 362-4290

Opened by innkeepers Jeanne and David Floyd in 1997, this elegantly decorated 1920 Victorian farmhouse offers two guest rooms, each with a private bath. A full breakfast is served. The Inn sits on two acres of land and is a popular spot for indoor and outdoor weddings, parties, luncheons and teas.

Chapel Hill

Fearrington House Country Inn
$$$$ • Fearrington Village, Pittsboro • 542-2121 • www.fearringtonhouse.com

A luxurious 31-unit Inn, Fearrington evokes images of an 18th-century country retreat, complete with cozy suites, exquisitely landscaped gardens and Belted Galloway cows grazing in the pasture.

Each room is uniquely decorated with antiques. In addition to the country charm, there are plenty of civilized touches: stereo music, modern baths, a full gourmet breakfast and a complimentary afternoon tea. The Country Inn is located at Fearrington Village, a 1,100-acre planned residential development located on a former dairy farm about 6 miles south of Chapel Hill.

In addition to the Inn and restaurant, there is the Fearrington Market, where you'll find fresh bagels and breads, gourmet coffee, wines, cheeses and a wide assortment of gifts. You may spend time strolling through the gardens or shopping at The Fearrington Village Shops.

The Inn at Bingham School
$$-$$$$ • 6720 Mebane Oaks Rd., Orange Cty. • 563-5583, (800) 566-5583 • www.chapel-hill-inn.com

Located 10 miles west of Chapel Hill in the countryside on the site of the old Bingham Preparatory School (1845-65), the Inn offers a convenient and comfortable retreat. Meticulously restored, the former headmaster's home (listed on the National Historic Registry) is now a cozy bed and breakfast getaway. The owners received an award from Preservation North Carolina for the restoration.

Furnished in period antiques, the Inn offers five spacious guest rooms with fireplaces and private baths, including one with a whirlpool. One room is located away from the main house in a building called The Milk House.

During your stay, you'll be invited to relax by the fire, roam the surrounding farm and woodlands, enjoy complimentary wine and

Photo courtesy of The Arrowhead Inn

Built in 1775, The Arrowhead Inn offers a wide variety of accommodations, including a private cabin in the backyard.

cheese or join in a game of croquet. A complete gourmet breakfast is served in either the formal dining room or the outside patio.

Windy Oaks Inn
$$ • The Paul Green Homeplace, 1164 Old Lystra Church Rd., Chatham Cty. • 942-1001

A century-old farmhouse that once served as the home of Pulitzer Prize-winning playwright Paul Green (*The Lost Colony*), The Windy Oaks Inn has been lovingly renovated. Located on 25 oak-shaded acres about 4 miles south of Chapel Hill, the Inn has four guest rooms, including one with a shared bath. Each room is furnished with period antiques. Full country breakfasts, featuring delicious homemade biscuits, are served. Guests also enjoy afternoon refreshments. The Inn can also accommodate weddings, parties and luncheon meetings.

Durham

Arrowhead Inn
**$$$-$$$$ • 106 Mason Rd. • 477-8430
• www.arrowheadinn.com**

The five-foot-high arrowhead marker that sits in front of the Arrowhead Inn commemorates the Great Trading Path to the Smoky Mountains. Situated on six acres north of town, the Inn is an elegant plantation home built in 1774. It features nine guest rooms, all furnished in antiques and country primitives. Fireplaces, spa whirlpool tubs, TV/VCRs, phones and data ports are found throughout the Inn. Downstairs in the Keeping Room, guests can sit by the fireplace, play the piano, watch TV or relax with an assortment of games.

Each guest receives a hearty gourmet breakfast prepared by the innkeeper chefs,

Phil and Gloria Teber. The Inn can also accommodate small meetings and weddings.

The Blooming Garden Inn
**$$$-$$$$ • 513 Holloway St. • 687-0801
• www.bbonline.com/nc/bloominggarden/index.html**

The Blooming Garden is an 1892 yellow Victorian Inn that features leaded, beveled and stained-glass windows, a custom picket fence, a wraparound porch and lots of blooms in season. The Inn boasts four beautifully appointed rooms, including two luxury suites with whirlpool baths, lace curtains, antiques and artwork set in a tasteful mix of warm colors. In addition, the popular "Holly House" cottage across the street from the Inn, is available for a minimum stay of one week. The Southern hospitality of innkeepers Dolly and Frank Pokrass makes this place a special treat. Guests enjoy a full gourmet breakfast on a relaxed schedule. Children are also welcome. Convenient to Duke University, Ninth Street and Brightleaf Square, The Blooming Garden Inn is a pleasant place to spend a few days.

Morehead Manor Bed & Breakfast
**$$$-$$$$ • 914 Vickers Ave.
• 687-4366 • www.moreheadmanor.com**

Morehead Manor, which opened in 1997, offers elegant accommodations in a splendidly decorated 8,000-square-foot, 1910 Colonial Revival style home. The Inn provides four common areas and four large guest rooms with private baths, including a honeymoon suite with a fireplace and sitting area.

The Inn is conveniently located within walking distance to the Durham Bulls Athletic Park, Brightleaf Square, Duke University's East Campus and downtown Durham. Innkeepers Daniel and Monica Edwards can

---

FYI

Unless otherwise noted, the area code for all phone numbers listed in this guide is 919.

INSIDERS' TIP

Insiders believe that in addition to Aaron Burr and Lord Cornwallis, George Washington also slept at Hillsborough's Colonial Inn. He had black-eyed peas and country ham for dinner. Really.

Hillsborough's Colonial Inn, built in 1759, is one of the 10 oldest inns in continuous operation in the United States.

Photo by Rich Weidman

assist guests with their sightseeing, shopping and dinner plans, if asked. The Morehead Manor is also available for weddings, private parties, corporate retreats and receptions.

Old North Durham Inn
$$$-$$$$ • 922 N. Mangum St. • 683-1885
• www.bbonline.com/nc/oldnorth

An intimate bed and breakfast located in the heart of Durham less than a mile from Duke University, the Old North Durham Inn offers 19th-century charm in one of Durham's oldest residential neighborhoods. In addition to the four lovely guest rooms with private baths, a family suite with two rooms is available. Amenities include fireplaces, televisions, VCRs, a whirlpool tub and complimentary refreshments. Relax on a rocking chair on the Inn's inviting wraparound porch. Innkeepers Debbie and Jim Vickery truly make visitors "welcome" by offering a full breakfast and free tickets to Durham Bulls home games at the nearby Durham Bulls Athletic Park.

Hillsborough

Colonial Inn
$$ • 153 W. King St. • 732-2461
• www.colonialinn.citysearch.com

Built in 1759, the Colonial Inn is one of the 10 oldest inns in continuous operation in the United States. It has provided lodging for the likes of Aaron Burr, Dolley Madison and Lord Cornwallis from our Colonial Period. It welcomes today's guests with quality service and Southern charm.

Located in historic Hillsborough about 10 miles north of Chapel Hill, the Inn, operated by Carlton and Sara McKee, has eight guest rooms. Throughout the building you'll see many antiques, including some of the original furnishings.

Guests will enjoy dining on Southern-style food in the Inn's restaurant, antique hunting in downtown Hillsborough or just sitting on rocking chairs on one of the porches overlooking this historic town.

Hillsborough House Inn
$$$-$$$$ • 209 E. Tryon St. • 644-1600
• www.hillsboroughinn.citysearch.com

The Hillsborough House Inn has six charming guest rooms. One is a suite in a renovated 1790's kitchen building, perfect for a romantic getaway. Guests may enjoy the pool, as well as a full breakfast and afternoon refreshments. Children over 10 are welcome. Pets may be boarded at a nearby kennel if prior arrangements are made.

The Inn at Teardrop
$$-$$$$ • 175 W. King St. • 732-1120

Located in the historic district of Hillsborough, this 18th-century Inn offers a charming retreat. Proprietor Tom Roberts—who opened the six-room Inn in 1987—invites guests to stroll in his gardens and relax in the elegantly furnished parlor or on the back veranda.

Occupied alternately as a residence and an inn since 1767, this lovely 2 1/2-story home is furnished in antiques and features reproductions by local craftsman Stephen Jones. Rates include a deluxe continental breakfast.

Raleigh

Cameron Park Inn
$$$-$$$$ • 211 Groveland Ave.
• 835-2171 • www.cameronparkinn.com

Built in 1916, this newly renovated, three-story home close to NCSU and downtown Raleigh has four bedrooms, two of which are suites. Beautifully appointed with private baths, the Inn has front porch, rocking chair charm along with FAX and copy machines and complimentary soft drinks and snacks. (This is the South, you know.) It is located in one of Raleigh's nicest neighborhoods and offers precious off-street parking. The innkeepers have worked all their lives in Raleigh, so they know the place. (Don't tell them that their prices are a bargain.)

Oakwood Inn Bed & Breakfast
$$$-$$$$ • 411 N. Bloodworth St.
• 832-9712 • members.aol.com/ oakwoodbb

Opened in 1984, this bed and breakfast is located in historic Oakwood, a neighborhood behind the Governor's Mansion in downtown Raleigh. Business travelers with appointments in North Carolina's capital city will find the Oakwood Inn a welcome respite. Built in 1871 as the Raynor Stronach House, the Inn is listed on the National Register of Historic Places and has a wraparound porch and six rooms, all with private baths and telephones. The rooms are exquisitely furnished, entirely in Victorian decor. Guests get the "chef's choice" breakfast and afternoon refreshments. Each room has a TV and fireplace. Fax and copy machines are also available.

William Thomas House
$$$-$$$$ • 530 N. Blount St.
• 755-9400 • www.williamthomashouse.com

Built in 1881 as an office and home for a prominent Raleigh attorney on Raleigh's finest residential row, this bed and breakfast is within walking distance of many downtown attractions, including the Executive Mansion, State Capitol, Museum of History and Museum of Natural Sciences. The Inn is operated by former Secretary of Administration Jim Lofton and his wife, Sarah, who know government and state history from an Insider's view.

Today, the elegant Victorian house offers four guest rooms named after the Thomas' family members. Rooms come with private baths, cable TV and refrigerators. The porch has rocking chairs and a swing. A full breakfast and turndown service are also included. The Inn offers a library and business amenities such as fax and copy machines. The Inn is also available for weddings, receptions and small private luncheons and dinners.

Kidstuff and Camps

The Triangle area contains a multitude of places, events and activities that appeal to the kid in all of us. Museums, historic sites, art centers, arcades, water parks, planetariums, zoos, skating rinks, parks and more beckon youngsters to play, learn and explore. The possibilities here are almost limitless.

New and improved attractions for kids seem to be sprouting up everywhere. For example, the N.C. State Museum of Natural Sciences in downtown Raleigh recently opened its new 200,000-square-foot facility, the largest museum of its kind in the Southeast. Also downtown, Exploris, the world's only interactive global experience center, opened its doors in the fall of 1999. Durham's Museum of Life and Science added a three-story Magic Butterfly House with a state-of-the-art insectarium.

The Triangle also boasts an abundance of outdoor recreational opportunities at hot spots like Bond Park in Cary, Eno River State Park in Durham and Pullen Park in Raleigh.

Free specialty publications such as *Carolina Parent* and *Kidsville News, The Triangle's Fun Family Newspaper* are good sources for information on upcoming family events and activities. *Carolina Parent* also publishes a special annual edition on summer camps. Also check out the weekly *Independent* and *Spectator*, as well as the Friday entertainment sections in the *News and Observer* and *Herald-Sun*.

For more fun-filled ideas for kids, browse through our chapters on "Attractions," "Annual Events," "Arts and Culture," "Daytrips and Weekend Vacations," "Spectator Sports" and "Parks and Recreation."

Clubs

Boy Scouts
3231 Atlantic Ave., Raleigh • 872-4884
Girl Scouts
6901 Pinecrest Dr., Raleigh • 782-3021
Boys & Girls Clubs of Wake County
701 Raleigh Blvd., Raleigh • 834-6282
John Avery Boys & Girls Club, Inc.
808 E. Pettigrew St., Durham • 688-7315

Educational Explorations

Chapel Hill

Ackland Art Museum
South Columbia St. at E. Franklin St.,
UNC-CH Campus • 966-5736
• www.ackland.org

The Ackland Art Museum's small but very fine collection spans the ages, from ancient Greek and Roman sculptures to modern paintings, and the variety will keep children interested. The museum usually hosts a display of a lovely hand-built Victorian doll house during November and December. Admission is free.

ArtsCenter
300-G E. Main St., Carrboro
• 929-ARTS

The ArtsCenter offers classes, Saturday morning "Kids Cabaret" performances, family concerts and summer day camp programs. It is a great resource, providing almost limitless entertainment and educational services for children and parents. Call for a current schedule of classes and upcoming events.

Chapel Hill Public Library
100 Library Dr. • 968-2777
Children's Room • 968-2778

The public library is truly a delight for children of all ages. The library's Children's Collection contains thousands of books. One of its special programs for children is the "Dial-a-story" service (968-0222).

Horace Williams House
610 E. Rosemary St. • 942-7818

The Horace Williams House, the restored home of a former UNC-CH professor, occasionally hosts exhibits of interest to children. Shows change monthly. The house is located on a big lawn, perfect for rambling. The huge magnolia tree is an ideal hideout for little ones. The Chapel Hill Preservation Society maintains the house and sometimes sponsors events such as an afternoon of storytelling. Admission to the house is free. A Historic Trolley Tour is offered every Wednesday afternoon at 2 PM from April through November.

Morehead Planetarium
250 E. Franklin St. • 962-1236
For show times: 549-6863
• **www.morehead.unc.edu**

The Morehead Planetarium offers a changing schedule of shows throughout the year, from UFOs to the age of the dinosaurs to black holes and much more. Four new exhibits were added recently: "The History of Astronomy at UNC-CH," "How Big are the Planets?," "What Causes Daytime and Nighttime?" and "Why Does the Moon Change Shape?" On Friday afternoon and evenings, Sky Rambles gives a look at the current night sky. A small gift shop has a nice selection of astronomy and science-related toys, most less than a couple of dollars. There are also Saturday classes (like model rocket launching) and summer day camp programs for kids.

Durham

Bennett Place
4409 Bennett Memorial Rd.
• **383-4345**

Bennett Place is the site of negotiations that led to the largest troop surrender of the Civil War, when Confederate General Joseph Johnston surrendered his troops to General William Tecumseh Sherman. Now a state historic site, Bennett Place offers exhibits, historic buildings and a video presentation for visitors. A highlight of the site's annual calendar is the April Civil War reenactment, complete with period costumes and replicas of Civil War era weapons. Admission is free.

Duke Homestead & Tobacco Museum
2828 Duke Homestead Rd. • 477-5498
• **metalab.unc.edu/dukehome**

Duke Homestead, another state historic site, is the restored home and tobacco farm of Washington Duke. The house, curing barn, pack house and other outbuildings on the grounds are all part of the living history program offered here. Staff members re-create late 19th-century farm life with special programs each fall and spring. The Homestead hosts a Tobacco Harvest Festival in July and a Christmas by Candlelight tour each December. Admission is free.

Duke University Museum of Art
East Campus • 684-5135
• **www.duke.edu/web/duma**

Duke's Museum of Art houses several art collections of interest to children. While downstairs exhibits periodically, the upstairs displays statues of Classical heroes. It is open daily, except Monday. Admission is free.

Durham Arts Council
120 Morris St. • 560-ARTS
• **www.durhamarts.org**

DAC sponsors year-round classes in all art disciplines, with special classes for children. In

---

INSIDERS' TIP

Some activities to keep kids busy on rainy days: bowling, movies, indoor skating and soccer, museum classes and library storytimes.

THEME PARKS & DAYTRIPS FOR CHILDREN

Battleship North Carolina	Wilmington	910-350-1817
Busch Gardens	Williamsburg, VA	757-253-3350
Cape Fear Museum	Wilmington	910-341-7413
Celebration Station	Greensboro	336-316-0606
Cherokee Fun Park	Cherokee	828-497-5877
Chimney Rock Park	Chimney Rock	828-625-9611
Colonial Williamsburg	Williamsburg, VA	800-999-4485
Diamond Shoals Family Fun Park	Kill Devil Hills	252-480-3553
Discovery Place	Charlotte	704-372-6261
Emerald Pointe Water Park	Greensboro	336-852-9721
Emerald Village	Spruce Pine	828-765-6463
Fascinate-U Children's Museum	Fayetteville	910-433-1573
Fort Macon State Park	Atlantic Beach	252-726-3775
Gem Mountain	Spruce Pine	828-765-6130
Ghost Town in the Sky	Maggie Valley	828-926-1140
Grandfather Mountain	Linville	828-733-2013
Greensboro Children's Museum	Greensboro	336-574-2898
Hill Ridge Farms	Youngsville	919-556-1771
Imagination Station	Wilson	252-291-5113
Jockey's Ridge State Park	Nags Head	252-441-7132
Jubilee Amusement Park	Carolina Beach	910-458-9017
Jungle Rapids Family Fun Park	Wilmington	910-791-0666
Kings Dominion	Doswell, VA	804-876-5000
Linville Caverns	Marion	828-756-4171
Museum of Coastal Carolina	Ocean Isle Beach	910-579-1016
Mystery Hill	Blowing Rock	828-264-2792
National Railroad Museum	Hamlet	910-582-3317
Natural Science Center	Greensboro	336-288-3769
North Carolina Aquarium	Fort Fisher	910-458-8257
North Carolina Aquarium	Manteo	252-473-3493
North Carolina Aquarium	Pine Knoll Shores	252-247-4003
North Carolina Maritime Museum	Beaufort	252-728-7317
North Carolina Railroad Museum	New Hill	919-362-5416
North Carolina Zoo	Asheboro	800-488-0444
Old Salem	Winston-Salem	888-328-5360
Pack Place	Asheville	828-257-4500
Paramount's Carowinds	Charlotte	800-888-4386
Roanoke Island Festival Park	Manteo	252-475-1500
Santa's Land Park & Zoo	Cherokee	828-497-9191
Sciworks	Winston-Salem	336-767-6730
Soco Gardens Zoo	Maggie Valley	828-926-1746
Tote-'em-In Zoo	Wilmington	910-791-0472
Tryon Palace	New Bern	252-514-4900
Tweetsie Railroad	Blowing Rock	800-526-5740
Wilmington Children's Museum	Wilmington	910-254-3534
Wilmington Railroad Museum	Wilmington	910-763-2634
Wright Brothers National Memorial	Kill Devil Hills	252-441-7430

Photo courtesy of Exploris

Exploris, the world's first interactive global experience center, offers dynamic hands-on and interactive exhibits for children of all ages.

the summer, DAC sponsors longer classes for kids. Check out the Young People's Performing Company, a theater troupe for younger people.

Durham County Library System
300 N. Roxboro St. • 560-0100

One of our favorite recommendations for a children's activity, libraries now boast a lot more than just books. There are branches located throughout Durham County and they even have bookmobiles that bring books to you. Each library offers a variety of children's programs and activities. Call your closest branch to obtain current information.

Hayti Heritage Center
804 Old Fayetteville St. • 683-1709
• www.hayti.org

Hayti is housed in a historic church building. It has a gallery featuring African-American art and hosts concerts, plays, programs and events for children and adults. The First Saturday (of most months) family program is a free arts, crafts and activity program designed for school-aged children. Call for information on upcoming events.

Museum of Life and Science
433 Murray Ave. • 220-5429
• www.ncmls.org

The Museum of Life and Science is a great place for science exploration and fun. The 70-acre regional science-technology center, with two floors of hands-on exhibits, is located in the heart of Durham, off I-85. Exhibits include Aerospace, ABC News Channel 11 Weather Exhibit, Small Science (for the little ones), Geology, Carolina Wildlife, Data Earth and Discovery Rooms. Outdoor exhibits include Loblolly Park, Water Play, Farmyard Animals and an outdoor Nature Park with black bears, endangered red wolves and hawks.

The outdoor MegaMaze is filled with delighted kids and adults in warm weather and the Ellerbee Creek Railway ride around the grounds is a perennial favorite. Special exhibits rotate through the Duke Power Gallery—such as "MarsQuest," a fascinating exhibit that takes visitors on an exploration of planet Mars. Outside on the grounds, there are climbing structures, wind chimes, water play and farmyard.

The Museum's new three-story Magic Wings Butterfly House, one of 10 permanent year-round butterfly houses in the United States, features about 1,000 exotic butterflies from Africa, Asia and Central and South America. A state-of-the-art insectarium opened at the museum in spring 2000 as part of Magic Wings Butterfly House.

Museum hours are 10 AM to 5 PM Monday through Saturday and noon to 5 PM on Sunday. Call for extended summer hours.

A family membership gives unlimited admission for a year and may be used for admission at other science museums around the country.

Raleigh and Cary

Cary Cultural Resources
318 N. Academy St. • 469-4061

Call for information on lessons and special summer activities on arts and crafts.

Exploris
201 E. Hargett St. • 834-4040
• www.exploris.org

The $37.5-million Exploris interactive global experience center opened its doors in downtown Raleigh in the fall of 1999. The state-of-the-art, 84,000-square-foot facility offers dynamic hands-on and interactive exhibits for children of all ages. Highlights include the "Look In-Look Out" window, the "Marbles Wall" (comprised of more than one million marbles) and a piece of the Berlin Wall. One of the newest Exploris exhibits is the popular "One Voice: From the Pen of Anne Frank." Plans are in the works for a 270-seat, $11.9-million IMAX theater to open here in 2001. Exploris is open Tuesday through Saturday from 9 AM to 5 PM and Sunday from 12 PM to 5 PM. Call for summer hours.

N.C. Museum of Art
2110 Blue Ridge Rd. • 839-6262
• www.ncartmuseum.org

The North Carolina Museum of Art has several collections that fascinate children—among them the Egyptian mummies and the shimmering silver of the Judaica exhibit. There are also changing special shows that often

appeal to younger ones. The museum offers classes, movies, concerts and puppet shows for kids some weekdays and Saturdays each month. The museum also has several Family Festivals each year. There is a charge for special classes.

N.C. Museum of History
5 E. Edenton St. • 715-0200
• nchistory.dcr.state.nc.us

Children will enjoy the more than 250,000 items in the museum's collection, including Indian artifacts, folk art and crafts, old-time transportation and the N.C. Sports Hall of Fame, which boasts a race car originally owned by Richard Petty. The museum also hosts classes, films, concerts, dramatic presentations, lectures and family nights. Admission is free.

N.C. State Museum of Natural Sciences
102 N. Salisbury St. • 733-7450
• www.naturalsciences.org

The new $70.5-million, $200,000-square-foot Museum of Natural Sciences—the largest museum of its kind in the Southeast—opened its doors in April 2000 with a 24-hour extravaganza that drew thousands of people. The museum is expected to draw approximately 500,000 people a year. Exhibits in the state-of-the-art facility include "North Carolina's Natural Treasures," "Mountains to

Photo courtesy of N.C. Museum of Natural Sciences

The new Museum of Natural Sciences in downtown Raleigh is a great place for educational exploration.

BIRTHDAY PARTY IDEAS

ENTERTAINMENT

Abracadabra the Magic Clown	Durham	544-6770
Androgeena (puppeteer)	Durham	286-0002
Art N' Soul/Sky Blue: A Clown From Cloud 9	Carrboro	968-8704
Ba Tumbler's Tumblebus (gymnastics in a bus)	Raleigh	878-9893
Birthday Magic	Raleigh	266-5945
Bruce Stevenson (draws caricatures & sings)	Raleigh	872-3609
Calvin Klown and Tutu (comedy magic show)	Raleigh	782-4701
Cotton the Clown	Triangle	872-0400
Eyes on "U" Moonwalk	Triangle	490-5516
F & M Entertainment (costumed characters & clowns)	Raleigh	787-7742
Grimbo the Clown	Durham	361-3000
Jelly Bean the Clown	Durham	286-9431
Keith's Comedy Magic	Raleigh	233-1005
Kinderfeste (music, stories & activities)	Raleigh	783-7341
Mad Science	Triangle	845-1426
Molly Anne's Clown House	Triangle	852-1718
Musicaleigh Inclined (games & sing along music)	Chapel Hill	933-1683
Party Pros (clowns, magicians, face painting & puppeteers)	Durham	361-3000
Tate the Great (magic show)	Cary	469-2441
Theatrical Birthday Parties	Triangle	363-6799
Theme Parties in a Box	Triangle	845-1657
Whisper (magic show)	Raleigh	932-1388

PARTY PLACES

Adventure Landing (miniature golf, video games, food)	Raleigh	872-1688
AMF Capital Lanes	Raleigh	832-3747
AMF Durham Lanes	Durham	489-9154
AMF Pleasant Valley Lanes	Raleigh	783-0080
AMF South Hills Lanes	Cary	467-2411
Amazing Glaze (ceramics studio)	Cary	851-2500
Amazing Glaze (ceramics studio)	Raleigh	856-1234
Best Wishes (theme parties)	Cary	468-0684
Buffaloe Lanes of Cary	Cary	468-8684
Buffaloe Lanes of North Raleigh	Raleigh	876-5681
Buffaloe Lanes of South Raleigh	Raleigh	779-1888
Bullwinkle's Family Food 'n' Fun	Cary	319-7575
Busy Street (hands-on museum)	Durham	403-3743
Capital Skate (rollerskating parties)	Raleigh	875-1994
Carolina Soccerplex	Morrisville	319-9910
Cary Family YMCA (summer swimming party)	Cary	469-9622
Cary Parks & Rec. (rooms & picnic shelters for rent)	Cary	460-4965
Chapel Hill Parks & Rec. (gyms, ball fields, pool, tennis cts.)	Chapel Hill	968-2784
Chuck E. Cheese's	Durham	493-6084
Chuck E. Cheese's	Raleigh	850-9922
Dream Sports Center	Apex	387-2955
Durham Bulls Baseball Club	Durham	687-6500
Durham Parks & Rec. (picnic shelters, ball fields & more)	Durham	560-4358
Exploris	Raleigh	834-4040
Falls Golf Complex	Raleigh	870-6475
Family Golf Center	Wake Forest	554-1600
Funtasia Family Fun Center (mini golf & bumper boats)	Durham	493-8973

BIRTHDAY PARTY IDEAS

Ganyard Hill Farm	Durham	596-8728
Glaze & Blaze	Durham	286-6757
Glazed Expectations	Chapel Hill	933-9700
Grand Slam USA	Raleigh	233-7522
GymCarolina (gymnastics parties)	Cary	467-0946
GymCarolina (gymnastics parties)	Durham	620-7788
GymCarolina (gymnastics parties)	Raleigh	848-7988
Gymboree of Cary	Cary	469-8988
Gymboree of Raleigh	Raleigh	870-0739
Ice House, The (ice skating parties)	Cary	467-6000
Jellybeans Skating Rink	Cary	467-5283
Kazoom's Children's Theatre	Raleigh	829-0822
Kids' Kingdom	Clayton	550-3332
Kids' Town (theme parties)	Cary	468-1080
Kindermusik Kids of Cary (participatory music)	Cary	467-4398
Little Gym of Durham (gymnastics parties)	Durham	403-5437
Little Gym of North Raleigh	Raleigh	876-1391
Little Gym of Raleigh/Cary (gymnastics parties)	Cary	481-6701
Mardi Gras, The (bowling, party room)	Chapel Hill	489-1230
Morehead Planetarium	Chapel Hill	962-1236
Museum of Life and Science (super science parties)	Durham	220-5429
N.C. Museum of Natural Sciences	Raleigh	733-7450
North Raleigh Gymnastics (trampoline & obstacle course)	Raleigh	790-9400
Owlbert's Fun Factory	Raleigh	790-0470
Paint the Earth (ceramics studio)	Chapel Hill	968-0400
Paint Your Pot (ceramics studio)	Cary/Apex	363-9333
Party Machine, Ltd. (video games, dancing room, hostess)	Cary	461-0800
Playspace (educational, creative parties)	Raleigh	832-1212
Putt-Putt (miniature golf, video games, food)	Durham	479-5773
Putt-Putt (miniature golf, video games, food)	Raleigh	832-0600
Raleigh Family Golf	Raleigh	554-1600
Raleigh IcePlex (ice skating parties)	Raleigh	878-9002
Raleigh Little Theatre (discounted group tickets)	Raleigh	821-3111
Raleigh Parks & Rec. (comm. ctrs., pools, picnic shelters)	Raleigh	890-3285
Raleighwood Cinema Grill (special party packages)	Raleigh	847-8370
Raleigh YWCA (gym or swimming pool & party room)	Raleigh	828-3205
Ryan's World Skate Park	Raleigh	788-8536
Science Safari (electricity, safari & chemistry parties)	Cary	460-6051
Scrap Exchange (pick a theme & make a project)	Durham	688-6960
Silver Lake Water Park	Raleigh	851-1683
Skate Ranch of Garner	Garner	772-4297
Soccer Dome America (rent field, referee avail.)	Raleigh	859-2997
Sounds & Motion (participatory music)	Raleigh	874-0708
Swensen's (birthday parties in the "Greenhouse" room)	Chapel Hill	929-3121
Triangle SportsPlex	Hillsborough	644-0339
Triple J Stables	Chapel Hill	967-4980
Ultrazone	Raleigh	847-4263
Utopia Park (skateboarding)	Raleigh	856-0906
Village Lanes (bowling)	Durham	682-9145
Wayne Gretzky's Roller Hockey Center	Morrisville	319-9910
Western Lanes	Raleigh	832-3533
Wheels Family Fun Park (roller skating, go-carts, arcade)	Durham	598-1944
Wood's Hole Miniature Golf (golf & pizza)	Cary	233-7189
ZooFauna	Wake Forest	562-8899

the Sea," "Coastal North Carolina" and "Living Conservatory." Perhaps the most popular exhibit, "Terror of the South," stars the ferocious predator Acrocanthosaurus dinosaur, once a native of the Southeast. Kids will enjoy lunch at the Acro Cafe. The museum also hosts special events on weekends several times a year such as Reptile and Amphibian Day (usually in March). Admission is free.

Playspace
400 Glenwood Ave. • 832-1212

A magical place for budding imaginations, Playspace is a nonprofit children's museum staffed by volunteers. Housed here are a pretend hospital, a grocery store, a cafe, a puppet theater, a dress-up area and a stage, as well as an exploration area designed for infants and toddlers. Play sessions begin on the hour and last for 50 minutes. It's a good idea to arrive a few minutes before the hour in case there's a crowd. Playspace is appropriate for children ages six months to seven years and their adult care-givers. Admission is $2 for a 50-minute session. It is closed on Sunday and Monday afternoons.

Raleigh Arts Commission
• 857-4372

Call for information on year-round and summer classes, camps and activities.

Wake County Public Libraries
Cameron Village Regional Library, Raleigh • 856-6710
Eva Perry Regional Library, Apex • 387-2113
North Regional Library, Raleigh • 870-4000
Southeast Regional Library, Garner • 662-2250

Once again, libraries are our favorite recommendation and offer a lot more than just books. There are branches located throughout Wake County in addition to the regional branches. Each library has a variety of children's programs and activities.

Entertainment
Durham

Chuck E. Cheese's
3724 Mayfair St. • 493-6084

Located next to South Square Mall, Chuck E. Cheese's is an eatery/entertainment complex that provides fun for the entire family. Kids will enjoy the games and rides, as well as an entertaining show featuring Chuck E. Cheese and friends. Pizza, sandwiches and a salad bar are available.

Funtasia Family Fun Center
4350 Garrett Rd. • 493-8973

Funtasia is a commercial family fun center that offers a 36-hole miniature golf course, bumper boats, video arcade, go carts, batting cages, two-story maze and a 14-acre paintball field.

The Mardi Gras
N.C. 54 at I-40 • 489-1230

A 24-lane bowling alley and video arcade, The Mardi Gras is a good venue for entertainment for southwest Durhamites and Chapel Hillians. Food is available and birthday parties and group outings are welcome by reservation. Bowling fees are lower during certain weekday hours.

Pleasure Horse Farm
8311 Fayetteville Rd. • 544-5867

If you want your child to learn the basics of how to care for a horse as well how to ride, this is the place. Lessons, boarding and training are available here.

Putt-Putt Golf & Games
5261 N. Roxboro Rd. • 479-5773

Highlights at this family fun complex include 36 holes of miniature golf, batting cages, a video arcade and a full-service grill. It's a popular spot for birthday parties.

INSIDERS' TIP

Amusement parks aren't the only place to catch a ride on a carousel—check out the 1911 hand-carved Dentzel carousel at Pullen Park in Raleigh and the Italian carousel at Northgate Mall in Durham.

Children of all ages enjoy Cary's
Kids Together Playground.

The Scrap Exchange
548 Foster St. • 688-6960

Formerly located at Northgate Mall, this nonprofit organization recycles cloth, ribbons, lace, paper, foam, tubing and plastic squirls donated from area companies. Creative workshops are available as well as bags of scraps for craft and school projects.

Triangle SportsPlex
One Dan Kidd Dr., Hillsborough
• 644-0339

Ice skating, hockey, and kiddie, lap and recreational swimming pools are available in this state-of-the-art facility. A number of youth leagues compete here. SportsPlex is located just outside downtown Hillsborough.

Vertical Edge Climbing Center
2422 U.S. 70 • 596-6910

Indoor rock climbing center teaches team building and self reliance.

Wheels Family Fun Park
715 N. Hoover Rd. • 598-1944

Wheels Family Fun Park is a full-service entertainment complex that offers go-carts, bumper cars, batting cages, mini-golf, a three-story jumbo gym, video arcades and a roller skating rink.

Raleigh and Cary

Adventure Landing
3311 Capital Blvd., Raleigh • 872-1688

Three miniature golf courses, go-karts, batting cages, laser tag, a human slingshot, video games and fast-food are offered at this location in North Raleigh.

Bullwinkle's Family Food 'n' Fun
1040 Buck Jones Rd., Cary • 319-7575

Kids will love this combination eatery and entertainment center that boasts a Rocky and Bullwinkle animatronics show, water and light show, indoor playground, rock climbing wall and video arcade, as well as a full-service restaurant that serves pizza, sandwiches and burgers. It is located next to Jellybeans skating rink.

Chuck E. Cheese's
3501 Capital Blvd., Raleigh • 850-9922

Chuck E. Cheese's is a national chain that serves pizza and provides rides and video games for entertainment while you wait.

Dream Sports Center
1016 Investment Blvd., Apex • 387-2955
• www.dreamsportscenter.com

The new $2.5-million, 56,000-square-foot Dream Sports Center contains space for indoor soccer and hockey.

Falls Golf Complex
8515 Falls of Neuse Rd., Raleigh • 870-6475

Formerly known as Carolina Custom Golf, Fall Golf Complex offers 36 holes of miniature golf for kids and a driving range and pro shop for adults. It's a popular spot for birthday parties.

Grand Slam U.S.A.
4500 Western Blvd., Raleigh • 233-7522

Four indoor batting cages and two basketball courts make this a children's year-round sports center. Grand Slam also has a video arcade.

Ice House
1410 Buck Jones Rd., Cary • 467-6000

Experience the coolest entertainment in the Triangle. The Ice House features skating, lessons and team sports, as well as a game room, birthday room and pro shop.

Jellybeans
1120 Buck Jones Rd., Cary • 467-5283

Jellybeans skating rink is very popular with both in-line and regular skaters. Conveniently located near Bullwinkle's Family Food 'n' Fun, it provides well-supervised, family fun.

Owlbert's Fun Factory
Millbrook Shopping Center, Raleigh • 790-0470
• www.owlbertsfunfactory.com

A 10,000-square-foot family fun center, Owlbert's offers kids ages 2 to 10 an indoor playmaze, games, rides and fresh-baked pizza. Owlbert's is located on the corner of Millbrook Road and Atlantic Avenue.

Putt-Putt Golf & Games
4020 Tryon Rd., Raleigh • 832-0600
• www.putt-putt.com/raleigh

Experience over seven acres of fun and excitement at the Triangle's newest entertainment park. Attractions include two 18-hole miniature golf courses, the Swiftcreek Speedway with three go-kart tracks, a video arcade, snack bar and ice cream shop.

Raleigh Family Golf
9820 Capital Blvd., Raleigh • 554-1600

Raleigh Family Golf boasts a miniature golf course, batting cages, a video arcade and a kids' playspace.

Raleigh IcePlex
2601 Raleigh Blvd., Raleigh
• 878-9002 • www.iceplex.com

The Raleigh IcePlex offers daily public skating, ice hockey, figure skating, a birthday party room and a pro shop.

Science Safari
Saltbox Village, Cary
• 460-6051

Science Safari is a quality toy store that offers both classes in science as well as birthday parties with science themes. There is usually a waiting list, so sign up early.

Silver Lake Water Park
5300 Tryon Rd., Raleigh • 851-1683

Silver Lake, near Swift Creek, is one of the area's most popular swimming parks. The water park boasts a five-story waterslide (known as "The Beast"), swimming areas, paddleboats, a playground, a game room and picnic areas. Admission is charged.

FYI

Unless otherwise noted, the area code for all phone numbers listed in this guide is 919.

SUMMER DAY CAMPS

ACADEMIC & CULTURAL

Carolina Friends School	Durham	Coed	4-15	919-384-9089
Duke Computer Explorations	Durham	Coed	3-5 Gr.	919-684-6259
Durham Academy	Durham	Coed	4-15	919-489-9118
Hill Center	Durham	Coed	K-6th Gr.	919-489-7464
Imagineering Center	Pittsboro	Coed	8-15	919-932-1215
Jr. Statesman (Politics & Gov.)	Various	Coed	14-17	800-334-5353
Meredith's Computer Camp	Raleigh	Coed	7-12	919-829-8353
N.C. Museum of History	Raleigh	Coed	K-8	919-715-0200
N.C. Museum of Life & Science	Durham	Coed	4-14	919-220-5429
N.C. Museum of Natural Sciences	Raleigh	Coed	4-14	919-733-7450
Ravenscroft	Raleigh	Coed	5-16	919-847-0900
Saint Mary's Summer Odyssey	Raleigh	Coed	3-7 Gr.	919-424-4020
Schoolhouse of Wonder	Durham	Coed	7-15	919-471-1623
Summer Peace Camps	Carrboro	Coed	6-12	919-929-9821

ARTS & MUSIC

American Dance Festival	Durham	Coed	12-16	919-684-6402
Artsquest	Durham	Coed	6-12	919-683-1709
Arts Together	Raleigh	Coed	4-18	919-828-1713
Artspace Summer Arts Program	Raleigh	Coed	8-16	919-821-2787
Brightleaf Music Workshop	Durham	Coed	7-12 Gr.	919-493-0385
Chapel Hill Arts & Music	Chapel Hill	Coed	6-12	919-933-7278
Durham Arts Council	Durham	Coed	5-16	919-560-2726
Expressions! Duke's Fine Arts Camp	Durham	Coed	10-13	919-684-6259
Jordan Hall Arts Center	Cary	Coed	6-14	919-469-4069
Maple Meadows Art Camp	Chapel Hill	Coed	12-18	919-942-6696
Meredith's (Art, Music, Theatre)	Raleigh	Coed	6 & up	919-829-8536
Raleigh Little Theatre	Raleigh	Coed	6-18	919-821-4579
Raleigh School of Ballet	Raleigh	Coed	7-18	919-834-9261
Raleigh School of Dance	Raleigh	Coed	5-11	919-850-9030
The Scrap Exchange	Durham	Coed	5-12	919-688-6960

GYMNASTICS & CHEERLEADING

Artistic Gymnastics	Raleigh	Coed	3-18	919-772-9463
Carolina Gymnastics Academy	Raleigh	Coed	5-16	919-848-7988
Champion Cheer Gym	Raleigh	Coed	5-12	919-859-1511
North Raleigh Gymnastics	Raleigh	Coed	4-12	919-790-9400

HORSEMANSHIP CAMP

Ballentine Farm Riding Academy	Fuquay-Varina	Coed	5-18	919-552-7869
Brasswood Summer Horse Camp	Durham	Coed	7-13	919-403-0758
Camp Cheval (MacNair's)	Raleigh	Coed	6-16	919-851-1118
Pleasure Horse Farms	Durham	Coed	6 & up	919-544-5867
Quail Roost Stables	Rougemont	Coed	6 & up	919-477-8932
Tamryss Farms	Raleigh	Coed	6 & up	919-847-3080
Triton Stables	Raleigh	Coed	5-16	919-847-4123

SUMMER DAY CAMP

A.E. Finley YMCA	N. Raleigh	Coed	3-15	919-848-9622
Cary Parks & Recreation	Cary	Coed	4-18	919-469-4062
Cary YMCA	Cary	Coed	1-8 Gr.	919-469-9622
Central YMCA	Ral. & Garner	Coed	4-14	919-832-6601
Chapel Hill/Carrboro YMCA	Chapel Hill	Coed	5-15	919-942-5156
Chapel Hill Parks & Recreation	Chapel Hill	Coed	6-12	919-968-2784
Durham Parks & Recreation	Durham	Coed	5-18	919-560-4355
Durham YMCA	Durham	Coed	4-14	919-493-4502
Garner YMCA	Garner	Coed	3-15	919-773-3621
Raleigh Parks & Recreation	Raleigh	Coed	3-18	919-831-6640
Triangle SportsPlex	Hillsborough	Coed	7-13	919-644-0339

SUMMER SPORTS CAMPS

Duke, N.C. State and UNC offer more than 20 different sports camps. Call their Sports Information Offices for details on individual camps.
Duke: 684-2633   N.C. State: 515-2102   UNC: 962-2123

BASEBALL

Duke Baseball Camp	Durham	Boys	1-12 Gr.	684-2358
Duke Youth Baseball Camp	Durham	Coed	7-14	687-6500
Durham Bulls Youth Baseball	Durham	Coed	7-14	687-6520
N.C. State Baseball Camp	Raleigh	Boys	9-18	515-3613
UNC Baseball Camp	Chapel Hill	Boys	6-18	962-2351

BASKETBALL

Campbell University Basketball	Buies Creek	Boys/Girls	8-18	800-760-8962
Dave Odom Basketball Camp	Winston-Salem	Boys	7-18	336-759-5622
Duke Univ. Basketball Camp	Durham	Girls	9-17	613-7527
Duke Univ. Basketball Camp	Durham	Boys	9-17	684-8515
N.C. State Basketball Camp	Raleigh	Boys	8-17	828-7100
N.C. State Basketball Camp	Raleigh	Girls	7-18	859-1511
UNC Basketball Camp	Chapel Hill	Boys	10-17	962-1154
UNC Basketball Camp	Chapel Hill	Girls	9-18	408-0221

FOOTBALL

Doug Evans Football Camp	Charlotte	Boys	8-18	800-555-0801
Duke University Football Camp	Durham	Boys	13-18	684-2635
N.C. State Football Camp	Raleigh	Boys	13-18	515-2114
NCCU Football Camp	Durham	Boys	10-16	530-5315
UNC Football Camp	Chapel Hill	Boys	9-18	966-2575

GOLF

Duke Golf School	Durham	Coed	11-17	681-2494
Duke University Golf Club	Durham	Coed	9-18	681-2288
N.C. State Golf Camp	Raleigh	Coed	6-18	846-1536

SOCCER

Capital Area Soccer League	Raleigh	Coed	6-16	834-3951
Duke Soccer Camp	Durham	Coed	6-12	493-2287
N.C. State Soccer Camp	Raleigh	Boys	6-12	851-1627
Soccer Dome America	Raleigh	Coed	7-15	859-2997
UNC Soccer Camp	Chapel Hill	Boys	10-18	408-0770
UNC Soccer Camp	Chapel Hill	Girls	13-17	962-4100

TENNIS

Duke Tennis Camp	Durham	Coed	8-18	479-0854
Mary Lou Jones (St. Mary's)	Raleigh	Coed	5-18	839-4015

MISCELLANEOUS

Campbell U. Sports Camp	Buies Creek	Coed	8-18	910-893-1325
Carolina Hurricanes Camp	Raleigh	Coed	6-16	467-7825
NC Track & Field/Cross Country	Chapel Hill	Coed	8 & up	962-5210
NCCU Sports School	Durham	Coed	6-14	530-7057
North Raleigh Sports Camp	Raleigh	Coed	6-14	790-0596
Outward Bound, USA	Various	Coed	14-up	877-826-9702
Pembroke State All-Sports Camp	Pembroke	Coed	6-12	910-521-6343

Twin Towers Stables
319 Green Level Rd., Apex • 303-5020

Twin Towers is a full-service equestrian facility that offers quality instruction for beginning and advanced riders and a Pony Club for kids ages 8 to 15.

Ultrazone
8311 Creedmoor Rd. • 847-4263
• www.ultrazone-raleigh.com

Billed as "The Ultimate Laser Adventure," Ultrazone features high-tech laser team games in a 5,000-square-foot, two-level arena. A video arcade and concession stand are on the premises.

Wayne Gretzky's Roller Hockey Center/Carolina Soccerplex
3717 Davis Dr., Morrisville
• www.gretzkyrollerhockey.com

A new $5-million, 72,000-square-foot facility, the Center contains space for hockey and indoor and outdoor soccer.

Wood's Hole Miniature Golf Club
5815 Holly Springs Rd., Cary
• 233-7189

Experience miniature golf in a family setting. Wood's specializes in birthday parties.

ZooFauna
U.S. 1 A, Wake Forest • 562-8899
• www.zoofauna.com

More than 30 acres of exotic animals from all over the world can be viewed at this nature park located north of Wake Forest.

Outdoor Recreation

Chapel Hill and Carrboro

N.C. Botanical Garden
Fordham Blvd. (U.S. 15-501 Bypass)
• 962-0522 • www.unc.edu/depts/ncbg

The Botanical Garden's 600-plus acres are a part of the University of North Carolina.

Here you will discover collections of native plants, grouped in coastal plain, piedmont and mountain sections, herb and wildflower gardens, goldfish ponds and a series of trails to walk throughout the garden property. Admission is free.

Durham

Duke Forest
For Information: 613-8013

Duke Forest consists of more than 8,000 acres of woods, part of the research lab for the School of Environmental Sciences (formerly the School of Forestry) at Duke. There are trails to hike and bike, picnic areas, streams and fishing holes in the forest, which straddles Durham and Orange counties. Duke Forest has a number of entrances. The most widely used are along N.C. 751 and Erwin and Whitfield roads. The forest is a great spot for a family walk (bring the dog along!) or a solo stroll when you need to clear your mind. Admission is free.

Eno River State Park
6101 Cole Mill Rd. • 383-1686
• www.geo.duke.edu/enowelco.htm

The Eno River State Park was established in 1973 and runs along a 14-mile stretch of the river. There are a number of access points to the park, including Cole Mill and Few's Ford, where the park office is located. There are hiking and bridle trails, creeks to fish and picnic spots. Admission is free.

Sarah P. Duke Gardens
Anderson St., Duke West Campus
• 684-3698
• www.hr.duke.edu/dukegardens

The Sarah P. Duke Gardens are glorious in the springtime, but worth a visit any time of the year. There are 55 acres of lawn, flowers and foliage divided into three major sections: the original Terraces, the Blomquist Garden of Native Plants and the Culberson Asiatic

---

INSIDERS' TIP

Two public playgrounds in the Triangle, All Children's in Raleigh and Kids Together in Cary, have been designed for all children, including those with physical disabilities.

SUMMER RESIDENT CAMPS

PIEDMONT

All-Arts & Sciences Camp (UNCG)	Greensboro	Coed	7-15	800-306-9033
Betsy-Jeff Penn 4-H Center (4-H)	Reidsville	Coed	8-12	336-349-9445
Camp Cheerio (YMCA)	High Point	Coed	7-15	800-226-7496
Camp Chestnut Ridge (Methodist)	Efland	Coed	7-17	919-304-3900
Camp Graham (Girl Scout)	Henderson	Girls	6-17	252-492-1478
Camp Kanata (YMCA)	Wake Forest	Coed	6-15	919-556-2661
Camp Mary Atkinson (Girl Scout)	Selma	Girls	6-17	919-782-3021
Camp New Hope (Presbyterian)	Chapel Hill	Coed	6-15	919-942-4716
Camp Oak Hill (Christian)	Oxford	Coed	7-17	919-782-2888
Camp Thunderbird (YMCA)	Lake Wylie, S.C.	Coed	7-16	800-732-3855
Camp Willow Run (Christian)	Littleton	Coed	8-18	252-586-4665
Duke Action: Science-Forestry	Durham	Girls	10-12	919-684-6259
Duke Creative Writers' Workshop	Durham	Coed	16-18	919-684-6259
Duke Drama Workshop	Durham	Coed	15-17	919-684-6259
Duke Young Writers Camp	Durham	Coed	11-17	919-684-6259
Gifted and Talented Develop. Ctr.	Charlotte	Coed	11-15	704-366-6052
Keyauwee Program Ctr. (G.Scouts)	Sophia	Girls	7-17	336-861-1198
Lutheran Outdoor Ministries	Fuquay-Varina	Coed	5-12	919-552-9421
Millstone 4-H Center (4-H)	Ellerbee	Coed	6-18	919-515-3244
Mount Shepherd (Methodist)	Asheboro	Coed	6-18	336-629-4085
Mountain Top Camp (Christian)	Pinnacle	Coed	8-20	336-767-7158
New Life Camp (Christian)	Raleigh	Coed	8-18	919-847-0764
N.C. School of the Arts	Winston-Salem	Coed	12-adult	336-770-3204
NCSU (Challenge & Champions)	Raleigh	Coed	10-13	919-515-7061
NCSU (Math & Science-Gifted)	Raleigh	Coed	15-18	919-515-6118
Payne Woodmen Camp	Greensboro	Coed	8-15	336-275-5949
Rockfish (Christian)	Parkton	Coed	6-16	910-425-3529
Sertoma 4-H Center (4-H)	Westfield	Coed	9-18	336-593-8057
Summer Ventures (Science & Math)	Durham	Coed	Jrs./Srs.	919-286-3366
Talent Identification Program (TIPS)	Durham (Duke)	Coed	12-16	919-684-3847
The Summit (Episcopal)	Brown Summit	Coed	7-18	800-448-8775
The Vineyard (Christian)	Westfield	Coed	6-16	336-351-2070
YMCA Camp Hanes	King	Coed	7-15	336-983-3131

COAST

Camp Albemarle (Presbyterian)	Newport	Coed	7-18	252-726-4848
Camp Don Lee (Methodist)	Arapahoe	Coed	7-17	800-535-5475
Camp Hardee (Girl Scout)	Blounts Creek	Girls	6-16	800-558-9297
Camp Seafarer (YMCA)	Arapahoe	Girls	7-16	252-249-1212
Camp Sea Gull (YMCA)	Arapahoe	Boys	7-16	252-249-1111
Camp Pretty Pond (Girl Scout)	Winnabow	Girls	7-17	800-558-9297
Duke Action: Science-Coast	Pine Knoll Shores	Girls	10-12	919-684-6259
Lutheran Outdoor Ministries	Kure Beach	Coed	5-18	919-552-9421
Mitchell 4-H Center (4-H)	Swansboro	Coed	6-18	919-515-3244
Roanoke Christian (Church of Christ)	Washington	Coed	5-18	252-946-2203

MOUNTAINS

Brevard Music Center (Audition req.)	Brevard	Coed	14-35	828-884-2975
Camp Arrowhead	Tuxedo	Boys	7-15	828-692-1123
Camp Broadstone (ASU/Gifted Prog.)	Boone	Coed	9-14	828-963-4640

SUMMER RESIDENT CAMPS

MOUNTAINS cont.

Camp Carolina Backcountry	Brevard	Boys	7-17	828-884-2414
Camp Celo	Burnsville	Coed	7-12	828-675-4323
Camp Chosatonga	Brevard	Boys	8-17	828-884-6834
Camp Ginger Cascades (Girl Scout)	Lenoir	Girls	5-17	800-328-8388
Camp Green Cove	Tuxedo	Girls	6-17	828-692-6355
Camp Greystone (Christian)	Tuxedo	Girls	7-17	828-693-3182
Camp Grier (Presbyterian)	Old Fort	Coed	7-18	828-668-7793
Camp High Rocks	Cedar Mt.	Boys	8-16	828-885-2153
Camp Highlander	Horse Shoe	Coed	7-16	828-891-7721
Camp Hollymont	Black Mountain	Girls	6-15	828-686-5343
Camp Illahee	Brevard	Girls	6-16	828-883-2181
Camp Kahdalea	Brevard	Girls	8-17	828-884-6834
Camp Kanuga (Episcopal)	Hendersonville	Coed	7-15	828-692-9136
Camp Living Water (Christian)	Bryson City	Coed	7-16	828-488-6012
Camp Merri-Mac	Black Mountain	Girls	6-16	828-669-8766
Camp Mishemokwa	Bat Cave	Coed	6-16	828-625-9051
Camp Mondamin	Tuxedo	Boys	6-17	828-693-7446
Camp Pinnacle	Hendersonville	Coed	7-16	828-692-3591
Camp Pisgah (Girl Scout)	Brevard	Girls	7-17	828-252-4442
Camp Rockbrook	Brevard	Girls	6-16	828-884-6151
Camp Rockmont	Black Mountain	Boys	7-16	828-686-3885
Camp Sky Ranch	Blowing Rock	Coed	6-17	828-264-8600
Camp Tekoa (Methodist)	Hendersonville	Coed	6-17	828-692-6516
Camp Timberlake	Black Mountain	Boys	7-16	828-669-8766
Camp Ton-A-Wandah	Hendersonville	Girls	6-15	800-322-0178
Camp Winding Gap	Lake Toxaway	Coed	6-14	828-883-8720
Christ School Sports Camp	Arden	Coed	9-13	828-684-6232
Cullowhee Experience (A. Gifted)	Cullowhee	Coed	9-15	828-227-7249
Deep Woods Camp	Brevard	Boys	10-17	828-885-2268
Eagle's Nest Camp	Pisgah Forest	Coed	6-17	336-761-1040
Falling Creek Camp	Tuxedo	Boys	7-16	828-692-0262
Green River Preserve	Cedar Mtn.	Coed	9-13	828-885-2250
Gwynn Valley	Brevard	Coed	5-12	828-885-2900
Holston Presbytery (Presbyterian)	Banner Elk	Coed	8-18	828-898-6611
Johns River Valley (Church of Christ)	Blowing Rock	Coed	8-18	828-264-1516
Keystone Camp	Brevard	Girls	7-17	828-884-9125
Laurel Ridge (Moravian)	Laurel Springs	Coed	6-18	336-359-2951
Lutheridge (Lutheran)	Arden	Coed	6-18	828-684-2361
Lutherock (Lutheran)	Newland	Coed	8-18	828-733-3309
Merriwood	Sapphire Valley	Girls	6-16	828-743-3300
Mountaincamp	Highlands	Coed	6-18	828-526-4505
N.C. Outward Bound School	Asheville	Coed	14-18	828-299-3366
Oak Ridge Military Academy	Oak Ridge	Coed	10-17	800-321-7904
Ridgecrest (Southern Baptist)	Ridgecrest	Coed	7-16	828-669-8051
Skyland Camp	Clyde	Girls	6-15	828-627-2470
South Mountain Baptist Camp	Connelly Springs	Coed	6-17	828-437-9475
South Mountain Christian Camp	Bostic	Coed	7-15	828-247-1168
Talisman Summer Camp	Black Mountain	Coed	9-17	828-669-8639
TVR Christian Camp	Plumtree	Coed	8-18	828-765-7860

Arboretum. It's a prime place for families, Duke students and others to picnic or just hang out. The gardens contain ponds with goldfish, paths to follow and woodlands to explore. Concerts are held here in the spring and fall. The Doris Duke Visitors Center is set to open at the Gardens in the spring of 2001. A children's amphitheater is also in the planning stages. Admission is free.

West Point on the Eno
5101 N. Roxboro Rd. • 471-1623

West Point on the Eno is part of the Durham City Parks and Recreation system. The park includes a reconstructed mill, the 1880's Greek Revival McCown-Mangum house and the Tobacco Barn and Pack House. West Point has trails to hike, a picnic area and a blacksmith shop. The park hosts the annual Fourth of July Festival for the Eno, Hallow-Eno, a special Halloween celebration for families, and other special programs like nature classes for children throughout the year. Admission to the park is free.

Raleigh and Cary

All Children's Playground
Laurel Hills Park, 3808 Edwards Mill Rd.
• 430-2383

Designed more than a decade ago with the help of many children, 1,500 volunteers built this playground in 4 days. Discovery, adventure and fun are available to all children. Children with disabilities will find sights, sounds and textures to excite their senses.

Blue Jay County Park
3200 Pleasant Union Church Rd.
• 870-4330

Located on the shores of Falls Lake, this 236-acre park is the home of the Blue Jay Center for Environmental Education. It features exhibits, demonstration areas, educational programs, hiking trails, picnic areas, playgrounds and ballfields.

Bond Park
801 High House Rd., Cary • 469-4100

The largest park in Wake County offers a playground, boat rentals, fitness trail and more

than five miles of hiking trails. The park is home to several annual kid's events such as a "haunted house" at Halloween and a community Easter Egg Hunt.

Durant Nature Park
8305 Camp Durant Rd. • 870-2871

Durant Nature Park is a little gem in the Raleigh Parks and Recreation Department's crown. There are trails to explore, a butterfly and bird garden (best in spring and summer) and many wonderful weekend nature programs for children and families. Durant has picnic facilities, too, if you want to make a day of it. One highlight of the park's yearly schedule of programs and events is the Halloween Trail each October. Call for more information about the park and its classes and activities.

Hemlock Bluffs
2616 Kildaire Farm Rd., Cary
• 387-5980

A 150-acre nature preserve, Hemlock Bluffs boasts a grove of Canadian hemlocks, hiking trails and the Stevens Nature Center, which offers exhibits, classes and lectures. Park tours are available on weekends.

J.C. Raulston Arboretum
4301 Beryl Rd. • 515-7641

The J.C. Raulston Arboretum at North Carolina State University is small and worth discovering. It is near Meredith College and the N.C. State Fairgrounds and covers about 8 acres. It is a delightful place for a quiet stroll through Japanese and English-style gardens. If you and the kids need a respite from the high-tech world, the Arboretum may be a solution. There are places to picnic. Admission is free.

Kids Together Playground
Cary Pkwy. & Thurston Dr., Cary

Similar to Raleigh's All Children's Playground, this public playground at Kids Together Park was designed for all children, including those with physical disabilities. Completed in the summer of 2000, it is located near the corner of Cary Parkway and Tryon Road, behind the Wellington Park Shopping

The 1911 Dentzel Carousel at Pullen Park is a favorite among kids.

Photo courtesy of N.C. Division of Tourism

Center. The site also includes a basketball court, picnic areas, hiking trails and traditional playground equipment.

Lake Crabtree
Off Aviation Pkwy. • 460-3390

A popular county park, Lake Crabtree contains playgrounds, hiking trails and rentals of canoes, rowboats and sailboats.

Pullen Park
408 Ashe Ave. • 831-6468

The highlight of 65-acre Pullen Park (at least to this Insider) is the carousel. One of only 25 hand-carved Dentzel carousels still in operation, it was constructed in 1911 and restored in 1982. You can ride a horse, an ostrich, a cat or a rabbit—or perhaps all of them, since you'll undoubtedly ride it more than once. The park also has a train and a boat ride for little ones, a large playground, a concession stand, picnic areas, paddle boats on the small man-made lake and an aquatic center. Admission to the park is free. There are charges for rides and the pool.

Shelley Lake and Sertoma Park
1400 West Millbrook Rd. • 420-2331

One of the best playgrounds in the Triangle is Sertoma Park. Fifty-three-acre Shelley Lake is just located down the hill from the playground where paddle boats, sailboats, canoes and rowboats are available for rent from April through September.

William B. Umstead State Park
8801 Glenwood Ave. • 571-4170
• ils.unc.edu/parkproject/wium.html

William B. Umstead and adjoining Reedy Creek State Parks offer 5,000-plus acres of trails, fishing, picnic sites, campgrounds and woodlands to explore right in the middle of the Triangle (just minutes from RDU International Airport). The parks contain bridle trails, a self-guided nature trail, a lake with boat rentals in warm weather, camping and picnic sites and more. It's worth a stop, especially if you need a place to let the kids run loose on a sunny afternoon. The Umstead State Park Visitors Center features a museum and other educational exhibits relating to the park. Admission is free.

Summer Camps

There is so much to be considered that picking a summer camp is difficult, at best. A good resource is the *North Carolina Resident and Sports Camp Directory* published each year by the NCSU College of Natural Resources. Call 515-7118 to order a copy. There is a charge. *How to Choose a Summer Camp* is available at no charge from the National Camp Association's Camp Advisory Service by calling 800-966-CAMP. If you are looking for camps throughout the United States, pick up a copy of *Peterson's Summer Opportunities for Kids and Teenagers* at your local bookstore.

Triangle residents enjoy the convenience of a variety of local and national publications.

Media

Read on. Listen up. Watch it. Plug in. We've got the media for your daily information fix.

The Triangle is part of a strong North Carolina tradition of solid news reporting, whether it's in print or broadcast. And it's been a proving ground for Internet journalism as well as the revolutionary High Density Resolution Television (HDTV). The local newspapers have produced Pulitzer Prize winning news and commentary, and the hometown television stations have a string of Emmy and Peabodys for issue and breaking news coverage. You will not run short on mediums from which to pick the message of your choice.

This chapter profiles as nowhere else the menu of Triangle media and their respective histories and outlooks. Here's where you can also find which radio station is the Voice of the (NCSU) Wolfpack or broadcasts Duke Blue Devil or Tar Heel sports. Here, too, you can read about our sassy weeklies and their entertaining personal ads. If you require a daily dose of Bob Edwards or Linda Wertheimer, we tell you where to find a fix—WUNC-FM, 91.5. (And if you listen there long enough, you'll hear one of the co-authors comment on subjects as varied as terrible toilets and book titles.)

Cary Newspapers

The Cary News
212 E. Chatham St. • 460-2600

Published on Wednesday and Saturday, this newspaper has grown with the city and keeps its 28,000 readers focused on Cary. It is owned by the California-based McClatchy chain and sometimes serves as a stepping stone for reporters or managers who move up to the *N&O*. It does a good job of covering Cary city news, local school news and sports.

Chapel Hill Newspapers

The Chapel Hill Herald
106 Mallette St. • 967-6581
• www.herald-sun.com

If you subscribe to the *Durham Herald-Sun* and you live in the Chapel Hill area, you'll receive *The Chapel Hill Herald* edition, with its impressive front page coverage of local news, including coverage of adjacent Chatham County as well as Hillsborough and northern Orange County. With more than 12,000 readers, this edition has local features, national columnists and plenty of scoop on everything from the courthouse to campus.

The Chapel Hill News
505 W. Franklin St.
• 932-2000
• www.chapelhillnews.com

Owned by the California-based McClatchy chain, this local paper in Chapel Hill is published on Wednesdays, Fridays and Sundays to more than 25,000 Chapel Hill-Carrboro households. The newspaper got its start as a weekly in 1923 and has undergone numerous changes in both name and format prior to its present status as a thrice-weekly paper. It also has an online edition that contains a searchable archive of past stories.

Under publisher and editor Ted Vaden, the paper keeps readers up to date on local government, university news and town tidbits. You'll find coverage of Chapel Hill, Carrboro, Orange County and UNC-CH, as well as state and regional news. The editorial page features commentary by local, regional and nationally syndicated columnists. Comprehensive local sports coverage, entertainment pages, book reviews, features on the thriving local arts community and a food and dining column round out the paper.

Durham Newspapers

The Carolina Times
923 Old Fayetteville St. • 682-2913

The Carolina Times, published weekly on Thursdays, emphasizes local, state and national news affecting the black community. The paper was established in 1926 by long-time civil rights activist Louis Austin, whose goal was to offer a voice to blacks at a time when they clearly had no say in local, state or national politics. Austin died in 1971, but his objectives continue to be carried out today under the leadership of his daughter, Vivian Austin Edmonds, the current editor and publisher. *The Carolina Times* emphasizes local news, sports and features, but provides state, national and international news from the Associated Press wire service.

The Herald-Sun
2828 Pickett Rd. • 419-6500
• www.herald-sun.com

It all started back in 1889 when the Durham and Northern Railroad found itself without any editorial support in its right-of-way battle with the Durham and Clarksville line. At the urging of several alarmed aldermen, the *Durham Daily Sun* was established, eventually taking its place as an afternoon paper. In 1929, just before the stock market crashed, Edward Tyler Rollins purchased *The Sun* and merged it with his morning paper, *The Herald*.

Today, the paper is headed by president and publisher David Hughey. *The Herald-Sun* emphasizes local news, with state, national and international news coverage provided by the Associated Press wire. In addition to local editorials, you'll find the opinions of nationally syndicated columnists James J. Kilpatrick and George Will, as well as local editorial writers such as Gregory Childress. The paper also provides comprehensive coverage of Duke University sports. *The Herald-Sun* has a daily circulation of about 64,000. The paper recently started a Friday page called *Nuestro Pueblo* ("Our Town") that provides news, features and columns for the area's growing Hispanic community. *The*

Photo by Rich Weidman

The Durham *Herald-Sun* keeps readers informed about activities in the "Bull City."

The Raleigh *News and Observer* is the state's most influential newspaper.

Herald-Sun also publishes an Orange County daily edition, *The Chapel Hill Herald*.

The Triangle Tribune
119 Market St. • 688-9408

The weekly *Triangle Tribune* made its debut in 1998, covering the black communities in Chapel Hill, Durham and Raleigh with a focus on business, education, health and politics. It is published on Sundays. The paper's owners also publish *The Charlotte Post* and *The Chronicle* in Winston-Salem.

Raleigh Newspapers

The Carolinian
649 Maywood Ave. • 834-5558

Published twice a week, *The Carolinian* targets the capital city's southeast black community and has its greatest influence there. It has been a voice for Raleigh African-Americans since 1940 and its current principal writer sets his own agenda when reporting the news. Articles are oriented toward African-American issues and personalities, religious commentary, arts and entertainment.

The News and Observer
215 S. McDowell St. • 829-4500
- **www.newsobserver.com**
- **www.triangle.com**

Established in 1865, the *N&O* is THE daily morning newspaper in Raleigh, and many in Chapel Hill and Durham subscribe to it in addition to—or instead of—their local newspapers. The paper, which is owned by the California-based McClatchy chain, has a tradition for outspoken opinions dating back to founder Josephus Daniels' campaigns for prohibition. Publisher Fred Crisp recently retired and was replaced by Orage Quarles III, the paper's first black publisher. Former Executive Editor Frank Daniels III pushed the paper into computer technology and the *N&O* is recognized nationally for its use of such wizardry in investigative and general news reporting. It also boasts a comprehensive daily online edition, as well as a recently launched

INSIDERS' TIP
The Durham *Herald-Sun* is the largest locally owned family newspaper in the state. And like every major daily in the state, including the *News & Observer*, it is a morning newspaper.

regional arts and entertainment web site, www.triangle.com.

The news coverage, separate from the newspaper's editorial opinions, is tough but fair. Its onetime chief investigative sleuth, Pat Stith, still strikes fear in the hearts of bureaucrats. Former editor Claude Sitton won the Pulitzer Prize for commentary in 1983 and former book editor Michael Skube won it in 1989. The 1996 Pulitzer was awarded to the paper for its series on the environmental threats on the Neuse River. Its prize-winning cartoonist, Dwane Powell, deserves a Pulitzer and his caricatures are coveted trophies even by his victims.

With veteran reporters and writers such as Rob Christensen, Joe Neff, Wade Rawlins and Jerry Allegood and columnists Barry Saunders, Dennis Rogers and Ruth Sheehan, the *N&O* is the most influential newspaper in the state with a daily circulation of 186,000 (207,000 for the Sunday edition). Sports fans look to columnists Caulton Tudor and Ned Barnett for insightful commentary. Nationally syndicated columnists include William Safire, Molly Ivins and William Raspberry.

The *N&O* publishes a number of regular features throughout the week, including a Tuesday recreation page, a Wednesday food section and a Friday "What's Up" entertainment section. Another special section, *The North Raleigh News*, goes out with the *N&O* to North Raleigh residents every Friday.

Triangle Publications

The Business Journal
1305 Navaho Dr., Suite 401, Raleigh • 878-0010
• www.bizjournals.com/triangle

The weekly *Business Journal* and Editor Dave Mildenberg work hard and effectively to keep members of the business community in touch with each other. People, company dynamics, commercial real estate, finance,

investments and other aspect of business are reported in an attractive, concise format. Owned by Charlotte-based American City Business Journals, it also publishes an annual business reference guide called the *Book of Lists.*

Business Leader
3801 Wake Forest Rd., Ste. 102, Raleigh
• 872-7077 • www.businessleader.com

Business Leader is a monthly magazine published by Business to Business, Inc. It offers the local business community features on area businesses, marketing strategies, industry trends, business law and commercial real estate, as well as an annual corporate relocation guide.

Carolina Parent
103 W. Main St., Suite. 210, Durham
• 956-2430
• www.carolinaparent.com

A parent and child-oriented publication, *Carolina Parent* was begun in 1987 by publishers and editors Barbara Matchar and Gita Schonfeld. In 1993 it was purchased by *The News & Observer,* which sold the monthly publication to Carolina Parenting, Inc., in 1998. The paper features well-written pieces, both humorous and informative, by and for parents. It includes a comprehensive calendar of events of interest to parents and kids in each issue. It is distributed free throughout the Triangle and has a circulation of more than 35,000. Annual subscriptions are available for $15. *Carolina Parent* also publishes special annual guides about babies, schools, summer camps and birthday parties, as well as a handy "Family Survival Guide."

Carolina Woman
P.O. Box 52687, Durham • 852-5900

Founded by Editor and Publisher Debra Simon in 1993, *Carolina Woman* provides quality feature articles on subjects such as business and health, as well as recipes, a calendar of events and horoscopes. The monthly publication is distributed free throughout the Triangle at businesses, grocery stores and public libraries.

The Independent Weekly
2810 Hillsborough Rd., Durham • 286-1972
• www.indyweek.com
The *Independent*, which began publishing in 1983, hails itself as the Triangle's "news alternative" and it does, indeed, take on some big assignments that others often miss. It was started by Harvard graduate and Nieman Fellow Katherine Fulton. The weekly has settled into a Triangle niche after first trying to be a statewide publication. That niche is a newspaper that's long on crusading opinions and politically correct reporting. It publishes the most entertaining "personals" in the Triangle. *The Independent* has berated local slumlords, state prisons, highway building and General Assembly high-handedness. It also publishes a great entertainment calendar, a comic page of national cartoonists and zany features. Several national journals have cited it as one of the best of its kind in the country. Film critic Godfrey Cheshire provides witty and comprehensive critiques on the latest blockbusters, as well as more obscure independent features. *The Independent's* biggest treat is the wild, brilliant writing by award-winning columnist, Hal Crowther, husband of novelist Lee Smith. Crowther is far and away the state's best newspaper columnist—and a big reason 180,000 "Indy" readers pick it up free at newsstands and racks everywhere on Wednesdays. Other popular columnists include Dan Neil, Melinda Ruley and Derek Jennings.

La Conexion
327 W. Morgan St., Raleigh • 832-1225
The Hispanic community is a growing, dynamic part of Triangle business and culture. *La Conexion* is a free publication that spotlights international, national, statewide and local news of special interest to the Hispanic community. Copies of *La Conexion* may be picked up at area businesses.

MetroMagazine
P.O. Box 6190, Raleigh • 831-0999
• www.metronc.com
One of the Triangle's newest magazines, this slick monthly publication contains in-depth feature articles on politics, business, art, travel and entertainment for the Triangle and Eastern North Carolina. *MetroMagazine's* Editor and Publisher R.B. "Bernie" Reeves founded two other successful Triangle ventures: *The Spectator* and *The Business Journal.*

The Spectator
1318 Dale St., Raleigh
• 828-7393
• www.spectatoronline.com
The Spectator fills an entertainment void that the staid and serious *N&O* misses. The publication, which was founded in 1978 by R. B. Reeves, is currently owned by Creative Loafing, an Atlanta-based publisher. Over the years, it has succeeded not so much by competing with the *N&O*, but by going around it. The weekly specializes in a calendar of events, as well as opinions and reviews on the Triangle's political and nonpolitical life, especially movies, restaurants, music and art, including architecture. Its crop of talented writers has earned a local following and its list of "The Triangle's Best" restaurants, shopping, attractions, etc., is widely read.

The Sun
107 N. Roberson St., Chapel Hill
• 942-5282 • www.thesunmagazine.org
Billed as "A Magazine of Ideas," *The Sun* is a literary publication full of essays, interviews, fiction and poetry. Started by Sy Safransky in 1974, it is distributed to 40,000 subscribers across the country.

Triangle Lifestyle
P.O. Box 12826, Raleigh • 839-0785
• www.trianglelifestyle.com
Triangle Lifestyle magazine offers trendy and traditional features on local arts and

FYI

Unless otherwise noted, the area code for all phone numbers listed in this guide is 919.

entertainment, area restaurants and night life, shopping, fashion, health and fitness and gardening. Publisher Margaret Webb introduced this bimonthly magazine in 1997.

Triangle Newcomer Magazine
5512 Brickhaven Dr., Raleigh
• 878-6151 • www.sigpubs.com

The semiannual *Newcomer Magazine* is published by Signature Publishing, Inc. It includes profiles on area cities, tips on selecting a neighborhood, home buying, building and decorating, utility hookups and pet licensing, as well as information on public and private schools, colleges and universities. Health care options, leisure activities, retirement communities and religious choices are included along with a Triangle business perspective. Charts and maps direct the newcomer to utilities, financial services, accommodations and radio and TV stations.

Triangle Pointer
88 McClamroch Cr. • Chapel Hill
• 968-4801, (800) 400-1901
• www.trianglepointer.com

Triangle Pointer is the Triangle's oldest guide and calendar magazine for lodging, restaurants, entertainment and a number of other items such as sporting events, art exhibits, museums and shopping. This handy little guide is free and distributed at area motels. Published monthly, each issue includes a handy guide map to Chapel Hill, Durham, Raleigh and RTP.

The Urban Hiker
904 Lancaster St., Durham • 416-3174
• www.urbanhiker.net

Started in 1999, this eclectic monthly publication provides features on music, travel, artists, local politic issues and much more, as well as fiction and poetry from local writers. Submissions to *The Urban Hiker* are always welcome.

Television

The Triangle is currently the nation's 29th largest television market. The Triangle's TV stations all see themselves as regional media and have helped foster the idea that the Triangle is one metropolis probably more than any other institution. Cable connections are available in most parts of the Triangle and bring in a number of outside stations, including A&E, AMC, E!, MTV, TBS and TNT. The stations based in the Triangle are listed here alphabetically, along with network and channel number. The numbers may be different, however, if you are a cable subscriber. Both the *Herald-Sun* and the *N&O* provide weekly TV guides.

WKFT-40
3117 Poplarwood Ct., Raleigh • 872-7440
Fayetteville • (910) 323-4040
• www.wkft-tv.com

WKFT is an independent affiliate of Charlotte-based Bahakel Communications, which acquired the station in 1997. Some of its most popular shows are reruns of *Matlock*, *Hunter* and *In the Heat of the Night*.

WLFL-22, WB
3012 Highwoods Blvd., Raleigh
• 872-9535 • www.wlfl.com

Formerly an affiliate of Fox, WLFL became the new Warner Brothers affiliate in 1998. The station, which is owned by Baltimore's Sinclair Communications, offers a popular 10 PM newscast with anchor Bob Vernon. WLFL-22 also features a number of popular new shows for the young set, including *Buffy, the Vampire Slayer*, *Felicity* and *Dawson's Creek*. Other fare includes movies

Photo by Rich Weidman

Whether it be the Blizzard of 2000 or ACC basketball, WRAL-TV in Raleigh provides up-to-date information about events in the Triangle.

and popular reruns, such as *Friends*, *Frasier* and *The Drew Carey Show*.

WNCN-17, NBC
1205 Front St., Raleigh • 836-1717
• www.nbc17.com

WNCN took up the NBC affiliate that WRDC dropped back in 1995 when it switched to UPN. The station features a personable news staff, including co-anchors Byron Day and Donna Gregory, along with comprehensive local news, and weather and traffic reports.

WRAL-5, CBS
2619 Western Blvd., Raleigh
• 821-8555 • www.wral-tv.com

WRAL became an affiliate of CBS in 1985 and before that, had established itself as the premier station in the Triangle and one of the best stations in the country. Though finding the airwaves more competitive these days, the station continues to compete for the top spot among

Triangle viewers. The station's veteran news team features co-anchors David Crabtree and Pam Saulsby, chief meteorologist Greg Fishel and sportscaster Tom Suiter. WRAL goes the extra mile to provide coverage on local newsmakers no matter where they go, be it Hurricane Floyd, the Blizzard of 2000, the state governor's race or the NCAA men's basketball tournament. Its parent company is Jim Goodmon's Capitol Broadcasting.

WRAZ-50, FOX
2619 Western Blvd., Raleigh • 821-8550
• www.fox50.com

Formerly known as WRAZ-50 WB, this station became the new Fox affiliate in 1998. Owned by Carolina Broadcasting System, which leases it to Capitol Broadcasting, WRAZ broadcasts from WRAL's facility. Fox 50, as it calls itself, relies on the Fox network's hit shows, such as *Ally McBeal*, *The X-Files* and *The Simpsons*. It also has a 10 PM newscast. During the season, Fox airs NFL football.

TRIANGLE RADIO STATIONS

Station	Programming Format	Request Line	Special Programming
WAUG 750 AM	Gospel, News, Talk	546-9284	Tom Pope Show
WBBB 96.1 FM	Adult-oriented Rock	860-9600	All Rock All The Time
WCHL 1360 AM	Contemporary Standards	683-6200	Tar Heel Sports, Chapel Hill News
WCLY 1550 AM	Gospel	821-1550	All Gospel All The Time
WCPE 89.7 FM	Classical	556-5178	Opera House, BBC World News, Weekend Classics
WDCG 105.1 FM	Contemporary	860-1051	Bob & Madison
WDNC 620 AM	News, Talk, Sports	683-6200	Bulls, Hornets, Duke Sports, G. Gordon Liddy
WDUR 1490 AM	Gospel	941-1096	All Gospel All The Time
WFXC 104.3 FM	Urban Contemporary	821-1043	Tom Joyner Morning Show
WKIX 96.9 FM	New Country	860-9549	Mad Dog & Morgan Show
WKNC 88.1 FM	Alternative	515-2400	Chainsaw Rock, Strictly Reggae Sunday
WNCU 90.7 FM	Jazz, News	560-9628	8-Track Flashback, Gospel Connections
WNNC 103.9 FM	Gospel	845-1039	The Breakfast Club
WPTF 680 AM	News, Talk, Sports	878-1724	NCSU Sports, Rush Limbaugh, Dr. Laura
WQDR 94.7 FM	Country	860-9470	Pinecone Blue Grass, Country Countdown USA
WQQK 97.5 FM	Contemporary, R&B	848-9765	Gospel Live, Russ Parr Morning Show
WRAL 101.5 FM	Adult Contemporary	860-1015	Cornerstone, Bill & Schatzie in the Morning
WRBZ 850 AM	Talk, Sports	875-9100	Imus, Mike Solarte Show, Sports Babe
WRDU 106.1 FM	Rock	860-1061	John Boy and Billy, Rock Line
WRSN 93.9 FM	Soft Rock	361-0939	Love Songs After Dark
WRTP 1000 AM	Christian Contemporary	471-9787	Focus on the Family
WSHA 88.9 FM	Jazz	546-8430	All Jazz All The Time
WTRG 100.7 FM	Oldies	860-1007	Mike & Oz in the Morning
WUNC 91.5 FM	NPR News, Classical	966-5454	Morning Edition, All Things Considered, Back Porch Music
WWND 102.9FM	Jazz	860-1029	All Jazz All The Time

WRDC-28, UPN
3012 Highwoods Blvd., Raleigh
• 872-2854 • www.upn.com

This local UPN affiliate runs such high-rated shows as *Star Trek Voyager*, *WWF Smackdown!* and popular syndicated reruns. WRDC switched from NBC to UPN in 1995 and no longer sponsors a local newscast. Original programming is limited, as UPN is a developing network. Like WLFL, WRDC is owned by Sinclair Communications.

WRPX-47, PAX
3209 Gresham Lake Rd., Raleigh
• 872-4748 • www.paxtv.com

The Triangle's newest television station, WRPX-47, hit the airwaves in 1998. Owned by Paxson Communications Corporation of West Palm Beach, Florida, PAX-TV features family fare such as *Touched by an Angel* and *It's a Miracle*.

WTVD-11, ABC
411 Liberty St., Durham • 683-1111
• www.abc11tv.com

WTVD has been trading the No. 1 spot with WRAL over the years. It is the home of solid, veteran North Carolina reporter, Larry Stogner, and news anchor Miriam Thomas.

The station gives more attention to political coverage than the competition and its veteran reporters have good noses for news and scoops. It broadcasts 90 minutes of local news and sports starting at 5 PM. Its sports coverage team has attracted national notice. WTVD has a bureau in Fayetteville that keeps us updated with operations at Ft. Bragg. The station's coverage of the weather is excellent.

WUNC-4, PBS
10 T.W. Alexander Dr., RTP
• 549-7000 • www.unctv.org

The state's university system operates the public television channels in North Carolina. The main studio is in Research Triangle Park. Founded in 1955, UNC-TV is one of the best PBS affiliates in the country and has a large following. WUNC has launched several programs that have become national PBS shows. Its local coverage of public affairs includes daily reviews when the North Carolina General Assembly is in session. Award-winning programs that UNC-TV produces include *North Carolina Now*, *North Carolina People* and *The Woodwright's Shop*, among others.

Unlike many public television operations, WUNC has a seasoned staff. The station broadcasts popular programming such as *Antiques Roadshow*, *National Geographic*, *Nova*, *Frontline* and British mysteries and comedies. The Sesame Street gang also lives here.

Time Warner Cable
Carrboro • 967-7068
Cary • 832-2225
Chapel Hill • 968-4631
Durham • 220-4481
Raleigh • 832-2225
Wake Forest • 556-6011
• www.twc-nc.com

Time Warner Cable serves Triangle viewers and offers several levels of service. You can get the networks, ESPN, CNN, TNT, Headline News, USA, BET, TBS, WGN and some others, including local access for about $34 a month.

Night Life

Tired of sitting at home night after night watching *Who Wants to be a Millionaire?* Maybe it's time to get out of the house and check out the area's burgeoning night life scene. From unpretentious neighborhood pubs to upscale trendy bars and everything in between, the Triangle offers something for everyone.

Catch the hottest regional and national acts at ALLTEL Pavilion at Walnut Creek, the new Raleigh Entertainment and Sports Arena, The Ritz and The ArtsCenter. Groove to the latest, loudest live rock at the Brewery, Cat's Cradle or Local 506. Boogie the night away to top-40 dance tunes at The Cellar, Jillian's and Bowties. Dance the Texas two-step at The Longbranch. Mellow out to acoustic guitar or jazz at Skylight Exchange, Cappers or the West End Wine Bar. Learn how to shag at Red's Beach Music. Grab a pint of ale at authentic pubs such as The Fox and Hound, James Joyce, RiRa or Tir Na Nog. Enjoy up-and-coming comedians at Charlie Goodnight's or ComedySportz. Cheer your favorite college team to victory at sports bars like Woody's, North Carolina Sports Bar and Devine's.

Movie buffs have a variety of choices as well. State-of-the-art theaters with stadium seating include the Raleigh Grande 16, Park Place 16 and Crossroads 20. The restored Carolina Theatre in downtown Durham specializes in independent films. Raleigh's Blue Ridge 14 offers second-run films at budget ticket prices, while Raleighwood Cinema Grill allows you to eat a meal and drink a beer during the feature. There's even a drive-in theater, the Starlite in Durham.

For more information on what's happening in the Triangle, see our chapters on "Attractions," "Annual Events" and "The Arts." Also check out the weekly periodicals, *Independent* and *Spectator*, and the Friday entertainment section of your newspaper.

Cary

While most night life in suburbia remains G-rated, there are a handful of places where you can kick up some excitement.

Coyote Cafe
1014 Ryan Rd. • 469-5253
• www.coyotecafe.citysearch.com

Coyote Cafe serves up Southwestern fare and features classic rock, jazz, blues or acoustic music on weekend nights. Local favorite Kim Hale usually takes the stage on Friday nights. The low-key action moves outside on the patio during warmer months.

The Fox and Hound
MacGregor Village • 380-0080
• www.foxandhound.citysearch.com

On Thursdays, musicians play blues, jazz or acoustic music as the good English fare is served at this authentic pub.

Newton's Southwest
1837 N. Harrison Ave. • 677-1777

The Newtons made a hit with a bit of Texas in north Cary. At the Southwest, the music gets loud and from March 'til October, the feet kick out on a heated, outdoor dance floor called The Pepper Patio. Thursday night is reserved for beach music.

Woody's Cary Tavern and Grill
928 W. Chatham St. • 467-1816

Once known as Wivi & Me, this eclectic pub and grill features Karaoke Thursday and Saturday nights, and live entertainment every Friday. It also offers four pool tables, eight TVs and pinball and video games.

Woody's Sports Tavern & Grill
8322 Chapel Hill Rd. • 380-7737

Woody's has two oak bars, 11 satellite systems that feed 25 TV screens, pool tables

Photo by Rich Weidman

The best of new local and touring bands take the stage at the legendary Cat's Cradle.

and dartboards. The menu features burgers, spicy chicken wings, sandwiches and late-night munchies. On Friday and Saturday nights, bands perform blues, rock and classic rock. During the week, dart leagues compete and tournaments are held on a regular basis. A number of area sports fan clubs meet here.

Chapel Hill

Although Chapel Hill is a small town, there's always been a large interest in music here. It's a regular stop for young and alternative bands on tour. The live music in night spots in town is often innovative and occasionally astounding. Here's our guide to a few places that regularly feature live music, usually for a modest cover charge.

The ArtsCenter
300-G East Main St., Carrboro • 929-ARTS

The ArtsCenter often sponsors jazz shows, including a Sunday night open jam once a month. You can also catch scheduled performances by well-known musicians and singers like David Wilcox and Livingston Taylor. The ArtsCenter offers table seating for some shows and refreshments are available. You're in for a treat at a reasonable admission price.

Cat's Cradle
300 E. Main St., Carrboro
• 967-9053
• www.catscradle.com

The old favorite, Cat's Cradle keeps on keepin' on, tucked away near the ArtsCenter in Carrboro. Popular with the twenty- and thirty-somethings for the past few decades, the Cradle is open seven nights a week, with the best of new local and touring bands. In addition, the Cradle hosts an annual Reggae Jam in April. Advance tickets are available for some shows at local independent music stores. If you call the Cradle, a recorded message will give you current information on hours and upcoming bands and musicians. Shows usually begin at 10 PM.

The Cave
452 1/2 W. Franklin St.
• 968-9308
• www.caverntavern.com

The Cave is a basement pub below Franklin Street that has been around forever (well at least since the 1960s). A true local haunt, it features everything from folk to rock 'n' roll, blues, alternative, bluegrass and acoustic. Music begins nightly around 10 PM. Early shows take place Thursday and Friday nights. The Cave is a great place for a cold beer and a game of pool.

He's Not Here
112 1/2 W. Franklin St. • 942-7939

The name of this popular gathering place comes from an old cartoon, in which the bartender answering the phone says, "He's not here," while all the customers shake their heads. A Chapel Hill landmark well known to Insiders, He's Not Here features bands at 9 PM on Friday and Saturday nights and Karaoke Night for would-be stars on Sunday at 9:30 PM. Dart leagues also compete here. He's Not Here is known for its famous giant blue cups of beer.

Local 506
506 W. Franklin St. • 942-5506

Local 506 has become an institution among local music fans for providing a great place to see great bands. In August, Local 506 hosts Sleazefest, an annual multi-night extravaganza of questionable taste. National and regional touring bands as well as the best local artists ply their trade here. Local 506 has all ABC permits and a membership is required. There is almost always a cover charge.

North Carolina Sports Bar
504 W. Franklin St. • 929-6978

A local favorite, especially among grad students, the Sports Bar offers 19 satellite feeds that beam in about every sport imaginable. The premises include pool tables, air hockey and hoop games. Enjoy burgers, sandwiches, appetizers and desserts from the Carolina Grill while you root the Tar Heels to victory. Many area fan clubs meet here.

Skylight Exchange
405 1/2 W. Rosemary St. • 933-5550

The Skylight Exchange is a coffeehouse/music club/restaurant and a used book and record store business. There is music Thursday through Saturday (mostly folk, jazz and bluegrass) and open mike nights on Monday and Wednesday, most often without a cover. The Skylight Exchange is always good for a sandwich or light snack, cup of coffee and several hours of browsing through old paperbacks, records and tapes.

Top of the Hill
Corner of Franklin & Columbia Sts.
• 929-8676
• www.topofthehill.citysearch.com

Top of the Hill is a popular downtown restaurant that offers live music on Thursday nights from 8 to 11 PM. In good weather, the music moves out to the third-floor heated patio, which provides a spectacular view of downtown. Even on nights without music, this is definitely a "hot" night spot for Chapel Hill.

West End Wine Bar
450 West Franklin St. • 967-7599

The West End Wine Bar offers a reprieve from the typical noisy and rowdy Chapel Hill bar environment. It features 80 wines by the glass and 200 bottle selections. Live jazz takes place on Tuesday and Thursday nights.

Durham

If you're looking for late night music, Durham has several night spots, where you'll find mostly jazz, folk or reggae-rock, for a modest cover charge. A number of popular restaurants and bars are clustered in and around Brightleaf Square and along Ninth Street near Duke University's East Campus.

Devine's Restaurant & Sports Bar
904 W. Main St. • 682-0228
• www.devinesrestaurant.com

Opened in 1978, Devine's offers live rock 'n' roll, R&B or blues music a couple of nights a week during the winter and about five nights a week during the summer. Wide-screened TVs are tuned to the day's sporting events.

INSIDERS' TIP

Aspiring musicians can showcase their talents in front of live audiences at night spots that feature open mike nights such as the Skylight Exchange in Chapel Hill and Berkeley Cafe in Raleigh, among others.

Down Under Pub
802 W. Main St. • 682-0039
• www.downunderpub.citysearch.com

A popular hangout for Duke students, the Down Under Pub offers occasional live music, from folk to alternative. It has a pool table, foosball and two dartboards. Enjoy pub fare and choose from a wide selection of European ales and lagers. The Pub is located along Main Street across the street from Brightleaf Square.

Duke Coffeehouse
Duke University, East Campus
• 684-4069

Duke students and locals alike flock to the Duke Coffeehouse to hear live bands playing everything from acoustic guitar to alternative rock. It's also packed during Duke basketball games with students who were not lucky enough to get a ticket.

Durham Alive!
Durham Civic Center Plaza
• 682-2800

Durham Alive! is a free concert series that takes place from 5:30 PM to 7:30 PM on the last Thursday of every month during the summer just outside the historic Carolina Theatre. Enjoy the sounds of rock 'n' roll, beach music and R&B.

George's Garage
737 Ninth St. • 286-4131
• www.georgesgarage.com

George's Garage is a popular upscale restaurant on Ninth Street that contains a 40-foot bar, wide-screened TVs and a dance floor. It features live music Friday and Saturday nights. Duke students can be found at the Garage on Thursday nights.

The Green Room
1108 Broad St. • 286-2359

One of the best billiard spots in the Triangle, The Green Room features 10 regulation size pool tables, as well as dartboards, shuffleboards, video poker and a foosball table.

James Joyce
912 West Main St. • 683-3022

The author of *Ulysses* himself would have felt right at home in this cozy Irish pub, billed as "A Little Bit of Ireland in Durham." Photos of Joyce line the walls. James Joyce is located across the street from Brightleaf Square.

Duke students flock to Tobacco Roadhouse, a restaurant and brew pub located in a converted warehouse in Durham's downtown tobacco district.

Talk of the Town
108 E. Main St. • 682-7747

Talk of the Town specializes in jazz and rhythm and blues Thursday through Saturday night. There is a cover charge.

Tobacco Roadhouse
115 North Duke St. • 688-4505
• www.tobaccoroadhouse.citysearch.com

Located in a converted warehouse near Brightleaf Square, Tobacco Roadhouse Restaurant and Brewpub features live entertainment on its outside deck Wednesday through Saturday, a large dance floor ("The Asylum"), a late-night menu, pool tables and video games.

Raleigh

Raleigh has a reputation as a waystation for bands, solo artists and comedians working toward the big time. You can see these people at places like The Ritz, Berkeley Cafe, The Longbranch, The Brewery and Charlie Goodnight's Comedy Club. Raleigh itself attracts big-name performers to the ALLTEL Pavilion at Walnut Creek, including Bob Dylan, Jimmy Buffett, James Taylor, Shania Twain and Britney Spears.

Raleigh was once touted as a city with everything but a night life. True no longer. The West End, a developed section of old warehouse space downtown, might change some minds. Here you'll find retail establishments, restaurants and clubs popping up around and between Hargett and Cabarrus streets. Individual business owners here have enlivened the downtown area and offered the city a variety of places to be seen after dark.

City Market boasts the city's first brewery, Greenshield's, as well as ComedySportz comedy club and Yancey's Jazz and Blues Cafe. The nearby Warehouse District is home to the hip retro Vertigo Diner; Jillian's Billiards Cafe; The Warehouse; and Humble Pie, as well as Flying Saucer Draught Emporium, Club Oxygen, Kings and Berkeley Cafe. In addition, the so-called Powerhouse Square or "Glenwood South" area off Glenwood Avenue offers such lively night spots as Southend Brewery, RiRa Irish Pub, The

Enjoy pub fare, a wide selection of ales and occasional live music at The Down Under Pub in Durham.

Rhinoceros Club, 42nd Street Oyster Bar and 518 West Italian Cafe. Another new and happening nightspot is Time, a dance club catering to the 25-and-over crowd in the former Have A Nice Day Cafe location at 901 Tryon Street. The Raleigh Entertainment Trolley runs downtown Thursday, Friday and Saturday nights from 6:40 PM to 1:40 AM.

Keep your eye on downtown Raleigh. New night clubs are sprouting up all over the place.

42nd Street Oyster Bar
508 W. Jones St. • 831-2811

A downtown landmark, this restaurant and bar is a place to be seen among the single's set. It has all ABC permits and live music on weekends—and an interesting decor, including a bar mural that celebrates the late restaurateur Thad Eure Jr. and friends. If you're interested in meeting people, then go on Friday or Saturday night. You will definitely meet people—waiting to get in!

Alive After Five
Fayetteville Street Mall,
Civic Center Plaza • 831-6011

Alive After Five is an after-work event sponsored by the city and others to get people downtown. Surprise ... it works! It happens only in the summer and only on Thursdays, but it has become popular with the younger professionals and working crowd as a place to hear free live music and mingle. The bands are rock 'n' roll and R&B.

ALLTEL Pavilion at Walnut Creek
Rock Quarry and Sunnybrook Rds.
Concert Line: 831-6666
Ticketmaster: 834-4000
• www.alltelpavilion.com

When there's a hot concert in town, this is the night life for the Triangle and eastern North Carolina. It is the latest in multimillion-dollar outdoor amphitheaters built with public and private funds. Built in 1991, the $13.5 million amphitheater has a capacity of about 20,000, 7,000 under the roof. Walnut Creek has seen tremendous sellout performances over the years, including the Dave Matthews Band, Pearl Jam and perennial favorite Jimmy Buffett and the Coral Reefer Band, a hit with Triangle "parrotheads."

Berkeley Cafe
217 W. Martin St. • 821-0777

No, this is not where expatriate Californians sip coffee and get down. However, poetry is read here during the Monday night "Poetry Slam" (8 to 11 PM) and an open mike night takes place on Tuesday or Wednesday nights. Berkeley is a small cafe and club facing Nash Square downtown and the live music won't blow you out in the street. Good bands on the rise as well as local folks play here. Because of its R&B and local grass roots rock acts, one critic described the cafe as "a little bit of Memphis in downtown Raleigh." Most shows start at 10 PM.

Bowties
Hilton North Raleigh, 3415 Wake
Forest Rd. • 872-2323

Bowties draws some of the yuppie crowd and features high-energy dance music. The big screen and four TV monitors for music videos or ACC basketball make this a popular place on game nights. It offers half-price appetizers and has all ABC permits.

The Brewery
3009 Hillsborough St. • 834-7018
• www.breweryrocks.com

If your heart is in alternative rock and rock and roll, this is the place for you. Opened in 1983, The Brewery brings in the best of the original rock groups and features good local and regional bands. Its proximity to NCSU gives the crowd a student flavor. Beer is served and the cover charge is usually modest. The crowd—300 is the limit—likes music. It's one of the more popular stops on the rock tour for working bands. Music usually starts around 10:30 PM.

Cappers
4421 Six Forks Rd. • 787-8963

Located across the street from North Hills Mall, this North Raleigh restaurant is a hit among Triangle jazz buffs. Cappers often leads *The Spectator* magazine's annual "Best List" as the best place for jazz. Musicians such as Lindsay Rosebrock, Joshua Bland and Norb Bleau are featured most of the week. Cappers' popular "Icons of Jazz Series" includes such legendary performers as Chuck Mangione and Stanley Jordan.

The Cellar
Dawson & Cabarrus Sts. • 836-9966
• www.warehouserestaurant.com

After enjoying a relaxing gourmet meal at The Warehouse Restaurant, head downstairs to The Cellar. A lively, 18,000-square-foot nightclub, it contains video gaming machines

---

INSIDERS' TIP

Movie buffs should check out the 3,700-title video rental store at downtown Durham's Carolina Theatre, which boasts a great selection of classic, cult and foreign films.

TRIANGLE COFFEEHOUSES

CARY

Barnes & Noble Cafe	760 S.E. Maynard Rd.	467-3866
Caribou Coffee Company		
Preston Corners	4214 N.W. Cary Pkwy.	462-0690
Maynard & Kildaire	109 S.W. Maynard Rd.	319-6265
The Ground Finalé	1287 N.W. Maynard Rd.	460-4747
Java Jive	919 N. Harrison Ave.	481-3838
Jitters Drive-Thru Espresso	920 Kildaire Farm Rd.	481-1002
Outer Banks Coffeehouse	976 High House Rd.	462-3320
Jumpin' Java Coffee Shoppe	122 N. Salem St., Apex	362-6207
Paradigm Coffee House	Waverly Place	859-8099

CHAPEL HILL

A Southern Season	Eastgate Shopping Center	929-7133
Caffe Driade	1215-A E. Franklin St.	942-2333
Caribou Coffee	110 W. Franklin St.	933-5404
Carolina Coffee Shop	138 E. Franklin St.	942-6875
Coffee Mill Roastery	161 E. Franklin St.	929-1727
Cup A Joe	1129 Weaver Dairy Rd.	967-2002
Java Cafe	231 S. Elliott Rd.	967-4888
P.J.'s Coffee & Tea Cafe	1289 N. Fordham Blvd.	967-5411
Starbucks	103 E. Franklin St.	932-3824

DURHAM

Barnes & Noble Cafe	New Hope Commons	489-3012
The Coffee Beanery	4001 Chapel Hill Blvd.	489-1866
Francesca's Dessert Caffe	706 Ninth St.	286-4177
Starbucks	1817 Martin Luther King Pkwy.	403-6676

RALEIGH

Barnes & Noble Cafe	Crabtree Valley Mall	782-0030
Caribou Coffee Company	6511 Falls of Neuse Rd.	790-5397
Classic Coffees	7451 Six Forks Rd.	848-9878
Coffee Beanery	4325 Glenwood Ave.	782-3820
Cream & Bean	2010 Hillsborough St.	828-2663
Cup A Joe		
Hillsborough	3100 Hillsborough St.	828-9665
Mission Valley	2109 Avent Ferry Rd.	828-9886
North Raleigh	5039 Falls of Neuse Rd.	876-4588
New World Coffee House	4112 Pleasant Valley Rd.	786-0091
Starbucks Coffee		
University Grille	2500 Hillsborough St.	836-0814
Falls of the Neuse	900-101 Spring Forest Rd.	873-9615
Pleasant Valley Promenade	6282-104 Glenwood Ave.	785-0111
Cameron Village	501 Oberlin Rd.	856-9444
Olde Raleigh Village	3101 Edwards Mill Rd.	789-4422
Stonehenge Market	7498 Creedmoor Rd.	846-0633
Third Place Coffee House	1811 Glenwood Ave.	834-6566

Conveniently located on bustling Hillsborough street across from NCSU, Mitch's Tavern is a legendary student hangout.

Photo by Rich Weidman

(winners receive gift certificates), pool tables and snooker tables. Catch sports action on The Cellar's mega screen TVs, and enjoy music and dancing at this late-night hotspot. Live music can be heard Thursday nights.

Charlie Goodnight's Comedy Club
861 W. Morgan St. • 828-5233
• www.charliegoodnights.com

Opened in 1981, Charlie Goodnight's is considered one of the best comedy clubs on the East Coast. It's been a stop for familiar acts and now features famous names like Richard Jeni, Pam Stone and Carrot Top, as well as scores of up-and-coming comedians. Charlie Goodnight's restaurant downstairs serves Mexican fare and the club serves drinks and snacks. It has all ABC permits. Shows run Tuesday through Saturday with one show a night during the week, two on Friday and three on Saturday.

ComedySportz
City Market, Raleigh • 829-0822
• www.comedysportz.com

ComedySportz offers live competitive improv comedy every Friday and Saturday night. Two teams of comedians battle against each other for points and laughs. A second ComedySportz location is at 128 East Franklin Street in Chapel Hill. Shows take place Friday and Saturday nights. Call for reservations.

Crowley's Old Favorites Restaurant & Lounge
3071 Medlin Dr. • 787-3431

There are three Crowley's and this was the first one. It attracts some of the young and beautiful and boisterous bunch, and the food is good, too. The other two locations are Crowley's Courtyard at 3201 Edwards Mill Road, 783-5447, and Crowley's of Stonehenge at 7330 Creedmoor Road, 676-3431—the latter which offers live music on weekends.

East Village Grill and Bar
Hillsborough St. and Dixie Tr. • 821-9985
• www.eastvillagegrill.com

East Village's outside deck, with its laid-back atmosphere, is the perfect spot to meet and mingle. It was voted the Triangle's "Best Deck" in *The Spectator* magazine's annual reader survey.

Expressions
110 E. Hargett St. • **835-0565**
• **www.welcome.to/expressions**
Expressions features live blues, jazz and reggae acts. Wednesday is open mike poetry night, Thursday is reserved for live jazz, Friday is a reggae dance party and Saturday is live reggae. Call for current schedule.

Flying Saucer
Draught Emporium
Harrington & Morgan Sts. • **821-PINT**
• **www.beerknurd.com**
Flying Saucer is a 4,000-square-foot pub that boasts nearly 200 varieties of beer, including 80 beers on tap. The menu includes typical pub fare. Thousands of plates and saucers line the walls. Enjoy TVs, darts and pool tables.

Hillsborough Street Hangouts
NCSU strip along Hillsborough St.
This is no combat zone, but with the 40+ bars and clubs that line Hillsborough Street between Oberlin Road and Gorman Street, it's a busy part of the city for night life. Some of the hottest spots where you will find the young, beautiful and generally impoverished student crowd are the Comet Lounge, the Five-O Cafe, the Cantina, Boo's Hideaway,

TRIANGLE CINEMAS

CARY & MORRISVILLE
Crossroads 20	Crossroads Plaza	226-2000
Park Place 16	9525 Chapel Hill Rd.	481-9686

CHAPEL HILL
Carolina Theatre	108-B E. Franklin St.	933-8464
Chelsea Theater	1129 Weaver Dairy Rd.	968-3005
The Lumina	Southern Village	932-9000
Movies at Timberlyne	Timberlyne Shopping Ctr.	933-8600
Plaza Theatres	Village Plaza Shopping Ctr.	967-4737
Varsity Theatres	123 E. Franklin St.	967-8665

DURHAM & RTP
Carmike 7	2000 Avondale Dr.	220-3393
Carolina Theatre Cinemas	309 Morgan St.	560-3060
Starlite Drive-In	2523 E. Club Blvd.	688-1037
Willowdaile Cinema 8	Willowdaile Shopping Ctr.	477-4681
Wynnsong 15	1807 Martin Luther King Pkwy.	489-9020

RALEIGH & GARNER
Blue Ridge 14	600 Blue Ridge Rd.	828-9003
Carmike Cinema 15	5501 Atlantic Springs Rd.	878-8778
Colony Twin Theatre	5438 Six Forks Rd.	847-5677
Garner Towne Square 10	2600 Timber Dr.	779-2201
Raleigh Grande 16	U.S. 70 and Lynn Rd.	226-2000
Raleighwood Cinema Grill	Falls Village Shopping Ctr.	847-0326
Rialto	1620 Glenwood Ave.	856-0111

Mitch's Tavern, Cup A Joe, Pantana's Pool Hall and Saloon, and Sadlack's. The Comet Lounge serves liquor, so it's a private club. It has DJs and a dance floor. The Five-O Cafe is above Studio I Theater, serves only beer and is a popular dance bar. Tucked in under the Cafe is Boo's Hideaway, which offers live music, usually alternative country. The Cantina crowd is younger and sits on the porch outside in good weather. An upstairs dance floor also features live bands. Mitch's Tavern is a favorite among students and locals alike. It's packed during NCSU football and basketball games. A scene from *Bull Durham* was filmed here. Cup A Joe is a coffee house that features live music some nights. Across the street is Pantana's, a pool hall with dartboards and video games that serves beer. It features live music—"Southern rock," alternative, rock and Top 40. Sadlack's is a laid-back sub shop that serves beer. Located across from the NCSU bell tower, Sadlack's has served as a local gathering place for years.

Humble Pie
317 S. Harrington St. • 829-9222

Billed as "Downtown Raleigh's Oldest Fine Dining Restaurant," Humble Pie hosts local and regional rock 'n' roll acts on the weekends. Shows take place Friday and Saturday from 11 PM to 2 AM. Dinner is served Tuesday through Saturday from 6 to 10 PM and there is also a Sunday brunch.

Irregardless Cafe
901 W. Morgan St. • 790-4304
• www.irregardless.citysearch.com

Irregardless offers live jazz, classical and acoustic music most nights of the week. Except for special performances, there is usually no cover charge. Call for details. Don't miss "Irregardless After Dark"—dancing and live bands every Saturday night after 9 PM.

Jillian's
117 S. West St. • 821-7887
• www.jillians.com

Billed as "Your Food and Entertainment Universe," Jillian's entertainment complex contains a sports bar, Hibachi Grill, a dance floor in "The Groove Shack," outdoor deck, 16 pool tables, ping-pong, darts, outdoor volleyball court and video games. An outdoor beach party is held most Sundays.

Kings
424 S. McDowell St. • 831-1005
• www.kingsbarcade.com

If you're seeking cold beer, a rockin' jukebox, classic video games, foosball and pool tables, look no farther than King's. Live music—usually showcasing local talent—can be heard most nights of the week. Kings is open from 8 PM to 2 AM every night. It's located next door to the Vertigo Diner.

Lakeside Lounge
227 S. Wilmington St. • 833-6557
• www.lakesideloungeraleigh.com

A small private club for members and their guests, Lakeside Lounge offers a wide variety of beer, an eclectic jukebox, an outdoor patio and live rock 'n' roll most nights of the week. Shows start at 10:30 PM.

The Longbranch
600 Creekside Dr. • 829-1125
• www.longbranchsaloon.com

The Longbranch is one of the four or five places in town where you can find name entertainment. Country legends such as George Jones, Merle Haggard and Emmlou Harris have all taken the stage here. It's a membership club with all ABC permits. Despite its name, it features Top 40 acts, some "beach music" and rock. The Longbranch also offers a room for country and western and country rock groups, so you won't feel out of place in your cowboy boots and hat. You can meet and mingle and even take line dancing and country dance lessons.

O'Malley's Tavern
5228 Holly Ridge Dr. • 787-1234

Open seven days a week until 2:30 AM, O'Malley's Tavern is a friendly neighborhood pub in Oak Park Shopping Center that features live bands Thursday through Sunday and open mike night on Wednesdays. It also offers wide-screen TVs, pool tables and dart boards.

Players Retreat
105 Oberlin Rd. • 755-9589

A Raleigh institution since 1951, the PR is a true-blue neighborhood pub or tavern that is rumored to be the oldest of its kind between Washington and Atlanta. Near the NCSU campus, many a State student has grown wise watching the fish behind the bar and debating the finer points of ACC basketball. Pool, darts and video games are available. The PR also boasts one of the best hamburgers in town. If you plan to live in Raleigh, you need to visit the PR at least once to appreciate the culture.

Playmakers
3801 Hillsborough St. • 743-5544
• www.playmakers-sports-cafe.com

A relatively new addition to the Raleigh night life scene, Playmakers is billed as "The Saucy Sports Cafe." Enjoy ribs and wings with eight signature sauces while you view sports action from more than 20 TVs. Relax on the 2,000-square-foot patio and listen to live music most nights of the week. It is located in a renovated warehouse across the street from Meredith College.

Raleighwood Cinema Grill
6609 Falls of the Neuse Rd. • 847-8370
24-Hour Movie Hotline • 847-0326
• www.raleighwood.citysearch.com

Raleighwood's logo says it all, "Great Movies, Food & Spirits!" Basically, the idea is to combine great food, a fun atmosphere and Hollywood's newest movies to create an enjoyable and affordable evening out. The contemporary decor is upbeat and the wide beverage selection and tempting food is served by a friendly and hospitable staff. The menu features pizza, burgers, chicken wings, subs and salads, as well as beverages, including beer, wine and soft drinks.

Red's Beach Music
4400 Craftsman Dr. • 876-7337

If you live in North Carolina, you should know about beach music—easy moving rock 'n' roll/soul of the late 1950s and early '60s. It took root on the Carolina campuses and is

The dueling piano players at Rum Runners tropical night spot in Raleigh encourage audience participation during their lively shows.

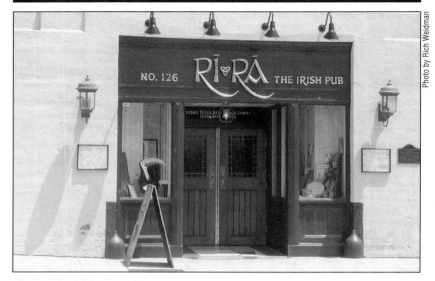

For genuine Irish atmosphere and award-winning food, look no farther than RiRa pub.

an institution now. Red's capitalizes on the nostalgia and the crowd there will reflect the age of the music. It's relaxed and a good place to take the spouse to shake up the metabolism. Red's is a private club located in North Raleigh and has all ABC permits. Shag lessons are offered on the first Monday and Tuesday of each month.

The Rhinoceros Club
410 Glenwood Ave., Ste. 140
• 831-0400 • www.rhinoclub.com

Open seven nights a week, Rhino Club is an upscale members-only club located in the old Pine Street Creamery building on Glenwood Avenue. The Club bills itself as "an honest drinking bar for members and their guests." It's a great spot to mingle and enjoy drinks, a game of billiards and live music. Rhino is part of a chain that includes clubs in Charlotte, Greensboro and Wilmington.

RiRa
126 N. West St. • 833-5535
• www.rira.com

Billed as the "Best of Ireland's Food, Music and Merriment," RiRa offers a Sunday Jazz Brunch, Open Mike Night on Monday, live music on Thursday and crowds of partygoers on Friday and Saturday nights.

The Ritz
2820 Industrial Dr. • 836-8535
Ticketmaster: 834-4000

The Ritz has had many lives and the latest incarnation may be its liveliest. It has the best in tour music, from country to rock, and there's plenty of room and lively dancing. Past performers include Dave Matthews Band, Bare Naked Ladies, Foo Fighters, Live, Hootie and the Blowfish, Elliott Smith and Sonic Youth. The Ritz features Latino music every other Friday night.

INSIDERS' TIP

Looking for a game for darts? Check out Fox & Hound, Upper Deck Sports Pub and Woody's in Cary; He's Not Here and N.C. Original Sports Bar in Chapel Hill; Down Under Pub, The Green Room and Tobacco Roadhouse in Durham; and Blinco's, O'Malley's, Player's Retreat and Tir na nOg in Raleigh, among others.

Rum Runners
City Market • 878-1959
• www.rumrunnersusa.com

Enjoy outrageous live entertainment at this tropical-themed restaurant and rock-and-roll singalong bar that features dueling piano players. The piano show takes place Wednesday through Sunday nights. A full dinner menu is served nightly.

Second Empire Tavern
$$$$ • 330 Hillsborough St., Raleigh
• 829-3663 • www.second-empire.com

Second Empire features fine dining in the elegant but relaxed atmosphere of the historic Dodd-Hinsdale House. Its casual, pub-like Tavern is the perfect spot to unwind in a relaxing atmosphere after a long day at work. It has an inviting bar, a dining area and an outside covered and heated patio area where you can listen to live entertainment every Friday night. The Tavern menu features items such as Chicago Baby Back Ribs, Angel Hair Pasta and Seafood Paella.

Southend Brewery & Smokehouse
505 W. Jones St. • 832-4604

Southend, which is housed in a renovated warehouse at Powerhouse Square in the burgeoning Glenwood South district, offers live music Thursday through Sunday. Dance the night away in the Powerhouse Lounge Dance Club. Wednesday is Karaoke Night.

Time
901 Tryon St. • 831-9222

Time is a new nightclub located in the former Have a Nice Day Cafe spot next to Charlie Goodnight's Comedy Club. It has a spacious dance floor and caters to the over-21 crowd.

Tir na nOg
218 South Blount St. • 833-7795
• www.tirnanogirishpub.com

Tir na nOg is Gaelic for "land of eternal youth." An authentic Irish pub and restaurant located at Moore Square, it features delicious food and live music Tuesday through Saturday. Patrons can relax with a cold draft beer or enjoy a competitive game of darts. Tir na nOg also has a Sunday brunch with a make-your-own Bloody Mary Bar.

The Warehouse
Dawson and Cabarrus Sts. • 836-9966
• www.warehouserestaurant.com

The Warehouse complex is located in downtown Raleigh's "West End" district. The Warehouse Restaurant serves innovative new American cuisine, while The Warehouse's bustling nightclub features a sports bar, music and dancing, wide-screen TVs and pool tables. Wednesday is Swing Night and Thursday is College Night. A second nightclub, The Cellar, is located downstairs (see separate write-up in this chapter).

Photo by Rich Weidman

Housed in the historic CP&L powerhouse building, Southend Brewery and Smokehouse offers dining, live entertainment, a dance floor and banquet facilities.

Lights, Camera . . . On Location in the Triangle

According to the North Carolina Film Commission, the state has attracted more than 500 features, six network TV series and more than $5 billion in production revenues. In 1999 alone, the state's film industry was the site of 65 major productions with estimated revenues of $300.2 million.

Although the Screen Gems Studio in Wilmington (known these days as "Hollywood East" or "Wilmywood") has captured much of the attention surrounding North Carolina's burgeoning film industry, the Triangle (mostly Durham) has also been the site of a number of classic— and not so classic—movies over the years. In fact, Durham as a subject for Hollywood dates all the way back

to a 1950 film called *Brightleaf* that starred Gary Cooper and Lauren Bacall. Here is a list of some of the more notable films to have had scenes shot in the Triangle:

Brainstorm [1983]—Scenes for this "virtual reality" thriller were shot at the Burroughs Wellcome (now known as Glaxo SmithKline) facility in Research Triangle Park. The film served as the directorial debut of Douglas Trumball, who had created the special effects for *2001: A Space Odyssey* and *Close Encounters of the Third Kind*. *Brainstorm* is notable for being Natalie Wood's last movie; she died in a boating accident during production. A double was used to finish some of her scenes. The film also starred Christopher Walken, Cliff Robertson and Louise Fletcher.

Weeds [1987]—Nick Nolte portrayed an ex-con turned playwright who organizes the "Barbed Wire Theatre" acting troupe of other ex-cons who perform plays at area prisons. Scenes were filmed at North Carolina Central University and Duke University. *Weeds* was based on a true story.

Bull Durham [1988]—The historic 1926 Durham Athletic Park at 426 Morris Street served as the main setting for this comedy about life on a minor league baseball team. In fact, the success of this flick brought worldwide stardom to the Bulls and their hometown. Kevin Costner portrayed aging ballplayer "Crash" Davis (named after Lawrence "Crash" Davis, a legendary Bulls catcher during the 1940s). The film also starred Tim Robbins as reckless young pitcher "Nuke" LaLoosh and Susan Sarandon as philosophic love interest Annie Savoy. In addition to the ballpark, scenes were shot in downtown Durham, at a Queen Anne-style house on North Mangum Street and at Mitch's Tavern across from North Carolina State University in Raleigh. The D.C. May Warehouse at 215 Morris Street in Durham was also used as a location for baseball offices and locker rooms.

The Handmaid's Tale [1990]—A futuristic feminist film starring Natasha Richardson, Faye Dunaway and Robert Duvall, *The Handmaid's Tale* was filmed at a number of downtown Durham locales, including Duke University and the nearby Forest Hills neighborhood. The film was scripted by playwright Harold Pinter from the novel by Margaret Atwood.

Once Around [1991]—The Forest Hills neighborhood near downtown Durham simulated Boston, Massachusetts, in this comedic fable starring Richard Dreyfuss and Holly Hunter. A wedding scene was shot at the Governor's Mansion in downtown

Raleigh. The film was directed by Swede Lasse Hallstrom (*My Life as a Dog*) and also starred Danny Aiello, Gena Rowlands and Laura San Giacomo.

The Program [1993]—Duke University served as the setting for fictional "Eastern State University" in Pennsylvania for this inside look at the sordid world of big-time college football. All the bases are covered: unscrupulous boosters, academic fraud and steroid abuse. The film starred James Caan as "Coach Winters," as well as Omar Epps, Halle Berry and Kristy Swanson. *The Program* generated controversy involving a scene where a drunken player lies down in the middle of the road at night as part of a dare. Believe it or not, some teenagers who watched the movie tried to copycat the scene— with tragic results. As a consequence, the scene was cut from the movie once it hit the video store shelves.

Kiss the Girls [1997]—This controversial film starred Ashley Judd and Morgan Freeman. Both UNC-CH and Duke denied the film crew access to shoot on-campus scenes because of the film's violent story matter about a serial killer stalking college campuses. However, Research Triangle Park and old tobacco warehouses in downtown Durham are featured prominently in the movie.

Photo by Rich Weidman

Historic Durham Athletic Park

Patch Adams [1998]— The UNC-CH campus doubled as Virginia Medical University in the 1970s for this comedy/drama starring Robin Williams as an unorthodox physician who treats his patients with humor. It was the first major motion picture to be filmed on the campus. About 3,500 extras were used during the six-week shoot, most sporting long hair, sideburns and funky clothing. The film also generated some controversy involving a huge pair of legs draped over the doorway of Murphey Hall. Purported sightings of Williams spread rampantly around downtown Chapel Hill during the six-week shoot. Williams did make an unannounced appearance one night at Charlie Goodnight's comedy club in Raleigh, performing a 45-minute routine. *Patch Adams* eventually opened to generally mediocre reviews.

Other notable films shot in North Carolina include *Being There* (Biltmore Estate, Asheville), *Firestarter* and *Blue Velvet* (Wilmington), *Dirty Dancing* (Lake Lure), *Billy Bathgate* (Durham), *Last of the Mohicans* (Chimney Rock Park), *The Green Mile* (Moses Cone Mansion, near Blowing Rock) and *Hannibal*, the controversial sequel to *Silence of the Lambs* (Asheville).

For more information about the North Carolina film industry, visit the North Carolina Film Commission's website at www.ncfilm.com.

Parks and Recreation

The Triangle's parks and its recreational programs are two big factors in the area's highly rated quality of life. New residential communities, for instance, incorporate green common areas for neighborhood play and many offer walking or jogging trails. The same is found in some of the more lavishly landscaped commercial and research parks, too.

Triangle cities and towns have records of strong support for leisure activities: to wit, the combined parks and recreation budgets of Cary, Chapel Hill, Durham and Raleigh—$29.6 million for fiscal year 2000—are more than the state's own park's spending. These recreational opportunities mix with the state's moderate climate to make the Triangle's good life even better.

In the following pages, you will find details about public as well as private recreational places and programs. This chapter is for readers who are interested in or having their families participate in such activities. For information about golf or spectator sports such as professional hockey or college basketball, check out the chapters on those subjects.

Here, you'll find the trails and paths in our favorite parks and who to call when you want to break in a bat or shoot some hoops. You will see that there's plenty to choose from—bocce and hockey are now Southern activities! Also, your local park or recreational center may be an affordable alternative for a wedding or anniversary reception or company picnic. Check out your respective Parks and Recreation Department for details. Meanwhile, start your workout by turning these pages.

Recreation Areas

With numerous bodies of water in the vicinity, swimming, boating, sailing, fishing, picnicking and camping are popular activities throughout the year. Jordan Lake, Falls Lake and the Eno River are among the best known of these recreation areas and are maintained by the state. However, there are numerous accessible sites for those who enjoy water sports, camping or just being outdoors. Some of these parks are included in the "Parks of Special Interest" section of this chapter—Hemlock Bluffs, Occoneechee Mountain, Pullen Park, Umstead State Park and West Point on the Eno. In addition, the mountains and coast are just a couple of hours away. Here's an overview of a few of the most popular locations.

Eno River State Park
6101 Cole Mill Rd., Durham • 383-1686
Main access: Northern end of Cole Mill Rd.
• www.geo.duke.edu/enowelco.htm

The Eno River State Park was established in 1973 and runs along a 14-mile stretch of the river. There are a number of access points to the park, including Cole Mill (off the road by the same name) and Fews Ford (at the end of Cole Mill Road), where the park office is located. You'll discover hiking trails, creeks to fish, picnic areas, primitive camping and, of course, the river itself (for experienced canoeists only). Hiking trails range from easy (the 1.3-mile Pea Creek Trail) to more strenuous (the 2.6-mile Holden's Mill Trail or the 3.75-mile Cox Mountain Trail).

Falls Lake State Recreation Area

13304 Creedmoor Rd., Wake Forest
• 676-1027
• ils.unc.edu/parkproject/falaindex.html
Access: N.C. 50 north of N.C. 98; Rolling View Marina, S.R. 1807; Sandling Beach, 3.5 miles north of N.C. 50 and N.C. 98 intersection.

The 22-mile-long Falls Lake is one of Raleigh's reservoirs, formed when the Neuse River was dammed at the tiny village of Falls, north of the city. Since it opened in 1983, Triangle residents have streamed to its shores and waters for swimming, picnicking, fishing, water skiing and camping. It is one of the area's biggest attractions with 12,490 acres of water and 230 miles of shoreline.

There are four boat ramps with free access, and one of the park's impoundments, Beaver Lake, is restricted to non-motor-driven boats and reserved for fishing.

The state maintains several wildlife resources at Falls Lake, including Falls Lake Trail on Falls of the Neuse Road, Ledge Rock Boat Access on Cheek Road and Upper Bartons Creek Access on North Six Forks Road.

Harris Lake County Park

2112 County Park Dr., New Hill • 387-4342

Located in southern Wake County off U.S. 1, this new 25-acre park will eventually encompass 680 acres. It provides opportunities for hiking, biking, waterskiing and fishing (largemouth bass are in abundance here). Picnic areas and a playground are also on the premises.

Jordan Lake

U.S. 64 and Fearrington Rd., Chatham County • 362-0586
• ils.unc.edu/parkproject/jordindex.html
Access: Crosswinds Boat Ramp off U.S. 64 E. at B. Everett Jordan Bridge; Ebenezer Church on S.R. 1008 S.; Crosswinds Marina off U.S. 64 E. on S.R. 1008; Parkers Creek west of B. Everett Jordan Bridge; Vista Point west of B. Everett Jordan Bridge on S.R. 1700.

On summer weekends, rural Chatham County south of Durham draws thousands of

Eno River State Park offers more than 18 miles of hiking trails, ranging from easy to strenuous.

visitors from all over the Triangle to Jordan Lake, the 14,000-acre lake and recreation area built by the U.S. Army Corps of Engineers. Jordan Lake offers hiking, boating, windsurfing, fishing, swimming, picnicking and camping opportunities. There are several beaches, boat ramps and campgrounds available to users for a modest fee. Backcountry camping is not permitted. Call for a detailed map and more information about boat ramps and beaches.

The Jordan Lake Educational State Forest encompasses 400 acres of Piedmont forest, offering nature trails, programs and a picnic area.

Lake Crabtree County Park

Off Aviation Parkway • 460-3390

A Wake County park located in Cary, this popular, 71-acre park surrounds 520-acre Lake Crabtree, which you can see off I-40. The lake is not deep—from 3 to 10 feet—but it is stocked with largemouth bass, bluegill, red-eared sunfish and channel catfish. Sailboats are available for rent at $8 an hour. Canoes, kayaks and rowboats cost less. All rentals have a $20 deposit. The park includes picnic shelters for rent, a playground and hiking and biking trails. Enter off Aviation Parkway.

Lake Johnson
4600 Avent Ferry Rd., Raleigh • 233-2121

A 301-acre park in southwest Raleigh, Lake Johnson provides paved and unpaved trails that loop around the lake, as well as picnic areas. Paddleboats, rowboats and canoes are available for rent seasonally. A new boathouse was recently constructed here. Lake Johnson is also known as a quality largemouth bass and crappie fishing spot.

Lake Michie
Roxboro Rd., Bahama
Boating and fishing: 477-3906
Spruce Pine Lodge: 560-4358

Lake Michie (pronounced like the Mouse), a small lake located 10 miles north of Durham on Roxboro Road, is a great getaway spot. Here you can rent boats, fish or just spend the day hiking or picnicking. Primitive camping is also available (by permit). The lake offers some of the finest largemouth bass fishing in the area. Spruce Pine Lodge, a 1940's vintage log building, may be reserved for parties and meetings. The official address is Bahama, but the area is easily accessible from Durham.

Lake Wheeler
6404 Lake Wheeler Rd., Raleigh
• 662-5704

The biggest of Raleigh's city parks, 635-acre Lake Wheeler lies just south of the city limits. Lake Wheeler is aimed at the watersports crowd and offers boating, water skiing, windsurfing and fishing. It is the base of the NCSU Sailing Club and is also home to the annual Tar Heel Regatta in June when powerboats from all over come to race.

The park offers a Waterfront Program Center, which includes a park office, classroom, concession stand, restrooms and large outdoor deck. The Center schedules a variety of programs, including boating safety instruction, fly-fishing clinics, windsurfing and waterskiing courses and even a waterski boat operators class.

Shelley Lake
1400 W. Millbrook Rd., Raleigh • 420-2331

Take a quiet stroll around this scenic 50-acre lake located in North Raleigh. The two-mile trail, which includes sections of boardwalk, links up with other surrounding greenway trails. Pedal boats can be rented here seasonally. The park also provides opportunities for biking, fishing and picnicking.

Parks

City, county and state authorities often overlap in matters of park jurisdiction. Under normal circumstances, this makes little difference to those of us who enjoy them. However, reservations are needed to utilize some park facilities, so you need to know who to call.

Cary Parks

Cary has 15 public parks with more on the planning board. Many Cary residents are closer to some Raleigh parks than some Raleigh residents—Lake Johnson and Lake Wheeler, for example.

The showpiece of Cary's parks—with picnic shelters, athletic fields, a lake for fishing, hiking trails, an amphitheater, a new community center and a new senior center on the way—is the 310-acre Fred Bond Park. The park also offers—for a fee—a D.A.R.E. ropes course. The Hemlock Bluffs nature preserve (see "Parks of Special Interest" section in this chapter) is maintained by the town of Cary and Lake Crabtree County Park (see "Recreation Areas" section in this chapter) is located nearby.

The 30-acre North Cary Park opened in 2000 just off Cary Parkway with a soccer and T-ball field, volleyball courts, a playground and picnic shelters.

Chapel Hill-Carrboro Parks

Both Chapel Hill and neighboring Carrboro have their own separate parks and recreation departments, providing acres of park land and a wide variety of activities for Orange County residents of all ages. Together the two towns provide 10 ball fields, 21 lighted tennis courts, three gymnasiums and two swimming pools. University Lake, at 400 South Old Fayetteville Road, encompasses 213 acres for fishing and boating. Rowboats and canoes are available for rent. Call 942-8007 for more information. Located 8 miles west of Carrboro at 8705 Stanford Road, Cane Creek Reservoir is also a popular spot for fishing and boating, as well as hiking. Call 942-5790 for more information.

Durham Parks

The Durham Parks and Recreation Department oversees more than 1,300 acres of park land throughout the county, including more than 62 parks within the city limits. Durham offers 18 lighted athletic fields. A dozen parks provide 72 hard-surfaced tennis courts, 68 of them with lights, and there are four public swimming pools. What's more, there are plenty of hiking, biking, jogging and horse trails as well as fishing and boating opportunities.

Two of Durham's most popular parks are the Lake Michie Recreational Area (see "Recreation Areas" section in this chapter) and the unique, historic West Point on the Eno (see "Parks of Special Interest" section in this chapter).

The new Durham Central Park currently being constructed downtown on Foster Street will eventually feature a playground, amphitheater and wading pools.

Raleigh City Parks

Raleigh takes particular pride in its parks system, which helped it earn the nickname "a park with a city in it." The city regularly wins national awards for its parks and recreation programs and recognition in publications such as National Geographic for its greenway program that connects neighborhoods, parks and streams in a network that stretches more than

40 miles. There is a weekly update on the city's recreational programs on cable television. Access to local and statewide information is available on the Internet.

Raleigh residents have voted consistently for bond issues that have increased parklands to more than 4,300 acres, 156 parks and open spaces, and thousands of recreational activities. If you want to plan a special event for a city park, you will need to call for specific dates and a reservation permit. Also check with the staff concerning availability of water, restrooms and electricity. A fee is charged to reserve city picnic facilities—$30 for all-day.

Raleigh offers several parks with special attractions, such as Pullen Park (see the "Parks of Special Interest" section in this chapter)—home to both a celebrated Dentzel Carousel and a miniature passenger train. Of special note, Laurel Hills Park in west Raleigh (Glen Eden Drive and Edwards Mill Road) offers a unique playground for all children, including those with special needs.

Jaycee Park is the site of Raleigh Beach, home of the city's outdoor volleyball addicts. There is a BMX bicycle course at Lions Park. The Sertoma Arts Center at Shelley-Sertoma Park is the de facto arts center in the city's park system and hosts a number of study programs and summer concerts. Durant Nature Park is home for the city's popular summer day camp, Ranoca, as well as Camp Friendly, a special day camp for children with special needs.

Also part of the city's park system are both the entertainment jewel, ALLTEL Pavilion at Walnut Creek (see our "Attractions" chapter), which seats 20,000 and contains a nine-field softball complex and Lake Wheeler (see "Recreation Areas" section in this chapter), which caters mainly to watersports enthusiasts.

A 612-acre educational park is being developed around historic Yates Mill, the only remaining grist mill in Wake County. A section of the park, which is located at the

---

INSIDERS' TIP

To test your Appalachian Trail boots, hike up 700-foot Cox Mountain in Durham County's Eno River State Park. The park has more than 18 miles of hiking trails, too.

TRIANGLE HIKING TRAILS

Name	Location	Distance	Difficulty
Chestnut Oak Trail	Hemlock Bluffs	1.2 Miles	Moderate
Cole Mill Trail	Eno River State Park	1.2 Miles	Moderate
Company Mill Trail	Umstead State Park	4.5 Miles	Moderate
Cox Mountain Trail	Eno River State Park	3.75 Miles	Strenuous
Cross-Country Trail	Duke Forest	3.0 Miles	Easy
Dunnagan's Trail	Eno River State Park	3.1 Miles	Moderate
Falls Lake Trail	Falls Lake	13.2 Miles	Moderate
Holden's Mill Trail	Eno River State Park	4.1 Miles	Moderate
Lake Crabtree Trail	Lake Crabtree	5.4 Miles	Moderate
Lake Johnson Trail	Lake Johnson	3.5 Miles	Moderate
Lake Lynn Trail	Lake Lynn	2.5 Miles	Easy
Lake Trail	Bond Park	2.5 Miles	Moderate
Lakeside Trail	Durant Nature Park	1.2 Miles	Easy
Old Beech Nature Trail	Lake Crabtree	0.5 Miles	Easy
Pott's Branch Trail	Umstead State Park	1.0 Miles	Easy
Rock Quarry Trail	Rock Quarry Park	1.2 Miles	Easy
Sal's Branch Trail	Umstead State Park	2.2 Miles	Moderate
Shelley Lake Trail	Shelley Lake	2.0 Miles	Easy
South Eno River Trail	West Point on the Eno	1.7 Miles	Moderate
Sycamore Trail	Umstead State Park	6.5 Miles	Moderate

intersection of Lake Wheeler and Penny roads, should open in the fall of 2000. A visitors center and education building are planned for the park.

Parks of Special Interest

There are a few parks in the Triangle area that you should make a special point of visiting. Each has a unique characteristic and offers special features or activities that are worth the short drive that may be involved.

Hemlock Bluffs
2616 Kildaire Farm Rd., Cary • 387-5980

Hemlock Bluffs is a nature preserve in southern Cary, located between Tryon and Penny roads. It covers about 150 acres along Swift Creek and features a grove of Canadian hemlocks, which are viewed from a series of trails winding around the distinctive 90-foot bluffs. The preserve is not for picnicking or camping, but for hiking and observing.

Park tours are available on weekends and guides will tell you that 10,000 years ago hemlocks used to be common in this part of the country. But time flies and so did the hemlocks, except in special places like Hemlock Bluffs, which the good citizens of Cary and North Carolina have preserved for your hiking pleasure. The Stevens Nature Center offers exhibits, classes and lectures.

Occoneechee Mountain State Natural Area
Virginia Cates Rd., Hillsborough • 383-1686

Hike the Eno Mountain Loop Trail to reach the 860-foot summit of Occoneechee Mountain for a spectacular view of Hillsborough and the surrounding countryside. Picnic areas are also on the premises.

Pullen Park
520 Ashe Ave., Raleigh • 831-6468

Pullen Park is the grandaddy of Raleigh's parks with 65 acres that lie between the NCSU campus and the state's School for the Blind off Western Boulevard. A train ride through the park and around its lake offers a great view of the amenities, including children's boat rides and even pedal boats on the serene lake, as well as the region's top indoor aquatics center.

The crown jewel of the park is the 1911 Dentzel Carousel, which has been restored to its original grandeur with great skill and hundreds of thousands of dollars. Put your child on a carved masterpiece and watch him or her go round and round. It's also a great place to picnic and has several covered pavilions that may be reserved for large groups.

A $4 million indoor aquatics center opened in 1992. It is connected to a Special Programs Center that offers classes and activities such as senior citizen dancing. A concession stand offers the usual hot dogs, sodas and cotton candy. Six tennis courts and, across the railroad tracks, two ball fields and the city's Theatre in the Park are located here. The park also includes the Pullen Art Center, which offers a variety of art classes—even weaving on traditional overshot colonial-patterned warped looms.

Umstead State Park

8801 Glenwood Ave., Raleigh • 571-4170
• ils.unc.edu/parkproject/wium.html

Right in the heart of the Triangle, next to the Raleigh-Durham International Airport, William B. Umstead State Park offers visitors an opportunity to trade the bustle of everyday life for the beauty and serenity of nature. North Carolina's third-largest park, 5,413-acre Umstead has two sections and two entrances. The Reedy Creek section can be accessed from Harrison Avenue off I-40 in Cary and the Crabtree section from U.S. 70 in Raleigh. Although the sections are connected, you cannot drive across the park.

The park has nature trails, fishing and rental rowboats and canoes, 19 miles of horseback riding and bicycling trails, 28 campsites and three large group campsites that are available to nonprofit organizations. Popular hiking trails include the 2.2-mile Sal's Branch Trail, 4.5-mile Company Mill Trail and the 6.5-mile Sycamore Trail. In the spring, go

Photo by Rich Weidman

Kids enjoy the miniature train that winds its way around Pullen Park in Raleigh.

for a Sunday walk in the Reedy Creek section down by the creek where you will see a spectacular display of blooming rhododendron blossoming throughout the park. The Umstead State Park Visitors Center houses a museum and nature exhibits related to the park.

West Point On The Eno
5101 N. Roxboro Rd., Durham • 471-1623

West Point on the Eno is unique among Durham's city parks. This 388-acre setting represents the joint efforts of a group of citizens (The Friends of West Point) and the city to restore and preserve a part of the 19th-century community that existed before Durham.

West Point was a thriving community of about 300 families with a post office, general store, blacksmith shop, saw mill and cotton gin. Its inhabitants depended on water power generated by the West Point Mill, which operated continuously along the river from 1778 to 1942. Today, you can visit the park and see corn and wheat grinding demonstrations. The cornmeal and flour produced are bagged and sold in the park's mill country store.

You will also see a traditional timber-frame blacksmith shop, a tobacco barn typical of the sort used to cure brightleaf tobacco (which now houses the Hugh Mangum Museum of Photography) and the restored Greek Revival country house of longtime mill owner John Cabe McCown.

Every year, West Point on the Eno is the site of a Fourth of July Festival for the Eno, which attracts musicians, artists and craftspersons from all over North Carolina. There are also annual events at Halloween and Christmas.

The park also sponsors two-hour guided trips in inflatable boats led by naturalist "River Dave." A moonlight "wafting trip" is also available. Call 471-3802 to make reservations.

Recreational Activities
Cary

Cary keeps getting bigger and its recreational programs keep growing as well. The

A reconstruction of the West Point Mill, which operated from 1778 to 1942, can be viewed at West Point on the Eno.

town currently has more than 20 Planned Unit Developments (PUDs) that offer their own recreational amenities to residents. Kildaire Farms, for example, has its own swimming pool with team swimming, a tennis complex and a nearby private racquetball club. The community is laced with jogging and walking trails that connect neighborhoods and include exercise stations along the way. Lochmere and Preston offer a similar menu of activities and have championship golf courses in the middle of their neighborhoods.

Because Cary is so close to Raleigh, many of its residents belong to Raleigh clubs and organizations, such as the famed YMCA on Hillsborough Street or the Raleigh Racquet Club (swimming and serious tennis). Many of Raleigh's recreation programs are open to Cary residents, too, for a slight fee, such as the Pullen Park Aquatic Center. Cary has no public swimming pool.

A Kids Together Playground recently opened near the corner of Cary Parkway and Tryon Road. The new 29,000-square-foot Bond Park Community Center offers a variety of recreational programs for all ages.

Photo by Rich Weidman

Sailboats, kayaks, canoes and rowboats can be rented at Lake Crabtree County Park.

The Town of Cary has made every reasonable effort to make facilities accessible to individuals with disabilities and accommodation can be made for most programs. If you have questions about a facility or need special assistance, contact Cary's Parks, Recreation and Cultural Resources located at 111 James Jackson Avenue, Suite 201, 469-4061. The administrative office hours are 8 AM to 5 PM during the week.

Baseball & Softball

Cary operates seven different youth baseball leagues, starting with T-ball for 6- to 7-year-olds and going up to senior league for players ages 17 to 18. The coaches are volunteers and the emphasis is on sportsmanship. Registration is held in February. Fees are determined annually, so call for information, 469-4062.

The girls' softball program has four leagues: ponytail (ages 8 to 10) through senior league (ages 16 to 19). Registration times, places and fees are the same as for the baseball leagues.

In addition to the youth leagues, the town operates adult softball leagues for women and men. It also coordinates a slow-pitch church league and a coed league in the fall. There is also a men's fall league. For information on registration times and places, call 469-4063. Games are played in one of the dozen or so town parks with baseball/softball fields. For older leagues and more competitive play, check with the Cary Softball Club at 467-4223.

Basketball

The town sponsors boys and girls leagues, starting at age 7 and going through age 18. Registration for ages 7 to 10 is held in July with games starting in mid-September. Registration for ages 11 to 18 is held in October with games beginning in November. Costs are usually the same as in youth basketball. There are three adult basketball leagues, one in the summer, one in the fall and one in the winter for men ages 35 or older. Call 469-4062 for more information.

The Cary YMCA on Cary Parkway, 469-9622, offers seven basketball leagues for children in kindergarten through grade 12 and adult men. They play at the YMCA and at Kingswood Elementary.

Dancing

There are a number of dance groups in the Triangle area. To get more information, consult the Wake County Library's referral services or the "Arts and Culture" chapter of this book. In Cary, there is a Plus Level square dance group, the TNT Twirlers, which meets weekly on Mondays at 7 PM. While it is not a town-sponsored group, The Parks and Recreation Department, 469-4065, provides contact information. Many types of dance lessons, including Shag, Two-Step, line dancing, ballroom dancing and jive/swing adult dance are offered on a continuing basis at the Cary Community Center, 460-4965. Clogging and tap dancing are offered at Jordan Hall Arts Center on North Harrison Avenue, 469-4069.

FYI

Unless otherwise noted, the area code for all phone numbers listed in this guide is 919.

Day Camps

The town offers a summer day camp for children ages 6 through 11. It meets weekdays from 7:30 AM until 5:30 PM. Activities include arts and crafts, drama, field trips, games, music and sports. There are four 1-week sessions, starting in mid-June and going through the first week in August. The Athletics Division offers several youth instructional camps throughout the summer in baseball, volleyball, softball, basketball, tennis and golf. Camps are structured to develop the young athlete's skills. For more information, call 469-4062.

The Cary YMCA on Cary Parkway, 469-9622, has two summer day camps for children in kindergarten through grade 5. Camp Rising Sun meets at the Y and Camp Outer Limits meets at the West Cary Middle School. Kindercamp for ages 3 to 5 meets at the Y two half days a week.

Football

The town can provide you with information on the Pop Warner youth football program, but it is operated by the Cary Booster Club, 376-3558. It has six different divisions separated by age and weight. Youths can begin play as young as 7 or as old as 15, provided they don't weigh more than 125 pounds. Call for registration information.

Golf

Like Raleigh, Cary has no municipally owned golf course. Golfers do not want for courses, however. There are reportedly at least 20 courses open to the public in and around Raleigh and Cary. For a short list, see our "Golf in the Carolinas" chapter.

Ice Hockey, Ice Skating & Roller Hockey

The Ice House, located at 1410 Buck Jones Road behind Borders bookstore, has been a big hit since it first opened. Admission includes skate rental and the Ice House has open skating as well as lessons. The rink has a well-stocked snack bar and a game room. The Ice House is open to the public seven days a week. To check for specific hours and for information on lessons, call the information line at 467-6000. For information on Raleigh Youth Hockey, which practices at the Ice House, call 233-8210.

The new 72,000-square-foot, $5-million Wayne Gretsky Roller Hockey Center and Carolina Soccerplex recently opened at 3717 Davis Drive in Morrisville. Call 319-9910 for more information. The Raleigh/Cary Inline Hockey Association sponsors youth and adult leagues at Jellybeans on Buck Jones Road in Cary. Call 467-1448 for more information.

TRIANGLE LAKES & RECREATION AREAS

Name/Authority	Activities Available
ENO RIVER (State of N.C.) *Three miles northwest of Durham, off S.R. 1569.*	Boating, sailing, fishing, hiking, picnicking, rock hounding, bird watching.
FALLS LAKE (State of N.C.) *Seven miles north of Raleigh, off N.C. 50 and N.C. 98.*	Beaches, boating, swimming, water skiing, picnicking, fishing, bird watching. Boat rentals available.
FLAT RIVER *Bahama Rd. at Veasey Rd., Durham.*	Boating, sailing, fishing, hiking, rock hounding.
HARRIS LAKE (Wake County) *6 mi. south of Apex off S.R. 1130 nr. Shearon Harris Nuclear Power Plant.*	Boating, fishing, hiking, biking, water skiing.
JORDAN LAKE (State of N.C.) *Twenty miles southwest of Raleigh off U.S. 1/64.*	Boating, swimming, sailing, picnicking, camping and full-service marina.
KERR LAKE (State of N.C.) *Eleven miles north of Henderson off I-85 to S.R. 1319.*	Camping, swimming, fishing, boating, sailing, water skiing.
LAKE BENSON (City of Raleigh) *Off Buffaloe Road in southwest Raleigh.*	Fishing only. No swimming.
LAKE CRABTREE (Wake County) *Aviation Parkway in Wake County*	Boating, camping, hiking, picnicking, fishing, nature trails.
LAKE JOHNSON (City of Raleigh) *Off Avent Ferry Rd. in southwest Raleigh.*	Jonboats, paddle boats, paved greenway trails, boardwalk across lake. No swimming.
LAKE LYNN (City of Raleigh) *Off Lynn Road in north Raleigh.*	Biking, inline skating, jogging, paved greenway trail. No swimming.
LAKE MICHIE *Off U.S. 501, 10 miles north of Durham.*	Boating, fishing, hiking, picnicking. No swimming.
LAKE WHEELER (City of Raleigh) *Off Lake Wheeler Road in Raleigh.*	Fishing, sailing, canoeing, rowing, kayaking, picnicking. No swimming. Rental boats.
LITTLE RIVER *Johnson's Mill Road off U.S. 501 N.*	Boating, sailing, hiking, fishing.
NEW HOPE CREEK *Duke Forest in Durham.*	Canoeing, hiking.
SHELLEY LAKE (City of Raleigh) *W. Millbrook Road in Raleigh.*	Fishing, canoeing, sailing, rowboating, pedal boating, hiking, biking. No swimming.
SILVER LAKE (Private) *5300 Tryon Road in Raleigh.*	Paddle boat rides, swimming, picnicking, water slide.
UNIVERSITY LAKE *Off Jones Ferry Road, one mile west of Carrboro.*	Non-engine boating, canoeing, fishing. No swimming. Boat rentals available.

Racquetball

Cary Fitness and Racquetball Club at 302-A Pebble Creek Drive, 467-1852, offers racquetball, wallyball, volleyball and basketball courts; a Nautilus room and free weights; and exercise and aerobics classes. It is conveniently located near the Kildaire Farms tennis and swimming pool complex. Memberships are open to the public and it also has corporate memberships.

The Cary YMCA on Cary Parkway also contains racquetball courts. Call 469-9622 for more information.

Running, Jogging

Many of the PUDs have their own jogging and running trails. The town has its own greenway network, designed to connect existing facilities such as schools with parks, churches and lakes. Existing trails total more than 12 miles and include the Tarbert-Gatehouse Trail, Pirate's Cove, Hinshaw, Swift Creek, Parkway, White Oak Creek, Black Creek, Oxxford Hunt, Symphony Lake, Coatbridge, Lake Pine, McCloud and Higgins Greenway. The Town has formulated an ambitious plan to create 20 miles of greenway trails by the year 2010. Cary is home to the Cary Road Race, sponsored by Cary Parks, Recreation and Cultural Resources and *The Cary News*. The race usually is scheduled in April and features a 5K and 10K course, as well as a one-mile fun run. It is one of the early races in the year and serves as a good warm-up for some of the longer runs.

Soccer

The Capital Area Soccer League (CASL) is the largest recreational soccer program in the Southeast. With more than 800 youth and adult teams (about 12,000 participants) CASL runs fall and spring seasons for boys' and girls' teams. Children can begin playing in the 3 v 3 Mini League as early as age 4. Applications are available at local sports stores or the CASL office in Raleigh (one block from Meredith College). There is a fee per individual participant. Children under 8 years of age receive uniform shirts; all older children must purchase their uniforms. Volunteer coaches are offered free training clinics semiannually, and soccer camps are scheduled in Raleigh and Cary every summer for children 12 years old and younger. An adult league consisting of Women's Open, Men's Open, Men's Over 30 and Men's Over 40 is available for all outside the youth league.

The 136-acre CP&L Soccer Training Center, set to open in the fall of 2001 between Apex and Holly Springs, includes 13 soccer fields that will be used mostly by CASL players. For more information, call 546-6189.

The State Capital Soccer Park, a new 5,000-seat stadium that will be managed by CASL, is scheduled to open in 2001 at the intersection of I-40 and East Chatham Street. The complex will eventually include 15 additional soccer fields and eight baseball fields as well as other recreational areas. CASL's office is at 3344 Hillsborough Street in Raleigh, 834-3951.

The Wayne Gretsky Roller Hockey Center and Carolina Soccerplex opened at 3717 Davis Drive recently with indoor and outdoor soccer fields. Call 319-9910. In addition, the new $2.5-million, 56,000-square-foot Dream Sports Center at 1016 Investment Boulevard in Apex contains space for indoor soccer and roller hockey. Call 387-2955.

Swimming

Cary has no municipal swimming pool, so most of the swimming is done at the many private swimming clubs connected to residential developments. Many of these clubs will accept members from outside their particular development. Some to check are Kildaire Farms, 467-4314, and Scottish Hills Recreation Club, 469-8109.

The Cary YMCA offers an extensive summer swimming program. Swimming privileges are included in Y Memberships, but you can also join just for summer swimming. Call 469-9622 for further information. Silver Lake, 851-1683, near Swift Creek Elementary School on Tryon Road, is a favorite swimming hole for Cary and Raleigh residents.

Tennis

In addition to the many private tennis clubs in Cary's planned communities, the town maintains many lighted tennis courts. The town has also opened the new Cary Tennis Center beside Green Hope High School. It will eventually feature 30 courts, including a championship court, as well as meeting space and a pro shop. Reservations are permitted during certain times of the year by calling the recreation office, 469-4062. The department sponsors tennis lessons for a fee from March through October. There are four seasons for team tennis with four levels of play. The town sponsors two tournaments: the Polar Doubles in March and Cary Town Championships in September. A popular league is the "Ladies Morning Tennis Team" play.

Volleyball

Cary offers three seasons of adult volleyball. The Spring league registration is held in March with matches beginning in April. Summer league registration takes place in June with play in July. Fall league registration is held in August and play begins in September. Men's, women's and coed leagues are offered.

Walking

You can go walking around the town's parks or along the town's more than 12-mile greenway network, but there's a special walking tour and architectural guide of Cary's historical places. You can pick up a tour folder from the Chamber of Commerce on Academy Street or at the Page-Walker Arts and History Center.

Chapel Hill-Carrboro

The Chapel Hill Parks and Recreation Department oversees 15 parks or playgrounds, including four community centers (two with pools), fitness and nature trails, two small play areas and one separate athletic field. It also offers an amazing assortment of activities, including adult volleyball as well as youth and adult tennis, swimming, basketball, baseball, softball and lacrosse. You can sign up for outdoor programs and trips involving rock climbing, kayaking or skiing, or take classes in everything from martial arts to pottery. The department sponsors special activities for senior citizens and handicapped persons.

In addition, Carrboro's own Recreation and Parks Department has a number of recreation facilities and activities. It maintains more than 72 acres of park land at six locations, providing ball fields, basketball courts, playgrounds, tennis courts, picnic shelters, nature trails and a lake. Like Chapel Hill's recreation department, it offers a wide range of athletic programs for both youth and adults

Photo by Rich Weidman

Wake County's largest park, 310-acre Bond Park in Cary, provides boat rentals, hiking trails, playgrounds, a community center and a senior center.

including basketball, softball, baseball, volleyball and football. You can sign up for classes and workshops on all sorts of activities, like aerobics, tumbling, tennis, basketry and craft classes, or you may participate in the annual fishing rodeo or kite-flying field day. In Chapel Hill and Carrboro, some activities are free but most require a nominal charge or registration fee.

Here's a handy guide to help you sort it all out. For a schedule of activities and more information, contact the Chapel Hill Parks and Recreation Department at 968-2784 or the Carrboro Recreation and Parks Department at 968-7703.

Triangle SportsPlex is at the intersection of N.C. 86 and Business 70 in historic Hillsborough in northern Orange County, creating a multitude of activities for the area's enjoyment. This $11 million multisports center offers ice skating, swimming, camps for kids and ice hockey on its official NHL-sized rink. For more information about hours and activities, call 644-0339.

Baseball & Softball

Both Chapel Hill and Carrboro sponsor youth and adult baseball and softball leagues. Girls ages 8 through 15 play in softball leagues. Boys have baseball leagues for Pee Wees (ages 6 to 8) and ages 9 to 14. In addition to its Spring program, Carrboro offers a Fall baseball program for youth ages 9 to 14. There is a coed softball league for high school students, and for Chapel Hill adults, there are separate competitive and recreational co-rec softball leagues. There is co-rec (coed) softball in Carrboro and a fall girls' fast pitch softball league. For further information, call the parks and recreation departments in either location.

Basketball

Newcomers may find it difficult adjusting to the basketball fever that suddenly strikes otherwise perfectly healthy adults here sometime after Thanksgiving. One way to get involved is to go down to the gym and shoot a few hoops.

The Chapel Hill Parks and Recreation Department offers two men's basketball leagues. The "recreational" league is for men 18 years old and older; but don't worry, former college players are not allowed. Then there's the "competitive open" league for the same age group in which the action is a bit more fierce. Carrboro also offers a men's league and some open gym playing times for men and women.

There are also youth leagues in both Chapel Hill and Carrboro. For information on teams and registration, call the parks and recreation department in the appropriate town.

If you just want to practice your jump shot or play a few pickup games, there are basketball hoops and willing participants available all over town. You can play at any one of the following locations in Chapel Hill: Hargraves, Umstead, North Forest Hills and Ephesus parks and the Lincoln and Community Center sites—some are indoors and some are outdoors. In Carrboro, there are basketball courts at the following sites: Community Park, Brewer Lane Mini-Park and Carrboro Elementary School Park.

Biking

Bicycle enthusiasts may be interested in meeting fellow cyclists for weekend rides. For information, contact one of the local bicycle shops or the Carolina Tarwheels Bicycle Club at 687-5066.

Carrboro boasts one of the most extensive bikeway systems in the state. Call the Carrboro Recreation and Parks Department at 968-7703 for more information.

Bocce

Believe it or not, they've been playing this Italian game of lawn bowling in the Chapel Hill area for a great while. Bocce is played on a court next to the Community Center on Plant Road every Tuesday and Friday morning starting around 9 AM. You can start pickup games anytime. Balls are available at the

Community Center. There are two more bocce courts located at the Fearrington development, about 8 miles south of Chapel Hill on U.S. 15-501.

Canoeing & Kayaking

The Haw River, about 10 minutes south of Chapel Hill, is a great place to put in a canoe or kayak and spend a day shooting rapids or dodging rocks, depending on the level of the water and your skill level. The Haw is best in the early spring or after a good rain. Take care—any river at flood stage can be a deadly adversary.

Pittsboro's Rock Rest Adventures, 542-5502, offers canoe, whitewater kayak and sea kayak instruction and guided excursions. In addition, the Chapel Hill Parks and Recreation Department usually cosponsors a couple of trips a year. For information, call the department at 968-2784.

Golf

There are four places to play golf in Chapel Hill: the (private) Chapel Hill Country Club, the (private) Governors Club, the (public) Finley Golf Course and the (public) Twin Lakes Golf Course, just south of town in Chatham County. You can take private lessons at Finley; call 962-2349 for details. Twin Lakes Golf Course, 933-1024, is located on Willow Way, off of Manns Chapel Road from U.S. 15-501 South.

Health Clubs

The YMCA and a handful of private health clubs provide a range of exercise facilities for residents of Chapel Hill and Carrboro.

The Women's Workout Club (formerly known as The Club for Women Only) in Rams Plaza, 929-8860, offers equipment, sauna and steam, whirlpool, aerobics and a pool. The Chapel Hill-Carrboro YMCA on Airport Road, 942-5156, features Nautilus equipment, racquet sports, a pool, sauna, whirlpool, a gym, aerobic classes and massage. The Spa Health Club on Elliott Road, 942-1182, has Nautilus equipment, a pool, sauna, whirlpool and aerobic classes. There are also several places that offer step, toning and aerobic exercise classes, including The

Body Shop, 933-9281. Other health clubs include Millennium Health and Fitness on Farrington Road, 401-2959, and AC Fitness Center on Main Street in Carrboro, 960-9910.

Horseback Riding

Triple J Stables offers riding lessons, guided trail rides and boarding on its 75 acres. It is located at 2301 Mt. Sinai Road. Call 967-4980 for more information. Collins Creek Farm, at 910 Dawson Road, also offers riding lessons and year-round boarding. Call 968-4541.

Horseshoes

That most Southern of sports, horseshoes, still thrives in small towns, including Carrboro. Carrboro's Recreation and Parks Department sponsors horseshoe tournaments with men's, women's and youth divisions, several times a year. Call 968-7703 for information.

Ice Hockey, Ice Skating & Roller Hockey

Triangle SportsPlex, located near Hillsborough, has a beautiful rink offering open skating and lessons. This rink is where Triangle Youth Hockey, 644-0339, is based. Skateboarders and rollerbladers can enjoy the skating park at Homestead Park.

Lacrosse

Lacrosse has seen an increase in popularity in Chapel Hill over the last decade, due in part to the successful record of the UNC lacrosse team. Culbreth, McDougle and Phillips Middle Schools and Chapel Hill High field competitive teams. The Chapel Hill Parks and Recreation offers junior and senior lacrosse.

Soccer

The Chapel Hill area has a thriving coed soccer program with activities for all ages and skill levels. In 1972, Rainbow Soccer was founded as a private, nonprofit organization. If you or your child want to play in a Rainbow Soccer league, all you have to do is sign up and pay the registration fee. This is a "noncompetitive" league. Everybody gets to play

Photo courtesy of N.C. Division of Tourism

Jordan Lake has gained a reputation as an inland paradise for windsurfers.

and everyone receives plenty of encouragement. Coed leagues—divided by age in two-year increments—are available for preschoolers (ages 3 and 4) all the way through 9th graders. The adult league, from high school age on up through adults, is called Sunset Soccer. There are also three all-girls leagues: for grades 1 and 2, 3, 4 and 5 through 9. Rainbow Soccer leagues play during the fall and spring seasons. Practice is twice a week and games are on Saturdays. Rainbow Soccer also sponsors special summer day camps for youths up to age 15 and for coaches and goalkeepers. For more information, call 967-8797.

If your kids want highly competitive play, they should try out for the Central Carolina Youth Soccer Association teams.

The Carolina United Soccer Club recently joined with the Triangle Soccer Academy to form the Triangle Futbol Club. The organization provides an atmosphere where children can receive soccer instruction from its experienced staff. Call 644-6800, ext. 1135, for more information.

Swimming

In Chapel Hill, you can swim year round in the indoor pool at the Community Center. The phone number is 968-2790. Since open swim times vary, call the pool hours hotline at 685-8316. There are special times for aquacize, senior swim, masters swimming and lessons. Fees range from $1.25 for children 6 to 17 and $2.50 for ages 18 and up; kids 5 and under swim free. Annual, family and 20 punch passes are available.

There is an outdoor pool open during the summer at Hargraves Community Park, 968-2794. Pool passes are valid at either pool.

Indoor pools are also available at three private membership facilities: the YMCA on Airport Road, 942-5156; the Spa Health Club on Elliott Road, 942-1182; and The Women's Workout Club at Rams Plaza, 929-8860.

Tennis

Tennis lessons are available for youths ages 8 to 17 and for adults through Chapel Hill's Parks and Recreation Department. Chapel Hill also has a youth tennis league and a men's and women's singles league. Further information is available from the Chapel Hill Parks and Recreation Department at 968-2784. Tennis may be played at public courts at the following locations: in Chapel Hill—Hargraves, Umstead, Oakwood, Cedar Falls, Ephesus Park and Phillips Parks; in Carrboro—Community and Wilson parks. Carrboro offers instructional tennis classes for youth and adults.

Members and guests can play at the Chapel Hill Tennis Club, 929-5248, which boasts 28 courts, an Olympic-sized pool, a fitness center and clubhouse. There are also private courts at the Stoneridge Racquet and

Photo by Rich Weidman

The Spruce Pine Lodge, a 1940's vintage log building at Lake Michie, can be reserved for parties and meetings.

Swim Club, the Chapel Hill Country Club, the Faculty-Staff Recreation Association facility (owned by UNC-CH with membership open to permanent UNC-CH faculty and staff) and several other private tennis clubs.

Volleyball

Coed volleyball leagues are open to players at all competitive levels, ages 18 and up. Teams play regularly at Culbreth Middle School from August to November. Registration is on a team basis. Call the Chapel Hill Parks and Recreation Department at 968-2784 for more information. Carrboro offers Fall and Spring leagues.

Windsurfing

Jordan Lake was created after the U.S. Army Corps of Engineers dammed up the Haw River. In doing so, the Corps inadvertently created an inland windsurfer's paradise. There are so many wide open spaces on the lake that just about anywhere is a good place to practice windsurfing. You can rent a sailboard and get information about lessons at Water World in Durham, 596-8185.

Durham

Though some folks think Durham's a little too quiet at night, there's an abundance of daytime activities available at public and private facilities all over town.

The Durham Parks and Recreation Department's 12 recreation centers offer a range of individual and team sports for children and adults, including baseball, basketball, boxing, soccer, softball, racquetball, handball, swimming, tennis and volleyball. Four regional recreation centers offer expanded programs: Edison Johnson District Recreation Center, 600 West Murray Avenue, 560-4270; Irwin R. Holmes Sr. Recreation Center at Campus Hills, 2000 South Alston Avenue, 560-4444; W.D. Hill Recreation Center, 1308 Fayetteville Street, 560-4292; and Weaver Street Recreation Center, 3000 Weaver Street, 560-4294. These and other centers sponsor a variety of arts, dance and crafts classes and other special programs for all ages, including senior citizens and the handicapped.

Here's a handy guide to how and where you can participate in these activities. Those facilities operated by the Parks and Recreation Department are noted. For more information, contact the City of Durham Parks and Recreation Department at its office located at the Durham Bulls Athletic Park on Blackwell Street, 560-4355.

Baseball

Little League Baseball is played at a number of city parks, including Lakeview, Red Maple, Long Meadow, Oval Drive and Lake Michie Recreation Area. Baseball is also offered at Woodcroft, and Pony and Colt Baseball for 13- to 16-year-olds at the Southern Boundaries ballfield. Contact the Parks and Recreation Department at 560-4355 for more information.

The Lakewood YMCA also offers a youth league, 493-4502.

Basketball

You can probably find a good pickup game at any one of the 50 full-size outdoor courts (30 of them lighted) located at city parks or at the gyms at the regional recreation centers. Courts are located at the following city parks: Old Farm, Lakeview, Red Maple, Sherwood, East Main Street, Lyon/Ramseur, East End, Long Meadow, East Durham, Birchwood, C.R. Wood, Burton, Hillside, Elmira Avenue, Unity Village, Southern Boundaries, White Oak, Rockwood, Forest Hills, Lyon, Morreene, Crest Street, West Durham, Oval Drive and Whippoorwill. There is a lighted court at Walltown Center. There are half-courts at Rocky Creek, Carroll Street and Albany/Sovereign parks.

For youth and adult league play, contact the Parks and Recreation Department, 560-4355.

The Downtown YMCA, 667-9622, and the Lakewood YMCA, 493-4502, also offer youth and adult leagues.

Biking

Durham's Trails and Greenways Commission is working on providing hiking, biking and jogging trails throughout the city. In addition, there are plenty of paved secondary roads ideal for biking through the surrounding countryside. For more information, contact the Durham Trails and Greenways Commission, 101 City Hall Plaza, 560-4137.

Join the Carolina Tarwheels Bicycling Club for weekend recreational rides, 687-5066. The Club offers rides for beginning as well as experienced cyclists and sponsors the annual Bikefest Heritage Tour.

Eagle Watching

The northern section of Jordan Lake is home to the largest population of bald eagles in the eastern United States. You can spot them from several bridges passing over the lake, but the best vantage point is from a special observation deck built by the New Hope Audubon Society. This site is located along N.C. 751 south of Durham, 6 miles south of I-40. Turn right after the "Wildlife Observation Site" sign, park your car and enjoy a pleasant 15-minute walk through the woods to the deck. Best observation times are dawn and dusk.

Flag Football

The Parks and Recreation Department offers men's, women's and co-recreational flag football leagues. The season begins in April. Call 560-4355 for more information.

Golf & Disc Golf

There are a handful of public and private golf courses in Durham—all of them 18 holes. The public facilities include Duke University Golf Club at N.C. 751 and Washington Duke Inn, 681-2288; Hillandale Golf Course at Hillandale Road, 286-4211; Lakeshore Golf Course at Lumley Road, 596-2401; and semi-private Lake Winds Golf Course at U.S. 501 North, 471-4653.

Championship courses are available to members and their guests at the country clubs serving some of Durham's most prestigious neighborhoods: Croasdaile, Willowhaven and Treyburn north of town and Hope Valley to the southwest.

Every spring Croasdaile, the Washington Duke Golf Course and Perry Como host the Duke Children's Classic, a golf/tennis benefit for Duke University Medical Center's pediatric facilities. Celebrities abound, often drawing more than 20,000 spectators during the three-day event. The annual Herald-Sun Golf Tournament takes place at Willowhaven Country Club in June.

Disc golf—complete with tees, greens and pars—can be played at Cornwallis Road Park, which is located at 2800 Wade Road. Call 560-4355 for more information.

Health & Fitness

The Lakewood YMCA at 2119 Chapel Hill Road, 493-4502, is a complete fitness center, offering separate men's and women's free-weight rooms, Nautilus equipment, saunas and steam rooms. The Y features an indoor 25-meter pool, two full-size indoor basketball courts and four indoor racquetball courts. Behind the main facility is a 1/5-mile graded outdoor track. The Y offers men's, women's, coed and senior aerobic classes for all levels. Child care is available for those exercising or taking classes. Call for more information.

The Irwin R. Holmes Sr. Recreation Center at 2000 South Alston Avenue, 560-4444, has a weight and exercise room with free weights, stairclimbers, Airdyne bikes, a treadmill and a rotary torsion hip machine. There is also a heated, indoor pool, racquetball/handball courts, a lighted softball field, a pond, playground and picnic shelters.

The $9 million, 46,000-square-foot Downtown YMCA, 667-9622, contains state-of-the-art exercise equipment, two swimming pools, regulation-size basketball court, indoor running track, aerobics/dance studio and daycare center.

Hiking & Jogging

The Durham Trails and Greenways Commission has plans for 170 miles of hiking, jogging and biking trails throughout the city.

A portion of the projected 12-mile North/South Greenway Trail is open from Trinity Avenue to Club Boulevard through Northgate Park into Rock Quarry Park. The 3.5-mile Quarry Trail will eventually join at its southern end with the Pearl Mill Trail, providing a connection to downtown and eventually a network of trails and greenways throughout Durham. A 3.2-mile portion of the American Tobacco Trail has opened along the old Norfolk & Southern Railroad line. It will eventually run 23 miles from the Durham Bulls Athletic Park south all the way through Chatham and Wake counties. Other popular trails include the 2-mile New Hope Creek Trail and the Ellerbee Creek Trail, which runs from Stadium Drive at Duke Street to Club Boulevard and Washington Avenue.

Meanwhile, some local developers have been persuaded to set aside land for hiking and jogging trails through their residential neighborhoods. Woodcroft in southwest Durham has an extensive network of paved trails in place.

For getting away from it all, the best hiking opportunities are at Duke Forest, 613-8013; Lake Michie, 477-3906; Eno River State Park, 383-1686; and West Point on the Eno city park, 471-1623.

Horseback Riding

You may go horseback riding in some of the same places recommended for hiking. In addition, riding and stables are available at the following private facilities: Pleasure Horse Farm on Fayetteville Road, 544-5867; B-Bar Farms on Bivins Road, which also has public riding, 477-3750; Longwood Farm on N.C. 751, 387-9400; and Quail Roost Stables on U.S. 501 North, 477-8932.

Ice Hockey & Ice Skating

Triangle SportsPlex located between Durham and Hillsborough has a beautiful rink offering open skating and lessons. This rink is where Triangle Youth Hockey, 644-0339, is based.

DEPARTMENTS OF PARKS AND RECREATION

Carrboro Recreation and Parks	968-7703
Cary Parks, Recreation and Cultural Resources	469-4061
Chapel Hill Parks and Recreation	968-2784
Durham Parks and Recreation	560-4355
N.C. State Parks and Recreation	733-7275
Orange County Parks and Recreation	732-6147
Raleigh Parks and Recreation	831-6640

Racquet Sports

Racquetball and handball can be played at two facilities run by the city's Parks and Recreation Department: the Edison Johnson Center at 600 West Murray Avenue and Duke Park at 1530 Acadia Street. Courts for racquet sports are also available at the following private facilities: MetroSport, 501 Douglas Street, 286-7529, and the Lakewood YMCA, 2119 Chapel Hill Road, 493-4502.

Scuba Diving

Water World in Durham, 596-8185, rents and sells scuba equipment, organizes trips and offers certification courses. Basic scuba classes are held two nights a week for three weeks. Open water tests are taken at Fantasy Lake Scuba Park, 556-1803, located north of Raleigh near Rolesville, depending on the season. The shop organizes trips to exotic dive spots like Curacao, Bonaire and Cozumel.

Soccer

The city's Parks and Recreation Department oversees youth and adult soccer teams. Seven playing fields (five of them lighted) are available at the following parks: Old Farm, Rock Quarry, Northgate, C.R. Wood, Southern Boundaries, Weaver Meadow and Erwin. Call 560-4355 for information on registration and schedules. The Downtown YMCA offers a youth soccer league. Call 667-9622 for more information. Other Triangle soccer clubs include the Triangle Futbol Club, 644-6800, ext. 1135, and the Capital Area Soccer League, 834-3951.

Softball

The city Parks and Recreation folks supervise hundreds of youth and adult softball teams playing at area parks, including the following: Old Farm, Rock Quarry, Sherwood, Long Meadow, Edgemont, East Durham, Birchwood, Hillside, Elmira Avenue, Campus Hills, Southern Boundaries, Lyon, Wrightwood, Morreene, Walltown and Whippoorwill. There are also neighborhood and teen softball teams in some city parks. Call the Parks and Recreation Department for registration information, 560-4355.

The Downtown YMCA offers an Adult Softball League. Call 667-9622 for more information.

Swimming

Public outdoor pools are open in the summer at these city parks: Forest Hills (outdoor) at 1639 University Drive, 560-4782; Hillside (outdoor) at 1300 South Roxboro Road, 560-4783; and Long Meadow at 917 Liberty Street, 560-4202. I.R. Holmes Center at Campus Hills, 2000 South Alston Avenue, 560-4781, and Rock Quarry Park at 600 West Murray Avenue, 560-4265, have indoor pools that are open year round. In addition, there are several private membership clubs available only to members and their guests.

A significant number of residential developments have private swimming facilities for residents and, if you're brave, check out the swimming holes on the Eno River.

Tennis

Finding a place to play tennis in Durham is easy to swing. There are more than 70 hard-surface courts at these city parks: Rock Quarry, Northgate, Sherwood, East End, W. D. Hill, Elmira Avenue, Southern Boundaries, Garrett Road, Forest Hills, Morreene, Oval Drive and Whippoorwill. The main facilities are at Garrett Road, 489-6873; Rock Quarry, 471-2681; and Morreene Road parks, 560-4405.

Or you may want to join one of the following private facilities: Croasdaile Country Club, 383-1591; Eno Valley Swim and Racquet Club, 477-9042; Hollow Rock Racquet and Swim Club, 489-1550; Hope Valley Country Club, 489-6565; and Willowhaven Country Club, 383-5511.

Tennis classes are available through the Parks and Recreation Department. Under a city program, instructors have also provided classes at public housing complexes.

Volleyball

More than 100 volleyball teams for youth and adults compete through the Parks and Recreation Department. For times and registration information, contact the department at 560-4355.

Windsurfing

Thanks to Durham's proximity to both Falls and Jordan Lakes, windsurfing has become very popular in the area. For more information, contact the Triangle Boardsailing Club at 596-8185.

Raleigh

The city maintains an active recreation program for all ages and sizes. There are also some programs—the most notable being the Capital Area Soccer League (CASL)—that are independent of municipal administration but an integral part of metropolitan recreation.

Because of the favorable climate, recreational programs are active year round. In addition to the city's eight public swimming pools, the Aquatic Center in Pullen Park is one of the finest indoor swimming pools on the East Coast. Optimist Park Swimming Pool wears an inflatable dome during winter to accommodate competitive swimmers.

The city has 20 staffed community centers that offer everything from indoor basketball courts to handcrafts. Following is a list—by activity—of some of the recreational programs available. For more information about city programs, call 831-6640.

The Parks and Recreation Department also offers an integrated package of fitness and recreational services to area businesses called Corporate Leisure Services, 890-3298, which includes fitness classes, company picnics, corporate team sports, outdoor adventure programs and meeting sites.

For information on snowskiing, hiking, camping, rafting and other excursions, contact the Raleigh Ski and Outing Club at 847-RSOC. The club contains more than 2,000 Triangle area members of all ages and skill levels.

Baseball

Five youth leagues are operated by the city Parks and Recreation Department, starting with T-ball for 6- to 8-year-olds and including Little League. The senior league is for students ages 15 to 16. A midsummer city tournament ends each season. Games are played on fields throughout the city and local businesses underwrite team expenses for uniforms. Contact Raleigh Parks and Recreation, Athletics Department, 2401 Wade Avenue, 831-6836.

The Salvation Army, 902 Wake Forest Road, 832-6918, operates its own youth athletic program, including baseball, where the emphasis is on fundamentals. There's no tournament and each participant—boy and girl—must play during the games. Registration begins in March and the season ends before school is out in June. The registration fee for one sport is $55; each additional sport costs $40. There are 30 teams in the 5 to 10 age group (T-ball, coach-pitch and machine pitch) and five teams for Little League-age children. Games for the 5 to 10 age group are played on the three fields at the Salvation Army Center on Wake Forest Road. The Little League teams play at nearby Oakwood Park.

Basketball

The Raleigh Parks and Recreation Department runs an active youth league 12-game schedule in the fall, plus a tournament for city champions. It's a competitive league with lots of teams. Players, ages 10 to 18 in the youth programs, sign up at their respective neighborhood recreation centers. Call the Athletics Department, 2401 Wade Avenue, 831-6836, for the center nearest you. Registration is in October, practice in November and play starts in late December. Most facilities also have free time for pickup games, but call first.

The city also operates an adult league that follows a 16-game schedule with registration starting in October. Play begins in November.

The Salvation Army's 9-week basketball league fields 32 teams for ages 5 to 10, which are divided into three leagues. Every child gets to play and parents are recruited as coaches. The $55 registration fee is good for baseball and soccer also. Sign-up begins around November with December practices and leagues play in January on Friday nights and Saturday mornings at the Army's center at 902 Wake Forest Road. Call the Salvation Army at 832-6918.

The Hillsborough Street YMCA, 832-6601, and the North Raleigh "Finley" YMCA at 9216 Baileywick Road, 848-9622, sponsor youth leagues in the fall and members-only adult leagues. Call the YMCA for the cost. Hundreds of kids from kindergarten to grade 12 participate in the Hillsborough Street league and hundreds more at Finley, which serves the tribes of North Raleigh suburbanites. Each child gets to play, with much emphasis on the fundamentals. Sign-ups start in early fall, practice in December and play begins in January and runs through March. Most games are played at the Y, but some have moved to public and private school gyms.

The adult leagues are competitive and sometimes include past ACC stars. Eight teams play in the summer and 12 teams in winter at the Hillsborough Street and Finley YMCAs. Cost is about $25 over and above membership fees.

Biking

The city adopted a comprehensive bicycle plan in 1991 and has an active bicycle lobby pushing for designated bikeways. More than 40 miles of greenways are currently available to bikers. For an excellent $1 bikeway map, contact the Planning Department in City Hall, 890-3125. The North Carolina Bicycle Club sponsors rides, mostly aimed at experienced riders.

Lions Park at 516 Dennis Avenue is the center for BMX racing. Teams compete there on Sundays most of the year and on Wednesdays during the summer. Bikers come from all over and races are organized through the Capital City BMX Association. For information and race times, call 790-4BMX or Lions Park at 831-6995.

The North Carolina Bicycle Club sponsors rides mostly aimed at more experienced riders. Write NCBC, P.O. Box 32031, Raleigh, NC 27622 for more information.

Football

The city operates a league with three divisions for ages 7 to 13. There are weight limitations to make things even. Registration starts in July and games run from September through mid-November, when a Superbowl champion in each division is crowned. Call Raleigh Parks and Recreation, Athletics, 831-6836.

Photo by Rich Weidman

Located in North Raleigh, Shelley Lake is the perfect place to spend a lazy afternoon fishing, boating or strolling along the greenway trails.

Lake Johnson's boardwalk serves as a gateway to the park's 5.5-mile stretch of greenway trails.

Golf & Disc Golf

In a state known for world-class golfers and courses, its Capital City has no publicly owned golf course. However, it does have a number of excellent public and semiprivate club courses (described in our chapter on "Golf in the Carolinas"). The semiprivate courses are Hedingham, 250-3030, part of the Hedingham planned community and Raleigh Golf Association at 1527 Tryon Road, 772-9987, one of the older courses and a favorite among NCSU students. The other courses open to the public are all out of the city and include: Wil-Mar Golf Club on Route 5, Knightdale, 266-1800; Eagle Crest Golf Course near Garner, 772-6104; and Pine Hollow near Clayton, 553-4554. The city maintains two disc golf (Frisbee golf) courses at Kentwood and Cedar Hills parks. A course is also available at Zebulon Community Park in Zebulon. The Raleigh Area Disc League can be reached at 876-0937. The annual Canine Frisbee Disc Championship takes place at Millbrook Exchange Park during the spring.

Health Clubs

There are plenty health and fitness clubs around, including franchise operations like Gold's Gym or Spa Health Club and established local operations such as the Pulse Athletic Club at Celebration at Six Forks and Research Triangle Park and The Club For Women Only with locations in Raleigh and Cary. Both the YMCA and the YWCA have extensive programs, including indoor pools.

The face of the YWCA has changed and it's not just for women anymore. The recently renovated YWCA at 1012 Oberlin Road, 828-3205, has a pool, Nautilus equipment and aerobics classes, as well as other fitness and recreation programs. The basic membership fee is $25. An additional monthly or annual fee gives you access to the use of the particular facilities in which you are interested. Call for more information and a copy of the YWCA's schedule. The location at 554 East Hargett Street, 834-7386, has no pool or gym and its programs focus on southeast Raleigh community needs such as day care, summer camp, adolescent pregnancy issues and activities for older citizens.

Horseback Riding

There is no publicly owned riding stable in Raleigh, although the State Fairgrounds maintains one of the best show-horse arenas and schedules in the state. MacNair's Country Acres Stables probably is the best known of the private stables and offers lessons and boarding. Call 851-1118 for information. Other stables include Tamryss Farms in North Raleigh, 847-3080; J&H Stables, 782-9830; and Triton Stables, 847-4123.

Ice Hockey, Ice Skating & Roller Hockey

After years of sharing Cary's successful Ice House, 467-6000, Raleigh residents finally got their own ice skating rink in 1996.

Raleigh IcePlex, 878-9002, is located at the corner of Brentwood Road and Raleigh Boulevard. It offers public skating, figure skating instruction, ice hockey, skate camps and a fitness center.

The Raleigh/Cary Inline Hockey Association, 467-1448, sponsors youth and adult leagues at Jellybeans in Cary. Skateboarders flock to Ryan's World Skate Park, 788-8536, and Utopia Park, 856-0906.

Jogging, Running, Walking

If you're a jogger, you probably will want to map out your own course, but you'll have company because Raleigh is a running town. Its premier Great Raleigh Road Race, for instance, draws up to 2,000 runners and joggers each April.

Two of the more popular courses are the paths around Shelley Lake in northwest Raleigh and NCSU's track stadium on the main campus near Pullen Road. The city's award-winning Capital Area Greenway system is one of the best in the country and it laces the city like a spider's web, generally running beside the city's creeks and streams. The master plan shows a 200-plus-mile system of which more than 40 miles are complete.

The Shelley Lake to Sawmill Road Trail is the most popular, followed by the Lake Johnson and Buckeye paths. A pedestrian bridge across Lake Johnson allows walkers and joggers to make a 3.5-mile circular course around the lake. The Lake Lynn trail, completed in 1994, won a Sir Walter Raleigh Award for Community Appearance in 1995. The trail's five boardwalk sections are its most unusual and costly feature. Motorized vehicles are not allowed. Some of the trails are paved and are shared by bicyclists, but other parts are strictly for walking or jogging. The Crabtree Creek Greenway Trail runs behind Crabtree Valley Mall from North Hills Trail to Creedmoor Road. Greenway maps with a description of the system are available through Raleigh Parks and Recreation for a small fee. Call 890-3285.

The city's Parks and Recreation Department also co-sponsors the 5K Run for the Oaks in early March as well as other youth races. It also can put you in touch with the people who coach the city's formidable Junior Striders, which are comprised of boys and girls ages 6 to 18. For information, call 878-0335. Finally, a number of the newer planned communities have met the demand for jogging and walking by installing their own trails.

Racquetball

Despite the interest in racquetball, the city still has no public courts. If you want to play, you'll have to join a club or the YMCA on Hillsborough Street. The YMCA has the best courts; they're solid and give you a lively bounce, but you have to share them with handball players. Other places where you will find strong racquetball crowds are Pulse Athletic Club at Celebration at Six Forks, 847-8189, and the Pulse Athletic Club at 4700 Emperor Boulevard in RTP, 941-9010.

Scuba Diving

Located north of Raleigh between Rolesville and Wake Forest, Fantasy Lake Scuba Park is a unique scuba diving recreational park that provides a full-service dive shop, training facilities and recreational diving at a former rock quarry. Call 556-1803 for more information.

Soccer

The Capital Area Soccer League, 3344 Hillsborough Street, 834-3951, is known as the league for soccer players of all ages, sizes and sexes. Last season, more than 12,000 youth and adults participated as active players. It is a nonprofit organization built on volunteers within the Raleigh/Cary community and has been the training program for some of the area's best players and coaches. It sponsors more than 800 classic, challenge, recreational and adult teams. Mini soccer (3 v 3) begins with 4-year-olds and the youth league goes up to age 19. An adult league consisting of Women's Open, Men's Open, Men's Over 30 and Men's Over 40 is available for all outside the youth league. The 118-acre WRAL Soccer Complex located on Perry Creek Road off U.S. 1 North has 25 heavily used fields. The Cedar Fork Park Complex, located in Morrisville off Aviation Parkway, has 10 active fields.

CASL has two playing seasons—fall and spring—each consisting of nine scheduled weekly games. Tournaments highlight the beginning and end of each season. The highly competitive First Union Raleigh Shootout is in November and the CASL Cup (one of the largest recreational tournaments in the country with over 300 participating teams) is in May. Soccer camps are available in the summer for children ages 5 to 17.

The Salvation Army, 832-6918, sponsors soccer in its athletic program and it organizes teams for boys and girls ages 5 to 10. There's a $55 registration fee (and then you can add baseball and basketball for $40 each). Sign-ups begin in July. The season runs from August to October.

The Triangle Soccer Academy was created to enhance the development of the classic level players in the Triangle. Tryouts are held in early June and teams begin competing in August. Raleigh tryouts are held at Method Road Soccer Stadium and Durham tryouts take place at Duke Soccer Stadium. For more information, call 684-5180 (boys' soccer) and 681-3456 (girls' soccer).

Soccer Dome America, an indoor soccer facility at 5600 Hillsborough Street, offers leagues for players of all ages and skill levels. Call 859-2997 for more information.

Softball

The city has fields for hundreds of teams. City officials can put you in touch with the Raleigh Amateur Softball Association and, among others, a very active church league and some company team leagues. Altogether, the city coordinates play among a variety of leagues, including medium pitch, slow pitch, fast pitch, coed and 40-and-older leagues. It also sponsors a slow-pitch softball league for girls ages 12 and under and a girls' fast-pitch softball league for ages 8 to 18. Registration for most leagues begins in mid-February and play starts in April. Call the city's Athletic Office, 831-6836, for information.

Swimming

There are a number of private clubs in Raleigh, but Candler Swim & Gym Club at 1013 Jones Franklin Road, 851-3935, is one of the oldest and best known. You can learn about competitive teams here. Its founder is a former Olympian and the quality of his diving program and swim teams has won the club national attention. It has an Olympic-size diving tower and a 25-meter pool.

The city runs an active aquatics program, from teaching babies how to swim to hosting some of the region's top swimming competitions. The centerpieces of its swim program are the $4 million indoor Pullen Park Aquatic Center and the Optimist Park pools, which are open year round, too. The Pullen Center is home to a number of area swim clubs and has a diving board. Optimist includes a diving pool, a shallow baby's pool and a competitive, 50-meter Olympic-size swimming pool. The city also has pools at the following locations: Biltmore Hills, Chavis Park, Lake Johnson, Longview, Millbrook Exchange and Ridge Road. The city offers season passes if you plan to swim often; otherwise, there is an admission charge for everyone over the age of six. Diving lessons are taught as well as American Red Cross courses. For information on swim clubs and teams, call 831-6852.

A favorite swimming hole for Cary and Raleigh residents is Silver Lake, east of Cary and south of Raleigh, at 5300 Tryon Road, 851-1683. It has developed into one of the area's popular privately operated swimming parks open to the public. It features a 400-foot-long waterslide, white sand beach, pedal and motorized boats, snack bar and picnic areas. Call 851-7782 for special group rates.

All three Raleigh YMCAs sponsor competitive coed swim teams and also have pools for instructional and lap swimming for members. The Finley YMCA in North Raleigh at 9216 Baileywick Road, 848-9622, has the largest program for children and like the Hillsborough Street YMCA, 832-6601, competitive swimming is a year-long program but can be taken on a month-by-month basis. Swim classes are available for toddlers, too. The third YMCA location is on Garner Road, 833-1256.

The YWCA at 1012 Oberlin Road, 828-3205, offers swimming programs and classes for children and adults. The pool is available for members' use for lap swimming and recreational swimming. The basic membership fee at the YWCA is $25; call for more information on fees and types of memberships that include the use of the pool.

Tennis

Raleigh was caught napping when the tennis boom hit in the mid '70s, but it has recovered since then and maintains 100 courts today—95 of which are lighted. Operation Central for city tennis programs is the Millbrook Exchange Park at 1905 Spring Forest Road, 872-4129, which has 23 lighted courts and hosts city tournaments. The old clay courts have been converted and all courts today are hard surface. There is plenty of league play and tournaments run into December.

Play at all parks is free unless you sign up for a tournament or league or reserve courts at Millbrook Exchange. League play, by the way, is a good way to meet people.

Raleigh Racquet Club at 5516 Falls of the Neuse Road, 876-0565, is a private membership club with clubhouse and swimming pool attached. It is also home to some of the best tennis in town and features composition (soft surface) as well as hard-surface courts, 29 total, including eight indoor courts. It also

has a stadium court and its tournaments attract some of the stars of tomorrow. In addition, the club hosts a number of charity tournaments, such as the annual BTI Champions Tournament, part of the Worldwide Seniors Tennis Circuit, in the spring. The BTI attracts such big-name stars as John McEnroe, Jimmy Connors and Mats Wilander.

Volleyball

The city sponsors several leagues at different park centers and co-sponsors, with the Inland Beach Volleyball Association, tournaments at Raleigh Beach in Jaycee Park on Wade Avenue. Lions Park has a power volleyball league with six-person teams that begins registration in August. Other centers with volleyball programs include Millbrook Exchange, Biltmore Hills, Chavis Center, Robert Park and Jaycee Park. For a taste of California, two-man ball under the sun or under the lights, stop by Jaycee Park's Raleigh Beach on the weekend or during warm summer nights. The park boasts six sand volleyball courts and hosts a Sand Volleyball League. It's where some of the East Coast's championship teams work out. For more information, check with Raleigh Parks and Recreation at 831-6836.

Staff Photo

Soccer is by far the most popular recreational activity among kids in the Triangle.

TRIANGLE SPORTS CLUBS & FACILITIES

American Singles Golf Association	843-3366
Backwoods Orienteering Klub	828-6068
Broken Arrow Archery Club	942-2716
Bull City Dart League	477-0684
C.C. Pacers Track Club	942-2583
Capital Area Darts League	571-1917
Capital Area Soccer League	834-3951
Cardinal Track Club	932-7491
Carolina Canoe Club	682-6343
Carolina Copperheads Youth Football League	319-9184
Carolina Eagles Track Club	552-0206
Carolina Fencing Club	968-1064
Carolina Godiva Track Club	732-5074
Carolina Sailing Club	779-6890
Carolina Tarwheels Bicycle Club	687-5066
Cary Fitness & Racquetball Club	467-1852
Cary YMCA	469-9622
Chapel Hill Area Volleyball Club	967-7564
Chapel Hill/Carrboro Pacers	942-2583
Chapel Hill-Carrboro YMCA	942-5156
Chapel Hill Masters Swim Club	968-2790
Chapel Hill Tennis Club	929-5248
Dream Sports Center	387-2955
Durham Aquatic Masters Swim Club	560-4781
Durham Downtown YMCA	667-9622
Durham-Orange Bowling Association	471-4795
Durham-Orange Community Tennis Association	547-4354
Durham Pistol & Rifle Club	248-9449
Durham Softball League	493-1238
Durham Striders Track Club	477-9445
Durham Volleyball Club	471-0438
Durham County Wildlife Club	544-1306
Eno River Women's Rugby Club	816-9343
Executive Women's Golf Association	380-7715
Fantasy Lake Scuba Park	556-1803
Finley YMCA	848-9622
Great Atlantic Lacrosse Club	361-1354
Hargett Street YWCA	834-7386
Hillsborough Street YMCA	832-6601
Hot Wheels Roller Hockey	981-0737
Ice House	467-6000
Junior Striders Track & Field Club	851-8320
Lakewood YMCA	493-4502
Mid-Atlantic Cricket Conference	392-2975
N.C. Aquatic Masters Swim Club	933-4905
N.C. Australian Rules Football Club	845-1068
N.C. Bicycle Club	851-2009

TRIANGLE SPORTS CLUBS & FACILITIES

N.C. Fats Mountain Bikers	961-3865
N.C. Flag Football Association	894-7976
N.C. Rifle & Pistol Association	477-0845
N.C. Roadrunners Club	833-4808
N.C. Saltwater Fishing Club	790-8088
N.C. Ultra Running Association	847-7613
New Wave Swim Team	981-0644
Oberlin Road YWCA	828-3205
Rainbow Soccer	967-8797
Raleigh Aquatic Masters Swim Club	787-8324
Raleigh/Cary Inline Hockey Association	467-1448
Raleigh Disc League	876-0937
Raleigh IcePlex	878-9002
Raleigh Oars Rowing Club	772-7658
Raleigh Racquet Club	876-0565
Raleigh Rugby Club	833-9678
Raleigh Saltwater Sportfishing Club	839-8261
Raleigh Ski & Outing Club	847-7762
Raleigh Vipers Rugby Team	833-9678
Raleigh Water Polo	831-9676
Raleigh Youth Hockey Association	233-8210
Ravens Aquatic Club of Raleigh	877-0675
Research Triangle Ultimate Frisbee	676-3791
RTP Kayak Racing Club	846-4966
Silver Lake Waterpark	851-1683
Soccer Dome America	406-9722
Sunset Soccer	942-9272
Tar Heel Aqua Racers Swim Team	873-9434
Tri-City Blazers Track Club	772-6119
Tri-City Panthers Youth Football League	687-6945
Triangle Area Youth Lacrosse League	484-2938
Triangle Boardsailing Club	933-6549
Triangle Dive Club	834-3483
Triangle Fly Fishers	286-5666
Triangle Futbol Club	852-3959
Triangle Senior Babe Ruth Baseball League	303-7435
Triangle Seniors Golf Association	383-4749
Triangle Sports & Outings Club	405-9577
Triangle SportsPlex	644-0339
Triangle Table Tennis League	787-3788
Triangle Trailblazers	676-8587
Triangle Troglodytes (caving)	967-8957
Triangle Youth Hockey	933-5268
Tricyclists Racing Team	969-7173
Wake County Volleyball Club	894-2274
Wake County Wildlife Club	848-3694
Wayne Gretsky Roller Hockey Center	319-9910

PHONE NUMBERS FOR NEWCOMERS

Newcomers' Clubs
Cary 233-4737
Chapel Hill 942-9241
Durham .493-6810
Raleigh .359-2853

Colleges & Universities
Chapel Hill:
UNC-Chapel Hill 962-2211
Durham:
Duke University 684-8111
Durham Technical Comm. College .686-3300
NC Central University 560-6100
Raleigh:
Meredith College 829-8600
NC State University 515-2011
Peace College 508-2000
Shaw University 546-8200
St. Augustine's College 516-4000
Wake Technical Comm. College . .662-3400

Hospitals
Cary:
Western Wake Medical Center . . .233-2300
Chapel Hill:
UNC Healthcare System 966-4131
Durham:
Duke Univ. Health System 684-8111
Durham Regional Hospital 470-4000
NC Eye & Ear Hospital 682-9341
Oakleigh at Durham 470-6600
VA Medical Center 286-0411
Raleigh:
Holly Hill/Charter Hospital 250-7000
Raleigh Community Hospital 954-3000
Rex Hospital 784-3100
Wake Medical Center 350-8000

Licenses
Business License:
Cary 460-4952
Chapel Hill 968-2759
Durham .560-4070
Raleigh .890-3200
Division of Motor Vehicles:
Chapel Hill 929-4161
Durham .560-6896
Raleigh/Cary 715-7000
Hunting/Fishing License 662-4370
Marriage License:
Chapel Hill 967-9251
Durham .560-0494
Raleigh/Cary 856-5460

Postal Services
Chapel Hill 967-6297
Durham .683-1976
Raleigh/Cary 420-5333

Public Library
Chapel Hill 968-2777
Durham .560-0100
Raleigh/Cary 856-6710

Recycling
Cary 469-4090
Chapel Hill 968-2788
Durham .680-4150
Raleigh .831-6522

Schools
Chapel Hill-Carrboro Schools 967-8211
Durham Public Schools 560-2000
Orange County Schools 732-8126
Wake County Public Schools 850-1600

Senior Citizen Services
Chapel Hill 968-2070
Durham .688-8247
Raleigh .872-7933

Taxes
State Tax Info 733-4682
City, County Tax:
Chapel Hill 968-2759
Durham .560-0300
Raleigh/Cary 856-5400

Utilities
Chapel Hill/Carrboro:
Duke Power Co. 967-8231
PEMC. 1-800-222-3107
PSNC Energy 877-776-2427
BellSouth 780-2355
Water & Sewer 968-4421
Durham:
Duke Power Co. 382-3200
PSNC Energy 877-776-2427
Verizon 1-800-483-4300
Water & Sewer 560-4411
Raleigh/Cary:
Carolina Power & Light 508-5400
BellSouth 780-2355
PSNC Energy 877-776-2427
Water & Sewer (Raleigh) 890-3245
Water & Sewer (Cary) 469-4050

Voter Registration
Chapel Hill/Carrboro 732-8181
Durham .560-0700
Wake County 856-6240

Public Services and Utilities

Getting established in a new area can often be an overwhelming experience. It usually involves a mad scramble to accomplish a myriad of chores in a short period of time. First, you have to get hooked up to electricity, gas, water and telephone service. Then you have to apply for a new driver's license, register the car and make sure it passes a safety inspection. If you have a cat or dog, they need tags too. And, most importantly, don't forget to call the cable guy! Last—but certainly not least—remember to register to vote at your local board of elections or at any driver's license office.

This chapter was designed to help you ease your way into establishing residency. We provide you with the information you will need to accomplish all of the above, as well as details on other Triangle services, ABC laws, garbage pick up, recycling and taxes.

ABC Laws

In North Carolina, the state controlled Alcoholic Beverage Commission operates ABC stores, outlets where liquor is purchased. ABC stores are open from 9 AM to 9 PM Monday through Saturday. You can buy beer and wine at most supermarkets and convenience stores seven days a week, but keep in mind that alcoholic beverages may not be purchased on Sunday until noon. You must be at least 21 years of age to purchase beer, wine and liquor in North Carolina.

Liquor by the drink is available at many restaurants throughout the Triangle. State laws prohibit the establishment of facilities open to the public designed only for imbibing spirits; therefore, places that serve alcohol must also serve food.

Voters in each county and municipality in North Carolina decide if alcoholic beverages will be available and in what fashion. For example, in rural Chatham County just south of Chapel Hill, you can sip beer and wine in several restaurants, but liquor is illegal.

North Carolina has stiff Driving While Impaired (DWI) laws. If your blood alcohol concentration reads 0.08 percent on the Breathalyzer test and you are convicted of DWI, there is a mandatory revocation of your license for one year. You will also spend at least one night in jail, be required to pay a fine and perform community service. Restaurant owners and hosts of private parties can be held liable if someone drinking at their place has an accident involving property damage, personal injury or death.

Automobile Information
Driver's License

If you're moving to North Carolina, you have 30 days in which to get a license after establishing residency. You must apply in person at the nearest driver's license office. Appointments may be made but are not necessary. However, call ahead to make sure you have the exact documents and method of payment required. The only way to avoid a line is to be at the door when the office opens. If you already have a license, you will be asked to take written, road sign recognition and vision tests. A road test may be required. The tests are not difficult, but it helps to first read over the *North Carolina DMV Driver's Handbook*. It is free and available at all driver's license offices. Take cash ($10-$20) to the office. In-state personal checks printed with the correct name and address are accepted at most locations, but call first. Licenses are good for five years and expire on your birthday.

Drivers under 18 have to successfully complete an 18-month probation period before they are issued a regular license. Call 715-7000 for more information.

Cary
211 N. Academy St. • 468-0319
Chapel Hill/Carrboro
Carrboro Plaza Ctr. • 929-4161
Durham
101 S. Miami Blvd. • 560-6896
Homestead Market • 560-3378
Raleigh
4004 District Dr. • 733-4540
6081 Capital Blvd. • 850-2892

The Division of Motor Vehicles provides a 24-hour, seven days a week telephone service, DMV *directAccess*. Just dial 715-7000 for information regarding driver's licenses, vehicle registrations and insurance requirements.

Auto Plates

New residents must register their motor vehicle within 30 days of moving to North Carolina. Plates cost $25. Motorists can obtain plates and renewal decals by mail. For an extra $20, the state also permits "vanity" plates so you can put your name, message (keep it clean!) or favorite number on your plate.

Newcomers also have to obtain a N.C. title ($35) for their car and registration, which usually ranges from $40 to $150, but can cost more. Before your auto can be registered, you must provide a title to the vehicle, your insurance company's name and a policy number, an odometer reading and photo identification. You must also complete a title transfer application and have it notarized, so don't forget to bring cash for the Notary Public. Applications are available at the plate office. The State Division of Motor Vehicles (DMV) is headquartered in Raleigh at 1100 New Bern Avenue, 733-7573, and there are offices throughout the Triangle where tags can be purchased. A new service allows

Photo by Rich Weidman

The downtown Cary Depot doubles as a driver's license bureau.

residents to renew their vehicle registration online at NC@YourService. Visit ncgov.com for more information.

Cary
South Hills Mall • 469-1444
Chapel Hill
University Mall • 929-0204
Durham
Northgate Shopping Mall • 286-4908
1920 N.C. 55 • 544-6607
Raleigh
North Hills Shopping Ctr. • 781-4967
1100 New Bern Ave.
• 733-7573

Auto Safety Inspections

Safety inspections are required 10 days after initial plates are purchased and on an annual basis thereafter. Inspections are done at service stations, automobile dealerships and vehicle repair garages licensed by the state. Because of varying requirements, they should be done in the county in which your vehicle is registered. Safety inspections cost $9.25. Wake, Durham and Orange counties also require an emissions inspection, which can be conducted during the safety inspection. Emissions inspections cost $19.40.

Auto Tax

Within a few months of registering the vehicle, owners will receive a personal property tax bill from the county showing an assessment on the vehicle's value. Property tax bills are collected by the county in which your vehicle is registered. Call for more information.

Durham County • 560-0380
Orange County • 732-8181
Wake County • 856-5400

Pet Regulations

Cary
Cary requires licenses for dogs and cats. The onetime license fee for neutered pets is $10. For non-neutered pets the fee is $20. For information on pet licenses, call the Cary Town Hall at 469-4052.

Chapel Hill
Chapel Hill ordinances require dog leashes, tags and rabies vaccination. All dogs must be leashed, in a vehicle or in an enclosure when off the dog owner's property. Dogs and cats older than 4 months must have a current rabies vaccination. Dogs older than 3 months are required to have current dog tags ($3 for neutered or under 9 months; $5 for all others). For more information, call the Orange County Animal Shelter at 967-7383.

Durham
When you list your personal and real estate property holdings with the city and county tax offices, you will be asked if you own a dog. If you do, you will be assessed a licensing fee. Dogs are also required to have all the appropriate shots, including a current rabies vaccination. There is a yearly fee for cats as well, which drops dramatically when your cat is neutered. You can call the animal control department at 560-0630.

Raleigh
Pet owners are required to purchase tags for their dogs and cats. You can obtain these through the mail. The tags are issued once you show evidence that your pet has had a rabies shot. Neutered animals are cheaper than non-neutered to encourage residents to help reduce the stray dog and cat population. The pet tags must be renewed annually and can be obtained at City Hall, 222 West Hargett Street; call 890-3200. For stray dogs or cats

FYI
Unless otherwise noted, the area code for all phone numbers listed in this guide is 919.

INSIDERS' TIP

For more information about North Carolina state government services, visit the official web site, www.ncgov.com.

TRIANGLE SERVICES & UTILITIES

Service	Name	Area Serviced	Telephone #
Electric Power	Duke Power Company	Chapel Hill	967-8231
	Duke Power Company	Durham	382-3200
	Carolina Power & Light	Raleigh/Cary	508-5400
Natural Gas	PSNC Energy	Triangle	877-776-2427
Water and Sewer	Town of Cary	Cary	469-4050
	OWASA	Chapel Hill	968-4421
	City of Durham	Durham	560-4411
	City of Raleigh	Raleigh	890-3245
Telephone	BellSouth	Chapel Hill	780-2355
	Verizon	Durham	800-483-4300
	BellSouth	Raleigh/Cary	780-2355
Cable Television	Time Warner Cable	Cary	467-2800
	Time Warner Cable	Chapel Hill	968-4631
	Time Warner Cable	Durham	220-4481
	Time Warner Cable	Raleigh	832-2225
Cellular Telephone	Verizon Wireless	All Areas	888-466-4646
	ALLTEL	All Areas	233-3000

to be picked up, call 831-6311. The city also has a leash law for dogs, although your pooch is not likely to get picked up unless it becomes a nuisance. If your dog does get collared, you can retrieve him from the SPCA kennel on U.S. 70 South in Garner.

Recycling Information

Cary

Cary's award-winning recycling program is a leader in recycling rates, participation rates and the variety of materials recycled. Much of the town's solid waste is diverted from landfills through curb-side recycling, yard waste composting, drop-off center recycling and town departmental recycling efforts. The participation rate in the curbside program is estimated to be 99 percent with more than half of all eligible residents setting out recyclable materials each week.

The Town of Cary is unique among its Triangle neighbors in the variety of materials collected in its curbside program. These include aluminum cans, steel cans, clear glass, brown glass, green glass, plastic bottles (#1, #2, #5 and #7), newspapers, glossy magazines, corrugated cardboard, milk and juice cartons, drink boxes, six-pack rings, aluminum foil and aluminum pie plates. The town also provides fall leaf collection and weekly yard waste collection for composting.

Cary operates a recycling drop-off center for apartment and condominium residents. Items collected at the Citizens Convenience Center on North Dixon Avenue include aluminum cans, steel cans, newspapers, glossy magazines, corrugated cardboard and #1 and #2 plastic bottles. In addition, the town's Public Works Department collects motor oil, phone books and Christmas trees for recycling. Contact the Town of Cary Recycling Program at 469-4090 for more information.

Durham County

Durham residents recycle newspaper, glass bottles and jars, steel and tin food cans, aluminum beverage cans, soft drink and other #1 plastic bottles, and milk jugs and other #2 plastic bottles at curbside. If you live within the city limits, call Durham's Solid Waste Management Department, 560-4185, to obtain a bin and collection information. Additional recycling services include collections at select Durham apartment complexes, Durham Public School System buildings, North Carolina Central University and more than 200 area businesses.

Durham County residents have curbside service provided every other week by Tidewater Fibre. If you live in the county, call Tidewater Fibre, 680-4150, to obtain a bin and a collection calendar.

Tidewater Fibre also manages a number of public drop-off sites in Durham that accept the same items recyclable through the curbside service. In addition, glossy magazines, mixed paper and corrugated cardboard at certain sites.

Orange County

Orange Community Recycling provides weekly curbside recycling of newspapers, glossy magazines, glass bottles and jars, aluminum and steel cans, plastic soda and other #1 bottles and milk and other #2 bottles to all single family residences and most apartment complexes within the town limits of Carrboro, Chapel Hill and Hillsborough. The same service is provided on a biweekly basis to roughly one-half of the homes in the unincorporated area of the county.

There are drop-off recycling locations throughout the county that collect the same materials as curbside, plus corrugated cardboard, aluminum foil and pie plates, paper milk cartons and juice boxes, other plastic bottles and six-pack rings. Six of the drop-off sites are at staffed solid waste centers with restricted hours and seven are unstaffed 24-hour recycling sites. Waste oil, car batteries, latex paint and hazardous waste are handled separately.

For more information from Orange Community Recycling, call 968-2788.

Raleigh

All Raleigh homeowners have curbside recycling service twice a month. The city collects aluminum, newspapers, glass, and plastic milk jugs and soft drink bottles. Check with your neighbors to learn which week and which day is your pickup day and call the city's Sanitation Division, 831-6522, to obtain your green recycling container.

The city also manages eight drop-off sites for apartment dwellers and those not currently served by curbside pickup. The county maintains additional sites at various schools in the city and county. Reynolds Aluminum also operates a center at which you can take your aluminum cans for reimbursement and BFI operates a recycling facility, The Recyclery, at Eastridge Commerce Park off U.S. 64 E., at which tours are conducted. The city also offers certain days per year when it accepts hazardous wastes such as engine oil, old paint, pesticides and pet flea collars at designated drop-off sites.

For information about Wake County solid waste reduction programs that promote reuse and/or increase recycling, contact the Wake County Solid Waste Management Division at 856-6186.

Taxes

No Triangle municipality has an income tax. The state does have an income tax that has a 7 percent cap. The state's sales tax is 4 cents and all counties have the option to tack on an additional 2 cents. All do; so the rate is 6 cents per dollar of merchandise. Local governments raise money primarily through the property tax. This tax is levied against real estate as well as personal property, so renters have to pay personal property taxes (on such items as automobiles) just as homeowners do. If you live in the county, you pay only the county property tax.

Politics Play a Big Role in Triangle Life

As North Carolina's Capitol City, politics play a big part of Raleigh's life and by proximity, the Triangle. The largest employers in the Triangle, for example, are local, state and federal governments. For the media, some of the best known local newsmakers are our elected officials, most of whom live here. This also means that during election years, most of the political headquarters are located here, too. So, if you like politics, the Triangle serves a full-course meal (the entree almost always is barbecue!).

Close-up

We assume that anyone who reads also wants to be a good citizen, so here's the deal: North Carolina elects its governor in presidential election years, every four years. Until the 1990s, North Carolina was the only state in the union that had not given its governor the veto. Now he has it as well as permission to run for a second term. All state legislators, members of the Senate as well as the House, must run for office every two years and elections are held in even years, e.g., 2000. The power in the House is in the Speaker's office; in the Senate where the Lt. Governor presides, the real power is in the Senate Majority leader's position. The people who run county government, the boards of commissioners, run in partisan elections every four years. Judges are also elected, although the length of their terms differ. The lowest court is the District Court; then Superior Court, which takes on serious crimes such as murder and defacing an Insider's Guide; then comes the Court of Appeals; and best and last, the Supreme Court. (Incidentally, Insiders know that if you want to catch one of the Honorables at lunch, a good place to look is the Mecca Restaurant in downtown Raleigh.)

State Capitol
———

Photo by Tim Johnson

Local municipal elections in the Triangle are held in odd years, e.g., 2001, and are nonpartisan, although some candidates have tried to make them partisan in recent years, especially in Raleigh municipal elections. Most cities allow their councillors four-year, staggered terms; Raleigh's mayor and councillors, however, must face the voters every two years. School Board elections are also nonpartisan and members serve four-year, staggered terms. Wake County has one county-wide district as does Durham. Chapel Hill and Carrboro share one school system. There is a flaw in the system in regard to school boards and county commissioners. School leaders, who generally holler for more money to meet parent demands, cannot levy local taxes for schools; that responsibility falls to the county commissioners who look at tax increases the way Dracula fears daylight. This can make for embarrassing shouting matches between school leaders and county office holders.

If you want to see politics in action, spend a day in the halls of the General Assembly when it's in session. You can also introduce yourself to some of the state's capital press corps who have offices on the first floor. They're the scruffy bunch over in the corner in the House and Senate chambers. If you want to get involved at the grass roots, show up at your neighborhood's annual party precinct meeting and tell them you're a generous contributor or stop by state party headquarters in Raleigh. Both the Democratic and Republic parties maintain offices on Hillsborough Street.

Cary

Cary residents pay Wake County taxes at the 0.564 rate and Cary town taxes at the rate of 0.42 per $100 assessed value.

Chapel Hill

If you live within the town limits of Chapel Hill and Carrboro, you will pay property tax to those municipalities in addition to the property tax you pay to the county. Tax rates are assessed at 0.919 cents per $100 value for Orange County; an additional 0.498 cents per $100 for Chapel Hill residents and an additional 0.675 cents per $100 value for Carrboro residents. Hillsborough is an additional 0.57 cents per $100. There is also a school district tax to supplement state funding for the Chapel Hill-Carrboro schools. Motor vehicles are subject to a 3 percent highway use tax, which is billed annually. The minimum tax is $40 and the maximum tax is $1,500.

Durham

If you live anywhere inside the Durham city limits, you have to pay a city property tax in addition to the county property tax. Check with a real estate agent, map or the county tax office to determine exactly what rate applies to you. Current rates for the county, per $100 assessed value, are 0.9297 cents; additional city taxes are assessed at 0.68 cents per $100. The rates are subject to change each summer.

Raleigh

If you live in Raleigh, you pay both the city and the county property tax. The tax rate for Wake County (per $100 assessed value) is 0.564 cents; the city rate is 0.385 cents. A Raleigh resident with a house assessed at $100,000 can expect to pay a combined property tax bill of about $949 annually. Property is reevaluated every eight years.

Voter Registration

Don't forget to register to vote. To register, you must be a U.S. citizen, a non-felon, at least 18 years of age by the date of the upcoming election and a resident of North Carolina and your precinct for 30 days prior to the next election. You can register at various locations, including your local library, by simply showing some identification that contains your permanent, local address. You may also register at the local board of elections in your community or at any bureau of the Division of Motor Vehicles while doing business there. Once registered, you will receive a postcard from the board confirming that you are a registered voter and the location of your polling place. Call your local board for more information. The N.C. State Board of Elections can be reached at 733-7173.

Chapel Hill and Carrboro
Orange County Board of Elections
110 E. King St., Hillsborough
• 732-8181, Ext. 2350

Durham
Durham County Board of Elections
200 E. Main St., 3rd Floor • 560-0700

Raleigh and Cary
Wake County Board of Elections
339 S. Salisbury St. • 856-6240

Human Services Numbers

Look in the front pages of the current edition of your local phone book for comprehensive listings of human services, including crisis hotlines, family planning, mental and physical health services.

MORTGAGE COMPANIES

Bank of America	829-6990
www.bankofamerica.com	
Branch Banking & Trust Mortgage	716-9570
www.bbandt.com/mortgage	
Central Carolina Bank and Trust Co.	683-7777
www.ccbonline.com	
Coastal Mortgage	490-4420
www.coastalmortgage.net	
Countrywide Home Loans	870-5070
www.countrywide.com	
CTX Mortgage	783-7890
www.ctxmortgage.com	
First Citizens Bank and Trust	716-7000
www.firstcitizens.com	
First Union Mortgage	571-3818
www.firstunion.com/mortgage	
FM Lending	781-7809
www.fmrealty.com	
Great Southern Mortgage Corp.	571-8444
www.greatsouthernmtg.com	
Irwin Mortgage Corp.	878-5722
www.irwinmortgage.com/raleigh.htm	
Mortgage Choice Inc.	489-4949
www.mfbonline.com	
National City Mortgage Co.	848-2117
www.nationalcitymortgage.com	
Northstar Mortgage Corp.	806-4606
www.forthebestrate.com	
Southeastern Residential Mortgage	468-9255
www.southeaternres.com	
SouthTrust Mortgage Corp.	874-1810
www.southtrustmortgage.com	
State Employees Credit Union	839-5012
www.ncsecu.org	
Wachovia Bank, N.A. Mortgage	676-1800
www.wachovia.com/mortgage	
Wells Fargo Home Mortgage	676-9500
www.wellsfargo.com	

Real Estate and Neighborhoods

This is one of the practical chapters, especially for those planning to move here or planning to move from here to there within the Triangle. This guide includes the names and numbers of people who will help you buy a house, inspect a house and sell a house. Our lists don't compete with the Yellow Pages, but rather help you find some of the reliable companies that Insiders might employ.

Next is one of the best parts of the book—the neighborhoods. Some are historic and have a definite place in their respective city's profile. Others have become part of the Triangle lexicon and define a lifestyle as much as a location. Hayes Barton in Raleigh or Hope Valley in Durham, for instance, speak of Establishment as well as traditional architecture. But we don't limit the list to older places—there are new neighborhoods that have attracted notice because of design such as Southern Village in Chapel Hill or the Triangle's new wealth such as Preston in Cary.

Be aware that each county must value property at least every eight years for tax purposes and the valuations provide the prosperous if painful truth that real estate almost anywhere in the Triangle is a good investment. You have a variety of choices, from traditional single-family homes to condominiums to townhouses and the new planned communities. One of the signs that the Triangle is growing up is the interest in living downtown. While that's always been a choice in Chapel Hill, both Durham and Raleigh are seeing a lively market in the return of residential property in the center city. The proposed American Tobacco Historic District project near the Durham Bull's baseball park is a case in point.

This is the place to start your hunt for those three most important things in real estate: location, location and location.

Builders

If you are shopping for a house, you may want to know who built it, or maybe you're looking for a custom-built home. Finding that perfect fixer-upper might mean you need a trustworthy remodeler. A great way to get a list of reputable builders is from the Home Builders Association in your chosen area. Association officials will refer you to a short list of builders, depending on location, type of house you want to build and price range.

**Home Builders Association
of Durham & Orange Counties**
20 W. Colony Place, Ste. 180 • 493-8899
• www.hbadoc.com

**Home Builders Association
Raleigh-Wake County
(Includes Cary)**
6510 Chapel Hill Rd. • 233-2033
• www.hbawake.com

*New Home Builders
& New Home Guide*
2626 Glenwood Ave., Raleigh • 782-7819
• triangle.newhomesguides.com
• builders.newhomesguides.com

TRIANGLE CUSTOM BUILDERS

Name	Phone #	$ Range	Areas Served	Homes	Est.
American Heritage Homes, Inc.	233-9666	$250s-$1M	Apex, Cary, Raleigh, Wake Co.	15	1990
Ammons Building Corp.	847-1994	$150s-$300s	Wake County	30	1994
W.T. Barker Construction Co.	859-0044	$180s-$350s	Apex, Cary, S. Wake Co.	18	1989
D.G. Baron Co.	858-5000	$100-$600s	Cary, W. Wake Co.	15	1989
Beaman Building and Realty, Inc.	828-8484	$400s-$1M	Cary, Raleigh, Wake Co.	6	1990
Benchmark Homes	847-8924	$370s-$550s	Cary, Raleigh	15	1979
Biltmore Homes	303-3303	$130s-$300s	Wake County	10	1995
Brentwood Homes	462-3135	$400-$1M	Triangle	12	1988
Buildmaster Homes, Inc.	881-4300	$90s-$600s	Cary, N. Raleigh, N. Wake Co.	30	1987
Cady Construction	847-7000	$90s-$400s	Raleigh, Wake Forest	50	1970
J.H. Carter Builder, Inc.	878-6660	$330s-$1M	Raleigh	10	1972
Tom Charnetzky Custom Homes	554-2199	$100s-$250s	Granville, Franklin, Wake Co.	45	1983
Creech Construction Co.	781-2929	$320s-$500s	Apex, Cary, Raleigh, Wake Co.	14	1952
Crist-Chapman Builders, Inc.	848-3030	$300s & up	Triangle	18	1979
Steve Dickson Builders, Inc.	829-0022	$130s-$400s	Cary, Raleigh, W. Wake Co.	21	1974
Stephen Dilger, Inc.	848-0342	$300s-$1M	Wake County	10	1983
Dixon/Kirby & Associates	461-0394	$250s-$800s	Wake & Orange Counties	30	1984
T.L. Evans Builders, Inc.	848-9852	$250s-$700s	Wake County	10	1979
Jeff Fike Builders, Inc.	363-4868	$90s-$900s	Wake County	45	1984
Richard Gaylord Homes, Inc.	783-5777	$235s-$310s	Cary, Chapel Hill, N. Raleigh	25	1980
Charles Grantham	562-7027	$200s-$490s	Raleigh	10	1987
Hurst Built, Inc.	460-1192	$500s & up	Cary, Raleigh, Wake County	12	1985
Isenhour Enterprises, Inc.	932-2821	$250s & up	Orange and Chatham Counties	4	1991
McClure & Associates	878-8006	$130s-$750s	Triangle	25	1987
N.C.W. Development, Inc.	467-3927	$300s-$500s	Apex, Cary, Wake Co.	25	1989
Oaks Construction Co.	469-3555	$200s-$700s	Wake County	12	1983
Olde Heritage Builders	269-4555	$160s-$750s	Wake County	25	1982
John J. Palczuk Builders, Inc.	847-5161	$450s-$1M	N. Raleigh, Wake Co., Chapel Hill	12	1983
Park Homes	876-4788	$100s-$400s	Wake County	125	1988
Premiere Homes, Inc.	781-4177	$200s-$350s	Wake County	35	1980
Prestige Associates	932-5800	$400s-$850s	Chapel Hill	20	1990
Bryant Roberts Builders	383-8518	$125s-$500s	Durham & Orange Counties	50	1973
Rufty Custom Built Homes	460-8550	$400s-$2M	Cary, Chapel Hill, Durham, Raleigh	15	1988
Sheffield Builders, Inc.	510-0011	$150s-$500s	Durham, Orange & Wake Co.	8	1985
Skywater, Inc.	846-7597	$150s-$600s	N. Raleigh, Wake Co.	23	1987
Sparrow Construction Co.	833-7341	$400s-$700s	Wake County	15	1969
Spectrum Homes	848-2041	$400s-$1M	Raleigh, Wake Co.	30	1980
Starmount Realty, Inc.	848-0228	$375-$550s	Cary, Raleigh, Wake County	14	1929
Tall House Building	878-7121	$400s-$3M	Triangle	10	1976
Upright Builders, Inc.	462-8383	$150s-$450s	Wake County	25	1988
Whitney Blair, Inc.	967-7196	$195s-$395s	Chapel Hill, Durham	15	1983
Williams Construction Co.	471-1308	$150s-$1M	Triangle	42	1972
Williams Realty & Building Co.	781-7107	n/a	Raleigh	12	1954
Williams-Russell Building Co.	848-0799	$350s-$500s	Wake County	24	1993
Witt-Banks Homes	851-5111	$200s-$750s	Apex & Cary	40	1973
Woodard Builders	779-1417	$200s-$600s	Wake County	25	1983
Lance Youngquist Construction	460-0047	$400s & up	Apex, Cary, W. Wake Co.	15	1984

Home Inspectors

Before you buy your new home, you will want to be certain everything is in top condition. Due to the widespread damage caused by recent hurricanes, particular attention ought to be paid to the structural integrity of any home you are considering buying in the Triangle. A qualified home inspector can give you peace of mind about the structure of your home. Most of these companies provide full structural and mechanical inspections. Many offer specialized services such as tests for radon, lead, carbon monoxide and gas leaks. The American Society of Home Inspectors is a national certification organization. You can be assured of a home inspector's qualifications if he or she displays the ASHI symbol.

Buyers' Agents

The fastest-growing trend in Triangle real estate has been the use of buyers' agents. These agents represent the buyer in the negotiation and purchase of homes and other real estate. Some companies now provide buyer representation exclusively, while other traditional listing companies offer both buyer and seller services. Buyers' agents are licensed in the full spectrum of real estate transactions and provide multiple listing services as all Realtors do. We have included information on two of the Triangle's best-known buyers' agents.

FOR HomeBUYERS
4000 Wake Forest Rd., Raleigh
• 878-1110, (800) 333-2893
• www.forhomebuyers.com
Ann Davis, an experienced real estate agent, established FOR HomeBUYERS in 1991 to serve only buyers. All agents exclusively negotiate and close deals for buyers and are certified Buyers Representatives.

Home Buyer's Choice
219 E. Chatham St., Cary
• 481-0116, (800) 444-1442
• www.hbccary.com
Home Buyer's Choice in Cary was founded in 1993 by Margit Gratzl. It provides

a truly customer-oriented full-service relocation department.

Realtors

Membership in the Triangle MLS allows any Realtor to access information on homes anywhere in the Triangle. The companies listed in this guide are a sampling of the real estate firms in the Triangle. A good resource for information is the appropriate Board of Realtors listed below.

Chapel Hill Board of Realtors
501 W. Franklin St. • 929-4032

Durham Association of Realtors
3200 Croasdaile Dr. • 383-2117

Raleigh/Wake Board of Realtors
1301 Annapolis Dr.
• 834-0359 • www.triangle-realtor.com

Ammons Pittman Realtors
911-A Paverstone Dr., Raleigh • 847-5555
307 S. Salem St., Apex • 362-6848
1008 Big Oak Ct., Knightdale • 266-9999
2000 S. Main St., Wake Forest • 556-2900
• www.ap-realtors.com
Jud Ammons is one of the more imaginative developers in the Triangle and his partner, George Pittman, is a former president of the Board of Realtors. Their relocation department will send you a Relocation Package.

Arbor Realty
431 W. Franklin St., Chapel Hill
• 942-9937 • Relocation: (800) 849-4422
• www.arborrealty.com
Arbor Realty is a small but unique real estate company. It donates all its profits to local and state land preservation efforts and offers quality service to its customers.

Block & Associates
204-C Colonades Way, Cary • 859-6300
6736 Falls of Neuse Rd., Raleigh
• 850-0501 • www.homes4you.com
Established in 1996, this local company uses innovative technology to meet the needs of its clients.

Century 21

These are independently owned affiliates of Century 21:

Becky Medlin Realty
1233 E. Academy St., Fuquay-Varina
• 552-4517
• www.beckymedlinrealty.com

Four Star Realty
301 Ashville Ave., Ste. 111, Cary
• 816-8770
• www.FourStarRealtyInc.com

Haywood Davis Realtors
1011 Broad St., Durham • 286-2121

J.K. Sherron & Associates
4021 Barrett Dr., Raleigh • 510-5000
• www.raleighishome.com

Park West Realty
1708 N.C. 54 E., Durham • 361-5752
• www.c21parkwest.com

Russell Gay & Associates
6817 Falls of Neuse Rd., Raleigh
• 848-5600

Vicki Berry Realty
5312 Six Forks Rd., Raleigh
• 782-9797
• www.century21.raleigh.citysearch.com

Chapel Hill Realty Group, Inc.
151 E. Rosemary St., Chapel Hill
• **942-4149**

Another locally owned real estate firm, it specializes in the Chapel Hill area.

Coldwell Banker

These are independently owned affiliates of Coldwell Banker:

Coldwell Banker Realty Center
501 W. Franklin St., Chapel Hill
• 942-4482

Coldwell Banker Advantage
6 Consultant Pl., Ste. 100, Durham
• 493-3300
150 Cornerstone Dr., Ste. 101, Cary
• 467-5711

TRIANGLE PRODUCTION BUILDERS

Name	Phone #	$ Range	Areas Served	Homes	Est.
Anderson Homes	828-6000	$ 80s-$270s	Durham & Wake Counties	280	1980
Centex Homes	781-1952	$100s-$450s	Triangle	600	1987
Cimarron Homes	382-2888	$110s-$280s	Durham County	100	1982
Bill Clark Homes, Inc.	852-5999	$ 80s-$400s	Wake County	175	1977
Country Lane Development Corp.	783-0095	$120s-$180s	Wake County	100	1990
Dave Servoss Homes	828-6015	$120s-$200s	Durham & Wake Counties	100	1994
David Weekley Homes	844-9150	$190s-$400s	Wake & Orange Counties	90	1995
Engle Homes/NC	387-9016	$130s-$250s	Apex, Cary, Raleigh	100	1974
Fortis Homes/NC	872-5252	$100s-$400s	Durham & Wake Counties	290	1965
Homes by Huff & Co.	998-8500	$110s-$250s	Durham & Wake Counties	200	1981
John Wieland Homes	481-3309	$250s-$500s	Triangle	50	1994
Landwright Homes	383-2121	$100s-$300s	Triangle	35	1982
McNeil-Burbank Homes	781-5225	$150s-$220s	Triangle	60	1989
M/I Homes	828-1106	$110s-$270s	Triangle	190	1987
HJ Morris Construction, Inc.	876-9004	$100s-$200s	Wake County	150	1988
Pulte Homes	677-0122	$120s-$300s	Triangle	600	1985
Robuck Homes	876-9200	$180s-$250s	Wake County	70	1957
Squires Homes	881-9350	$ 90s-$300s	Wake County	350	1991
St. Lawrence Homes	676-8980	$150s-$330s	Triangle	450	1989
Sunstar Homes	469-1316	$130s-$400s	Wake County & Durham	200	1985
Timberline Builders, Inc.	387-7540	$200s-$300s	S. Wake County & Durham	60	1992
Toll Brothers	233-0939	$200s-$700s	Cary, Wake County	45	1994
Torrey/Dobson Homes	877-9557	$ 90s-$300s	Triangle	700	1996
Westminster Homes	462-0070	$110s-$250s	Wake County	200	1967
Zaring Homes	844-9288	$190s-$340s	Wake County	800	1994

4800 Six Forks Rd. Ste. 150, Raleigh
• 783-6066
6736 Falls of Neuse Rd., Raleigh
• 847-2222
• www.realestate-advantage.com
Coldwell Banker Preferred Properties
2555 Capital Dr., Hwy. 56, Creedmoor
• 528-4888

Distinctive Properties
605 Jackson St., Durham • 688-9314
Since 1980, Eugene and Signe Brown have specialized in historic residences in Durham's Trinity Park and other neighborhoods in the "Bull City."

Fonville Morisey
Relocation: (800) 846-7356
3600 Glenwood Ave., Raleigh • 781-7731
523 Keisler Dr., Cary • 859-8889
1903 High House Rd., Cary • 469-6300
2395 Kildaire Farm Rd., Cary • 859-0800
1149 Kildaire Farm Rd., Cary • 467-3232
1243 N.W. Maynard Rd., Cary • 469-6300
1738 Hillandale Rd., Durham • 383-1341
1304 N.C. 54 W., Durham • 493-4434
1004 Vandora Springs Rd., Garner
• 772-7240
5925 Falls of Neuse Rd., Ral. • 872-4450
100 Sawmill Rd., Raleigh • 847-9300
6301 Creedmoor Rd., Raleigh • 781-4452
8100 Creedmoor Rd., Raleigh • 847-2511
• www.fmrealty.com
Tommy Fonville and Johnny Morisey are two UNC fraternity brothers who teamed up in the early '70s during a year in which the market dried up. They persevered and today are one of the largest agencies in the Triangle. Both Fonville and Morisey are active in the Raleigh real estate community. They have kept their company in the forefront and were among the first to offer relocation services, a full-service mortgage company and a training school for agents.

Franklin Street Realty
1525 E. Franklin St., Chapel Hill
• 929-7174 • Relocation: (800) 849-2226
• www.franklinstrealty.com
This company is comprised of experienced agents knowledgeable in the Chapel Hill/Carrboro market and is conveniently located one block from the Siena Hotel on Franklin Street. Clients can expect that "hometown" difference with this agency.

Hodge & Kittrell Realtors
3200 Wake Forest Rd., Ste.101, Raleigh
• 876-7411
• www.hodgekittrell.citysearch.com
This independently owned company enjoys a loyal following and is considered one of the better agencies in the area. It offers a corporate relocation division, financial counseling and buyer assistance.

The Home Team
1721 E. Franklin St., Chapel Hill
• 967-6363 • Relocation: (800) 326-3577
• www.home-team.com
The Home Team opened in late 1989 and its agents pride themselves on selling Chapel Hill's most distinctive homes.

Howard Perry and Walston/ Better Homes and Gardens
Relocation: (800) 868-7653
4112 Blue Ridge Rd., Ste. 200, Raleigh
• 782-5600
981 High House Rd., Cary • 467-1882
1130 Kildaire Farm Rd., Ste. 100, Cary
• 380-8585
1600 E. Franklin St., Chapel Hill
• 967-9234
490 N.C. 42 W., Clayton • 553-0744
5285 N. Roxboro Rd., Durham • 479-1020
8 Consultant Place, Durham • 490-9000
1002 Vandora Springs Rd., Garner
• 772-9410
112 W. King St., Hillsborough • 732-6101
7048 Hwy. 64 E., Knightdale • 266-5500
7320 Six Forks Rd., Raleigh • 847-6767
5000 Falls of Neuse Rd., Raleigh
• 876-8824
5509 Creedmoor Rd., Raleigh • 781-5556
• www.hpw.com
HP&W/Better Homes and Gardens began in 1973 and is the largest residential real estate company serving the Triangle. HP&W runs a number of on-site sales offices for developers, as well as for its own projects. It maintains a relocation office, real

estate school, property management operation and commercial division.

Prudential Carolinas Realty
Relocation: (800) 334-8161
7500 Six Forks Rd., Raleigh
• 846-8101
1815 Kildaire Farm Rd., Cary
• 859-3300
1407 E. Franklin St., Chapel Hill
• 929-2186
921 Morreene Rd., Durham
• 383-4663
3933 Arrow Dr., Raleigh
• 782-5502
5821 Falls of Neuse Rd., Raleigh
• 876-7030
• www.prutriangle.com

With more than 17 offices in North and South Carolina, the company is one of the largest independently owned and operated real estate companies in the Carolinas. The company offers in-house mortgage services and operates a real estate school and a relocation department.

RE/MAX

These real estate companies are independently owned affiliates of RE/MAX.

RE/MAX One Realty
209 W. Millbrook Rd., Raleigh
• 781-9883
RE/MAX Preferred Associates
7101 Creedmoor Rd., Raleigh
• 676-9766
• www.preferredassociatesnc.com
RE/MAX Property Associates
1140 Kildaire Farm Rd., Cary
• 469-4700
1230 E. Academy St., Fuquay-Varina
• 557-1522
6801 Falls of Neuse Rd., Raleigh
• 518-8100
• www.trianglelistings.com
RE/MAX Realty 2000
14 Consultant Pl., Durham
• 401-4667
3000 Village Park Dr., Ste. 101, Knightdale • 217-9600
4601 Six Forks Rd., Ste. 106, Raleigh
• 571-9822

Realty Executives-Triangle
6308 Falls of Neuse Rd., Raleigh
• 872-6660
Hwy. 64 E., Knightdale • 266-3666
Hwy. 70, Garner • 772-7574
3713 University Dr., Durham • 490-1944
• www.realtyexecutives.com

Owner, Patrick Crawford, has this national franchise on the fast growth track.

Simpson and Underwood
3700 Computer Dr., Raleigh
• 782-6641 • www.simpsonunderwood.com

Simpson and Underwood is well connected to old Raleigh and knows that market. It has gained a reputation for representing many of the better homes. The company plans to merge with York Properties in early 2001 to form York Simpson Underwood.

Tony Hall & Associates
311 W. Rosemary St., Chapel Hill
• 933-8500 • Relocation: (800) 382-0673
• www.tonyhallassociates.com

Tony Hall is a very experienced Chapel Hill real estate agent. He and his staff of five agents specialize in relocation.

Tripointe Properties
201 Timber Hill Place, Chapel Hill
• 929-7100 • www.tripointe.com

This firm is located in the Timberlyne shopping center. The office's agents handle a lot of residential resales and new developments.

Weaver Street Realty
116 E. Main St., Carrboro • 929-5658
96 East St., Pittsboro • 542-7122
• www.weaverstreetrealty.com

Weaver Street founder Gary Phillips and his partners and associates believe that ecologically sound land development also makes good business sense.

Phyllis Wolborsky, CRS
HP& W/Better Homes & Gardens
6504 Falls of Neuse Rd., Raleigh
• 876-2372 • www.phyllisone.com

As one of the top Triangle Realtors serving clients since 1969, Phyllis has sold nearly $1 billion in residential sales.

York Residential

1127 Kildaire Farm Rd., Cary • 467-1811
801 Oberlin Rd., Raleigh • 821-7177
Relocation: (800) 334-3010
311 Oberlin Rd., Raleigh • 832-8881
8312 Creedmoor Rd., Raleigh • 846-7100
• www.yorkproperties.com

This company is a division of the York companies, a business name that has been in the Triangle building and development market since 1910. As the residential arm of the York companies that include commercial brokerage, property management and construction, it offers relocating companies a full range of real estate services, including Christie's Great Estates sales and auction services. The company plans to merge its residential arm with Simpson and Underwood in early 2001 to form York Simpson Underwood.

Neighborhoods

You've probably heard the advice about the three most important things to consider when looking for a new home—location, location, location. While the purveyors of this advice were probably talking about resale value, choosing a location or neighborhood that suits your personality and lifestyle is equally important. Developers today are trending toward "neighborhood amenities," such as championship golf courses, clubhouses, swim and tennis clubs, jogging trails and private lakes. Here is an overview of some of the area's favorite neighborhoods—old, new, big and small.

Cary

With nearly 100,000 residents, Cary is currently the seventh-largest city in North Carolina. Many of the neighborhoods are Planned Unit Developments, or PUDs, and they are built as complete communities. They contain a mixture of housing, from apartments to single-family homes on conventional lots. Some even include neighborhood shopping centers and office and industrial sections. Most have their own recreation centers and complexes. These planned communities are designed to help newcomers get to know their neighbors in a hurry. You can meet neighbors on the jogging or walking paths that may run past your back yard. You'll meet others at the homeowners association, community clubhouse, swimming pool or tennis courts.

This Guide lists a number of the established as well as some of the newer neighborhoods of Cary. Our list is not inclusive. It is a sampler and highlights some of the communities that have gained special attention. They are located throughout Cary and are convenient to Research Triangle Park or the I-440 Beltline around Raleigh. Many of the newest neighborhoods are being developed along N.C. 55 and in southwest Cary.

Cary has been the strongest housing market by far for most area real estate companies. Because of Cary's reputation as a prime residential area, prices reflect its popularity: $100,000 homes are rare and most start at $140,000 or more. Community spirit in Cary is high and children, active adults and senior citizens are a vital part of this town's arts, cultural and athletic synergy.

If you are looking for a new home priced from $100,000 to $130,000 you will have to consider a cluster or townhome. For $130,000 to more than $200,000, consider production builders' communities, such as Fieldstone, Coventry Glen, Brookgreen Forest, Forest Creek, Lochmere Forest, Devereaux and Park Village. Other home communities to be considered in the area are The Reserve, Cambridge, Camden Forest, Fernwood, Glenridge, Landsdowne, Normandie, Oak Chase, Ashley Woods, Riggsbee Farm, Sherwood Greens, Silverton, Somerset, Tatton Place, Wellsley, Wessex, Weston Estates, Whitebridge, Windsmere and Wyndfall. If you can't find

Triangle

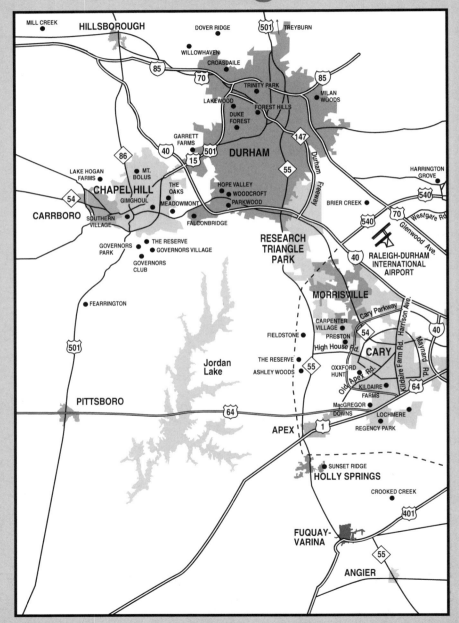

MILL CREEK
HILLSBOROUGH
DOVER RIDGE
501 TREYBURN
WILLOWHAVEN
CROASDAILE
85
70
85
TRINITY PARK
MILAN WOODS
LAKEWOOD
FOREST HILLS
DUKE FOREST
147
GARRETT FARMS
86
40
501
DURHAM
15
55
LAKE HOGAN FARMS
MT. BOLUS
HARRINGTON GROVE
540
THE OAKS
HOPE VALLEY
CHAPEL HILL
GIMGHOUL
WOODCROFT
MEADOWMONT
PARKWOOD
BRIER CREEK
54
Durham Freeway
540
70
Westgate Rd.
CARRBORO
SOUTHERN VILLAGE
FALCONBRIDGE
Glenwood Ave.
RESEARCH TRIANGLE PARK
40
RALEIGH-DURHAM INTERNATIONAL AIRPORT
GOVERNORS PARK
THE RESERVE
GOVERNORS VILLAGE
GOVERNORS CLUB
MORRISVILLE
Cary Parkway
Harrison Ave.
FEARRINGTON
CARPENTER VILLAGE
PRESTON
54
40
FIELDSTONE
High House Rd.
Maynard Rd.
CARY
501
Jordan Lake
THE RESERVE
55
ASHLEY WOODS
OXXFORD HUNT
Old Apex Rd.
Kildaire Farm Rd.
KILDAIRE FARMS
64
PITTSBORO
MacGREGOR DOWNS
LOCHMERE
64
REGENCY PARK
APEX
1
SUNSET RIDGE
HOLLY SPRINGS
CROOKED CREEK
401
FUQUAY-VARINA
55
ANGIER

REMAX

"#2 in the
Carolinas,

#17 in the
United States,

#20 in the
World–

Time to
Call Pat…

Time's Flying."

Pat Cross, CRS
Broker

RE/MAX Realty 2000
4601 Six Forks Rd., Suite106
Raleigh, NC 27609

Toll Free: 800-727-7281
Direct: 919-786-4148
Fax: 919-571-9881
E-mail: PHCr@aol.com
www.patcross.com

"Call me–
I will care about
you. I build
relationships one
buyer at a time
through outstanding
personal service–
I've been selling
homes in Cary and
the RTP area
since 1972."

Lillian L. Smith, CRS, GRI
Accredited Buyer's Agent

RE/MAX Property Associates
1140 Kildaire Farm Rd.
Suite 101, Cary, NC 27511

Toll Free: 800-326-3562
Mobile: 919-272-2550
Home: 919-467-6592
E-mail: ncrebroker@aol.com
www.lilliansmith.com

"A
seasoned
professional…
the first
ingredient for a
good move is
my personal
commitment to
quality service
for everyone."

Bill Edwards, CRS, GRI
Broker

RE/MAX Preferred Associates
7107 Creedmoor Road • Suite 115
Raleigh, NC 27613

Toll Free: 800-506-6329
Voice Mail: 919-845-2164
Fax: 919-676-3114
Mobile: 919-649-8200
E-Mail: williamedwards@remax.net
www.bedwards.com

If land is
what you
want, I'm
the realtor
to call!

Linda Jacobs, CRS GRI
Broker

RE/MAX Realty 2000
4601 Six Forks Rd., Suite106
Raleigh, NC 27609

Message
Center: 919-545-9907
Toll Free: 888-863-1581
Pager: 919-501-2864
E-Mail: lcj@horizons.net

Do you want to increase sales to new homeowners?

Please accept our invitation to join the area's most prominent merchants and professional service providers in welcoming new homeowners to your area.

Welcome Home! the area's premier community-oriented welcoming service provides one of the most effective direct marketing opportunities available. Your business will reach new homeowners in your local area *before* they establish new buying patterns and professional loyalties.

Our sponsorships are exclusive and your business will be the only sponsor in its category.

A full page, 2-sided ad placed in the *Welcome Home!* gift certificate book will introduce your business to the new family.

You will be supplied with a list of families welcomed each month for your follow-up.

Call 919-467-4035 to reserve your exclusive category and begin attracting new homeowners to your business.

Welcome Home
8085 Chapel Hill Road, Cary
919-467-4035 • 800-777-4843

Neighborhoods

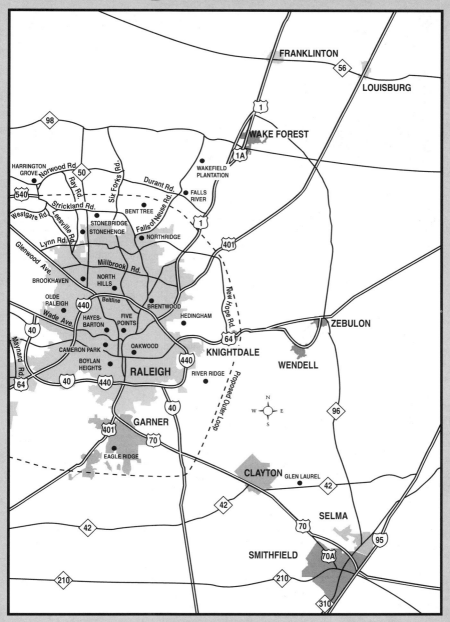

Located on Morrisville-Carpenter Road across from Preston, Carpenter Village is Cary's first "neotraditional" community.

the home of your dreams in Cary, many families are now looking at nearby communities in Apex such as Abbington, Ashley Downs, Beckett Crossing, Haddon Hall and Haddon Place, Pearson Farms, Scotts Mill and Walden Creek.

Braeloch

Braeloch is a Squire's Homes community conveniently located off N.C. 54, one mile west of I-40. These attractive traditional homes have the feel of custom-built houses. Prices start in the upper $100,000s.

Carpenter Village

Cary's first "neotraditional" community, Carpenter Village is a 400-acre community located on Morrisville-Carpenter Road across from Preston. It includes a swim and tennis club, walking trails and a playground. A village center, complete with shops, restaurants and a dinner theater, is in the construction stages. A total of 575 townhomes, single-family homes and Charleston-style homes will be constructed in Carpenter Village. Prices range from $140,000 to the $600,000s.

Downtown

This is the older part of town and it retains much of Cary's small-town flavor. The Town Hall and Chamber of Commerce are nearby, as is Ashworth Drugs on the corner, where you can get a first-rate milkshake. The library and Cary Elementary are within walking distance, as is Russell Hills, a downtown subdivision. Older homes in the downtown area, some in the process of restoration, come in a mixture of styles. Prices vary, but although the larger homes with the spacious yards will sell for more than $200,000, you might find a bargain in the $100,000s.

Greenwood Forest

Greenwood Forest was one of Cary's first large subdivisions, once on the southeast outskirts of town, but now right in the middle. The neighborhood is bounded by the slanting Walnut Street from the northeast and the curving East Maynard Street that wraps around its southern border. It is a typical 1950's, early 1960's neighborhood (no sidewalks) and has a mixture of home styles. Cary High School is nearby—some would say within walking distance—as are Cary Village Square and Cary Towne Center, the town's largest enclosed mall. Prices on these conventional homes start in the low $100,000s. Other neighborhoods of this vintage and price range are Greenwood Acres, Pirate's Cove, Tanglewood and Walnut Hills.

Kildaire Farms

Kildaire Farms was Cary's first Planned Unit Development and was hailed with lavish praise during the 1970s. It was named after the 927-acre farm owned by the Kilgore family. The development is located at Kildaire Farm Road and Cary Parkway. About 2,600 residential units fill the PUD. It includes a 230-acre greenway system winding throughout the community, with jogging trails and bike paths. The Kildaire Farms Racquet and Swim Club has 13 lighted tennis courts and an 8,500-square-foot swimming pool. There's a membership fee for Kildaire Farm residents and, unlike most PUDs, nonresidents may also join. The Cary Fitness and Racquetball Club is also located here. Prices vary, depending on the project. For example: homes in Royal Ridge go for more than $250,000 and Fox Chase homes start at around $140,000, while some townhouses can be found in the low $100,000s.

Lochmere

The 1,000-acre Lochmere development began in 1981 and became a textbook example of a successful PUD. It offers a variety of neighborhoods and is located on the southern end of Kildaire Farm Road, east of U.S. 1, not far from Regency Park. Lochmere has three man-made lakes big enough for sailing, canoeing and fishing. In the center is its 18-hole golf course—Lochmere Golf Club. A swim and tennis complex is also available to residents, along with jogging trails, including a path around the larger lake. The Homeowners Association is extremely active in this community. There are several neighborhoods within the development, and they have names such as Fairways, Lochwood, Lochview, Windsong, The Greens, Williamsburgh Commons and Lochridge. Homes range from more than $200,000 to $1 million. Homes located in the Birkhaven neighborhood start at $340,000. Condominium prices start at about $130,000.

The Highlands is a neighborhood within Lochmere that started in 1987. It contains 343 homes, most of which are single-family detached homes. It has its own swim and tennis club, but members have access to Lochmere also. Homes range between $200,000 to $350,000.

MacGregor Downs

MacGregor Downs lit the fuse that led to Cary's growth explosion. It boasts a lake, a championship golf course and private country club and a tournament-caliber tennis complex as well as a pool. Townhouses and condominiums are built on property closer to the club and tennis complex.

An adjacent but separate neighborhood is MacGregor West. It is especially upper-end in price range—starting around $350,000—and reflects the sumptuous amenities that newer homes offer today, such as extravagant master bedroom suites and elaborate bathrooms. The MacGregor West mini-estates—those homes sitting on 2- to 3-acre lots—go as high as $1.5 million.

Oxxford Hunt

Oxxford Hunt is another residential community with English sounding neighborhoods such as Trafalgar. It is located off West Chatham Street and includes about 450 homes and apartments. Oxxford Hunt has a mix of housing, from single-family homes to condominiums and apartments. Prices are moderate, from $150,000 and up for the single-family homes. This is a family neighborhood. Residents pay modest homeowners dues to maintain common areas such as jogging trails, playground, tennis courts and swimming pool. This development is adjacent to Fred Bond Park.

Park Village

Park Village is a popular family community of more than 620 homes built by Sunstar Homes. It is located off Davis Drive, 1.5 miles south of High House Road. Amenities include a swimming pool, clubhouse, mini-parks, walking trails and a children's playground. Prices range from $135,000 to $300,000.

The Parkway

This development stretches along Cary Parkway and has become a popular Cary address. It is located in west Cary and contains 20 separate neighborhoods with names like Arlington Ridge, Candlewood and MacArthur Park. Prices range from $150,000 to more than $250,000.

Preston

Preston is the Triangle's largest golf course community and one of the state's top-selling country club communities. Located off High House Road and only 10 minutes from the Research Triangle Park and RDU International Airport, Preston is at the heart of the area's booming residential market. Thoughtful planning that emphasizes beauty, privacy and convenience has allowed the community to respond to the tremendous growth of the area.

More than 20 neighborhoods make up this development, offering a diversity of home styles and a variety of price ranges—from $375,000 to $1,500,000. Preston Village boasts a two-acre Great Lawn, athletic field, putting greens, sheltered picnic areas, gazebos overlooking the lake and a huge play area designed for kids.

The centerpiece of the community is Prestonwood Country Club. The clubhouse complex and ballroom includes an expanded Olympic-size pool (with poolside dining), a fitness center and composition tennis courts. The championship golf course has 54 holes and is home to the Jimmy V Celebrity Golf Classic each August.

Regency Park

Regency Park is located near the intersection of U.S. 1 South and U.S. 64. Although approved in the late '70s, development of Regency Park did not begin until the '80s, but when it did, it established itself as one of the Triangle's classiest developments. It also marked a change from previous PUDs because it did not focus entirely on residential projects. It contains some of the Triangle's best office buildings and has helped change Cary's image from that of a bedroom community to a professional work center. The residential area is made up of single-family detached homes, cluster homes, townhouses and estate houses.

Regency Park Estates is an exclusive enclave of only 55 residences; each homesite is 1-acre or larger.

Photo by Rich Weidman

Preston consists of more than 20 neighborhoods, making it the largest golf course community in the Triangle.

Weatherstone

Weatherstone is an upscale community conveniently located off High House Road near Weatherstone Elementary School. It includes a pool, tennis courts, a playground and a 22-acre lake. Prices range from $260,000 to more than $300,000.

Weston Pointe

Located between Weston Parkway and Cary Parkway, the Weston PUD was first developed as an employment center. Weston Pointe is the residential part of the development and offers new homes built by well-known and respected area builders. Prices range from $260,000 to more than $360,000. As with most of the new planned communities, Weston Pointe has walking trails and a swim and tennis club.

Chapel Hill

Chapel Hill has come a long way from the day in 1793 when an auctioneer offered the first 22 lots for sale in the new university village. Today this growing town of about 45,000 residents and 24,600 students is considered one of the most desirable addresses in the Southeast.

Despite the pressures of new commercial and residential development, Chapel Hill still exudes the charm of a historic university village. Add to that some of the best public schools in the state and access to RTP, Raleigh and Durham, and it is no wonder Chapel Hill has become a haven for young families, professionals and retirees.

The demand for housing translates into some of the highest home prices in the Triangle. The average home price is more than $200,000. Large older homes or custom-built new homes in some of the finer neighborhoods can easily cost $450,000 or more.

Both Chapel Hill and Carrboro also offer a wide range of condominiums and townhomes, from $40,000 to $50,000 for a small one-bedroom unit to $175,000 and up for a luxury apartment unit. Townhomes were in generous supply just a few years ago. Today, they are a very hot item for retirees, small families, singles and students. In addition to the communities described below, some other home communities you may want to check out with a Realtor include Highland Meadows, Meadow Ridge, Northwoods, Parkside, Silver Creek, Southbridge, Springcrest, Windsor Place, Wexford.

Historic Districts

Chapel Hill has three historic districts. The first, the Franklin-Rosemary District, was established in 1976 and includes sections of the town's main thoroughfares, Franklin Street (Chapel Hill's main business street, named for Ben) and Rosemary Street, a block to the north. (It is said that Rosemary Street was so named to honor a Lady Rose who lived at one end and a Lady Mary who lived at the other.)

The Cameron-McCauley Historic District was established in 1990. It takes in an area ranging from just south of West Franklin Street up to the University Drive area, and includes the area around the landmark Carolina Inn.

The newest historic district, which was established in 1993, is the Gimghoul area. This neighborhood is named for the "medieval and mysterious-looking" Gimghoul Castle, built by Masons as the meeting place of the Secret Order of the Gimghouls, a university society that continues today.

In these neighborhoods, you'll find rambling brick, cedar shake or wood-frame colonials, many built in the 1920s and '30s, as well as smaller homes tucked behind hedges and old stone walls. Expect to pay more than $200,000 for a home that needs work and from $350,000 to $650,000 for one that's been remodeled and updated. Also close to downtown and campus is a unique neighborhood around Cobb Terrace, a narrow winding circular road. This neighborhood features a mix of larger colonials and more modest wood-frame homes and cottages on smaller lots.

All three of the historic districts are within walking distance of the campus and many restaurants and stores. They are the most convenient neighborhoods for university faculty and medical center personnel.

Booker Creek

Northeast of Lake Forest is Booker Creek, a 1970's neighborhood that features one- and two-story traditional homes. Most homes in Booker Creek are 1,800 to 2,500 square feet in size, and prices range from $185,000 to $250,000.

Cedar Hills and Timberlyne

Farther up the road are two neighborhoods offering traditional and contemporary homes from 1,800 to 3,000 square feet in size. These neighborhoods are popular with families, and homes here sell from $190,000 to $300,000 and up. This area offers convenient access to I-40 and to shopping at Timberlyne Shopping Center.

Chesley and Chandler's Green

Chesley and Chandler's Green are neighborhoods along Weaver Dairy Road that feature large, elegant homes in the $300,000 to $500,000 range. Chesley adjoins Cedar Falls Park. Both neighborhoods are a stone's throw from East Chapel Hill High School.

Countryside

Heading north, just above Cedar Falls Park, is Countryside, a neighborhood of one- and two-story homes, mostly in the 1,500 to 2,500 square feet range. These homes sell for about $160,000 to $225,000.

Culbreth Park/Tandler

These two developments in Chapel Hill are designed to provide affordable housing in a marketplace that has very few "starter homes" left. Culbreth Park is next to Culbreth Middle School. Tandler is a bit closer to the UNC-CH campus off Merritt Mill Road. Home prices start in the low $100,000s.

Dogwood Acres

A few miles south of town, between U.S. 15-501 and Smith Level Road, is this older neighborhood of small cottages and ranch-style homes, many on lots of almost an acre. One of the more affordable neighborhoods in town, Dogwood Acres is a good place to look for a first home. Homes start at about $125,000.

Downing Creek/Downing Woods

The Downing Creek and Downing Woods neighborhoods are located off N.C. 54, east of Chapel Hill. These neighborhoods offer homesites amid buffered forests, custom-built transitional homes and a private swim and tennis club. Homes are convenient to Chapel Hill, Research Triangle Park and I-40, and are priced from $195,000 to $300,000.

Falconbridge

Located midway between Chapel Hill and Durham on N.C. 54, Falconbridge offers townhomes and single-family residences convenient to both towns. It's also located minutes from Jordan Lake and RTP. Falconbridge offers traditional and contemporary single-family homes from $175,000 to $325,000 and townhomes starting at about $120,000. There is a private clubhouse with tennis courts and a swimming pool.

Forest Hills

The neighborhood of Forest Hills is located near UNC Hospitals. Here you'll see a variety of home styles and sizes from modest wood-frame cottages to larger traditionals and a sprinkling of newer homes. Prices are in the mid-$100,000s to mid-$200,000s range.

Franklin Hills

Franklin Hills, which is located off East Franklin Street, boasts stately two- and three-story homes with plenty of custom features: gourmet kitchens, formal dining rooms, whirlpool baths, vaulted ceilings, winding stairwells, porches, upper balconies and more. Expect to pay $300,000 to more than $400,000.

Glen Lennox

Heading east of Chapel Hill, off the U.S. 15-501 Bypass is a neighborhood built in the 1950s known as Glen Lennox. In Glen Lennox, you'll find mostly frame and brick ranches starting in the high $100,000 range.

Glendale

If you like the idea of owning a home near Franklin Street, but you favor more contemporary architectural styles, Glendale is for you. Glendale features newer, more contemporary homes, some built into the sides of hardwood-covered bluffs overlooking the woods. You'll see a variety of styles including ranches and split-levels on hillside lots large enough to convey the feeling that you are in the wooded countryside, though Chapel Hill's bustling downtown is just a minute away. Here homes built in the 1960s sell for $190,000 to more than $300,000.

Greenwood

Greenwood is just southeast of Glendale and still a pleasant walk to campus. This neighborhood features a mix of traditional and contemporary homes. Prices here are in the $190,000 to $525,000 range for large custom homes.

Heritage Hills

Like Dogwood Acres, Heritage Hills is south of the town limits but within the Chapel Hill-Carrboro School District. Homes here start in the $135,000 to $197,500 range. Heritage Hills offers a private swim and racquet club.

Hidden Hills, Estes Hills, Coker Hills and Coker Hills West

These family neighborhoods are located in the wedge-shaped area between East Franklin Street and Airport Road. They feature a variety of ranch, contemporary and colonial homes on midsize to large lots and are convenient to elementary and middle schools, downtown and University Mall. Prices range from $155,000 to more than $350,000.

Homestead Village

Homestead Village is located off Homestead Road only minutes from downtown Chapel Hill. Built by Landwright Homes, prices start in the $190,000 range.

Ironwoods

Just 2 1/2 miles north of town off Seawell School Road and Estes Drive, this development offers wooded lots and spacious traditional and contemporary homes with custom features. Prices begin around $205,000.

Lake Forest

What's special about this neighborhood is that it has its own private lake, Eastwood Lake, large enough for fishing and boating. Lake Forest offers a variety of housing styles from New England and American colonials to ranches, split levels and other contemporaries, most built in the 1960s and '70s. Prices range from about $200,000 to $600,000 or more for a special large property with a pool and perhaps its own dock on the lake.

Lake Hogan Farms

Located off Homestead Road, this development consists of 438 homesites on more than 310 acres. Homesites range from estates to townhomes. The Commons includes a swim and tennis club. A 12-acre spring-fed lake offers light boating and fishing. Single-family homes are featured in Bolin Ridge, Shadow Ridge, The Woods and Lake Hogan Estates. The Greenfields neighborhood offers more than 90 patio homes. Prices range from $230,000 to more than $600,000.

Meadowmont

East West Properties has started development on the massive 435-acre Meadowmont community, which is located off N.C. 54 in eastern Chapel Hill. The project was designed in the "neotraditional" mode and will eventually contain about 1,298 housing units and 785,000 square feet of commercial space, as well as a 70-acre park.

Mill Race

Located close to Bolin Creek, but within walking distance of Downtown Chapel Hill, this community is in the heart of Chapel Hill. Mill Race has 25 homes with prices starting in the $400,000s.

Morgan Creek Hills, Farrington Hills and Laurel Hill

These three neighborhoods offer a mix of home styles on large, wooded lots in the rolling countryside off Mount Carmel Church Road south of town. Homes here start at about $215,000 and go to $350,000 or more.

Mt. Bolus/Winding Ridge

Heading north of town off Airport Road, you'll turn east into Mt. Bolus. This magnificent hill rising above Bolin Creek was named for Joseph Caldwell, the first official UNC president whom the students affectionately called Diabolus (devil) or Bolus for short. Today Mt. Bolus offers a mixture of traditional, ranch and contemporary homes clinging to the sides of steep hardwood-shaded bluffs.

Just south of Mt. Bolus Road is a neighborhood called Winding Ridge. It features spacious homes with an abundance of custom details such as oak panelling, granite kitchen counters and wine cellars. These neighborhoods offer lots of privacy and wooded views, all just minutes from UNC and

Photo by Rich Weidman

Lake Hogan Farms is located in Orange County just
minutes from downtown Chapel Hill and Carrboro.

downtown. Prices vary with the size and location of each home, but generally range from $275,000 to $400,000.

The Oaks and
The Oaks II and III

East of Glen Lennox is this neighborhood built in the 1980s, surrounding the Chapel Hill Country Club and its golf course. It features a mix of traditional and contemporary homes. In The Oaks II and III, you'll find sprawling custom homes of brick, stone, stucco and wood on spacious lots with greenway views. Most feature large living rooms, spacious master suites, cathedral ceilings, arched windows, detailed woodwork and two- or three-car garages. Expect to pay $350,000 and up to $1 million.

Old Forest Creek

Just off Piney Mountain Road, this development runs along Rock Creek within walking distance of Estes Hills Elementary and Phillips Middle schools. Larger traditional and contemporary homes feature wood, stucco and stone exteriors, cathedral ceilings, formal dining rooms and spacious master bedrooms. All are within walking distance of

town and UNC-CH. Prices are in the $250,000 to $350,000 range.

Southbridge

Just south of Chapel Hill, across from Culbreth Middle School, Southbridge features two-story traditional and transitional homes on hilly terrain. This is a popular neighborhood for university faculty due to its proximity to UNC-CH. Most homes sell for $215,000 to $325,000.

Southern Village

Developed by Bryan Properties, Southern Village is located in south Chapel Hill along U.S. 15-501. This "neotraditional" community of 535 homes has been built in the style of a village, where sidewalks, porches, a greenway, a bus stop and a corner store help bring neighbors together. The Village includes a swim and tennis club, a market and deli, and a four-screen movie theater. Southern Village Elementary and Culbreth Middle schools are within walking distance. Houses are designed away from the "cookie-cutter" mode, with styles ranging from long, narrow Charlestons, to Georgetown and "Courtyard" style homes. With the variety of

Photo by Rich Weidman

A neotraditional community in south Chapel Hill, Southern Village includes a market and deli, swim and tennis club and a four-screen movie theater.

home styles comes a variety in home prices—$200,000 to $700,000. Condominiums and townhomes are also available.

Stoneridge and Sedgefield

On the northernmost edge of Chapel Hill, on the other side of I-40, are these two developments of gracious contemporary and traditional homes with the privacy afforded by wooded lots of 1-acre or more. Stoneridge also has a private racquet and swim club in the neighborhood. This location provides easy access to Research Triangle Park, Durham, Raleigh and RDU International Airport. Prices range from $300,000 to $600,000 and up.

Westwood

Until 1950, the town of Chapel Hill was composed of 850 acres. Another 289 acres were annexed east of town that year, and in 1951 the town added 61 acres, which today make up the neighborhoods of Westwood and Forest Hills just to its south.

Westwood is located along a winding, hilly drive across Columbia Street from the UNC Hospitals. Here you'll find large two- and three-story traditional homes of brick or wood, many built in the 1950s. They feature hardwood floors, high ceilings, sweeping porches and spacious yards framed by low stone walls. Prices go from about $245,000

for a fixer-upper to $450,000 plus for a recently remodeled home.

Carrboro

Real estate prices in Carrboro are generally somewhat lower than in Chapel Hill. You may still be able to find single-family homes in the $120,000 to $175,000 range for a new three- to four-bedroom home. Some other communities are Bel Arbor, Berryhill, Sunset Creek and University Station.

Bolin Forest and Quarterpath Trace

Just off North Greensboro Street are two neighborhoods filled with young families. Bolin Forest is a neighborhood of two and three bedroom homes ranging from about $200,000 to $250,000. Homes in Quarterpath Trace are traditional styles with three to four bedrooms. Prices range from $200,000 to more than $225,000.

Cobblestone and Barrington Hills

Travel north out Hillsborough Road and you'll come to Cobblestone and Barrington Hills. In Barrington Hills, you'll find modest contemporary homes built in the late 1970s, starting at over $125,000. Cobblestone's homes are in the $200,000 to $265,000 range.

Morgan Glen

Morgan Glen is a pastoral residential development consisting of eleven 10-acre tracts, with restrictions against further subdivision. A 150-foot swath along Morgan Creek was given to the Triangle Land Conservancy for a perpetual wildlife conservation easement. All property owners have access to the creek that runs through the development and the easement allows wildlife to coexist with people. Resale homes on the large lots are in the $300,000 to $450,000 range.

Plantation Acres

Wedged between North Greensboro Street and Old N.C. 86 is Plantation Acres, a family neighborhood of ranch-style homes built in the 1960s. Most are three-bedroom houses that sell for $150,000 to $185,000.

Spring Valley

If you drive through Webbwood, you will come to a development called Spring Valley, featuring two-story rustic-contemporary homes, many with a view of a man-made pond. Homes here start at about $155,000 to $200,000.

Weatherhill Pointe

These award-winning cluster and patio homes are adjacent to the Chapel Hill Tennis Club. In the $130,000 to $175,000 range, these are among the more affordable homes to be found in Chapel Hill and Carrboro.

Webbwood

A bit further from downtown Carrboro is Webbwood, a neighborhood featuring a blend of modest traditional and contemporary homes built in the 1970s. Prices start in the mid-$100,000s.

Windwood

West of downtown Carrboro is Windwood, another neighborhood of ranch homes built in the 1960s. These are smaller houses in a price range of low to high $100,000s.

Chatham County

The lower property taxes and often lower home prices of Chatham County have helped this area prosper. Excellent schools like North Chatham Elementary and Northwoods High School serve these communities. You can find a three-bedroom home in one north Chatham community for under $100,000. There are also still many 2- to 10-acre tracts to build on. For more information on home and land sales in Chatham County, follow the real estate listings in *The Chapel Hill News*, as well as *The Chatham Record* in Pittsboro.

Fearrington

Fearrington is located about 8 miles south of Chapel Hill on U.S. 15-501 in rural Chatham County. This planned development features rustic-contemporary homes, townhomes and condominiums clustered around greenways, tennis courts and a market area. The Fearrington Village Center includes a cafe, bookstore, crafts shop, gardening store and jewelry store. There is also an award-winning country inn and fine restaurant. Fearrington is very popular with retirees but is home to young families as well. Children living here attend Chatham County schools. Prices start at $150,000 and can be more than triple that for the larger homes in the newest phases of the development.

INSIDERS' TIP
According to one recent Home Price Comparison Index, a 2,200-square-foot, four-bedroom, 2 1/2 bath home that sold for $172,250 in the Triangle would sell for $124,000 in Binghamton, NY, $156,000 in Austin, TX, $200,375 in Atlanta, $265,675 in Hartford and $456,030 in San Jose.

Galloway Ridge, an innovative retirement community, is currently under development at Fearrington.

Governors Club

Governors Club is situated on 1,600 rolling acres adjacent to Jordan Lake on scenic Edwards Mountain, about 5 miles south of Chapel Hill. Among its many features are a 27-hole golf course designed by Jack Nicklaus, horse trails and footpaths, a 24-hour security gate entrance and a private country club. Developers of Governors Club have attracted executives with families, professionals and retirees. Plans call for about 1,250 single-family homes, golf villas, townhouses, patio homes and "club cottages," with home prices ranging from $350,000 to $3 million.

Governors Village

Governors Village is a 300-acre community that began development in 1996. It is located across from Governors Club and features a "neotraditional" neighborhood style. Amenities include swimming and tennis facilities and two parks. Home prices start at about $200,000. Prices at adjacent Governors Park range from $260,000 to more than $375,000.

Durham

When the influx of newcomers to the Triangle began in the late 1960s and early '70s, it seemed everybody wanted to live in North Raleigh, even though Durham was a shorter commute to many jobs in Research Triangle Park. Now Durham has been discovered by all sorts of folks, and they've learned what Insiders knew all along—it's a great place to live.

Thanks to Durham's recent popularity, home prices have gone up significantly over the past decade, placing the cost of housing here slightly above the national average. The average cost of a home in Durham is now about $157,000, still one of the best home values in the Triangle area. Durham is just 15 minutes from RTP or Chapel Hill, and offers homes, apartments and condominiums to suit just about any lifestyle and budget.

Durham has many new home communities under development. A 2,700-home development on 700 acres has recently been proposed for Southeast Durham. If you are looking for a home priced in the low $100,000s, consider Brighton, Creekside, Greystone, Marbrey Landing, Rolling Hills, Stratton Park, Stone Hill Estates and Twin Lakes. If your price range is from $100,000 to $150,000, you should look at Brittany Woods, Cedar Valley, Crooked Creek, Eastwood Park, Eno Trace, Greycliff, Lenox, Pickett Crossing, Ridgewood, Vantage Pointe and Wood Hollow. Between $150,000 and $200,000, ask to see American Village, Audubon Park, Autumn Ridge, Briardale, Dover Ridge, Grandale Forest, Green Mill, Heather Glen II, Sunningdale Wellington Forest and Whitehall. More than $200,000, Autumn Ridge, Cameron Woods, Coles Pond, Fairfield, Hardscrabble Plantation and Winstead are excellent communities.

Croasdaile

Croasdaile was developed in the '60s around its own 18-hole golf course and country club. Homes in Croasdaile usually sell for $300,000 or more, with some in the $600,000 plus range. Croasdaile Farm offers lots of 1/2 to more than 2 acres from $70,000 to $156,000 and luxury townhomes from $300,000.

Dover Ridge

Dover Ridge is a family community located north of I-85 on Guess Road with more than 200 homes. Dover Ridge offers 27 acres of recreation space, including a soccer field, volleyball court, playground and picnic area. Prices range from $150,000 to $200,000.

Duke Forest

Duke Forest was built in the 1930s adjacent to Duke University's own woodlands in southern Durham to provide comfortable housing for faculty and administration. Today residents include "civilians" as well. Here you'll find architectural styles ranging from the traditional homes of the 1930s to wood-and-glass contemporaries. Prices range from $150,000 to more than $350,000.

Duke Park

Duke Park is demographically and architecturally diverse. Located east of Trinity Park and just south of Interstate 85, it features a variety of homes built from the 1940s to '60s that sell for the low $100,000s. Duke Park has an active neighborhood association and baby-sitting co-op. An oak-shaded community park is complete with a swimming pool.

Falconbridge

Located midway between Chapel Hill and Durham on N.C. 54, Falconbridge offers townhomes and single-family residences convenient to the cultural, educational and employment opportunities afforded by both towns. Minutes from Jordan Lake and Research Triangle Park, it's within the Durham Public School System.

Falconbridge's traditional and contemporary single-family homes sell for $140,000 to $250,000 and townhomes are in the low $100,000 range. There is a private swim and tennis club in the Falconbridge neighborhood.

Fieldstone by the Eno

This charming community is nestled against the Eno River State Park and consists of the Buckwater Creek, Ridgestone and Cabes Mill neighborhoods. Prices range from $150,000 to $230,000.

Forest Hills

One of the most exclusive and picturesque of the old city neighborhoods, Forest Hills features gracious homes on winding, tree-shaded lanes adjacent to an expansive park. Large homes constructed in the 1930s and '60s of brick, stone and wood are nestled on carefully landscaped lots up to an acre in size. Homes sell for anywhere from $150,000 for a bungalow a street or two away from the park to $375,000 and more for a stately brick mansion. Forest Hills Park features tennis courts, a swimming pool, softball fields, open fields for frisbee tossing and other weekend sports. A seemingly endless greenway is flanked by gigantic willow oaks.

Garrett Farms

Garrett Farms is a popular neighborhood that contains approximately 300 homes. Home prices average around $200,000.

Grove Park

Grove Park consists of neighborhoods with names such as Cameron Place, Grove Crossing, Grove Ridge and Nichol's Landing. Amenities include a clubhouse, an

18-hole golf course, Junior Olympic-size swimming pool, tennis courts, a lake and playground. Very affordable homes range from $130,000 to the $300,000s.

Hope Valley

Hope Valley is located along N.C. 751, north of Interstate 40. Here you will find a variety of residences ranging from nicely landscaped, suburban ranches from $170,000 to $200,000, to some of the most colossal older homes in Durham. Flanking the Hope Valley Country Club's 18-hole golf course, tennis courts and swimming pool are Old English Tudors and Colonial mansions with price tags from $300,000 to $700,000 and up. Hope Valley neighborhoods include Arborfield, Carlton Crossings, Eagle Ridge, Greenbriar, Greyfield, Hunter's Forest, Oakbrook, Stonebridge and Windsor Oaks. Conveniently located midway between RTP and Chapel Hill, the area has experienced an unprecedented building boom in recent years. You'll find brick ranches, colonials, split levels and contemporaries in a wide range of prices.

Hope Valley Farms

Located in southwest Durham, Hope Valley Farms will eventually contain about 1,000 homes at build out. Amenities include a clubhouse, Olympic-size pool, tennis courts, fitness center and playground. Prices range from $150,000 to more than $300,000.

Lakewood

Of all the neighborhoods that grew up in the early 20th century, Lakewood was the most popular, thanks to the now defunct Lakewood Park, a rollicking amusement park known as "the Coney Island of the South." Today, Lakewood is a shopping center surrounded by bungalow homes dating from the 1890s to the 1930s. Homes can be found here in the low $100,000s.

Marydell and Bent Creek

These neighborhoods off Garrett Road near Jordan High School have a variety of spacious and attractive homes on wooded lots. Prices range from $200,000 to more than $300,000.

Milan Woods

Located in northeast Durham, off U.S. 70 at the Geer Street exit, Milan Woods offers affordably priced ($100,000 to $130,000) traditional and transitional homes on wooded home sites.

Morehead Hill

In the 1880s, some of Durham's industrialists and financiers began building their homes in a neighborhood developing adjacent to Forest Hills and near the hilltop residence of Eugene Morehead. The construction of the Durham Freeway saw the demolition of many fine homes. To this day, Morehead Hill remains a small island of wide tree-lined boulevards and well-landscaped yards. Its homes date from the turn of the century to more contemporary energy-efficient solar models. Prices range from $100,000 for a small home to $150,000 or more for a newer or restored larger home.

Old North Durham

If you want historic charm at a more reasonable price, North Durham may be your best bet. Built in the early 1900s, some of the city's most elegant and spacious homes, once fallen into disrepair, are now being returned to their former splendor. An active homeowners association in Old North Durham has helped draw new people into the neighborhood to participate in its renaissance.

Parkwood

One of the oldest residential subdivisions in southern Durham, Parkwood offers a range of appealing family homes in a neighborhood setting, priced in the $100,000 to $150,000 range. Located on N.C. 54 near I-40, it's convenient to Durham and Chapel Hill and only minutes from Research Triangle Park. An elementary school and a branch of the Durham Library are located in Parkwood.

Rockwood

Rockwood is a hilly, winding, tree-shaded neighborhood, located just south of Forest Hills. Contemporary homes are interspersed with those built in the 1940s. Residents also enjoy

TRIANGLE GOLF COURSE COMMUNITIES

Name	Location	$ Range	# of Holes	Opened
Brier Creek	Raleigh	$200s-$700s	18	2000
Croasdaile	Durham	$300s-$600s	18	1966
Crooked Creek	Fuquay-Varina	$200s-$400s	18	1994
Eagle Ridge	Garner	$150s-$350s	18	2000
Glen Laurel	Clayton	$190s-$500s	18	1993
Governors Club	Chapel Hill	$350s and up	27	1990
Grove Park	Durham	$100s-$400s	18	1997
Hedingham	Raleigh	$100s-$250s	18	1991
Lochmere	Cary	$200s-$1 million	18	1991
MacGregor	Cary	$180s-$600s	18	1968
Mill Creek	Mebane	$160s-$800s	18	1995
North Ridge	Raleigh	$190s-$1 million	36	1968
Preston	Cary	$300s-$1.5 million	54	1988
River Ridge	Raleigh	$200s-$450s	18	1997
Riverwood	Clayton	$150s-$250s	27	1995
Sunset Ridge	Holly Springs	$190s-$700s	18	1991
Treyburn	Durham	$200s-$2 million	18	1989
Wakefield Plantation	Raleigh	$130s-$2 million	18	2000
Willowbrook	Clayton	$140s-$200s	18	1997

a neighborhood park. Prices start in the mid $100,000s.

Treyburn

Situated on 5,300 rustic acres along the Little River north of Durham, Treyburn is the largest development in the Durham area. Treyburn has commercial and industrial tenants, including a medical facility and a satellite campus of Durham Tech. When completed, it will be about the size of RTP. The developers say it will eventually house 10,000 residents in 4,400 condominiums, apartments and single-family homes "oriented to provide golf, waterfront or open-space views." The membership-only Treyburn Country Club features a beautiful clubhouse, a 25 meter Olympic-size pool, a tennis facility and a 72-par golf course designed by Tom Fazio.

Many families already call Treyburn home and a 369-unit residential retirement community and condos adjacent to the clubhouse are planned. Home sites are selling for $75,000 for a half-acre lot to $175,000 for 2 acres on the waterfront. Homes sell from $200,000 to more than $2 million.

Trinity Park

Durham's older, in-town neighborhoods have enjoyed a comeback. The oldest and one of the most popular locales is Trinity Park. This community was developed in the early 20th century around Trinity College, now Duke University's East Campus.

Here you'll find medium to large homes on small city lots conveniently located between Duke University and downtown. A few homes contain apartments and condominiums, but most remain single-family residences. Prices usually start at more than $110,000 for a bungalow in good condition. Larger, restored homes are in the $150,000 to more than $200,000 range. Homes tend to go quickly for the asking price.

Watts Hospital-Hillandale

Directly to the north of Trinity Park is an area known as Watts Hospital, named for the facility that was once the focal point of the neighborhood. Today the old Watts Hospital building houses the North Carolina School of Science and Mathematics, a special public high school for students from across the state who are gifted in those fields.

Residents include young singles, families and senior citizens. The bungalows and larger houses were built in the 1940s and '50s and the lots are larger than in Trinity Park. The main streets are shaded by some of the most majestic willow oaks in Durham. Oval Park is a pleasant recreational retreat here for kids and adults. Most homes sell for $100,000 to $150,000.

Willowhaven

Located north of downtown, Willowhaven offers a variety of designs, from traditional to contemporary, on family-size lots larger than you'll find in the city. Begun in the 1950s, Willowhaven was developed on 1.5-acre lots around the Willowhaven Country Club. Homes sell for $150,000 and up.

Woodcroft

Perhaps the most successful development in southwest Durham is Woodcroft, an award-winning $300 million planned community and shopping center on 800 acres. Begun in 1981, Woodcroft offers more than 4,000 dwellings. The area is almost fully developed, but many homes are available for resale.

Woodcroft features a series of distinct "neighborhoods" offering a variety of housing options from $90,000 condos and $100,000 townhomes to single-family homes selling for $150,000 to more than $250,000. Each subdivision is surrounded by woods or open space. All residents have access to jogging trails, athletic fields and a community club, complete with a swimming pool and tennis courts. There is also a shopping center that serves the Woodcroft community and adjacent neighborhoods.

Woodlake

Woodlake is located on Fayetteville Road across from Woodcroft in southwest Durham. Woodlake is a unique community of more than a half-dozen neighborhoods such as Grayson Ridge, Chesden, Old Hickory, Candlewood, Shannon and Lake Village Townhomes, offering homes in a variety of styles, sizes and price ranges from $150,000

Photo by Rich Weidman

The Swim and Tennis Club at the Woodcroft community in southwest Durham is a popular gathering place for residents.

to more than $300,000. A lakeside swim club is one of the community's many amenities. Woodlake is also within walking distance of Piney Wood Park.

Raleigh

Raleigh is a city of neighborhoods, most of them filled with comfortable homes of traditional design. Visitors often are struck by how one lovely neighborhood simply leads to another. The city's steady growth has brought more contemporary styles, such as California cluster homes, and larger, luxury homes that sell for $500,000 and up.

If you divide the city into quarters with the Capitol building at the center, you will find that most of the recent growth has been in the northwest and northeast quadrants. The expected future growth of the city continues to be in these areas.

The average price for a new home today is rapidly approaching $200,000. If you are looking for a new home priced around $100,000 consider the Village at Beacon Hill and Timberidge at Parkside or one of the outlying towns such as Clayton, Knightdale, Wake Forest, Wendell or Zebulon. From $100,000 to $170,000 consider a top builder's new communities or Dominion Park, Durant Trace, Grove Park, North College Park and Winchester, where several builders are available. From $170,000 to $300,000 consider Breckenridge III, Bridgeton Park, LaCrosse Pointe and Umstead Ridge. From $300,000, ask to see Barclay Manor, Bartons Creek Overlook, Boulder Creek, Cross Gate, Macon's Path, Olde Creedmoor, Sheffield Manor IV and Woodspring. This Guide offers an insight into some neighborhoods.

Bent Tree

This development first appeared on the subdivision drawing boards in the 1980s as a neighborhood of mini-estates in North Raleigh. In the '90s the project was given a new name and developed as Bent Tree. It is off Strickland Road in North Raleigh, about a mile east of Six Forks Road. The homes are traditional in looks, but you will find

sumptuous modern master suites, bathrooms and grand landscaping. Prices start at $350,000.

Boylan Heights

Boylan Heights is an older neighborhood located within walking distance of the downtown complex. It was part of the Boylan Plantation and, as the name implies, occupies high ground. It has a mixture of low income housing on its periphery and lovely, larger homes at its core. Homes now sell for $135,000 and up, a bargain by Raleigh standards.

Brentwood

This area includes a number of neighborhoods, most of them with Brentwood in their names, and is located north of the I-440 Beltline and west of U.S. 1. The homes are affordable brick, single-story or split-level, and residents generally have been families with growing children. Homes start at about $125,000.

Brier Creek

A brand-new 2,000-acre community located adjacent to Research Triangle Park, Brier Creek boasts an 18-hole Arnold Palmer signature golf course surrounded by golf villas, townhouses and single-family homes. A total of 1,500 homes will eventually be built here. Prices range from the upper $200,000s to more than $700,000.

Brookhaven

Brookhaven is one of the 1940's suburbs outside of the I-440 Beltline and northwest, beyond Crabtree Valley Mall, off Glenwood Avenue. For years, Brookhaven residents lived outside the city limits, but today Brookhaven is protected by a neighborhood overlay zoning district reserved for older Raleigh neighborhoods. Its lots are spacious and its conventionally designed homes were well built. The average price for a home is about $235,000.

Cameron Park

Cameron Park is one of the co-author's favorite Raleigh neighborhoods, but not just because he lives there. It has big, old trees throughout and three neighborhood parks around which streets wind and curve and in which residents play, picnic and walk their dogs. Cameron Park was one of the city's first suburbs, started in 1910. It is located one mile west of the Capitol and is bounded by Hillsborough Street to the south, St. Mary's School and St. Mary's Street on the east, Oberlin Road and NCSU on the west, and Clark Avenue and Cameron Village Shopping Center to the north.

Cameron Village is within walking distance, as are Wiley Elementary and Broughton High schools. Homes range from some of the most contemporary in town to traditional, white-columned Southern manses, but most are comfortable structures with plenty of room. Prices run from $200,000 to more than $400,000.

Country Club Hills

As its name implies, Country Club Hills surrounds much of the golf course at the Carolina Country Club on Glenwood Avenue. The development is marked by large lots and hilly terrain and has some unconventional designs. It has a 1950's look about it with lower profile, ranch-style homes, although most are large and there are many conventional, two-story homes. The neighborhood has retained a woodland flavor, helped in part by its lack of sidewalks and a street matrix that is winding and twisting and as puzzling as a maze. Its location off Glenwood Avenue puts it close to both the I-440 Beltline and Crabtree Valley Mall as well as one of the main thoroughfares downtown. Many of its residents custom-built their homes and it is not a hotbed for sales. Prices range from $300,000 to more than $600,000.

Eaglechase

Located off Poole Road in east Raleigh, Eaglechase has been very popular with first-time home buyers and, for the money, it's one of the best buys in the Raleigh market.

You can find three- and four-bedroom homes with two baths for prices in the low $100,000s. The community is nicely landscaped with protective earthen berms at the entrances and along Poole Road. Amenities include a swim club.

Falls River

You should visit this planned neighborhood even if you don't decide to live here. Falls River is a 1,140-acre community that lies east of Falls of Neuse Road and north of Durant Road in North Raleigh. It is a "neotraditional" community that borrows planning themes from the early 20th century such as grid-like street patterns, sidewalks and village-type living. It offers a diverse mixture of residential homes, from multifamily apartments, condominiums and townhouses, to traditional single-family detached homes. Altogether, 2,975 residences will be built, and a population of 7,500 will live at Falls River at build out. There are extensive conservation and recreational commons—262 acres, much of it along the banks of the Neuse River. Amenities include a swim and tennis club as well as playing fields, jogging and greenway trails. Prices range from $140,000 to $350,000.

Five Points

This "inside the Beltline" community surrounds the five-way intersection of Glenwood Avenue, Fairview Road, Whitaker Mill Road and Glen Avenue. A favorite with artisans, musicians, politicians and writers, this neighborhood's prices range from the $100,000s to more than $250,000.

Foxcroft

Foxcroft is one of the few "equestrian" neighborhoods near Raleigh. The area is located east of the city, but not within the city limits. It is north of U.S. 64 and east of New Hope Church Road. Foxcroft was developed for people who wanted enough room to keep

INSIDERS' TIP
The average closing price for homes in spring 2000 in Orange County (Chapel Hill) was $200,903; for Durham County (Durham), $149,347; and for Wake County (Raleigh), $119,179.

their horses on their property. Homes vary in size and style, going back to the single-story ranch house popular in the 1960s and including some very contemporary designs. Starting prices are about $250,000.

Greystone

Greystone, which lies outside the I-440 Beltline to the northwest, began in 1980 and reflects the trend toward planned communities. Unlike many suburban developments that aim at the young or middle-aged family, Greystone appeals to the entire market and even includes a retirement village for older residents. It features a child-care center in the middle of the community. Amenities include two recreational lakes stocked with fish and a swim and tennis club. Prices vary, but they are aimed at middle-income buyers, from the $100,000s to more than $200,000.

Harrington Grove

Harrington Grove, located in northwest Raleigh, includes three distinct neighborhoods—The Woods, The Downs and The Oaks—and features popular transitional designs. Residents can join a neighborhood swim/tennis club. Prices at Harrington Grove start in the mid-$100,000s.

Hayes Barton

Named after Sir Walter Raleigh's homeplace in England, Hayes Barton has become the home for many of the city's "Establishment" since its development in the 1920s and '30s. The neighborhood is located close to downtown and is roughly bounded by Glenwood Avenue to the east and St. Mary's Street to the west, both of which curve around and intersect in the north. Wade Avenue serves as its southern boundary.

Photo by Rich Weidman

One of Raleigh's first suburbs, Cameron Park, is conveniently located near 65-acre Pullen Park, known as the grandaddy of Raleigh's parks.

Photo courtesy of N.C. Division of Tourism

Raleigh's downtown Mordecai neighborhood contains
the restored 1785 Mordecai House and Park.

This area is filled with large homes, some on spacious lots, as well as many of modest size. A winding stream runs beside Cowper Drive. It's at the center of a small park that leads to the neighborhood's entrance off Glenwood Avenue. So desirable is a Hayes Barton address that several builders bought smaller older homes, tore them down and built new, larger ones.

The hub of the Old Raleigh Establishment, the Carolina Country Club, is conveniently located nearby on Glenwood Avenue. Home prices range from $400,000 to more than $1 million.

Hedingham

A premier, planned community in northeast Raleigh, Hedingham sits on 553 acres between New Hope Road and the Neuse River. It contains a variety of homes and apartments. The centerpiece is the golf course development, Hedingham on the Neuse. The community has 62 acres of greenways and a riverfront park, plus the usual amenities that go with a golf course, such as a clubhouse, grill room, swim and racquet club, and basketball and volleyball courts. Homes start at the amazingly low price of $100,000 and go up to more than $250,000.

Hymettus Woods

This inside-the-Beltline neighborhood is a perfect example of residential "infill" where small parcels of property in desirable areas are developed. Fourteen lots are located on less than 5 acres adjacent to Hymettus Park, which occupies the corner of Wade Avenue and Dixie Trail. The homes are custom built with attention to detail. Price tags start at $450,000 and go up to $1,250,000.

Inman Park

A new planned community located only half a mile from Crabtree Valley Mall, Inman Park features townhomes, patio homes, estate homes and custom homes. Amenities include a pool and cabana. Prices range from $200,000 to more than $500,000.

Mordecai

Pronounced Mord'e-kee, this downtown neighborhood is within walking distance to state government complex jobs and Peace College. It also contains the restored Mordecai House and Park which, together, are one of the city's historical treasures. Mordecai's sturdy homes are survivors and it's a place for bargain hunting home buyers. Prices range from the low $100,000s and upward.

North Hills

Although there is a specific neighborhood called North Hills, many Raleigh residents consider North Hills Terrace, North Glen, North Ridge, North Bend and North Clift as part of North Hills. North Hills encompasses the broad stretch of North Raleigh suburbs roughly bounded by Wake Forest Road and Falls of Neuse Road to the east and North Hills Drive to the west.

Homes in North Hills vary in size and look, although most reflect the conventional styles of the 1960s and '70s. Trees abound and the city's Optimist Park Pool near Six Forks Road and Millbrook Road serves the area. Realtors consider the area a good value for the real estate dollar and homes sell for $155,000 to more than $220,000.

North Ridge

This North Raleigh neighborhood surrounds North Ridge Country Club, whose members are often connected to the Triangle's corporate establishment. It is also located close to Ravenscroft, a prestigious private school. The homes are big and impressive and many show the touch of an architect, so it's not stamped by any particular style. Some of the older homes may sell for $200,000, but a $600,000 price tag no longer raises eyebrows.

Oakwood

Oakwood is one of the city's oldest neighborhoods—one that has been improved by the efforts of its residents. It is located downtown, behind the Governor's Mansion, roughly bounded by Person, Franklin and Edenton streets and historic Oakwood Cemetery, where some of Raleigh's most famous citizens are buried. Oakwood is where the bankers and burghers and railroad managers who prospered in the years after the Civil War built Victorian homes with spacious rooms and high ceilings. Residents show off their restoration handiwork at the annual Historic Oakwood Candlelight Tour in December. The range of prices goes from $235,000 to more than $500,000, but bargains still come on the market for those willing to scrape wallpaper, refinish floors and restore supporting beams.

Olde Raleigh

This is anything but old Raleigh. It's one of the most lavish developments in the city, between Duraleigh and Edwards Mill roads in northwest Raleigh, not far from Rex Healthcare. It has more than 130 single-family homes, three small lakes, a swim and tennis club, and guarded, electronic gates. Prices range from $450,000 to $1 million. Empty nesters may want to check out the luxury townhome community, Olde Raleigh Villas, located between Duraleigh and Ebenezer Church roads, which start in the mid-$200,000s.

River Ridge

Located east of Raleigh off of Rock Quarry Road, River Ridge is a luxurious golf course community that features 18 holes, a clubhouse, pool, tennis and volleyball courts. Prices range from $200,000 to $450,000.

Springdale Estates

Springdale Estates is one of three Springdale neighborhoods in northwest Raleigh, located on either side of Leesville Road on a rolling, wooded countryside. Typical of

One of Raleigh's oldest neighborhoods, Oakwood dates back to the 1800s.

development in the 1970s, homes in Springdale Estates are built on large, 1-acre lots. It has a lake in the middle and it's one neighborhood where you will find contemporary designs mixed in with traditional and colonial styles. Located close to RDU and RTP, prices in this neighborhood range from $200,000 to more than $450,000.

Stonebridge

The entrance to this North Raleigh neighborhood is located off Six Forks Road. The houses are traditional in style and are large with three and four bedrooms being the norm. Expect to pay $150,000 to more than $400,000 for homes in Stonebridge.

Stonehenge

Located on both sides of Creedmoor Road, Stonehenge has been a favorite North Raleigh community among real estate agents. Begun in 1976, Stonehenge has continued to grow and add new neighborhoods, as well as townhouses and apartments. The homes are traditional in appearance and located on acre lots in the older sections. Seven Oaks Recreation Center, part of the Stonehenge community, has 12 acres of lighted tennis, basketball and volleyball courts as well as a competitive-size swimming pool. Prices range from $200,000 to more than $300,000.

Wakefield Plantation

Wakefield is a 2,260-acre "equestrian" community located adjacent to Falls Lake in northern Wake County on Falls of Neuse Road between Raleigh and Wake Forest. Wake County's largest development, Wakefield will include about 3,500 homes at build out. It features the Tournament Players Club at Wakefield Plantation, an 18-hole golf course designed by Hale Irwin, as well as a plantation-style clubhouse, an equestrian facility, 85-acre town park, tennis courts and an outdoor pool. Each estate homesite has from 2 to 10 acres. Prices for this new home community range from $130,000 to more than $2 million.

Wildwood Green

Wildwood Green is a northwest Raleigh community built around one of Raleigh's old private golf courses, Wildwood Green Golf Club, located off Strickland Road. The amenities include an 18-hole championship golf course, swimming pool and tennis courts. The homes are custom built and the average price is in the upper $200s.

Wakefield Plantation, Wake County's largest residential development, will eventually contain 3,500 homes.

Williamsborough and Drewry Hills

While there are a few contemporary styles in these neighborhoods, traditional and Williamsburg homes prevail. These neighborhoods are within the I-440 Beltline, near North Hills Mall. One of the city's greenways along Crabtree Creek forms the southern boundary. Older parts of Drewry Hills have homes that sell for $200,000, and in Williamsborough, prices go for well over $500,000.

Woods of St. Albans

This neighborhood came on the market in 1994 and is another example of "infill" that extends outside the I-440 Beltline. The neighborhood is located in a pocket of previously undeveloped land between North Hills Mall and Eastgate Shopping Center off St. Albans. Its convenient location close to shopping and employment centers, makes these traditional, Williamsburg-styled homes popular. Prices start in the high $100,000s.

Wyndfield

Wyndfield is a small development featuring expansive homes. Located out of the city limits west of Six Forks Road, it's actually closer to Falls Lake than Raleigh. Many of the original homes were custom built in the '70s and they have a personal touch.

Residents prize their spacious lots, narrow streets and quiet isolation. Swimming pools are not unusual. There are some neighborhood tennis courts and residents are close to the boating, fishing and recreation at Falls Lake. Wyndfield is one of a number of similar subdivisions with names such as Coachman's Trail, Martindale, Trappers Creek and Trotters Ridge. Home prices start at more than $200,000 and quickly escalate.

Other Wake County Communities

Crooked Creek

Located in Fuquay-Varina in southern Wake County, Crooked Creek is a beautiful golf course community that contains an 18-hole course and swim club. Prices range from $200,000 to $400,000.

Eagle Ridge Golf & Country Club

Located south of Raleigh and minutes from downtown, Eagle Ridge features an 18-hole golf course designed by Tom Kite, a clubhouse and a 200-acre nature preserve and park along Swift Creek. Single-family home prices range from $150,000 to more than $350,000.

Sunset Ridge

Sunset Ridge is located about 20 minutes south of Raleigh in Holly Springs. It is home to Devils Ridge Golf Club, an 18-hole course designed by John LaFoy, and a professionally staffed Aquatics and Recreation Park. Other amenities include a clubhouse, soccer field and playground. Prices range from $190,000 to $700,000 for single-family homes. Townhomes start at $150,000 and Charleston homes start at $230,000.

Johnston County Communities

Glen Laurel

Home of the 18-hole Neuse Golf Club, Glen Laurel is located off N.C. 42 East in Clayton, about a 20-minute drive from Raleigh. Amenities include a swim and tennis club, clubhouse, ball field, playground and walking paths along the Neuse River. Prices range from $190,000 to $500,000.

Riverwood

Riverwood offers golf course living amid the countryside of Clayton near the banks of the Neuse River. Home sites average more than 3/4 of an acre and home prices range from $150,000 to $200,000.

Willowbrook

Another popular development in Clayton, Willowbrook features an 18-hole golf course, tennis courts and a swimming pool. Prices range from $140,000 to more than $200,000.

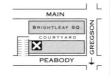

Restaurants and Caterers

Restaurants

Years ago, diners looking for a place to eat out in the Triangle had about three options: fried seafood, cheeseburgers and, of course, barbecue. Some of these "classic" barbecue eateries have become famous in their own right and well worth a road trip. Yes, we're talking about such hotspots as Mama Dip's Kitchen in Chapel Hill, Bullock's Bar-B-Cue in Durham and Cooper's Barbecue in downtown Raleigh.

Today, the Triangle dining scene is in a state of constant flux, offering a myriad of choices, from down-home country cooking to nationally acclaimed gourmet cuisine. You can still find family-friendly chain restaurants sprouting up everywhere, including Applebee's, Chili's, Golden Corral, Lone Star Steakhouse and Red Lobster. However, this chapter will lead you to some of the unique places to dine in the Triangle, whether you're looking for Eastern-style barbecue, shrimp and grits, coconut curry chicken, dim sum, paella, fish and chips, smothered pork chops, Texas-style chili, tropical pizzas, tapas, certified black Angus beef, souvlaki or sushi.

Those diners wishing to celebrate a special occasion have a variety of choices such as Angus Barn, Fearrington House, Four Square, Il Palio Ristorante, La Residence, Magnolia Grill, Margaux's, Nana's and Second Empire, among others. New upscale chain restaurants have also invaded the region, including Sullivan's Steakhouse. You're sure to satisfy your appetite at one of the following restaurants, which are listed alphabetically by type of cuisine.

Price Code

The dollar signs ($) beside a restaurant entry are an indication as to what your bill for dinner for two might be, assuming that you don't order a bottle of Chateau Lafite-Rothschild with your meal. Lunch at many of the fancier places will be about half the cost of evening fare. If a restaurant has all ABC permits, it means the place serves mixed drinks as well as beer and wine. The cost code dollar signs ($) can be deciphered as follows:

$	Under $20
$$	$21 to $35
$$$	$36 to $50
$$$$	$51 and up

AMERICAN

Abbey Road
$-$$ • 1195 W. Chatham St., Cary • 481-4434

The walls of this lively neighborhood bar and grill are covered with collages of familiar images from the '60s, dominated of course by Beatles memorabilia. Enjoy burgers, sandwiches, pasta dishes, salads and appetizers. Abbey Road is open for lunch and dinner seven days a week. Live entertainment is offered on weekends.

Carolina Coffee Shop
$$ • 138 E. Franklin St., Chapel Hill • 942-6875

Conveniently located on the edge of the UNC-CH campus, this is a traditional Southern

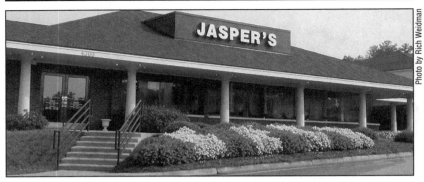

Photo by Rich Weidman

Conveniently located near Preston in Cary, Jasper's American Eatery offers a constantly changing menu that highlights regional cuisine.

restaurant and coffee shop that is reminiscent of the coffee shops in Europe. Opened in 1922, it is the type of spot you can hang out for a leisurely breakfast or grab a quick bite to eat for lunch or dinner. The menu includes steaks, seafood, pasta dishes, sandwiches and homemade soups. Ask about the daily specials. It has all ABC permits. It is open daily for breakfast, lunch and dinner.

Chambers Food & Spirits
$$-$$$ • 19 W. Hargett St., Raleigh
• 834-1938

Located in downtown Raleigh, Chambers is a jazzy eatery with an art deco atmosphere reminiscent of the Prohibition Era. The changing seasonal menu specializes in new American cuisine such as Stuffed Filet of Beef, Pan-Fried Chicken, Oysters Rockefeller and Sea Scallops. Order a classic cocktail with your meal. Chambers includes a cozy piano bar. It is open for dinner Monday through Saturday. Reservations are recommended.

Darryl's Restaurant & Bar
$$ • 4603 Chapel Hill Blvd., Durham
• 489-1890
$$ • 6008 Glenwood Ave., Raleigh
• 782-1849
$$ • 1906 Hillsborough St., Raleigh
• 833-1906
$$ • 4309 Old Wake Forest Rd., Raleigh
• 872-1840

Darryl's expansive menu includes steaks, chicken, seafood, ribs, burgers, sandwiches,

salad bar and late-night snacks. It draws a large lunch crowd and is popular in the evenings with students and families. Each site is open for lunch and dinner daily.

Elaine's on Franklin
$$$-$$$$ • 454 W. Franklin St.
• 960-2770

One of Chapel Hill's newest and most popular eateries, Elaine's serves new American cuisine in a bistro atmosphere. The menu changes frequently. Elaine's boasts an eclectic wine list. Dinner is served Tuesday through Saturday. Reservations are recommended.

Enoteca Vin
$$$-$$$$ • 410 Glenwood Ave.,
Raleigh • 834-3070

Set in the renovated Pine State Creamery building within the "Glenwood South" District in downtown Raleigh, Enoteca Vin is a happening bistro that serves cured meats and an assortment of cheeses, as well as delicious tapa-like appetizers for sampling. Of course, diners also can choose from an extensive wine list. Dinner is served Tuesday through Sunday.

Frazier's
$$-$$$ • 2418 Hillsborough St.,
Raleigh • 828-6699

A true gem hidden along bustling Hillsborough Street across from North Carolina State University, this laid-back eatery is popular with professors, students and the theater-going crowd (there's a late-night menu). Entrees include such delicacies as Pan-Seared Ribeye, Roasted Chicken and Stuffed Pork Loin, as well as pasta dishes, pizza cooked in a wood-fired oven, sandwiches and salads. The restaurant's walls are covered with the colorful works of local artists. A quiet bar can be found in back. Lunch is served Monday through Friday and dinner is served nightly. Frazier's has all ABC permits.

Gypsy's Shiny Diner
$ • 1550 Buck Jones Rd., Cary • 469-3663
$ • 335 Tryon Rd., Garner • 773-3663

Because of its unique stainless steel decor, Gypsy's ran afoul of zoning codes, but finally opened a couple of years ago to rave reviews from Cary residents. A second location recently opened its doors in Garner. Open from early morning until late at night through the week and 24 hours on the weekend, Gypsy's offers traditional diner fare accompanied by deep-fried butterfly chips.

Houlihan's
$-$$ • 2007 Walnut St., Cary • 859-0668
$-$$ • 6004 Falls of Neuse Rd., Raleigh • 874-0505
$-$$ • 6711 Glenwood Ave., Raleigh • 783-0700 • www.houlihans.com

Houlihan's is a lively eatery that specializes in a diverse selection of American cuisine. Enjoy chicken and shrimp platters, pasta dishes, fajitas, steaks, ribs, seafood, sandwiches, burgers, salads and soups. Each location is open for lunch and dinner daily.

Jasper's American Eatery
$$-$$$ • 4300 NW. Cary Pkwy., Cary • 319-3400

Jasper's menu changes every six weeks, highlighting regional cuisines. Lunch and dinner are served seven days a week, and brunch is served on Sunday.

Jillian's
$$ • 117 S. West St., Raleigh • 821-7887
• www.jillians.com

Jillian's is a lively dining and entertainment complex. The Sports Video Cafe & Bar features classic American favorites, including steak, salmon, barbecue ribs, pizza and sandwiches. It is open for lunch and dinner daily.

Lucky 32
$$-$$$ • 832 Spring Forest Rd., Raleigh • 876-9932

The art deco grill room and bar offer several dining options. The menu changes monthly and offers innovative appetizers, salads, sandwiches, grilled fresh seafood and meats, gourmet pizzas, pastas and burgers. Lucky 32 has all ABC permits. It is open for lunch and dinner daily. A second Lucky 32 is set to open in Cary in late 2000.

Michael Dean's Seafood Grill, Wood Oven & Bar
$$$-$$$$ • 1705 E. Millbrook Rd., Raleigh • 790-9992
• www.michaeldeans.citysearch.com

A popular North Raleigh eatery, Michael Dean's features the best of new American cuisine, with entrees such as Shrimp Pizza with Spinach and Basil Pesto, Grilled Beef Tenderloin and Roasted Lobster Tail. Michael Dean's offers lunch Monday through Friday, dinner Monday through Saturday and live music Thursday, Friday and Saturday.

Michael Jordan's 23
$$-$$$ • 200 W. Franklin St., Chapel Hill • 960-9623

Legendary basketball star Michael Jordan opened this trendy restaurant within strolling distance from his alma mater, the University of North Carolina, in 1999. 23 is named after the lucky number Jordan wore on his jersey throughout most of his career as a member of the Tar Heels (1982 NCAA national champs) and Chicago Bulls (winners of six NBA championships). The 9,000-square-foot restaurant, located in the Pavilion building, specializes in innovative American cuisine, featuring local ingredients. 23 is decorated with memorabilia from Jordan's playing days. Even his diploma from UNC-CH is on display (by the way, he majored in geography). There's also a gift shop, of course. It serves lunch Monday through Saturday, dinner nightly and brunch on Sunday. Arrive early or be prepared to wait.

Mo's Diner
$$-$$$ • 306 E. Hargett St., Raleigh
• 856-9938

Located in a more-than-century-old house in the Moore Square Arts District, Mo's Diner serves new American cuisine, including such dishes as Garlic and Herbed Shrimp on Angel Hair Pasta, Pan Seared Beef Tenderloin, Paella and Spicy Jambalaya. It is open for dinner Tuesday through Saturday. Call ahead for reservations.

Owen's 501 Diner
$$ • 1500 N. Fordham Blvd., Chapel Hill
• 933-3505

Owen's Broad Street Diner
$$ • 1802 Main St., Durham • 416-6102

Owen's two restaurants serve traditional diner fare that includes hamburgers, meatloaf and mashed potatoes and other "blue plate specials," as well as house specialties such as Jamaican-Jerked Salmon, Brie and Chicken Fettuccini and Grilled Eggplant. Daily specials and homemade desserts round out the menu. Both diners have ABC permits and are open for breakfast, lunch and dinner Tuesday through Saturday and for brunch on Sunday.

Pantana Bob's
$-$$ • 300 W. Rosemary St., Chapel Hill
• 942-7575

Pantana Bob's specializes in casual dining, featuring fajitas, gourmet burgers and sandwiches and late-night snacks. Eat inside or out on the deck. Live music is an occasional treat. It is open for dinner nightly.

Piney Point Grill and Seafood Bar
$$$ • Doubletree Guest Suites
I-40 at N.C. 55 (Exit 278), RTP
• 361-4660

Piney Point Grill offers filet mignon, North Carolina Mountain Trout, Wild Mushroom Pasta, Blackened Tuna, fresh oysters and a variety of fresh North Carolina coastal seafood. Be sure to ask about the daily "blue-plate special." Piney Point Grill is open for lunch and dinner seven days a week. It has all ABC permits.

Ram's Head Rathskeller
$-$$ • 157-A Franklin St., Chapel Hill
• 942-5158

Since 1946, "The Rat" has been a major hangout for students, faculty, sports fans and alumni. It's always packed on home football weekends. The recently renovated Rat features a selection of steaks, sandwiches, its famous lasagna, pizza, salads and daily specials. Scrumptious desserts include apple pie and cheesecake. The Rat is open daily for lunch and dinner. Beer, wine and mixed drinks are available.

The Rathskeller
$-$$ • 2412 Hillsborough St., Raleigh
• 821-5342 • www.cris.com/~ratwork

The Rathskeller sits across the street from NCSU and is popular with students, faculty and local business people. Despite its name, the menu is not the same as "The Rat" in Chapel Hill. The menu offers an excellent selection of vegetarian, seafood, poultry and beef entrees; an extensive soup and sandwich selection; and homemade daily specials. It is open for lunch and dinner Tuesday through Sunday.

Spanky's Uptown
$-$$ • 101 E. Franklin St., Chapel Hill
• 967-2678
• www.spankys.citysearch.com

A downtown Chapel Hill landmark, the recently renovated Spanky's is open for lunch Monday through Saturday and dinner nightly. The eatery is most noted for its wide variety of menu selections such as weekly pasta, steak and seafood specials, burgers, sandwiches, grilled chicken, salads, quiche and homemade desserts. Spanky's has evolved into a casual meeting place for college students, locals and visitors alike. It has all ABC permits.

Tobacco Roadhouse
$-$$ • 115 N. Duke St., Durham
• 688-4505
• www.tobaccoroadhouse.citysearch.com

A converted warehouse across the street from Brightleaf Square in Durham is the home of this lively restaurant and brewpub. Tobacco Roadhouse has an extensive menu that includes chicken, seafood, steaks, ribs and pan-style pizzas, as well as burgers, sandwiches and salads. Live entertainment can be heard on the spacious outdoor patio Wednesday through Saturday. It is open Monday through Saturday for dinner. A popular nightspot, Club Shakers, is also here.

Top of the Hill
$$-$$$ • 100 E. Franklin St., Chapel Hill
• 929-8676
Top of the Hill Grille
$$-$$$ • 601 W. Peace St., Raleigh
• 856-0999

The floor-to-ceiling windows of this third-floor restaurant provide a spectacular view of Chapel Hill on one side and a view of the copper and stainless steel brew tanks on the other. The food is American, featuring pasta, chicken, beef, pork loin, grilled-teriyaki salmon and brick-oven pizzas. The Top of the Hill Grille in Raleigh also boasts an outdoor deck. Both sites are open for lunch and dinner daily.

Winston's Grille
$$-$$$ • 6401 Falls of the Neuse Rd., Raleigh • 790-0700

Located in the Sutton Square Shopping Center in Raleigh, this restaurant and bar is one of "the" places for a power lunch or special dinner. The bar is packed on weekends as the young and single crowd checks out the scene and the "grazing menu," which features crab dip and popcorn shrimp. The dinner menu offers steaks, ribs, live Maine lobster, fresh seafood and pasta.

The Top of the Hill Grille in Raleigh provides a spacious outdoor deck.

Patio seating is available. It is open for lunch and dinner daily and for brunch on Sunday.

BAKERY

Big Sky Bread Company
$ • Cameron Village, Raleigh • 828-8389

This incredible bakery makes the best rolls, croissants, muffins, cookies and breads you can imagine. The bakery mills its organic whole wheat flour every day, using only the finest natural ingredients. A variety of sandwiches is served at lunch, all delicious. It is open Monday through Saturday.

The Croissant Cafe and Bakery
$ • 3901 Capital Blvd., Ste. 177, Raleigh
• 981-0032

C'est bon! This is a pleasant surprise in northeast Raleigh. The owner and baker takes his pastries—the best chocolate eclairs in town—and breads seriously. The Cafe offers breakfast and lunch. The quiche has a flaky, tasty crust and the salads and soups could be served on the Left Bank, while the sandwiches are more American in style. The Cafe is located in Tarrymore Square.

The Mad Hatter's Bake Shop
$ • 2200 W. Main St., Durham • 286-1987
• www.madhatters.citysearch.com

The Mad Hatter is a great breakfast and lunch spot. Come for cappuccino and fresh-baked muffins or pastries, for a midday meal or a late-night snack. Also, enjoy burgers, sandwiches and salads. The Mad Hatter is also a great source for delicious custom cakes for birthdays and other special occasions. While you're waiting for your food, marvel at the incredible hats on display. The Mad Hatter is open daily.

BARBECUE

Allen & Son Bar-B-Que
$ • Airport Rd., Chapel Hill • 942-7576
$ • U.S. 15/501, Pittsboro • 542-2294

Satisfy your barbecue cravings at these no-frill eateries that serve hickory-smoked specialties and fresh seafood, along with the usual sides of baked beans, french fries or fried okra. Take-out and catering are available at both locations. Both sites are open for lunch and dinner Monday through Saturday.

Bullock's Bar-B-Cue
$-$$ • 3330 Quebec Dr., Durham
• 383-3211 • No Credit Cards

Bullock's offers a no-nonsense decor, veteran waitresses and the most extensive barbecue menu in town. You can get it chopped or sliced, plain or spiced, with the usual sides of hushpuppies, slaw, Southern-style vegetables, French fries and, of course, a big glass of sweet tea. If you've still got room, there's plenty of home-style desserts.

Takeout and catering are available. Bullock's is closed on Sunday and Monday.

Cooper's BBQ & Catering
$ • 109 E. Davie St., Raleigh • 832-7614

Opened in the 1930s, this downtown restaurant serves some of Raleigh's best Eastern Carolina pork barbecue. You can get your pork chopped or sliced, and it comes with fried hushpuppies, crisp pork skin and coleslaw. Eastern Carolina barbecue has a vinegar, not tomato-based, sauce. You can sit at the counter or in one of the booths and mingle with blue collar workers or politicians. Cooper's is open for lunch and dinner Monday through Saturday.

Dillard's Bar-B-Que
$ • 3921 Fayetteville St., Durham
• 544-1587

Enjoy authentic barbecue doused in a homemade spicy sauce at this popular southern Durham eatery just down the road from NCCU. It is open for lunch and dinner Tuesday through Saturday.

Don Murray's Barbecue
$ • 2751 Capital Blvd., Raleigh • 872-6270

Open for lunch and dinner seven days a week, Don Murray's serves authentic North Carolina barbecue. Catering and Pig Pickin's are available.

Pork 101: Know the Basics of Barbecue

Food often marks a region's personality. If you're in Louisiana, for example, you will get invited more than once to a party or political function that serves crab boil, a steaming pot of crawfish. In Virginia, every traditional wedding reception serves thinly sliced and super salty Virginia ham biscuits. Boston bakes beans, and the catfish fry is popular in Arkansas and Mississippi. In North Carolina, it's barbecue and pig pickin's. More specifically, it's barbecue pork, coleslaw and hushpuppies.

State authors write books on barbecue, and UNC's public TV airs documentaries on the subject. One of the ritual tests for every new, local newspaper columnist, for

instance, is the treatise on North Carolina barbecue. Family reunions serve it; neighborhood picnics spread it; churches celebrate homecomings with it; and politicians rally around it. This is serious cultural business.

Start with the fundamentals. When you say barbecue, just plain, simple barbecue, you're talking about pork—Not chicken, not beef, not fish. If someone says, "We're having a barbecue in the backyard. Come on over," it is understood that he or she is cooking pork.

Next, and you need to underline this, there are two basic types of barbecue in North Carolina, and it remains unsettled as to which is better. Legislators have debated it, and families have divided over it. And, when the talking stops, fights have been fought over it. In short, there is Eastern Barbecue and Western Barbecue. Note that these are proper nouns.

• Western Barbecue uses a red, tomato-based sauce. It's not bad. Some is downright tasty—even excellent—depending on the family recipe. And, tomato-based barbecue sauce is what you get in the 49 other states.

• Eastern Barbecue is basted with a distinctive vinegar-based sauce. It is truly a North Carolina creation, found nowhere else except in enclaves where transplanted eastern North Carolinians have settled. Some claim that it is an "acquired taste." It is sharp and tangy and brings out the flavor of the pork.

Photo by Tim Johnson

Eastern-style barbecue

While the dividing line between these two barbecue sauces is unclear, you should be aware that the Triangle, for the most part, is considered Eastern Barbecue territory. For the full barbecue experience, you must attend a pig pickin'. Some families still put on their own pickin', but most people hire outside cookers. The best ones seem to come from outlying Triangle towns such as Dunn, Benson or Bunn. These fellows have their own rigs, and they will start cooking before dawn. The pig is split down the middle and basted throughout the day. By late afternoon, the pig will be ready (sometimes, the cooking team is pretty basted, too, if they're sippin' along with the basting). The side dishes include coleslaw, hushpuppies, boiled potatoes and Brunswick stew. Coleslaw is another item that is subject to special treatment, and the best tasting hushpuppies are the fat short ones. Brunswick stew is a meal unto itself, but it has been sanitized and modernized in that chicken now replaces squirrel as the meat of choice.

The cooking team usually carves off chunks of the best meat and chops them into shreds, which are served from a platter. But, do not deny yourself the succulent pleasure of actually picking morsels directly off the pig with your fingers. The ribs are especially prized. Are we getting hungry, yet?

Ole Time Barbecue
$ • 6309 Hillsborough St., Raleigh
• 859-2544

For delicious Eastern-style barbecue at an economical price, look no farther than Ole Time. Owner Jerry Hart jokes with all the regulars to keep the atmosphere lively. It is open for breakfast, lunch and dinner Monday through Friday and for breakfast and lunch on Saturday. Ole Time also offers catering.

Red Hot & Blue
$$ • Waverly Place, Cary • 851-2282
$$ • 115 S. Elliott Rd., Chapel Hill
• 942-7427
$$ • 6615 Falls of Neuse Rd., Raleigh
• 846-7427
• www.redhotblue.citysearch.com

Red Hot & Blue is the local home of Memphis barbecue, whether it's ribs, wet or dry, a tasty barbecue sandwich, delicious chili, authentic hickory smoked chicken, pulled pork or beef brisket. It's worth a trip just to try the homemade desserts. Blues memorabilia cover almost every inch of wall space, and there is nonstop background blues music that ranges from upbeat and sassy to downright moody. This is a good place to bring the kids. Each Red Hot & Blue is open daily for lunch and dinner and has all ABC permits. Catering is also available.

BREAKFAST, BRUNCH & LUNCH

Breadmen's
$ • 324 W. Rosemary St., Chapel Hill
• 967-7110

Breadmen's, long an Insiders' favorite, has good food and character. It's the kind of place where, no matter what time of the day it is, you can order breakfast and take your time reading the newspaper while you drink a bottomless cup of coffee. Besides breakfast anytime, Breadmen's offers the basics: delicious cheeseburgers, sandwiches, salads, and meat and vegetable plates. After a movie, it's a good place to get a piece of homemade pie. Beer and wine are also available. Breadman's is open daily.

Brigs
$-$$ • 1225 N.W. Maynard Rd., Cary • 481-9300
$-$$ • 4900 N.C. 55, Durham • 544-7473
$-$$ • 8111 Creedmoor Rd., Raleigh • 870-0994

Billed as "The Ultimate Brunch and a whole lot more," Brigs serves brunch items, sandwiches and salad platters. Since the full menu is served all day, it's one of the few places you can order breakfast for dinner.

Cary Cafe
$ • 904 N.E. Maynard Rd., Cary • 469-9415

An unassuming, family-operated cafe that serves delicious freshly made food, Cary Cafe is located in a corner of the Reedy Creek Plaza. Omelettes, quiches, soups, salads and baked goods are among its specialties. It is open for breakfast and lunch Monday through Saturday. The Cary Cafe Market offers delicious and healthy take-home entrees, sides, sauces, breads, soups, quiches and appetizers. Cary Cafe is also an excellent caterer.

Courtney's
$ • 685 Cary Towne Blvd., Cary • 469-8410
$ • 407 Six Forks Rd., Raleigh • 834-3613
$ • 2300 Gorman St., Raleigh • 859-3830

Courtney's offers breakfast, brunch and lunch daily. Omelettes, waffles, pancakes and sandwiches are its specialties.

Gregory's Grand Occasions
$-$$ • Waverly Place, Cary • 852-3694

Decorated with a casual elegance, this popular restaurant is a great place for brunch and lunch. Insiders like Gregory's for family parties. It's also a place where you can visit over a cup of coffee and croissant for as long as you want. Gregory's contains a two-story main dining room with a separate club room available. It is open for breakfast, brunch and lunch every day except Monday. Gregory's is also an excellent caterer for Christmas, corporate and theme parties.

Honey's
$ • 2700 Guess Rd., Durham • 477-2181
• www.honeys.citysearch.com

Honey's serves breakfast and country cooking 24 hours a day, seven days a week. It is

Wine Cellar Dining at the Angus Barn

The Ultimate Culinary Experience

For parties of 12-28, reserve an elegant five or six course French Country Cuisine wine dinner with classic white glove service.

Upon descending the winding staircase, you will experience not only the rare Bordeaux wines of France and the signed, oversized bottles from California's greatest wine makers, but also the antiques, the artwork and the other unique appointments that make our wine cellar the finest dining room in the Triangle area.

You will dine surrounded by nearly 35,000 bottles of wine, offering over 1,100 selections. The Angus Barn is recognized as having one of the top 100 wine lists in the world. Our classically trained Chef will spend days preparing the courses of your choice and, if you so desire, you are invited to join the Cellarmaster in the pairing of the evening's wines.

the ANGUS BARN ltd.®

Hwy. 70 at Aviation Parkway, Raleigh
919-787-3505 • www.angusbarn.com

*T*he Angus Barn is a fine dining restaurant with a casual atmosphere. Whether you are out for a nice, quiet meal, a business dinner or an elegant evening on the town, the Angus Barn's goal is to make the dinner one that will be long remembered. We feature three separate dining rooms and luxurious accommodations in the Wine Cellar. We also offer spacious banquet facilities for any occasion. Whenever dining at the Angus Barn, we encourage you to look around and tour our kitchen and wine cellar.

Monday-Saturday 5-11pm • Sunday 5-10pm
The Wild Turkey Lounge opens at 4pm
For Reservations Call 919-787-3505

Reservations are not required, but are recommended. No reservations are taken on Saturdays or holidays.

the **ANGUS BARN** ltd.®
9401 Glenwood Avenue (US Hwy. 70), Raleigh
www.angusbarn.com

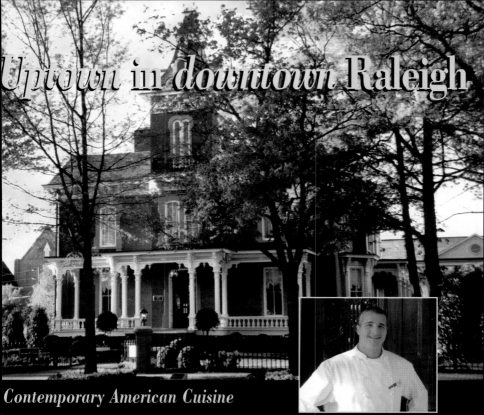

THE AREA'S PREMIERE GREEK RESTAURANT.

BRIGHTLEAF SQUARE • DURHAM, NC • (919) 682-0043

www.tavernanikos.citysearch.com

Fine Dining in the Continental Tradition for Over 20 Years

Seasonal Continental Cuisine

Open Patio Dining

Luncheons and Private Parties

Rooms Available for Receptions

La Residence
RESTAURANT & BAR

MONDAY THROUGH SATURDAY 6:00-9:30PM
202 WEST ROSEMARY ST. • CHAPEL HILL, NC (919) 967-2506
www.laresidence.citysearch.com
Reservations by Email: larez2@juno.com

WHERE HOME GROWN CAROLINA CUISINE MEETS GRACIOUS SOUTHERN HOSPITALITY

The Carolina Crossroads Restaurant specializes in creative interpretations of traditional Southern fare. Using fresh, locally produced ingredients, Chef Brian Stapleton prepares seasonal dishes that are imaginative, delicious, and artfully presented.

The restaurant's atmosphere of casual elegance is perfectly suited to its home, The Carolina Inn, a Chapel Hill landmark listed on the National Register of Historic Places.

Call for reservations. Serving lunch from 11:30 a.m. to 2:00 p.m. and dinner from 5:30 p.m. to 10:00 p.m. daily. Sunday brunch from 11:30 a.m. to 2:00 p.m. Complimentary valet parking for lunch and dinner.

CAROLINA CROSSROADS RESTAURANT AND BAR

Four Diamond Award

211 Pittsboro Street, Chapel Hill, NC 27516 • 919-918-2777 • www.carolinacrossroads.citysearch.com

conveniently located off I-85, northwest of downtown Durham.

Mecca
$ • 13 E. Martin St., Raleigh • 832-5714

The Mecca has been an American success story for three generations of the Dombalis family. It is a downtown lunchtime restaurant, with fading photographs on the wall. A room upstairs is available when the wooden booths downstairs are full. The food is solid, good fare—the lightly fried trout and the juicy burgers are excellent. Mecca buys its produce fresh at the State Farmers Market. The rice pudding, when available, is one of the best in the Triangle.

Sunflower's Sandwich Shop
$ • 315 Glenwood Ave., Raleigh
• 833-4676

Sunflower's is a bright, corner sandwich shop that serves what may be the best chunky chicken salad sandwiches in town. It's small and open for lunch Monday through Saturday and for dinner Tuesday through Saturday. Because the noon crowd knows one another, waiting usually turns into a time to visit. Sunflower's also provides catering.

CAFE

Blue Ridge:
The Museum Restaurant
$-$$$ • 2110 Blue Ridge Rd., Raleigh
• 833-3548 • www.ncartmuseum.org

An upscale cafe located on the ground floor of the North Carolina Museum of Art, Blue Ridge offers a varied menu that changes regularly. For the popular "Festival Rodin" exhibit, the cafe's menu showcased the French culinary tradition. Save room for one of the delicious desserts. The Saturday and Sunday brunches are very popular.

The Cafe at Weaver Street Market
$ • 101 E. Weaver St., Carrboro • 929-0010
• www.weaverstreetmarket.com

The Cafe at Weaver Street Market features fresh house-baked breads, ethnic and regional vegetarian food, fresh seafood and meat entrees, and a large selection of fine wines and beers. You can dine indoors, outside on the lawn or choose from the extensive takeout menu. Lunch and dinner are served Monday through Saturday, and a wholesome brunch is served on Sunday, complete with live jazz.

Photo by Rich Weidman

Weaver Street Market in Carr Mill Mall hosts a jazz brunch every Sunday morning.

Fearrington Market Cafe

$-$$ • Fearrington Village Ctr., Pittsboro
• 542-5505
• www.fearrington.com/Market/cafe.html

Homemade entrees, delicious breads (best bran muffins around), fresh salad platters and deli-style sandwiches are served in a quaint setting of Fearrington Village. In warm weather, you can sit outdoors, admire the flower beds and enjoy your food. Lunch and dinner are served Monday through Friday, and brunch is served weekends.

Foster's Market

$ • 750 Airport Rd., Chapel Hill
• 967-3663
$ • 2694 Chapel Hill Blvd., Durham
• 489-3944
• www.fostersmarket.com

Open daily, Foster's serves deli sandwiches, pastas, steaks and salads. It also has a coffee bar. The market area sells gourmet packaged gifts, wine and other culinary delicacies. Patio seating is available. Both sites are open daily for breakfast, lunch and dinner.

Fowler's Market

$ • 112 S. Duke St., Durham
• 683-2555

Established in 1925, Fowler's is a gourmet grocery store that also serves sandwiches and salads daily. A coffee bar is also on the premises. Located in Durham's Brightleaf Square District, it is open daily.

Irregardless Cafe

$$-$$$ • 901 W. Morgan St., Raleigh
• 833-9920, 833-8898
• www.irregardless.citysearch.com

Chef and owner Arthur Gordon has never been afraid to test convention since he opened his Raleigh restaurant in 1975 with a vegetarian menu. The changing menu now offers delicious fish, poultry, and beef along with vegetarian and vegan dishes. The produce arrives fresh from the State Farmers Market. The homemade desserts are wonderful, and if the Chocolate Kahlua Fantasy Cake is on the menu, be sure to order it. The ambience is metropolitan and live entertainment is provided nightly. Don't miss "Irregardless After Dark"—dancing and live music every Saturday night after 9 PM. The Irregardless Cafe serves lunch Monday through Friday, dinner Monday through Saturday, and brunch on Sunday. Catering is also available.

Second Nature Cafe

$-$$ • Olde Raleigh Village Shopping Ctr., Raleigh • 571-3447

The Second Nature Cafe in Raleigh is known for healthy and delicious dishes made with no preservatives, artificial ingredients or red meat. The menu includes pitas, quesadillas, salads, soups and smoothies. An espresso bar is also on the premises. It is open for breakfast, lunch and dinner every day except Sunday.

Simple Pleasures Market & Cafe

$-$$ • Glenwood Village, Raleigh
• 782-9227
• www.simplepleasuresmarket.com

Located off Glenwood Avenue, in one of Raleigh's favorite specialty food stores, Simple Pleasures offers sandwiches, salads, daily specials and homemade zesty soups in a smoke-free environment. Lunch is served daily, and brunch is provided on weekends. Catering is also available.

The Weathervane Cafe At A Southern Season

$$-$$$ • Eastgate Shopping Ctr., Chapel Hill • 929-9466
• www.asouthernseason.com

The Weathervane in Chapel Hill offers a delightful place to sit down and sample some of the delicious homemade fare turned out by the kitchen. The Cafe serves entrees like Paella, Grilled Chili-Rubbed Ribeye, Roasted Halibut and Grilled Pork Tenderloin, as well as great sandwiches, salads and luscious desserts. Try the Italian Tiramisu Cake or the Belgian Chocolate Blackberry Pate. During nice weather, an outdoor patio offers a special dining experience. The Weathervane is open daily for lunch and dinner and has all ABC permits.

CAFETERIA

The Capital Room Cafeteria
$ • Crabtree Valley Mall,
4325 Glenwood Ave., Raleigh
• 782-7010

A Raleigh landmark that opened in 1972, the Capital Room Cafeteria is tucked in a corner on the second floor of the Hudson Belk in Crabtree Valley Mall. Open for lunch and dinner Monday through Saturday, it serves hearty Southern fare.

K & S Cafeteria
$ • 1177 Buck Jones Rd., Cary • 462-8404
$ • 3620 Bastion Ln., Raleigh • 231-8040
$ • 3101 Edwards Mill Rd., Raleigh • 783-7791
$ • 9420 Forum Dr., Raleigh • 676-7781

These local cafeterias offer a wide variety of Southern food and are well known for their turkey and dressing, fried chicken, fresh vegetables, salads and delicious homemade desserts.

K & W Cafeteria
$ • University Mall, Chapel Hill • 942-7809
$ • Cameron Village, Raleigh • 832-7505

A Triangle mainstay for decades, K & W Cafeteria is very popular with local residents, especially senior citizens.

Picadilly Cafeteria
$ • South Square Mall, Durham
• 489-1041

Another excellent cafeteria, Picadilly is a wonderful place to eat after a busy day of shopping at Durham's South Square Mall. It is open daily.

CARIBBEAN

Bahama Breeze
$-$$ • 3409 Wake Forest Rd., Raleigh
• 872-6330 • www.bahamabreeze.com

Experience a taste of the tropics at this lively and colorful Caribbean-themed chain restaurant. Unique appetizers and entrees range from seafood pasta to tropical pizzas and coconut curry chicken. The wait staff is dressed in shorts and colorful island shirts, adding to the ambience. The outdoor patio and bar serve island drinks such as the frozen Bahamarita and the Bananaberry Daiquiri. It is open for dinner nightly.

Ben's Jamaican
$-$$ • 8306 Chapel Hill Rd., Cary
• 380-1818
• www.bensjamaican.citysearch.com

Ben's in Cary does not compromise when it comes to the preparation of its authentic Jamaican cuisine. Jerk chicken and pork, patties, and curried chicken and goat keep Ben's food lovers coming back for more. Ben's is open for lunch and dinner Monday through Saturday.

Jamaica Jamaica
$-$$ • 4853 N.C. 55, Durham
• 544-1532
• www.jamaicajamaica.citysearch.com

Jamaica Jamaica is the place to go for authentic West Indian cuisine in Durham. Among the offerings are curried chicken and goat, jerk chicken, jerk pork and Caribbean shrimp. Live jazz takes place on Thursdays. Lunch and dinner are served Monday through Saturday. Catering is available.

Rum Runners
$-$$ • City Market, Raleigh
• 878-1959 • www.rumrunnersusa.com

The dueling piano players at this popular tropical Raleigh night spot keep the crowd entertained with rock 'n roll singalongs Wednesday through Sunday. Caribbean-style fare is served nightly.

Una's Jamaican Restaurant & Bar
$-$$ • 1909-11 Poole Rd., Raleigh
• 231-3288

Enjoy authentic Jamaican cuisine such as jerk chicken or fish, curry goat and roast

INSIDERS' TIP
Most restaurants are booked solid in late May during weekends when area colleges and universities hold graduation ceremonies.

fish. Una's serves lunch and dinner Monday through Saturday.

CHINESE

35 Chinese
$$ • 1135 Kildaire Farm Rd., Cary • 467-4262
$$ • University Square, Chapel Hill • 968-3488

35 Chinese is best known for its extensive lunch and dinner buffet offering 60 to 70 items, including vegetables, shrimp, chicken, pork, soups and desserts. Both locations are open seven days a week.

China Chef
$-$$ • Eastgate Shopping Ctr., Chapel Hill • 942-2688

Cozy and attractively decorated, China Chef in Chapel Hill serves well-prepared Chinese food at reasonable prices. Some house specialties include Ivory Shrimp and Chicken with Black Bean Sauce. There is a daily special that includes soup and an egg roll with an entree. Lunch and dinner are served seven days a week, and takeout is available. Wine and beer are offered.

China Inn
$-$$ • 2701 Hillsborough Rd., Durham • 286-2444

Located close to Duke University and the medical center, this restaurant gladly prepares food for people with special dietary requirements. For health conscious diners, this restaurant never uses MSG. China Inn is open for lunch and dinner seven days a week.

China One
$-$$ • 4325 N.C. 55, Durham • 361-3388

Convenient for RTP workers, this popular restaurant offers a fabulous weekday lunch buffet. For a weekend brunch, China One is the place for dim sum. Carts wheeled throughout the dining area allow you to preview the appetizer-sized entrees of dumplings, buns and noodle rolls filled with shrimp, pork and other Chinese delicacies. It is open seven days a week for lunch and dinner.

China Pearl
$$ • Waverly Place, Cary • 851-0358

China Pearl in Cary serves Hunan, Szechuan, Mandarin and Cantonese dishes, and it's a family place, so don't hesitate to take the kids. Open for lunch Sunday through Friday and dinner every night, it also has all ABC permits.

Crystal Palace
$$ • 4011-161 Capital Blvd., Raleigh • 878-9699
• www.crystalpalace.citysearch.com

Fortunately, almost every section of Raleigh has its own favorite Chinese restaurant. This popular, inexpensive spot is located in Tarrymore Square. The recently expanded all-you-can-eat buffet is one of the best, including General Tso's Chicken, Vegetable Lo Mein, Chicken Teriyaki and Steamed Crab Legs. Crystal Palace serves lunch and dinner daily. A take-out menu, catering and banquet facilities are available.

Hing Ping
$$-$$$$ • North Ridge Shopping Center, Raleigh • 876-6988

Hing Ping (which means "celebration of peace") offers a more extensive and authentic menu than the typical neighborhood Chinese restaurant. Enjoy duck, seafood and beef dishes. This Raleigh restaurant is open for lunch Monday through Friday and for dinner nightly.

Main Garden
$-$$ • 1353 Kildaire Farm Rd., Cary • 481-9009

Main Garden in Cary features a diverse buffet with more than 100 items and a Mongolian Stove. Lunch and dinner are served seven days a week.

Neo-China
$$ • 4015 University Dr., Durham • 489-2828
$$ • 6602-1 Glenwood Ave., Raleigh • 783-8383

Authentic Chinese cuisine is served in an upscale, contemporary setting. You may even order takeout from the extensive menu of this elegant restaurant. Both Neo-China locations are open for lunch Monday through Friday and for dinner seven days a week. A Sunday lunch buffet is available.

Shanghai
$$ • 3433 Hillsborough Rd., Durham
• 383-7581
• www.shanghai.citysearch.com

Shanghai has a relaxed atmosphere where you can enjoy tasty Chinese cuisine prepared with the freshest ingredients. This established Durham restaurant takes pride in the dishes it serves and has all ABC permits. It is open daily for lunch and dinner.

Ten Ten
$ • 3812 Western Blvd., Raleigh
• 856-1818

Located near the North Carolina State University campus, Ten Ten boasts "the largest Chinese buffet in the Triangle" with about 100 items. It is open daily for lunch and dinner.

CONTINENTAL

The Fairview at The Washington Duke Inn
$$$-$$$$ • 3001 Cameron Blvd., Durham
• 493-6699 • www.washingtondukeinn.com

The Fairview, in the elegant Washington Duke Inn, is a wonderful place to entertain friends or out-of-town guests. The menu features continental cuisine and regional specialties. Salads, fresh homemade soups, steaks and seafood specialties highlight the menu. It is open for breakfast daily, lunch Monday through Saturday, brunch on Sunday and dinner nightly. Reservations are highly recommended on weekends.

Foster's
$$-$$$ • Cameron Village, Raleigh
• 832-9815

Foster's features an American Continental menu with fresh fish, choice beef, pastas and daily specials. The wine bar, open kitchen and outdoor patio add to the atmosphere. Foster's is open for lunch, dinner and late night Monday through Saturday. It has all ABC permits and is a popular late night spot for college students.

The building that once served as the Cary Library now houses Serendipity Gourmet-Deli.

Galeria
$$$$ • Radisson Governors Inn, I-40 (Exit 280) at Davis Dr., RTP • 549-8631

Located in the Radisson Governors Inn, the Galeria's noontime buffet is generous and varied, but it has made its reputation as an evening dining spot. The menu offers some of the best seafood, veal and pasta in the Triangle. The Galeria has all ABC permits. Reservations are recommended.

The Melting Pot
$$$-$$$$ • 3100 Wake Forest Rd., Raleigh • 878-0477

Enjoy sizzling beef, chicken and seafood at Raleigh's original fondue restaurant. For dessert, try one of the spectacular Chocolate Fondue delights. The Melting Pot is open seven nights a week and reservations are suggested.

Rubens
$$-$$$ • Sheraton Chapel Hill, Europa Dr. and U.S. 15-501 Bypass, Chapel Hill • 968-4900

Located in the luxurious Sheraton Chapel Hill Hotel, Rubens is named for the famous Flemish painter. Here you'll find nicely prepared regional American cuisine as well as a wide variety of seafood dishes. Rubens is open daily for breakfast, lunch and dinner, and reservations are recommended. It has all ABC permits.

DELICATESSEN

Hotpoint Deli
$-$$$ • 1284 Buck Jones Rd., Cary
• 460-6299

After Maximillian's Restaurant in Cary was damaged by fire, the owners decided to repair and renovate the building, turning it into an eclectic deli. The menu features cold and hot subs, focaccia and grilled panini sandwiches, pasta dishes, salads and an array of pizzas, from Buffalo Chicken to Voodoo Chile. Hotpoint is open for lunch and dinner Monday through Saturday.

Piper's Deli
$ • 3219 Old Chapel Hill Rd., Durham
• 489-2481

Popular with students, professors and employees at Duke University, this deli has the atmosphere of a neighborhood tavern. The prices are modest and the food is homemade. Enjoy deli sandwiches, burgers, subs, salads and soups. It is open Monday through Saturday.

Serendipity Gourmet-Deli
$ • 118 S. Academy St., Cary
• 469-1655 • No Credit Cards

Serendipity in Cary offers creative sandwiches and a deli counter for takeout. It is open for lunch Monday through Saturday and dinner Tuesday through Friday.

ECLECTIC

Acme Food & Beverage Co.
$$-$$$$ • 110 E. Main St., Carrboro
• 929-2263

Enjoy regional cuisine at Acme, which offers a seasonal menu full of diverse entrees such as Pan-Fried North Carolina Soft Shell Crabs, Barbecued Baby Back Ribs, Angel Hair Pasta with Shrimp, Oven-Roasted Chicken, Jambalaya, Jerked Porterhouse Steak and Vegetarian Curry. Acme also boasts an impressive wine list. Located in downtown Carrboro, it is open for lunch Monday through Friday and for dinner nightly. A brunch is served on Sunday. It has all ABC permits.

Anotherthyme
$$-$$$$ • 109 N. Gregson St., Durham
• 682-5225

A Durham landmark since 1982, Anotherthyme offers a tantalizing array of delicious Mediterranean and Southwestern entrees in an elegant atmosphere. Diners will also enjoy creative appetizers, a 150-item wine list, homemade desserts and a friendly neighborhood bar that serves a variety of frozen drinks, imports and microbrewed beers. The walls are decorated with artwork from local artists. It is open for dinner seven nights a week. Reservations are recommended.

Henry's Bistro
$$-$$$ • 403 W. Rosemary St., Chapel Hill
• 967-4720 • www.henrysbistro.com

Henry's in Chapel Hill serves an eclectic selection of bistro fare in a relaxed atmosphere. Chef Curtis Vincent offers creative cuisine—often with a Mediterranean or Caribbean influence. Dinner is served Tuesday through Saturday and a late-night menu is available nightly. Live music can be heard Sunday, Monday and Tuesday.

New Oakwood Cafe
$-$$$ • 300 E. Edenton St., Raleigh
• 828-5994

The New Oakwood Cafe in Raleigh is not your ordinary diner. Of course you can still get eggs and grits here for breakfast and sandwiches for lunch. However, the Cafe's dinner menu offers a mix of traditional American fare with Italian, Cuban and Argentinian dishes. Breakfast and lunch are served daily and dinner is served Friday and Saturday.

Pyewacket
$$$ • 431 W. Franklin St., Chapel Hill
• 929-0297
• www.pyewacketrestaurant.com

Pyewacket has been a mainstay of the Chapel Hill restaurant scene since 1977. It is known for its vegetarian, pasta, fresh seafood, chicken and beef specialties. Original homemade dressings and freshly baked breads complement Pyewacket's seasonal menus. Desserts are not to be missed. Outdoor seating is available. It is open for lunch Monday through Saturday and for dinner nightly. A late-night menu is available on Thursday, Friday and Saturday.

Vertigo Diner
$$-$$$ • 426 S. McDowell St., Raleigh • 832-4477

Vertigo Diner in Raleigh offers upscale New American cuisine such as Roast Pork Chops and Shrimp and Grits. The menu changes every four weeks. It serves lunch Tuesday through Friday, dinner Tuesday through Saturday and brunch on Sunday.

Zest Cafe and Home Art
$$-$$$ • 8831 Six Forks Rd., Raleigh • 848-4792

Zest features light New American cuisine and in a contemporary setting. Roasted chicken, herbed salmon fillet, tacos, quesadillas and "pizzestas" are offered. It is open for lunch and dinner Tuesday through Saturday and Sunday for brunch.

ETHIOPIAN

Blue Nile
$$-$$$ • 2000 Chapel Hill Rd., Durham • 490-0462
• www.kirsten.net/thebluenile

For an exotic culinary adventure, nothing beats a visit to Blue Nile where diners sit at woven "basket" tables (known as mesobes) and sample traditional Ethiopian dishes with a spongy bread called injera. Blue Nile serves lunch Tuesday through Saturday and dinner Tuesday through Sunday.

FINE DINING

Bloomsbury Bistro
$$$$ • 509 Whitaker Mill Rd., Raleigh • 834-9011 • www.bloomsbury.citysearch.com

Located in the heart of Raleigh's Five Points neighborhood, Bloomsbury Bistro was named for Bloomsbury Park, an early 20th-century amusement park. It offers a creative

Staff Photo

Brightleaf 905 has received rave reviews for its delicious international cuisine.

menu of new American cuisine that changes seasonally and an extensive wine selection. Dinner is served Monday through Saturday. A private dining room is available.

Brightleaf 905
$$$-$$$$ • Brightleaf Square, Durham
• 680-8848
• www.brightleaf905.citysearch.com

Brightleaf 905 features international cuisine in a chic atmosphere where guests can dine comfortably and actually have a private conversation. Signature dishes range from their Argentine Sirloin Steak to what has been named the "best burger" in the Triangle. Brightleaf 905 serves lunch Tuesday through Friday and dinner Monday through Saturday and has all ABC permits. Reservations are recommended. A private dining room is available.

The Fearrington House
$$$$ • Fearrington Village Center,
Pittsboro • 542-2121
• www.fearringtonhouse.com

This charming restaurant lies about 8 miles south of Chapel Hill on U.S. 15-501 in Fearrington Village. The Fearrington House has been noted in *Food and Wine* and *Gourmet* magazines for its "new cuisine of the South."

Dinner is served as a five-course fixed price meal (excluding wine). It's served in elegant surroundings by an attentive and professional waitstaff. Desserts are a specialty and include chocolate souffle with warm chocolate sauce and whipped cream, fruit tarts and incredible homemade ice creams.

The menu changes daily, depending on the availability of ingredients. It has all ABC permits. Reservations are required.

Four Square
$$$-$$$$ • 2701 Chapel Hill Rd., Durham
• 401-9877

Located in the beautifully restored 1908 Bartlett-Mangum House, Four Square in Durham specializes in globally influenced contemporary American cuisine. It was named for the unique "four-square" style architecture of the house, which is listed on the National Register of Historic Places. The menu changes monthly, offering the freshest seasonal ingredients. Start with a tantalizing array of appetizers such as Grilled Duck and Duck Foie Gras on Sticky Rice Cakes with Cranberry Compote. Entrees include such innovative culinary creations as Rock Crabmeat-laced Grouper, Grilled Rosemary-scented Lamb, and Herb Crusted Salmon with Fried Green Tomatoes. Save room for one of the delicious homemade desserts.

Four Square also boasts a cozy bar, extensive wine list, eclectic selection of beers, seasonal outdoor dining and private dining facilities. Dinner is served Monday through Saturday. Reservations are recommended.

The Grill at Glen Lennox
$$-$$$$ • 1201 Raleigh Rd.,
Chapel Hill • 942-1963
• www.grillatglenlennox.citysearch.com

Located in Chapel Hill's Glen Lennox Shopping Center, The Grill serves delicious cuisine with California and Mediterranean influences. The menu changes seasonally. Enjoy hearty portions of fire-grilled fish and meats, thin-crust pizza cooked in a wood-fired oven, pasta specialties and a wide selection of wines. Try one of the delicious homemade desserts such as Vanilla Creme Brulee or Plum Honey Cheesecake. It serves lunch Monday through Friday and dinner Monday through Saturday. It has all ABC permits.

Il Palio Ristorante
$$$$ • Siena Hotel,
1505 E. Franklin St., Chapel Hill
• 929-4000 • www.sienahotel.com

At the Siena Hotel's gracious restaurant, Il Palio, internationally acclaimed Executive Chef Gennaro Villella creates exceptional Italian cuisine based on his food concept of simplicity. Fresh, seasonal ingredients are combined to give pure, healthy and flavorful dishes. The ambience is elegant and the level of service is high. Various special events are held throughout the year, focusing on the regional cuisines and wines of Italy. Enjoy after-hours cappuccino on the private, glassed-in terrace. Breakfast, lunch and dinner are served daily. There is also a Sunday brunch. Reservations are recommended. Il Palio has all ABC permits.

La Residence Restaurant & Bar
$$$-$$$$ • 202 W. Rosemary St.,
Chapel Hill • 967-2506
• www.laresidence.citysearch.com

La Residence has a long tradition of offering fine, innovative cuisine in the Triangle. This charming, elegant restaurant is located in the heart of Chapel Hill. The menu changes monthly and has included such items as seared tuna, filet mignon, pecan crusted pork tenderloin and lobster, all creatively prepared. The restaurant uses the freshest local produce for the seasonal vegetable side dishes and salads. Desserts include Kaluga—a divine chocolate creation—sorbets and fresh fruit, and berry specialties.

In warm weather, you may dine on the patio overlooking colorful gardens. It's no wonder the restaurant has won accolades through the years from *Food and Wine*, *Bon Appetit*, *Gourmet* and *The New York Times*. Private parties are a specialty. Dinner is served Monday through Saturday. Reservations are advised. It has all ABC permits.

Magnolia Grill
$$$$ • 1002 Ninth St., Durham • 286-3609

The Magnolia Grill in Durham is one of the Triangle's FINEST places to dine, with its commitment to innovative and absolutely delicious food. It features a daily menu composed of the freshest ingredients of the season. That means you're likely to find anything from Moroccan Eggplant Soup to Brunswick Strudel to Chile-Rubbed Cured Yellowfin Tuna to Grilled Georgia Quail with Blackberries on Creamy Stone-Ground Grits—tantalizing, eclectic fare that defies labels. Each menu features six to nine appetizers (like watercress and watermelon salad in raspberry vinaigrette), just as many entrees and incredible desserts (blueberry gingerbread with lemon cream, anyone?). Reservations are essential, especially during American Dance Festival season. It is closed on Sundays and Mondays.

Margaux's
$$$$ • 8111 Creedmoor Rd., Brennan Station, Raleigh • 846-9846

Be prepared for a special dining experience. From the cozy and eclectic atmosphere to the excellent service to the innovative menu, a meal at Margaux's is one you won't forget. The menu at this Raleigh restaurant changes frequently and offers a variety of daily and seasonal specials with an emphasis on seafood. If you are a fan of crabcakes, order them as an appetizer or as part of the seafood grille. The desserts are among the best in the Triangle, with many seasonal fresh fruit offerings. It is open for dinner nightly and has all ABC permits.

Nana's
$$$-$$$$ • 2514 University Dr., Durham • 493-8545
• www.nanas.citysearch.com

Nana's, named for owner-chef Scott Howell's grandmother, has gained national acclaim for its new American cuisine. The changing menu at this Durham establishment features entrees like Roast Quail with Dried Cranberries Cipollini Onions and Grilled Radicchio, Tomato Consomme with Smoked Salmon Ravioli, Filet of Beef over Braised Belgian Endive and Grilled Veal Chop over a Risotto Cake. Nana's recent renovations include an expansion of the dining room, a state-of-the-art kitchen and a new bar. Dinner is served Monday through Saturday. Reservations are requested. It has all ABC permits.

Second Empire Restaurant and Tavern
$$$$ • 330 Hillsborough St., Raleigh
• 829-3663 • www.second-empire.com

One of the hottest restaurants in Raleigh, Second Empire features fine dining in the elegant but relaxed atmosphere of the historic Dodd-Hinsdale House, which has a Victorian-style Mansard-roofed tower. Chef Daniel Schurr dishes up contemporary American cuisine, such as Striped Bass and Grilled Beef Tenderloin. A separate menu is available in the casual, pub-like Tavern, which features items such as Chicago Baby Back Ribs, Crispy Polenta and Seafood Paella. The Tavern also has an outside covered and heated patio area where you can listen to live entertainment every Friday night. The wine cellar features more than 150 varieties. Private dining rooms are available for large and small groups. Dinner is served Monday through Saturday. Reservations are strongly recommended.

The Warehouse
$$$-$$$$ • Dawson & Cabarrus Sts., Raleigh • 836-9966
• www.warehouserestaurant.com

Enjoy innovative American cuisine in this popular combination restaurant and dance club, which is located in downtown Raleigh's bustling warehouse district. Start your culinary adventure with one of more than 50 tapas—tantalizing appetizers such as Coconut Shrimp, Grilled Beef Tenderloin Kabob and Maryland Crabcakes. Then choose from a variety of delectable entrees, including Grilled New Zealand Lamb Chops, Pan Seared Sesame Crusted Tuna and Giant Sea Scallops. Cap it all off with one of

The Warehouse's spectacular desserts. Dinner is served nightly.

The Wine Cellar at Angus Barn
$$$$ • 9401 Glenwood Ave., Raleigh
• 787-3505 • www.angusbarn.com

The Wine Cellar is located in a downstairs dining room in the Angus Barn. Enjoy French country cuisine in an elegant atmosphere surrounded by nearly 35,000 bottles of wine offering more than 1,100 selections. Each of the five to six courses is matched with the appropriate wine selection. This unique culinary experience was designed for parties of 12-28. Call ahead for reservations.

FRENCH

Bistro 607
$$$-$$$$ • 607 Glenwood Ave., Raleigh
• 828-0840

Located in a restored 1912 house, Bistro 607 in Raleigh serves traditional French cuisine with fresh seasonal ingredients prepared daily. The menu changes monthly. Enjoy homemade breads and desserts. Bistro 607 is open for lunch Monday through Friday and dinner Monday through Saturday.

Photo by Rich Weidman

Second Empire is located in the historic Dodd-Hinsdale House.

Butterflies

$$$-$$$$ • 6325 Falls of Neuse Rd.,
Raleigh • 878-2020
• www.butterflies.citysearch.com

Butterflies specializes in innovative French cuisine with a Mediterranean influence. The seasonal menu features such delicacies as Pan Seared Grouper, Portabella Mushroom Napoleon, Hickory Spring Free Range Chicken and Roasted Australian Rack of Lamb. Dinner is served Monday through Saturday. Reservations at this North Raleigh restaurant are recommended.

Gaulart & Maliclet French Cafe

$$ • 957 N. Harrison Ave., Cary
• 469-2288
• www.citysearch.com/rdu/gandmcafe

G&M in Cary has been a hit with its food, wine and atmosphere. The food is not always French, but it is enthusiastically recommended by the customers. A glass of wine comes with weekend specials, which change weekly. The most popular dish is Seafood Normandy, with Chicken Provencale a close second. The Cafe is open for lunch and dinner Monday through Saturday.

Jean-Claude's French Cafe

$$ • North Ridge Shopping Ctr., Raleigh
• 872-6224 • www.jeanclaudes.com

Jean-Claude's in Raleigh offers a varied French menu in a cafe atmosphere. If you look over the counter, you might see the owner, Therese Freeman, at work fixing softshell crab or the daily special, which might be duck or fresh salmon, or a special crepe. The Beef Stroganof Crepe is highly recommended and the caramel flan is the best in town. A wine-tasting is held nearly every month. It's popular and relaxed, so get there on time or you may have to wait outside. Lunch and dinner are served Tuesday through Saturday. Banquet facilities are available. Live music can be heard Friday and Saturday nights.

Tartines Bistro Provencal

$$$-$$$$ • 1110 Navaho Dr., Raleigh
• 790-0091

Experience French Provencale cuisine in Tartines' intimate and comfortably elegant dining room. Save room for one of the excellent homemade desserts. This Raleigh restaurant is open for dinner Monday through Saturday and has all ABC permits.

GREEK

Mariakakis Gourmet Market and Deli

$-$$ • U.S. 15-501 Bypass, Chapel Hill
• 942-1453

This Chapel Hill deli offers stuffed sandwiches, salads and appetizers, as well as other Greek favorites such as stuffed grape leaves and baklava. It is open Monday through Saturday for lunch. The market features an extensive wine selection.

Papa's Grill

$$-$$$ • 1821 Hillandale Rd., Durham
• 383-8502
• www.papasgrill.citysearch.com

Located in Durham, Papa's Grill specializes in Greek cuisine, and offers a wide assortment of Greek appetizers such as Kalamari Saluta and Tiri a la Mikonos. It also serves steaks, seafood and pasta dishes. Try the chocolate mousse cake for dessert. Papa's is open for lunch and dinner Monday through Friday and only for dinner on Saturday.

Spartacus

$$ • Waverly Place, Cary • 852-5050
$$ • 220 W. Rosemary St., Chapel Hill
• 928-0300
$$ • 4139 Chapel Hill Blvd., Durham
• 489-2848
• www.spartacusrestaurants.com

Spartacus offers Greek, Middle Eastern, vegetarian and seafood specialties, and we heartily recommend the homemade rice pudding. The original location in Durham contains a spacious restaurant and bar decorated with hand-painted murals, and an outdoor deck. Each site is open for lunch Monday through Saturday and for dinner nightly.

Taverna Nikos

$$-$$$ • Brightleaf Square, Durham
• 682-0043 • www.fuzz.com/nikos

Taverna Nikos in Durham offers some of the most delicious and authentic Greek food to

Staff Photo

Enjoy authentic Greek cuisine at Taverna Nikos in Brightleaf Square.

be found in the Triangle. Moussaka, Souvlaki and other favorite Greek dishes fill the menu, along with huge salads and hearty soups. The atmosphere is friendly and it's a great place to go with a group of friends, when you can share platters heaped with food. It has all ABC permits and is open for lunch and dinner Monday through Saturday.

Zorba's
$$ • 105 S. Elliott Rd., Village Plaza, Chapel Hill • 967-5517

Zorba's in Chapel Hill features deliciously authentic Greek dishes, huge portions and reasonable prices. The Lemon Chicken is especially good and the Pastitsio and Moussaka melt in your mouth. The appetizer platter is a good way to sample some of the specialties; it features Stuffed Grape Leaves, Spanakopita, Gyros and Souvlaki to share. Zorba's is open for lunch Monday through Friday and nightly for dinner. Beer and wine are available.

GRILL- 50's Style

The Char-Grill
$ • 618 Hillsborough St., Ral. • 821-7636
$ • 3211 Edwards Mill Rd., Raleigh • 781-2945
$ • 4617 Atlantic Ave., Raleigh • 954-9556
$ • 9601 Strickland Rd., Raleigh • 845-8994

The Char-Grill is an enduring '50s-style, drive-in fixture that keeps the lunchtime and late-night crowd standing in line for burgers, fries and shakes.

Grill '57
$ • 4202 Fayetteville Rd., Raleigh • 779-5757

Grill '57 specializes in hamburgers, chicken sandwiches and hot dogs grilled over an open flame. Barbecue sandwiches, salads, french fries and onion rings are also available at the Grill.

HOME COOKING

Big Ed's City Market
$ • City Market, Raleigh • 836-9909

Every visitor or newcomer who wants to experience the Triangle's true flavor eventually ends up at Big Ed's in Raleigh's downtown City Market. Fresh vegetables from the State Farmers Market make this restaurant's country cooking truly down-home. Surplus food is donated to the Raleigh Rescue Mission daily. Breakfast is served Monday through Saturday and lunch is served Monday through Friday.

Elmo's Diner
$-$$ • 200 N. Greensboro St., Carrboro • 929-2909
$-$$ • 776 Ninth St., Durham • 416-3823
• www.elmosdiner.com

Elmo's Diner serves freshly prepared traditional food with family-friendly customer service. The menu features "Square Meals" such as meatloaf, salmon cakes and roast turkey as well as "Daily Specials" ranging from stir-fry to Italian entrees. A wide variety of sandwiches, burgers and salads is also available. Both diners are open daily for breakfast, lunch and dinner.

Farmers Market Restaurant
$ • 1240 Farmers Market Dr., Raleigh • 833-7973

Traditional homestyle cooking using local ingredients is served at this bustling little eatery located at the State Farmers Market in Raleigh. It is open for breakfast and lunch Monday through Friday and breakfast on Saturday.

Joe's Place
$ • 301 W. Martin St., Raleigh • 832-5260

Joe offers his mom's cooking and it's popular with the downtown Raleigh noontime crowd. Joe's provides home-cooked entrees, big sandwiches and vegetables. Joe's place is open Monday through Friday for lunch and dinner.

Mama Dip's Kitchen
$-$$ • 408 W. Rosemary St., Chapel Hill
• 942-5837 • www.mamadips.com

If you're seeking The Real Thing Southern-style, look no farther than Mama Dip's Kitchen in Chapel Hill. Started in 1976 by Mildred "Dip" Council, this is the place to get country fried chicken, smothered pork chops, chicken dumplings, catfish or even (if you can handle it) real chitlins, served up with okra, black-eyed peas, collards and cornbread. Dip's slogan is "put a little South in your mouth," and, boy, does she! Mama Dip makes up her daily specials with seasonal ingredients, so they are always fresh. For dessert, opt for the homemade pecan pie. Dip's serves breakfast, lunch and dinner daily. Beer and wine are available.

Melba's Country Kitchen
$ • 121 E. Chatham St., Cary
• 467-0929 • No Credit Cards

Melba has been working here since 1978. It's a downtown Cary eatery for working folks and a good place for newcomers to get a taste of small town Southern cooking. Specialties are barbecue, hushpuppies, chicken-fried steak and black-eyed peas.

Rick's Diner
$-$$$ • 4015 University Dr., Durham
• 419-0907

Rick's serves down-home cooking such as Southern breakfasts, "blue plate" specials and a variety of vegetables. Hot plates include ham steak, fried chicken, turkey with dressing, meatloaf, pork barbecue, steaks, seafood and pasta dishes. Located behind South Square Mall in the BB&T Plaza in Durham, Rick's is open for breakfast, lunch and dinner Monday through Saturday and brunch on Sunday. Patio seating is available.

Toot-N-Tell Family Restaurant and Catering
$ • 903 W. Garner Rd., Garner • 772-2616

Originally a drive-in, this country-cooking restaurant in Garner has been packing customers in since 1946. It still has a drive-up window for orders to go. The buffet lunch has a variety of meats and country vegetables, along with homemade desserts. The most unbelievable thing about this all-you-can-eat extravaganza is the price, just $5.15 for lunch. Lunch and dinner are served every day and there is a Sunday brunch.

Village Diner
$ • 600 W. King St., Hillsborough
• 732-7032

Located west of Hillsborough's historic downtown, the Village Diner is the town's oldest continuously operated restaurant. It features an extensive buffet lunch and is open Monday through Friday for breakfast, lunch and dinner.

INDIAN

Darbar Indian Restaurant
$-$$ • 423 W. Franklin St., Chapel Hill
• 968-8706

Authentic Indian appetizers, breads, vegetarian, chicken, lamb and seafood dishes are served in an unpretentious setting. Darbar Indian Restaurant is open daily for lunch and dinner.

India Garden
$-$$$ • Cary Towne Center, Cary
• 319-3722

Cary residents flock to India Garden for its popular lunch buffet, which features authentic Indian specialties. It is open for lunch and dinner daily.

India Mahal
$$ • 3212 Hillsborough St., Raleigh
• 836-9742

Serving delicious northern Indian food in an informal setting, India Mahal is close to N.C. State University. It specializes in vegetarian, lamb and tandoori entrees and offers a variety of Indian beers to go with your meal. India Mahal is open daily for lunch and dinner.

India Palace
$-$$ • 508-A W. Franklin St., Chapel Hill • 942-8201
$-$$ • 962-B Airport Blvd., Morrisville • 460-3339

Open for lunch and dinner daily, India Palace in Morrisville serves a variety of authentic northern Indian dishes, including a number of vegetarian choices. Enjoy the all-you-can-eat buffet for lunch.

Sitar India Palace
$$$-$$$$ • 3117-D Shannon Rd., Durham • 490-1326
• www.sitarindiapalace.citysearch.com

Sitar Indian Palace is the place to go for southern and northern Indian specialties, including curry dishes, Lamb Vindaloo, Chicken Tikka Masala and Malai Kofta. Located in Regency Plaza near South Square Mall in Durham, Sitar serves lunch and dinner daily. Catering is also available.

Tandoor Indian Restaurant
$$-$$$ • 1301 E. Franklin St., Chapel Hill • 967-6622
$$-$$$ • 5410 N.C. 55, Durham • 484-2102 • www.tandoorindian.com

Tandoor offers an extensive menu that features such delicacies as Tandoori Mixed Grill, Malai Kopta and Saag Paneer, along with 12 varieties of bread. Lunch and dinner are served daily.

ITALIAN

411 West
$$-$$$ • 411 W. Franklin St., Chapel Hill • 967-2782
• www.411west.com

411 West is consistently good and consistently crowded. We recommend that you go early or be prepared to wait in the bar, but it is worth the wait. This Chapel Hill restaurant's wood-burning pizza oven gives an authentic touch to the sun-dried tomato or fresh garden mozzarella "pizzettes." Homemade pasta dishes like Lemon Linguine

Photo by Rich Weidman

Contemporary Italian cuisine is the specialty at 411 West.

and Angel Hair Cream Primavera are offered. Dinner is served seven nights a week. Catering is available.

518 West
$$-$$$$ • 518 W. Jones St., Raleigh • 829-2518 • www.518west.com

Like its sister restaurant, 411 West in Chapel Hill, 518 West has gained a reputation for delicious Italian cuisine in a lively atmosphere. The renovated Raleigh warehouse has been beautifully redecorated to resemble a Roman piazza with terrazzo floors, wrought iron balconies and a trompe l'oeil sky ceiling. The menu offers Italian contemporary cuisine with fresh seasonal pastas, seafood, vegetarian dishes and pizzettes. In-house desserts are made daily. Dinner is served nightly.

Amedeo's
$ • 3905 Western Blvd., Raleigh • 851-0473

Amedeo's is an inside-the-Beltline Raleigh restaurant that has been serving homemade lasagna, pizza and veal since 1960. Located close to N.C. State University, the TV in the sports bar is tuned to the Wolfpack. Amedeo's is open for lunch and dinner daily.

Aurora
$$$ • N.C. 54, Chapel Hill • 942-2400
• www.aurorarestaurant.com

At Aurora in Chapel Hill, you can enjoy superb Northern Italian cuisine. Select tender veal, lamb, poultry or fresh seafood for the entree, then complement it with one of many handmade pastas. Or opt for a pizza from the wood-fired oven. Appetizers, fresh salads, irresistible desserts and a fine wine will complete your meal. Patio dining is available. Aurora serves lunch Monday through Friday and dinner nightly. Dinner reservations are advised. Aurora has all ABC permits.

Cafe Roma
$$$-$$$$ • 7361 Six Forks Rd., Raleigh • 846-6080 • www.cafe-roma.com

Traditional Italian multi-regional dishes are the specialty at Cafe Roma in Raleigh. The Cafe also boasts an impressive wine list and offers live blues and jazz most nights of the week, as well as a dance floor. It has all ABC permits and is open for lunch Monday through Friday and dinner Monday through Saturday.

Cafe Tiramisu
$$ • 6196 Falls of the Neuse Rd., Raleigh • 981-0305

Northern Italian cuisine is the speciality of this North Raleigh restaurant named for the dessert. It is open for dinner Tuesday through Sunday and has all ABC permits. Reservations are recommended.

Caffe Luna
$$-$$$$ • 136 E. Hargett St., Raleigh • 832-6090 • www.cafeluna.com

Enjoy superb Italian cuisine at this New York-style eatery, which offers a seasonally changing menu with such entrees as Pasta Primavera, Linguini Pescatore, Salmone alla Griglia and Parmigiana di Vitella. Choose from a variety of wines to accompany your entrée. It is open for lunch Monday through Friday and dinner Wednesday through Saturday. Reservations are recommended. Outdoor dining and private party rooms are available.

Casa Carbone
Ristorante Italiano
$$ • U.S. 70 W., Oak Park Shopping Ctr. Raleigh • 781-8750 • www.citysearch.com/rdu/casacarbone

The Carbones have been in the business for a long time. For years their cooking was the standard by which Raleigh measured its Italian food. Casa Carbone specializes in veal and pasta entrees, sauces and homemade bread. This is a family place, so don't worry about taking the little ones. It has all ABC permits and is open for dinner Tuesday through Sunday.

Casalinga Ristorante Italiano
$-$$$ • 4538 Capital Blvd., Raleigh • 873-1334 • www.casalinga.citysearch.com

This cozy Raleigh restaurant is perfect for a romantic evening. It serves homemade dishes made to order. Vegetarians will delight in the options. Casalinga is open for lunch Monday through Friday and for dinner nightly.

Daniel's
$$-$$$ • 1430 N.C. 55, Apex • 303-1006

Daniel's in Apex is not just another pizza restaurant. Creative Italian specialties, such as Mushroom Ravioli and Penne Ala Casa, keep customers waiting in line. Daniel's homemade desserts are incredible. The Cafe is located near the intersection of N.C. 55 and U.S. 64, and is open for dinner nightly.

Italian Chophouse
$$$-$$$$ • 8111-137 Creedmoor Rd. Raleigh • 847-4440 • www.theitalianchophouse.com

Formerly known as Vincenzo's, this North Raleigh restaurant has added steaks and chops to its menu of authentic Italian dishes such as eggplant, veal, mussels and a variety of homemade pasta and seafood dishes. You can dine on the outdoor enclosed patio or reserve the private room for large parties. Dinner is served nightly.

Nina's Ristorante
$$$-$$$$ • 8801 Leadmine Rd., Ste. 113, Raleigh • 845-1122 • www.ninas.citysearch.com

Nina's is a warm and inviting Italian ristorante that promises a memorable dining experience. The Raleigh restaurant, which specializes in Tuscan and Sicilian cuisine, was opened in the fall of 1999 by Nina and

Chris Psarros. A native of Palermo, Sicily, Nina is a member of the Italian Culinary Institute and also serves as Food Master for the Italian Table in the Triangle. Specialties include Osso Bucco, Gnocchi, Cannelloni Fiorentina and Pollo Scarpariello. The menu also offers seafood, chicken and veal. The extensive wine list is exclusively Italian. Nina's is open for dinner Monday through Saturday.

Panzanella
$$-$$$ • 200 N. Greensboro St., Carrboro
• 929-6626 • www.panzanella.com
Located in Carr Mill Mall in Carrboro, Panzanella is owned by the adjacent Weaver Street Market. It serves superb pasta dishes, pizzas and salads, as well as steak and seafood dishes. A full bakery is also on the premises. Panzanella is open for lunch Tuesday through Saturday and for dinner Tuesday through Sunday.

Piccola Italia
$$-$$$ • Cameron Village, Raleigh
• 833-6888
This Raleigh restaurant specializes in fresh Italian dishes prepared in an authentic Italian kitchen. It serves lunch Monday through Saturday and dinner daily.

Pop's
$$-$$$ • 810 W. Peabody St., Durham
• 956-7677 • www.pops.citysearch.com
If you think that a casual restaurant owned by Scott Howell (of Nana's) sounds intriguing, you're right. Pop's in Durham features exotic pizzas and homemade breads straight from the wood-burning brick oven and simple, delicious Italian fare. Prices are reasonable, the atmosphere is pleasantly bustling and the food is as good as you'd hoped for. It is open for lunch Monday through Friday and dinner nightly.

Pulcinella's Ristorante
$$-$$$ • 4711 Hope Valley Rd., Durham
• 490-1172
$$-$$$ • 4412 Falls of Neuse Rd.,
Raleigh • 954-8426
Located in southwest Durham's Woodcroft Shopping Center, the original

Pulcinella's is very popular with local residents. The cozy restaurant features Northern Italian cuisine and gourmet pizza. Lunch and dinner are served Monday through Saturday. A second Pulcinella's is located on Falls of Neuse Road in Raleigh.

Sorrento
$$-$$$ • Prime Outlets-Morrisville,
Morrisville • 380-0990
The food at Sorrento is rich, Northern Italian cuisine. Pasta, seafood and creative treatments of vegetables highlight the menu. Lunch and dinner are served Monday through Saturday at this Morrisville restaurant.

JAPANESE

Kanki Japanese House of Steaks
$$ • Crabtree Valley Mall, Raleigh
• 782-9708
$$ • 4500 Old Wake Forest Rd., North Market Square, Raleigh • 876-4157
• www.kanki.com
It may not be traditional "live entertainment," but the chefs put on quite a show. The menu features beef, pork and seafood, and the dishes are all prepared tableside with great flair. A Sushi Bar is available at both locations. Kanki has all ABC permits and is open for lunch and dinner daily.

Kurama Japanese Seafood & Steak House & Sushi Bar
$$ • 3644 Durham-Chapel Hill Blvd. Durham • 489-2669
Meals are prepared with a flash of a knife right before your eyes at Kurama (formerly known as Kyoto), which also features a sushi bar. This Durham restaurant is open for dinner nightly.

Sushi Blues Cafe
$$$-$$$$ • 301 Glenwood Ave.,
Raleigh • 664-8061
• www.sushibluescafe.com
Sushi Blues combines eclectic Japanese entrees with an American influence in an atmosphere of blues and jazz music. For instance, the menu includes such delicacies as the New Orleans Temaki and the B.B.

King Crab Roll. The Cafe in Raleigh is open for lunch Monday through Friday and for dinner nightly. Reservations are not accepted.

Tokyo House
$$-$$$$ • Crescent Commons, Cary
• 816-9595
$$-$$$$ • 7439 Six Forks Rd., Raleigh
• 848-3350

In addition to traditional offerings, Tokyo House serves eclectic dishes that include Tempura-Battered Oysters and Stir-Fried Giant Clams. Both locations have sushi bars and are open for lunch and dinner Monday through Saturday. Private party rooms are also available.

Yamazushi
$$ • Woodcroft Shopping Ctr., Durham
• 493-7748

Enjoy sushi, as well as Japanese cuisine such as seafood teriyaki, shrimp tempura and stir-fried vegetable dishes at Yamazushi in Durham. Yamazushi serves lunch Tuesday through Friday and dinner Tuesday through Sunday.

KOREAN

Korean Garden
$$$ • 748 E. Chatham St., Cary • 388-3615

Located in Cary's Chatham Square Shopping Center, Korean Garden offers authentic Korean and Chinese cuisine. Popular Korean beef barbecue dishes include Kal Bee, Bul Go Ki and Prime Short Rib in Sweet Barbecue Sauce. It is open for lunch Monday through Saturday and for dinner nightly.

LATIN AMERICAN

Blue Corn Cafe
$-$$ • 716-B Ninth St., Durham • 286-9600

Blue Corn serves authentic Latin American cuisine in a laid-back atmosphere.

Vegetarian and healthy entrees are also available. It is located on bustling Ninth Street near Duke's East Campus. Lunch and dinner are served Monday through Saturday.

MEDITERRANEAN

Cafe Parizade
$$$ • 2200 W. Main St., Durham • 286-9712
• www.parizade.citysearch.com

Seasonal Mediterranean cuisine is served in a contemporary setting at Parizade. There is an extensive wine list and Cafe Parizade has all ABC permits. This Durham cafe is open for lunch Monday through Friday and for dinner nightly.

George's Garage
$$$-$$$$ • 737 Ninth St., Durham
• 286-4131 • www.georgesgarage.com

George's Garage has some unusual big-city features, including a casual dining atmosphere with an upscale menu offering many seafood entrees; a fun, late-night bar; and a takeout market and bakery. Breakfast and lunch at this Durham restaurant are self-serve from a hot and cold buffet. It is open seven days a week for breakfast, lunch and dinner. George's is also a popular night club.

Neomonde Bakery and Deli
$ • 3817 Beryl Road, Raleigh • 828-1628
• www.neomonde.com

Since 1977, Neomonde in Raleigh has served authentic Middle Eastern and Mediterranean cuisine such as Hummus, Tabouli, Kibbeh, Falafel, Shawarma and Baba Ghanouj. Patio dining is available. It is open for lunch and dinner daily.

Saladelia Cafe
$ • 4201 University Dr., Durham
• 489-5776 • www.saladelia.com

Saladelia is a unique Greek and Lebanese cafe that offers specialties such as

INSIDERS' TIP
Looking for an outdoor dining experience? Check out Coyote Cafe and Serendipity in Cary; Pyewacket, Top of the Hill and The Weathervane Cafe in Chapel Hill; Devine's and Fowler's in Durham; and Greenshield's and Lilly's Pizza in Raleigh, among others.

Hummus, Tabbouleh and Falafel pockets, along with salads, soups and quiche. Catering is also available. Lunch and dinner are served daily at this Durham cafe.

MEXICAN

Bandido's Mexican Cafe
$-$$ • 159 1/2 East Franklin St., Chapel Hill • 967-5048
$-$$ • Woodcroft Shopping Ctr., Durham • 403-6285
$-$$ • 122 S. Churton St., Hillsborough • 732-8662

The original Bandido's in Chapel Hill proved to be so popular that owners Tony and Maria Sustaita opened a second in Durham and a third in Hillsborough. These restaurants all offer standard Mexican fare in addition to a variety of vegetarian and low-fat dishes. Bandido's is open for lunch Monday through Friday and for dinner nightly, except for the Hillsborough location, which is closed Sundays.

Carrburritos Taqueria
$-$$ • 711 W. Rosemary St., Carrboro • 933-8226

This popular spot in Carrboro features tacos, tostadas, burritos and quesadillas with a variety of meat and vegetarian fillings. Top them off with distinctive salsas and the best guacamole in town. All menu items are available to go. Carrburritos is open for lunch and dinner Monday through Saturday.

The Cosmic Cantina
$$ • 128 E. Franklin St., Chapel Hill • 960-3955
$$ • 1920 Perry St., Durham • 286-1875
• www.cosmiccantina.com

Durham's first burrito bar was so successful that a second site opened up in Chapel Hill. Cosmic Cantina features mostly organic and all natural Mexi-Cali food. The food is made fresh daily and low-fat items are available. Fresh fruit smoothies, margaritas and a large variety of Mexican and microbrewery beers are available. Eat in or take out. Cosmic Cantina is open daily for lunch and dinner. It has all ABC permits.

Dos Taquitos
$-$$ • 5629 Creedmoor Rd., Raleigh
• 787-3373 • www.dostaquitos.com

Located in Creedmoor Crossings Shopping Center, this colorfully decorated eatery offers the usual taco, burrito and enchilada entrees, as well as eclectic fare such as Pescado Maya and Mexican Beef Stew. Wash it all down with a "Monster Margarita." An outdoor patio is available. It is open Monday through Saturday for dinner.

El Dorado
$ • 990 High House Rd., Cary • 461-4900
$ • Wellington Park Shopping Ctr., Cary • 859-9334
$ • 1404 E. Franklin St., Chapel Hill • 929-6566
$ • 4900 Hwy. 55, Durham/RTP • 361-0302
$ • 2811 Brentwood Rd., Raleigh • 872-8440
$ • 8111 Creedmoor Rd., Raleigh • 848-0788

El Dorado is a local Triangle restaurant chain that offers a true Mexican experience. Delicious fajitas, burritos, tacos, enchiladas, vegetarian selections and Corona beer are served. Each site is open for lunch and dinner daily.

El Rodeo
$ • 1404 E. Franklin St., Chapel Hill • 929-6566
$ • Brightleaf Sq., Durham • 683-2417
$ • 4215 University Dr., Durham • 402-9190
$ • 4112 Pleasant Valley Rd., Raleigh • 571-1188
$ • 2400 Hillsborough St., Raleigh • 755-9697
$ • 2402 Wake Forest Rd., Raleigh • 833-1460
$ • 329 S. Blount St., Raleigh • 829-0777

El Rodeo is another authentic Mexican restaurant chain in the Triangle. Vegetarian dishes and traditional Mexican foods such as enchiladas, tacos, burritos and quesadillas can all be found on the menu. Each site is open daily for lunch and dinner.

Enjoy tasty Southwestern fare at Margaret's Cantina in Chapel Hill.

Flying Burrito
$-$$ • Town and Country Shopping Ctr., 746 Airport Rd., Chapel Hill • 967-7744 • No Credit Cards

Some of the finest Mexican/Southwestern cuisine in the area, with the best smothered burritos and the hottest burrito in North Carolina (the Ultimate Raging Bull), and fresh seafood specialties await you at the Flying Burrito in Chapel Hill. The restaurant is open for lunch Monday through Friday and dinner nightly. It has all ABC permits. Outdoor patio seating is available.

Margaret's Cantina
$-$$ • Timberlyne Shopping Ctr., Chapel Hill • 942-4745 • www.margaretscantina.com

This artfully decorated Southwestern cuisine cafe in Chapel Hill dishes up unique and tasty dishes with a Mexican flavor. Check out the impressive imported beer selection and the scrumptious desserts. Margaret's is open for lunch and dinner Monday through Saturday.

Taqueria La Zacatecana
$ • 805 W. Peace St., Raleigh • 821-7642

For tasty, cheap and authentic Mexican cuisine, check out this downtown Raleigh eatery. The menu includes tacos (made with soft corn tortillas), enchiladas, burritos, tamales and tortas. It is open daily for breakfast, lunch and dinner.

Tippy's
$ • 808 W. Hodges St., Raleigh • 828-0797

Tippy's was the first Mexican restaurant to open in Raleigh in 1968. To veterans, it's still Tippy's Taco Hut. The restaurant is bigger and fancier with bullfight scenes on the wall, but the refried beans, chili, tacos and hot enchiladas are as good as when it was a taco hut. It is open for lunch Monday through Friday and dinner Monday through Saturday.

Torero's
$-$$ • 1207 Kildaire Farm Rd., Cary • 468-8711
$-$$ • 800 W. Main St., Durham • 682-4197
$-$$ • 3808 Guess Rd., Durham • 477-3939
$-$$ • 4125 Chapel Hill Blvd., Durham • 489-6468

Torero's serves authentic Mexican food in a relaxed atmosphere. The menu offers a wide array of freshly made tacos, enchiladas, burritos and sizzling fajitas. A variety of Mexican beer is available and the margaritas are enormous. Each site is open daily for lunch and dinner.

The Wicked Burrito
$ • 214 W. Franklin St., Chapel Hill
• 967-8899

Popular with UNC-CH students and faculty alike, The Wicked Burrito is housed in the most colorful building on Franklin Street. It offers standard Mexican fare, along with an extensive salsa bar. The outdoor patio is always crowded. It is open for lunch and dinner daily.

PIZZA

Brothers Pizza Restaurant
$ • Kildaire Farm Rd., Cary • 481-0883
$ • 2508 Hillsborough St., Raleigh
• 832-3664

A family-owned, friendly neighborhood restaurant, Brothers serves homemade, hand-tossed pizzeria-style pizza and other hearty Italian dishes. The Raleigh location is open for lunch and dinner daily. The Cary location is open for lunch Monday through Saturday and for dinner seven nights a week.

CiCi's Pizza
$ • Cary Village Square, Cary
• 469-9988
$ • Oak Creek Village, Durham
• 403-2424
• www.cicispizza.com

One of the best meal deals in the Triangle, CiCi's features a $2.99 all-you-can-eat pizza buffet. Both locations are open for lunch and dinner seven days a week. Video games are available for the kids.

Italian Pizzeria
$ • 508 W. Franklin St., Chapel Hill
• 968-4671 • No Checks

This is an honest-to-goodness, no frills, family-owned New York-style pizza joint in Chapel Hill. If you are particularly fond of deep-dish Sicilian pizza, you can't go wrong. You can get freshly made slices with exactly the toppings you want.

This pizzeria also has Greek salads and great hot sandwiches like the Italian sausage and cheese on a submarine roll. The Italian Pizzeria is open daily for lunch and dinner.

J.S. New York Pizza
$ • 540 E. Williams St., Apex
• 363-0071

The owners of this popular pizza restaurant operated Silvio in Brooklyn before moving to Apex in 1995. J.S. offers delicious pizzas, pasta, calzones, hot and cold subs and salads. It is open seven days a week.

Lilly's Pizza
$ • 1813 Glenwood Ave., Raleigh
• 833-0226

Lilly's is a gourmet pizzeria in Raleigh's Five Points area on Glenwood Avenue and it's one of the hip places to go. The pizzas are as unconventional as the crowd who will sit at the sidewalk tables outside in 30-degree weather, eating and talking. The pizza is among the best in town. Lilly's is open for lunch and dinner daily.

The Loop
$ • Eastgate Shopping Center,
Chapel Hill • 969-7112
$ • 1207 Kildaire Farm Rd., Cary
• 657-0330

Although the Loop specializes in California- and Chicago-style pizza, diners can also enjoy fabulous burgers, sandwiches, hot dogs, soups and salads. It is open for lunch and dinner daily.

Pepper's Pizza
$ • 127 E. Franklin St., Chapel Hill
• 967-7766

You haven't been to Chapel Hill without a visit to Pepper's. A favorite among students, Pepper's offers some of the best pizza and Italian dishes around. It's also one of the best places in town to people-watch. Pepper's is open for lunch and dinner daily.

PieWorks
$$ • 201 Colonnades Way, Cary
• 233-8008

PieWorks in Cary's Waverly Place Shopping Center is a popular contemporary pizza restaurant that allows customers to design their own pizzas or order from the extensive menu of unusual pizzas. It is open daily for lunch and dinner.

Satisfaction

$ • Brightleaf Square, Durham • 682-7397

Located in Brightleaf Square, this restaurant is a favorite among Duke students. Gourmet pizza, sandwiches and salads are featured as well as an extensive selection of beer. There are three wide-screen TVs so the place is packed during Duke sporting events. It is open Monday through Saturday for lunch and dinner.

Vincent's

$ • 1305 Kildaire Farm Rd., Cary • 461-3799

$ • 3911 Capital Blvd., Raleigh • 876-6700

• www.vincents.citysearch.com

Established in 1990, Vincent's specializes in authentic New York-style pizza with a variety of toppings, as well as calzones, stromboli, pizza rolls, homemade pasta dishes, hot and cold subs, salads and desserts. The stuffed pizza is also popular. Both locations are open for lunch and dinner daily.

FYI

Unless otherwise noted, the area code for all phone numbers listed in this guide is 919.

PRIVATE DINING

Capital City Club

$$$-$$$$ • 411 Fayetteville St. Mall, Raleigh • 832-5526

Associated with Club Corporation of America, this is the Triangle's original private dining club. Located in downtown Raleigh at the top of the CP&L Building, the club offers an American menu served with a distinctive touch of class.

The Cardinal Club

$$$-$$$$ • 150 Fayetteville St. Mall, Ste. 2800, Raleigh • 834-8829

• www.cardinal-club.com

A luxurious dining club on the top two floors of the First Union Capitol Center, The Cardinal Club provides a breathtaking view of Raleigh and an elegant atmosphere for its members. It is also associated with Club Corporation of America. Members and their guests can enjoy superior cuisine, vintage

Photo by Rich Weidman

The outdoor patio at The Wicked Burrito on West Franklin Street is a favorite gathering spot among UNC-CH students.

Staff Photo

Located in Cary's MacGregor Village, the Fox & Hound serves authentic pub fare.

wines and reciprocal privileges with private clubs worldwide.

The Carolina Club
$$$-$$$$ • George Watts Hill Alumni Ctr. Stadium Dr. at Ridge Rd., Chapel Hill • 962-1101 • CarolinaClub.unc.edu

Established in 1993, The Carolina Club in Chapel Hill offers a haven where members may relax, socialize, entertain or conduct business and academic exchange in a comfortable atmosphere. The Club contains nearly 64,000 square feet of dining and meeting rooms, parlors, offices and a library. Although, membership in the Club is available only to members of the General Alumni Association, GAA membership is open to all alumni, faculty, staff and friends of UNC-CH. Non-alumni are welcome to join.

Prestonwood Country Club
$$$-$$$$ • 300 Prestonwood Pkwy., Cary • 467-2566

The service, atmosphere and cuisine are unequaled in Cary. Special dining events are planned monthly.

The University Club
$$$-$$$$ • 3100 Tower Blvd., Durham • 493-8099

Located on the top floor of University Tower in Durham, this club provides a lounge, a dining room and many private rooms for conducting business while enjoying a meal. Members have reciprocal privileges at more

than 150 clubs across the country, including the Cardinal Club in Raleigh.

PUBS & TAVERNS

Carolina Brewery
$$ • 460 W. Franklin St., Chapel Hill • 942-1800 • www.carolinabrewery.com

Chapel Hill's first microbrewery is also a fine place to dine for lunch or dinner. Try the Jambalaya Pasta, Brewerhouse Ribs, the Hickory Smoked Chicken Pasta or the Fish and Chips. A surprising number of desserts are made with beer brewed on the premises! You may be tempted by the Stout Cheesecake to complete your meal. This attractively decorated restaurant has all ABC permits. It is open for lunch and dinner daily. Enjoy live blues every Thursday night.

The Fox and Hound
$$-$$$ • MacGregor Village, Cary • 380-0080 • www.foxandhound.citysearch.com

The Fox and Hound in Cary is full of John Bull's favorites: Roast Beef with Yorkshire Pudding, Shepherd's Pie, Beefsteak and Kidney Pie, Roasted Lamb Chops, and Fish and Chips. Diners can also choose from a variety of creative entrees such as Spiced Venison, Blackened Mahi Mahi, Salmon Bombay and Pecan-Crusted Catfish. Cheerio! This is a bully handsome pub. It is open for lunch Monday through Saturday and dinner nightly.

Greenshield's Brewery & Pub
$$-$$$ • City Market, Raleigh • 829-0214
• www.greenshields.com

For the best beer in town, Raleigh's original brewpub is the place. Greenshield's brews its own and has light and dark varieties. The centerpiece restaurant in the old City Market building, Greenshield's has earned a following among the Anglophiles of the Triangle. The location is superb and the fare reasonably priced. Enjoy pub fare such as fish and chips and shepherd's pie, as well as steaks, seafood and sandwiches. It is open for lunch and dinner daily. Live music can be heard on weekends.

Players Retreat
$ • 105 Oberlin Rd., Raleigh • 755-9589

Opened in 1951, Players Retreat (known to regulars as the PR), is the Triangle's oldest tavern. A friendly, unassuming gathering place, the PR is a favorite among locals and NCSU students alike. The menu includes sandwiches, burgers and pizzas. Pool tables, dart boards and video games are available. The PR is open Monday through Saturday for lunch and dinner.

RiRa
$-$$ • 126 N. West St., Raleigh
• 833-5535 • www.rira.com

RiRa means a place "where exuberance and revelry prevail," according to the owners of this bustling Raleigh pub that features traditional and eclectic Irish fare. Its wooden bars were actually shipped from Ireland. RiRa is open for lunch and dinner daily. Outdoor patio seating is available.

Southend Brewery & Smokehouse
$$-$$$$ • 505 W. Jones St., Raleigh
• 832-4604

Housed in a renovated warehouse in downtown Raleigh, Southend Brewery offers a good selection of house-brewed drafts such as Carolina Blonde and Chocolate Ale. The menu includes such entrees as smoked chicken, baby back ribs and pasta dishes, as well as pizza cooked in a wood-burning oven.

It is open for lunch and dinner daily. The adjoining Powerhouse Lounge has a dance floor.

Tir na nOg
218 S. Blount St., Raleigh • 833-7795
• www.tirnanogirishpub.com

A popular Irish pub located off Raleigh's Moore Square, Tir na nOg serves authentic cuisine in a lively atmosphere. Enjoy live music most nights of the week. It is open for lunch Monday through Saturday, dinner nightly and brunch on Sunday.

W.B. Yeats
$$ • 306-G W. Franklin St., Chapel Hill
• 960-8335

W.B. Yeats pub, named after the famous 20th-century Irish poet, offers Irish and American pub fare such as Irish Pot Pie, Fish and Chips, Shepherd's Pie, Curried Chicken Breast, tuna melt, chicken sandwiches and burgers. The walls and tables are full of sayings and quotes from the author. This Chapel Hill pub is open for lunch and dinner daily.

SEAFOOD

42nd Street Oyster Bar
$$$-$$$$ • 508 W. Jones St., Raleigh
• 831-2811

The grilled swordfish and tuna are as good as you will get anywhere and the shrimp salad is a meal by itself. The meat dishes rival the city's best and the menu has Cajun specials and children's portions. It's also a great late night place to be seen and meet people. 42nd Street Oyster Bar in Raleigh is open for lunch Monday through Friday and for dinner nightly, and has all ABC permits.

Blue Marlin
$$$-$$$$ • 111 Shannon Oaks Cir.,
Cary • 469-3322
• www.bluemarlinfood.com

One of Cary's newest upscale eateries, Blue Marlin boasts Lowcountry cuisine, including She-Crab Soup, Pan-Fried Carolina Crab Cakes, Blue Marlin Oscar, Soft-Shell Crabs, Shrimp and Grits and Barbecued Jumbo Shrimp. Fresh fish arrives daily such

Photo by Rich Weidman

A unique pig sculpture beckons diners to Crook's Corner, which specializes in authentic Southern cuisine.

as mahi-mahi, catfish and tuna. Enjoy home-made desserts (you can't go wrong with the key lime pie). Dinner is served nightly and there is also a Sunday brunch.

Cappers
$$$-$$$$ • 4421 Six Forks Rd., Raleigh • 787-8963

Cappers is located across from North Hills Mall and is a popular lunch stop for North Raleigh business people. Diners will find an excellent selection of seafood, and it's one of the best places in the city for those who like live jazz with their food. Cappers has all ABC permits. It is open for lunch Monday through Friday and for dinner Monday through Saturday.

Captain Stanley's Seafood
$-$$ • 3333 S. Wilmington St., Raleigh • 779-7878

If you're willing to wait in line, this is the place for inexpensive seafood. Calabash seafood, named for a North Carolina coastal town, is dipped in batter and then deep fried. Lunch at this Raleigh restaurant is served Tuesday through Friday and dinner is served Tuesday through Saturday.

Fins
$$$-$$$$ • 7713-39 Leadmine Rd., Raleigh • 847-4119

Owner and chef William D'Auvray offers quintessential fusion cuisine, specializing in seafood with Californian and Asian flavors in a casual atmosphere. The menu, which changes bimonthly, features such entrees as Chilean Sea Bass and Sea Scallops, as well as some non-seafood items. Reservations are recommended on the weekends. Located in Raleigh's Greystone Village, Fins is open for dinner Monday through Saturday.

Fishmonger's Restaurant and Oyster Bar
$$-$$$ • 806 W. Main St., Durham • 682-0128 • www.fishmongers.net

Once primarily a fresh seafood market, Fishmonger's in Durham now serves lunch offering seafood salads, fish sandwiches and chowders, and dinner, featuring fresh steamed crabs, oysters, shrimp and lobster; broiled fish in season; and daily specials. Beer and wine are available. It's open for lunch Tuesday through Sunday and dinner nightly and is the closest you can get to the beach without leaving home.

Ocean Emmy's
$$-$$$$ • 2505 Chapel Hill Blvd., Durham • 419-1232 • www.oceanemmys.citysearch.com

Ocean Emmy's in Durham specializes in Chesapeake Bay style seafood in a casual setting. Fresh fish is brought in daily and the restaurant also boasts an oyster bar. Ocean Emmy's is open for lunch Tuesday through Friday, dinner Tuesday through Sunday and brunch on Sunday. It has all ABC permits.

Squid's Restaurant, Market & Oyster Bar
$$-$$$ • 1201 N. Fordham Blvd., U.S. 15-501 Bypass, Chapel Hill • 942-8757 • www.squidschapelhill.com

Squid's in Chapel Hill offers freshly shucked oysters, peel-your-own shrimp, and littleneck clams. A main menu of fresh seafood features specialties such as Honey Grilled Scallops and Blackened Tuna

Burritos. You'll also find steak, lobster, salads and chowder on the menu, and a variety of special desserts. Squid's also has a seafood market and oyster bar. It is open for dinner nightly and has all ABC permits.

Tony's Bourbon Street Oyster Bar
$$$-$$$$ • MacGregor Village, Cary • 462-6226 • www.tonysbourbonstreet.com

Tony's oyster bar in Cary features crawfish, oysters, clams, mussels and shrimp. It also offers fresh seafood, Cajun-style entrees, steaks, pasta and chicken—all in a Mardi Gras atmosphere. Live entertainment is available Friday and Saturday nights. Tony's is open for dinner nightly.

SOUTHERN CUISINE

Carolina Crossroads
$$$-$$$$ • 211 Pittsboro St., Chapel Hill • 918-2777 • www.carolinainn.com

Carolina Crossroads is an elegant restaurant located in the Carolina Inn in Chapel Hill. Chef Brian Stapleton dishes up innovative Southern-style cuisine with an Italian influence. The seasonal menu offers specialties like Catfish Encrusted in Smoked Pecans, Grilled Georgia Quail, Cherry-Wood Smoked Beef Tenderloin and Oven-Roasted Red Snapper Jambalaya. Save some room for the homemade desserts. Breakfast, lunch and dinner are served every day. A Sunday brunch is served from 11 AM to 2 PM. Reservations are recommended. Limited courtyard seating is available.

Crook's Corner
$$$ • 610 W. Franklin St., Chapel Hill • 929-7643 • www.crookscorner.citysearch.com

It is safe to say that there is no restaurant like Crook's anywhere else in the Triangle. The first thing you notice is the pig on the roof, the work of sculptor Bob Gaston, surrounded by a herd of wooden animal figures, made by Chatham County folk artist Clyde Jones. A changing menu features a wide choice of seasonal entrees along with ethnically and regionally authentic dishes such as Shrimp and Grits, Hoppin' John and Vegetarian Jambalaya. Dinner is served nightly and brunch is served on Sunday. Reservations are accepted but not required. Crook's has all ABC permits.

Glenwood Grill
$$$ • 2929 Essex Cr., Glenwood Village Shopping Ctr., Raleigh • 782-3102

Glenwood Grill in Raleigh has a flair for presentation and an innovative new Southern cuisine menu. Specialities range from Pan Seared Chicken Breast to prime filets and Shrimp and Grits. Glenwood Grill is open for lunch Monday through Friday and for dinner nightly. The Grill has all ABC permits.

SOUTHWESTERN

Cactus Flower
$$-$$$ • 5300 Edwards Mill Rd., Raleigh • 789-0125

Located behind Crabtree Valley Mall in Raleigh, Cactus Flower features specialties such as Red Chile Chicken Enchiladas, Southwestern wraps, and seafood, steaks and pasta dishes. It is open for lunch and dinner Monday through Saturday and brunch on Sunday.

Coyote Cafe
$$ • Cary Village Square, Cary • 469-5253 • www.coyotecafe.citysearch.com

Coyote Cafe in Cary offers such specialties as Pechuga Rellenos, Southwest Chicken Pasta and chimichangas, salads, and white bean chili. Popular with the business bunch, Coyote Cafe is open Tuesday through Friday for lunch and seven nights a week for dinner. Weather permitting, the Coyote Cafe presents live acoustic music on its 3,500-square-foot patio Friday and Saturday.

Newton's Southwest Restaurant & Bar
$$-$$$ • 1837 N. Harrison Ave., Cary • 677-1777

This Cary restaurant is hot off the Texas grill. Certified Angus steaks, barbecued beef ribs, brisket, chili and fresh fish are some of its specialties. The restaurant caters to groups. It has all ABC permits and a bar called The Trophy Room. Newton's is open Monday through Saturday for lunch and dinner. Live beach music takes place every Thursday during the season.

SPORTS BAR

Blinco's Sports Restaurant
$$ • 5009 Falls of Neuse Rd., Raleigh
• 790-3882 • blincossportsbar.com

Fourteen separate satellite feeds and more than 20 TVs make this a sports enthusiast's place to be in Raleigh. It serves terrific wings, pasta dishes, steaks and seafood. Blinco's has all ABC permits and is open for lunch and dinner daily.

Damon's Clubhouse
$$ • 3019 Auto Dr., Durham • 493-2574

Four 100-inch TV screens allow sport lovers in Durham to eat delicious food and enjoy their favorite game at the same time. Try Damon's signature ribs, as well as sandwiches, burgers and pasta dishes. Lunch and dinner are served every day.

Devine's Restaurant & Sports Bar
$ • 904 West Main St., Durham • 682-0228
• www.devinesrestaurant.com

Open since 1978, Devine's is a favorite among Duke students. Relax and enjoy great food and company inside or out on the patio seven days a week for lunch, dinner or late night. The menu includes burgers, sandwiches, spicy wings, appetizers and salads.

Raleigh Ale House
$-$$ • 512 Creekside Dr., Raleigh
• 835-2222
• www.raleighalehouse.citysearch.com

The Raleigh Ale House serves great food in a lively atmosphere full of wide-screen TVs, pool tables and video games. Choose from steaks, ribs, seafood, pizza, pasta dishes, burgers, sandwiches and salads, as well as a wide assortment of domestic, imported and microbrews on tap. It is open daily for lunch and dinner.

Scores Sports Bar & Grill
$ • 3050 Wake Forest Rd., Raleigh
• 876-8143

Located in Raleigh's Holly Park Shopping Center and connected to Sam's Steakhouse, Scores boasts about 30 TVs and eight separate satellite feeds. The menu includes burgers, sandwiches, salads and chicken wings. It is open daily for lunch and dinner.

Upper Deck Sports Pub
$ • 329 N. Harrison Ave., Cary • 460-9977
$ • 2235 Avent Ferry Rd., Raleigh
• 755-3880
$ • 625 E. Whitaker Mill, Rd., Raleigh
• 833-4527

No matter what the sport, you can find it televised at any Upper Deck location, with a variety of appetizers and sandwiches served on the side. All three sports pubs are popular with many of the area's fan clubs, and are open for lunch and dinner seven days a week.

Woody's Sports Tavern & Grill
$ • 8322 Chapel Hill Rd., Cary
• 380-7737
Woody's Tar Heel Tavern
$ • E. Franklin St., Chapel Hill
• 968-3809

At Woody's, you can enjoy good food and friends while you watch your favorite game on state-of-the-art TV screens. Both locations are open for lunch, dinner and late night daily.

STEAK HOUSE

Angus Barn
$$$$ • 9401 Glenwood Ave., Raleigh
• 781-3505 • www.angusbarn.com

Angus Barn is "THE" steak house in Raleigh and has been for more than 40 years. Located near the airport, it has always been popular with business travelers. The dining room is decorated in classic Americana with antiques, quilts, farm equipment, artwork and even a gun collection. Popular specialties include steak, prime rib, filet mignon and lobster. For the ultimate culinary experience, groups can reserve the wine cellar dining room, surrounded by nearly 35,000 bottles of wine. After dinner, enjoy a drink in the Wild

Turkey Lounge. Open seven nights a week for dinner, Angus Barn has all ABC permits. Reservations are recommended but no reservations are accepted on Saturday.

Capital City Chop House
$$$$ • 151 Airgate Dr., Morrisville
• 484-7721
• www.chophouserestaurants.com

Located in Morrisville just off I-40 at the Airport Boulevard exit, this Chicago-style steakhouse serves certified Angus beef, as well as fresh seafood, veal, lamp and pork entrees. Lunch and dinner are served Monday through Saturday. Reservations are recommended. Private banquet rooms are available for groups up to 60.

The Farm House
$$-$$$ • N.C. 86, Chapel Hill
• 929-5727

Set off the beaten path between Chapel Hill and Hillsborough, The Farm House is a welcome discovery for newcomers and long-time residents alike. Enjoy superb steaks, seafood and chicken entrees at this rustic eatery. Don't miss an opportunity to sample the homemade cheesecake or apple pie for dessert. The Farm House is open for dinner Wednesday through Saturday.

Hartman's Steak House
$$-$$$ • 1703 E. Geer St., Durham
• 688-7639

Hartman's opened in 1940 in Durham and was operated by the same family until 1998. The new owners have not made any major changes, although they did convert one of the rooms into a bar, the Bull City Tavern. Hartman's serves grain-fed beef and fine seafood. Prime Rib is a specialty Tuesday through Thursday. It is open for dinner Tuesday through Saturday. You can even get a table with a view of the backyard lake. Private dining rooms are available. It has all ABC permits.

It's Prime Only
$$$-$$$$ • 1742 N. Fordham Blvd.
at 15/501, Chapel Hill • 929-1518
$$$-$$$$ • 5509 Homewood Banks Dr.,
Raleigh • 420-0224

It's Prime Only serves filet mignon, New York strip and prime rib. Hearty appetites might opt for the 24-ounce porterhouse. The menu also includes grilled seafood, chicken and pasta dishes. Overlooking Crabtree Valley, the Raleigh location offers a panoramic view. At the Chapel Hill location, formerly known as The Prime Exchange, you can dine in the smoke-free dining room or relax in the

Photo by Rich Weidman

Angus Barn is the most popular steakhouse in the Triangle.

smoke-friendly lounge. It's Prime Only has all ABC permits and is open for dinner Monday through Saturday.

J. Gilbert's Wood-Fired Grill
$$$-$$$$ • 6464 Tryon Rd., Cary
• 852-2300

J. Gilbert's specializes in fresh, certified Angus steaks and also features pasta and seafood such as Herbed Marinated Swordfish, Caribbean Mahi Mahi, Sauteed Crab Cakes and Grilled Barbecue Salmon. Located in Cary's Wellington Park Shopping Center, the restaurant is open seven days a week and has all ABC permits.

Jimmy V's Steakhouse & Tavern
$$$-$$$$ • MacGregor Village, Cary
• 380-8210

Catering to business clientele, this Cary steakhouse serves certified Angus beef, prime rib, fresh seafood, Southern Italian specialties and homemade desserts. Dinner is served Monday through Saturday.

Outback Steakhouse
$$-$$$ • 1289 Kildaire Farm Rd., Cary
• 460-1770
$$-$$$ • 3500 Mount Moriah Rd., Durham
• 493-2202
$$-$$$ • 7500 Creedmoor Rd., Raleigh
• 846-3848
• www.outbacksteakhouse.com

The Outback is one of the most popular chains in the Triangle. Try its "blooming onion." The Outback is open for dinner nightly and has all ABC permits.

The Peddler Steak House
$$$ • 6005 Glenwood Ave., Raleigh
• 787-6980

Small, candlelit and cozy, The Peddler Steak House opened in 1969 in Raleigh's Oak Park Shopping Center on Glenwood Avenue. If you're a steak lover, you can choose your cut of meat right at your table. Lobster, seafood and chicken are other entrees. The restaurant is open for dinner Monday through Saturday and has two private dining rooms available for meetings.

Ruth's Chris Steak House
$$$$ • 1130 Buck Jones Rd., Cary
• 468-1133 • www.ruthschris.com

Known as the "home of serious steaks," Ruth's Chris is an upscale chain that specializes in custom-aged, corn-fed U.S. Prime beef. Banquet facilities at the Cary location are available for up to 200 people. Dinner is served nightly.

Simpson's Beef and Seafood
$$-$$$ • 5625 Creedmoor Rd., Raleigh
• 783-8818
• www.simpsonsrestaurant.com

Simpson's serves some of the best steaks and prime rib in the Triangle. The diverse menu also includes chicken and seafood dishes such as Lemon Chicken Fettucine and Chargrilled Salmon. Simpson's has live piano music during the week and jazz on the weekends. The delightful Raleigh restaurant is open for dinner nightly and has all ABC permits. Reservations are suggested. Banquet facilities are available.

Sullivan's Steakhouse
$$$$ • 414 Glenwood Ave., Raleigh
• 833-2888

Sullivan's in Raleigh is an upscale steakhouse named for the last bare-knuckle boxing champ, John L. Sullivan. Choose from the 20-ounce Kansas City strip, the 24-ounce porterhouse, the filet mignon or the New York strip. Seafood dishes are also available such as the salmon steak and the tequila-lime shrimp. Sullivan's is open for dinner Monday through Saturday. Live jazz can be heard Wednesday through Saturday nights. It boasts an extensive wine list and has all ABC permits. Reservations are strongly suggested.

Swain's Charcoal Steak House
$$$$ • 3201 New Bern Ave., Raleigh
• 231-6873

Swain's specializes in certified black Angus beef in an elegant atmosphere. The menu at this Raleigh restaurant includes seafood, chicken and pasta dishes. Enjoy piano music Tuesday through Saturday. Dinner is served nightly. Reservations are recommended.

The elegant Willow Oak Tea Room in Smithfield is located in the historic 1910 Dupree House.

Vinnie's Steakhouse & Tavern
$$$$ • 7440 Six Forks Rd., Raleigh • 847-7319
$$$$ • 3210 Yonkers Rd., Raleigh (adjacent to Thee Dollhouse) • 231-9030

Vinnie's has a loyal following for its pleasant atmosphere and well-prepared food. It features Italian specialties but grills some of the best steaks and chops in town. Watch out for the legislators when they're in town; it's a lobbyist's favorite. It is open nightly and has all ABC permits.

TEA ROOM

Gold Leaf Tea Room
$-$$ • 105 S. Main St., Fuquay-Varina • 567-9561

The Gold Leaf Tea Room in Fuquay-Varina provides delightful elegance in a hometown atmosphere. The menu includes sandwiches, soups and salads. The Tea Room is open for lunch Tuesday through Saturday and brunch on Sunday. Catering services are available.

Olde English Tea Room
$-$$ • 219 S. White St., Wake Forest • 556-6910

Step back in time at the Olde English Tea Room, which is located in Wake Forest's historic district. The Tea Room is open Monday through Saturday and serves sandwiches, salads, soups and homemade desserts.

Silk Road Tea House
$-$$ • 456 W. Franklin St., Chapel Hill • 942-1533

Located in downtown Chapel Hill and decorated with tapestries, Silk Road specializes in Middle Eastern vegetarian cuisine to accompany its list of more than 80 teas. It is open Tuesday through Saturday.

The Willow Oak Tea Room
$-$$ • 709 S. Third St., Smithfield • 934-3350

The restored 1910 Dupree House in Smithfield is home to Willow Oak, which serves a variety of teas along with sandwiches, salads, soups and the quiche of the day. It is open Tuesday through Saturday. Willow Oak is also available for private functions.

TEX MEX

Armadillo Grill
$ • 120 E. Main St., Carrboro • 929-4669 • www.armadillogrill.com

For quick, tasty and economical Tex-Mex cuisine, check out the Armadillo Grill, located in downtown Carrboro across the street from Carr Mill Mall. Enchiladas, fajitas, Texas-style chili, chalupas and guacamole tacos are just a few of the offerings. Patio dining is available. It is open daily for lunch and dinner.

Chevy's Fresh Mex
$$-$$$ • 4512 Falls of Neuse Rd., Raleigh • 981-0080 • www.chevys.com

Chevy's in Raleigh offers huge platters of Mexican delights, all made from scratch. Enjoy Texas-sized fajitas and hand-rolled tamales. It is open daily for lunch and dinner.

THAI

The King & I
$$ • 926 N.E. Maynard Rd., Cary • 460-9265

Located in Cary's Reedy Creek Plaza, The King and I offers a varied selection of Thai cuisine. Enjoy spicy curry or more milder fare. Lunch is served Monday through Friday and dinner is served nightly.

Thai Garden
$$ • 1408 Hardimont Rd., Raleigh • 872-6811 • www.citysearch.com/rdu/thaigarden
Located off Wake Forest Road, Thai Garden is North Raleigh's finest Thai restaurant. Many vegetarian choices are available. It is open for lunch Monday through Friday and for dinner every night.

Thai Palace
$$ • N.C. 54 E., Glenwood Square, Chapel Hill • 967-5805 • www.thaipalace.citysearch.com
The Thai Palace in Chapel Hill serves authentic Thai food and offers many vegetarian dishes. It's a pleasant place for a good meal and is open for dinner nightly except Monday.

VIETNAMESE

Dalat Oriental Restaurant
$ • 2109 Avent Ferry Rd., Mission Valley Shopping Ctr., Raleigh • 832-7449
Dalat's tasty and economical fare is popular with NCSU students. The unfried vegetable Dalat roll, pork dishes and pasta salad are excellent. Dalat also serves authentic Vietnamese subs. Lunch and dinner are served Monday through Saturday.

Kim Son
$$-$$$ • 2425 Guess Rd., Durham • 416-9009
Experience "traditional, healthy and fresh" Vietnamese cuisine at this family-operated eatery in Durham. Kim Son is open for lunch and dinner Monday through Saturday.

Caterers

Caterers provide everything from picnics and pig pickin's to private parties, banquets and weddings. Many of the restaurants mentioned in these pages also cater.

The Catering Company
2 Mariakakis Plaza, U.S. 15-501 Bypass, Chapel Hill • 929-4775
One of Chapel Hill's most established caterers, this company offers imaginative and delicious cuisine for any occasion.

Catering Works
905-106 Tryon St., Raleigh • 828-5932 • www.cateringworks.citysearch.com
Catering Works is one of the most reliable caterers in the Triangle. It provides high-quality food for weddings, corporate functions and theme parties.

Chefs Unlimited
1818 St. Albans Dr., Ste. 104, Raleigh • 873-9500 • www.chefsunlimited.citysearch.com
Chefs Unlimited caters weddings, parties, corporate gatherings and also provides holiday meals.

Durham Catering Company
2514 University Dr., Durham • 489-9535
A joint venture between Nana's and Pop's restaurants, Durham Catering Company offers full-service catering, including corporate events, pig pickings, private parties, receptions and weddings.

Foster's Market & Catering Company
**750 Airport Rd., Chapel Hill • 967-3663
2694 C.H. Blvd., Durham • 489-3944 • www.fostersmarket.com**
The Market has become a popular source for everything from homegrown fresh vegetables to delicious dinners and desserts to go. It's also a good spot for lunch, a light snack, espresso or afternoon tea. On weekends, brunch is served. Foster's catering service offers creative cuisine for both private and corporate affairs.

Gregory's Grand Occasions
Waverly Place, Cary • 852-3694
Gregory's in Cary is available seven days a week for private parties or business functions. It specializes in wedding receptions and intimate rehearsal dinners.

Grill '57
4202 Fayetteville Rd., Raleigh • 779-5757

If you're looking for Beach Music and great hot dogs and hamburgers for your next corporate or special event, give Grill '57 a call.

The Ground Finale
1287 N.W. Maynard Rd., Cary • 460-4747
• www.thegroundfinale.com

The Ground Finale offers a complete line of corporate catering options, from sandwiches to entrees such as roast beef, grilled salmon, pork tenderloin and paella.

Horwitz's Delicatessen
MacGregor Village, Cary • 467-2007

Horwitz's is one of Cary's most reliable caterers. The same quality that makes Horwitz's one of the best deli's in the Triangle also holds true for its catering platters. This deli works with corporate customers as well as mothers-of-the-bride.

LadyFingers
627 E. Whitaker Mill Rd. • Northside
Shopping Ctr., Raleigh • 828-2270

LadyFingers has been catering since 1980 and has developed a large corporate following. Located in Raleigh's Northside Shopping Center, the storefront offers salads, sandwiches and oven-ready gourmet entrees to go, as well as full-service catering.

Marlin Events, Inc.
8320 Litchord Rd., Ste. 108, Raleigh
• 874-0370 • www.marlinevents.com

Marlin Events specializes in corporate events, weddings, cigar and wine dinners, and semiprivate and private parties.

Mitchell's Catering & Events
6633 Falls of Neuse Rd., Raleigh
• 847-0135

Mitchell's is big-time catering, featuring smoked fish, shrimp, roast pig, fowl and much more. It is known throughout the Triangle for its ice sculptures.

Sandi's Catering
817 Bradley Rd., Fuquay-Varina
• 552-8964

Whether it's a corporate event, wedding reception or theme party, Sandi's Catering offers full-service catering to make yours a memorable occasion.

Savory Fare
908 W. Main St., Durham • 683-2185

Savory Fare proprietor Gary Wein started at the top when he was a Duke University student and offered to cook for then-Duke-President Terry Sanford and his wife. The Sanfords encouraged him to start a catering business and Gary is still at it, offering everything from simple box lunches to cocktail buffets to elegant six-course dinners, for any number from 10 to 500.

Sisters' Catering Company
2400 E. Millbrook Rd., Raleigh
• 872-2100
3300 Woman's Club Dr., Raleigh
• 782-0985
• www.sisterscatering.com

Established in 1976, Sisters' Catering Company has become one of the largest privately owned catering companies in the state. Sisters' main facility is located on Millbrook Road and it is the exclusive caterer for The Woman's Club. Sisters' caters to the burgeoning North Carolina film industry and corporate events and is also a wedding reception specialist.

Tripodi's Catering
Terrace at Calvander, Chapel Hill
• 933-9407

Tripodi's offers full-service catering for weddings, luncheons, cocktail parties and corporate entertaining.

A new place to call home.

A comfortable assisted living residence opens its doors in Apex.

You'll find it in a quiet residential neighborhood here in Apex, situated on a tree-lined street. Spring Arbor is an easy place to live, just one floor, with no long hallways. Residents will warm to its friendly atmosphere, with a cozy country kitchen and a library complete with fireplace —where people gather to talk, or read, or just pass the time of day with friends. And our staff prides itself on its passion for friendly and attentive care. As our residents move in, we'd like to show you what made them choose Spring Arbor. Come by any time to find out about our special benefits for new residents. Or call ahead and set up an appointment. We'd like to make our house your new home.

Spring Arbor of Apex
901 Spring Arbor Court
Just west of Hwy 55 and
Olive Chapel Rd.

SPRING ARBOR
OF APEX

Contact Aimee Kepler at 303-9990.

CHOOSE A RETIREMENT COMMUNITY WHERE THE RESIDENTS ARE ANYTHING BUT RETIRING

Carol Woods residents have been making a difference all their lives. And they're not about to stop just because they've retired.

In fact, living at Carol Woods gives you even more time for the things that really matter. Such as tutoring a child or leading a seminar. Organizing a recycling program or preserving a wildlife habitat. Teaching a computer class or advising a local charity. Supporting the arts or creating art.

Carol Woods residents contribute to the vitality of Chapel Hill in hundreds of ways. And they make Carol Woods the special, stimulating place it is. In fact, they're a big reason why New Choices magazine, for six years in a row, named Carol Woods one of America's 20 best retirement communities.

Carol Woods is a place where you can spread your wings, try new things and truly make a difference.

To learn more or to schedule a visit, call us at 800-518-9333.

CAROL WOODS
RETIREMENT COMMUNITY

EQUAL HOUSING
OPPORTUNITY

750 Weaver Dairy Rd., Chapel Hill, NC 27514 • 1-800-518-9333
info@carolwoods.org
Carol Woods Is An Accredited, Not-For-Profit Community

Would You Like Your Parents To Be Closer To You?

Independence Village, North Carolina's best kept retirement secret, is a wonderful place for your parents to begin a new life. In addition to taking advantage of our warm climate and spending time with you and their grandchildren, your parents can maintain their active, independent lifestyles.

- Independence Village adjoins one of Raleigh's most prestigious and gracious neighborhoods, Olde Raleigh
- Studio, one and two bedroom apartments
- Monthly rental—no entry fee or endowment
- Scheduled transportation
- 3 meals served daily
- 24-hour emergency assistance
- Weekly housekeeping and linen service
- Variety of activities and social events
- Beauty/barber shop
- Convenient to I-40, Rex Hospital and Crabtree Valley Mall
- Within Walking distance of Olde Raleigh Village Shopping Center

Call to schedule a personal guided tour and complimentary lunch.

919-781-8226

3113 Charles B. Root Wynd • Raleigh, NC 27612

www.seniorhousing.net/indepedenceolderaleigh • www.independence1.citysearch.com

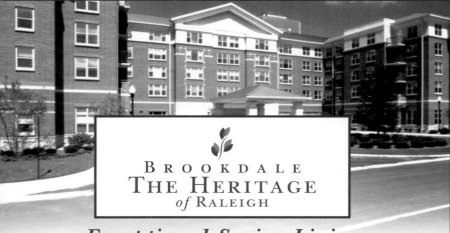

𝒢 lenaire's Residential Retirement Community is nestled within a private, yet inviting residential setting. Imagine a lifestyle of quiet companionship, friendly neighbors and a variety of activities. Indeed, life at Glenaire is about choices. A range of services and options is here for your benefit and enjoyment.

Glenaire's active, older adults take full advantage of living independently, participating in the programs offered and enjoying life to the fullest. Be it traveling to distant places or simply taking a stroll around the pond, at Glenaire your day is filled with the things you desire. In addition, peace of mind is provided by the availability of higher levels of care within the community.

Residential Assisted Living offers a level of care between our cottages and apartments (intended for those who are fully independent) and the next two higher levels of care within Glenaire's Health Care facility.

Glenaire
A Continuing Care Retirement Community
An Affiliate of The Presbyterian Homes, Inc.
www.glenaire.org

A major advantage to Glenaire's approach to assisted living is the continuum of care from residential into a licensed nursing facility that includes medical assisted living and skilled nursing, which is Medicare certified.

Residential Assisted Living opens a way into Glenaire for those who postponed the decision to enter a retirement community.

Call today for an appointment to visit and to learn more about the Glenaire advantage.

200 West Cornwall Road • Cary, NC 27511 • 919-460-8095 • 800-225-9573

At either of our specialized residences, Alterra Sterling House and Alterra Wynwood for assisted living, or Alterra Clare Bridge and Alterra Clare Bridge Cottage for memory care, our residents enjoy a life of choices, their choices. Each of our residents can keep their own schedule, enjoy their favorite hobbies and live each day to the fullest.

Aging with Choice.

www.assisted.com

Please call to discover all that Alterra has to offer.

ASSISTED LIVING RESIDENCES

ALTERRA WYNWOOD OF CHAPEL HILL
919-933-1430

ALTERRA STERLING HOUSE OF RALEIGH
919-844-9747

MEMORY CARE RESIDENCES

ALTERRA CLARE BRIDGE OF CARY
919-852-1355

ALTERRA CLARE BRIDGE OF CHAPEL HILL
919-929-5850

ALTERRA CLARE BRIDGE COTTAGE OF RALEIGH
919-844-2499

Alterra
AGING WITH CHOICE

EQUAL HOUSING OPPORTUNITY

356-2207-8/00

For information on Alterra residences nationwide, call toll free, 1-888-780-1200.

First In Cary!
First In Fun!

Heritage Pines Is The First Community Designed Just For Active Adults Like You!

- Cary's first active adult community offering low-maintenance living for those 55 and better!
- 7,000 sq. ft. country club with pool, spa, fitness center, library/computer center, tennis & more! Visit now!

Single Family Homes From The $180's & Villa Homes From The $140's

HERITAGE PINES
ACTIVE ADULT LIVING

Directions: Heritage Pines is located on the east side of Carpenter-Upchurch Rd., just south of Carpenter-Morrisville Rd. Open Mon.-Sat. 10-6 & Sun. 1-6.

(919) 469-5534

Westminster Homes™

US·HOME

PHASE I - 60% SOLD OUT!

THE CHESTNUT

Retirement and Senior Services

The Triangle is noted for its youthful profile, thanks to 11 colleges, universities and community colleges in the three principal counties. But it's the growth in the retirement age population that has marked the Triangle's last decade, a trend that continues into the 21st Century. In fact North Carolina is the nation's No. 3 retirement spot, behind Florida and Arizona. And those individuals 85 and older make up the fastest-growing group in the state. To Insiders, that's no surprise. Many of the same attributes—education, moderate climate, change of seasons, medical services, low crime and tax rates, active social and art scenes, metropolitan airport, etc.—that attract students and young families catch the eyes of those who wear bifocals. And in some cases, it's the younger families themselves that are the magnets drawing grandparents to the Triangle's burgeoning retirement communities.

This chapter provides specific information on these communities, which include some of the top rated retirement villages in the nation. We also give you an Insider's view of the services and activities that keep the heart pumping and the brain clicking. (Indeed, with all the medical research facilities in the neighborhood, you will find numerous ads in the media soliciting people of a certain age to participate in clinical trials that test all your favorite body parts.) As a group, older citizens are great volunteers. One state university study shows that 77 percent of our retired citizens volunteer an average of 7.4 hours a week in community service! So if you're thinking of retirement here, don't get too comfortable.

Retirement Communities

As the retirement community has grown, so have the number and levels of services. When choosing a retirement community, be certain that the level of care provided matches your lifestyle and needs:

Independent living retirement communities are for those who are able and willing to take care of themselves, but don't want the hassle of taking care of a big house. The convenience and activities of a retirement community are attractive to this group. Independent care housing can be a single, detached house, a condominium, a cottage or an apartment.

Assisted living is the next level in retirement, offering a wide range of services and amenities. It provides assistance with activities of daily living such as preparing food, providing local transportation and housekeeping. Many residents are capable of doing most things for themselves but, from time to time, need assistance. Room and board, activities, administration of medications, medical transportation, assistance with personal hygiene (such as bathing, grooming and dressing assistance) and 24-hour supervision are provided.

Intermediate care is appropriate for persons who may need nursing intervention, but not on a continuous basis. Rehabilitation programs, activities and personal care assistance are available. The care is provided under the direction of a physician.

Nursing care provides full-time, around-the-clock, long-term health care. While many nursing care tenants can do a lot of things for themselves, they need assistance with medication management and other issues. Such care is for those who are too ill or impaired to be ambulatory. Some retirement communities even offer on-site physicians and nurses with their nursing care facilities.

The Triangle offers retirement communities in all of these categories and some that offer a combination of all. These continuing care communities are ideal because the level of care is adapted to the needs of the resident. Now, the red flag warning! Some retirement communities offer assisted living care and nursing care only to those tenants who started with the community as independent living tenants. For additional information, contact Resources for Seniors, 872-7933, or the Department of Social Services in your county.

The following communities are listed according to the level of care provided.

Planned Communities

There are a number of neighborhoods and developments that are not exclusively for retirees, but do have a number of retired people in the community. They include Treyburn in Northern Durham County, Governor's Club in Orange County and Fearrington in Chatham County. A $65-million retirement community, Galloway Ridge, is scheduled to open at Fearrington in 2002 as an affiliate of Duke University Health System.

Continuing Care Retirement Communities

Carol Woods
750 Weaver Dairy Rd., Chapel Hill
• 968-4511, (800) 518-9333
• www.carolwoods.org

Carol Woods is a nationally accredited, not-for-profit community located 3 1/2 miles from UNC-CH and 10 miles from Duke University. Situated on 120 wooded acres, Carol Woods' campus is a bird sanctuary and a national backyard wildlife habitat.

A variety of cottages and apartments, as well as on-campus amenities, are offered, including a heated indoor pool, fitness center, computer room and 4,500-volume library. A resident-driven community creates resident participation in a range of activities, and four residents serve on the board of directors.

On-site licensed assisted living and Medicare-certified skilled nursing facilities continue to support resident autonomy and maximize quality of life. Expansion plans include two cluster homes for residents requiring 24-hour supportive care and an on-site child development center, which will enable intergenerational activities on a daily basis.

Carolina Meadows
100 Carolina Meadows, Chapel Hill
• 942-4014 • www.carolinameadows.org

Carolina Meadows is an accredited not-for-profit, fee-for-service retirement community located minutes from the charm and cultural activities of Chapel Hill. Floor plans range from studio apartments to 1,800-square-foot villas with garages. Construction was completed in 1997 and there are now 391 homes and approximately 600 residents. The community is located on 160 acres in a beautiful country setting surrounded by a hardwood forest. It provides privacy and security along with dining, health care and recreational facilities. An Ambulatory Services Clinic is located on site as is an assisted living facility called The Fairways. The 90-bed Health Center provides a residential environment to residents at all levels of care.

Croasdaile Village
2600 Croasdaile Farm Pkwy., Durham
• 384-2475
• www.umrh.org/croasdailevillage.htm

Croasdaile Village, a continuing care retirement community of The United Methodist Retirement Homes, Inc., opened in June 1999. Situated in the gently rolling hills north of downtown Durham, Croasdaile Village offers gracious, secure retirement living in a pastoral setting that once was home to a working family farm. The 110-acre site, adjacent to the planned community of Croasdaile Farm, includes walking trails, a scenic lake

Glenaire is a continuing care retirement community located on 30 beautifully landscaped acres in the heart of Cary.

and expansive green spaces where residents can enjoy the outdoors. The Village Commons, in the center of Croasdaile Village, houses common areas and amenities.

Croasdaile Village provides a wide selection of apartments, cottages and homes designed to complement residents' pursuit of a carefree, gracious and abundant retirement lifestyle, as well as a health care center that provides assistance and medical care for residents who require it.

The Forest at Duke
2701 Pickett Rd., Durham • 490-8000
• www.forestduke.com

The nonprofit Forest at Duke opened in 1992 on a 42-acre campus near Duke University. Now home to about 350 residents, it offers three levels of care: independent living, assisted care and nursing care. The community contains 80 cottages, 160 apartments and 60 health care rooms. Like other full-service continuing care villages, the Forest has housekeeping, security, transportation and maintenance for residents.

The Forest at Duke provides an attractive setting for residents and services such as community and private dining, beauty and barber shops, a library, a full-service bank, a 40,000-square-foot community center, an exercise room and even an indoor swimming pool. Moreover, there is an active schedule of events for residents, many of which are offered in the spacious auditorium.

Glenaire
200 W. Cornwall Rd., Cary • 460-8095
• www.glenaire.org

Opened in 1993, this retirement community in the heart of Cary has recently completed a major expansion of its facilities. Glenaire's 30 acres are beautifully landscaped. Well-designed accommodations and programs are offered for residents in cottages, a range of apartment options, two distinct levels of assisted living and three nursing sections, providing Medicare, Medicaid and dementia care.

Glenaire is home to 275 active adults beyond age 65 living in residential settings and 120 residents in progressive levels of care. The residents have relocated from the local area as well as from some 10 states, and many have family ties in the area. The Community Center is the focal point for activities, from the arts to exercise and educational experiences. Also available are game and craft rooms, a library, a bank, a gift shop, a barber and beauty salon, storage spaces and a postal service. Among the features provided for all residents are meal plans, housekeeping, maintenance and grounds services.

All residents are members of the Residents Association, which has an active role in the governance of the community and programming of campus life. The Association elects a Council that coordinates a broad range of committees and activities initiated by the residents and assisted by the Resident Services staff. The Council is also a channel of communication for the residents with Glenaire's management and voluntary Board of Trustees. Glenaire seeks to attract younger residents who look for opportunities for themselves in retirement and who value involvement in community life. The facility is an affiliate of the nonprofit Presbyterian Homes, Inc., which manages two other facilities, River Landing in High Point and Scotia Village in Laurinburg, North Carolina.

Springmoor
1500 Sawmill Rd., Raleigh
• **848-7080** • **www.springmoor.com**

Springmoor offers a full range of care, from independent living to nursing care. It is built on 42-wooded acres off Creedmoor Road, 3 miles north of Crabtree Valley Mall. The 600 residents are invited to use the walking and jogging trails as well as the indoor swimming pool in the 500-acre Greystone Village community of which Springmoor is a part.

The complex is a mixture of apartments, villas and private homes. In the apartment complexes, there are dining rooms, health centers and a nursing wing for those who need 24-hour care.

Springmoor maintains a clinic with a physician on duty and has a special wing for victims of Alzheimer's disease and related memory disorders. Residents have access to a wide variety of amenities, including a store, a bank, post office, beauty salon and library. The Activity Center provides social and recreational facilities. To live here, you must be at least 62 years old.

Whitaker Glen
501 E. Whitaker Mill Rd., Raleigh
• **839-5604** • **www.whitakerglen.com**

An attractive, locally owned community, Whitaker Glen is situated not far from Five Points. It offers independent living with support services. Whitaker Glen is a complex of four buildings containing 96 units, split between one- and two-bedroom apartments. The support building includes a dining room that serves three meals a day, library, craft room, exercise room, barber and beauty shop. Scheduled transportation, grocery stores and doctors' appointments are available. Personnel are available 24 hours per day to respond to security and emergency calls.

Apartment Retirement Communities

Abbotswood at Stonehenge
7900 Creedmoor Rd., Raleigh
• **847-3202**
• **www.kiscoretirement.com/ abbots_stone.html**

Abbotswood offers independent apartment living. It is designed for the "senior, middle-income adult" and does not require a large endowment fee. Its monthly membership fee covers the rent for the one- or two-bedroom apartments that includes maid service and all utilities except telephone.

The complex contains 120 units and is located on 10 acres off Creedmoor Road in North Raleigh. The "private quarters" have bedrooms, great rooms, kitchens, storage space and, with the two-bedroom units, two bathrooms. The service at Abbotswood includes a 24-hour security and emergency call system, breakfast and dinner, weekly housekeeping, additional storage space and scheduled transportation. Residents also have access to exercise rooms, activity rooms and a library. There is a Wellness Program that includes a health coordinator who helps residents keep in touch with their family physician, as needed.

Durham Regent
3007 Pickett Rd., Durham • 490-6224

Durham Regent offers apartment living with month-to-month rent and no buy-in fees or leases. It is owned and managed by

---

INSIDERS' TIP

In the 1996 elections, 23 percent of North Carolina voters were age 60 and older; in the 1998 mid-term election that number had leapt to 29 percent.

Holiday Retirement Corporation. Utilities are included in the monthly rent and residents are provided three meals a day, weekly housekeeping and free local transportation.

Apartment Retirement Communities Offering Assisted Living

The Heritage of Raleigh
5950 Falls of Neuse Rd. • 873-2400
• www.brookdaleliving.com

Reserve your space at The Heritage, Raleigh's newest luxury rental retirement community, which offers a maintenance-free lifestyle with all the familiar comforts of home. Spacious studio, and one- and two-bedroom apartments are available for one affordable monthly fee. Amenities include a dining room, indoor pool, on-site health clinic, housekeeping services, scheduled transportation, library, billiards room, full-service bank, 24-hour concierge service, and exercise programs.

Independence Village
3113 Charles B. Root Wynd, Raleigh
• 781-8226
• www.citysearch.com/rdu/independence

Independence Village is a monthly rental community that offers apartments and assisted living facilities. It opened in 1990 and is 1/2 mile from Rex Hospital off Duraleigh Road in Raleigh. Within walking distance of Olde Raleigh Village Shopping Center, it contains 165 units with a choice of studio, one- and two-bedrooms.

Independence Village provides meal service along with a variety of social and recreational activities. The community also has a crafts room, beauty salon and barber shop, library and a billiard room. Scheduled transportation, weekly housekeeping and 24-hour emergency assistance are included in Independence Village's monthly rental fee. The fees vary based upon the size of the unit, but in general are very reasonable. Although there is a waiting list, the community usually can accommodate a new resident within a year.

Windsor Point
1221 Broad St., Fuquay-Varina
• 552-4580 • www.windsorpoint.com

A continuing care retirement community, Windsor Point is located on 17 landscaped acres in the small but rapidly growing town of Fuquay-Varina in southern Wake County. Independent living, assisted living and Alzheimer's care are available here. Windsor Point offers studio and one- and two-bedroom units. Amenities include scheduled

Photo by Rich Weidman

Independence Village, a monthly rental community off Duraleigh Road in Raleigh, offers apartments and assisted living facilities.

Alterra Clare Bridge provides assisted living in three locations throughout the Triangle.

transportation, weekly housekeeping, an indoor pool and fitness center, walking paths, private dining and catering services, a wellness center, a doctor's office, a 24-hour emergency call system and a community center.

Woodland Terrace
300 Kildaire Woods Dr., Cary • 465-0356
• www.kiscoretirement.com/
woodlandterrace.html

Located in the heart of Cary, Woodland Terrace is a full-service retirement community that provides a variety of amenities geared to today's seniors. Independent living (90 units), assisted living (34 units) and Alzheimer's care (44 units) are available here. Spacious cottages and apartments surround the community lake, giving the 22-acre campus the appearance of a small Southern town. Woodland Terrace offers a variety of amenities, include weekly housekeeping, maintenance, scheduled transportation to shopping and medical appointments, an optional laundry service, a beauty salon, a barber shop and coordination of home health services.

Assisted Living Facilities
Alterra Clare Bridge of Cary
7870 Chapel Hill Rd., Cary • 852-1355
Alterra Clare Bridge of Chapel Hill
2230 Farmington Dr., Chapel Hill • 929-5850
Alterra Clare Bridge of North Raleigh
1110 Falls River Ave., Raleigh
• 852-1355 • www.assisted.com

Alterra Clare Bridge provides specialized assisted living for memory impaired residents in a homelike environment. Licensed nurses are available 24 hours a day. Alterra Clare Bridge also offers nutritious and well-balanced meals and snacks, ongoing health care monitoring, life enrichment programs, housekeeping and personal laundry and linen services. Each facility is owned by Alterra Healthcare Corporation.

Alterra Sterling House of Raleigh
1110 Falls River Ave., Raleigh
• 844-9747 • www.assisted.com

Opened in the summer of 1999, Sterling House provides a wide range of specially tailored services to meet the needs of its residents. Amenities include all nutritious meals, personal and medical assistance, emergency call systems, on-site worship, laundry and linen services, and housekeeping. Sterling House is owned by Alterra Healthcare Corporation.

Alterra Wynwood of Chapel Hill
2220 Farmington Dr., Chapel Hill
• 933-1430 • www.assisted.com

Wynwood offers assisted living through a variety of programs, including customized care programs. Residents receive individualized assistance with their unscheduled needs 24 hours a day, even as their needs change. Meals, housekeeping and personal laundry and linen services are included. Wynwood is equipped with a comprehensive emergency response system. The facility is owned by Alterra Healthcare Corporation.

Brighton Gardens
3101 Duraleigh Rd., Raleigh • 571-1123
• www.marriott.com/senior/bg_raleigh

A Marriott assisted living community, Brighton Gardens offers 115 residential suites, daily meals, planned social activities, weekly housekeeping, a beauty/barber shop and scheduled transportation. An on-site center provides specialized care for residents with Alzheimer's.

Carolina House of Cary
111 MacArthur Dr., Cary • 460-5959
Carolina House of Chapel Hill
100 Lanark Rd., Chapel Hill • 918-7600
Carolina House of Wake Forest
611 S. Brooks St., Wake Forest • 562-8400
• www.carolinahouse.com

The three Carolina Houses provide assisted living in a comfortable, caring residential atmosphere. Private studios and suites are available. A monthly fee includes all meals, housekeeping and daily assistance. Amenities include a library, landscaped courtyard, screened porches and gardening areas. The facilities also offer The Discovery Program, a self-contained, state-of-the-art Alzheimer's

and memory-impaired care program. Carolina House is locally owned and operated by Southern Assisted Living, Inc.

Heartfields Assisted Living at Cary
1050 Crescent Green Dr., Cary
• 852-5757 • www.lcsnet.com

Located just off Kildaire Farm Road, Heartfields offers assisted living with personalized services in a residential setting. Amenities include 75 spacious suites, transportation, on-site worship, wellness programs and meals. Nurses are on-site 24 hours a day. The separate HeartHaven program serves residents with Alzheimer's and related memory disorders.

Manorhouse
801 Dixie Tr., Raleigh • 828-5557
• www.manor-house.com

Manorhouse opened in 1991 in a landscaped, central location at the intersection of Wade Avenue and Dixie Trail. It is close to Rex Hospital, North Carolina State University and the State Fairground complex. Manorhouse offers an elegant lifestyle that surrounds its residents with personal care support, comfort and security. Residents receive assistance with bathing, dressing and medication management. A licensed nursing staff is on-site 24 hours a day. Housekeeping, laundry, transportation services and a full social schedule are also provided. Residents enjoy three meals a day in a traditional restaurant-style dining room. Manorhouse has also implemented a Life Connections program that offers specialized dementia care services.

Meadowbrook Manor of Durham
5935 Mt. Sinai Rd., Durham • 489-2361

Meadowbrook Manor offers complete assisted living services, providing peace of mind for seniors and their families. It features affordable monthly rates, private rooms, housekeeping and laundry services, dining, transportation and on-site worship. An on-site Alzheimer's Special Care Program provides specialized care for residents with Alzheimer's or related memory impairment.

Meadowbrook Terrace of Raleigh
4510 Duraleigh Rd., Raleigh • 781-6605
• **www.meadowbrook.citysearch.com**

Meadowbrook, which recently made renovations and is under new management, provides quality 24-hour care from a specially trained staff. Amenities include 120 units, three meals a day, special security features and a full schedule of activities. In addition to complete assisted living services, an Alzheimer's care program and rehabilitative services are available. No community fee is required.

Oakleaf Village
615 Spring Forest Rd., Raleigh
• **981-6100**

Oakleaf is a new assisted living community in North Raleigh set to open in the fall of 2000. In addition to basic services, advanced programs at Oakleaf include medication administration; assistance with bathing, dressing and grooming; special needs monitoring; mobility assistance; and more. Residents can choose from a variety of floorplans, including studios, one-bedroom and deluxe two-bedroom apartments. Three meals a day are included in the basic monthly fee.

Other amenities include 24-hour professional staffing, scheduled transportation, personal laundry services, housekeeping, beauty and barber shops, a library, a crafts center, a recreation room and a landscaped courtyard.

Outlook Pointe at Northridge
600 Newton Rd., Raleigh • 848-4906
• **www.outlookpointe.com**

Outlook Pointe provides assisted living in a comfortable, home-like environment. Amenities include 24-hour assistance, a wellness program, a fully equipped medical rehabilitation gym and treatment rooms, transportation and on-site worship services. Outlook Pointe's "Treasures" Program is designed for residents with Alzheimer's and related memory disorders.

Shepherd House Assisted Living
405 Smith Level Rd., Carrboro
• **929-7859**

Shepherd House offers a variety of services for seniors in Orange County. Amenities include well-balanced meals, transportation, shopping trips, daily scheduled activities, laundry and housekeeping services, a library and on-site worship. Shepherd House includes a special wing for residents with Alzheimer's and other memory-related disorders.

Spring Arbor of Apex
901 Spring Arbor Ct., Apex
• **303-9990**

One of the Triangle's newest assisted-living facilities, Spring Arbor opened in the spring of 2000 off Olive Chapel Road. The first and only assisted living residence in Apex, Spring Arbor offers 76 units. Amenities include meals and snacks, laundry and housekeeping services, scheduled transportation, a library, daily exercise classes, a beauty/barber shop and walking paths. Wellness programs, a therapeutic whirlpool bath, special diet menus, medical administration and specially designed exercise programs are just some of the services available. Spring Arbor is owned and operated by HHHunt Assisted Living.

A second Spring Arbor assisted living facility is located at 4523 Hope Valley Road near the Woodcroft residential development in Durham. Call 403-0055 for more information.

INSIDERS' TIP

If you've just retired to North Carolina, you will want to get a copy of *The Old North State Fact Book* from the state Division of Archives and History. This slim, entertaining volume includes such vital Insider Information as the state motto, "Esse Quam Videri" (To be rather than seem), the state song and the state dog . . . it's not the French poodle.

Photo by Rich Weidman

Spring Arbor is the first and only assisted living residence in Apex.

Summerville Assisted Living at Durham
4434 Ben Franklin Blvd., Durham
• 479-9966 • www.summervillehg.com

Formerly known as Chancellor Gardens, Summerville is an assisted living community located near Durham Regional Hospital. The three-story brick building, which encloses a beautiful courtyard, contains 96 studio and one- and two-bedroom apartments. A licensed nurse is on site 24 hours a day. Residents enjoy a state-of-the-art fitness program, nutrition counseling and regular health screenings. Amenities include an elegant dining room, formal living room, gift shop, ice cream parlor and library. Summerville's specialized SummerBrook program provides assistance for residents living with Alzheimer's disease or a related memory disorder.

Sunrise
4801 Edwards Mill Rd., Raleigh
• 787-0777 • www.sunrise-al.com

Sunrise is a national company founded in 1981 in Fairfax, Virginia. Its Raleigh facility, which overlooks Crabtree Valley Mall, opened in 1996. The attractive, small-scale complexes have won architectural awards and feature billiard rooms, libraries and rocking chairs on the front porch. Sunrise communities provide housekeeping services, dining facilities and nursing care. Sunrise also offers specialized programs for residents with memory disorders.

Willow Springs Rest Home and Retirement Center
624 Jones Ferry Rd., Carrboro
• 968-3072

This 120-bed retirement home offers assisted care for its residents. It provides 24-hour care and offers a range of services and activities: housekeeping, transportation, exercise classes and bingo. There are private and semiprivate rooms.

Nursing Homes

The Brian Center
6000 Fayetteville Rd., Durham • 544-9021

The Brian Center Health & Retirement Home of Durham provides skilled, intermediate and assisted-living care. It also offers rehabilitation services.

Carver Living Center
321 E. Carver St., Durham • 471-3558

Carver Living Center is a 120-bed nursing care facility with a solid local reputation. It has private and semiprivate rooms. There is a licensed geriatric nurse practitioner available and primary care physicians from Duke Medical Center on call. Carver Living Center also offers rehabilitation therapy for residents who need only short-term nursing care before returning home.

Mayview Convalescent Center
513 E. Whitaker Mill Rd., Raleigh
• 828-2348

Established in 1957, Mayview contains 139 private rooms with full baths on wooded landscaped grounds. The Center boasts an experienced staff that provides quality, 24-hour care. A variety of scheduled activities take place here daily, including craft sessions, films, parties, music and other learning opportunities. Amenities include a hair salon/barber shop, laundry service and TV lounges.

Rex Convalescent Care Center
4210 Lake Boone Tr., Raleigh • 782-6600
• www.rexhealth.com

Opened in 1991, this 140-bed facility is part of Rex Healthcare's total system. It is located on the Rex campus and provides assisted living and nursing care, including physical, speech and occupational therapy. Its medical director is on call 24 hours a day. While most of the residents are age 65 or older, it does have younger tenants. Proximity to the hospital campus and its various specialities makes Rex Convalescent Care Center especially convenient (see "Rex Healthcare" write-up in our "Health Care" chapter).

Special Services and Activities

As our population grays, the services and activities available for seniors are growing in quality and quantity.

Adult Day Care

Adult day care is a concept that is growing in popularity and provides seniors with supervision, meals and activities Monday through Friday. Call Resources for Seniors at 872-7933 for more information.

Encore Center for Lifelong Enrichment

The Encore Center at North Carolina State University provides enrichment opportunities for adults over 50 through short courses, study trips and social and volunteer activities. All courses are noncredit, have no prerequisites and cover topics such as literature, the arts, science, politics and computers. Most courses are held at the University's easily accessible McKimmon Center. For more information and to receive a free catalog of offerings, call 515-5782.

Fifty Plus
P.O. Box 51277, Durham, NC 27717
• 493-5900 • www.fiftyplus.com

Fifty Plus is a monthly tabloid produced by AdVenture Publishing, Inc., for the Triangle. As the name suggests, it is aimed at those readers who are 50 years old and counting and it is a good source for information. Fifty Plus features articles on travel, health and wellness, finance and local profiles—plus

a monthly calendar of events such as support group meetings, AARP chapter meetings, senior citizen center activities, entertainment and much more.

Home Health Care

Home health care is a fast growing service nationwide because it allows seniors to stay independent and in their own homes longer. Triangle home health care agencies include UNC Home Health, 966-4915; Durham Regional Home Care, 470-6550; Rex Home Services, 784-4474; WakeMed HomeCare, 350-7990; and In Home Health, 781-4357.

Senior Living
P.O. Box 31763, Raleigh, NC 27622
• 254-3603

A free, quarterly resource magazine for seniors, Senior Living contains feature articles, a summary of retirement community types, directories of area retirement communities and other valuable resources and hotline numbers. It is available at many Triangle grocery stores.

Cary

The new $2.7 million, 16,500-square-foot Cary Senior Center is scheduled for completion in the fall of 2000 at Bond Park. Call 469-4081 for more information.

Chapel Hill

Both the Chapel Hill Parks and Recreation Department and the Carrboro Recreation and Parks Department sponsor special activities for senior citizens. There is an AARP chapter in Orange County as well as a number of volunteer opportunities including the Retired Senior Volunteer Program (RSVP), 968-2054, and Service Corps of Retired Executives (SCORE), 967-7075. Four Senior Centers offer a variety of activities: Chapel Hill Senior Center, 968-2070; South Orange County Senior Center, 968-2080; Carrboro Senior Center, 968-2075; and Hillsborough Senior Center, 732-8181. The Carolina College of Learning in Retirement at UNC-CH and Elderhostel, 962-1123, both provide educational opportunities for seniors.

Contact Meals on Wheels at 942-2948. The Orange County Department of Aging can be reached at 968-2070.

Durham

The Parks and Recreation Department, 560-4355, provides a variety of activities of interest to senior citizens, including exercise classes, square dances, field trips and social clubs. The Durham Council for Senior Citizens can be reached at 688-8247; RSVP, 686-3663; SCORE, 541-2171; and Meals on Wheels, 682-7255.

The Duke Institute for Learning and Retirement at Duke University offers a variety of senior-oriented courses. Call 684-2703 for information on class schedules and rates.

Raleigh

As a capital city, Raleigh has a number of statewide services to help retired and senior citizens. Check the Department of Human Resources—Division of Aging, 693 Palmer Drive, 733-3983, for more information. The City of Raleigh also has a very active life for senior citizens, starting with its RSVP program, 831-6295. This is a good way for you to meet some very interesting people and do some good deeds such as reading news accounts over the Radio Reading Service for blind listeners. RSVP also sponsors the Foster Grandparents Program, 831-6102. SCORE can be reached at 856-4739.

If you like dancing and card playing, there's a group that regularly meets at the city's Golden Years Association at Pullen Park's Activity Center. Yes, there's a Meals on Wheels program in Wake County, too. Call 833-1749.

There are two AARP chapters in Raleigh and the Resources For Seniors is another good place to start for information on services as well as nursing homes. For a listing of community services and telephone numbers of the preceding, check the front of the telephone book under Community Services numbers.

DURHAM **DA** ACADEMY

THANK YOU,

UNC-CH, Duke, Stanford, Vanderbilt, Princeton, Davidson, Wake Forest, Washington Univ. (MO), Brown, Yale, Johns Hopkins, Northwestern, Virginia, Amherst, NYU, MIT, Univ. of Pennsylvania, Dartmouth, Oberlin, Harvard, Univ. of Chicago, Columbia, Cornell, Emory, Georgetown, Williams, Smith, Wellesley, Kenyon and Notre Dame

for enrolling **more than half** of Durham Academy's graduates over the past five years! We're quite proud of them, and we're confident you will be, too.

Founded in 1933, Durham Academy is an independent, coeducational day school with 1,025 students in Pre-K through Grade 12 and admits students of any race, creed, color or national origin. Durham Academy annually awards more than $600,000 in need-based financial aid.

To learn more about Durham Academy, please contact our admissions office at **919-489-9118.** You can also read more about us on the web at **www.da.org.** We accept new students at every grade level, Pre-K to 12th, every year, so newcomers are encouraged to apply!

Schools and Child Care

A commitment to quality educational opportunities has always been a deeply rooted tradition in the Triangle. In fact, the first state-assisted public high school in North Carolina opened in Cary in 1907. Today, the area boasts some of the most acclaimed educational institutions in the state and the country. For instance, Chapel Hill-Carrboro students regularly score higher on statewide tests than any other system. The innovative North Carolina School of Science and Mathematics draws the best and brightest students from across the state to its Durham campus. In addition, Durham's Jordan and Raleigh's Enloe high schools have received national recognition as two of the best high schools in the nation.

However, success also breeds new challenges. Over the past decade, each of the Triangle's school systems has had to make tough choices associated with rapid growth throughout the region. Redistricting and school overcrowding are main concerns. Another critical issue facing the school district is finding the source of funding for new school construction.

In addition to the public school system, there are a number of private schools from which to choose, as well as state-sanctioned charter schools. Many preschools and day-care programs are also available to keep pace with the vast number of working families relocating to the region.

This chapter provides comprehensive details on the three public school systems and offers sample descriptions of the diverse range of private schools located throughout the Triangle. We also take a closer look at public high schools and charter schools, and provide extensive information on local after-school programs, preschools and day-care facilities.

Public Schools
Chapel Hill-Carrboro

The Chapel Hill-Carrboro School System consistently ranks among the top public school systems in North Carolina and the United States, boasting one of the highest average end-of-course and end-of-grade scores in the state. In addition, the system has the lowest dropout rate in the state.

The system enrolls more than 9,300 students in nine elementary schools (K-5), three middle schools (6-8), two senior high schools (9-12) and a hospital school at UNC Hospitals for inpatients unable to attend school. A new middle school, Smith, is set to open in the fall of 2001.

Although Chapel Hill and Carrboro are separate towns run by two different mayors and town councils, they share one school system. Keep in mind that the boundaries of the Chapel Hill-Carrboro school district are not the same as the Chapel Hill and Carrboro town limits. Therefore, it's possible to live outside of either town and avoid paying city property taxes but still be within the Chapel Hill-Carrboro school system.

The average combined SAT score for Chapel Hill-Carrboro Schools' class of '00 was 1,175, the highest in the state. More than 85 percent of the system's graduates continue their formal education. In grades 3 through 8,

Photo by Rich Weidman

Located on the former campus of Watts Hospital, the North Carolina School of Science and Mathematics was founded in 1980 as the country's first statewide residential public high school.

more than 91 percent of students achieve proficiency in state-mandated tests.

It's not surprising that the Chapel Hill-Carrboro School System enjoys such an excellent track record. First of all, the system leads the state in per-pupil expenditure (approximately $7,788). Chapel Hill and Carrboro Schools also benefit from both the relative wealth and higher-than-usual education levels of local residents. With a public school system heavily populated by the sons and daughters of academics and professionals, many award- and scholarship-winning students emerge from the local school system each year.

A well-endowed tax base and parents who are concerned about excellence means that the system can afford to spend money on special programs. Chapel Hill-Carrboro Schools educate a larger-than-average percentage of "exceptional" students, particularly in programs for the academically gifted and learning-disabled. Enrichment programs augment elementary classroom teaching and classes for the "highly gifted" are offered in grades 4 through 8.

Honors courses are available in the language arts, math and sciences in grades 6 to 8, with advanced placement classes available at the high school level. Both Chapel Hill

High and East Chapel Hill High offer an impressive array of athletic and extracurricular activities, including team sports ranging from lacrosse and soccer to tennis, golf, football and basketball.

Dr. Neil Pedersen is the superintendent of the Chapel Hill-Carrboro Public School System.

More than 6,300 students in northern Orange County, including Hillsborough, are served by the Orange County School System, which contains seven elementary schools, two middle schools and one high school. Randy Bridges has been the superintendent since 1997. Call 732-8126 for more information.

For more information
Chapel Hill-Carrboro School System
967-8211
www.chccs.k12.nc.us

Durham

The Durham Public School System, which was created in 1992 through a merger of the former city and county school systems, enrolls more than 29,600 students in 27 elementary schools (K-5), eight middle schools (6-8), five senior high schools (9-12), two secondary schools, a school program for hospitalized students and two alternative learning centers. Four of the elementary schools—Easley, Eastway, Holt and Pearsontown—and two middle schools—Chewning and Rogers-Herr—operate as year-round programs.

The Durham Public School System offers excellent educational and recreational opportunities and has a reputation for innovative programs and stringent academic standards. Graduation requirements exceed state standards and include computer education and additional math and science courses. The school system enforces one of the state's toughest academic standards on student athletes.

The student-teacher ratio is about 26:1 for elementary and middle schools and 28:1 for high schools. More than 40 percent of the system's teachers hold advanced degrees. Approximately 85 percent of Durham high school graduates continue their educational studies.

Strong funding for the school district translates into a variety of innovative programs. For example, the school system expanded the state's definition of "academically gifted" with a local program for elementary students who are gifted in the arts and communication.

In addition, the system employs special academic programs for gifted, handicapped and learning-disabled students in grades K to 12. It also provides advanced courses such as Latin and foreign languages in the middle schools, an extensive cultural arts program and sophisticated audiovisual facilities, including cable television instruction to supplement classroom work.

A vocational education program offers instruction in 65 different courses, one of the most comprehensive in the state. The system also provides one of the best individualized services in the state for students with learning disabilities or with physical, emotional, speech, hearing, visual or mental handicaps. A special developmental reading program is

available for grades 1 to 5 followed by a supplemental program in basic skills for grades 6 to 8. A number of other programs, including elementary physical education, computer instruction and cultural arts, have been state and national models.

The school system includes eight magnet schools. Because of the high demand, new students are selected by random lottery. Parents must apply in person beginning in January for the following school year. For more information, call 560-3716.

The magnet school program includes the following study areas:

1. Geoworld: This program located at Burton Elementary is designed to prepare students for Shepard Middle School and focuses on communication and research, global studies, and languages and cultures.

2. Biosphere: C.C. Spaulding Elementary offers this program that enhances the basic curriculum by emphasizing the study of the life sciences through the ecosystems and by observing living environments.

3. Humanities: Club Boulevard Magnet School emphasizes thematic studies in children's literature and the arts, with a comprehensive curriculum in writing and research, reading, mathematics, social studies, science and computers.

4. Montessori: This program at Morehead Elementary promotes the development of social skills, emotional growth, physical coordination and cognitive ability while encouraging students to progress at their own rate in multi-age classrooms.

5. Integrated Arts/Core Knowledge: R.N. Harris Elementary offers a combined program of arts integration and a specific core studies system designed to give students the advantage of entering each grade level with a solid common base of knowledge.

6. Science and Technology: Y.E. Smith Elementary emphasizes the study of physical sciences through the use of high technology.

7. International Baccalaureate: Shepard Middle School provides a program with emphasis on foreign languages and law,

FYI

Unless otherwise noted, the area code for all phone numbers listed in this guide is 919.

preparing students for the study of the IB program at the high school level.

8. Durham School of the Arts: The School serves students in grades 6 to 12. It offers dance, theater, stage craft, photography, creative writing, vocal and instrumental music, as well as piano, strings and guitar.

The Durham Public School System is led by Dr. Ann Denlinger, who was named North Carolina Superintendent of the Year in 1999.

The Durham Schoolhouse Resource Center, which is located in Northgate Mall, serves as a welcome center for newcomers and residents of Durham who need more information about the county's public school system. The Center is open from 10 AM to 5 PM Monday through Friday. Call 286-4454 for more information.

For more information
Durham Public School System
560-2000
www.dps.durham.k12.nc.us

North Carolina School of Science and Mathematics

1219 Broad St. Durham, NC 27705
• 286-3366 • www.ncssm.edu

Founded in 1980 as the nation's first statewide residential public high school, this unique facility provides exceptional opportunities for 550 high school students in grades 11 and 12 who have a strong interest and potential in science and mathematics. Students live on the 27-acre campus of the former Watts Hospital and School of Nursing. Admission is extremely competitive and the process begins each October.

Wake County Schools

The Wake County Public School System, which was formed in 1976 with the merger of the former City of Raleigh and Wake County School System, serves the entire county, including Raleigh, Cary, Apex, Fuquay-Varina, Garner, Holly Springs, Knightdale, Morrisville, Rolesville, Wake Forest, Wendell and

Zebulon. Wake County students consistently score above national norms and individual schools within the system have earned national recognition for their cutting edge programs. In fact, the Wake County School System is the best successfully integrated large city system in the country.

With an enrollment of more than 97,500, the Wake County School System is the second-largest system in the state and the 27th largest in the nation. The school system contains 120 schools and employs more than 6,000 teachers, resulting in a teacher-student ratio of about 1 to 21.

Wake County students averaged 1,061 on their 2000 SAT scores, which is 42 points above the national average and 73 points higher than the state average. The school system has announced an ambitious goal of having 95 percent of third and eighth grade students tested at or above grade level on the state's end-of-grade tests by the year 2003.

In Wake County, school assignment for most students is based on the home address of the student's parent or legal guardian. The Wake County School System evaluates redistricting options frequently in an effort to accommodate population growth, so expect more changes in the coming years.

The Wake County Public School System includes 43 magnet schools that draw students from all over the county. Through the magnet program, parents can select area schools that emphasize a curriculum that best fits their child's talents. In addition to following the North Carolina Standard Course of Study, magnet schools use a variety of teaching approaches and curriculum offerings that help to customize a student's educational program.

To enroll your child in a magnet program, you must register him or her in a Wake County Public School first before submitting a magnet application. Applications are accepted every year in February and selections are made through a lottery process. To receive more information about the magnet application process and to learn more about the magnet programs, contact the Magnet Resource Center at 501-7900 or visit the Center Monday through Friday from 9 AM to 4 PM at 1600 East Millbrook Road.

Magnet elementary programs offer a variety of choices for the K-5 student. These programs include the following:

1. Classical Studies focuses on the basics of education with an emphasis on classical literature, writing skills and public speaking.

2. Community Model uses centers to mirror the local community such as a post office, bank, television station and publishing house.

3. Creative Arts and Sciences uses the "A+" approach to learning and merges the arts with academic subjects to explore students' multiple intelligences.

4. Extended Day provides before- and after-school care with planned activities.

5. Gifted and Talented is based on the belief that all students possess gifts and talents that need to be valued and nurtured.

6. Global Communications explores global studies using project-based learning in reduced class sizes and in technology connection classrooms.

7. International Baccalaureate (Primary Years Programme) uses an inquiry-based approach to teaching and learning, addressing three interrelated questions: "What do we want to learn? How best do we learn? How will we know what we have learned?"

8. International Studies teaches students about a variety of cultures, as well as to speak a foreign language and to use technology important to our global society.

9. Language Arts/Communication emphasizes the importance of communication, language arts and writing skills to all areas.

10. Montessori focuses on the philosophy of Dr. Maria Montessori that children will self-educate if allowed to do so naturally.

11. Year-Round takes the traditional 180-day school year and divides it into nine-week quarters with a three-week break at the end of the quarter.

Magnet middle schools continue the breadth of program choices for the 6th to 8th grade student. These choices include the following:

1. Centennial Campus is a collaboration of the Wake County Public School System and the 10 colleges of North Carolina State University, emphasizing math, science and technology, and following a modified year-round calendar.

2. Gifted and Talented features a variety of electives designed to challenge and encourage a student's special gifts and talents. In addition to the basic instruction of core courses, the electives vary from individual and performing arts to expanded academic offerings.

3. International Baccalaureate (Middle Years Programme) is a five-year program for grades 6 to 10. It integrates five areas of interaction throughout the academic courses: effective study skills, community services, health and social education, environment and homo faber (man the maker).

4. Year-Round continues the 45/15 calendar followed in the year-round elementary schools where children benefit from a continuous learning process and intermittent breaks.

Magnet high school programs offer 9th to 12th grade student the following choices:

1. Accelerated Studies emphasizes math, science and technology; links school-based learning with potential careers through School-to-School Connections; and follows a modified year-round calendar and block scheduling to allow students to move through their high school career at their own pace.

2. Gifted and Talented offers a vast array of electives in the visual and performing arts, video production, math, science, technology, engineering and the humanities. This program also offers eight foreign languages and an array of advanced placement courses.

3. International Baccalaureate Diploma Programme is a rigorous, pre-university course of studies for 11th and 12th graders.

Upon exiting the program IB Diploma holders have the opportunity to gain admission to selective universities throughout the world.

The Wake County School Board requires more credits in the basics such as English, mathematics, science and history. The state requires all students to pass a competency test of basic skills before they are awarded a diploma. The board, however, has attracted national attention with experimental programs such as the Writing to Read Program, which uses computers to help students develop writing skills at an early age and become familiar with computers. All middle schools also have computer labs and courses for students to learn about computers. Students have Internet access through an online service donated by the Raleigh *News & Observer*.

The public high schools that serve Raleigh and Cary students offer a broad range of courses, including foreign languages and higher mathematics.

As befits a large system, special programs are available for handicapped children, including educable mentally retarded and seriously emotionally and learning-disabled children. Project Enlightenment is an acclaimed service of the system that offers family therapy as well as individual therapy for young children, parents and teachers.

For More Information
Wake County Public School System
850-1600
www.wcpss.net

Private Schools
Chapel Hill and Durham

About 100 private schools serving more than 15,000 students are scattered throughout the Triangle.

With the relatively short distance between Durham and Chapel Hill, the private schools often attract students from both communities with a wide choice of excellent private and parochial schools. We advise that you visit these facilities, meet the principals, observe a few classes and activities and compare tuition costs before making a decision.

MONTESSORI SCHOOLS

Artgarden Montessori	1603 E. Franklin St., Chapel Hill	942-1339
Bryson Christian Montessori	6701 Garrett Rd., Durham	489-9394
Cary Montessori School	201 High House Rd., Cary	469-9406
Heartwood Montessori	5005 Western Blvd., Raleigh	859-4113
Joy Land Montessori Preschool	603 Lynn Rd., Durham	596-4702
Montessori Ctr. for Children	4817 Johnson Pond Rd., Apex	779-6671
Montessori Ctr. for Children	Sunset Lake Rd., Holly Springs	303-3636
Montessori Children's House	2400 University Dr., Durham	489-9045
Montessori Children's House	1501 N. Main St., Fuquay-Varina	557-5438
Montessori Children's House	824 N. Bloodworth St., Raleigh	832-3494
Montessori Children's House	802 Mill St., Wake Forest	556-2360
Montessori Community School	4512 Pope Rd., Durham	493-8541
Montessori Day School	1165 Weaver Dairy Rd., Chapel Hill	929-3339
Montessori Schl. of Raleigh	7005 Lead Mine Rd., Raleigh	848-1545
Morehead Montessori School	909 Cobb St., Raleigh	560-3954
New School: A Montessori Ctr.	133 Rand Rd., Raleigh	779-6671
Pinewoods Montessori	200 Davis Rd., Hillsborough	644-2090
Pittsboro Montessori Preschool	300 W. Salisbury St., Pittsboro	545-0691
Sterling Montessori Academy	202 Treybrooke Dr., Morrisville	462-8889

Carolina Friends School

4809 Friends School Rd., Durham
• 383-6602 • www.quaker.org/cfs
Summer Programs: 384-9089

Founded in 1963, Carolina Friends School enrolls approximately 490 students. The School's philosophy is rooted in Quaker values. Distinctive features include attention to the student as a whole person, respect for individual uniqueness, experiential learning opportunities and emphasis on cooperation, personal responsibility and community service. Three Early Schools (in Durham, in Chapel Hill and at the rural main campus) serve children through kindergarten; Lower School offers grades 1-4; and Middle School, grades 5-8.

The School offers strong academics, visual and performing arts, computer facilities, interscholastic sports, outdoor education, community involvement, trips and internships, and college counseling. The student-teacher ratio is 10 to 1. Ninety-five percent of graduates go to college. Twenty-five percent of families receive tuition assistance to Carolina Friends School.

Cresset Christian Academy

3707 Garrett Rd., Durham • 489-2655
• www.cressetchristian.org

Located on a beautiful 40-acre campus, Cresset Christian Academy provides instruction for nearly 350 students, from preschool through 12th grade. The preschool program includes toddlers through 4-year-olds and classes are small. Affiliated with Cresset Baptist Church, the school bases its instruction on Biblical concepts.

The program uses a mixture of a Beka curriculum and other quality materials to lead students in the development of character and intellectual excellence. The curriculum is college preparatory in nature.

Cresset provides instruction in the arts, drama and music. There is a competitive athletic program for the middle and upper schools and private music instruction is offered. The upper school boasts an award-winning concert choir.

A special program is offered for students with attention deficit disorder and learning disabilities as well as one for intellectually gifted students.

Getting Educated About Area High Schools

Triangle public high schools have established a tradition of academic and athletic excellence. Magnet schools, vocational programs, advanced placement courses, honors classes and extracurricular activities are just a few of the many options available to students in the Chapel Hill-Carrboro, Durham and Wake school systems.

The **Chapel Hill-Carrboro School System** has the highest average Scholastic Assessment Test (SAT) scores in the state. The School System requires students to accumulate 50 hours of service learning in the community. Students at **Chapel Hill** High School (929-2106) averaged 1,177 on the 2000 SAT. Chapel Hill High students consistently receive top honors in state competition in math, science and foreign languages.

East Chapel Hill High School (969-2482) opened its doors in 1996. It offers a variety of advanced placement and honors courses. The 2000 graduating class had a grade-point average of 3.5 on a 4-point scale and averaged 1,175 on their SATs. The Wildcats have also won state championships in a handful of sports. The school also boasts of nearly 60 campus clubs.

The **Durham Public School System** offers students a variety of educational opportunities. The state-of-the-art **Hillside** High School (560-3925) in southeast Durham opened in August 1995. In addition to the standard curriculum, Hillside offers several special programs, including the International Baccalaureate Program and several centers of specialization (including Business and Finance, and Law and Justice). The school also features cutting-edge technology and a number of vocational programs. Students scored an average of 883 on their 2000 SATs.

Jordan High School (560-3912), located in southwest Durham County, has a tradition of sending most of its students on to college. Approximately 90 percent of Jordan's graduates pursue further education. Jordan had one of the highest average SAT scores (1,065) in the district for 2000. The school offers a variety of advanced placement and honors courses. A national magazine recently ranked Jordan as one of the top high schools in the nation. Jordan is a frequent contender for the Wachovia Cup for overall excellence in high school athletics.

Northern High School (560-3956) offers a strong curriculum balance among academics, vocational and fine arts courses. The school's vocational program has been identified as a Model Program in a curriculum audit. Northern also established the first high school Habitat for Humanity in the world and is a center for International Studies. The average SAT score at Northern for 2000 was 991. The Knights are known as a football powerhouse that captured the 1993 state championship and continue to win PAC 4-A titles just about every year.

Students at **Riverside** High School (560-3965) in northern Durham had average SAT scores of 1,007 for 2000. The school's engineering center is a mini-magnet program. Through the program, students can take on highly technical independent projects. Riverside students publish a monthly newspaper, *The Pirate's Hook*, and an arts and literary magazine, *Reveries*, annually. The Pirates claimed the 1998 4-A state championship in volleyball and its wrestling team consistently ranks high in the conference.

Southern High School (560-3968), located just north of Research Triangle Park, provides its students a comprehensive educational program. It also offers classes and programs for the academically gifted, trainable mentally handicapped, behaviorally/emotionally handicapped and hearing impaired. Students can take advantage of the school's health sciences center of specialization. Students averaged 884 on their 2000 SAT scores.

High schools in the **Wake County Public School System** have made great strides over the past decade and the district's average SAT scores currently rank second among all state school districts. **Athens Drive** High School (233-4050) has shown the greatest gains: the school's average 2000 SAT score was 1,073, up 75 points since 1993. Athens Drive serves 1,500 students and features a community library, child development center, peer mediation program and courses in English as a Second Language.

Broughton High School (856-7810), which opened its doors in 1929, is Wake County's oldest high school. The school's 1,600 students can take advantage of a career center, two endowed teaching chairs and one of only two Air Force/Junior ROTC programs in the country. Students scored an average of 1,077 on their 2000 SATs. The Caps have been state champions in women's soccer, golf and men's tennis.

Opened in 1962, **Enloe** High School (856-7918) in east Raleigh is now a "Gifted and Talented" magnet school, offering nearly 2,400 students an opportunity to concentrate in fields such as visual and performing arts, video production, science, technical engineering and the humanities. The Eagles' average SAT score (1,157 in 2000) consistently ranks near the top of the Wake County School System. The school was ranked among the top 100 high schools in the country in a recent national magazine survey.

Green Hope High School (380-3700) opened in the fall of 1999. This state-of-the-art school is located off Carpenter-Upchurch Road, convenient for students in Morrisville, Cary and Apex. The school's mascot is the falcon and the school's colors are green and burgundy.

Photo by Rich Weidman

Wakefield High School

Leesville Road High School (870-4250) opened its doors in 1993 and currently serves approximately 2,000 students. It is part of the Leesville campus, which includes an elementary and a middle school. The three schools share two gyms, an auditorium and a theater. Leesville Road students averaged 1,096 on their 2000 SAT scores. The school has four networked computer labs, an automated media center and a fully functional television studio.

Millbrook High School (850-8787), which opened in 1967, offers a strong academic curriculum for its 2,000 students. The school has a career center; recently built fine arts, science and vocational wings; and a new media center, gym and cafeteria. Students averaged 1,045 on their 2000 SATs.

Built in 1968, **Sanderson** High School (881-4800), which is North Raleigh's oldest high school, serves approximately 1,800 students. The school boasts a high percentage of North Carolina scholars. About 82 percent of the graduating class pursues further education. Sanderson also features a 4-year curriculum in Air Force ROTC, a 3-year Academy of Finance program, English as a Second Language Program and a career center. The Spartans' average SAT score in 2000 was 1,070.

Southeast High School (856-2800) is an "Accelerated Studies" magnet school that features innovative teaching, unique learning opportunities, flexible schedules and academic support. Student form into academic teams that stay together with the same academic coach for four years. The school's challenging instructional programs emphasize math, science and state-of-the-art technology. Southeast students averaged 1,009 on their 2000 SATs.

Wakefield High School (562-3600), Wake County's newest high school served Sanderson students during the 1999-2000 school year while their building was being renovated. In August 2000, Wakefield officially opened to serve students in North Raleigh, including the adjacent Wakefield Plantation development. The Wakefield campus includes an elementary and middle school.

Cary High School (460-3549) has a long history dating back to the town's famous Cary Academy in the late 1800s. In 1907, Cary High became the first state-assisted public high school in North Carolina. The school recently underwent a $3.4 million renovation, which included a new career center, and it also has an Accelerated Learning Center. Cary students scored an average of 1,069 on the 2000 SAT. The school, which has an enrollment of approximately 1,800 students, is famous for its marching band and has hosted one of the state's noted music events, Cary Band Day, since 1960. In athletics, the Imps have won 10 state wrestling titles and are strong in other sports such as soccer and cross country.

With an enrollment of more than 2,000 students, **Apex** High School (387-2208) is one of the largest high schools in the state. The school's curriculum includes a full schedule of advanced placement courses, including biology, chemistry, physics, calculus, English, U.S. history, European history, French, Spanish and German. The average SAT score for 2000 was 1,077. The Apex baseball team captured the 2000 4-A State Championship.

Duke School For Children
1516 Hull Ave., Durham
(Preschool-4th Grade) • 416-9420
3716 Old Erwin Rd., Durham
(5th-8th Grade) • 493-2642

Founded in 1947, the Duke School for Children is run by a parent-owned corporation. The total enrollment of the school is 450 for students from preschool through 8th grade. Before- and after-school programs are available.

Durham Academy
3116 Academy Rd., Durham • 489-9118
(Pre-K-8th Grade)
3601 Ridge Rd., Durham • 489-6569
(9th-12th Grade)
• www.da.org

Founded in 1933, Durham Academy is the oldest primary-through-secondary private school in the area, providing instruction from preschool through 12th grade for more than 1,000 students. Admission is competitive, but students are admitted at every grade level, every year. The campus is located in Durham, about a 10-minute drive from Chapel Hill.

Enrichment courses include computers, wind ensemble, chorus, dance, drama, studio art, economics and comparative religions. The Academy's athletic teams have won more than 25 State Championships in the past 10 years. Recent graduating classes have averaged more than 1300 on their SATs.

The Emerson Waldorf School
6211 New Jericho Rd., Chapel Hill
• 967-1858
• www.emersonwaldorf.org

The Emerson Waldorf School is located on 30 wooded acres south of Interstate 40 off N.C. 86 and Mt. Sinai Road north of Chapel Hill. As one of more than 750 Waldorf schools worldwide, it is part of the world's fastest-growing independent school movement.

A typical day at Emerson Waldorf begins with a two-hour "main lesson" that focuses on a single theme. The selected subject may remain the same for several weeks. All history, spelling, mathematics and science problems are related to the main lesson subject. In addition to the basics, Waldorf students study foreign languages, music, handwork and other electives. The school has 220 students in kindergarten (ages 4 to 6) through 8th grade.

Greenbriar Academy
2502 N. Roxboro Rd. • 471-8968
• www.greenbriar.citysearch.com

A nonsectarian college prep school, Greenbriar enrolls about 130 students in prekindergarten through 12th grade. It offers small class sizes, a fully equipped computer lab, foreign language study, music and fine arts instruction, before- and after-school programs and local transportation. Technology is integrated into every classroom.

Hill Center
3200 Pickett Rd., Durham • 489-7464
• www.hillcenter.org

The Hill Center, affiliated with Durham Academy, offers a remedial program for approximately 150 students with learning disabilities or achievement difficulties in kindergarten through grade 12. The Hill Center program provides private instruction for children enrolled in schools in Durham and the surrounding counties in conjunction with regular classroom work. The student-teacher ratio is 4 to 1. The Hill Center is accredited by the Southern Association of Colleges and Schools and the North Carolina Department of Public Instruction.

Immaculata Catholic School
721 Burch Ave., Durham • 682-5847
• www.immaculate-conception-church.org

Immaculata is a 350-student Catholic school founded in 1909 to provide a unique learning program in a Christian environment. Class instruction, small groups and independent study are geared to meet the needs of both slower and more advanced students. The school enrolls students in prekindergarten through grade 8. Families with more than one child attending the school receive tuition discounts.

Montessori Community School
4512 Pope Rd., Durham • 493-8541
• www.mcsdurham.com

Established in 1981, this school is a nonprofit organization directed by parents, promoting child-centered and child-initiated learning. It has a part-time toddler program and an elementary program through grade 6. There are more than 200 students enrolled at the school, which is located on nine wooded acres near I-40 and U.S. 15-501. The school is a full affiliate of the American Montessori Society.

Montessori Day School
1165 Weaver Dairy Rd., Chapel Hill
• 929-3339

The Montessori school practices the methods of Marie Montessori, an Italian educator and physician who believed that children learn naturally if placed in an environment consisting of "learning games" suited to their individual abilities and interests.

The 3- and 4-year-olds attend until 11:45 AM, 5-year-olds until 2 PM and ages 6 through 10 until 2:30 PM. There are about 20 students in each of the preschool classes and about 30 students enrolled in the primary program.

The Sandra E. Lerner Jewish Community Day School
1935 W. Cornwallis Rd., Durham
• 286-5517 • www.ljcds-dch.org

The Jewish Community Day School of Durham/Chapel Hill (LJCDS) is a private, independent school offering integrated secular/Judaic studies from preschool through grade 5. LJCDS provides an environment where children develop a love of learning, positive Jewish identity and a healthy self-image while achieving the highest standards of academic excellence. Low student/teacher ratios allow for rapid individual progress. All teachers are experienced and certified. Hebrew is taught as a second language and the Judaic component is designed for families of diverse Jewish backgrounds and practices. LJCDS is conveniently located to Durham and Chapel Hill.

St. Thomas More School
920 Carmichael St., Chapel Hill
• 929-1546 • www.st-thomasmore.org

St. Thomas More School was built in 1964 as an outgrowth of St. Thomas More Catholic Church parish in Chapel Hill. The school's approximate enrollment of 460 students is open to non-Catholics as well. The philosophy at St. Thomas More School is "to help our students to integrate religious truth." Students from prekindergarten to grade 8 are served and there is an after-school program as well.

Triangle Day School
4911 Neal Rd., Durham • 383-8800

Triangle Day School opened in 1991 as a college preparatory day school. It has an enrollment of 150 students in kindergarten through grade 8 and a low student-teacher ratio. The program also emphasizes foreign language, physical education, computers, music and art.

Raleigh and Cary

The Triangle's private and parochial school tradition is a long one, dating back to Raleigh's early decades when Saint Mary's College was founded in 1842. Wake County offers a diversity of private and parochial school opportunities. Below is a list of some of the private schools and programs located in Raleigh and Cary. Call each school for current tuition.

The Achievement School
400 Cedarview Ct. • 782-5082
• www.achievementschool-ld.com

The Achievement School is a local private school founded in 1979 to help children with learning disabilities such as dyslexia and attention deficit disorder. The school offers children in grades 1 through 12 a highly structured program with close personal and positive teaching. With a total enrollment of 110, the school offers a favorable 1:4 teacher-pupil ratio. The accredited school offers half- and full-day instruction in a wide range of courses, including the basics—language

Cary Academy offers a rigorous college preparatory program to equip students for success in higher education.

and mathematics—as well as computers, art, physical education, science, drama and foreign languages.

Cardinal Gibbons High School
1401 Edwards Mill Rd. • 834-1625
• www.cghs.pvt.k12.nc.us

Cardinal Gibbons is the Triangle's only Catholic high school, providing coed instruction for up to 830 students in grades 9 through 12. The school provides a college preparatory curriculum and 99 percent of its seniors go on to a four-year college. The average SAT score for seniors at Cardinal Gibbons is more than 1,090, well above the state average of 986.

Uniforms are required and students must take religious instruction in all grade levels. There are about 64 full-time teachers at the school, which is administered by the Franciscan Brothers of Brooklyn. Sixty percent of the faculty possess at least a master's degree. The new Cardinal Gibbons High School opened in the fall of 1999. They welcome students of all faiths, ethnic origins and economic levels.

Cary Academy
1500 N. Harrison Ave., Cary • 677-3873
• www.caryacademy.pvt.k12.nc.us

Cary Academy is a co-educational, college preparatory day school for students in grades 6 through 12, offering a challenging education that effectively integrates technology into a curriculum firmly grounded in the humanities. There are more than 725 computers throughout the campus for use by the school's 625 students.

Strong programs in the performing and visual arts, athletics and extracurricular activities offer leadership opportunities and complement the students' academic lives. The 52-acre campus features a state-of-the-art Media and Administration Building, separate Upper and Middle schools, a Sports and Fitness Center, and a Fine Arts Building.

Cathedral School
204 Hillsborough St. • 832-4711

Proud of its tradition of academic excellence, Cathedral School is ideally located in the heart of historic Raleigh, offering its students the opportunity to experience the city's history firsthand with visits to cultural, historical and scientific facilities, which are all within walking distance. Cathedral School, a Catholic faith community since 1909, encourages students from all denominations and ethnic backgrounds to pursue academic excellence within the framework of Christian principles. With a current enrollment of 270, Cathedral School offers a 4-year-old program, a K-8 curriculum and a supervised after-school program.

Chesterbrook Academy
130 Towne Village Dr., Cary
• 319-9622 • www.nobellearning.com

Chesterbrook Academy is a Nobel Learning Community that opened in August 2000 for students from preschool through sixth grade. The school, which plans for an ultimate enrollment of just over 200 students, places an emphasis on social, emotional and academic growth. It features small class sizes and a comprehensive curriculum that includes foreign language study, computer instruction, art and music programs, and before and after school programs. The 4.2-acre campus boasts a multimedia center, pool, gymnasium, soccer field and playground.

Faith Lutheran School
1809 Capital Blvd. • 829-5899

Faith Lutheran serves approximately 300 students from kindergarten to eighth grade. It has a low student/teacher ratio of 18:1. After-school care is available.

Franciscan School
11401 Leesville Rd., Raleigh
• 847-8205
St. Mary Magdalene Catholic School
625 Magada Pl., Apex • 657-4800
St. Michael the Archangel Catholic School
High House Rd., Cary • 468-6150
• www.raldioc.org

The Roman Catholic Diocese of Raleigh recently embarked on a major expansion, opening three new schools in the Triangle during the fall of 2000. The K-8 Franciscan School in North Raleigh is associated with

Photo by Rich Weidman

Cathedral School is located on the campus of Sacred Heart Cathedral in downtown Raleigh.

St. Francis of Assisi Catholic Church. The preK-8 St. Mary Magdalene Catholic School is a mission school of St. Andrew the Apostle Catholic Church in Apex. The K-6 St. Michael the Archangel Catholic School is associated with the church of the same name in Cary (grades 7 and 8 will eventually be added).

Friendship Christian School
5510 Falls of Neuse Rd. • 872-2133

Organized in 1970, Friendship is a Baptist-affiliated school for boys and girls from 4-year-old kindergarten through grade 12. It was started as a day care and kindergarten and its current enrollment is 450 with a 20 to 1 student-teacher ratio. The school follows a traditional college preparatory teaching format and its students average more than 1,000 on their SAT scores. In addition to advanced-placement courses for college-bound students, the school offers a state-of-the-art computer lab.

Montessori School of Raleigh
7005 Leadmine Rd. • 848-1545
• www.montessori.org

Founded in 1974, MSR is one of the largest Montessori schools in the country. The school takes children from 18 months and goes through the 9th grade. Enrollment is about 400 and teachers follow the Montessori method, which emphasizes individual development at the child's own speed and meeting the needs of each child. Montessori School of Raleigh is accredited by both the Southern Association of Colleges and Schools and the American Montessori Society. Classes average about 25 students with two teachers per class. Day-care service for before- and after-school hours is available. MSR is accredited by both the Southern Association of Colleges and Schools and the American Montessori Society.

North Raleigh Country Day School
10200 Strickland Rd. • 847-3120
• www.citysearch.com/rdu/dolphins

North Raleigh Country Day School, with about 230 students, offers instruction for children from age 3 through the 5th grade. The 6-acre campus is convenient and offers excellent facilities. A member of Nobel Education Dynamics, it is accredited by the National Association for the Education of Young Children (NAEYC). It has an excellent reputation and is known for providing educational extras such as computer instruction, swim lessons in on-campus pools and before- and after-school day-care programs. Summer camp programs are also available.

Our Lady of Lourdes
2710 Overbrook Dr. • 782-1670
• www.olls.org

Founded in 1954, this is another Catholic elementary-middle school serving the Raleigh and Cary area. It goes through the 8th grade, and many of the students continue at Cardinal Gibbons. The school requires uniforms. Lourdes has more than 500 K-8 students and uses lay teachers.

Paideia Academy
2918 Kildaire Farm Rd., Cary
• 881-1100 • www.paideiaacademy.com

Founded in 1998, Paideia (pronounced pie-DAY-ah) provides Christian-centered education for kindergarten through ninth grade. The school uses a classical curriculum that divides education into three parts: grammar, logic and rhetoric. Class size is limited to 18 students. Soccer, basketball and roller hockey teams are available for students to join.

Raleigh Christian Academy
2110 Trawick Rd. • 872-2215

Sponsored by the First Free Will Baptist Church, this school began in 1977. It has all

Understanding Charter Schools

The North Carolina General Assembly passed the Charter Schools Act of 1996 in an effort to create an avenue for parents, teachers and community members to develop new and innovative methods of educating all children within the public school system. Charter schools are essentially deregulated public schools that operate as autonomous schools of choice within a school district. About 4,000 students in the Triangle currently attend charter schools, which are tuition free and typically smaller in both overall size and class size than your average public school. Some of the schools provide transportation and offer before- and after-school programs.

The State Board of Education is authorized to grant approval of all charter school proposals. If approved by the state, the charter school must sign a contract with the local school board that describes its educational objectives.

North Carolina has nearly 100 charter schools, 25 of which are in the Triangle. Here is a sampling of some of the area charter schools:

Durham County

Carter Community School (K-8) • 1305 W. Club Blvd., Durham • 416-9025
Healthy Start Academy (K-4) • 515 Dowd St., Durham • 956-5599
Kestral Heights School (6-9) • 1915 Chapel Hill Rd., Durham • 403-9194
Maureen Joy Charter School (K-3) • 320 Belvin Ave., Durham • 317-1711
Omuteko Gwamaziima (K-12) • P.O. Box 52072, Durham • 687-0870
Partnership Academy (K-5) • 3823 Guess Rd., Durham • 477-3570
Research Triangle Charter Academy (K-4) • Ellis Rd., Durham • 857-8770
Success Academy (7-12) • 4600 Chapel Hill Blvd., Durham • 680-8076
Turning Point Academy (K-8) • 4600 Chapel Hill Blvd., Durham • 680-8076

Orange County

New Century Charter School (9-12) • 3501-E, N.C. 54 W., Carrboro • 942-7722
Orange County Charter School (K-8) • 660 Cornelius St., Hillsborough • 644-1965
Village Charter School (K-6) • 630 Weaver Dairy Rd., Chapel Hill • 967-2606
The Woods Charter School (4-12) • Cole Park Plaza, Chapel Hill • 960-8353

Wake County

Community Partners Charter High School (9-12) • Holly Springs • 367-8263
East Wake Academy (K-9) • P.O. Box 65, Zebulon • 404-0444
Exploris Middle School (6-8) • 207 E. Hargett St., Raleigh • 821-3168
John H. Baker Jr. High School (9-12) • P.O. Box 550, Raleigh • 856-5929

Magellan Charter School (4-8) • 9400 Forum Dr., Raleigh • 844-0277
Northeast Raleigh Charter Academy (K-5) • 4030 Capital Blvd., Raleigh • 713-0997
Preeminent Institute of Learning (K-2) • 6711 Brookmeade Pl., Raleigh • 846-4104
Quest Academy (1-12) • 9650 Strickland Rd., Raleigh • 841-0441
Raleigh Charter High School (9-10) • 1111 Haynes St., Raleigh • 839-0600
The Sankore School (6-8) • P.O. Box 943, Raleigh • 834-2780
SPARC Academy (K-8) • 1315 Oakwood Ave., Raleigh • 835-2000
Sterling Montessori Academy (K-7) • 202 Treybrooke Dr., Morrisville • 462-8889

For more information about charter schools, contact the North Carolina Office of Charter Schools at 715-1730 or the North Carolina Charter School Resource Center at 461-8824. Or visit the charter school web site at www.dpi.state.nc.us/charter_schools/maincharter.html.

grade levels, from kindergarten to 12th as well as a day-care program that takes infants as young as one year. Enrollment is around 680. At the elementary school level, before-school day care starts at 7 AM and after-school care ends at 6 PM.

The Raleigh School
1100 Edwards Mill Rd. • 546-0788

The Raleigh School began as a preschool when North Carolina had no kindergarten in its public schools. It is a co-op, which means that parents have to help with some of the chores. Today, The Raleigh School serves students from preschool through grade 5.

Ravenscroft School
7409 Falls of Neuse Rd. • 847-0900
• www.ravenscroft.org

Ravenscroft School, one of the best known private schools in the Triangle, was founded in 1862 by members of Christ Episcopal Church and named for the first Episcopal bishop of North Carolina. The school offers a coed, college preparatory day school for students from preschool to 12th grade. While the school has no denominational affiliations, it maintains its

Judeo-Christian heritage and strives to help students understand basic values and pursue ideals of integrity, service, compassion and sportsmanship.

The school upholds rigorous academic standards in keeping with its college preparatory goals. All graduates go on to colleges or universities. SAT scores average about 1240. The school is located on an attractive, wood-fringed 127-acre campus in North Raleigh and enrolls more than 1,000 students with a 16:1 student-teacher ratio.

Saint Mary's High School
900 Hillsborough St. • 424-4100
• www.saint-marys.edu

Founded in 1842, Saint Mary's School is a four-year college preparatory school for girls in grades 9 to 12. Both boarding and day programs are available. The school, which has an enrollment of 240 students, boasts a student-teacher ratio of 10 to 1. Nearly 100 percent of the teaching faculty hold their master's degree in their academic fields. Saint Mary's offers students a variety of extracurricular activities, including clubs and athletic teams. Athletes participate in the North Carolina Independent Athletic Association in the

PRESCHOOLS & DAYCARE

CARY

Bright Horizons	Preston Corners	461-2382
Chesterbrook Academy	203 Gregson Dr.	469-2046
Chesterbrook Academy	201 MacKenan Dr.	469-8007
Chesterbrook Academy	610 Nottingham Dr.	467-6991
Chesterbrook Academy	3821 N.W. Cary Pkwy.	319-9400
Children's Discovery Center	409 Crossroads Blvd.	851-0630
Goddard School	1177 N.W. Maynard Rd.	466-0008
It's Academic	580 E. Chatham St.	388-3024
It's Academic	300 S.E. Cary Pkwy.	481-1744
Kids R Kids	150 Towne Village Dr.	467-1112
KinderCare	4 Locations	(888) 525-2780
La Petite Academy	104 Baines Ct.	469-5735
La Petite Academy	955 W. Chatham St.	467-5875
Little Pros Academy	551 James Jackson Ave.	481-6000
Primrose School	1500 Evans Rd.	481-3901
Primrose School	2511 N.C. 55	363-2700

CHAPEL HILL-CARRBORO

Amity United Methodist	825 Estes Dr.	929-6149
Binkley Preschool	1712 Willow Dr.	968-1427
Carrboro United Methodist	200 Hillsborough Rd.	929-5143
Chapel Hill Cooperative	106 Purefoy Rd.	942-3955
Chapel Hill Day Care	501 Kildaire Rd.	929-3585
Family Preschool	632 Laurel Hill Rd.	967-9684
Holy Family Day Care	200 Hayes Rd.	929-5004
KinderCare	210 S. Elliott Rd.	942-7223
Montessori Day School	1165 Weaver Dairy Rd.	929-3339
Preschool of the Arts	Village Plaza	402-0876
University Methodist	150 E. Franklin St.	967-8867
Wee Care Child Care	1702 Legion Rd.	942-8957

DURHAM

The Asbury Preschool	806 Clarendon St.	286-2668
Beth El Synagogue Preschool	1004 Watts St.	682-1238
Bethesda Baptist Child Care	1914 S. Miami Blvd.	596-5420
Briar Rose Kindergarten	912 Ninth St.	286-5663
Bright Horizons	Imperial Centre, RTP	941-6225
Bright Horizons	Independence Park	477-9296
Bryson Christian Montessori	2811 University Dr.	489-5539
Chesterbrook Academy	117 Woodcroft Pkwy.	489-8899
Cresset Christian Preschool	3707 Garrett Rd.	489-2655
Duke Memorial Preschool	504 W. Chapel Hill St.	688-5130
The Enrichment Center at RTP	10 T.W. Alexander Dr.	549-4802
Epworth United Methodist	3002 Hope Valley Rd.	489-6098
First Presbyterian Day School	305 E. Main St.	688-8685
Gorman Early Learning Ctr.	3315 E. Geer St.	682-0867

PRESCHOOLS & DAYCARE

DURHAM cont.

Grace Baptist Church	1004 N. Mangum St.	682-0671
Hope Valley Preschool	1600 Chapel Hill-Nelson Hwy.	493-0326
KIN, Too	1416 Broad St.	286-5432
KinderCare	3 Locations	(888) 525-2780
La Petite Academy	4 Locations	(800) 545-4005
Lakewood Ave. School	1701 Lakewood Ave.	493-5882
Little Paradise Preschool	1101 W. Main St.	682-6184
Montessori Children's House	2400 University Dr.	489-9045
Montessori Community	4512 Pope Rd.	493-8541
Mt. Tabor United Methodist	4200 Bahama Rd.	479-1614
Primary Colors Child Care	3008 Dixon Rd.	490-1173
Scarborough Nursery School	309 Queen St.	682-5037
Toddlers Academy	2811 Beechwood Dr.	489-4777
Triangle Children's Center	1900 Sedwick Rd.	544-2815
Westminster Kindergarten	3639 Chapel Hill Rd.	489-8432
Yates Baptist Preschool	2819 Chapel Hill Rd.	489-5760
YMCA Early Learning Center	218 W. Seminary St.	688-9622

RALEIGH & GARNER

Asbury Preschool	6612 Creedmoor Rd.	847-2561
Bright Horizons	3 Locations	(800) 324-4386
Chesterbrook Academy	2215 W. Millbrook Rd.	787-7568
Edenton St. United Methodist	228 W. Edenton St.	832-2029
Ernest Myatt Presbyterian	4926 Fayetteville Rd.	779-0316
First Baptist Church	99 N. Salisbury St.	832-4650
First Cosmopolitan Baptist	1515 Cross Link Rd.	833-3283
Highland Children's Center	1901 Ridge Rd.	787-2182
Hudson Memorial Preschool	4921 Six Forks Rd.	787-1086
KinderCare	5 locations	(888) 525-2780
La Petite Academy	4 Locations	(800) 545-4005
Learning Together	568 Lenoir St.	856-5200
Longview Christian School	2312 Milburnie Rd.	832-1636
Method Day Care Center	1801 Hillsborough St.	828-2926
New Hope Baptist	4301 Louisburg Rd.	876-5850
North Hills Child Care	4711 Six Forks Rd.	782-3380
Pleasant Day Preschool Ctr.	2601 Pleasant Pines Dr.	571-7469
Pleasant Grove Preschool	4415 Pleasant Grove Church Rd.	787-1652
Primary Beginnings	4001 Spring Forest Rd.	790-1178
Raleigh Preschool	1215 Ridge Rd.	828-5351
The School of Grace	5010 Six Forks Rd.	787-4740
St. Mark's Preschool	4801 Six Forks Rd.	787-1832
St. Michael's Day School	1520 Canterbury Rd.	782-6430
Tammy Lynn Center	739 Chappell Dr.	832-3909
YWCA	3 locations	828-3205

Photo courtesy of St. Mary's High School

St. Mary's is a four-year college preparatory school that offers a variety of extracurricular activities, including clubs and athletic teams.

following sports: tennis, soccer, basketball, volleyball, swimming, softball, field hockey, cross country and golf.

Saint Mary's is affiliated with the Episcopal Church and accredited by the Southern Association of Colleges and Schools. The beautiful 23-acre wooded campus, situated between the downtown State Government Complex and North Carolina State University, is listed on the National Register of Historic Places.

St. Timothy's School
4523 Six Forks Rd.
Admissions: 781-0531
School Office: 787-3011

St. Timothy's-Hale School
3400 White Oak Rd.
Admissions & School Office: 782-3331
• www.sttimothyshale.com

St. Timothy's School and St. Timothy's-Hale School are fully accredited coeducational Episcopal day schools for students in pre-first through grade 12. Located on two campuses in close proximity to the North Hills section of Raleigh, both schools enroll

students of all faiths from the Triangle and surrounding areas.

Established in 1958 by St. Timothy's Episcopal Church, St. Timothy's School enrolls 415 students in pre-first through grade 4. A challenging academic program emphasizes appropriate activities in reading, language arts, math, science, social studies and French. Art, music, drama, physical education and a cultural arts program complement the academic program. Technology is integrated through computers in the classroom, as well as several fully equipped labs. Low student-to-teacher ratios foster the development of close relationships between faculty and students.

St. Timothy's-Hale School enrolls 460 students in grades 5 to 12. Students pursue an accelerated college-preparatory program in classes small enough to permit individual attention. Graduates must successfully complete a minimum of 23 high school credits, which include English, foreign language, history, math, history, science, foreign language, religion and health/physical education. The curriculum includes a one-year

Excellence in Education

College Preparatory

Small Classes

Upgraded Facilities

Visual and Performing Arts

Competitive Sports (7-12)

Integrated Technology

Chapel Services

Honor Code

20 Acres on Two Campuses

SACS Accredited

ST. TIMOTHY'S SCHOOL
ST. TIMOTHY'S-HALE SCHOOL
Coeducational Episcopal Day Schools

ST. TIMOTHY'S SCHOOL
GRADES K-4

Ms. Cathy Clement, Director of Admissions
4523 Six Forks Road, Raleigh, NC 27609
(919) 781-0531
www.sttimothys.org

ST. TIMOTHY'S-HALE SCHOOL
GRADES 5-12

Mr. Chris Kelley, Director of Admissions
3400 White Oak Road, Raleigh, NC 27609
(919) 782-3331
www.sttimothyshale.com
email: admissions@sths.pvt.k12.nc.us

Please call to schedule a campus visit and interview.

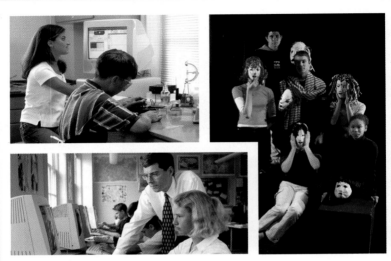

RAVENSCROFT SCHOOL
— FOUNDED 1862 —

As Wake County's only independent co-ed, preschool through twelfth grade college preparatory school, Ravenscroft offers an outstanding education with emphasis in academics, athletics, and the arts.

- The most comprehensive Advanced Placement course offering in Wake County

- Average SAT scores more than 200 points higher than the Wake County average

- 100% college acceptance

- Award winning faculty

- A competitive athletic program featuring 19 varsity and 17 junior varsity sports

- A wide variety of programs in both visual and performing arts including strings, band, drama, choral music, and studio art

- Numerous off-campus education programs

The purpose of Ravenscroft School is to promote the development of the total child.

Photos by Brenda Pegram

For more information about the educational program offered at Ravenscroft School please call **(919) 847-0900**, *or write the Admissions Office, Ravenscroft School, 7409 Falls of the Neuse Road, Raleigh, North Carolina 27615. Ravenscroft School does not discriminate on the basis of race, sex, ethnic or national origin. Financial aid based on need available.*
www.ravenscroft.org

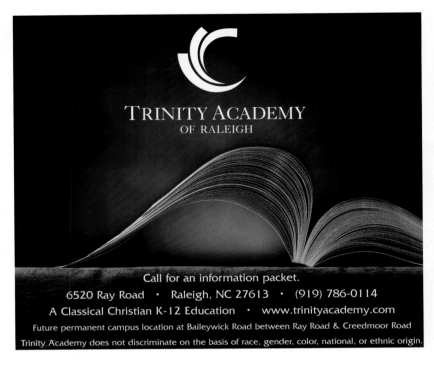
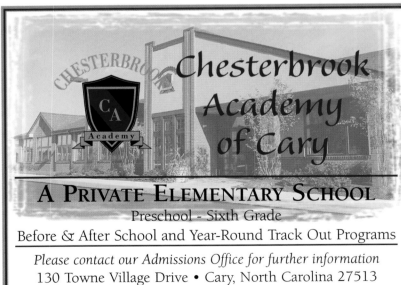

SAINT MARY'S SCHOOL
A TRADITION OF EXCELLENCE
Preparing girls—mind, body and soul—for college and life

**Saint Mary's School
is an Episcopal affiliated all-girls college
preparatory high school with day and
boarding programs—grades 9-12.**

**College preparation • Beautiful campus
Caring teachers • Small classes
Fine arts • Extensive extracurricular programs
JV and varsity sports • Home away from home
Friends for life**

Saint Mary's School
900 Hillsborough Street
Raleigh, NC 27603-1689
(919) 424-4100 • (800) 948-2557

E-mail: admiss@saint-marys.edu
Website: www.saint-marys.edu

I think. I can.

Teach a child to think, and they can do anything. That's what sets KinderCare apart. From our specially-trained teachers... our bright, energetic classrooms... to our age-appropriate curricula, we're improving the lives of children in the most important classroom they will enter — their first.

KinderCare®
Your child's first classroom.

FIRST CLASS
WE TEACH
CHILDREN.
BUT FIRST
WE TEACH
TEACHERS.

Our teachers are trained in traditional learning programs that provide a strong foundation for children 6 weeks to 5 years old. Our programs help your child grow academically and socially. Visit us and find out why we're "The Leader In Educational Child Care℠".

Primrose School of Cary
1500 Evans Road
481-3901

Primrose School of West Cary
2511 NC Highway 55
363-2700

Primrose School of Raleigh
6941 Hilburn Drive
783-8222

www.primroseschools.com

Each school is privately owned and operated. All trademarks named or illustrated are registered trademarks of Primrose School Franchising Company. ©2000 PSFC.

Now Enrolling
Limited Openings Available

To Play ● To Explore ● To Create ● To Develop Physically

Together with our well-trained and educated teaching staff, parent support and involvement, a curriculum designed especially for young children and our innovative physical development/sports program, Little Pros offers a complete educational program for the successful development of young children intellectually, emotionally, socially and physically.

● Low Ratios
● Spanish Classes
● Computer Classes
● State of the Art Security
● Sports and Movement Programs
● Degreed Teachers

New Location on corner of Highway 54 & Keybridge Dr. near Weston Parkway
Opening Early 2001

Call Today to Register Your Child! Caring for Children Ages 6 weeks-K
919-481-6000 ● www.littleprosacademy.com
551 James Jackson Avenue (near Preston) ● Cary, NC 27513

Latin requirement designed to improve reading, writing, grammar and vocabulary skills. Advanced Placement courses in all subject areas, as well as electives in music, art, drama and computer technology are offered. Students are also encouraged to participate in athletics and extracurricular activities. One hundred percent of St. Timothy's-Hale graduates are accepted into a college or university.

Trinity Academy
6520 Ray Rd., Raleigh
- **786-0114 (Lower School)**
- **846-7475 (Upper School)**
- **www.trinityacademy.com**

Trinity Academy is a college preparatory day school that offers an education grounded in Christian faith and the classical tradition. The Lower School (K-8) is currently located at the campus of Calvary Presbyterian Church at 6520 Ray Road. The Upper School (9-12) is located on the campus of Asbury United Methodist Church. A permanent campus will soon be constructed on Baileywick Road between Ray and Creedmoor roads.

Wake Christian Academy
5500 Wake Academy Dr. • 772-6264

One of the oldest and largest private Christian schools in Wake County, Wake Christian Academy enrolls students from kindergarten through grade 12. It offers a curriculum based on Christian values and has a full extracurricular program.

After-School Programs

After-school programs are designed for the older child who is in school, but who needs an activity to keep him or her busy until mom or dad gets home.

Chapel Hill-Carrboro

Affordable after-school care is available at all eight public elementary schools and all three middle schools. For more information, contact the Administrative Offices at Lincoln Center, 967-8211.

Some of the private schools we described also offer after-school care. For more information, contact the school.

Durham

The public schools in the Durham area offer before- and after-school care at many school sites. Call to inquire about the availability of transportation at your child's school. Several private schools also offer earlier and later drop-off and pickup times for students. Local day-care programs also offer transportation from some schools to the centers for after-school care.

After-school care is provided at various neighborhood centers run by the Durham Parks and Recreation Department. For more information on these after-school programs, contact the Durham Parks and Recreation Department, 560-4355. The Lakewood YMCA also offers an after-school "Kid's Club" for ages 5 through 12.

Raleigh-Cary

The Raleigh-Cary area offers three primary providers of after-school care: the public schools' extended-day program, the YMCA and YWCA and the diverse city recreation programs. Contact information can be found elsewhere in this chapter or in the "Parks and Recreation" chapter.

Preschools and Day-Care Programs

Since North Carolina has the highest percentage of working women in the nation and because many of these women are mothers, adequate day care for children has long been part of the state's social fabric. A higher-than-state average of working women, many in professional ranks, also work in the Triangle area. Therefore, the Triangle has a number of private and quasi-public day-care operations and several Triangle businesses—such as Cary software giant SAS—provide day care for

Cary Elementary stands on the site of the original Cary High School, which was chartered as the first state-assisted public high school in North Carolina in 1907.

employees' children as part of the company's benefit package.

North Carolina has enacted minimum standards for child-care facilities. All providers must be registered with the North Carolina Division of Child Development, 662-4499, located at 319 Chapanoke Rd., Suite 120. Ask your provider or center for its registration number to verify this registration. If you want to check out a center's record, you can go to this office in Raleigh and look in the state files to see if any complaints have been lodged against the center.

State standards also set the following adult-to-provider ratios: infants up to 1-year-old (1:5), 2 years (1:10), 3 years (1:15), 4 years (1:20) and 5 years and older (1:25). However, these standards allow fewer adults per child than federal standards permit.

Chapel Hill-Carrboro

There are more than two dozen preschools and many more child-care providers in Chapel Hill and Carrboro. One way to learn about which facility or home setting is right for your needs is to ask for recommendations from friends and neighbors, then go observe.

Or you can contact Child Care Networks, a private, nonprofit organization that assists people in matching their child-care needs with the right facility, home setting or provider. For more information, call Child Care Networks at 542-6644.

Another resource is the Child Care Services Association of Orange County, which is located at 1829 Franklin Street. Call 967-3272 for more information.

Durham

There are at least 150 child-care centers and preschools and 280 child-care homes in the Durham area. They include Montessori schools, church-affiliated centers, national chains, small independent operators and school-age programs. Daycare centers in Durham usually charge $75 to $175 a week. Child care in private homes usually costs $60 to $150 a week.

To learn more about choosing quality child care and child-care regulations, contact the Durham Day Care Council, a resource and referral agency at 115 Market Street, Suite 300. Or call the TOTLINE at 403-6955 for referrals and information on child-care centers and homes, preschool programs and school age child care in Durham. Another resource is the Child Care Services Association, 2634 Chapel Hill Boulevard, 403-6950.

Raleigh and Cary

There are several kinds of providers for full day-care service, which usually take infants from 6-weeks-old to kindergarten-aged children. The small in-home provider is at one end of the spectrum, yet regulations and insurance rates are making it more difficult for many such programs. At the other end are the national child-care centers such as KinderCare, La Petite Academy and Young World. They can be found in the Yellow Pages under "Child Care Centers."

In between are single-site providers, many of which, again, are in churches. Two of the best are First Baptist Church in downtown Raleigh and Pullen Memorial Baptist Church's Method Day Care. Some of the other churches with established programs for 2-year-olds and up are West Raleigh Presbyterian, Edenton Street United Methodist and First Cosmopolitan Baptist Church.

Learning Together is operated on contract with Wake County School System and Department of Social Services and it serves gifted and learning-disabled children. Tammy Lynn Center is a nonprofit school for the handicapped. Some of the city's housing projects also have day-care centers.

The Child Care Resource and Referral Center of Wake County at 4 North Blount Street (832-7175 for referrals), is not a day-care center but rather a nonprofit information center that helps families find day care suitable to them and their budgets.

The Growing Child at 1120 Sawmill Road (846-1164) is a program that supplies community oriented care—most children who attend Impressions live within a 3- to 4-mile radius of the center. Located within the Greystone neighborhood (see the "Raleigh Neighborhoods" section in our "Real Estate and Neighborhoods" chapter), the Center provides full day- and preschool care for infants (6 weeks) through age 2. Hours are from 7 AM until 6 PM. Call for tuition.

Spectator Sports

In the past, we've advised readers who are new to the Triangle that they should learn their sports. It's still good advice because the Triangle is not only the world capital of college basketball, but since our first edition way back in the 20th Century, the Triangle's sports business has boomed. And talking about the fortunes of a favorite local team remains a safe and acceptable introduction to local society.

This chapter looks at spectator sports and it includes information on the National Hockey League's Carolina Hurricanes who start in 2000 their second year in Raleigh's Entertainment and Sports Arena (ESA). This section highlights two of the best minor league baseball teams, the Durham Bulls and the Carolina (Zebulon) Mudcats. And starting this year, Arena Football's new Cobras began play in the ESA. Yes, we have professional soccer, too, and by the way, you can watch Triangle resident and track Superstar Marion Jones train at NCSU's Derr Field.

But college sports are what touch the hearts (and wallets) of Triangle Insiders. The rivalries between the state's two largest universities and the "special relationship" between Carolina and Duke give fire to the invigorating enthusiasm of college games. It is no different among the three historically black campuses of Shaw, St. Augustine's and North Carolina Central University. Raleigh's ESA will be the site for the next several years of the CIAA Basketball Tournament, a sport, fashion and social event like no other.

One final tip. Because the rivalries here are so intense, you want to avoid social faux pas such as confusing Carolina Blue with Duke Blue or talking about North Carolina University (there ain't no such place—it's North Carolina State University or the University of North Carolina). So get out your pompoms and Sis Boom Bah! Let's play ball!

Collegiate Sports
Chapel Hill

University of North Carolina at Chapel Hill
- **Tickets: 962-2296**
- **Information: 962-2123**
- **tarheelblue.fansonly.com**

UNC-CH is also known as Carolina, the Tar Heels, the Heels and Chapel Hill. Carolina fans are some of the most ardent in the ACC. If you don't believe it, just ask a fan why they say the sky is Carolina blue. Most of all, Carolina's athletic tradition is a winning one—Atlantic Coast Conference championships in a variety of sports every year.

In 1982, the school posted national championships in three different sports: basketball, lacrosse and women's soccer. The 1992-93 men's basketball team won the national NCAA championship and the women's team won it all in the 1993-94 season. UNC women have one of the best all-around sports programs in the country.

Basketball
Dean E. Smith Center, Manning Dr.

Under former head coach Dean Smith—for whom the 21,572-seat arena ("The Dean Dome") is named—Carolina basketball compiled a legendary record, including 13 ACC Tournament Championships, 11 Final Fours and two NCAA Championships ('82 and '93). Smith, a Kansas transplant, once led a United States Olympic team—with a number of Carolina players—to the gold medal.

After UNC captured the ACC Tournament title and advanced to the NCAA Final Four during the 1996-97 season, Smith shocked the Tar Heel faithful by retiring after 36 seasons and 879 victories—the most of any coach in NCAA Division I history. Long-time assistant coach Bill Guthridge stepped in during the 1997-98 season, guiding the team to a 34-4 overall record (the most wins by any first-year head coach in NCAA history), a second consecutive ACC Tournament Championship and a second consecutive Final Four appearance. During the 1998-99 season, the team finished with a solid 24-10 overall record but was defeated by an unheralded Weber State team in a stunning upset during the first round of the NCAA Tournament. The Heels struggled throughout the 1999-2000 regular season but made a spectacular run in the NCAA Tournament before falling 71-59 to the Florida Gators in the Final Four. Senior Ed Cota finished his collegiate career with 1,030 assists, which ranks third in both ACC and NCAA history. Freshman sensation Joseph Forte became the first rookie in UNC history to lead the team in scoring with 16.7 points per game. Guthridge retired as head coach in the summer of 2000 and was replaced by Matt Doherty, a former head coach at Notre Dame and a member of the 1982 UNC basketball team that won the national championship.

Carolina basketball tickets are so valuable that they sometimes have been mentioned in wills and as part of divorce settlements. If you go to preseason games, against non-ACC opponents, your chances for tickets aren't that bad. When available, these tickets cost about $25. Joining the alumni's Rams Club improves, but doesn't guarantee, your chances of obtaining basketball tickets.

If you're wondering why there's such a fuss over Carolina basketball, just look at the list of some of the pros who wore Tar Heel blue: James Worthy, Bobby Jones, Mitch Kupchak, Phil Ford, Walter Davis, Brad Daugherty, Sam Perkins, J.R. Reid, Antawn Jamison, Vince Carter and, of course, Michael Jordan.

In addition, the Heels are winners and behave accordingly as evident in the 1993 NCAA championships that brought UNC its third national title, defeating the highly touted "fab five" from Michigan. Tar Heel fans will never forget when Michigan's Chris Webber called the last minute "time-out" that sealed the Tar Heel victory.

The women's basketball team is also competitive year in and year out. The 1993-94 squad won the NCAA title in a dramatic three-point shot in the final second by Charlotte Smith. During the 1999-2000 season, the Tar Heels finished with an overall record of 20-13, falling to the Georgia Bulldogs 83-57 in the West Regional final of the NCAA Tournament. The Heels are led by head coach Sylvia Hatchell.

FYI

Unless otherwise noted, the area code for all phone numbers listed in this guide is 919.

Football
Kenan Stadium, Main Campus
You have to act fast to buy season tickets for UNC football games. In 1990, UNC's team kept national champ Georgia Tech from having an unblemished record. Since 1992, the Heels have been "bowling" most every

year, including the 1994 Sun Bowl, the 1995 CarQuest Bowl and the 1996 Gator Bowl. In 1997, the Heels defeated Virginia Tech 42-3 in the Gator Bowl, capping a stellar 11-1 season and a national Top 10 finish. Long-time head coach Mack Brown resigned at season's end to accept the head coaching position at the University of Texas and defensive coordinator Carl Torbush stepped in and led the team to the Gator Bowl victory. In 1998, the Heels finished 7-5 and captured a 20-13 victory over San Diego State in the Las Vegas Bowl. The 1999 squad struggled toward a 3-8 overall record that included wins over top rivals N.C. State and Duke. Torbush hired former Wolfpack head coach Mike O'Cain as his new offensive coordinator.

The football tradition is strong at Carolina with the likes of Charlie "Choo Choo" Justice among its great running backs. Some of its most notable graduates include Natrone Means, all-pro linebacker Lawrence Taylor and tailback Kelvin Bryant. Other Carolina greats include Chris Hanburger, "Famous" Amos Lawrence, Greg Ellis and Super Bowl champions Harris Barton and Dre Bly.

If you go to a Carolina football game, plan on making a day of it since pregame parties and tailgating are part of the ritual. Since tickets are retained by families year after year, you may see the same folks at the games, which makes the afternoon a neighborly get together. "Tar Heel Town" is the official pregame party for UNC football fans with live music, entertainment and children's activities. It takes place 2 1/2 hours before the game across South Road from the Bell Tower.

Don't get alarmed when you start running into bumper-to-bumper traffic as you approach Chapel Hill. It's that way before every home game. Finding parking in Chapel Hill on game day is like looking for a lost contact lens in a dark movie theater. Plan ahead. It is illegal to park on the sidewalk, especially during game days. Parking there will result in a ticketed or towed car during the game. A better option would be to park at University Mall and take the shuttle. If you don't know where the stadium is, just follow the crowd. Originally constructed in 1927 and renovated extensively over the years, Kenan Stadium

Photo courtesy of UNC Sports Information

Nothing beats cheering the UNC Tar Heel football team to victory on a crisp fall afternoon.

seats 60,000. A six-game season ticket package runs about $148.

Other Sports

Carolina is a championship competitor in a long list of other NCAA sports. In fact, the Heels have finished in the top-20 six successive times in the Sears Director's Cup standings, winning the award as the best overall sports programs in the country during the 1993-94 season. Carolina teams regularly capture ACC championships in such sports as women's soccer, field hockey, women's cross country, women's basketball, volleyball, men's and women's swimming, wrestling, men's and women's indoor track, men's golf and men's and women's outdoor track, among others. In fact, UNC teams won an astounding 83 ACC titles during the '90s. These sports always offer an exciting, low-cost entertainment option for families, students and young professionals in the area.

In addition, the lacrosse team won 11 ACC and four NCAA titles between 1981 and 1996. The field hockey team has won 14 ACC titles and four NCAA Championships since 1983 under the leadership of head coach Karen Shelton.

Likewise, the women's soccer program, led by head coach Anson Dorrance, is the best in the country. Past Tar Heel standouts include Mia Hamm, Cindy Parlow, Robin Confer and Kristine Lilly. The team captured its 15th NCAA national title in 18 years after defeating Notre Dame in 1999.

Track and field, wrestling and baseball are the school's other spectator sports. UNC has been the ACC wrestling champion for eight of the last nine years and was an NCCA champion in 1993. UNC won six straight ACC swimming titles from 1993 to 1998.

Durham
Duke University

Tickets: 681-2583
Information: 684-2633
• www.goduke.com

Duke continues to be among the top athletic programs in the nation each year, an amazing feat for a school with an undergraduate enrollment of 6,000. It's a private school with high academic standards and SAT scores that average around 1300—a difficult task for coaches recruiting 285-pound tackles or 7-foot basketball centers. Duke has been featured on the cover of *Parade* magazine for its success in promoting good grades and great athletes.

Duke teams soar—like the 1990-91 and 1991-92 Blue Devil basketball teams, which won back-to-back national championships. Duke won it all against UNLV, Kansas, Indiana and Michigan. Duke went to the Final Four five years in a row and was the first team since UCLA to repeat a championship.

Basketball
Cameron Indoor Stadium, West Campus

Duke's basketball teams have been one of the best shows in the nation for more than 20 years. Cameron Indoor Stadium is absolutely one of the best spots to watch college basketball in the country. If you can get a ticket—go! In 1978, 1986, 1990, 1991, 1992, 1994 and 1999, the Blue Devils advanced to the NCAA's Championship game. Duke won it all in 1991 and 1992. In 1999, Duke swept the ACC regular season and captured the ACC Tournament championship. After losing four starters to the NBA draft, Duke dominated the ACC again during the 1999-2000 season with the addition of freshmen sensations Jason Williams, Carlos Boozer and Mike Dunleavy combined with the leadership of upperclassmen Chris Carawell, Shane Battier and Nate James. The Blue Devils finished the season with an overall record of 29-5, capturing the ACC championship with a victory over Maryland and advancing to the Sweet Sixteen of the NCAA Tournament before falling 78-87 to the Florida Gators.

Duke stars who have moved into the NBA include Elton Brand, William Avery, Corey Maggette, Trajan Langdon, Roshown McLeod, Grant Hill, Christian Laettner, Bobby Hurley, Danny Ferry, Johnny Dawkins, Mike Gminski, Gene Banks, Jeff Mullins and Jack Marin, with more to come.

At Cameron Indoor Stadium (which seats 9,314), you get two shows for the price of one: you get to watch the basketball team and you get to see the notorious Duke fans—The Cameron Crazies. Long before TV broadcasters like Al McGuire and Dick Vitale compared them to Attila's hordes, the students were entertaining visiting teams with all sorts of digs, barbs and sarcasm. For instance, during one game against a crosstown rival, the Crazies held up hundreds of fake mug shots of a certain player who had run into trouble with the law earlier in the season. Another tried and true trick from the Crazies is to count down the wrong numbers on the shot clock.

Season tickets have been sold out since the early 1980s. To get basketball tickets, you can join the Iron Dukes, which supports Duke athletics, but that's no guarantee—the allocation of season tickets is based upon

Photo by Jeff Camarati, courtesy of Duke University

The Duke Blue Devils basketball team competes at 9,314-seat Cameron Indoor Stadium, home of the notorious "Cameron Crazies."

contributions to the Iron Duke organization. Single tickets cost $20 for non-conference games and $25 for all home ACC games. Holiday game tickets are sold when the students are away so check the Duke ticket office in September for availability. (No, it's not true that if you can spell Coach Mike Krzyzewski's last name, you get in free.)

Led by head coach Gail Gostenkors, the Blue Devil women's basketball team made it to the 1999 NCAA finals for the first time in school history, falling to Purdue in the championship game. In 2000, the team won the ACC Tournament, finished with an overall record of 28-6 and made it to the East Regional semifinals. Tickets for women's basketball are only $5 per game.

Football
Wallace Wade Stadium, West Campus

Blue Devil teams were once national powers in football starting back in the '30s when the famous 1938 Iron Dukes under Football Hall of Famer Wallace Wade went undefeated, untied and unscored on but lost the Rose Bowl, 7-3, to Southern California in

the last 40 seconds. The Blue Devils are one of only a handful of schools that have played in all four of the major bowl games: Rose, Cotton, Orange and Sugar. Former Blue Devil stars include quarterbacks Sonny Jurgensen, Ben Bennett and Dave Brown, running backs Ace Parker and George McAfee and linebackers Mike Curtis and Bob Matheson.

After the dream season of 1989 that included an ACC co-championship, Coach Steve Spurrier, Coach of the Year in 1988 and 1989, left for Florida's warmer climes. Coach Fred Goldsmith took the helm in 1994 and led Duke to an 8-4 season and Hall of Fame Bowl game. Current head coach Carl Franks, a former assistant offensive coordinator at the University of Florida, played tight end and running back for the Blue Devils and served as an assistant coach at Duke under Spurrier. His high-flying airborne offense spreads the field and allows Duke a chance to score on any possession.

On almost any autumn Saturday afternoon or evening that the Blue Devils are playing at 33,941-seat Wallace Wade Stadium, you can get a ticket at the gate. The price is $22 ($30 for the East Carolina and UNC games); preferred season tickets run about $100. Other season tickets cost $40 and $70, depending on the seat. Before the game, enjoy food and interactive games at the Blue Devil Tailgate Terrace.

Other Sports

Duke's national athletic prowess doesn't stop with basketball and football. During the 1998-99 school year, the Blue Devils tied for sixth place in the Sears Directors' Cup standings, winning the women's national golf championship and placing four other teams in the NCAA semifinals: men's and women's basketball, women's tennis and women's lacrosse.

Also in 1999, Duke swept the men's and women's ACC Tennis Championships. It was the men's eighth title in nine years and the women's 12th consecutive ACC championship.

You can watch some of the best college soccer at Duke's Koskinen Stadium in the fall. Its men's soccer team usually is ranked among the top 20 and it won the 1986 NCAA national championship. In 1995, the team advanced to the NCAA Final Four, finishing second in the nation with a 1-0 loss to Wisconsin. In 1994, the Duke women's team beat the juggernaut UNC women's soccer team, an unheard-of feat since UNC was undefeated at home in a stretch of about 20 years! The 1999 men's soccer team won the ACC title and finished ranked number one in the nation.

The Blue Devils also are ranked in men's and women's lacrosse and the men's and women's tennis teams are frequent ACC champs. The women's volleyball team has won the ACC championship four times in recent years. Track teams have included Dave Sime, once one of the world's fastest runners.

North Carolina Central University

Tickets: 560-5170
Information: 530-7054
• www.nccu.edu/campus/athletics

NCCU is a member of the NCAA Division II Central Intercollegiate Athletic Association and offers a number of sporting events to Triangle residents. The school became known in the '70s for its track teams, coached by now-retired Leroy Walker, who was the United States track coach at the Montreal Olympics. There are 12 schools—including St. Augustine's and Shaw in Raleigh—in the CIAA, a conference that has produced dozens of players in the pro ranks.

Basketball
McLendon-McDougald Gym, Main Campus

NCCU's basketball history includes John B. McLendon's then-dramatic fast-break teams of the 1930s and one of the game's first 7-foot players. Sam Jones of the Boston Celtics, who is a former Eagle star, was inducted into the NBA Hall of Fame in 1983.

In 1989, when Duke lost the championship to UNLV, Durham did not go without an NCAA national title—the Eagles brought home the NCAA Division II basketball

championship title instead! During the 1996-97 season, the Eagles compiled a 20-6 record, which included a fourth CIAA Southern Division Championship in five years and a return to the NCAA South Atlantic Regional playoffs. The Eagles finished with a solid 17-9 record during the 1999-2000 season.

Season tickets for NCCU basketball cost about $60, with single game tickets selling for $10. Games are played in the 3,200-seat McLendon-McDougald Gym.

Football
O'Kelly-Riddick Stadium, Main Campus

Like the larger ACC schools, football is one of the NCCU Eagles' biggest spectator sports. The team went to the NCAA quarterfinals in 1988 and has been a contender in the conference over the years. In 1999, the Eagles finished with a 5-5 overall record during a rebuilding year.

NFL Hall of Famer Larry Little was the Eagle head coach from 1993-98, compiling a 33-32 record. After three losing seasons in four years, NCCU decided not to renew Little's contract. He was replaced by former Livingstone coach Rudy Abrams. Past NCCU stars include John Baker of the Pittsburgh Steelers (now sheriff of Wake County) and John Brown, one of the first black pros, who played for the old Los Angeles Rams.

Season tickets go for about $60 for five home games or $10 per game at the gate. Constructed in 1975 and renovated in 1999, O'Kelly-Riddick Stadium seats about 11,000.

Other Sports

NCCU's track teams under Leroy Walker brought national attention to the Durham school, especially the Eagles' famed "six-pack" of sprinters who helped win the NCAA Division II national championship in the '70s. The team continues to get respect at national meets such as the Penn Relays.

In women's sports, NCCU's volleyball team made it to the NCAA playoffs in 1988 and won the 1999 CIAA Championship. Its basketball

INSIDERS' TIP

Hey, all you UCLA, Indiana, Kentucky and Kansas fans! THIS is the college basketball capital of the USA. Get over it. (Eight national NCAA championships since 1974.)

team is an annual contender for conference honors. The softball team captured the CIAA Championship in 1998 and 1999.

Raleigh
N.C. State University
Tickets: 515-2106
Information: 515-2102
• athletics.ncsu.edu

The powerhouse in the Raleigh-Cary corner of Triangle sports is North Carolina State University (also known as State, NCSU or the Pack), the sprawling campus between Hillsborough Street and Western Boulevard in Raleigh. It has a rich sports tradition and when it's winning, you can feel it in Raleigh's mood. Its teams, nicknamed the Wolfpack, have produced such famous athletes as quarterbacks Roman Gabriel and Eric Kramer, receivers Mike Quick and Torry Holt and running back Ted Brown; baseball pitchers Mike Caldwell, Tim Stoddard and Dan Plesac; basketball pros David Thompson, Tom Gugliotta, Thurl Bailey and Spud Webb; and in tennis, John Sadri. In addition, NCSU boasts a graduation rate among athletes that is higher than the university average.

Basketball
Entertainment & Sports Arena
1400 Edwards Mill Rd.

NCSU fans are some of the most fervent, especially those who call themselves "ABC" fans—Anybody But Carolina. State fans demonstrated their faith in celebratory bonfires in 1983 when the late Jim Valvano's "Team of Destiny" rallied from a lukewarm season record to first capture the ACC Tournament title and then win the NCAA Championship Game against Houston with a heart-stopping shot at the buzzer.

The Pack, led by head coach Norm Sloan, also won the NCAA championship in 1974 after beating UCLA and Bill Walton in two overtimes in what some consider the best NCAA tournament game ever. In 1996, Coach Herb Sendek, former head coach of Miami (Ohio) University, replaced Les Robinson as head coach, becoming the youngest coach in the ACC.

Sendek's teams are noted as fierce competitors and the Wolfpack surprised everyone by making it to the 1997 ACC Tournament Finals before being knocked off by a more talented UNC squad. During the 1999-2000 season, the Pack finished with a 20-14 overall record and qualified for the National Invitation Tournament for the fourth year in a row, falling 59-62 to Wake Forest in a thrilling overtime game in the semifinals.

Season tickets for 17 home games start at about $170 and they're only $20 for most non-conference games. Don't expect to get any tickets at the door when other ACC teams are in town.

The Wolfpack moved from Reynolds Coliseum to its new home at the $158 million, 21,600-seat "Entertainment and Sports Arena" near Carter-Finley Stadium and the State Fairgrounds in the fall of 1999. The arena is also

Photo by Roger W. Winstead, courtesy of NCSU

The NCSU Wolfpack basketball team plays its home games at the state-of-the-art Entertainment and Sports Arena.

March Madness: A Triangle Tradition

We know that CBS has trademarked March Madness and broadcast it into the national vocabulary, but the craziness started here, in what Triangle residents justifiably call the college basketball capital of the United States.

Big time college basketball arrived in the Triangle when Everett Case began recruiting talented athletes from "up north" to play at Raleigh's North Carolina State University during the 1950s. They whipped everybody on Tobacco Road and many teams beyond. At that time, the teams played in the Southern Conference and, believe it or not, the end of season conference tournament was played in Raleigh's Memorial Auditorium, which was smaller than it is now. (Carolina stopped Case's team in 1957 when the undefeated Heels won the NCAA national championship.)

Close-up

The conference evolved into the Atlantic Coast Conference (ACC) and the madness took hold in the 1960s when the ACC sent only one team to the annual NCAA tournament—that team was not the regular season champ, but the take-all winner of the ACC Tournament. By this time, too, the Triangle's ACC sports teams had acquired a strong sports tradition and thousands of alumni, thanks to the GI Bill and huge college enrollments following World War II. The crowds found themselves squeezed into two small basketball arenas at Duke and Carolina; only State's Reynold's Coliseum, which seats 12,000, was worthy of the name. Going to an ACC basketball game became a mark of social standing as much as sports loyalty. Why, you might even be on TV! Season tickets to Carolina games, in particular, were (and still are) items listed in wills or divorce settlements.

Photo courtesy of UNC Sports Information

Brendan Haywood

Add to this insatiable demand and fixed supply the heat of year-long bragging among fans who lived and worked cheek by jowl in the Triangle, and you had the ingredients for an ACC tournament. Three teams in less than three days. Remember, only one team could go to the NCAA. And beware the lowly team that found a rabbit's foot and pity the team that fell behind Carolina in the final minutes when Dean Smith administered the dreaded Four Corner Offense drip torture.

Today's ACC Tournament no longer produces that maddening tension because the NCAA now takes more than just the tournament champion to the Big Dance in March. The ACC contest remains a popular social event and the Last Chance Lottery to a team with a poor season record to win its way into the 64-team NCAA Tournament. The ACC has sent as many as six teams to the NCAA in recent years, although only three were invited in 2000. Of course, one of those, Carolina, made it to the Final Four, and in 1999, Duke was in the final game.

March Madness. Welcome to our asylum.

the home of the Carolina Hurricanes, as well as a regional entertainment showcase.

Football and men's basketball are the profit producers for State's athletic program, but women's basketball also draws a crowd. The Wolfpack women play in Reynolds Coliseum and the team's head coach, Kay Yow, is recognized as one of the best in the country. Yow is the winningest women's basketball coach in ACC history. It was Yow's USA basketball team that brought home the Olympic gold medal in 1988 from Seoul when the men couldn't. During the 1997-98 season, the Wolfpack advanced to the Final Four of the NCAA Tournament. The team finished with a 22-9 overall record during the 1999-2000 season. Wolfpack star Summer Erb was drafted by the Charlotte Sting. Tickets are $5 a game; season tickets run about $50. Youths under age 17 are admitted free.

Football
Carter-Finley Stadium, Trinity Rd.

Football gets the academic year off to a pulse-pumping start. Former head coach Dick Sheridan took the Pack to the 1988 Peach Bowl, the 1989 Copper Bowl, the 1990 All American Bowl, the 1992 heart-stopping Peach Bowl and the fogged-in 1993 Gator Bowl. Sheridan's successor, Mike O'Cain, led the Pack to the 1994 Hall of Fame Bowl and followed that with a dramatic win in the '95 Peach Bowl over Mississippi State. Over the next two years, the Pack stumbled with back-to-back 3-8 seasons, but bounced back during the 1997 season with a 6-5 record, winning its last three games. NCSU continued its winning ways during the 1998 season with a stunning 24-7 victory over then second-ranked Florida State—one of the biggest upsets in ACC history. After posting a 6-6 overall record in 1999, O'Cain was replaced by Chuck Amato, a former assistant head coach at Florida State University who played and coached for the Wolfpack in the late 1960s and early 1970s.

Home games are played at 51,500-seat Carter-Finley Stadium next to the State Fairgrounds, off Blue Ridge Road. Game tickets are $25 at the gate; season tickets run about $150.

Some consider the ritual tailgate feast before the game the best part of the contest and North Carolinians have raised the custom to culinary heights. Consider yourself a baptized Insider to the Triangle when you attend the home game that plays during State Fair Week. The football crowd and the State Fair crowd combine to create the biggest traffic jam in the state.

Other Sports

NCSU's other sports also put championship athletes on the field. The Pack's baseball team has made 12 NCAA Tournament appearances in the last 14 years. The team plays at Doak Field on Sullivan Drive. The team's coach is alumnus Elliott Avent. The Pack plays about 60 games a year and no admission is charged for non-conference games.

NCSU's swimmers have racked up 14 ACC titles and State boasts about alum David Fox, who wears a 1996 Olympic Gold medal as part of the USA's 4 x 100 freestyle relay contingent. He joins fellow alums Duncan Goodhew ('84 Olympics) and Steve Rerych ('68 Olympics) as Olympic Gold Medalists.

NCSU fields competitive teams in a number of other sports, including wrestling, track and field, men's and women's soccer, cross country and golf, among others. Track meets are held at Derr Field, which NCSU generously shares with the greater Raleigh community as one of the city's favorite jogging and running fields. The men's cross country team has won five consecutive ACC titles and finished third in the 1999 NCAA Championships.

Soccer is another sport where NCSU's women have shared ranking honors with the men. Both teams are usually ranked among the nation's top 20 and the men's team made it to the Final Four in 1990.

If you want to see some rising stars in the universe of golf, don't miss the BellSouth Intercollegiate at MacGregor Downs Golf Club in Cary. It is held the same week of the Masters Tournament in Georgia. NCSU is a co-sponsor of this college cattlecall of the best young players in the country. The tournament invites 12 teams, including the ACC's Big Four of NCSU, UNC, Duke and Wake Forest, and it's a place where you may see the next golf superstar on his way to the pro tours.

In 2000-01, NCSU will also field a women's golf team.

Professional Sports
Arena Football

Carolina Cobras
Entertainment & Sports Arena
• **(877) 4COBRAS (426-2727)**
Ticketmaster: 834-4000
• **www.cobrasfootball.com**

Experience the thrill of "in-your-face, smash-mouth" arena football with the Triangle's newest professional team, the Carolina Cobras. The nonstop action takes place on a 50-yard indoor field with a total of eight players on each side of the ball battling it out during four 15-minute quarters. The 17-team Arena Football League is known for its high-powered offenses, loud music and pyrotechnics. Other teams in the Arena Football League include the New England Sea Wolves, Florida Bobcats, Orlando Predators, Nashville Kats, Tampa Bay Storm, Buffalo Destroyers, Albany Firebirds, Arizona Rattlers, Grand Rapids Rampage, Houston Thunder Bears, Iowa Barnstormers, Los Angeles Avengers, Milwaukee Mustangs, Oklahoma Wranglers, San Jose Saber Cats and New Jersey Red Dogs. The season runs from April through August, culminating with

the ArenaBowl Championship. Season tickets for eight home games run $70 for end zone seats to $700 for first row sideline seats.

Baseball
Carolina Mudcats Baseball
Five County Stadium, Zebulon
• **269-2287** • **www.gomudcats.com**

Steve Bryant, owner of the Mudcats, long ago heard a voice say, "Build it and they will come." Bryant, who is a billboard advertising executive, wanted Raleigh to have its own baseball team. Since he was kept out of the city by the 30-mile rule (he had to be at least 30 miles from the Durham Bulls, the Triangle's other pro team), Bryant built his stadium on an old tobacco field outside Zebulon. The stadium opened in mid-season of 1991, and the Double-A Mudcats draw some of the largest crowds in the Southern League.

The Mudcats' logo is a grinning catfish, and the Mudcat baseball hat is one of the hottest souvenir items in the league among collectors. Now affiliated with the Colorado Rockies, the Mudcats were formerly a farm

Photo courtesy of the Carolina Cobras

The Carolina Cobras of the Arena Football League set attendance records during their first season.

team of the Pittsburgh Pirates and almost half of the Pirates squad got their training here. They've put graduates such as pitcher Esteban Loaiza, catcher Jason Kendall, infielders Kevin Young, Tony Womack, Kevin Polcovich and Freddy Garcia, and outfielder Jermaine Allensworth into the Big Leagues. In 1995, The Mudcats won the Southern League championship for the first time with a minor-league winning record of "95 games in '95."

In the Southern League, the Mudcats compete against the likes of the Greenville Braves, Jacksonville Tigers, Tennessee Blue Jays and Orlando Devil Rays.

A $16 million renovation of Five County Stadium recently has been completed to eliminate bleacher seating and create box and reserved seating for 6,500 fans. The renovation also upgraded the press box, concession areas and restrooms. Tickets range from $4.50 to $8. You can get the usual baseball fare at the concession stand, or for $3.25, you can treat yourself to a catfish sandwich!

Durham Braves

Durham Athletic Park • 956-9555
• **www.coastalplain.com/braves.htm**

A summer college baseball team that plays its home games at historic Durham Athletic Park, the Durham Braves compete in the Coastal Plain League. The roster includes players from Duke, UNC and N.C. State. The Braves compete against teams like the Wilson Tobs, Edenton Steamers, Florence Red Wolves, Outer Banks Daredevils, Asheboro Copperheads, Thomasville Hi-Toms, Peninsula Pilots, Petersburg Generals and Wilmington Sharks. Kids love Bravey the Bear, the team's ubiquitous mascot.

Durham Bulls

**Durham Bulls Athletic Park,
409 Blackwell St.**
• **956-BULL, Information: 687-6500**
• **www.durhambulls.com**

The Durham Bulls have been a Triangle tradition since the first Bulls' team took the field in 1902. Nearly a century and several leagues later, the Bulls are a worldwide

The Durham Bulls are the Triple-A affiliate of the Tampa Bay Devil Rays.

phenomenon. A good bit of that success is due to the 1988 movie *Bull Durham* in which Kevin Costner and Susan Sarandon brought stardom to the Bulls and their hometown.

The 1994 season was the last in the venerable old Durham Athletic Park—the "DAP"—before the team was moved to the country's best minor league ballpark just off the Durham Freeway. The recently renovated, 10,000-seat Durham Bulls Athletic Park or "DBAP" is a brick stadium that evokes baseball memories even though it offers such modern amenities as corporate skyboxes and an in-house television system to broadcast all games. The facility is surely one reason the Bulls drew approximately 464,000 fans for the 1999 season.

From 1980 until 1997, the Bulls were the Class A affiliate for the Atlanta Braves and played a large role in the team's success during the '90s. Steve Avery, Ron Gant, David Justice, Jeff Blauser, Chipper Jones, Mark Lemke, Andruw Jones and Javy Lopez are among players who spent time in a Bulls uniform before advancing to Atlanta.

In 1998, the Bulls embarked on their inaugural season as the Triple-A affiliate of the Tampa Bay Devil Rays, moving from the Carolina League to the International League. More than 2,000 seats were added behind the right field wall to comply with Triple-A requirements and the famous "snorting bull" was moved to left field.

The Bulls won the division championship in 1998 and 1999, advancing to the International League Championship Series both seasons.

At the bargain prices of $5.50 for reserved seats and $4.50 for general admission, it's no wonder that Bulls' fans return again and again to watch some baseball and partake of ball park *haute cuisine* such as El Toro beer, hot dogs, pizza, popcorn, barbecue sandwiches, burritos and soda pop.

Hockey

Carolina Hurricanes
Season tickets: (888) NHL-TIX1
Ticketmaster: 834-4000
Information: 467-PUCK
• **www.caneshockey.com**

The Triangle's first major league franchise, the Carolina Hurricanes, officially introduced National Hockey League action to Raleigh on October 29, 1999, when the team played its first home game of the 1999-2000 season against the New Jersey Devils. The game also marked the first event in the Entertainment and Sports Arena and was the first NHL game in the Triangle. The Hurricanes (originally the Hartford Whalers) compete in the Southeast Division of the Eastern Conference of the NHL and won the Southeast Division Title in the 1998-99 season. During the 1999-2000 season, the Canes finished with an overall record of 37-35-10 and came one point short of making the Stanley Cup playoffs.

After playing their first two seasons in Greensboro, the Hurricanes moved into the Entertainment and Sports Arena just weeks prior to opening night. The Arena is built on a 140-acre tract, adjacent to Carter-Finley Stadium and the North Carolina State Fairgrounds. It is set to host about 160 events annually, including the home games of the Hurricanes, North Carolina State University Wolfpack men's basketball and Carolina Cobras of the Arena Football League. The arena seats 18,700 fans for hockey games, 19,700 for basketball games, 21,000 for center stage concerts and 20,500 for arena end

Photo courtesy of Carolina Hurricanes

The Carolina Hurricanes compete in the Southeast Divison of the NHL's Eastern Conference.

performances. It features three concourses, 61 luxury suites, 2,000 club seats, 10,000 lower bowl seats and 6,600 upper bowl seats.

The Hurricanes' schedule consists of a total of 82 games, including 41 home games. The regular season runs from October to April. Evening games traditionally start at 7:30 PM and afternoon games start at 1:30 PM. Ticket prices in the upper level start at $12, while prices in the lower bowl start at $35. Make sure to purchase tickets early for such high-profile opponents as the New York Islanders and the New Jersey Devils. Games can be heard on the Carolina Hurricanes Radio Network, which includes WRBZ-850 "The Buzz" in Raleigh.

The Hurricanes are led by head coach Paul Maurice. Standouts on the Hurricanes squad include Ron Francis, Sami Kapanan, Jeff O'Neill, Glen Wesley and goalie Arturs Irbe, a native of Latvia.

The Hurricanes have also made a positive impact on the community through charity events and service. The team has formed the Kids n' Community Foundation, a nonprofit organization that raises funds year-round for charities throughout the state. The Hurricanes hold several major events to benefit the foundation during the year, including the Hurricanes charity golf tournament, the FedEx Super Skills Contest and Skate with the Hurricanes.

Soccer

Raleigh Capital Express
WRAL Soccer Complex
Perry Creek Road, Raleigh • 781-RALX
• www.raleighexpress.com

Started in 1993 as an amateur group, the Capital Express (formerly known as the Raleigh Flyers) are now affiliated with the United States Soccer Federation's 30-team A League. Capital Express soccer is great family fun and a good chance to see some exciting, hard-hitting soccer played by future Major League Soccer stars. The roster is full of standout players from area colleges such as NCSU, UNC-CH and Duke. The team competes against the likes of the Wilmington Hammerheads, Atlanta Silverbacks, Charleston Battery, Hershey Wildcats, Maryland Mania and Richmond Kickers. The team struggled during the 1998 season, finishing with an overall record of 5-23. However, it showed dramatic improvement in 1999 under the tutelage of head coach John Dugan, finishing with a record of 11-17. In 2000, the team made the playoffs and finished with an overall record of 12-13-4.

The season, which includes about 14 home games, runs from mid-April to mid-September. Most games start at 7:30 PM. Tickets are about $8 for adults, $7 for youth and $12 for VIP seating.

Raleigh Wings
Flyers Stadium, WRAL Soccer Complex
Perry Creek Road, Raleigh
• 848-3063 • www.raleighwings.com

The Raleigh Wings, a professional women's soccer team, celebrated its inaugural year in 1998. The team features a lot of home-grown talent, including players from North Carolina State, Duke and the University of North Carolina. For the 1998 season, the Wings achieved a 17-0 overall record and captured the league championship with a 4-3 victory over the Boston Renegades. The Wings captured the league championship once again during the 1999 season with a dramatic 3-2 victory over the Chicago Cobras. In 2000, the Wings were defeated 2-1 by the Cobras in the league championship.

The season runs from late May to late July. Tickets are $7 for adults, $5 for youths (18 and under) and $10 for VIP seating.

Stock Car Racing

Orange County Speedway
9740 N.C. 57, Rougemont • (336) 364-1222
• www.orangecountyspeedway.com

Over the years, Orange County Speedway has seen the likes of Jeff Gordon, Bobby Labonte and a host of other Winston Cup drivers compete on its 3/8-mile, high-banked oval track. The Speedway is located north of Durham on N.C. 57 and offers racing events on most Saturdays from late March to late October. Races usually start at 7:30 PM. Tickets cost $12 for adults, $10 for students, $6 for children 10 to 14 and children under 10 are admitted free. The Speedway is home to the infamous Orange County "Bologna Burger."

Wake County Speedway
2109 Simpkins Rd., Raleigh • 779-2171
• www.wakecountyspeedway.com

Built in 1962 as a dirt track, Wake County Speedway is now a 1/4 mile, semi-banked oval track made of asphalt. Catch the action of exciting track racing every Friday night at 8 PM from mid-April to mid-September. Drivers compete in four divisions: Late Model Sportsman, Modified Four Cylinder, Street and Economy Four Cylinder. The Wake County Speedway is located south of Raleigh off U.S. Hwy. 401 South.

INSIDERS' TIP
For all you folks who don't understand hockey, can't get a basketball ticket and ain't attending no Dance Festival, go to a Bulls or Mudcats baseball game. It's the best sports bargain in the Triangle.

Triangle Shopping

Come on down! The cities of the Triangle have a long history as the places where eastern North Carolinians go shopping. Where, for example, are you going to find petite sizes in Tickbite, Shoeheel or Lizard Lick? That shopping tradition continues, and national chains, from Talbots to Lord and Taylor, Nordstrom to Barnes & Noble, have or will open doors here. You will find that some of the most familiar names in the Triangle lexicon belong to shopping centers and malls: Crabtree, Franklin Street, Northgate, Brightleaf, Crossroads, Cameron Village and soon-to-be Streets at Southpoint.

This chapter lists the small and large shopping centers familiar to Insiders. Enjoy the best national retail stores at megamalls like Crabtree Valley, Cary Towne Center and Northgate. Visit regional shopping complexes like Crossroad Plaza for discounts on a wide range of clothes, sporting goods, office supplies and gifts. Browse specialty shops, upscale boutiques and galleries along Franklin Street in Chapel Hill and Ninth Street in Durham for that one-of-a-kind item. Stroll through renovated textile mills and tobacco warehouses such as Carr Mill Mall and Brightleaf Square that have been converted into shops, galleries and restaurants. Choose fresh produce at the State Farmers Market in Raleigh. Explore small area towns like Hillsborough, Pittsboro and Selma for great buys on a variety of antiques.

But as any veteran shopper knows, the malls and centers listed below don't have it all. So launch your own expedition and discover your own gold nuggets!

Oh, by the way, don't take your shoes off. Two major regional malls are on the drawing boards and promise to add more than two million square feet of retail shopping pleasure.

Regional Malls

Cary Towne Center
Maynard and Walnut Sts., Cary
• 460-1053 • www.shopyourmall.com

Cary Towne Center, which opened its doors in 1979, is Cary's largest enclosed mall with 135 stores and restaurants. As the second largest enclosed mall in Wake County, it truly is a regional shopping center. Anchor tenants are Hudson Belk, Sears, JCPenney, Hecht's and Dillard's. National apparel and shoe stores include Lerner of New York, Gap and GapKids, The Limited and Limited Too, Casual Corner, Eddie Bauer, Lane Bryant, Talbot's, Structure, Victoria's Secret, Frederick's of Hollywood, Rack Room Shoes, Foot Locker and Lady Foot Locker. There are specialty stores such as Bath and Body Works, Cyber Station, Kay-bee Toys, The Disney Store, Candleman, Kirklands, Gypsy's Candyland, The Allen Montague Collectors Gallery, North Carolina Remembered, Camelot Music, Select Comfort Air Bed Company and Aggie's Gifts and Collectibles. Jewelers include Kay, Zales and Bailey Banks & Biddle. In addition to the food court, Ragazzi's, India Garden and Spinnakers restaurants are located here. Across the street you'll find a large Barnes & Noble, complete with a coffee shop.

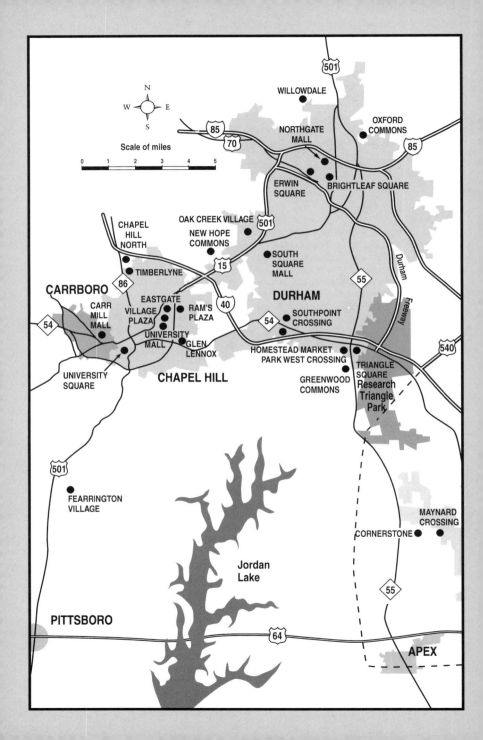

Triangle Shopping

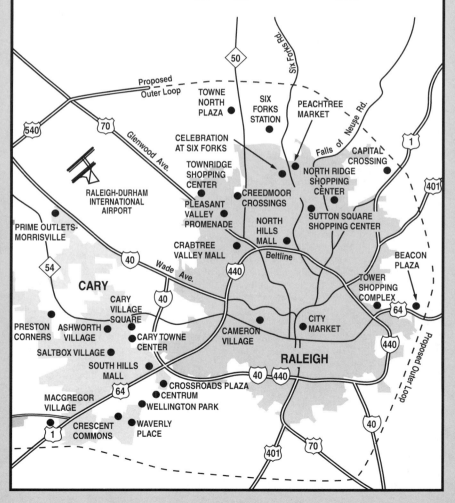

Proposed Outer Loop

50

Six Forks Rd.

540

70

Glenwood Ave.

TOWNE NORTH PLAZA

SIX FORKS STATION

PEACHTREE MARKET

Falls of Neuse Rd.

1

CELEBRATION AT SIX FORKS

CAPITAL CROSSING

401

RALEIGH-DURHAM INTERNATIONAL AIRPORT

TOWNRIDGE SHOPPING CENTER

NORTH RIDGE SHOPPING CENTER

PRIME OUTLETS-MORRISVILLE

PLEASANT VALLEY PROMENADE

CREEDMOOR CROSSINGS

NORTH HILLS MALL

SUTTON SQUARE SHOPPING CENTER

CRABTREE VALLEY MALL

Beltline

BEACON PLAZA

54

40

Wade Ave.

440

TOWER SHOPPING COMPLEX

64

CARY

CARY VILLAGE SQUARE

40

CITY MARKET

440

PRESTON CORNERS

ASHWORTH VILLAGE

CAMERON VILLAGE

SALTBOX VILLAGE

CARY TOWNE CENTER

RALEIGH

Proposed Outer Loop

SOUTH HILLS MALL

40 440

MACGREGOR VILLAGE

64

CROSSROADS PLAZA

CENTRUM

WELLINGTON PARK

40

1

CRESCENT COMMONS

WAVERLY PLACE

401

70

Crabtree Valley Mall
U.S. 70 at I-440, Raleigh • 787-8993
• www.crabtree-valley-mall.com

Opened in 1972, Crabtree Valley Mall is Raleigh's largest enclosed mall with more than 240 stores, restaurants and services. Anchor stores include Lord & Taylor, Hudson Belk, Hecht's and Sears. Crabtree has a number of national, name-brand stores such as Pottery Barn, Crate and Barrel, Smith and Hawken, Brooks Brothers, Laura Ashley, J. Crew, Ann Taylor, Banana Republic, Abercrombie and Fitch, Williams Sonoma, The Disney Store, The Museum Company and Select Comfort.

A few of the specialty stores you will find at Crabtree include: This End Up, Garibaldi & Bruns jewelry store, Gymboree, Successories, North Carolina Remembered, The Great Train Store, Sam Goody, Sharon Luggage & Gifts, Suncoast Motion Pictures, Ross-Simons, Nine West, Pacific Sunwear, The Body Shop, Crabtree and Evelyn, Luggage and Leather, Victoria's Secret, Papyrus (fine stationery), Great Outdoor Provision Company, Brookstone, Fallons Creative Flowers, Wolf Camera, Babbage's, Electronics Boutique, Restoration Hardware, Coconut Traders, Yankee Candle and Pier 1 Imports. Popular apparel stores include: Cache, Casual Corner, Gap, Eddie Bauer, The Limited, Limited Too and Lane Bryant. Barnes & Noble's bookstore serves lifestyle along with the titles. Thomas Kinkade Art Gallery is truly worth visiting to see why Thomas Kinkade has become the most collected artist in America. Deck the Walls is a locally owned frame shop and gallery that provides beautiful custom framing.

Crabtree Valley Mall is also home to a food court and several popular eateries: The Capital Room cafeteria at Hudson Belk, Ruby Tuesday, Mr. Dunderbak's, Kanki Japanese House of Steaks, P.F. Chang's China Bistro, Remington Grill and Panera Bread Company.

Crossroads Plaza
U.S. 1 and I-440, Cary • 233-8087

Crossroads is a regional shopping complex that offers the convenience of front door parking since it is not a traditional enclosed mall. The anchor tenants are OfficeMax, Marshalls and SteinMart. Of interest to readers is Bookstar, a book superstore that carries more than 100,000 titles at a discount. Crossroads Plaza has some specialty discounters such as Dick's Sporting Goods, REI (the membership store for outdoorsmen), Toys 'R Us, Classical Clocks, Linens 'n' Things, Best Buy and Bed Bath & Beyond. Visit Pier 1 Imports for unique gift items. An Old Navy is scheduled to open at Crossroads by the spring of 2001. In addition, Michael's Arts and Crafts plans to relocate here from South Hills Mall. There are restaurant chains, too, such as Ryan's Family Steakhouse, Red Lobster, Olive Garden, Ruby Tuesday, Remington Grill, Atlanta Bread Company and Chick-Fil-A. Crossroads 20, a huge cinema with stadium seating, is also located here.

Walnut Plaza is adjacent to Crossroads and includes Target, Home Depot, Office Depot, National Tire & Battery and the popular Houlihan's restaurant franchise. Located across the street are Lowe's Plaza, a home building supplies and hardware megastore; a Circuit City; and the new Centrum Shopping Center.

Northgate Mall
Off I-85 at Gregson on W. Club Blvd.
Durham • 286-4400
• www.ngatemall.com

Durham's first large shopping mall, which opened as a shopping center in 1960 and converted to a mall in 1974, currently boasts 900,000 square feet of space with more than 160 stores and services. Its anchor stores are Hecht's, Sears and Hudson Belk.

The many specialty shops in the mall include Ann Taylor, Talbot's, The Gap, The Disney Store, Victoria's Secret, Sharon

INSIDERS' TIP
The upscale Nordstrom department store will soon have its first location in the Triangle in Durham's new 1.3-million-square-foot Streets at Southpoint regional mall, set to open in spring 2002.

Luggage and Gifts, The Bombay Company, Waldenbooks, Footlocker, Aerosole's Shoe Store, Old Navy, Great Outdoor Provision Company, Hungates Arts and Crafts, Thomas Kinkade Signature Gallery and a number of unique, locally owned and managed stores such as SoHo Shoes and Cherokee Art and Jewelry. A full-size Italian Carousel is a permanent fixture and a favorite of children. Northgate Mall includes a Food Gallery as well as popular restaurants Ruby Tuesday, Yamato Japanese Seafood and Steak and Cafe Carolina.

North Hills Mall
Six Forks Rd. and I-440, Raleigh
• **787-8896**
• **www.shopnorthhillsmall.com**

Built in 1967, North Hills is Raleigh's original enclosed mall. Since that time, it has been updated and currently offers a diverse range of shops where you can find just about everything. The mall is anchored by two department stores, Dillard's and JCPenney, but it has found a niche by providing smaller specialty shops and national name shops such as Structure, The Limited, Limited Too, Gap, Lane Bryant, Footlocker, Express and Victoria's Secret.

Other stores include Globetrotter Luggage, Added Dimensions Fashions, Zales jewelry, Storehouse Furniture, Gallery and Gifts, Lynn's Hallmark, Kay-Bee Toys and Little Art Gallery. There are numerous eating establishments, including Bruegger's Bagel Bakery, Andy's Pizza and Chick-Fil-A. North Hills Plaza is a small shopping center across Lassiter Mill Road from the mall. It is geared strongly toward service with merchants such as a U.S. Post Office, Blockbuster Video and the N.C. Division of Motor Vehicles. It has specialty shops as well, such as Dan Howard's Maternity Factory Outlet, Audio Book World and Hickory Hams, as well as the popular Cappers restaurant.

Prime Outlets-Morrisville
1001 Airport Blvd., Morrisville • 380-8700
• **www.primeoutlets.com**

Conveniently located near the airport and directly off I-40 at exit 284, Prime Outlets offers over 40 manufacturers outlets such as Off 5th Saks Fifth Avenue, Corning Revere, Nine West and Samsonite Company Stores in a beautiful enclosed center. The center features a food court, fine dining at Sorrento and casual dining at the Grandstand Grille and Tavern, all within walking distance of many of the Research Triangle Park businesses. Customer Service can assist with free coupon books, complimentary wheelchairs and strollers and tourist information.

South Square Mall
U.S. 15-501 N./Bus., Durham
• **493-2451**
• **www.southsquaremall.com**

The other of Durham's two mega-malls, South Square is anchored by Hudson Belk, JCPenney and Dillard's. Popular national chains include: The Limited, Abercrombie & Fitch, Eddie Bauer, Gap, Paul Harris, Ashley Stewart, Structure and Express. Visit The White House for women's fashions and Moondance Gallery for gifts and jewelry. Shop Deck the Walls for frames and prints and Lechter's for household goods and gadgets. Both B. Dalton and Waldenbooks are also located in the mall. Picadilly Cafeteria is a great place to eat.

South Square is located adjacent to Toys 'R Us store. Next door is Circuit City, the discount stereo, TV and appliance chain.

University Mall & Plaza
U.S. 15-501 & Estes Dr.
Chapel Hill • 967-6934

Featuring more than 50 stores, restaurants and services, University Mall and Plaza offers Chapel Hill its most varied array of shopping possibilities. This mall is anchored by Dillard's and Hudson Belk. A host of apparel and specialty shops ranging from athletic apparel to maps to electronic equipment add to the diversity of University Mall.

Some Insiders' favorites are Pleasing Mona, a stylish women's wear shop; Kitchenworks; Cameron's, filled with wonderful gifts and things that defy description; and The Children's Store and The Toy Corner for quality clothing, toys and games. Other special shops are Minata jewelry and De Gustibus

TRIANGLE ANTIQUE STORES

APEX
Antiques on Salem Street	114 N. Salem St.	362-1332
That Unique & Wonderful Place	104 N. Salem St.	387-9550

CHAPEL HILL & ORANGE COUNTY
Countryside Antiques	U.S. 15-501 S.	968-8375
Daniel Boone Village	I-85, exit 164, Hillsborough	732-2361
Touchwood Antiques	100 E. Main St., Carrboro	967-6078
Whitehall at the Villa	1213 E. Franklin St.	942-3179

DURHAM
Chelsea Antiques	2631 Chapel Hill Blvd.	683-1865
Fargo-Hanna Oriental Rugs	4422 Chapel Hill Blvd.	419-0963
James Kennedy Antiques	Brightleaf Square	682-1040
Patterson's Mill Country Store	5109 Farrington Rd.	493-8149
The Persian Carpet	5634 Chapel Hill Blvd.	489-8362

FUQUAY-VARINA
Bostic & Wilson Antiques	105 S. Main St.	552-3248
Hoke Powell Interiors	101 S. Main St.	552-2004

RALEIGH & WAKE FOREST
A.H. Danielson	1101 Wake Forest Rd.	828-7739
Antique Emporium	Cameron Village	834-7250
Antiques at Five Points	2005 Fairview Rd.	834-4900
Carolina Antique Mall	Cameron Village	833-8227
Carolina Collectibles	11723 Six Forks Rd.	848-3778
Classic Antiques	319 W. Davie St.	831-0306
Edith Medlin Antiques	2931 Essex Cir.	781-9908
Fairgrounds Flea Market	State Fairgrounds	829-3533
Gresham Lake Antique Mall	6917 Capital Blvd.	878-9381
Highsmith Antiques	106 Glenwood Ave.	829-5999
Legacies	2012 S. Main St., Wake Forest	562-6890
Oakwood Antique Mall	1526 Wake Forest Rd.	834-5255
Regan Lewis Antiques	5300 Atlantic Ave.	872-8177
Woodleigh Place	610 W. Peace St.	834-8324

SELMA*
Alice's Wonderland Antiques	110 W. Anderson St.	202-0092
Collected Treasures	202 N. Raiford St.	965-9774
Railroad St. Antiques	107 E. Raiford St.	965-9659
Savannah's Antiques	1105 S Pollock St.	965-9055
Simpler Times	110 N. Raiford St.	202-0700

*For information about other antique stores in Selma, contact the Johnston County Visitors Bureau at 989-8687.

(fine cigars, wines and other delicacies). Other stores include Roses, The Print Shop, Zales Jewelers, Kerr Drug, Waldenbooks, Camelot Music, Burlington Shoes and Bath and Body Works. One of our favorite places to eat is located in University Mall, the K & W Cafeteria.

Shopping Centers

Cary

Cary's record-breaking residential growth has driven its retail growth. The biggest attractions are the Cary Towne Center, an enclosed mall with 130 stores and restaurants that rivals Raleigh's Crabtree Valley Mall in space, and Crossroads Plaza, a collection of large, mostly discount, national chains. Centrum Shopping Center was recently constructed across the street from Crossroads with a discount grocery store warehouse, specialty stores and restaurants.

Ashworth Village Center
115 W. Chatham St.

Located in downtown Cary, this village center is a collection of specialty shops and restaurants. Some of our favorite shops include Ordinary and Extraordinary; Once Upon a Time children's boutique; Panache distinctive home accents and fine gifts; and Adria's fashion, gifts and accessories. Also check out Ashworth Drugs, an old-fashioned corner drugstore that serves delicious milkshakes. Serendipity Gourmet Deli serves creative sandwiches, soups and salads. In addition, Ashworth Village Center includes Vespa Italian restaurant, Once in a Blue Moon Bakery and Cafe, Danielle Hunter Limited jewelry and Annie's Attic, a fine consignment shop.

Cary Village Square
Cary Towne Blvd. and Walnut St.

Cary Village Square includes a consignment marketplace that contains about 120 showspaces full of art, furniture, fine antiques, pottery, garden accessories and more. Other stores include T.J. Maxx, Real Wood Furniture, Wicker Beach Imports, Mailboxes Etc. and The Frame Up Gallery. For dining, you'll find Coyote Cafe, CiCis Pizza, Courtney's,

Asahi Asian Restaurant, Jersey Mike's, McDonald's and others.

Centrum
Walnut St., directly across from Crossroads Plaza

Cary's newest shopping center, Centrum offers 400,000 square feet of space and includes BJ's Warehouse Club, JoAnn Fabrics, PetSmart, Cost Plus World Market, Ethan Allen furniture and abraKIDabra Toys. Enjoy dining at Golden Corral, Sweet Tomatoes and Panera Bread, among others.

Cornerstone
Corner of High House Rd. and Davis Dr.

The primary anchor here is a Lowes Foods superstore. Locally owned Carbonated Video, Eckerd Drug, Rudino's Pizza, Connolly's Irish Pub, Art Connection Art Gallery, Goodberry's and PostNet postal and business services are also located here.

Crescent Commons
Kildaire Farm Rd. at Tryon Rd.

Across the street from Waverly Place is one of the area's most attractive shopping centers. Here you'll find a Harris Teeter superstore and Cary's first Wal-Mart, with a brick front. The center also has many locally owned businesses, including Wild Birds Unlimited, The Paper Company, Affinity Gifts and Frame Masters & Awards (specializing in unique framing of family treasures). Tokyo House and TGI Fridays are also here.

Kroger Plaza
Kilmayne Dr.

Kroger Plaza is a neighborhood shopping center located off Kildaire Farm Road that features a Kroger supermarket, open 24 hours. The center also includes the popular Brother's Pizza restaurant, Sewing Solutions, Zero's Subs and Sushi-Thai authentic Japanese and Thai cuisine.

MacGregor Village Shopping Center
Near U.S. 64 and U.S. 1

MacGregor Village is a neighborhood shopping center best known for its

restaurants. Along with established favorites Jimmy V's Steakhouse, Fox and Hound, Horwitz's Deli and Honey Baked Ham Company and Cafe, you will find Tony's Bourbon Street Oyster Bar, Canton Buffet and Santa Lucia. It also has an Eckerd Drug, Artistic Hair Designers and Spa Health Club.

Maynard Crossing
Maynard Rd. and High House Rd.
Anchored by a Kroger superstore, Maynard Crossing also contains Bayleaf Peddler, Jerry Miller Art Gallery and Blockbuster Video. Restaurants include The Ground Finale coffee shop and catering, Philly Steak Factory, Il Sogno Italian cuisine, Brigs and Dosa Inn Indian cuisine.

Park Place
N.C. 54, Morrisville
Park Place boasts a 16-screen movie theatre complex with stadium seating, Park Place 16, a Golden Corral, Food Lion, Bear Rock Cafe, Amante Pizza and other specialty shops, including Pets Warehouse and Qwik Pack and Ship.

Preston Corners
Corner of Cary Pkwy. and High House Rd.
Made up of four corners of retail shops and professional buildings, Preston Corners also offers bank branches of BB&T, CCB, First Citizens, First Union and Wachovia. For dining, you'll find McDonald's, Jersey Mike's Subs, El Dorado, Jasper's, Back 9 Pub and Roly Poly rolled sandwiches, among others. Lowes grocery store is one of the anchors, and you'll also find an ABC Store, a Howard Perry & Walston real estate office, The Flower Basket, Manhattan Bagel, Edy's Ice Cream, Rion's Shoes and Bruegger's Bagels, Jitter's and Caribou Coffee Company, and The Wine Merchant.

Saltbox Village
Kildaire Farm Rd.
Saltbox Village is home to some of Cary's unique shops. Cary Insiders soon find out about The Fresh Market; Possibilities, a women's clothing boutique; Pattywhacks, an upscale children's boutique; Advanced Audio; Science Safari; The Spin Cycle; The Write Image specialty stationery; Schoolkids Records; and Saltbox Valet, a very popular local dry cleaner. Outback Steakhouse and Bear Rock Cafe are also located here.

South Hills Mall and Plaza
U.S. 1 and Buck Jones Rd.
South Hills is a community mall and adjacent service plaza that features several unique stores, specialty shops, services and eateries. This shopping center is anchored by the recently remodeled and expanded Burlington Coat Factory. Country Sonshine offers a wide variety of home decor choices. South Hills also has a host of locally owned businesses such as Cary Office Supply, George Bryant's Florist & Gifts, American Nostalgia collectibles and Carolina Sew-N-Vac, to name a few. Other specialty shops include Carolina Custom Golf, Rugged Wearhouse and Grand Asia Market. The mall also contains Kerr Drug, Mitchell's Hairstyling and United Fabrics. A branch office of the N.C. License and Title Agency also makes South Hills its home. A K&S Cafeteria is also located here.

Waverly Place
Kildaire Farm and Tryon Rds.
Waverly Place is a uniquely designed bi-level shopping plaza with an outside escalator, fountain and outdoor sculpture. It is conveniently located near Lochmere and Regency Park. Here you'll find a new Wellspring grocery store, Merle Norman, Eckerd Drug, Amazing Glaze, Workbench, Sundram Rug Gallery, Cary Travel and several restaurants

INSIDERS' TIP
Yes, we have a sales tax in North Carolina. The state gets 4 cents per dollar and counties can take up to two cents more . . . and all do. Local governments must get permission from the state legislature to levy any new kind of tax such as the one Wake County charges on restaurant meals and hotel rooms.

such as China Pearl, PieWorks, Red Hot and Blue, Paradigm Coffee House, AspenRock (fondue) and Gregory's Grand Occasions for breakfast, lunch and brunch.

Wellington Park
Cary Parkway and Tryon Rd.

Wellington Park, one of Cary's newer strip shopping centers, is anchored by Lowes Foods and also contains Bedroom and Sofa Emporium, Carbonated Video, Learning Express, Discount Pet Supply and Wellington Animal Hospital. Dining options include El Dorado, J. Gilbert's Wood-Fired Grill and Cool Mountain Creamery and Cafe, among others.

Chapel Hill

From boutiques to malls, Chapel Hill offers the range of shopping choices you might expect to find in any growing, university community. Here's a quick guide to Franklin Street, the major shopping centers and malls.

Downtown Franklin Street

Franklin Street is Chapel Hill's main thoroughfare, the first place UNC students and visitors hit when they wander off campus or drive through town. As a result, it has its fair share of places for cheap eats, Carolina paraphernalia and basic collegiate clothing. Though many Franklin Street businesses are designed with the college community in mind, they also have plenty to offer the over 25 crowd.

Favorite clothing stores on East Franklin include Anjana's, Mia, Gap and Barr-Ee Station, which specializes in catalog clothing (J. Crew and Tweeds among them), and Julian's for top-quality menswear. Designer Alexander Julian has also opened Julian's Home an upscale furnishings store. If you need a special gift or a fine new watch, try longtime jewelers Wentworth & Sloan. Visit Franklin Street Cycles for bikes, accessories and service. University Florist and Gift Shop offers flowers, gifts, balloons and unique accessories.

The downtown area also has three cinema houses with six screens: The Varsity I and II, which offer first runs and foreign films, The Ram Triple on Rosemary Street and the Carolina Theatre on the corner of Franklin and Columbia streets. Ice cream and frozen yogurt aficionados can choose from Ben and Jerry's and The Yogurt Pump. Restaurants include Spanky's, Top of the Hill, Carolina Coffee Shop, Rathskeller, Woody's Tar Heel Tavern and Grill, Franklin Street Pizza, Pepper's Pizza and Bandido's.

The west end of Franklin Street features specialty shops like Time After Time, which sells vintage clothing, small decorative items and jewelry. Toktumee Art Gallery is the Triangle's own showcase for original American and international art. Close by is Modern Times, where local clothing designer Lisa Heyward purveys her creations. Further down the block are Paint the Earth ceramics and Uniquities, featuring Betsy Johnson and Nicole Miller fashions. Another shop you'll want to visit is Hill Country Woodworks for handmade contemporary furniture. For authentic Middle-Eastern food like stuffed grape leaves and tabouli, The Mediterranean Deli is delicious, fast and friendly. Other favorites include Michael Jordan's 23, Ham's, 411 West, Wicked Burrito and Patio Loco.

West Franklin is also home to a couple of secondhand bookstores such as The Bookshop and The Avid Reader. They're both great places for an hour's browse.

Further down East Franklin, heading toward Durham, lies Dickinson Garden Center.

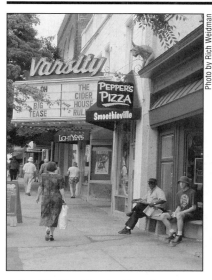

Franklin Street is a bustling shopping district across the street from UNC-CH.

Photo by Rich Weidman

Carrboro's Main Street

If you continue west on Franklin Street, you will eventually run into Carrboro's Main Street. Just as you enter Carrboro, you'll see Nice Price Books in the white and hot pink little house. On the right, a block or so before you cross the railroad tracks, you'll find Surplus Sids, a good source for military gear, rain slickers and old jeans. Further down is Carr Mill Mall.

Keep heading west and at the corner of Main Street and Greensboro you'll find Sanctuary Art and Furniture Gallery and Cliff's Meat Market, an independently owned butcher shop offering an assortment of quality meats and fresh seafood. The Clean Machine bike shop boasts the largest selection of mountain and road bikes in the Triangle. Southern States and Fitch Lumber and Hardware lie north on Greensboro Street. Continuing on Main Street, don't miss the North Carolina Crafts Gallery, showcasing ceramic pieces, jewelry, woodwork and more, all made in the Tar Heel state.

Popular Carrboro restaurants include Tyler's Restaurant and Tap Room, Acme Food and Beverage Company, El Chilango, The Spotted Dog Restaurant and Bar, The Trains Cafe and Armadillo Grill.

Carr Mill Mall
Downtown Carrboro

Some year's ago, Julian Carr's old cotton mill was converted into an upscale shopping village. A group of local citizens and businesses banded together to preserve and transform the dormant mill into one of the area's most unique shopping centers, the Carr Mill Mall. The careful restoration of the original brick exterior, heart-pine interior and other fine architectural details highlight the original structure. It now houses more than two dozen businesses including fine specialty shops like The Clock Works Again (antique and contemporary clocks and clock repairs), Mandarin Gazebo (a gift shop), Monire's Jewelers, Shades of Blue gifts, The Original Ornament, Mulberry Silks, O'Neill's (for menswear), Ali Cat Toys, Animation and Fine Art Galleries and A New Attitude, a women's clothing boutique.

The mall is anchored by a Harris Teeter supermarket (open 24 hours) and CVS, a drug store on one side and Weaver Street Market on the other. Restaurants here include Elmo's Diner and Panzanella Italian cuisine.

Chapel Hill North
Airport Rd. and I-40 (Exit 266)

One of Chapel Hill's newest shopping centers is anchored by a Harris Teeter grocery store and includes Blockbuster Video, Forever Young Spa, Bayleaf Peddler, Optical Reflections, Wolf Camera, GNC and Zero's Subs. It is conveniently located near I-40 north of downtown Chapel Hill.

The Courtyard
W. Franklin St.

You won't believe that this office and retail complex tucked into Chapel Hill's West Franklin Street was once a milk processing plant. Today, The Courtyard features Pyewacket restaurant, The Stock Exchange (an upscale consignment clothing store for women), Pipes by George, a hair salon, and a number of offices.

Eastgate Shopping Center
E. Franklin St. and U.S. 15-501

Eastgate has many noteworthy features that set it apart from the run-of-the-mill shopping center. First, there's A Southern Season, offering a dazzling assortment of fine wines, coffees, nuts, cheeses, crackers, chocolates and other gourmet goodies, as well as The Weathervane Cafe. Other Eastgate attractions are the Potted Plant, for a wide array of house plants, and Workbench, a locally owned store belonging to the largest contemporary furniture chain in the country.

There's also Gallery Americas, for contemporary furniture and accessories for the home; the fashionable Talbot's clothing store; Steinway Gallery, offering everything from art prints to oil paintings; Joe Rowand's Somerhill Art Gallery; Domicile Home Furnishings; and Black Mountain Gallery for handwrought gold and silver jewelry. The Wild Bird Center and Womancraft are great for gifts and Minta Bell Interior Design can help with furnishing and decorating your home. Eckerd Drug, Wherehouse Music, Play It Again Sports, Lynn's Hallmark and Eastgate BP are some other tenants. Good places to eat at Eastgate include The Loop Grill, a casual place with something for the whole family, Sal's N.Y. Pizza (for family dining), Bruegger's Bagel Bakery and China Chef.

Fearrington Village
Chatham County • www.fearrington.com

Eight miles south of Chapel Hill, in rural Chatham County, lies a village complete with its own quaint post office, a pasture with grazing Belted Galloway cows, a market/cafe and an elegant inn and restaurant. Amid this pastoral setting, you'll find a collection of unique shops, including Pringle's for pottery and gifts, A Stone's Throw for jewelry and gemstones, The Potting Shed for plants and accessories, Dovecote Home and Garden and McIntyre's Fine Books and Bookends.

Glen Lennox Shopping Center
N.C. 54 E.

Located across from Glenwood Square, Glen Lennox Shopping Center is home to The Grill at Glen Lennox, one of Chapel Hill's most popular restaurants. Other stores include Pace Gifts, Traditions Bridal Store and All Things Good gourmet take-out. At Glenwood Square is a Harris Teeter, Eckerd Drug and the Thai Palace restaurant.

Photo courtesy of N.C. Division of Tourism

An early 20th-century tobacco warehouse has been carefully restored to house specialty shops and restaurants at Brightleaf Square in downtown Durham.

Ram's Plaza
U.S. 15-501

Across U.S. 15-501 from Eastgate, Ram's Plaza features several interesting places to shop. Dance Design is the store to go for dancewear and for costumes for parties and Halloween. There's also Women's Workout Club, a tanning salon and Serenity Day Spa. Other businesses include a Framer's Market, Fred's Beds, a CVS drugstore, Tire King, Nantucket Cafe and Bailey's Pub and Grille. Just behind Ram's Plaza is Yarnell-Hoffer, a locally owned hardware store that stocks or will special order almost anything you need to fix up your home.

Timberlyne
Weaver Dairy Rd.

A bustling shopping center on Weaver Dairy Road, Timberlyne includes a Food Lion, Eckerd Drug, Tsing Tao restaurant, True Value Hardware and the Chelsea Theatres. Other shops and businesses include Framemakers, Small World Travel, VisArt Video, Mama's Pasta Cafe, Cup A Joe, Margaret's Cantina, Bud and Eb's Grill and J & J Deli. The U.S. Post Office also has a branch here. Movies at Timberlyne, a seven-theatre complex, plays first-run features.

University Square
W. Franklin St.

University Square is a small shopping center located on West Franklin Street, just a few steps away from the UNC campus. Built on the site of the old Chapel Hill High School, it offers a diverse mix of shops and restaurants, geared to a wide range of tastes and budgets. You can find quick fried chicken and biscuits at Time Out, open 24 hours, or designer clothes at Fine Feathers, with a lot in between. There's The Painted Bird that sells imported clothing for women and children and Central and South American crafts; Shoes at the Square with fine footwear for

women; Peacock Alley, purveyor of fine gifts and accessories for the home; and Sizl Gallery. Browse at T'boli imports and The Whistlestop, both great sources for inexpensive and always unusual gift ideas. Stop at the Swensen's Ice Cream Factory, GranCafe or 35 Chinese for a bite to eat.

Village Plaza
Elliott Rd.

The Village Plaza, located on Elliott Road, is anchored by Wellspring Grocery. Penguin's Cafe is located inside the store. There is a mini-mall here with The Cotton Boll for fine fabrics, the Design Workshop offering upholstery fabrics and design services, Lacock's Shoe Repair and other shops and services. Viking Travel and the Plaza Theatres, Great Harvest Bread Company, Plaza Dry Cleaners and VisArt Video are here, as well as Red Hot & Blue and Zorba's restaurants. You'll also find Java Cafe and Monterrey Mexican Restaurant.

Across the street is the Galleria with specialty shops such as the Purple Puddle I and II, Plum Gardens, The World Traveller, The Lighting Place, Silk Quarters, Baum Jewelers and Mina's salon. Cafe Parvaneh is located here as well. The Chapel Hill Senior Center is adjacent to the Galleria shops. Located nearby are Charles Hopkins jewelers and Vacuum Cleaner Hospital.

Durham

With several dozen shopping centers and malls in and around Durham, it's a shopper's paradise. The area offers hundreds of retail outlets, from major department stores, like Dillard's, Hecht's and Belk's to discount houses, and specialty boutiques. In addition, a regional mall of 1.3-million square feet is in the construction stages at Fayetteville Road and I-40 in south Durham. Scheduled to open in spring 2002, The Streets at Southpoint will contain

---

FYI

Unless otherwise noted, the area code for all phone numbers listed in this guide is 919.

INSIDERS' TIP

The best time to go to Triangle shopping malls during the traffic-jammed Christmas season is suppertime. But don't tell anyone.

TRIANGLE BOOKSTORES

CARY

Barnes & Noble	760 S.E. Maynard Rd.	467-3866
Bookstar	Crossroads Plaza	859-9933
Borders	1751 Walnut St.	469-1930

CHAPEL HILL & CARRBORO

The Avid Reader	462 W. Franklin St.	933-9585
The Book Market	Carr Mill Mall	929-7264
The Bookshop	400 W. Franklin St.	942-5178
Bull's Head Bookshop	Daniels Bldg., UNC-CH	962-5060
McIntyre's Fine Books	Fearrington Village, Pittsboro	542-3030
Nice Price Books	Main St., Carrboro	929-6222
Skylight Exchange	405-1/2 W. Rosemary St.	933-5550
World Traveller Books	400 S. Elliott Rd.	933-5111

DURHAM

Barnes & Noble	New Hope Commons	489-3012
The Book Exchange	107 W. Chapel Hill St.	682-4662
Books Do Furnish A Room	1809 W. Markham Ave.	286-1076
The Know Book Store	2520 Fayetteville St.	682-7223
Nice Price Books	3415 Hillsborough Rd.	383-0119
Regulator Bookshop	720 Ninth St.	286-2700
Wentworth & Leggett	Brightleaf Square	688-5311

RALEIGH

Barnes & Noble	Crabtree Valley Mall	782-0030
Books-A-Million	4031 Old Wake Forest Rd.	790-8784
Books at Stonehenge	7414 Creedmoor Rd.	846-1404
Borders	8825 Six Forks Rd.	755-9424
Edward McKay Used Books	3501-127 Capital Blvd.	790-9299
Nice Price Books	3106 Hillsborough St.	829-0230
Quail Ridge Books	Ridgewood Shopping Center	828-1588
The Reader's Corner	3201 Hillsborough St.	828-7024

five anchor department stores, including Nordstrom, about 120 specialty shops, five restaurants and an 18-screen movie theater.

Here's our guide to the major malls as well as some other special places to browse and shop in Durham.

Brightleaf Square
Gregson and West Main Sts.
www.brightleaf.citysearch.com

In 1980, a couple of local businessmen saw potential beauty in the twin giant American Tobacco Company warehouses at the corner of Gregson and West Main streets. They worked painstakingly to preserve and display the all-heart-pine beams, 20-inch-thick brick walls and ornate chimneys. Several years later, what had become a symbol of economic decline was resurrected as an upscale shopping center called Brightleaf Square.

Here, you'll find upscale woman's clothing boutiques such as Collections and Simply Hip, as well as Millennium Music. The Glassworks Gallery at Goldworks, Horizon and Tyndall galleries offer fine art and crafts. Antique stores include LaFayette Galleries

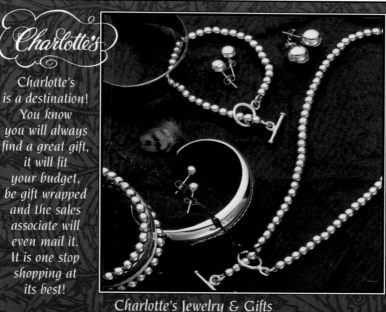

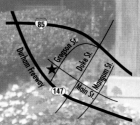

Cameron Village

THOMPSON·LYNCH COMPANY

Fine Lamps, Shades, Repairs,
Accessories, Antiques

439 Daniels St.
Cameron Village, Raleigh
919-821-3599

Falls of the Neuse Rd.
Northridge Shopping Center, Raleigh
919-872-7253

The Globetrotter
LUGGAGE, LEATHERGOODS AND GIFTS

Our Customers Are
Going Places

417 Daniels St.
Cameron Village, Raleigh
919-828-1226

The Beltline at Six Forks Rd.
North Hills Mall, Raleigh
919-782-6936
www.theglobetrotter.com

Nowell's

The Best Fit,
The Latest Fashion in
Corporate or Casual Clothing

435 Daniels St.
Cameron Village, Raleigh

919-828-7285
www.nowellsclothing.citysearch.com

Shop in the Village...

JILL FLINK FINE ART
framing·gallery·art supplies

Custom Framing
Everything in Art Supplies
Same-day Photo Processing

2018 Clark Ave.
Cameron Village, Raleigh
919-821-7172
www.citysearch.com/rdu/jffineart

doodlebugs
furniture, linens & gifts for children

Offering custom-designed linens,
lamps, rugs, cribs, twin beds, artwork, hand-painted furniture &
unique gifts for the new baby.
We make decorating child's play!

419-A Daniels St.
Cameron Village, Raleigh

919-832-7467

Lavender and Lace

The Finest Selection of Linen,
Lingerie, Toiletries and Baby Gifts.

400 Daniels St.
Cameron Village, Raleigh
919-828-6007
www.lavenderlace.citysearch.com

Follow the Cobblestones to City Market

Sally Huss Gallery

For Gifts That Touch The Heart
This Upbeat Gallery Has
Something For Everyone

309 Blake Street, Raleigh
919-833-0809

Magnolia Marketplace, Cary
919-319-0505

Magnolia Marketplace, Raleigh
919-841-1103

Sweet Tea & Grits, Inc.

Southern Pottery At Its Best…
And Other Neat Stuff!
Specializing in Regional Art
Pottery • Jewelry • Art
Coffee and Dessert Bar

307 Blake Street, Raleigh

919-834-7752
www.sweetteaandgrits.com

The Brass Key Inc.

Baldwin Brass 30% Off
The Triangle's Best Selection
of Home Accessories,
Collectibles and Fine Gifts

317 Blake Street, Raleigh

919-828-9126

LOCATION, LOCATION,

85

→ FROM MEBANE

15-501

As every smart home buyer knows,
where is just as important as anything else.
And Northgate Mall is **where** you need to shop.

Conveniently located off of I-85 in Durham, it's only
20 minutes away from just about everything in the Triangle!

Featuring over 160 stores, including The Food Gallery
and Carousel, Hecht's, Hudson Belk,
Old Navy, and Sears.

DURHAM FREEWAY

YOU ARE HERE

15-501
CHAPEL HILL

← TO CHAPEL HILL **40**

LOCATION!

501 ← TO ROXBORO

85 NORTH RICHMOND

TO HENDERSON →

85

TO AIRPORT

70

GREGSON ST.

NORTHGATE
MALL

NORTHGATE
MALL

CLUB BOULEVARD

RESEARCH
TRIANGLE
PARK

TO RALEIGH →

40

and James Kennedy Antiques. Don't miss Wentworth & Leggett Old Rare Books, Goldworks jewelry and City Lights for Tiffany and unique lighting. Food is plentiful as well with El Rodeo, Satisfaction, Taverna Nikos, one of the best Greek restaurants in the Triangle, and Brightleaf 905, which serves delicious world cuisine. Across the street in the Brightleaf Shopping District you will find Fowler's Market and Morgan Imports. Free validated parking is available for Brightleaf Square visitors in a lot across Gregson Street.

Erwin Square
W. Main St.

Erwin Square is located in the First Union Building Plaza within walking distance of historic Ninth Street. Shops here include Jewelsmith and K. Peterson for leathergoods. Restaurants are The Market Place, Cafe Parizade and The Mad Hatter's Bake Shop.

Homestead Market
N.C. 54 and Fayetteville Rd.

Homestead is anchored by a Harris Teeter supermarket, Eckerd Drug and Rose's department store. Other tenants include David Michael jewelers, Kitchen and Bath Galleries, Carbonated Video, Optometric Eye Care Center and Fitness World Health Club. You can also take your driver's license exam or get your license renewed at the N.C. Driver's License Examiners office here. Dining options include Subs, Etc. and El Inca Cafe.

Loehmann's Plaza
1821 Hillandale Rd.

The Plaza is home to the anchor store Loehmann's, offering great discounts on women's designer clothes, Kerr Drug and a number of small shops, including Michelle's Fine Jewelry and Gifts and Jo's Hallmark Shop. Loehmann's Plaza also features Papa's Grill, a casual cafe, Sal's Pizza and El Vaquero Mexican Restaurant. FitSouth fitness center is also located here.

New Hope Commons
U.S. 15-501 and I-40

Strategically located off Interstate 40 between Chapel Hill and Durham, New Hope Commons provides shoppers of both cities with quite a choice of discount shops. Anchor tenants Wal-Mart, Best Buy, Marshall's and OfficeMax offer low prices and huge selections. Other stores include a Barnes & Noble bookstore, Old Navy Clothing Company, Chesapeake Bagel Bakery, Michael's craft supply store, Zany Brainy, Party City, Dick's Sporting Goods, The Men's Wearhouse and Linens 'n Things. There's ample parking and the shops offer something for everyone.

Ninth Street
West Durham
• www.ninthst.com

Ninth Street is neither a shopping center nor a mall. It is a charming commercial block in west Durham that grew up around the Erwin Cotton Mill, a neighborhood that in the past two decades has made a comeback. Mosey on down to the two blocks of Ninth Street running between Hillsborough Road and West Main Street, within walking distance of Duke University's East Campus. Here's a sample of what you'll find.

Shops include Earth & Spirit, with gifts from the earth; Vaguely Reminiscent, a boutique featuring stylish natural-fiber garments and fun accessories; and Look Out!, with catalog clothing for men and women at outlet prices. An Insiders' favorite is The Regulator Bookshop, offering a great selection of books and the best assortment in town of left-liberal newspapers, magazines, bizarre postcards and more. Check out One World Market (on Perry Street) and Zola for art, crafts and jewelry. Keep on walking and you'll find an exotic ice cream, pastry and chocolate shop called Francesca's Dessert Caffe. In the old Wachovia Bank Building, you'll find Bruegger's Bagel Bakery. Nearby is Schoolkids Records, Lisa Kaye and Company Fine Jewelry (just off Ninth on Perry Street), The Play House (a wonderful toy store), North Carolina Anglers and Outfitters, Bernard's Formal Wear and The Duck Shop for Duke memorabilia. Be sure to stop at McDonald's Drug Store, a fixture on Ninth Street since 1922 that one local writer called "the beating heart of Ninth Street." Here you

Raleigh's Cameron Village opened in 1949 as the first outdoor shopping center in the Southeast.

can ask for an old-fashioned soda (or even an egg cream, if you please) while you wait for your prescription to be filled. Popular restaurants include George's Garage, Elmo's Diner, Magnolia Grill and Blue Corn Cafe.

Two blocks away on Broad Street is Owen's Broad Street Diner and Wellspring, a market of natural, organic and gourmet foods, including naturally grown meats and whole-grain baked goods.

Oak Creek Village
U.S. 15-501 and Garrett Rd.

Oak Creek features T.J. Maxx (the designer-label discount clothing and housewares store), Rack Room Shoes, Payless Shoes and Jo-Ann's Fabrics and Crafts. Other stores include a Funcoland computer games, Sleep World and a cellular phone outlet. Oak Creek also has an On the Border, Chili's Grill & Bar, Panda Inn, CiCi's Pizza and Subway sandwiches.

Park West Crossing
N.C. 54 and N.C. 55

Park West and its neighboring stores serve as service centers for RTP employees on weekdays. Here you'll find just about every fast-food restaurant imaginable (and they're all packed during lunch hour). Park

West itself includes a Food Lion, CVS Pharmacy, Kinko's Copies and C&M's Hallmark. Dining options include Fuji, Brigs, Schlotsky's and El Dorado. Across N.C. 55, you'll find a Winn Dixie and Eckerd Drug, as well as popular restaurants such as Jamaica Jamaica, Ginger Inn and Parkside Restaurant and Bakery.

Southpoint Crossing
N.C. 54 and Fayetteville Rd.

Located across the street from Homestead Market, the relatively new Southpoint Crossing shopping center is anchored by a Kroger grocery store. Other tenants include Blockbuster Video, Packaging Express, Wolf Camera, Ruby Tuesday, Rudino's Pizza and Grinders, Souper! Salad, Orient Garden and Quizno's Subs.

Woodcroft Shopping Center
Hope Valley Rd. and N.C. 54

There are many shopping centers in Durham about the size of Woodcroft: 20 stores anchored by a chain supermarket, a bank and a fast-food eatery. We're making a fuss over this one because it was done with style and sensitivity to its location. The entire mall is done in earth-toned brick. The awnings are uniform evergreen.

The reason may be that Woodcroft has a captive shopping audience located conveniently next door in the planned residential development by the same name. Woodcroft Optical, Kerr Drug, Martyn's fly fishing supplies, Fallons Creative Flowers and Triangle True Value Hardware can be found here. Restaurants include Bandido's, Pulcinellas, West 94th Street Pub, Yamazushi and Cafe Momo.

Raleigh

Raleigh has long served as a regional shopping area for eastern North Carolina and it continues to hold that reputation. It is where people come to buy the fancy shoes and special dress or the delicate dessert and dry wine they can't find in Smalltown, NC. Raleigh is also where many people come for their "big ticket" items at discount prices. The trend of off-pricing or discount buying of brand names has made it a more competitive market. The adventurous shopper will not be disappointed with Raleigh.

A new regional mall, the 1.2-million-square-foot Triangle Towne Center, is under development at the intersection of Capital Boulevard and Old Wake Forest Road. It is scheduled to open in early 2002 and will feature five anchor department stores, 120 specialty shops, restaurants, a 16-screen theater, an ice skating rink and a food court. Plans are also in the works for a 226,000-square-foot cinema and retail entertainment complex off Capital Boulevard called the MarqE. It is set to open during the summer of 2001.

Cameron Village Shopping Center
Oberlin Rd. and Clark Ave.
• **www.shopsofcameronvillage.com**

Cameron Village is the city's third largest shopping center. When it opened on November 17, 1949, Cameron Village was the Southeast's first outdoor shopping center. One of the most popular shopping destinations in the Triangle, the Village underwent extensive renovation in the '90s.

Cameron Village is known for its large number of locally owned, family stores and shops. Recently, however, the Village has made moves to attract national retailers such as Victoria's Secret, Bath and Body Works, Ann Taylor, Gap and Banana Republic.

Some families have been affiliated with the Village since the '50s, such as Nowell's a fine clothing store; Thompson-Lynch Company, which in addition to selling fine lamps, shades and accessories can make your old lamp new again; The Hobby Shop; and Medlin-Davis, cleaners of distinction. Dina Porter offers fine crafts and women's fashions. Tyler House offers some of the smartest styles for women of all ages. Other specialty women's clothing stores include Beanie & Cecil, Cameron Clothing, Christian's, Galatea, Pea in the Pod, Razooks, SoHo, Talbot's and Uniquities. Georgiano's shoe salon carries the finest European ladies shoes, handbags and accessories. The expert shoe fitters at The Athlete's Foot will help you find the perfect fit. Lavender and Lace carries an incredible selection of fine linens, lingerie, toiletries and baby gifts. Nowell's and Joseph A. Bank Clothiers offer a wide selection of quality men's suits and apparel for all occasions. Gentleman's Choice carries an extensive line of formal wear. Ten Thousand Villages specializes in international gifts handcrafted by skilled artisans, as well as Oriental rugs.

For estate and one-of-a-kind fine jewelry, the Elaine Miller Collection is unsurpassed. Other Village jewelers include: Jolly's Jewelers, Monte Cristo's, Bailey's Fine Jewelry and Charlotte's Jewelry & Gifts.

Cook's Choice is literally a dream store for the home chef, where you can find just about anything for the kitchen from unique utensils and gadgets to designer dinnerware. Discover solutions to home organization and storage problems at Hold Your Own.

Antiques Emporium offers an array of traditional antiques. Together with Carolina Antique Mall and George McNeil Antiques, the Village is a popular stop for antique shoppers looking for something different.

Accipiter is the place to find eclectic gifts and custom made furniture. The Globetrotter will meet all your luggage and leathergoods needs. Jill Flink Fine Art features contemporary and original local artists, as well as framing, photo developing and hard to find art supplies. Doodlebugs carries furniture, linens and gifts for children. Other Village favorites include: Frances T. King Stationery, Quintessentials, Danneberg Galleries, The Pine Box, Dolls Plus, Party Shop, Main and Taylor Shoe Salon, Animal Quacker Toys, Sam Bass Camera, Junior League Bargain Box, CEO's Executive Gifts, Richey and Company footwear, Stride Rite Shoes, Home Economics Accessories Market and Parsley, Sage & Rosemary. The Village also includes Blockbuster Video, Waldenbooks and Wherehouse Music.

Big Sky Bread Company bakes fresh specialty breads, muffins and cookies and is a great place to have lunch in the Village. The Fresh Market is a specialty food store. Foster's, The Village Deli, Leon's Deli, Piccola Italia, Second City Grill, Mandarin House, Cafe Carolina and Bakery and K & W Cafeteria are some of the favorite eating places located in Cameron Village. It has the city's most popular library branch, too. Check it out.

Capital Crossing
Capital Blvd. and Millbrook Rd.

Known for its unique traffic circle and clock tower, Capital Boulevard Center is home to a number of popular discount chains such as Service Merchandise, Staples, Sam's Club, Target, Lowes and PetSmart. A Lowes grocery store can also be found here.

City Market
Downtown, Moore Square
• www.citymarket.citysearch.com

Two blocks east of the Fayetteville Street Mall in the Moore Square Art District is the City Market complex that has attracted artists and craftspeople as well as new customers to downtown. Historic old buildings house unique establishments with collectible antiques. Artspace offers artisans both a place to work and to sell their goods. For adult fun, laugh it up at ComedySportz. Also don't miss The Brass Key for unique gifts, The American Indian Company, Sweet Tea & Grits for Southern pottery, Sally Huss Gallery, Maximilian Home Accents and Amazing

Glaze Ceramics. Some of the most popular restaurants in the Triangle are located in City Market, such as Big Ed's City Market Restaurant, Greenshield's, Vic's Italian Cafe and Pizzeria, Peppercorns, Yancey's Jazz and Blues Cafe and El Rodeo.

"Music in the Market" features live entertainment at City Market every Friday night from 7:30 PM to 10:30 PM during the summer.

The Falls Centre
Old Wake Forest and Falls of Neuse Rds.

The Falls Centre offers a variety of stores to meet your family's shopping needs, including Stein Mart, Office Depot, Party City, GNC and Jo-Ann Fabrics. Popular restaurants include Chevy's Fresh Mex, Cooker and Boston Market.

Greystone Village
Leadmine and Sawmill Rds.

The quaint stone architecture makes this center remarkable. Anchored by Food Lion, Greystone Village is home to several popular restaurants such as Imperial Garden, Fins, Casa Doria and Sawmill Tap Room.

North Ridge
Falls of Neuse and Spring Forest Rds.

Built in 1980 at a key intersection near North Ridge Country Club, this strip shopping center includes a Winn Dixie; a locally owned French restaurant, Jean-Claude's; and the popular Hing Ping Chinese restaurant, which serves the best lunch buffet in this part of town. Thompson-Lynch Company has a fine selection of lamps, shades and accessories. Other tenants include Houlihan's, Kerr Drug, Ace Hardware, Spa Health Club and Schoolkids Records.

Oak Park
U.S. 70 W. and Holly Ridge Rd.

A vintage, late '50s shopping center, Oak Park was built to accommodate its namesake residential development nearby. For shoppers, it has a diverse lineup including Bernina's World of Sewing, Tuesday Morning gifts, Hertzberg Furs and Dan's Fan City. Maus Piano, which sells Baldwins and provides tuning, has been around since 1934.

Oak Park also has a friendly tavern, O'Malley's, with the atmosphere of a neighborhood pub. The Peddler steakhouse and Casa Carbone, one of the oldest Italian restaurants in town, are both located here.

Olde Raleigh Village
Edwards Mill and Duraleigh Rds.

Anchored by a Harris Teeter supermarket, Olde Raleigh Village contains more than 25 stores, including Serotta's, women's fine fashions; Sparrowood Jewelers; Johnson's Jewelers; The Bare Wall, frame shop and gallery; Trillium gift shop and art gallery; The French Knot, a unique needlepoint shop; K & S Cafeteria; Crowley's Courtyard restaurant; Second Nature Cafe; and an Eckerd Drug store.

Pleasant Valley Promenade
Glenwood Ave.

Best Buy, Marshall's, Office Max, Michael's, Pleasant Valley Cinema, Zany Brainy, Hold Your Own, The Bike Rack and a host of specialty shops and restaurants can all be found at Pleasant Valley Promenade. Across Pleasant Valley Road lies another shopping center, Townridge, home to a Wal-Mart, Winn Dixie, Lone Star Steakhouse, Neo-China and other specialty shops and restaurants.

Six Forks Station
Strickland and Six Forks Rds.

This neighborhood shopping center in North Raleigh includes a Food Lion, Home Depot, Eckerd Drug, Borders bookstore and K-mart as major tenants. Another big attraction is Waccamaw's Homeplace. A Fallons Creative Flowers shop is also located at Six Forks Station. You won't go hungry here either with the K & S Cafeteria, O'Charley's, Zest Cafe and Char-Grill, as well as a variety of fast-food restaurants.

State Fairgrounds Flea Market
Hillsborough St. at Blue Ridge Rd.
• 829-3533

The permanent flea market at the State Fairgrounds boasts more than 200,000 square feet of antiques, collectibles, jewelry, furniture, crafts and much more. The market is one of the best on the East Coast and draws vendors from all over the state. It is open every Saturday and Sunday from 9 AM to 5 PM.

State Farmers Market
Lake Wheeler Rd. & I-440, Raleigh • 733-7417

Located near the southern half of the Beltline interchange and Lake Wheeler Road, this state-operated market provides shoppers from across the state with the garden bounty of area farmers as well as seasonal produce, such as citrus fruits, trucked in from neighboring states. It's open year round every day except Christmas. Saturday is usually the busiest day. It's the place to go in season to get fresh produce, often from the person who grew it: strawberries, blueberries, black-eyed peas, sweet corn, tomatoes, yams, watermelon, you name it. Here you'll find your Halloween pumpkin or Christmas tree.

In April, Buildings One and Two are in full bloom with flowers and bedding plants.

The Garden Center features Family Home & Garden, which has stores in Apex and Raleigh.

In the market specialty shops you'll find Ford's Fancy Fruits "The North Carolina Store" and The Fudge Master's Factory and Candy Garden. For those who want their fresh produce or seafood already prepared, The Farmers Market Restaurant serves breakfast and lunch and N.C. Seafood, famous for its fried shrimp, serves lunch and dinner daily.

As the sign leading into the Farmers Market proclaims, it's "more than fresh vegetables, it's a family adventure." Indeed, for some, Saturday morning at the Farmers Market is a family tradition.

Stonehenge Market
Creedmoor Rd.

A bustling shopping center located along Creedmoor Road, Stonehenge contains more than 40 stores, including Harris Teeter, Eckerd Drug, Stein Mart, Discount Pet Supply and a

Photo courtesy of N.C. Division of Tourism

Saturday morning at the State Farmers Market in Raleigh has become a family tradition for many Triangle residents.

post office. A Crowley's restaurant, Outback Steakhouse, Cozumel Mexican Grille, Wildflour Pizza, Starbucks coffee shop and Bruegger's Bagel Bakery are located here. Stonehenge hosts Twilight Tunes, a free concert series, during the summer.

Tarrymore Square
Capital Blvd. & New Hope Church Rd.

Located on bustling Capital Boulevard, Tarrymore Square includes a Marshall's, Fashion Bug, Rack Room Shoes, Hobby Town USA and Payless Shoes. Dining options include Vincent's and Crystal Palace.

Tower Shopping Complex
U.S. 64 and I-440

Built at Raleigh's main gateway to the east, this strip center quickly established itself in the late '50s as a shopping place for east Raleigh residents as well as commuters from suburbs such as Knightdale and Wendell. Behind the Tower center is another discount shopping center. Fast-food restaurants proliferate in and around the strip. A Hamrick's, Casual Male Big and Tall shop, K&S Cafeteria, Kimbrell's Furniture, Food Lion, Eckerd Drug and Oh! Brian's ribs can be found in and around the Complex.

TRIANGLE FARMERS MARKETS

CARRBORO *Seasonal*	Town Commons Wednesday 4-7 PM Saturday 7 AM-Noon
CARY *Seasonal*	Downtown Tuesday 3-6 PM Saturday 8 AM-12:30 PM
CHAPEL HILL *Seasonal*	Cedar Falls Park Tuesday 7-11 AM
CITY MARKET *Seasonal*	333 Blake St. Thursday-Saturday 7 AM-6 PM
DURHAM *Seasonal*	Durham Athletic Park Saturday 8 AM-Noon
FEARRINGTON VILLAGE *Seasonal*	Chatham County Tuesday 4-6:30 PM
FUQUAY-VARINA *Seasonal*	S. Main St. Wednesday 3-6 PM Saturday 8:30 AM-1 PM
HILLSBOROUGH *Seasonal*	Downtown Saturday 7 AM-1 PM
PITTSBORO *Seasonal*	Chatham County Fairgrounds Thursday 3:30-6:30 PM
RALEIGH (State Farmers Market) *Year Round*	Lake Wheeler Rd. Monday-Saturday 5 AM-6 PM Sunday 12-6 PM

RELIGIOUS ORGANIZATIONS

Anglican
The Anglican Church of America • www.acahome.org

Assemblies of God
190 Campground Rd., Selma, NC 27576 • 965-0225 • www.ncdcag.org

Baptist
American Baptist Church, 5124 Greenwich Ave., Baltimore, MD 21229-2393
• (410) 947-0100 • www.abc-usa.org
Southern Baptist Convention, P.O. Box 1107, Cary, NC 27512-1107 • 467-5100
• www.sbc.net

Buddhist
Buddhist Kadampa Center, 7404-G Chapel Hill Rd., Raleigh, NC 27607 • 859-3433
• www.kadampa-center.org

Catholic
Diocese of Raleigh, 715 Nazareth St., Raleigh, NC 27606-2187
• 821-9700 • www.raldioc.org

Episcopal
201 St. Alban's Dr., Raleigh, NC 27619-7025 • 787-6313 • www.episdionc.com

Greek Orthodox
2480 Clairmont Rd., N.E., Atlanta, GA 30329 • (404) 634-9345 • www.atlanta.goarch.org

Jewish
Raleigh-Cary Jewish Federation, 8210 Creedmoor Rd., Raleigh, NC 27613
• 676-2200 • www.rcjf.org

Lutheran
Evangelical Lutheran Church in America, 1988 Lutheran Synod Dr.,
Salisbury, NC 28144 • (704) 633-4861 • www.elca.org

Orthodox
Antiochian Orthodox Christian Archdiocese of North America
• (201) 871-1355 • www.antiochian.org

Presbyterian
Presbyterian Church in America • (404) 320-3303 • www.pcanet.org
Presbyterian Church USA • (800) 872-3283 • www.pcusa.org

United Church of Christ
• (216) 736-2100 • www.ucc.org

United Methodist
N.C. Conference of the United Methodist Church, 1307 Glenwood Ave.,
Raleigh, NC 27605 • 832-9560 • www.nccumc.org

Worship

New places of worship keep opening their doors in response to the spiritual needs of the Triangle's ever-growing population. The spiritual heritage of North Carolina runs deep and a few area churches have already celebrated their 100th- and even 200th-year anniversaries. The majority of these older congregations can be found in downtown Chapel Hill, Durham and Raleigh. Triangle congregations include all those denominations conventionally represented in most cities. Chances are, no matter what your beliefs, the Triangle will have a congregation to satisfy you.

Today's ministries extend to community outreach, mission trips, and even health and fitness training. Southern Baptists and Roman Catholics, ultraconservatives, moderates and liberals all contribute to a healthy community of faith. Many churches are experiencing rapid growth and are ready to welcome and incorporate new members into their community of faith.

Contemporary ministries also abound here—full of upbeat music, multimedia and interactive study groups. The Triangle's religious community has indeed grown very diverse over the past 10 years. For instance, the area now includes such places of worship as the Buddhist Kadampa Center in Raleigh, the Hindu Society of North Carolina in Morrisville and the Islamic Center of Durham. Apex is the site of North Carolina's only Morman Temple, an imposing $5-million structure on N.C. 55. Other congregations include Quaker, Eastern Orthodox, Evangelical, Pentecostal, Assembly of God, Mennonite, Unitarian Universalist, Moravian and Seventh-Day Adventist, among others.

Some area churches are worth a visit just to experience their historical and architectural value. For example, Duke University Chapel has earned a reputation as the most stunning church facility in Durham.

The 1,800-seat Gothic Revival structure was built to fulfill James B. Duke's dream of "a great towering church which will dominate all the surrounding buildings." The 210-foot tower, patterned after Canterbury Cathedral, contains a 50-bell, four-octave carillon. Inside, the double doors are flanked by portal figures of churchmen Girolamo Savonarola, Martin Luther, Thomas Cooke and John Wesley, as well as Thomas Jefferson and fellow Virginian Robert E. Lee. Also in Durham, St. Joseph's AME Church was founded in 1869 as one of the first autonomous African-American churches in the United States. Located adjacent to the Hayti Heritage Center, the church is in the process of being converted into a performance hall. Raleigh's Wake Cross Roads Baptist Church was founded in 1789, a few short months after George Washington was inaugurated as the country's first president.

For more information about area churches, contact the organizations in the chart on the preceding page. Also check out the *N&O's* "Faith" section, which can be found in the Friday edition of the paper. It includes an extensive calendar of events. You may also want to contact your local chamber of commerce to see if it has a list of area faith groups. Other helpful ways to find a suitable place for worship include visiting religious web sites, consulting with neighbors and coworkers, perusing the Yellow Pages and driving around your community.

It's a good idea to call first for time of worship, especially during the summer when many churches change their schedules. During the remainder of the year, most mainline Protestant churches hold at least one Sunday service at 11 AM; Catholic services will vary, but the early mass is normally at 8 AM. Many churches now offer two to three services to meet the schedules of their growing congregations.

Index

Index of Advertisers

BLACK & WHITE ADVERTISERS:

COLOR ADVERTISERS:

Inside Front Cover

Road Runner High Speed Online

Inside Back Cover

Sprint

Getting Around
Between Pages 12-13

Amtrak
Blockade Runner Resort
Daytrips & Weekend Vacations in N.C.
Midway Airlines

Overview of the Triangle
Between Pages 44-45

Allstate Insurance-George Marshall
American Music Jubilee
Nationwide Insurance-Barbara Logsdon
Raleigh Entertainment & Sports Arena
State Farm Insurance-W. Don Cox
Time Warner Cable

Accommodations & Temporary Housing • Between Pages 76-77

A Rental Solution
Alexan Farms
Apartment Finder, The
Strickland Farms

Arts & Culture
Between Pages 108-109

Jane Filer, Artist
North Carolina Symphony
North Carolina Theatre
Thomas Kinkade Signature Gallery
Toktumee Art Gallery

Colleges & Universities
Between Pages 140-141

Campbell University
Mount Olive College
N.C. State University
Wake Forest University

Employment Opportunities
Between Pages 172-173

Bank of America
Cisco Systems
Northwest Mutual
Verizon Wireless

Real Estate & Neighborhoods
Between Pages 300-301

Today's Fireplace
Welcome Home!

Howard Perry & Walston

Vince Carey, Anne Kern Carpenter, Edna Cole, Steina DeAndrade

Remax

Pat Cross, Bill Edwards, Linda Jacobs, Lillian Smith

Restaurants
Between Pages 332-333

four eleven west
five eighteen west
Angus Barn
Angus Barn-The Wine Cellar
Aurora
Brightleaf 905
Carolina Crossroads
Crook's Corner
Daniel's Pizza Pasta Cafe
Fox & Hound
Grill at Glen Lennox, The
Il Palio
La Residence
Mama Dip's Kitchen
Margaret's Cantina
Nina's
Panzanella
Second Empire
Shanghai
Simpson's Beef & Seafood
Spanky's
Squid's
Taverna Nikos
Weaver Street Market
Willow Oak Tea Room

Retirement & Senior Services
Between Pages 364-365

Alterra
Carol Woods
Croasdaile Village
Glenaire
Heritage of Raleigh, The
Independence Village

Meadowbrook Terrace
Oakleaf Village
Westminster Homes

Schools & Childcare
Between Pages 396-397

Cary Academy
Chesterbrook Academy
Kids R Kids
KinderCare
Little Pros Academy
Nobel Learning Centers
Primrose School of Cary
Primrose School of Raleigh
Ravenscroft
Saint Mary's School
St. Timothy's School
Trinity Academy

Triangle Shopping
Between Pages 428-429

Brightleaf Square
Crossroads Plaza
ECKO International Furnishings
New Hope Commons
Northgate Mall
Rynde & Co. Decorative Rugs & Orientals
Smithfield's Ham Shop

Brightleaf Square

City Lights
James Kennedy Antiques
Tyndall Galleries

Cameron Village

Charlotte's
Doodlebugs
Globetrotter, The
Jill Flink Fine Art
Nowell's
Thompson-Lynch Company
Tyler House

Carr Mill Mall

Clock Works Again, The

City Market

Brass Key, The
Sally Huss Gallery
Sweet Tea & Grits

More Information

What you think is important. Please share your ideas.

IN APPRECIATION, WE WILL SEND YOU A COUPON FOR **$10.00 OFF** A COPY OF ONE OF OUR GUIDES.

Name _____

Title _____

Company _____

Address _____

City, State, Zip _____

Phone _____ **Fax:** _____

E-mail _____

Age: ❏ Under 25   ❏ 25-35   ❏ 36-50   ❏ 51-65   ❏ Over 65

Annual Household Income: ❏ Under $25K   ❏ $25 to $35K
❏ $35 to $50K   ❏ $50 to $75K   ❏ $75 to $100K   ❏ Over $100K

Triangle Area: ❏ Newcomer   ❏ Resident   ❏ Student   ❏ Visitor
❏ Planning to Relocate   Date move projected: _____

How did you obtain *The Insiders' Guide To The Triangle?*

❏ Bookstore ❏ Chamber of Commerce ❏ Publisher ❏ *Welcome Home!*

❏ Employer ❏ Friend ❏ REALTOR® ❏ Other _____

Will the book be used by: ❏ Individual   ❏ Family   ❏ Business

How many times do you refer to your guide per month?

❏ 1–3 ❏ 4–6 ❏ 7–9 ❏ 10–15 ❏ 16 and up

Suggestions for future editions: _____

_____

_____

Please send more information on the following:

❏ Cary ❏ Chapel Hill ❏ Durham ❏ Raleigh ❏ Surrounding Areas

❏ Accommodations   ❏ Banks in the area   ❏ Chamber of Commerce
❏ Child Care   ❏ Employment   ❏ Mortgage Companies
❏ Private Schools   ❏ Retirement   ❏ Shopping
❏ Apartments & Temporary Housing—Mo. Rent: _____
❏ REALTOR®   ❏ Builders—Price Range: _____
❏ Development amenities desired: ❏ Pool ❏ Tennis ❏ Golf Course

The Insiders' Guide to The Triangle

Please take a moment to fill out our reader survey and you will receive a coupon good for **$10.00 off** the purchase of your next *Insiders' Guide To The Triangle.* Your comments are very important. In appreciation, we will enter your name in our Grand Prize drawing. Thank you!

$500 GRAND PRIZE
In Entertainment and Dining Gift Certificates

$100 SECOND PRIZE
In Entertainment and Dining Gift Certificates

FIVE $25 THIRD PRIZES
In Entertainment and Dining Gift Certificates

UNLIMITED $10.00 FOURTH PRIZES
Coupon good toward purchase of next Insiders' Guide

EVERYONE'S A WINNER!